Tahiti &
French Polynesia

Jean-Bernard Carillet
Tony Wheeler

LONELY PLANET PUBLICATIONS
Melbourne • Oakland • London • Paris

Tahiti & French Polynesia
5th edition – May 2000
First published – October 1985

Published by
Lonely Planet Publications Pty Ltd A.C.N. 005 607 983
192 Burwood Rd, Hawthorn, Victoria 3122, Australia

Lonely Planet Offices
Australia PO Box 617, Hawthorn, Victoria 3122
USA 150 Linden St, Oakland, CA 94607
UK 10a Spring Place, London NW5 3BH
France 1 rue du Dahomey, 75011 Paris

Photographs
Many of the images in this guide are available for licensing from
Lonely Planet Images.
email: lpi@lonelyplanet.com.au

Front cover photograph
Traditional Polynesian canoe, Moorea, Tony Wheeler, Lonely Planet
Images.

[handwritten inscription:] Tahiti here we come! Love Joan & Dick

ISBN 0 86442 725 5

text & maps © Lonely Planet 2000
photos © photographers as indicated 2000

Printed by Craft Print Pte Ltd, Singapore

Although the authors and Lonely Planet try to make the information as accurate as possible, we accept no responsibility for any loss, injury or inconvenience sustained by anyone using this book.

Modern tiki at Hatiheu, Nuku Hiva (Marquesas)

Reclining tiki at Puamau, Hiva Oa (Marquesas)

Vaikivi petroglyph, Ua Huka (Marquesas)

One of the tiki at Puamau, Hiva Oa (Marquesas)

Petroglyph at Vaiote, Tahiti Iti

Modern art at Taiohae, Nuku Hiva (Marquesas)

Raivavae tiki, Gauguin Museum (Tahiti)

The well-restored Marae Taputapuatea (Raiatea) is the largest in French Polynesia.

Contents – Text

Contents – Maps

The Authors

Jean-Bernard Carillet

After a degree in translation and in international relations, Jean-Bernard joined Lonely Planet's French office in 1995 and is now a full-time author. Diving instructor and incorrigible traveller, he will decamp at the slightest opportunity to travel round the world, but always returns to his native Lorraine in the east of France. As well as coauthoring the last edition of *Tahiti & French Polynesia*, Jean-Bernard has contributed to Lonely Planet's *South Pacific*, *Corsica*, and the French-language guides to *Martinique*, *Dominique et Sainte Lucie* and *Guadaloupe et ses îles*.

Tony Wheeler

Tony was born in England but grew up in Pakistan, the Bahamas and the USA. He returned to England to study engineering, worked as an automotive design engineer, completed an MBA then set out with his wife, Maureen, on an Asian overland trip that ultimately led to them founding Lonely Planet in Australia in 1973. They have been travelling, writing and publishing guidebooks ever since.

FROM THE AUTHORS

Jean-Bernard Carillet Thank you from the bottom of my heart to Yan, my *faaamu* brother, for his constant support and princely welcome. May there soon be more *kaina* times! If Polynesia became my *fenua faaamu*, I owe it to him. I'm also grateful for his generous contribution to the surfing section. Heartfelt thanks for Hubert and Majo's delicious *maa*. Also from my heart's depths come thanks to Patricia, who preferred Papeete to the mining cities of Lorraine, and to whom I owe my 'home sweet home' welcome in Papeete. Thanks also to Sandra, Tahiti's Chinese fairy, who will no doubt be the star of an upcoming Heiva.

I'm also thankful to Eric, to the Tikisoftc@fé, to Jeanne Lecourt, to Karim Cowan, to Pierre Ottino, whose passion remains intact, de Gaétan and Veerna, to Luc and Isabelle Izquierdo, to Chimé and Bab's, to Sylvie and Nathalie, to Ludovic Berne, and to Jacques Mendiola, who kindly enlightened me about the *maquisien* language. Acknowledgments to Rodrigue Ah-Min, Louise Kimitete and Fabien Dinard, the lords of the dance, who shared some of the sacred fire that consumes them – the *ori tahiti*.

I also take my hat off to my diving instructor colleagues with whom I shared some unforgettable moments.

Thanks to the whole LP team for its kindness and logistical support, and to Tony for his last-minute information.

My apologies to Chris and Éva for moments stolen.

Tony Wheeler My thanks go to Jonathan Ray and to the dive staff at Tahiti Plongée, Bathy's Club and the Bora Bora Diving Centre. Geoff Green and the other expedition staff and the Russian crew of the good ship *Akademik Shuelykin* deserve a special thank-you for a fascinating trip that took me to Mangareva, Rapa, Raivavae and other islands in the Pacific.

This Book

This 5th edition of *Tahiti & French Polynesia* was entirely updated by Jean-Bernard Carillet. Tony Wheeler, coauthor of the 4th edition, contributed supplementary material and some of the last-minute information as well as clarifications on the Australs and the Gambier Archipelago. He also translated parts of the text from French.

From the Publisher

This book was edited and proofed by Jane Thompson, with the help of Joanne Newell and Sally O'Brien. Mapping credits go to Chris Lee Ack and Jenny Jones, and Jack Gavran steered the whole thing through layout. Tim Uden was particularly clever with Quark, Quentin Frayne took care of the Language chapter, and Michael Janes translated several of the special sections. Thanks to Alex Landragin and Laurence Billiet for their good humour in providing spot-translations, and to Errol Hunt for sharing his knowledge of things Pacific.

Acknowledgments

THANKS
Many thanks to the travellers who used the last edition and wrote to us with helpful hints, useful advice and interesting anecdotes:

Alberto Livia Lazzeri, Alexander Pfennig, Alexandra Walge, Allegra Marshall, Anne Kathrin Just, Ariane Joannou, B A Howarth, Ben So, Bernd Buchmaier, Berta Gardner, Carol Geishman, Catriona Glendinning, Charles d'Arailh, Chris Hau, Christian Kober, Claudio Strepparava, Comothe Nukuhiva, Daniel Joli, David McCauley, David Newton, Devra Doiran, Elizabeth Gschwandtner, Fabian, Patricia & Julieta Lores, Fabio Barella, Frithjof Kuepper, Giancarlo Galavotti, Gour Sen, Gretchen Grawunder, Heidi Hoffmann, Ian Mackersey, Ian Wood, J C Welch, Jenny Stenhouse, Jeremy & Francesca Pennant, John Anderson, Keith Hetherington, Kent Lester, Kevin Crampton, Kimberly MacDonald, Kristin & Michael Wohlers-Reichel, Lene Kjerri, Lindsey Gant, Lisa Carlosn, Lucy Shanahan, Marilyn Hawkings, Marina Zwittlinger, Mark Pannekoek, Mary McCormick, Matt Cox, Maurice Wilson, Melissa Hockey, Michael Wingenroth, Moira Minoughan, Nicole Kenward, Nicole Lester, Paul Runyon, Peg Smith, Peggy Bendall, Pepita Bos, Peter & Rhonda Turner, Peter Mayes, Peter Norrington, Peter Skinner, Peter Wakeman, Prof Gour C Sen, R D Wicks, R E McGeorge, R J Honer, Rakoczi Katalin, Ralph Mayer, Reinmar Hager, Rex Burrown, Rob Smallwood, Robert Wallace, Robin Patchett, Roger & Hilda Sturge, Roland J O'Driscoll, Rolf Ernst, Rosselli Trindade Costa, Sarah Pottin, Susan McCartney, Susan Strelioff, Suzanne Bermingham, T Thorley, Ted Davis, Tim Earling, Tom Brannigan, Tom Milligan, Troy Henkels, Uli Schlapfer, Vicky Kemp, Wayne Jordan, William P Main and Yorka Bosisio.

Foreword

ABOUT LONELY PLANET GUIDEBOOKS

The story begins with a classic travel adventure: Tony and Maureen Wheeler's 1972 journey across Europe and Asia to Australia. Useful information about the overland trail did not exist at that time, so Tony and Maureen published the first Lonely Planet guidebook to meet a growing need.

From a kitchen table, then from a tiny office in Melbourne (Australia), Lonely Planet has become the largest independent travel publisher in the world, an international company with offices in Melbourne, Oakland (USA), London (UK) and Paris (France).

Today Lonely Planet guidebooks cover the globe. There is an ever-growing list of books and there's information in a variety of forms and media. Some things haven't changed. The main aim is still to help make it possible for adventurous travellers to get out there – to explore and better understand the world.

At Lonely Planet we believe travellers can make a positive contribution to the countries they visit – if they respect their host communities and spend their money wisely. Since 1986 a percentage of the income from each book has been donated to aid projects and human rights campaigns.

Updates Lonely Planet thoroughly updates each guidebook as often as possible. This usually means there are around two years between editions, although for more unusual or more stable destinations the gap can be longer. Check the imprint page (following the colour map at the beginning of the book) for publication dates.

Between editions up-to-date information is available in two free newsletters – the paper *Planet Talk* and email *Comet* (to subscribe, contact any Lonely Planet office) – and on our Web site at www.lonelyplanet.com. The *Upgrades* section of the Web site covers a number of important and volatile destinations and is regularly updated by Lonely Planet authors. *Scoop* covers news and current affairs relevant to travellers. And, lastly, the *Thorn Tree* bulletin board and *Postcards* section of the site carry unverified, but fascinating, reports from travellers.

Correspondence The process of creating new editions begins with the letters, postcards and emails received from travellers. This correspondence often includes suggestions, criticisms and comments about the current editions. Interesting excerpts are immediately passed on via newsletters and the Web site, and everything goes to our authors to be verified when they're researching on the road. We're keen to get more feedback from organisations or individuals who represent communities visited by travellers.

> Lonely Planet gathers information for everyone who's curious about the planet – and especially for those who explore it first-hand. Through guidebooks, phrasebooks, activity guides, maps, literature, newsletters, image library, TV series and Web site we act as an information exchange for a worldwide community of travellers.

Research Authors aim to gather sufficient practical information to enable travellers to make informed choices and to make the mechanics of a journey run smoothly. They also research historical and cultural background to help enrich the travel experience and allow travellers to understand and respond appropriately to cultural and environmental issues.

Authors don't stay in every hotel because that would mean spending a couple of months in each medium-sized city and, no, they don't eat at every restaurant because that would mean stretching belts beyond capacity. They do visit hotels and restaurants to check standards and prices, but feedback based on readers' direct experiences can be very helpful.

Many of our authors work undercover, others aren't so secretive. None of them accept freebies in exchange for positive write-ups. And none of our guidebooks contain any advertising.

Production Authors submit their raw manuscripts and maps to offices in Australia, USA, UK or France. Editors and cartographers – all experienced travellers themselves – then begin the process of assembling the pieces. When the book finally hits the shops, some things are already out of date, we start getting feedback from readers and the process begins again ...

WARNING & REQUEST

Things change – prices go up, schedules change, good places go bad and bad places go bankrupt – nothing stays the same. So, if you find things better or worse, recently opened or long since closed, please tell us and help make the next edition even more accurate and useful. We genuinely value all the feedback we receive. Julie Young coordinates a well travelled team that reads and acknowledges every letter, postcard and email and ensures that every morsel of information finds its way to the appropriate authors, editors and cartographers for verification.

Everyone who writes to us will find their name in the next edition of the appropriate guidebook. They will also receive the latest issue of *Planet Talk*, our quarterly printed newsletter, or *Comet*, our monthly email newsletter. Subscriptions to both newsletters are free. The very best contributions will be rewarded with a free guidebook.

Excerpts from your correspondence may appear in new editions of Lonely Planet guidebooks, the Lonely Planet Web site, *Planet Talk* or *Comet*, so please let us know if you *don't* want your letter published or your name acknowledged.

Send all correspondence to the Lonely Planet office closest to you:

Australia: PO Box 617, Hawthorn, Victoria 3122
USA: 150 Linden St, Oakland, CA 94607
UK: 10A Spring Place, London NW5 3BH
France: 1 rue du Dahomey, 75011 Paris

Or email us at: talk2us@lonelyplanet.com.au

For news, views and updates see our Web site: www.lonelyplanet.com

HOW TO USE A LONELY PLANET GUIDEBOOK

The best way to use a Lonely Planet guidebook is any way you choose. At Lonely Planet we believe the most memorable travel experiences are often those that are unexpected, and the finest discoveries are those you make yourself. Guidebooks are not intended to be used as if they provide a detailed set of infallible instructions!

Contents All Lonely Planet guidebooks follow roughly the same format. The Facts about the Destination chapters or sections give background information ranging from history to weather. Facts for the Visitor gives practical information on issues like visas and health. Getting There & Away gives a brief starting point for researching travel to and from the destination. Getting Around gives an overview of the transport options when you arrive.

The peculiar demands of each destination determine how subsequent chapters are broken up, but some things remain constant. We always start with background, then proceed to sights, places to stay, places to eat, entertainment, getting there and away, and getting around information – in that order.

Heading Hierarchy Lonely Planet headings are used in a strict hierarchical structure that can be visualised as a set of Russian dolls. Each heading (and its following text) is encompassed by any preceding heading that is higher on the hierarchical ladder.

Entry Points We do not assume guidebooks will be read from beginning to end, but that people will dip into them. The traditional entry points are the list of contents and the index. In addition, however, some books have a complete list of maps and an index map illustrating map coverage.

There may also be a colour map that shows highlights. These highlights are dealt with in greater detail in the Facts for the Visitor chapter, along with planning questions and suggested itineraries. Each chapter covering a geographical region usually begins with a locator map and another list of highlights. Once you find something of interest in a list of highlights, turn to the index.

Maps Maps play a crucial role in Lonely Planet guidebooks and include a huge amount of information. A legend is printed on the back page. We seek to have complete consistency between maps and text, and to have every important place in the text captured on a map. Map key numbers usually start in the top left corner.

Although inclusion in a guidebook usually implies a recommendation we cannot list every good place. Exclusion does not necessarily imply criticism. In fact there are a number of reasons why we might exclude a place – sometimes it is simply inappropriate to encourage an influx of travellers.

Introduction

From the time the first European explorers returned from Tahiti with reports of a paradise on earth, the islands of Polynesia have exerted a magnetic attraction for visitors. Of course, like all good travellers' tales, those first reports contained much fantasy. Louis-Antoine de Bougainville, the aristocratic French explorer who narrowly missed the honour of being the first European arrival, started the game by musing about 'noble savages' and dubbing the island 'New Cytheria', after the legendary birthplace of Aphrodite, goddess of love.

There was no shortage of followers, succeeding visitors bringing back vivid descriptions of exotic temples where human sacrifices and other strange rites were practised, chieftains with fleets of magnificent *pirogues* (outrigger canoes) and, far from least important to European interests, beautiful women and erotic dances. Tahiti became a popular haven for passing explorers, and then a retreat for whaling ships, a profitable port for Pacific traders and provided a treasure trove of lost souls for missionaries to convert.

The effect on the Polynesians was disastrous. Within a generation, traditional culture had been all but obliterated. Besieged with new weapons that turned partly ceremonial wars into deadly clashes, new poisons like alcohol, and new diseases to which the islanders had no natural immunity, the population was soon in free fall. As a final indignity, the islands became pawns on the European colonial chessboard.

Yet the myth of paradise persisted and attracted writers such as Herman Melville and Robert Louis Stevenson and artists such as Paul Gauguin, for reasons that are incredibly simple. One glance out of your aircraft window as it gently spirals down over the lagoon to an island like Bora Bora tells it all. This is a place of incredible, wildly varying beauty, from the postcard greens and blues of the mountainous Society Islands to transparent lagoons edged by white-sand *motu* (islets) in the

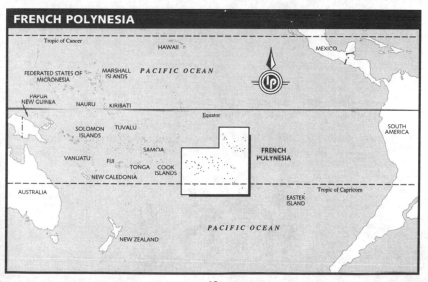

FRENCH POLYNESIA

What's in a Name?

Ask where French Polynesia is or what it consists of and many people will have some difficulty in giving you an answer. Ask about Tahiti, however, and the vision of a beautiful tropical island rising from a deep-blue sea immediately materialises on the map. The reality is that Tahiti is just one island in one of the five island groups that make up French Polynesia. It's the largest island, the best-known, and very historically interesting, but it's just one part of a larger picture. French Polynesia, in turn, is only part of the Polynesia (or 'many islands') region of the South Pacific. The Cook Islands are the other major Polynesian island group, but the Maoris of New Zealand, the native Hawaiians, and the people of Easter Island are also Polynesians.

low-lying atolls of the Tuamotus. Farther north-east are the savage and mysterious Marquesas, to the south the remote and rarely visited Austral Islands and the Gambier Archipelago.

For most visitors, the natural beauty of the islands is the major attraction. Sophisticated restaurants and luxurious resort hotels can add to the experience, but, if you find their prices rather painful, there are cheaper options. These include economical backpacker havens, friendly family *pensions* (guesthouses), and cheap snack bars under palm trees.

You'll never be short of something to do. A small fleet of ships waits to carry adventurous travellers from island to island, and while you can certainly laze on beaches, you can also climb mountains, embark on 4WD expeditions, ride bicycles, and dive beneath the surface to find some of the most exciting scuba diving in the Pacific.

Facts about the Islands

HISTORY

The Society Islands came into existence sometime between one and three million years ago, the product of huge volcanic eruptions under the sea. Human settlement came much later – the islands of Polynesia and New Zealand were the last places on earth to be settled by humans and 'discovered' by Europeans.

Polynesian Migration

Archaeologists, linguists and anthropologists have argued for years about where the ancestors of today's Polynesians came from and *why* they came to the islands of the Pacific. Was it all just a mistake, some great voyage that went astray? Or was it a carefully planned movement, perhaps an escape from land pressures and overpopulation? Because the settlement of the Pacific is, comparatively speaking, so recent, the area holds great interest for academics.

Despite the theories of a South American source, which propelled Thor Heyerdahl's 1947 *Kon-Tiki* expedition, it's generally agreed that the Polynesian people started from South East Asia and began to move eastwards about 3000 to 4000 years ago. The direct ancestors of the Polynesians, now known as the Lapita, moved from the islands scattered off the north coast of the island of New Guinea (in modern-day Papua New Guinea) to the Solomon Islands and Vanuatu about 1600 BC. From there

Mass Migration & the Polynesian Canoe

Two factors were crucial to the success of the mass migrations of the Polynesians: the boats themselves and the art of navigation. Ancient Polynesians had a very detailed knowledge of the paths of heavenly bodies, wind direction, and sea and current movement.

Nothing remains of the boats that were used to make these fascinating voyages. We have to make do with descriptions given by 18th century Europeans of *va'a* (canoes) that were in use at the time of their arrival. During the Cook period, three types of boats were used: simple monohulls, monohulls with outrigger (float), and double canoes (two canoes firmly joined by a large platform). Monohulls were always paddled, while *pirogues* (outrigger canoes) and double canoes could be driven by sail or paddle, or both. All materials in the canoes and woven sails were of plant origin, and construction tools were of stone, shell or bone.

Each type of canoe had a precise role. The smallest monohulls (5 to 10m long), either with or without an outrigger, were paddled over short journeys and used for lagoon fishing. Somewhat larger pirogues (10 to 15m) were sailed on short inter-island trips. The longest paddle-driven single canoes (often 30m long) could carry well over 100 people and were used in battle or for ceremonies. Double canoes, forerunners of the catamaran, had two parallel hulls fused together by cross beams or platforms into an integral structure. They could carry up to 70 people and were used for long migration journeys – on the connecting platform could be carried the plants, seeds and animals (chickens, pigs and dogs) needed to colonise the new land.

Nowadays the canoe is still highly valued symbolically even though it is often made of synthetic materials. It naturally appears as the centrepiece of the French Polynesian flag with five figurines on board, each one representing one of the archipelagos. A major yearly sporting event in French Polynesia is the Hawaiki Nui canoe race, at the beginning of November, in which there are several hundred participants (see the boxed text 'Hawaiki Nui Canoe Race' in the Facts for the Visitor chapter).

they moved on to Fiji, Tonga and Samoa around 1000 BC.

A millennium passed before the next great migration wave, which moved east from around the start of the Christian era to 600 AD. This wave of voyages landed on both what are known as the Society and Marquesas islands in modern-day French Polynesia. Again there was a pause before the next migratory movement, which headed in all directions: south-west to Rarotonga and the southern Cook Islands, south-east to Easter Island (300 AD), north to Hawaii (400 AD) and south-west past Rarotonga to New Zealand (900 AD).

These long voyages were phenomenal feats of navigation and endurance. The coconuts, *uru* (breadfruit), taro, sugar cane, dogs, pigs and chickens carried on the great canoes all originated in South-East Asia.

The Polynesian triangle has its points at Hawaii, Easter Island and New Zealand. Within this immense area, the people of French Polynesia, native Hawaiians and the Maori of New Zealand and the Cook Islands all come from common Marquesan and Society ancestors, and all speak very similar languages, known collectively as Maohi.

European Exploration

The idea that a place did not exist until 'discovered', and preferably named, by a European visitor has been thoroughly discredited in recent decades. Nevertheless the story of the early European explorers and their daring visits to the Pacific is a fascinating one. Finding islands in the Pacific was a needle-in-a-haystack operation, and the navigational instruments were so primitive that, having chanced upon an island, it was equally problematic to locate it on a return trip.

Magellan Vasco Núñez de Balboa was the first European to set eyes on the Pacific, but just seven years later, in 1520, Ferdinand Magellan was the first European to actually sail across the vast island-dotted ocean. Sprinkled with islands the Pacific may be, but Magellan managed to miss nearly all of them. The Philippines was his main find and he also came across Guam,

but his one sighting in Polynesia was remote Puka Puka, the farthest north-east of the Tuamotus.

Mendaña & Quirós Magellan was Portuguese, but in the service of the Spanish, and it was Spanish expeditions that made the next major forays into the Pacific. From Acapulco, their Mexican Pacific coast port, the Spanish established trade with Manila. In 1567, Alvaro de Mendaña de Neira set out from Acapulco to search for the Great Southern Continent that was to be the holy grail of European exploration for the next two centuries. He came across the Solomons on that first voyage and in 1595 set out on a return trip. This time he was not able to locate them, but en route he came upon the farthest north-east of the Polynesian island groups, which he named Las Marquesas de Mendoza after his patron, the Viceroy of Peru. His visit was a bloody affair as Mendaña was of the 'shoot first and ask questions later' school when it came to encounters with 'savages'.

His chief pilot, Quirós, followed with his own expedition in 1606, and discovered a number of the Tuamotus before continuing to the Cooks and other island groups of the Pacific. This, however, was the end of serious Spanish exploration in the Pacific.

Le Maire & Roggeveen The Dutch, already firmly established in the Dutch East Indies (now Indonesia), took up the banner and in 1615-16 Jacques Le Maire sailed through the Tuamotus. Other Dutch explorers started to trace in the boundaries of Australia, New Zealand and other islands of the western Pacific, but it was not until 1722 that the first of the Society islands, the most significant group in modern French Polynesia, was sighted. Jacob Roggeveen came to Easter Island during Easter of that year and continued west through the Tuamotus, passing the island of Makatea on his way to the Society Islands, where he came across Maupiti, the most westerly of the group's high islands. Since other islands of the group are clearly visible from Maupiti and the Maupitians were well aware of their existence, it's a mystery why Roggeveen did not 'discover' other islands as well.

Byron, Carteret & Wallis The Dutch were followed by the British, led in 1765 by John Byron, an English admiral and grandfather of the poet. Byron found more of the Tuamotus. He was followed in 1767 by the expedition of Philip Carteret, in command of HMS *Swallow*, and Samuel Wallis, in HMS *Dolphin*. As they rounded Cape Horn, they lost contact, so the small fleet became two separate expeditions both searching for the great southern continent. Carteret found Pitcairn Island, later to be the refuge of the *Bounty* mutineers, and went on to rediscover Mendaña's long lost Solomons. But Wallis was to carry the real prize home when he became the first European to visit Tahiti.

The *Dolphin* anchored at Matavai Bay in Tahiti's lagoon in late June, but a quarter of the crew were down with scurvy and poor Wallis was incapacitated below decks during most of his visit. Initially their arrival was greeted with fascination as up to 500 canoes with 4000 men on board surrounded the ship, not to mention many canoes each carrying 'a fair young girl ... who played a great many droll wanton tricks.' Then fascination turned to fear and an attack was launched on the *Dolphin*. Stones rained down upon the ship's crew and when the Tahitians made an attempt to board the vessel, the *Dolphin's* cannons, loaded with deadly grapeshot, were turned upon them. Two days later the havoc was followed by a further fusillade, on this occasion unprovoked, and a British raiding party went ashore and destroyed 80 canoes.

Surprisingly, this violent show of force did not turn the Tahitians against the explorers and from then on a friendly trade was carried on each day. The crew were desperate for fresh supplies and the Tahitians, who had not yet discovered metals, were delighted to receive knives, hatchets and nails in exchange. At this point the *Dolphin's* crew also took the first steps towards creating the long-lasting image of Tahiti as a sexual paradise, when they discovered a

single nail would buy sex just as readily as it would buy a pig.

Wallis only stayed in Matavai Bay for a few weeks and his short visit was soon forgotten when two much better-known explorers arrived on the Tahitian scene. Wallis did, however, move on from exploration to empire-building when he renamed the island King George's Land and claimed it for Britain.

Bougainville With his ships *La Boudeuse* and *L'Etoile*, Louis-Antoine de Bougainville, the first great French Pacific explorer, arrived at Tahiti in April 1768, less than a year after Wallis. At this time Wallis was still homeward bound, so Bougainville had no idea that he was not the first European to set eyes on the island. His visit was for only nine days but Bougainville was a more cultured and observant man than Wallis. It was Bougainville who coined the expression 'noble savage' and he who inspired Jean-Jacques Rousseau's vision of a new earthly paradise.

Bougainville had no unfriendly clashes with the Tahitian locals, in fact quite the reverse. Perhaps it was Bougainville's rather cultured outlook on life, but he did not complain of 'droll wanton tricks' by half-naked nymphs. In fact, he wryly noted, the Tahitians 'pressed us to choose a woman and come on shore with her; and their gestures, which were not ambiguous, denoted in what manner we should form an acquaintance with her'.

When he returned to Europe, his reports of Venus-like women with 'the celestial form of that goddess', and of the Tahitians' uninhibited attitude towards matters sexual, swept through Paris like wildfire.

Bougainville also discovered a less attractive side to the Tahitian character: they were expert thieves. A year later, James Cook's expedition was also to suffer from these skilful pickpockets, who quickly carried off anything not closely watched. In part, this proclivity to theft was simply a different attitude towards private property, but equally it may have been due to the fact that one of the most enduring figures

FRENCH POLYNESIA

The Tuamotus

- **Rangiroa:** Dive with the sharks in the passes or discover the lagoon on a boat excursion

- **Manihi:** Enter the mysterious world of black pearl culture at a pearl farm

- **Fakarava:** Live like Robinson Crusoe on a remote motu

0   200   400 km

THE TUAMOTUS

THE SOCIETY ISLANDS

Leeward Islands

Bellingshausen

Scilly

Mopelia

Tupai
Bora Bora
Maupiti
Tahaa
Huahine
Raiatea
Malao
Moorea
PAPEETE
Tetiaroa
Windward Islands
Mehetia
TAHITI

Manihi
Ahe
Takaroa
Takapoto
Mataiva
Tikehau
Tikei
Arutua
Apataki
Aratika
Rangiroa
Kaukura
Kauehi
Toau
Taiaro
Makatea
Niau
Raraka
Fakarava
Katiu
Faaite
Tahanea
Anaa
Motutunga

The Society Islands

- **Papeete:** Experience the lively market and waterfront

- **Tahiti:** Cross the mountainous interior by 4WD, enjoy the tranquil atmosphere of Tahiti Iti and study the Museum of Tahiti & Its Islands

- **Tetiaroa:** Visit Marlon Brando's island with its bird sanctuary

- **Moorea:** Marvel at the magnificent Cook's and Opunohu bays and dive with rays and sharks

- **Huahine:** Admire the Maeva archaeological site and bask on the beaches of the south coast

- **Raiatea:** Examine the important Marae Taputapuatea and walk on Mt Temehani

- **Bora Bora:** Discover the most beautiful lagoon in the world on a pirogue excursion

Hereheretue

THE AUSTRALS

Rimatara

Rurutu

SOUTH
PACIFIC
OCEAN

Tubuai

Tropic of Capricorn

Raivavae

The Australs

- **Rurutu:** Swim with the whales or visit a limestone cave

- **Raivavae:** Enjoy the most beautiful beaches in the archipelago

Rapa

To Rapa
(420km)

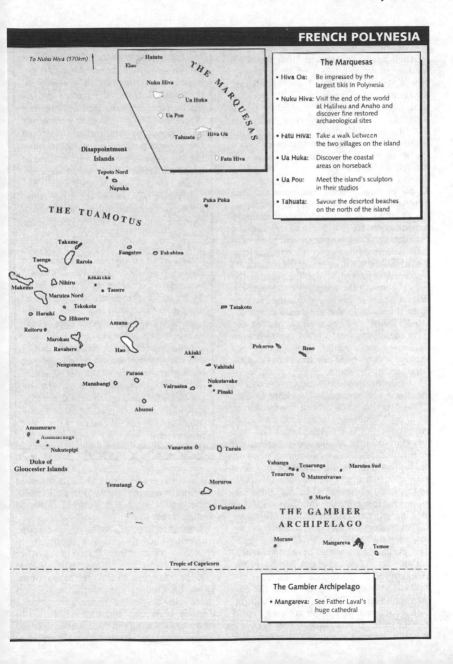

FRENCH POLYNESIA

To Nuku Hiva (170km)

Hatutu
Eiao

THE MARQUESAS

Nuku Hiva

Ua Huka

Ua Pou

Tahuata   Hiva Oa

Disappointment
Islands

Fatu Hiva

Tepoto Nord

Napuka

Puka Puka

THE TUAMOTUS

Takume

Fangatau   Fakahina

Taenga   Raroia

Kauehi

Makemo   Nihiru

Marutea Nord   Tauere

Tekokota

Haraiki   Hikueru

Reitoru   Amanu

Marokau

Ravahere   Hao   Akiaki

Pukarua   Reao

Nengonengo   Vahitahi

Paraoa

Manuhangi   Vairaatea   Nukutavake
Pinaki

Ahunui

Anuanuraro

Anuanurunga

Nukutepipi

Vanavana   Tureia

Duke of
Gloucester Islands

Vahanga   Tenarunga   Marutea Sud
Tenararo   Matureivavao

Tematangi   Moruroa

Maria

Fangataufa

THE GAMBIER
ARCHIPELAGO

Morane

Mangareva   Temoe

Tropic of Capricorn

The Marquesas

- **Hiva Oa:** Be impressed by the largest tikis in Polynesia

- **Nuku Hiva:** Visit the end of the world at Hatiheu and Anaho and discover fine restored archaeological sites

- **Fatu Hiva:** Take a walk between the two villages on the island

- **Ua Huka:** Discover the coastal areas on horseback

- **Ua Pou:** Meet the island's sculptors in their studios

- **Tahuata:** Savour the deserted beaches on the north of the island

The Gambier Archipelago

- **Mangareva:** See Father Laval's huge cathedral

of the Polynesian religion was Hiro, the god of thieves.

Anchorage problems at Bougainville's landing place, well east of Matavai Bay where Wallis, and later Cook and Bligh, all anchored, cut short his visit. Unaware that the Union Jack had already flown over the island, Bougainville took time out to claim Tahiti for France but, like Wallis, he was soon overshadowed when the greatest Pacific explorer of them all arrived on the scene.

Cook In three great expeditions between 1769 and 1779, Cook filled out the map of the Pacific so comprehensively that future expeditions were reduced to completing the fine details. Cook had been sent to the Pacific with two great tasks. One was for the Royal Society, to observe the transit of Venus as it passed across the face of the sun. By timing the transit from three very distant places it was hoped that the distance from the earth to the sun could be calculated. Tahiti was selected as one of the three measuring points (the other two were in Norway and Canada). Cook's second objective was to hunt for the elusive great continent of the south.

The instruments of the time proved to be insufficiently accurate to achieve Cook's first objective and, of course, the Great Southern Continent was never to be found, but otherwise Cook's arrival on Tahiti was the start of one of the most impressive scientific expeditions of all time. Cook was the perfect man for the task, an expert seaman, a brilliant navigator, a keen observer, an inspiring leader and an indefatigable explorer. Furthermore he was ably supported by endlessly enthusiastic and inquisitive associates, most notably the wealthy young Joseph Banks. As a result Cook's expedition brought the wonders of not only Tahiti, but also New Zealand and Australia, home to an appreciative European audience.

Cook arrived at Tahiti on board the *Endeavour* in April 1769 and stayed for three months before sailing south to New Zealand and Australia. If Bougainville brought back a poet's view of paradise, the pragmatic

The Island of Love

The first European visitors to Tahiti brought back descriptions of beautiful islands populated by a handsome people who were superb navigators. But the part of the tale that really intrigued London and Paris was simple: sex. The official report from Wallis' *Dolphin* was dull and matter-of-fact, but below-decks gossip was already constructing the great Tahitian dream: an island of beautiful women and handsome men, where love was unconstrained.

If Wallis was uncommunicative, Bougainville compensated with his tales of a New Cytheria and Dr Commerçon's gushing avowals that the Tahitians knew 'no other god than love'. Cook was less florid, but his prosaic reports confirmed suspicions about Tahiti, where young girls would 'dance a very indecent dance' while 'singing most indecent songs' all the while 'keeping time to a great nicety'. Furthermore they enjoyed recounting 'the most indecent ideas in conversation without the least emotion'.

Sex, it would appear, was simply part of everyday Tahitian life, to be enjoyed just like a good meal. However, visiting sailors began buying sex with nails (coveted by the locals for making fish hooks), thereby jumping the gap to prostitution and contributing to the rapid decline of the Polynesian culture.

Cook with his scientists and artists surveyed the flora and fauna and described traditional society and Polynesian customs in words and pictures.

Cook's comprehensive survey of the Australian east coast ended in a disastrous encounter with the Great Barrier Reef. After emergency repairs, the *Endeavour* limped into Batavia (now Jakarta), the capital of the Dutch East Indies. The enforced stop for repairs in the desperately unhealthy city was a disaster – dysentery and malaria killed seven of the crew during the three-month stop and 23 more died on the way home. Nevertheless the voyage was considered a resounding success and Cook returned to Tahiti during a second expedition in 1772-75 and a third in 1776-80. Cook was killed during a clash with Hawaiians in early 1779.

Boenechea The Spanish, firmly established in South America, looked upon the Pacific as their backyard and were less than happy to hear of the visits to Tahiti by other European navigators. In 1772 the *Aguilla*, under Don Domingo de Boenechea, sailed from Peru, anchored in the lagoon off Tautira on Tahiti Iti and, for the third time, the island was claimed by a European nation. Boenechea took four Tahitians back with him to Lima for a short indoctrination course, but while he was away Cook returned on his 1774 visit and this time also paused off Tautira. Boenechea came back later in the year with two of the four Tahitians. (One had died in Lima and one opted to remain there.) Boenechea established Tautira as the first long-term European settlement on the island with two missionaries and two military men. He died on Tahiti during the course of his second visit.

Twelve months later, in 1775, the *Aguilla* returned from Peru. The Spanish missionaries, who had been spectacularly unsuccessful at converting the heathen, were more than happy to scuttle back to Peru. Thus ended the Spanish role on Tahiti, and Cook had the last word. At Tautira in 1777 he found a Spanish cross in front of the abandoned mission house, carved with the 1774 year of its establishment. On the back of the cross Cook added the far more impressive list of Tahitian visits by his own and Wallis' expeditions.

The Mutiny on the *Bounty*

After 1779 there was a pause of nearly 10 years before Europeans returned to Tahiti. It was an important break because it marked the transition from exploration to the first phase of exploitation. Perhaps the first whaling ship turned up during this time but the next recorded visit to Tahiti took place in 1788, when the *Lady Penrhyn*, part of the First Fleet carting convicts

to Botany Bay (Australia), dropped in to Tahiti on its way home. Quite why it stopped there is a mystery – the entire crew was in the final throes of scurvy but perhaps they were simply the first tourists? They didn't stay long and no sooner had they sailed off than a boat that was to be much more famous turned up.

European involvement in Tahiti's history has had some colourful chapters but none more so than the *Bounty* incident. It made HMS *Bounty* one of the most famous ships in history, made William Bligh's name a byword for bad-tempered cruelty and was certainly the most famous naval mutiny in history. It also inspired three Hollywood extravaganzas, almost the sum total of cinematic interest in Tahiti.

Separating myth and reality when it comes to the *Bounty* and Bligh is nearly impossible. Some of the facts are fairly simple. Food was needed to sustain the African slaves working the profitable plantations of the Caribbean. Someone had the bright idea that the breadfruit of Polynesia would make a fine substitute for bread, rice, bananas and any other starch food you care to mention. Sir Joseph Banks, botanist on Cook's first expedition and then Britain's number one man of science, agreed that breadfruit was the ideal plant, and Bligh was sent off to convey it from Tahiti to the Caribbean. He was perfectly qualified for the job, an expert navigator who had learnt his trade under Cook and had already visited Tahiti once.

His expedition started late in 1787. He found it impossible to round stormy Cape Horn and had to double back and sail right around the world eastbound to Tahiti. As a result the *Bounty* arrived at Tahiti, after an arduous 10-month voyage, at a time when breadfruit-tree saplings could not be immediately transplanted. This meant they had to remain on Tahiti for six long, languorous months. Eventually, with the breadfruit trees loaded on board, the *Bounty* set sail, westbound, for the Caribbean. Three weeks later, on 28 April 1789, when passing by Tonga, the crew, led by the mate, Fletcher Christian, mutinied and took over the ship.

Bligh was pushed on to the *Bounty's* launch with 18 faithful crew members and set adrift. That might have been the end of Bligh, but whatever the controversy about his management style nobody has ever denied that he was a champion navigator and sailor. With consummate skill he sailed his overloaded little boat across the Pacific and past islands inhabited by hostile cannibals, threaded it through the dangerous complexities of the Great Barrier Reef and through Torres Strait, rounded the north-east coast of Australia and eventually made landfall in Dutch-controlled Timor after a 41 day, 5823km voyage that was promptly written into the record books.

By early 1790 Bligh was back in England; an inquiry quickly cleared him of negligence and a ship was despatched to carry British naval vengeance to Tahiti. Christian and his mutineers had not meekly waited for justice to catch up. After dumping Bligh in late April, the *Bounty* returned to Tahiti and hung around for less than a month before sailing off to find a more remote hideaway. Two attempts were made to settle on Tubuai in the Australs. After the second Tubuai interlude had ended without success, Christian returned briefly to Tahiti, where the mutineers split into two groups. A larger group remained there while a smaller group left with Christian and the *Bounty* in late September and simply ... disappeared.

So what happened to the two bands of mutineers? Well, the 16 who remained on Tahiti met exactly the fate Christian had predicted. Vengeance arrived in 1791 in the shape of HMS *Pandora*. Captain Edward Edwards, who made Bligh look like a thoroughly nice guy, quickly rounded up the 14 surviving mutineers (two had already been killed in disputes) and told the men's new Tahitian wives they were going back to Britain to get their just desserts. They then stuffed the mutineers into a cage on deck to travel home in considerable discomfort. Arriving at the Great Barrier Reef, Edwards proved to be nowhere near the navigational equal of Bligh and sent his ship to the bottom on Pandora's Reef. Four of the mutineers went with it, as the key to 'Pandora's Box' was only 'found' at the last moment. Back in Britain the surviving 10 mutineers were put on trial. Six of them were eventually sentenced to death but three were reprieved. Some of these 'mutineers' probably had no part in the mutiny as Bligh's overloaded getaway boat was close to foundering with 19 men aboard, and there were probably other crew who would have followed their captain had there been room.

As for Christian, he led eight British seamen, together with six male and 12 female Tahitians and one child, all the way to uninhabited Pitcairn Island, from where, many years later, reports trickled back of a strange little English-Tahitian colony, where half the residents bore the surname Christian. Today, thanks to Fletcher Christian's mutiny, Pitcairn Island is one of the last vestiges of the British Empire.

Bligh himself was back on Tahiti in 1792, this time in command of HMS *Providence* and with 19 marines to make sure there was no possibility of similar problems second time round. Bligh duly picked up his breadfruit saplings and transported them in record time to the Caribbean. Of course the ungrateful slaves never developed a taste for the fruit.

Surprisingly, given all the trouble spent trying to take breadfruit to a new home, Bligh's voyages did manage to successfully transfer two other plants to a much more appreciative audience. On his first voyage he picked up pineapples in Rio de Janiero and introduced them to Tahiti, where they remain popular to this day. On his second voyage he brought the apple to Tasmania, which even today is known as Australia's 'Apple Isle'.

The Mutineers & the Pomares

The effects on Tahiti of the *Bounty* mutiny lasted long after the mutineers had been rounded up and carted back to England. Prior to the arrival of Europeans, Polynesian power had essentially been a local affair. Certainly the war-like rulers of Bora Bora, propelled by their lack of arable land, frequently sailed off to wreak havoc on neighbouring Raiatea, but essentially no ruler was strong enough to extend control very far. Tahiti was in fact divided into a number of squabbling groups, who, when they tired of fighting with each other, sailed off to take on Moorea. European arms soon changed all this.

The Tahitians quickly realised the importance of European weaponry and pressed the early explorers to take sides in local conflicts. Cook and others had strenuously resisted this, but to the *Bounty* mutineers it was a different proposition. They offered themselves as mercenaries to the highest bidder, and the highest bidders were the Pomares, one of a number of important family power centres, but by no means the most important and certainly not the most prestigious.

The first of the Pomare dynasty, Pomare I, was Tu, the nephew of Obarea, the 'fat, bouncing, good looking dame' who befriended Wallis, Cook and particularly Banks and whom the early explorers thought was the 'queen' of Tahiti.

The mutineers and their weapons were the first step towards one group controlling all of Tahiti and the Pomares were destined to become the most important rulers of the islands. Pomare I already controlled most of Tahiti when he died in 1803, and his son, Pomare II, took over.

Missionaries, Whalers & Traders

The early explorers were portents of the dangers to come and the mutineers were a murderous, but brief, revelation of the impact of European technology. But the real disaster arrived in the early 19th century in the form of missionaries and traders. The double-pronged attack was insidious, and for the Polynesians it proved to be utterly disastrous.

Descriptions of Tahiti and its people had European intellectuals speculating on theories of the noble savage, but before long devout church-goers were planning to do something about the savages, noble or not. Thirty members of the London Missionary Society (LMS) set out on the *Duff* to bring Christianity to the Pacific. In March 1797, 25 of them landed at Point Venus and set to

work. Their eventual success is evident in the Protestant churches that dot islands throughout the Society group, the Tuamotus and the Australs.

Success, however, was not immediate and within a few years most of the original missionaries had drifted off. Pomare II fell from power in 1808 and the remaining Tahitian missionaries, too closely associated with him to be safe, also had to flee the island. Pomare II took refuge on Moorea and when he returned to power on Tahiti in 1815, Christianity came too.

The missionaries may have had the best intentions, but the effects were often disastrous and the new beliefs killed off the old ones. Soon dancing was forbidden, singing indecent songs was certainly out, tattoos – and even wearing flowers in the hair – were banned, cover-all clothing was decreed, silence on Sunday was enforced and, most importantly, indiscriminate sex was outlawed. A century later, the English writer Robert Keable, who had been a vicar with the Church of England, commented about the pioneering missionary William Ellis that: 'it was a thousand pities that the Tahitians did not convert Mr Ellis'.

Whalers started to appear in Polynesian waters in the 1790s, even before the first missionaries arrived. Sailing from England, and later from the New England region of the newly independent USA, and crewed by uncompromisingly tough men, they hunted whales in southern waters during the summer months, then retreated to islands like Tahiti during the winter, escaping their harsh shipboard life, buying supplies, introducing alcohol and spreading diseases. Traders also started to appear from the convict colonies in Australia, exchanging weapons for food supplies, encouraging prostitution, and establishing stills to produce alcohol.

Listless, disinterested and plagued by diseases against which it had no natural immunity, the population began to plummet. Cook had estimated the population of Tahiti at 200,000, although it's felt that 40,000 was probably a more accurate figure. In 1800 another estimate put the population at less than 20,000 and by the 1820s it was certainly down to around 6000. In the Marquesas the situation was even worse – it has been estimated the population dropped from 80,000 to only 2000 in one century.

The Pomares & the Missionaries

After 1815 the Pomares ruled Tahiti but the English Protestant missionaries were the power behind the throne, advising on government and laws and doing their best to keep unsavoury influences, like whalers and Australian traders, at arm's length. Pomare II extended his power over the Leeward Islands in 1815 at the time of the Battle of Fei Pi, when he forced the traditionally hostile chiefs to form a Christian alliance. The Code of Pomare was instituted in 1819, but Pomare II had adopted Christianity more as a convenience than a real belief, and probably drank himself to death, in 1821. In 1827, his

The Reign of the Pomares	
King Pomare I	ruled to 1803
King Pomare II	1803-21
King Pomare III	1821-27
Queen Pomare IV	1827-77
King Pomare V	1877-91

son Pomare III also died and was succeeded by the young Queen Pomare IV.

The new queen's missionary advisers saw her only as an interim ruler until the next king and as a result they turned a blind eye to some of her youthful excesses. The new queen was not averse to a little singing and dancing of the old premissionary-day flavour, and even visiting passing ships was not unknown. But Queen Pomare was not a passing fancy; she ruled over Tahiti for 50 years, extended her control to other islands in the Austral group and forged strategic alliances with other islands in the Society group. Unhappily, she also lived to see her islands fall into the hands of the French.

Perhaps it was Tahiti's very isolation that was the problem. Spain's era as a colonial power had ended and the British had their hands full with Australia, New Zealand and other assorted islands in the Pacific. Places like Tahiti were simply in a vacuum, waiting to suck in some would-be colonial power. The missionaries were effectively that colonial power; the LMS missions reigned supreme in the Societies, the Australs and the Tuamotus, while French Catholic missionaries were in control in the Gambier Archipelago from 1834 and the Marquesas from 1838.

In 1836, Father Honoré Laval and François Caret, French missionaries from the Gambier Archipelago, were quietly dropped off near Tautira at the eastern extremity of Tahiti Iti (see the Gambier chapter for more on their extraordinary activities). The reason for this clandestine landing at a remote backwater was very simple: they knew the last people the English Protestants wanted on Tahiti were French Catholics. Sure enough, when they arrived in Papeete they were arrested and deported.

The long-serving Queen Pomare IV (1827-77) was the last to rule an independent Tahiti.

The French Takeover

France was already effectively in control of the Marquesas, and the enforced departure of the two French missionaries from Tahiti was treated as a national insult. Demands, claims, counterclaims, payments and apologies shuttled back and forth until 1842, when Admiral Dupetit-Thouars turned up in the ship *La Reine Blanche*, pointed his guns at Papeete and took over. The unhappy Tahitian queen was forced to yield to the French, and soldiers and Catholic missionaries were promptly landed.

The French moved quickly and George Pritchard, the British missionary, consul and unofficial chief adviser to the queen, was arrested and forced to leave the islands. The queen, still hoping for British intervention, fled to Raiatea in 1844 and a guerrilla rebellion broke out on Tahiti and other islands. French forts around Tahiti confirm that it was a fierce struggle, but eventually the rebels were subdued, and by 1846 France had control over Tahiti and Moorea. In 1847 the queen was persuaded to return to Tahiti, but she was now merely a figurehead.

Queen Pomare died in 1877 and was succeeded by her son, Pomare V. He had little interest in the position, effectively abdicating power in 1881, and drank himself to death in 1891. French power did not initially extend to all the Society islands, which remained with local rulers and their mission advisers. Most of them came under French control in 1888, although rebellions rumbled on in Raiatea until almost the end of the century. The Gambier was annexed in 1881 and the Australs in 1900-01. In 1903 the five archipelagos officially took the name Établissements Français d'Océanie (ÉFO).

Still, it's possible the Protestant missionaries had the last laugh; Catholicism has never made serious inroads on the islands originally converted by the Protestants.

20th Century & Beyond

The foundations of the colonial system, laid during the 19th century, were consolidated at the turn of the 20th century. At the outbreak of WWI, the economy was flourishing and local products like vanilla, cotton, copra, mother-of-pearl and fruit were exported in exchange for manufactured goods. This rapid economic and commercial expansion required a larger workforce than was locally available, and colonists, the majority of them French, settled in Polynesia. In 1911, there were about 3500 Europeans in the ÉFO. Chinese immigration, which began in 1864 with the production of cotton at Atimaona, continued, and the foundations of a multiethnic society were in place.

The island of Makatea was exploited for its phosphate deposits from 1911 until the supplies were exhausted in 1966 (see the 'Makatea' boxed text in the Australs chapter).

Although removed from the main theatres of operation, Polynesia was directly involved in both world wars. In WWI, almost 1000 Tahitian soldiers fought in Europe, and on 22 September 1914, two German cruisers patrolling the Pacific sank the French cruiser *Zélée* and shelled Papeete Market.

Polynesia acquired strategic significance in WWII with the entry of the USA into the war in December 1941. To thwart the Japanese advance in the Pacific, the Americans used Bora Bora as a supply base. Five thousand soldiers set foot on the island in February 1942 and completed a 2000m-long runway in April 1943. At the same time, young Tahitian and half-Tahitian (mixed race) volunteers in the Pacific Battalion fought from April 1941 with the forces of the Free French in North Africa, Italy and France.

In 1946 the ÉFO became an overseas territory within the French Republic but the first signs of a push for emancipation from France also took shape. A political party, the Democratic Assembly of Tahitian Populations (RDPT), founded in 1949 by nationalist Pouvanaa a Oopa, took centre stage on the political scene for about 10 years (see the boxed text 'Pouvanaa a Oopa – a Tahitian Leader' in the Huahine chapter).

The 1960s were a real turning point. Three events in quick succession had a considerable impact on Polynesian society. On 22 July 1957, the ÉFO officially became French Polynesia. In the September 1958 referendum, 65% of Polynesians demonstrated their wish to remain linked to

French Nuclear Testing

French nuclear testing started in the Sahara desert, but Algerian independence forced France to look for a new testing site. In 1963 it was announced that Moruroa and Fangataufa, atolls in the Tuamotus, were to be the lucky sites, and testing commenced with atmospheric nuclear explosions in 1966. The Centre d'Expérimentations du Pacifique (CEP), the euphemistic name for the nuclear-testing program, soon became a major component of the French Polynesian economy.

In 1963 the USA, USSR and Britain agreed to stop patently unsafe atmospheric testing (although they continued testing underground), but in 1973 France refused a World Court request to halt above-ground testing. In that year the New Zealand government sent a naval ship to Moruroa in protest, the first Greenpeace protest vessels were boarded by French forces, and Peru broke off diplomatic relations with France.

In 1981, in the face of continuing international opposition to all forms of nuclear testing, the French drilled bomb shafts under the central lagoon rather than on *motu* (islets) around the reef edge, and moved the tests underground.

International and local opposition to nuclear testing in the Pacific has grown stronger and stronger over the years. In 1985 French commandos, in what can only be called a terrorist operation, sank the Greenpeace ship *Rainbow Warrior* in Auckland harbour, New Zealand, killing a Portuguese photographer on board. Dominique Prieur and Alain Mafart, two of the terrorists, were captured, tried and sentenced to 10 years' imprisonment on reduced charges of manslaughter. The French government pressured New Zealand to allow Prieur and Mafart to be transferred to serve reduced sentences on the island of Hao in the Tuamotus. France soon reneged on the agreement, the Club Med-style prison sentence was ended, and the two were returned to France to be rewarded for their parts in the fiasco.

In 1995, French president Jacques Chirac announced a new series of underground tests, and a storm of protest broke out worldwide. Pacific and Pacific-rim nations uniformly condemned the announcement and Greenpeace vessels were once again sent into the fray. The first test was conducted in September and in another round of international protests, Chile and New Zealand recalled their ambassadors from Paris. Severe rioting broke out in Papeete, but in Europe, far from the strong antinuclear sentiment in the Pacific and around the Pacific rim, the French government turned a deaf ear. The tests were finally concluded in early 1996 and it was announced there would be no further testing in the Pacific.

The French government has consistently denied that the tests have posed any ecological threat. In 1998 it admitted that plutonium had leaked into Moruroa's lagoon; at a press conference on Tahiti in May 1999, the director of France's Atomic Energy Commission admitted, for the first time, the existence of cracks in the coral cones of Moruroa and Fangataufa. French officials maintain that there's no cause for concern and, as international observers have never been permitted to inspect large parts of the sites, ask that we take their word for it.

France. In 1961, the construction of Faaa international airport helped to make Polynesia less of an enclave. Shortly after, the filming of the superproduction *Mutiny on the Bounty* with Marlon Brando called on thousands of extras and poured millions of dollars into the island's booming economy.

In 1963, with the establishment of the Centre d'Experimentations du Pacifique (CEP) at Moruroa and Fangataufa, Polynesia came straight into the nuclear age (See the boxed text).

In addition to the international controversy raised by these 'experiments' – violent protests shook Papeete in 1987 and 1995 – the CEP totally overturned the socioeconomic structures of Polynesia, thrusting it straight into a market economy. In 1993 France agreed to continue its aid until 2005, but the final end to nuclear testing in February 1996 sounded the death knell for the artificial prosperity of the previous 30 years.

In two stages, in 1977 and 1984, French Polynesia took over internal management and autonomy and these powers were widened and reinforced in 1990 and 1996. Independence is still a future possibility but it would bring with it great social and economic challenges.

GEOGRAPHY

French Polynesia is 6000km west of Chile, 5200km east of Australia, 6500km south-west of the Californian coast and 15,700km from Paris, to the east of the International Date Line. The nearest islands to the west are the Cooks, 900km away, while solitary Easter Island is the nearest land to the east. The 118 islands, only six of them larger than 100 sq km, are scattered over a vast expanse of ocean stretching more than 2000km from Hatutu in the north to Rapa in the south. In European terms they would occupy a quadrilateral marked by Stockholm, London, Madrid and Bucharest.

French Polynesia is divided into five archipelagos with a total land area of barely 3500 sq km, not even half that of the French Mediterranean island of Corsica. The Society group, the farthest west, is subdivided into the Windward and Leeward islands and is home to over three-quarters of the population. The administrative capital of Polynesia, Papeete, is on Tahiti (1043 sq km), which also has the Territory's highest point, Mt Orohena (2241m). The Tuamotus, between Tahiti and the Marquesas, consists of 77 atolls and, stretches more than 1500km north-west to south-east and more than 500km east to west. The Marquesas, 1400km north-east of Tahiti and not far from the equator, comprises about 15 islands and islets, six of which are inhabited. The Australs straddles the Tropic of Capricorn. It consists of five high islands and an atoll, each a great distance from the others and lying between 575 and 1275km south of Tahiti. Finally the tiny Gambier Archipelago, 1600km from Tahiti, is an appendage to the south-east continuation of the Tuamotus.

GEOLOGY

The islands of French Polynesia are all the result of volcanic activity but they can be subdivided into high islands and atolls:

High Islands

These are mainly found in the Society, Austral and Marquesas archipelagos. They are essentially mountains rising above the surface of the ocean, often surrounded by a coral ring that forms a barrier reef. Between the barrier reef and the island proper is the lagoon, a sort of shallow buffer zone with a gentle aquatic environment where the calm turquoise waters contrast with the darker blue of the ocean. The Marquesas are a consistent exception – they have no barrier reef and no lagoon.

The reefs are often pierced by passes: openings that allow water to flow between the lagoon and ocean and, if they are wide and deep enough, permit boats to go back and forth. The high islands often have impressive calderas (ancient volcano craters), sharp peaks and knife-edged ridges, even plateaus. These rugged interiors are rarely populated; the urban centres are almost always along the coast. Some coastlines are smooth and regular, some cut by deep and magnificent bays.

Atolls

Atolls are the chronological continuation of high islands and are particularly common in the Tuamotus. Varying in shape and size, they are ring-shaped coral reefs emerging above the surface of the water and surrounding a lagoon. They can be any shape from circular to neatly rectangular, and vary from 70km in length to just 4km across.

The strips of land formed around the reef, made of coral debris and calcareous substances, can reach a height of 3 to 6m and are usually covered in bushes and coconut palms. The ring is generally, but not always,

High Islands to Atolls

From a fixed point in the asthenosphere, called a hot spot, a rising column of magma produces an oceanic volcano or, if the eruption is not sufficiently violent to rise above the surface of the ocean, a seamount (underwater mountain). In accordance with plate tectonics, the newly formed island drifts westwards at an average rate of 10cm a year. The stationary hot spot meanwhile continues to erupt periodically and another island is formed and in turn moves westwards and so on. The result is a string of islands positioned on the same axis and stretching from south-east to north-west.

As an island drifts to the north-west, it sinks about 1cm a year (subsidence). Other geological processes are also at work: as soon as the volcano is extinct, the vent through which the magma was expelled is no longer fed and therefore empties. Under the weight of the lava accumulated on top, it collapses and fills in, creating a huge basin (caldera), which may be several kilometres in diameter. Erosion continues to shape its relief, and water courses cut into the caldera and form valleys.

Clear, warm waters allow coral constructions to form (from a depth of 70m). The coral grows on the rocky underwater substrata of the island and gradually builds up a fringing reef adjoining the island. As the island erodes, the coral continues to grow, seeking to stay at the ocean surface to catch the light it needs to live. It then forms a circular crust, known as a barrier reef, around the volcano. Between the fringing reef and the barrier reef is the lagoon, a channel of variable width. Finally the original volcano disappears completely under the water, and only the coral ring remains, encircling the lagoon. The atoll has been created.

Under the combined effect of these geological forces, over several million years the island passes gradually from the high volcanic island stage to the atoll stage. The Society Archipelago perfectly illustrates these different stages of development: Mehetia, near the hot spot, is a young island with no coral reef; Moorea is a high island with a coral reef; Bora Bora is nearly an atoll with a barrier reef; and Scilly is an atoll.

Over time, the atoll continues to break up. If the coral's rate of growth cannot compensate for this sinking, the atoll gradually disappears and dies.

Step 1
A new volcano rises from the sea bed high enough to become an island.

Step 3
As the island erodes and sinks, the coral grows to stay near the water's surface; a lagoon forms between reef and island (eg Bora Bora).

Step 2
The volcano becomes extinct; meanwhile a coral reef forms around its coast (eg Tahiti).

Step 4
The old volcano sinks entirely, leaving a ring of coral to mark the ancient coastline.

broken by channels or passes. Smaller, shallower passages *(hoa)*, connect the lagoon and the ocean only at high tide. The lagoon is often shallow, rarely exceeding 40m in depth. On the ocean side the reefs often fall directly to great depths.

CLIMATE
Seasons & Temperatures

Contrary to the popular ideal, the climate is not always beautiful in French Polynesia. The temperatures may always be pleasant but sunny, clear skies are not guaranteed. Keep in mind that French Polynesia is between the Tropic of Capricorn and the Equator, where the climate is humid and tropical. El Niño can also disrupt the pattern so that some years are nothing like the overall averages.

Although the contrasts are not great, there are two seasons. The summer rainy season runs from November to April with maximum temperatures in February-March (24 to 31°C in March at Faaa on Tahiti). This leads to considerable evaporation over the ocean so that the air is very humid and, there is plenty of cloud cover. Three-quarters of the annual rainfall occurs during this period, generally in the form of brief, violent storms, although torrential rains lasting several days are not uncommon.

The winter dry season lasts from May to October. This is the ideal time to visit, as a vast anticyclone is positioned over the South Pacific. Rain is less frequent, the air is dry and temperatures are slightly cooler (21 to 28°C in August at Faaa).

The difference in temperature between day and night is limited (about 5 to 8°C), with the ocean acting as a thermal regulator. The water temperature is relatively constant throughout the year (between 26 and 29°C). For local weather reports phone ☎ 36 65 08 (96 CFP per minute).

Regional Variations

The climate across the region is far from uniform, with relief and latitude playing a major role in the variances. In the Tuamotus the trade winds are more noticeable due to the low-lying relief and there are, on average,

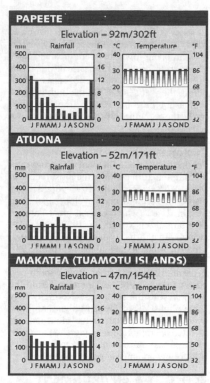

3000 annual hours of sunlight. The Marquesas, close to the Equator, is the driest archipelago in Polynesia. Ua Huka gets barely 600 to 900mm of rain per year. In other archipelagos the rain is concentrated between June and August. The Australs, the southernmost islands, have a high annual rainfall of about 2500mm a year. Winter in the Australs is cool: the mercury can drop to 10°C.

On some islands rainfall can vary with altitude, the exposure to wind and the profile of the valleys. The windward coasts are often wetter, while those sheltered to leeward are drier. Temperatures drop with the altitude and it tends to get hazier as you get closer to the mountain tops, due to the heavier rain.

Prevailing Winds

French Polynesia is subject to trade winds that blow from the north-east sector to the south-east with a force of 40 to 60km/h in all seasons. The *maraamu* (south-east trade wind) is common throughout the dry season and can bring lower temperatures and rain. The *toerau* (north-north-east wind) is often followed by rain and blows occasionally during the wet season. On the high islands, a pleasant morning breeze, the *hupe*, relieves the sometimes suffocating heat of the coastal plain.

Cyclone Risk

Polynesia suffered a litany of disastrous cyclones in the 20th century, the most recent in the 1982-83 season. In 1997-98, El Niño disruptions brought eight cyclones including Martin, Oséa (which caused great damage on Maupiti in November 1997) and Alan (which did enormous damage to Bora Bora, Raiatea, Tahaa and Huahine in April 1998).

In the Pacific, cyclones generally originate in the area between Samoa and the south-east edge of French Polynesia, moving from the north-west to the south-east. Normally they spare almost all of French Polynesia. However, it is assumed that each cyclone that has affected the region formed more to the north-east and that currents and air masses caused it to follow an unusual path.

ECOLOGY & ENVIRONMENT

Atolls and high islands are ecologically fragile places, easily susceptible to damage, and unfortunately French Polynesia has been slow in implementing environmental protection. Because tourism is the region's main resource and it rests squarely on the integrity of the natural heritage, it's fundamentally important. Pollution steadily chips away at that picture of paradise.

Garbage & Wastewater Treatment

Garbage is one of the less appealing aspects of French Polynesia. It's not unusual to see garbage dumps spoiling the natural setting, even right by the lagoon. It's a problem that will not go away.

On Tahiti an incinerator was closed in 1994 because of local complaints, and a carefully planned garbage disposal project

---

An Ecological Curse

Miconia calvescens was introduced in 1937 as an ornamental plant, for its attractive green leaves and crimson sheen. It has, however, overgrown parts of the landscape of Tahiti and Moorea. Highly prolific, it is gradually forcing out the rest of the plant cover. It has been declared a harmful species and is being closely monitored by political and scientific authorities, which are trying to stop the progress of this formidable enemy of biodiversity.

---

for the Taravao area has met the same problem. Garbage pollutes watercourses, which in turn pollute the lagoons. After heavy rain the forceful run-offs on the high islands certainly don't help.

Only Bora Bora has a state-of-the-art sewerage plant that meets all the requirements. In other places, private septic tanks and small sewerage stations are often badly maintained and unreliable, and inevitably the poorly treated outflow ends up in the lagoon. A 1996 survey of swimming areas found that 45% of the places checked on Moorea and 40% of the places on Tahiti were polluted. Coral reefs are especially vulnerable, and the situation is a particular concern in urban areas of Tahiti and the other Leeward islands.

Problems exist on the other archipelagos but are not as great, simply because the populations are so small.

Tourist infrastructure is strictly controlled and has not been a contributor to this problem. Big hotels are built to very strict standards, with their sanitary facilities as part of the basic architectural plan. Blending harmoniously with the landscape is also a major requirement.

Protection of Flora & Fauna

With the exception of Scilly, there are no marine or terrestrial reserves, although several species are protected, notably rays and turtles.

[Continued on page 38]

CIVILISATION & ARCHAEOLOGY

Ancient Polynesian civilisation almost disappeared with the arrival of Christianity and the first Europeans. Nowadays, it has been given the consideration it deserves and has come back into the limelight. Polynesian culture was essentially based on oral tradition, and the only written records of it are the accounts of the first westerners to arrive in French Polynesia. It is mainly through archaeological heritage that visitors can discover the different facets that make up this society.

The sheer overpowering pleasures of the lagoons are enough to occupy most tourists, and it is often by chance that they become aware of the wealth of this heritage. The sites possess nothing like the imposing character of the *moai* (sacred statues) of Easter Island, and their exploitation is, for the time being, limited to restoration works. However, they present a unique opportunity to discover another aspect of Polynesia.

Polynesian Myths

The Polynesians were polytheistic, worshipping various important *atua* (guardian divinities) surrounded by a pantheon of secondary gods. The main gods were Taaroa (God of Creation), Tane (God of Craftsmen) Tu (Man God), Oro (God of War) and Hiro (God of Thieves and Sailors). Gods competed with each other and could be ousted. Moreover, their power was geographically limited – they were not recognised in all the archipelagos. Tane, for instance, was ousted by Taaroa who was in turn replaced by his son Oro, whose cult never extended beyond the limits of the Society Islands. Hiro was worshipped on Raiatea and on Huahine (his finger – or his sexual organ) can be admired as a backdrop to Maroe Bay at Huahine). All these legends were handed down via spoken legends relating the exploits and adventures of the gods.

The image of the gods was symbolised by the *too*, a wooden stick wrapped in plaited coconut fibres and decorated with red feathers.

Social Organisation

Ancient Polynesian society was far removed from the pleasantly sweet and naive description given by the French explorer Bougainville. It was fundamentally aristocratic: an extremely hierarchical and structured caste system governed relationships between members of the communities, which were feudal in nature and organised around chieftaincies. In this heavily ritualised society, the practice of human sacrifice, as offerings to the gods, was commonplace.

Political Authority: the Arii

The *arii* were the high chiefs who held sway over a portion of an island. The rank was hereditary and was passed to the eldest son. Their supremacy and legitimacy were sanctioned by the recital of their genealogy on festival days by the *orero* (orators), whose origin could be traced back to the illustrious god-like ancestor who founded the clan.

The attributes of the arii status and dignity were represented by an adornment comprising the *maro ura* (belt of red feathers), a head-dress, a ceremonial stick and a fan. Deemed to be holy people, they possessed *mana* (supernatural power). The arii controlled the major activities connected with the life of the clan: fishing, harvesting and warfare. Sometimes an island was governed by an *arii rahi* (supreme chief), usually from the dominant clan, who had succeeded in impos-ing his authority upon the other arii.

Spiritual Authority: the Tahua

Also belonging to the aristocracy, the *tahua* (priests) were allied to the arii. In charge of liturgy and the *marae* (traditional temples), these priestly dig-nitaries were assisted by a host of officiating priests including the *haere po* (reciters of oral traditions) and the orero. As trustees of mana, they con-sulted and invoked the gods, practised divination, attended to the obser-vance of rites, pronounced *rahui* (temporary restrictions affecting the consumption of farm produce), and presided over ceremonies.

Pleasures & Festivals: the Arioi

Joined in brotherhood, the *arioi* enjoyed a very special status. They too were holy figures descended from the god Oro, and were connected with the itinerant artist-troubadours whose role it was to entertain Polynesian society with dancing and theatrical shows, sometimes with erotic overtones. Selected from within one or other of the castes for their physique and talent for dancing, arioi went through a long initia-tion period. They were not allowed to have children; infanticide was practised if their wives gave birth, but children who managed to utter a shout before being killed were spared.

The Landowners: the Raatira

Raatira belonged to the middle caste, comparable to the European bourgeoisie at the close of the Middle Ages. Their status was derived from the ownership of land.

The Common People: the Manahune

Manahune was the lowest rank in the social pyramid and grouped together the lower classes. It comprised various subclasses, among them fishermen, servants, farmers, slaves and prisoners of war. The only social advancement possible was to become an arioi. For the benefit of the arii they had to carry out menial duties and produce offerings. It was from this caste that human sacrifices were drawn.

Daily Life
Religion

Refer to Polynesian Myths earlier in this section, and to Archaeological Remains later, for information about ceremonies and places of worship.

War

Battles between clans were frequent. When unable to extend their kingdoms by virtue of an alliance by marriage, the various arii of an island would resort to military conquest. There would be ceremonies on the marae, after which the chief and his warriors would go off to fight on land or sea. The outcome was cruel: the defeated were often massacred and their marae destroyed. The victors would take possession of the defeated clan's land, and new investiture ceremonies would take place.

The weapons used included clubs, lances, whips and slings. At sea, the warriors would travel in dugout canoes.

Art & Craft

Little remains of traditional Polynesian art, which was created exclusively for religious and utilitarian purposes.

Before the arrival of Europeans, metal was unknown. Craftsmen worked with stone, coral, bone, wood, shells, mother-of-pearl and plant matter. They made weapons, utensils and tools (dishes, pestles, adzes, paddles, fishhooks), *tapa* (fabric made from pounded bark), ceremonial costumes (of animal fur and feathers), and tiki. Petroglyphs (patterns engraved on stones) are also considered a form of artistic expression.

Sports

Polynesians traditionally engaged in many games of skill and strength. Archery was a form of aristocratic entertainment, practised on specially constructed platforms – there are some to be admired on Moorea, in the Opunohu Valley. Surfing, which was also highly popular, is a sport of Polynesian origin. Javelin-throwing (in the Tuamotus), dugout-canoe racing, stone lifting and wrestling were equally commonplace.

Music & Dance

Music, dance and singing were inextricably linked. Many different forms of *heiva* (celebration) featured in the life of the community, and many celebrations would last several days. The instruments played were *pahu* (drums) and *vivo* (nasal flute).

Resources

The livelihood of the ancient Polynesians was based on fishing, animal husbandry, farming and fruit picking. *Uru* (breadfruit), which was eaten fermented, was a staple food, together with taro and sweet potato. Turtle was reserved for members of the higher castes. Dog was eaten in the Tuamotus.

Rahui, the temporary bans on eating specific products, were issued by the priests or arii in order to regulate the supply of food.

Mana & Tapu

Mana and *tapu* are the essential ingredients of holiness. The term mana is difficult to translate: it may be defined as a supernatural power, force or aura surrounding a person or object. For instance, the priests and the arii possessed mana, as do some tiki.

Tapu (taboo) is a word that has entered many western languages in various forms, and signifies that something has a complete ban on it. Anyone who transgresses incurs a curse and consequent punishment. Places and things can be tapu. Anything to do with the arii was tapu.

The Marquesas

Although belonging to the same melting pot as other Polynesians, the Marquesans have, over the centuries, developed their own distinct culture. The practice of cannibalism, officially outlawed in 1867, was concealed for many years since it was, to western thinking, considered repulsive. The victims were warriors who were captured or killed in battle. Only chiefs and warriors were allowed to seize the mana of the enemy in this way.

Social organisation also differed from the Polynesian model. Every *huaka* (clan) lived in a valley considered to be exclusive territory and which was jealously defended. Fighting between clans was frequent and bloody.

A *hakaiki* (chief), either male or female, exerted authority and enforced the clan's social and religious laws.

Taua (high priests), endowed with powerful mana, acted as intermediaries between the tribe and the gods. The role of the *toa* (chief warrior) was to lead the soldiers. Finally there were the *meie* (common people), among whom were the *tuhuna*, specialists in certain activities such as tattooing, sculpture and architecture.

Art and craft reached a very high degree of perfection, especially tattooing. Warriors' bodies were tattooed more extensively as they performed ever-increasing acts of bravery.

It was in the Marquesas that sculpture took on its most accomplished form, with the most imposing tiki in Polynesia.

Musical instruments were similar to those used in the other archipelagos. However, dances and traditional singing were different from those on Tahiti.

Archaeological Remains
State of Preservation

Evangelising Polynesia has resulted in the complete loss of the ancient religion and abandonment of places of worship. Fortunately, excavations have unearthed many sites that had been completely forgotten and overgrown. These are mainly places of worship built out of stone, including stone-carved patterns and statues. All evidence of plant matter – dugout canoes, dwelling-places, clothes and woodcarvings – have disappeared.

The state of preservation of the sites varies. In some places there are piles of stones, completely surrounded by vegetation, which have little meaning for visitors. In others, the sites are well looked-after and regularly visited. Unfortunately, they almost always lack explanatory signs. In order to appreciate their full historical and cultural significance you will need the services of a competent local guide who will make sure the site 'comes to life' before your very eyes and will explain it within its context. Although this is strangely amateurish, it is not without charm.

Geographical Distribution

There are remains in every archipelago. In the Leeward Islands the sites are well cared-for and easy to reach. The Tuamotus' heritage is more restricted. The Marquesas are the best provided-for: every island is an open-air archaeological museum containing several sites. In this archipelago, the emergence of small-scale 'archaeological tourism' in the medium term would not be beyond the bounds of possibility.

Marae

Marae were places of worship, cloaked in tapu, built in the open air for the purpose of celebrating the religious and social life of the clan. Within their confines, the gods were honoured and invoked, the chiefs formally installed, wars prepared, rituals performed, offerings and human sacrifices made. Marae were set up either along the coast or on the sides of mountains. Usually the trees surrounding them, especially the banyan, were considered holy.

There were several types of marae, of varying importance. The simplest type of marae were the family ones, where events affecting the life of the entire clan, such as births and deaths, were celebrated. The most complex were the royal marae, such as Marae Taputapuatea on Raiatea, which had worldwide influence, attracting Maohi chiefs from several islands of Polynesia, who would come to pledge allegiance to the arii. The most important religious symbols and objects, such as the too, were placed out of sight in a tabernacle-like recess.

Marae are like large paved rectangular platforms, sometimes more than 50m long. They were built of blocks of basalt and slabs of coral. The smaller stones or pebbles were coarsely shaped and assembled. Their design varies from island to island but there are certain architectural features in common, namely a paved level space, a sort of open rectangular platform, surrounded by a wall. At one end is the *ahu*, a sort of altar and the marae's most holy place, which was reserved for the priest and the arii. Depending on the type of marae, the ahu may have several levels. Some contain three or four tiers like a stepped pyramid, while others are on one level only. The latter consists of a simple facing of coral slabs placed vertically, the inside of which is filled with broken stones.

On the front of the ahu facing the platform there are three vertical slabs of coral known as 'upright stones'. The centre of the platform is adorned with several 'sitting stones', intended for the chiefs and priests, symbolising their social rank. The design of the family marae is simpler: they only have one upright stone and three sitting stones. Various adjoining wooden structures, such as the *fare tupapau*, where the dead were laid out, were built around the marae. None has survived to this day.

Petroglyphs

Petroglyphs are designs carved on stones; their significance has not yet been clearly established. The pictures feature octopuses, turtles, dugout canoes, suns, geometric designs, anthropomorphic figures and extremely schematic facial features. The best-known are those on Tahiti and in the Marquesas.

Tiki

At the meeting point of art and religion, tiki are human-like statues, of enigmatic appearance, carved in basalt or *keetu* (volcanic tuff), or in wood, though the wooden ones have not withstood the ravages of time.

They nearly all conform to the same model: the legs are short and bent and the elbows held close to the sides. Some have been only very roughly carved out, making it very difficult to identify them. Others have a head that is quite visible but the upper and lower limbs are hardly discernible. The head is a direct extension of the trunk. The highly stylised mouth and eyes are the most striking features. The disproportionate mouth is represented by an extremely long but narrow rectangle, and the eyes are large concentric circles.

Tiki vary in size considerably. The tallest, located in the Marquesas, stands 2.7m high. Since they were generally erected on or near a holy place, experts believe tiki had a religious and symbolic function, representing deified ancestors or protective power. Providing an interface between men and gods, they also marked the boundaries of properties or places that were tapu. Sculpted in the form of statues, tiki can also be carved in bas-relief, on weapons (clubs), paddles, dugout canoes, and utensils. The most significant remains are found on the Marquesas.

Shrouded in mana, the ancient tiki continue to instil some degree of fear among Polynesians. Tiki have a potential for evil, so it's said, that can manifest itself if they are moved or handled.

The Marquesas

Tohua The *tohua* is a paved rectangular level space with stepped rows of stone seats on either side, where festivals were held and public events such as dancing took place. They can be up to 100m long. At one end is a platform reserved for sacrifices and offerings. Flat boulders form a sort of stage on which one-man dances took place, and that was also used by young chiefs to show off their tattoos.

Pae Pae *Pae pae* are platforms of stone blocks, on which *hae* or *fae* (dwellings) were built of plant matter. The pae pae is divided into two parts. The front part forms a level that was reserved for daily activities. The back section, which was covered and slightly raised, served as a sleeping area. The roof was constructed of leaves from the uru tree and coconut palm. The front portion was also made from leaves and the whole structure was held up by several wooden stakes.

Only the stone foundations have survived. The covered areas, which contained plant matter, have been destroyed. You will find models of reconstructed hae at Nuka Hiva, Hiva Oa and Ua Pou.

Meae On the Marquesas the term used is not marae, but *meae*. Meae are religious sites built from basalt blocks placed side by side and piled up, and are similar to marae. Generally found in the valleys and away from secular places, the meae was the sacred precinct par excellence. It was a place of worship, burial and offerings, and was strictly tapu. Access was restricted to a few initiated individuals endowed with mana, such as the priest or chief. Cannibalistic rites, restricted to chiefs, priests and warriors, also took place there when human sacrifices were made. Meae were generally built near a banyan, the sacred tree.

[Continued from page 30]

There are size and seasonal limits for some fish and crustaceans, particularly lobsters. Nevertheless fish continue to be caught indiscriminately and shells collected for purely decorative purposes.

Visitors definitely have a responsibility and should particularly avoid collecting shells. Divers and swimmers should take care to avoid untimely fin movements that damage the fragile coral. Yachts should ensure that the anchor does not drag on madreporian coral banks. Although turtles are highly protected, they continue to be poached for their flesh and their shells, which are used as ornaments. Do not encourage this practice in any way. Scilly's role as a reserve is particularly important for turtles.

Finally there's the question of the nuclear tests and their repercussions. The belief of experts that Moruroa Atoll was fissured by tests and that radioactivity has been allowed to escape was confirmed in 1999, when the French government admitted, for the first time, the existence of cracks in the atoll's coral cones. See the boxed text 'French Nuclear Testing' in this chapter.

FLORA & FAUNA

It is thought that the Pacific flora and fauna originated in Austronesia and spread towards Polynesia, becoming less varied the farther east you travel. Numerous plant and animal species have been introduced by humans at different times.

Flora

The luxuriant flora, particularly on the high islands, is recent and introduced. In the course of their migrations to the east, Polynesian navigators brought plants and fruits that easily became acclimatised. In the 19th century, missionaries and settlers imported other plants of ornamental and commercial value.

Vegetation varies significantly from one archipelago to another. On the atolls, where the soil is poor and winds constant, bushy vegetation and coconut palms predominate. On the high islands, plant cover is more diverse and varies with altitude. The plants most often found are the following:

Ahi (sandalwood) – A species essentially indigenous to the Marquesas, it was systematically plundered in the 19th century by westerners. The sawdust from its wood, renowned for its subtle fragrance, is mixed with coconut oil to make Marquesan *monoi* (fragrant oil; see Arts later in this chapter).

Auti or **ti** *(Cordyline fructicosa)* – This member of the Lilieaceae family used to have a sacred function and was planted near traditional religious buildings. Very decorative, it's also used as a hedge to mark property limits. Its foliage opens in a V shape and its colour ranges from yellow to green or purplish red.

Banana *(Musa sapientum,* meia) – Its leaves are used in traditional Tahitian ovens to wrap food for cooking. One variety is the *fei,* similar in appearance to the plantain, the fruit of which grows upwards and can only be eaten when cooked.

Banyan *(Ficus prolixa,* ora) – This Indian fig tree has numerous aerial roots that form a dense tangle. A sacred tree, its ghostly silhouette is often seen near traditional religious buildings. It was an ancient Marquesan custom to put the long bones and the skull of a deceased person in among the banyan roots along with a conch shell.

Breadfruit *(Artocarpus altilis,* uru or maiore) – This impressive grey-trunked tree, of which there are several dozen varieties in Polynesia, has a large grainy fruit that forms the basis of local cuisine. Its whitish fibrous flesh is rich in starch and can be eaten cooked or as a fermented paste. The bark is used to make *tapa* (barkcloth; see the Tapa entry under Arts later in this chapter).

Coconut palm *(Cocos nucifera,* tumu haari) – Found everywhere, this is Polynesia's most important tree. It is thought to have been introduced by the first Polynesians, then cultivated by the missionaries last century. Its uses are many: the coconut water is sterile and is a favourite drink, the young coconut flesh is squeezed to produce coconut milk, and when mature and dried it produces copra. The coconut oil is the basis of monoi. The coconut wood is used to make containers, the palm fibres make rope, *niau* (plaited palm) for roof coverings or *peue* (braided palm) for basketwork.

Flamboyant *(Delonix regia)* – This majestic tree that forms an umbrella shape originated in

Madagascar and has vivid crimson flowers at the beginning of the wet season in December.

Frangipani (*Plumeria acuminata*, tipanie) – This bush has very strongly scented white flowers with yellow or pink shading and is used to make crowns and flower *lei*.

Hibiscus (*Hibiscus rosinensis*, aute) – Very widespread, this plant has strongly scented flowers of varying colours, generally orange-yellow.

Hotu (*Barringtonia asiatica*) – This tree can be recognised by its pear-shaped fruit with protruding ridges. The grated kernel of the fruit mixed with hora root and shaken underwater near coral formations has the effect of paralysing fish, which can then be caught by hand.

Ironwood (*Casuarina equisetifolia*, aito or toa) – This tree, which grows on the seashore or in the mountains, can reach a height of 20m and looks like a pine. Its wood, which is very solid, is used to manufacture weapons (clubs, spears), tools and canoe parts.

Mango (*Mangifera indica*) – Widely cultivated in Polynesia, where several varieties are found, this tree is smothered in delicious fragrant fruit with a fibrous orange flesh. The trunk is used to make canoes.

Mape (*Inocarpus fagiferus*) – This white-wood tree, often grown in plantations, used to be found near traditional religious buildings. Its roots form buttresses around the base of the trunk. It produces an edible fruit, a sort of chestnut.

Miconia calvescens – Introduced in the 1930s, this plant is now a threat to Tahitian flora, which is in danger of being smothered. See the boxed text 'An Ecological Curse' in this chapter.

Miki miki (*Pemphis acidula*) – Typical of the flora of the atolls, this bush grows to 3 to 5m and is found mainly on the ocean side, where it forms a bush.

Monette (*Allamanda cathartica*) – It's hard to miss the magnificent yellow flowers of this rather decorative bush that is often grown close to dwellings.

Myrobalan (*Terminalia cattapa*, auteraa) – Quite widespread near beaches or at the mouth of valleys, the branches of this tree have a widened appearance. The leaves acquire a red or yellow tinge before falling. The kernel of the fruit is edible.

Noni or **nono** (*Morinda citrifolia*) – The yellowish fruit of this tree looks like a bloated soft potato. It is edible but its nauseating goat's cheese smell and acidic taste are not very appealing. It has medicinal properties.

Pandanus (fara) – This tree, with a span of 5 to 7m, is easily recognised by its aerial roots, which grow obliquely from the trunk and look like arches. The strong leaves are dried to make traditional roofing, wickerwork and woven articles. The flower is called *hinano*. It is found on the atolls and on the high islands up to an altitude of 800m.

Purau (*Hibiscus tiliaceus*) – Extremely widespread, it sometimes forms tangled clusters due to its contorted branches. The wide heart-shaped leaves are used in the Tahitian oven. The bark, cut in strips, is used to attach fish by the gills. It is also used to make *more* (purau fibre skirts), worn in traditional women's dances.

Rosewood (*Thespesia populnea*, miro) – This is often used in craftwork and carving.

Tamanu or **ati** (*Calophyllum inophyllum*) – The reddish-brown wood of this tree is very strong and rot-resistant. It is used to make canoes and for carving.

Taro (*Colocasia esculenta*) – The purplish-red rhizome of this plant is commonly eaten in Polynesia.

Tiare (*Gardenia tahitiensis*) – Its flower is the emblem of Polynesia. Snowy-white in colour, it gives off a subtle fragrance, and is used to make garlands or is woven into the hair. Wrapped in aluminium foil and a banana-tree leaf it lasts for several days.

Tiare apetahi – Found only on Mt Temehani on Raiatea, this rare and protected white flower is shaped like a half-corolla with five petals on one side only.

Tou (*Cordia subcordata*) – Extremely common in the Marquesas, this medium-sized tree with heart-shaped leaves gives a dark, hard, grained wood that is greatly valued by sculptors.

Vanilla (*Vanilla tahitiensis*, vanira) – This epiphytic orchid produces a pod 20cm long. It is cultivated particularly on Tahaa, Huahine and Raiatea and has to be hand-fertilised because the insects that do the job in its original home are not found in French Polynesia.

Along the paths of French Polynesia you will certainly encounter sumptuous porcelain roses, heliconias, ginger and birds of paradise. Among the fruit trees, you are bound to find soursop (the surface of the fruit is covered with soft spines), pineapple (grown in plantations on Moorea), guava, avocado, tamarind, lemon, lime (in the Marquesas), grapefruit, pacayer (with green pods), cashew, papaya and custard apple. Melons and watermelons are also grown. *Mati* (the

Loads of Noni

The best-known fruit in Polynesia is the noni (sometimes called nono – not to be confused with the insect common in the Marquesas). It has always been a traditional medicinal drug in Polynesia but since 1995 it has enjoyed enormous success in the American market.

Following work done by an American researcher, who is reported to have highlighted its anti-ageing virtues, a network is being rapidly put in place to supply the American market with nono juice. Large numbers of Polynesians, especially on the Marquesas, are abandoning some of the traditional agricultural activities to devote themselves to the much more lucrative activity of growing nono, which thrives in the wild. The crop is puréed on Tahiti, then shipped off to the USA, where it is processed by the Morinda company, which also holds exclusive marketing rights. Due to a very peculiar distribution system known as pyramid selling, the price of the product may be increased a hundredfold.

The risk for the Polynesian farmers is that this sudden craze might die as quickly as it started. Most people are, however, aware of the very fragile nature of the market and that it may be little more than a passing fad.

berries of which provide a red colouring), acacia and kapok trees are fairly common.

At higher altitudes, in addition to *puarata* (which has red flowers), you will note several types of *maire* (fern). The *Albizia falcata* has recently been introduced to counteract the effects of erosion, particularly in the Marquesas.

Motoi (ylang-ylang), with strongly scented flowers, also grows in Polynesia, as does *pitate* (jasmine) and bougainvillea.

Fauna

Like French Polynesia's flora, its fauna is rather limited compared to regions in the west Pacific, due to the distance from the great continents.

At the time of the great migrations, the first Polynesians brought pigs and dogs in their canoes. The rat arrived on the westerners' ships. Reptiles include the harmless, insectivorous gecko, a small lizard with a translucent colour. There are no snakes in French Polynesia.

There are few insect species. You are certain to meet with wasps, cockroaches and their predators, centipedes. The latter can be up to 20cm long and the spikes at the front of the head inject a venom that causes inflammation. Mosquitoes are there in profusion and can transmit dengue fever and filariasis. The *nono* (black or white) is a minute midge that is a particular problem on the Marquesan coasts, where eradication campaigns are being carried out (see the boxed text 'Nono a Gogo' in the Marquesas chapter). It is not a disease carrier, but its bite causes itching and inflammation.

Horses, which originated in Chile, were introduced on Tahuata by Dupetit-Thouars in 1842 and have bred on the Marquesas. Goats are also a familiar part of the landscape on this archipelago, where they roam around in semi-freedom. Sheep were introduced for rearing, notably on Tahiti, the Australs and the Marquesas.

The waterways are home to eels and freshwater shrimps, which are highly valued in the local cuisine.

Bird Life There are about 100 species of *manu* (birds) in Polynesia. On the low islands, many nest on the ground or in the bushes. The feathers of certain birds were once much sought-after as costume accessories (eg headdresses, chieftains' belts).

Sea birds include terns, petrels, noddies, frigatebirds, boobies and the superb tropicbirds (phaethons) with long red or white feathers in their tails. All of them live on fish. The sheltered Tetiaroa Atoll is home to several species. The number of *kaveka* (sooty terns) nesting on Ua Huka is estimated at nearly one million. In the Tuamotus there are numerous 'bird islands'.

The pigeon and the buzzard were introduced, as was the chicken, brought at the time of the first migrations and now partly reverted back to its wild state.

Lagoon, Reef & Ocean Fauna The coral constructions of the high islands and atolls are favoured environments for diverse fauna.

Crustaceans Greatly prized for their flesh, lobsters and other shellfish live on the outer slope of the reef (on the Tuamotus) or carpet the bottom of caves in the cliffs (in the Marquesas). Hermit crabs, which are common on reefs, wedge their abdomens inside the empty shells of gastropods.

In the Tuamotus, the kaveu (coconut crab), which can reach an impressive size, feeds at night. Its flesh is highly prized. The tupa (land crab) infests coconut plantations, where it digs a network of tunnels.

Echinoderms Sea urchins hide in cracks in the reef. The two most common species are the black vana (sea urchin) with long spines, and the fetue (pencil urchin) with long cylindrical spines. Their gonads, eaten raw, are greatly prized.

Long and cylindrical, the rori (sea cucumber) looks like a fat black or grey sausage. It sucks in sand and filters it to feed on micro-organisms.

Molluscs Shells, which were once used as decorative or ceremonial jewellery, are now used to make ornaments. Most shellfish are edible.

They have a diverse habitat: reef crevices, coral pinnacles and the sandy bottom of lagoons. The most numerous are gastropods and bivalves, including the symbol of the Tuamotus, mother-of-pearl (pearl oyster) and the pahua (giant clam). Pearl shells were once used to make fish hooks, lures, utensils, tools and, during the 19th century, buttons. Giant clams have brightly coloured, velvety-looking mantles, which they draw in when threatened. The outer edges of the shells are crinkled. Troca shells are used for mother-of-pearl work.

Cone shells can be dangerously venomous, the beautiful porcelain cones are particularly valued by collectors. The conch shell is often used as a wind instrument in traditional ceremonies.

Fish Among the ocean, or pelagic, fish that come to hunt near the reef are sharks. Very common in the Tuamotus, the grey shark (*Carcharhinus amblyrhinchos*, raira), powerful, streamlined and about 2m in length, is found in abundance near channels and shelves. The lemon shark *(Negaprion acutidens,* arava) has a slightly yellowish skin and can reach 3m in length. It swims around near the bottom, including in lagoons, and can be aggressive. The white-tip reef shark (*Carcharhinus albimarginatus,* tapete) can be recognised by the white mark at the tip of its dorsal fin. It frequents the shelves around the Tuamotus at greater depths than the grey shark but may come up if enticed by food. It can reach more than 3m in length. The black-tip reef shark (*Carcharhinus melanopterus,* mauri) and the white-tip lagoon shark (*Trianodon obesus,* mamaru) are small, harmless and found primarily in lagoons and channels. Tiger, hammerhead and sleeper sharks are occasionally seen.

Ono (barracuda), with its tapering profile and metallic sheen, is also a predator, and swims close to the channels, alone or in shoals.

Three types of *fafa piti* (rays) are found in Polynesian waters: manta rays, easily recognised by the horns on either side of the mouth, can be as much as 4m across; leopard rays are smaller and have dark spots; and whip-tailed stingrays live on the sandy bottom, where they partially bury themselves.

Among the hundreds of species of smaller fish, the moray eel is the most impressive. Hidden in the coral crevices of the shelf, only its half-open mouth, edged with sharp fangs, can be seen. The good-natured *mara* (napoleon wrasse), with its blue-green livery, thick-lipped mouth and bump on its forehead, is often more than 1m in length. The loach and *roi* (grouper) families are well represented, as are the *maito* (surgeonfish), especially the black and convict varieties.

Clownfish and damselfish have a symbiotic relationship with anemones. Duckbills and trumpetfish are very streamlined. *Uruti* (scad) often move around in shoals. Parrotfish have beaks that they use to graze the coral. *Ume* (unicornfish) have rostrums, which project above the mouth. Soldierfish and squirrelfish, with their orange-red skin, shelter in compact groups in the faults in the reef.

The perch family includes several species, among them the blue-striped perch, almost always encountered in groups. The filefish family is diverse, and includes the picasso fish, which is highly territorial and will fearlessly bite the fingers of an intruding diver. Chaetodons are devoted to a diet of coral paste. The most attractive specimens are the coachman with its long dorsal fluke, the whipfish, emperorfish and butterflyfish. The stonefish, which is difficult to see because of its camouflage, can give a dangerous sting, as can the scorpionfish. The porcupinefish, and the aptly named pufferfish, puff themselves up like a balloon when in danger.

Mahi mahi (dolphin fish), bonito, *thazard* (wahoo) and tuna, greatly prized for their meat, are generally found in the open sea.

Reptiles Sea snakes are very rare in French Polynesia. *Honu* (turtles) are an endangered species but are often encountered around the reefs.

Dolphins & Whales Dolphins are encountered in all the archipelagos, particularly around the reef passes. Electra dolphins *(Peponocephala electra)*, also known as pygmy orcas or melon-headed whales, are a major attraction of Nuku Hiva in the Marquesas. They gather in groups of several hundred, a phenomenon found nowhere else in the world. In the Australs, whales are the stars – you can even swim with them. See the Australs chapter for details.

GOVERNMENT & POLITICS

French Polynesia is not an independent state, but a Territoire d'Outre-Mer (TOM), which has autonomous status within the French Republic.

French Polynesia was given internal management autonomy in 1977 with further powers added in 1984, 1990 and 1996. The Territory itself looks after territorial administration, education (elementary, primary and secondary), taxation, prices, foreign trade and the regulation of maritime resource exploration and exploitation. The French state remains in control of territorial defence and law and order, foreign affairs, nationality and immigration, justice, higher education and research, audiovisual communications and currency.

The Territory's institutions are the government of French Polynesia, the Assembly of French Polynesia and the Economic and Social Committee (CES). The Republic of France is represented in the Territory by a high commissioner, appointed by the French government. He or she controls the legality of acts of authorities of the Territory, and can submit matters to the administrative court.

The Assembly of French Polynesia is composed of 41 territorial councillors from the five archipelagos, elected by direct universal suffrage every five years. The assembly elects the president of the government of French Polynesia, head of the Territorial administration, who appoints a council of ministers. The president represents the authorities of the Republic of France before regional Pacific organisations, and negotiates and signs agreements with Pacific states on matters for which the Territory has responsibility. The assembly sits in Papeete, the Territory's capital.

French Polynesians participate in all French national elections, and elect two deputies and a senator to represent them in the French parliament. Institutional changes under consideration include the establishment of French Polynesian citizenship.

Political Parties

Political life in French Polynesia concentrates around two principal poles. On one side is the autonomist but loyalist Tahoeraa Huiraatira (Gathering of the People) party, which is currently in power. On the other side is Tavini Huiraatira (To Serve the People), the pro-independence party led by Oscar Temaru, mayor of Faaa, who wants to break all ties with France as soon as possible, and who extols a return to basic Maohi principles. Between these two heavyweights smaller parties attempt to make themselves heard – without much success. Only the autonomist Fetia Api (New Star), which is opposed to the Tahoeraa party and was created in 1995 by Boris Léontieff, the mayor of Arue, has had much success in proposing a third way.

Local political practices are often disconcerting for foreign observers. Political meetings start with a prayer, speeches are dotted with biblical quotes, U-turns are frequent and fail to shock anybody, and cronyism – which sometimes drifts towards corruption – is everyday currency. Local politics is essentially based on personality rather than on ideology or policy.

ECONOMY

Far from the myths of a carefree paradise, French Polynesia faces many economic challenges. As a result of the nuclear testing era the region has become heavily financially dependent upon France, although this dependence is programmed to be reduced as the local government modernises and makes better use of its own resources.

Economic Indicators

French Polynesia is one of the richest countries in the South Pacific with a per-capita GNP comparable to that of Australia. This elevated standard of living is, of course, somewhat artificial since it depends on lots of input from France. Exports may be increasing but they still don't amount to one-fifth of the imports. The main trading partners are metropolitan France (38% of imports and 25% of exports), the USA, Japan, Australia and New Zealand. Exports include pearl products (pearls, mother-of-pearl) and agricultural and food products (vanilla, noni, flowers, fruits, monoi, copra oil, fish). Imports include consumer durables, equipment and food.

Unemployment is officially 13.2% of the active population and is particularly difficult for women and young people without qualifications. Of course that figure is virtually meaningless in the local context. On some atolls there is really no job market at all and the population is primarily engaged in self-sufficiency. Combine that with the *fetii,* or extended family, concept and employment levels don't have the same impact as they do in the industrialised nations of the west. Papeete is the one exception, and

---

Cultural Renewal & Identity Problems

Polynesian leaders of the post-CEP era are worried about little else other than economic indicators and performances, and run the risk of neglecting fundamental cultural issues. Young people are the first to suffer. Torn between the lure of the modern world and a return to their roots steeped in Polynesian culture, they have difficulty finding their way. The revival of Maohi symbolism (eg tattooing, traditional dance, canoeing and surfing) is clear evidence of the will of the people to reclaim their culture. At the same time, young people longing for mobile phones, Big Macs and motorcycles cast envious eyes towards America, especially Hawaii and California, which are fast becoming the dominant cultural icons. Trying to manage these obviously opposing aspirations is not the least of the challenges facing Polynesian society.

unemployment has brought it the same social problems experienced elsewhere.

The End of the CEP Era

The establishment of the CEP in 1963 and the subsequent flood of finance into the Territory artificially inflated the standard of living. The change encouraged many outer-islanders to quit traditional activities and migrate en masse to Papeete. This in turn led to economically depressed sections of the city where there was strong support for political parties pressing for independence. These stresses led to a Polynesian identity crisis and a search for Maohi roots (see the boxed text 'Cultural Renewal & Identity Problems' in this chapter). The close of the CEP has meant a return to reality and the announcement of an end to the assistance.

France has undertaken to compensate the loss of financial resources linked to the cessation of CEP activities during a transition period, and provides assistance in the fields of education, training, research, health and transport infrastructure, agriculture, tourism and housing. Financial transfers to the Territory will amount to 18 billion CFP (US$150 million) per annum until 31 December 2005.

Areas of Activity

The new economic orientations gave priority to the use of the Territory's own internal resources.

Agriculture The spectacular boom in the services sector and the public service during the CEP period caused a huge rural exodus and a marked decline in agricultural output. This sector is vital for the Territory's social and economic stability – French Polynesia is not self-sufficient in food production – and strong support is being given.

The development of the agricultural sector is handicapped by some fundamental problems including small plot sizes, difficult climatic conditions and poor distribution.

Copra production is the main source of income for more than 12,000 people, particularly in the Tuamotus (50% of production) and the Marquesas. Aware of the social issues at stake, the Territory guarantees a price

per kilogram which is considerably higher than that on world markets. Market gardening and vegetable production is concentrated in the Leeward Islands and the Australs. Vanilla is grown on Tahaa, Raiatea and Huahine and is considered to be the best in the world. Production is increasing, reaching 34 tons in 1997, but this is still far below the pre-CEP annual level of 150 tons. Fruit production is mainly bananas, pineapples, coconuts and citrus fruit but only Moorea's intensively grown pineapples are exported. Staples – taro, sweet potatoes, cooking bananas – are grown entirely for local consumption. Flower exports, mainly to Europe, have been recording good results.

Chicken, pork and beef production (at Taravao on Tahiti Iti and Nuku Hiva in the Marquesas), goats (the Marquesas) and dairy products only meet a small part of the local demand and there are extensive imports from Australia, New Zealand and France.

Fishing Polynesia's huge marine areas have been notoriously under-exploited, but that situation is rapidly changing. Small-scale fishing in lagoons and offshore using small boats, fish traps and spearfishing has always been important for meeting local demand but a semi-industrial fishing fleet for exports is also being developed and has achieved good results.

Pearl Culture The real locomotive of the French Polynesian economy, the pearl business, is booming. In 1997 it accounted for 28% of exports – only tourism provided more income. In that year Japan bought 58% of the production, but this proportion is falling as French Polynesian producers reduce their single-market dependency by opening outlets in North America, Europe and other parts of Asia. Production is mainly concentrated in the atolls of the Tuamotus and the Gambier, where it plays an important part in local life. It's also being developed in the Leeward Islands, particularly Huahine, Raiatea, Tahaa and Maupiti.

The apparent buoyancy of this sector does not, however, conceal certain basic weaknesses. There's little organised merchandising despite a professional union overseeing the business. The many small pearl cultivators' professional practices are sometimes rather amateurish, wildly selling pearls cheaply, which drives prices downwards and tarnishes the image of black pearls. Overproduction is another consequence of this relative anarchy, and again depresses prices. In 1994 black pearls were worth 4103 CFP per gram, but by 1997 that figure had fallen to 2938 CFP. It was hoped that increased regulation of the business, introduced in 1998, would rationalise operations.

Tourism As the main source of income in the Territory, tourism is the principal lever by which the government intends to achieve its objectives of economic independence. The ambitious objectives – 300,000 visitors a year – seem rather utopian. The number of tourist arrivals has been increasing regularly but there's certainly no sign of the growth suddenly exploding. The long distance from principal markets, the cost of life on the islands, competition from other tropical destinations and a lack of professionalism in some areas all combine to restrain demand.

In 1997, French Polynesia welcomed 180,000 visitors, mainly French (31%), American (22%), Japanese, Australian, New Zealanders, Italian and South American. Thanks to some attractive but artificial tax breaks there's been a boom in luxury hotel construction in Papeete and on Bora Bora. Similarly, small inns and guesthouses have also been developing in more remote locations, making for some democratisation of the accommodation possibilities.

The most visited islands are Tahiti, Moorea, Bora Bora and Rangiroa, but recently there has been increased promotion the other islands. Cruise ships, honeymoon visits, aquatic activities (sailing, scuba diving, pirogue tours of the lagoons) and contact with local culture (handicrafts, traditional feasts) are all growth areas. Ecotourism (archaeology, walking, horse riding, whale watching) are other potential growth areas that are currently under-exploited.

Industry The industrial sector is little developed in French Polynesia; there are just some small-scale agro-food businesses and specialised clothing and textile operations.

Taxation The fiscal system is the main reason for the elevated prices in French Polynesia. The taxation system is totally unbalanced in favour of indirect taxes, particularly import taxes. All goods entering the Territory are weighed down with import duties that vary according to the type of product and can be as much as 160% of the product's value. Customs duties are added, except to goods from the European Union (EU).

Bearing in mind the Territory's extreme dependence on imports, it is easier to understand why the cost of living is exorbitant. Locally manufactured goods do not escape this implacable logic as they include imported components. On the other hand income taxes are derisory.

Reforms introduced in 1998 brought in a value-added tax (VAT), which is intended to balance the system and progressively replace customs duties.

POPULATION & PEOPLE

The total population of French Polynesia is now estimated at about 220,000, and is characterised by its youth and uneven geographic distribution. Of the total population, 43% are under 20 years of age, compared to 28% in Australia and 26% in France. With a birth rate of 22 per 1000 (13.7 in Australia, 12.6 in France) the demographic growth is high, although it has dropped markedly over the last two censuses.

The Society group has more than 86% of the total population, the Tuamotus 7%, the Marquesas 3.6% and the Australs not even 3%. In fact, everything is completely unbalanced by Papeete, with its dense urban zone that is home to more than 100,000 people.

The isolated Marquesas and Australs have lost large parts of their populations to Papeete but between 1988 and 1996 the Tuamotu-Gambier region, long considered 'backward', has seen its population grow by 25%, due to the boom in cultured pearls. In the same period, the population of the Lee-ward Islands has increased by 20%, due to better transport infrastructure and the development of tourism. Tahiti and Moorea recorded an unsurprising 15% jump.

On all the islands, the majority of the population lives in coastal zones but this was not always so, as archaeological evidence indicates.

Ethnicity

French Polynesia is a multiethnic society of four major groups: Polynesians, *demis* (of Polynesian-European or Polynesian-Chinese mixed race), *popaa* (Europeans) and Chinese (or French of Chinese origin). In fact these distinctions may be purely theoretical since the population is very mixed indeed. Surnames certainly indicate this melting-pot characteristic. You will hear names ranging from very Maohi (Teariki), to English (Brotherson), French (Buillard), French-Chinese (Chungue, Langy), right through to German and Russian.

Polynesians comprise 66.5% of the population, demis 16.3%, popaa 11.9% and Asians 4.7%. Demis are mainly the descendants of mixed marriages around the turn of the 19th century between colonial administrators and traders and the women of important Polynesian families. Today they seem to have integrated the two cultures and sail from one to the other with disconcerting ease, even though this cultural duality is sometimes a problem. Mastering western culture as well as traditional references (the Maohi language, dance) and with a high educational standard, demis occupy some of the most important positions in public – especially political – life, banks and maritime transport.

Pure Polynesians are less fortunate, engaged mostly in traditional fishing and agricultural pursuits and in the building and construction industry. They tend to live in the outlying districts and on the islands whereas the demis are concentrated in Papeete.

The first Chinese landed in the mid-19th century to work on the cotton plantations. A second wave arrived in the early 20th century but they were only granted French citizenship in 1964. Self-made, they've excelled in the trade and business sectors, and unlike other overseas Chinese are not concentrated in a Chinatown. In fact they're perfectly integrated in French Polynesian life, although that hasn't stopped them from preserving their own traditions. Chinese New Year, the Buddhist temple at Mamao, the annual election of Miss Dragon and involvement in various cultural associations illustrate this will to retain their heritage.

The popaa are essentially French people who have stayed in French Polynesia for years as teachers, military or medical personnel, civil servants, restauranteurs and other tourist industry workers.

French Polynesia has enjoyed an extraordinary ability to assimilate people throughout its history and Papeete is a cultural crucible with all the communities represented. Nevertheless racial tensions have developed because of the rise of inequalities and fading of traditional solidarity. A gulf has emerged between the Chinese and demis, the big winners in the region's westernisation, and the Polynesian population, which has failed to find its place in the new western model.

EDUCATION

The basic educational structures are identical to those of metropolitan France. School is compulsory between the ages of five and 16. The school program was essentially conceived by and for westerners, so in primary school the teachers are Polynesian but by secondary school they're almost all French. Teaching is in French only; a few hours a week of Tahitian is provided in primary and secondary schools. This causes great difficulties for Maohi children, who have greater difficulty integrating than demi, Chinese and Popaa children.

There are primary schools in each community, but the six high-schools (of which two are private and one is an agricultural school) are all in the Society Islands. This certainly complicates things for teenagers from the other island groups who have to go to boarding school in order to continue their studies. School holidays are one month from mid-December to mid-January, seven weeks in July-August, two weeks in March and one week for All Saints' Day (Toussaint, on 1 November).

The French University of French Polynesia (UFP) has about 600 students and is aimed at developing a pool of local talent to run the region. It has not been an outstanding success; many students drop out at the end of the first year.

ARTS

The pioneering missionaries endeavoured to wipe out all forms of Polynesian art and culture. They destroyed temples and carvings, banned tattoos and dancing, and generally took a lot of the joy out of Polynesian life. Fortunately some traditions did survive and in recent years there has been a real revival of Polynesian culture, particularly in music, dance and tattooing. This book has separate sections on tattooing, Tahitian dance, and civilisation and archaeology. See the Shopping section in the Facts for the Visitor chapter for more information on crafts.

Dance

Early explorers all commented on the excitement and erotic explicitness of Polynesian dancing so, naturally, it was one of the first things the missionaries banned. It continued clandestinely, and since the 1950s has revived to become one of the best ambassadors for Polynesian culture. See the 'Ori Tahiti – Tahitian Dance' special section for more information.

Music

Traditional music has not been replaced by modern western music. You'll particularly find traditional music as an accompaniment to dance performances. Guitars, ukuleles and percussion instruments play a large part. See the Tahitian Dance section for more information. Song, both secular and religious, is also important and Sunday *himenes* (hymns) feature wonderful harmonies.

Modern Polynesian music by local artists is part of the daily background noise, whether it's in a *le truck* (bus) or on the

Bringues & Kaina Music

You might perhaps take part in a family gathering, or *bringue*, often with lots of Hinano to drink and *kaina* (local) music to listen to. Improvisation and spontaneity are the main features of this type of event. Someone grabs a ukulele, someone else a guitar, while another person plays percussion using drums or two spoons banged together. A plastic garbage bin rigged up with a stick and a wire is used as double bass. The whole event is accompanied by singing, and some people dance.

radio. The themes can be anything from lightweight romance on the lagoon to more important celebrations of cultural matters. Some groups perform in hotels and discos; the best-known local names are Andy Tupaia, Gabilou, Esther Tefana, Michel Poroi, Maruia, Barthélémy, Bobby, Te Ava Piti, the Royal Band and the Trio Kikiriri (which plays at the Royal Kikiriri). Special mention must be made of Angelo Ariitai Neuffer, whose high-pitched voice will quickly become familiar and who distinguishes himself with his very committed lyrics. He's even done a song denouncing nuclear testing.

The Marquesan colours are defended by Rataro and the Kanahau Trio. The Fenua group has for its part managed to fairly successfully fuse traditional music with techno while defending Polynesian culture.

Architecture

The *fare* (house) is the traditional dwelling. It is constructed entirely from plant materials and is built directly on the ground, without foundations. The framework is of coconut wood and the roof of woven coconut palms or pandanus leaves, which are waterproof. Unfortunately new construction techniques and designs are supplanting the traditional *fare*. Today, *fare* made of plywood or cement with corrugated iron roofs to better withstand cyclones have largely replaced the traditional designs.

These utilitarian designs have little style, and beautiful Polynesian-designed homes are predominantly found among the wealthy. On some islands, such as Maupiti, the cyclone-proof '*fare* MTR' has appeared. Paradoxically it's at luxury hotels that you are most likely to be able to admire traditional architecture with frames and rafters in ironwood, roofs thatched with niau and walls covered in plaited bamboo. Colonial-era buildings have also become rare while Christian religious architecture, with certain exceptions, is not particularly interesting.

Painting
In Gauguin's wake a number of predominantly European artists – working in media ranging from water colour to line drawing – have sought inspiration in French Polynesia. They've contributed to the very characteristic style of the region. Essentially representational, their work shows everything from scenes of everyday life to still life and can be found in shops and galleries in Papeete.

Apart from Matisse, who made a short stay on Tahiti, the best-known is certainly Jacques Boullaire and his magnificent watercolours. Mention must also be made of Christian Deloffre, François Ravello, Michèle Dallet, Bobby (also known as a singer and musician, he died in 1991), André Marere, Jean Masson, Yrondi, Noguier and Erhart Lux.

Sculpture & Wood Carving
Traditional sculptural craftwork is particularly dynamic in the Marquesas (see that chapter) where fine tiki, bowls, mortars and pestles, spears and clubs are carved from rosewood, tou wood or in stone. They are displayed twice a year in Papeete.

The best-known contemporary sculptor is the potter Peter Owen, who lives on Huahine. The work of Woody on Moorea is also well known.

Clothing & Decoration
Pareu The mission dress is a long dress-style that arrived in the region with the missionaries. It's generally worn by older women and is decorated in floral styles, often trimmed with lace.

Like the South-East Asian sarong, the *pareu* is a cool, comfortable, all-purpose piece of attire, directly descended from that made from pre-European tapa. A modern pareu is 180cm by 90cm (about six feet by three feet) and is often imported from Asia, although brightly painted Polynesian pareu are becoming more common. Hibiscus flowers and uru leaves are the most popular Polynesian designs but motifs vary from island to island.

Men usually wear the pareu like a wraparound skirt for casual wear or around the house. Tucked up like shorts it becomes workwear. Women have a variety of ways of wearing a pareu. It can be worn as a wrap-around skirt with a blouse, halter top or bikini top. Alternatively it can be worn tied above the breasts or with two corners tied behind the neck.

Tifaifai Brilliantly coloured *tifaifai* are appliquéd or patchwork blankets produced on a number of islands, including Rurutu. The craft was introduced by the missionaries and a tifaifai blanket now has several important uses. Wrapping someone in a tifaifai is a sign of welcome. Traditionally, it's an important wedding gift and a tifaifai may also be used to cover a coffin. Flowers or fruit are often used in tifaifai patterns and production can be a very sociable community activity.

Monoi Monoi is the local fragrant oil, made from coconut oil and perfumed with crushed flowers (tiare, jasmine and the like). It's used as hair oil, ointment, sunscreen and even mosquito repellent.

Tapa The ancient technique of tapa making, practised throughout the Pacific, consists of making nonwoven fabric from the bark of uru, banyan or *aute* (paper mulberry) trees. The colour depends upon the wood used, varying from white through to chestnut.

Collecting the bark is the men's job, while the preparation of the tapa falls to the women. The bark of young trunks or branches is slit and removed from the wood using a sharpened stick. It is then soaked in water to soften. The outer layer is scraped away with a shell, leaving just the sapwood. The sheets of bark, about 15cm wide, are spread out on a flat, elongated stone anvil positioned in front of the operator, who sits cross-legged. Using a square-shaped ironwood beater with parallel slots, she pounds it repeatedly for several hours, during which time the bark becomes thinner and gradually stretches. When the piece is finished, it is put to dry then dyed with the sap of various plants or decorated with traditional designs. Tapa clothing is generally in the form of pareu or the poncho-like *tiputa*.

Tapa rapidly disappeared when European cloth became available but it is still produced, particularly on Fatu Hiva in the Marquesas, for ceremonial use and for collectors.

Plaiting & Basketwork This craft is the domain of women, who make baskets, hats and the panels used for roofing and the walls of houses. Coconut-palm leaves are used for the more rough-and-ready woven work, such as the woven walls of *fare*, but pandanus leaves are used for finer hats, bags and mats, and this is one of the best examples of a true local craft. Hats made of woven pandanus leaves or thin strips of bamboo look very elegant on Polynesian women, particularly at the Sunday church services. They are often decorated with flowers or shells.

Some of the finest work comes from Rurutu in the Austral Islands, where hillside pandanus rather than common lagoonside pandanus is used.

Flowers & Shells Plants and flowers play a big part in everyday life in French Polynesia, whether it is for utilitarian or decorative use, and the annual displays in Papeete in September testify to their importance. They contribute to the visual – and olfactory – appeal of hotel rooms and restaurant tables, are presented to new arrivals at airports and are worn in the hair or as necklaces or crowns. Tiare, jasmine, hibiscus and frangipani are the flowers most often used for necklaces and crowns.

Engraved mother-of-pearl is another decorative element, which is often used to decorate dance costumes. Shells are used to make necklaces, and it's traditional to use them to garland people arriving and departing the islands.

Tattoos See the 'Tattooing' special section for information on this ancient technique, which has been adapted to modern tastes.

SOCIETY & CONDUCT

French Polynesia is generally very easygoing and there are few pitfalls for the unwary visitor. Despite this you will still sometimes encounter people who are *fiu* (have the blues) and are distant and unreceptive. Don't show your impatience – it won't get you anywhere.

Remember the standards of conduct today are often a blend of Polynesian and French customs – you'll see Polynesian friends

Mahu & Rae Rae

Do not be surprised if you take *le truck* in Papeete on a weekend evening and an exceptionally tall and ravishing Tahitian woman steps onto your bus. She is not, in fact, a woman at all, but a *mahu* or *rae rae* – a transvestite.

Transvestites have always held an important place in Polynesian society, as can be seen in the writings of European explorers, and are considered perfectly acceptable members of it. The number of transvestites in French Polynesia is linked to a family practice that is still common: In many families the eldest son is raised as a girl and adopts the behaviour of a girl.

In everyday speech a distinction is made between the mahu, who are the effeminate men, and the rae rae, who are the transvestites engaging specifically in prostitution in the hot spots of Papeete. The mahu are highly valued in the restaurant and hotel business for their refinement and the quality of the service they provide.

greeting with a kiss on both cheeks, just as if they were in Paris. The body language you're most likely to notice is raised eyebrows as a sign of compliance.

Dress standards are generally relaxed, and coats and ties are not necessary even at the fanciest Papeete restaurants. Religion permeates everyday life and, contrary to popular mythology, Polynesian women are very chaste. Half-naked *vahine* (women) cavorting on white-sand beaches only exist in locally produced calendars. Except around westernised Papeete, local women usually wear shorts and T-shirts in the water, and nudity on the beach is only generally permissible on isolated motu. Unlike Fiji and other more straight-laced Pacific Islands, women are allowed to 'go topless'(not wear a bikini top) in French Polynesia at big hotel beaches and swimming pools. Elsewhere, however, this is inappropriate.

Avoid public demonstrations of affection or intimacy, which are not normal in Polynesia. You won't see local couples kissing or embracing in public, or even holding hands.

The Polynesians are very religious so it's wise to avoid criticism of the subject. Attending church on a Sunday can be an interesting insight into their lives, but always dress and behave politely.

At archaeological sites, don't move stones or tiki. For many Polynesians, these are living places and such actions would be very bad mannered. Respect these sites.

If visiting a Polynesian home, the first rule, as in Japan, is to take your shoes off at the front door. Your hosts may insist that it's unnecessary but you'll win friends if you refuse their entreaties and insist that you would be more comfortable shoeless. At the table simple politeness and watching what others do will usually work. Offer to fill other glasses before your own, for example. Some Tahitian foods are eaten with fingers, so don't always expect utensils. Respect private property signs, which often indicate that entry is *tapu* (taboo).

Most waterfront land is privately owned so before trying to make your way down to the water, ask permission. Similarly, fruit trees are almost always private property; never pick fruit without asking first.

Note that tipping is not expected in French Polynesia and also that bargaining (except for pearls) is not practised.

RELIGION

The arrival of Protestant missionaries at the end of the 18th century, followed soon after by Catholic priests, marked the end of traditional religious beliefs and practises. Rituals, gods, religious buildings and symbols were all obliterated. The missionaries even dictated what people could wear.

Women were required to wear the all enveloping Mother Hubbard, or mission dress, once they reached maturity. See the 'Civilisation & Archaeology' special section for more on the traditional religion.

French Polynesia has a surprising number and variety of churches relative to its population. It's an indicator of the struggle for influence by the various missionary movements during the 19th century. Half of the population follows the Protestant Evangelical Church of Polynesia, which is particularly strong in the Society Islands and the Australs. Catholics represent 30 to 35% of the population and live mostly in the Marquesas, the eastern Tuamotus and the Gambier Archipelago as well as on Tahiti among the demis and Chinese. The balance is made up of Mormons, Seventh-Day Adventists, Sanitos (the local name for the reorganised Church of Jesus Christ of the Latter Day Saints, a dissident branch of the Mormons), Jehovah's Witnesses and Jews (Papeete has a synagogue). Most Chinese converted to Catholicism in the 1950s and 60s.

On some islands, where attending mass is almost the only distraction, the variety and number of churches and the religious devotion of the inhabitants is quite remarkable. Cemeteries, on the other hand, are rare because most people bury their dead in front of their houses. Try to attend a church service if only to hear the wonderful hymn-singing and admire the immaculate white outfits of the women.

The churches are very influential, wield strong financial power and play a major role in the social life, politics and culture of the islands. Biblical references pepper political speeches, and grace often precedes a meal. Pastors and priests are not hesitant about playing a part in public life and the Protestant church took a strong position against nuclear testing. Curiously, the churches today actively promote the olden-day Polynesian culture, particularly when it comes to language – Tahitian and Marquesan are the languages of church services.

Paradoxically, some pre-Christian rituals and superstitions survive and thrive. In some dwellings a light is always left on overnight for fear that *tupapau* (spirits of the dead) or a *varua ino* (malevolent spirit) might be on the prowl. In the same way, Polynesians respect and fear ancient *tapu* sites. Nothing would persuade them to move a tiki or marae stone, and on occasion they will consult a *tahua,* or faith healer.

LANGUAGE

Tahitian and French are the official languages of French Polynesia although Tahitian is spoken much more than it is written. Much of the tourist industry uses English but, if you venture to the more remote and less touristy islands where the Tahitian dialects are spoken, it's definitely useful to know some French. Fortunately, bad French is readily accepted in French Polynesia – you won't be ignored just because your accent is poor! See the Language chapter for more information, and for useful Tahitian and French phrases. For more-extensive Tahitian-language tips, pick up a copy of Lonely Planet's *South Pacific phrasebook.*

Facts for the Visitor

HIGHLIGHTS
Landscapes
French Polynesia is naturally well endowed – the sheer cliffs of Tahiti Iti, the smaller end of the Tahiti dumb-bell; the nearly 2000m-high volcanic peaks of Tahiti Nui, the larger end; the stunning Cook's and Opunohu bays of Moorea; the Maroe and Bourayne bays of Huahine; mountainous Bora Bora with its idyllic lagoon and *motu* (sandy islets in the lagoon or on the outer reef); picture-postcard Tetiaroa; the wild motu of the Tuamotu atolls; the impressive peaks and bays of the Marquesas; and the amazingly varied Australs are just some examples.

Activities
Scuba diving and snorkelling, among multi-coloured fish, dolphins, rays and the islands' famously accessible sharks, are prime activities in French Polynesia. Beginners and experienced divers are welcome at a host of dive sites around the islands. Surfing is popular on Tahiti, Moorea and Huahine. With a local guide there are some surprisingly testing hikes to be made on Tahiti, Moorea, Raiatea, Bora Bora and Maupiti. Yachts can be chartered from Raiatea, the yachting centre of Polynesia, or you can explore many of the lagoons with smaller *pirogues* (outrigger canoes) or outboard-powered dinghies. Or you could just play Robinson Crusoe on a deserted motu.

Culture
Many archaeological sites have been restored and you can visit marae (sacred religious structures) on Tahiti, Moorea, Huahine and Raiatea, and see tiki, tohua (esplanades of stone) and petroglyphs (pictograms incised into stone) on many islands – particularly in the Marquesas. There are many interesting handicrafts, including wood and stone Marquesan sculptures, shell work, flower necklaces, tapa (bark-cloth), hand painted pareu (sarongs), basketwork and tifaifai (appliqué).

Food
The food is always fresh and includes French, Chinese and, of course, Polynesian specialities. Try *poisson cru*, the famed raw fish of Polynesia; prawns (shrimp) in coconut milk; *mahi mahi* (dolphin fish – not a dolphin) seasoned with Tahaa vanilla; chow mein; lobster; poe (plantain-like bananas); coconut bread; tuna sashimi; and a wide variety of luscious exotic fruits. Don't miss an opportunity to try a meal prepared in an ahi-maa (traditional Tahitian oven).

Pearl Farms
The full story of Polynesia's famed black pearls can be explored at pearl farms on Manihi, Rangiroa, Fakarava and Tahaa, or at the Pearl Museum in Papeete. Numerous jewellery shops sell mounted and unmounted pearls.

Festivals
Heiva in Papeete in July celebrates the Maohi culture, the culture of the peoples of Polynesia. It's the biggest festival of the year with dance, song and traditional sports. All year round, the Polynesian dance performances in the big hotels are not be missed.

Off the Beaten Track
Voyage to the Tuamotus on a cargo ship, swim with whales at Rurutu or with dolphins at Nuku Hiva. Flightsee over an island in a helicopter or parasail over Nuku Hiva. Get married in a traditionally kitsch ceremony at the Tiki Village on Moorea. Or bring home a permanent souvenir, a traditional tattoo from the place where the word was invented.

SUGGESTED ITINERARIES
Don't expect to see everything; French Polynesia consists of five archipelagos spread over an expanse of ocean larger than Europe. If you only allow two or three days for each island – one to tour the island, one to tour the lagoon and one to do something

like scuba diving or hiking – you'll soon run through a lot of time.

One Week
A stay as short as this will still allow you to visit Tahiti, Moorea and Bora Bora, with a quick visit to Rangiroa or Tikehau in the Tuamotus, thanks to direct flights from Bora Bora to Rangiroa.

Two Weeks
This is the minimum time to get a taste of all the major Society group islands and continue to an atoll in the Tuamotus. Allow two days for Tahiti, two for Moorea, two for Huahine, three for Raiatea and Tahaa, two for Bora Bora, one for Maupiti and, if you're a scuba-diving or lazing-about enthusiast, two to three for Rangiroa in the Tuamotus.

Three Weeks
Three weeks will allow you to explore several islands in depth. You could visit all the main islands of the Society group, by air or sea, and continue on to the Tuamotus (Rangiroa, Tikehau and Manihi) or the Australs (Rurutu and Tubuai) by air. Another possibility is to allow a week and a bit for the Society Islands and then take a 10 to 12 day cruise with the *Aranui* to the Marquesas.

Four Weeks
A whole month will give you time to do the Society Islands, two or three atolls in the Tuamotus and several islands in the Marquesas if you use flights from Bora Bora to Rangiroa and from Rangiroa to Nuku Hiva in the Marquesas.

PLANNING
When to Go
French Polynesia is an outdoor destination. Many tourist activities require good weather, and the period from November to April statistically gets lots of rain. You're likely to see lots of clouds, and tropical downpours that can last for days. In theory heavy rain should be followed by hot sun but there are lots of variations and uncertainties – one island can be drowning day after day while a close neighbour is enjoying radiant sunshine. May to October is drier and slightly cooler, but from June to August the intermittent *maraamu* tradewinds can bring blustery weather and rain from the south. During that period it's often better on the more sheltered northern sides of the high islands.

French Polynesia is south of the equator but school holidays still fall in line with France's, so adding to crowds at resorts and making flights more difficult to get. This means that from Christmas to early January, late February and early March, the Easter period, early May, the longer northern-summer holiday in July-August, and early October are likely to be busiest.

The month of activities in July combines the local Heiva festivities with the French Bastille Day celebrations on 14 July. There are dance, music, all sorts of sporting and cultural events, beauty contests and big crowds. It's not only popular locally but is also one of the most popular times of year for international visitors to French Polynesia, so plan ahead. March is a popular holiday month in the Australs, Marquesas and Tuamotus.

Diving is popular all year round and each season brings its share of discoveries. See the 'Diving' special section following the Outdoor Activities chapter for more details. Surfing is also a year-round activity, but sailing is best if you avoid the November to March tropical depressions – they can be depressing! Walking is also better in the dry season, as some of the trails are simply impassable when it's wet.

What Kind of Trip
There are all sorts of ways to visit French Polynesia, and styles of travel to suit every budget. At one extreme there are organised tours, stunning hotels and luxury island-to-island cruises. At the other are the backpackers who may spend two or three weeks exploring the Society Islands and perhaps an atoll of the Tuamotus. For these long-distance explorers, French Polynesia may be just one stop in a longer journey across the South Pacific.

Maps
The map *Tahiti Archipel de la Société* (IGN No 3615) at 1:100,000 is readily available in Papeete and at map specialists abroad. It covers the whole of the Society Archipelago and is the one really useful map for tourists. IGN also publishes maps at

Where Are the Beaches?

It's a cruel disillusion! You get off your plane, dreaming of lounging on a beach, cocktail in hand, only to find Polynesia is a *lagoon* destination, not a *beach* destination. Those long white-sand beaches are in the Seychelles and Caribbean, not in Polynesia. Don't be fooled by the lagoon-side definition – it doesn't necessarily mean it's close to a beach.

There are a few small beaches on Tahiti (usually black sand), Moorea, Huahine, Bora Bora and Maupiti, as well as on the Marquesas and the Tuamotus, but none to match that postcard dream. Worse still, the beaches on the Marquesas are plagued by *nono*, an insect far more annoying than mosquitoes.

Some luxury hotels have created their own artificial beaches, but a continuous barrier of properties along the coastlines can make them difficult to get to.

So where are those postcard beach-scapes? Well ... on the *motu*, the sandy islands around the barrier reef that fringes a lagoon. Some luxury resorts are situated on motu, but otherwise you will generally need a boat to get to them. Many excursion tours make motu stops, or you can arrange to be marooned on a motu for the day.

1:50,000 for each island in the archipelago. The SHOM navy maps are the best available of the Tuamotus. There are SHOM maps or IGN maps at 1:50,000 for Hiva Oa, Nuku Hiva and Ua Pou in the Marquesas. You can find these maps in Papeete at Prince Hinoi Centre, Ave Prince Hinoi, or at Klima, Rue Jeanne-d'Arc. In Paris, try Librairie Maritime et d'Outre Mer (☎ 01-46 33 47 48).

What to Bring

The climate is mild and dress rules are relaxed so you don't need to bring much with you. Coats and ties are not required except on the most formal business occasions and it would take a cold day in the Australs, the most southerly group, to need more than a short-sleeved shirt. Shorts, swimsuits and lightweight cotton clothes are the order of the day.

This is the tropics, and visitors should be prepared for the intense sun (bring sunscreen, sunglasses and a hat) while not forgetting that it can disappear to be replaced by heavy (but usually short) downpours. The temperatures will remain high, however, so an umbrella is probably wiser than a raincoat. Insect repellent can be near vital, particularly if you have any sensitivity to mosquito bites, and a small first-aid kit (see the Health section later in this chapter) is always wise. Plastic shoes or an old pair of sneakers are a good idea for avoiding cuts. To keep your camera gear protected from water and humidity, bring a plastic bag and desiccating sachets.

Imported goods are always expensive in French Polynesia so bring sunscreen, film, toiletries and any other consumables. If, however, you find you need a swimsuit or a new T-shirt, there are lots on sale, often at not too-excessive prices. Such items are imported from Europe, the USA and Asia.

If you're backpacking or travelling to the more remote islands, you'll need to pack some essentials that are unnecessary for those staying at the big hotels. Small family-run *pensions* (guesthouses) may not supply towels or soap, so bring both. Laundrettes are rare outside of Papeete, where they're very expensive, so come prepared to wash your own clothes.

Although overseas visitors are often given some leeway, the official baggage-weight limit on Air Tahiti flights is just 10kg, so pack light. You can always leave things behind in Papeete, but bring something to pack the leftovers in. If you're going to be travelling extensively, jumping on and off inter-island boats, riding *le trucks* (public buses) and so on, then a soft bag, like a backpack or a travel pack, will be easy to travel with.

If you're going hiking, bring good shoes and a light jacket or sweater; it can get surprisingly cool on top of the mountains. Don't forget your mask, snorkel and fins for exploring the lagoons, and your dive card if you're a certified diver.

TOURIST OFFICES
Local Tourist Offices
The main tourist office is on the quayside in Papeete. For information, contact GIE Tahiti Tourisme (☎ 50 57 00, fax 43 66 19, email tahiti-tourisme@mail.pf), BP 65, Papeete, Tahiti; or visit its Web site at www.tahiti-tourisme.com. This office centralises information for the whole of French Polynesia.

The more touristed of the other islands will often have some sort of tourist office or counter, but they vary widely in usefulness and dependability. These offices are generally run by local government or businesses, and even finding them open is a hit-and-miss affair. Local guesthouse operators are often the best source of information.

Tourist Offices Abroad
Overseas representatives of Tahiti Tourisme include:

Australia
(☎ 02-9281 6020, fax 9211 6589, email paramor@ozemail.com.au)
The Limerick Castle, 12 Ann St, Surry Hills, NSW 2010

Chile
(☎/fax 2-251 28 26, email tahiti@cmet.net)
Ave 11 De Septiembre 2214, OF-116, Box 16057, STGO 9, Santiago

France
(☎ 01 55 42 61 21, fax 01 55 42 61 20, email tahitipar@calva.net)
28, Blvd Saint-Germain, 75005 Paris

Germany
(☎ 69-9714 84, fax 7292 75)
Bockenheimer Landstr 45, D-60 325 Frankfurt/Main

Hong Kong
(☎ 2525 1367, fax 2845 9560, email pacific@cary.com)
15th Floor, United Overseas Bank Bldg, 54-58 Des Voeux Rd, Central

Indonesia
(☎ 021-727928546, email gsa@pacific.net.id)
JL Panglima Polim Raya, No 127/10 C, Jakarta 12150

Italy
(☎ 02-66 980317, email staff@aigo.com)
Piazza Caiazzo 3, 20 124 Milano

Japan
(☎ 03-3265 0468, fax 3265 0581, email tahityo@mail.fa2.so-net.ne.jp)
Sankyo Bldg (No 20) 8F-802, 3-11-5 Iidabashi, Chiyoda-Ku, Tokyo 102
(☎ 06-6635 3266, fax 6635 5025, email tahitosa@fa2.so net.ne.jp)
Osaka City Air Terminal Bldg (OCAT) 3F, 1-4-1 Minato-Machi, Naniwa-Ku, Osaka 556-0017

New Zealand
(☎ 09-360 8880, fax 360 8891, email renae@tahiti-tourisme.co.nz)
Villa Tahiti, 36 Douglas St, Ponsonby, Auckland

Singapore
(☎ 732 1904, fax 732 3205, email cti-network@pacific.net.sg)
c/o CTI Network Pte Ltd, 321 Orchard Rd, #09-01 Orchard Shopping Centre, Singapore 238 866

Taiwan
(☎ 02-593 5279, fax 591 9345, email knaintl@mail.ttn.com.tw)
c/o K & A International Co Ltd, 9F, No 9, Ming-Chuan E Rd Sec 2, Taipei

Thailand
(☎ 02-652 05 07, fax 652 05 09, email eckard@plgroup.com)
c/o Pacific Leisure, 8th Floor, Maneeya Centre Bldg, 518/5 Ploenchit Rd, Bangkok 10 330

USA
(☎ 310-414 8484, fax 414 8490, email tahitilax@earthlink.net)
300 Continental Blvd, Suite 160, El Segundo, CA 90 245

VISAS & DOCUMENTS
Passport & Visas
Except for French citizens, everyone visiting French Polynesia needs a passport, and the regulations are much the same as for France itself: if you need a visa to visit France then you'll need one to visit French Polynesia. Anyone from a European Union (EU) country can stay for up to three months without a visa. So can Australians and citizens of a number of other European countries, including Switzerland.

Citizens of Argentina, Canada, Chile, Japan, Mexico, New Zealand, the USA and some other European countries can stay for up to one month without a visa. Other nationalities need a visa, which can be applied for at French diplomatic missions. Visa regulations for French Polynesia can change at short notice so visitors should be sure to check with a French diplomatic office or with a travel agent shortly before departing.

Apart from permanent residents and French citizens, all visitors to French Polynesia must have an onward or return ticket.

Visa Extensions & Exemptions Travellers who must have a visa, or those who have a one month exemption and wish to extend their stay, should contact the Frontier Police (Police aux Frontières, formerly known as DICILEC) at Faaa international airport on Tahiti, open weekdays from 8 am to noon and from 2 to 5 pm, at least one week before the visa or exemption expires. The extension granted is for a maximum of two months, and incurs a tax of 3000 CFP.

Travellers with a three month visa exemption and all other foreign travellers who wish to extend their stay beyond three months must complete a form at the Direction de la Réglementation et du Contrôle de la Légalité (DRCL, ☎ 54 27 00), Blvd Pomare, Papeete. You must apply with plenty of time to spare, during the second month of your stay in the Territory, and extensions are not given automatically. One to three additional months may be granted. If you are successful, a tax of 3000 CFP is payable.

Stays by foreign visitors may not exceed six months in any 12. For longer periods, you must apply to the French consular authorities in your own country for a residence permit; you cannot lodge your application from French Polynesia. See Work later in this chapter for information on permits to work in the Territory.

Travel Insurance

A travel insurance policy to cover theft, loss and medical problems is a good idea. There are a wide variety of policies and your travel agent will have recommendations. The international student-travel policies handled by STA or other student-travel organisations are usually good value. Some policies offer lower and higher medical-expenses options, but the higher one is chiefly for countries like the USA that have extremely high medical costs. Check the small print.

Some policies specifically exclude 'dangerous activities', which can include scuba diving, motorcycling, even trekking. If such activities are on your agenda you don't want that sort of policy.

You may prefer a policy that pays doctors or hospitals directly rather than you having to pay on the spot and claim later. If you have to claim later, make sure you keep all documentation. Some policies ask you to call back (reverse charges) to a centre in your home country where an immediate assessment of your problem is made.

Check whether the policy covers ambulances or an emergency flight home. If you have to stretch out you will need two seats and somebody has to pay for them!

Other Documents

In practice, car rental agencies only ask to see your national driving licence but an international driving permit can be useful. It's a good idea to bring your scuba certification card if you plan to do any scuba diving in French Polynesia.

Photocopies

All important documents (passport data page and visa page, credit cards, travel insurance policy, air/bus/train tickets, driving licence etc) should be photocopied before you leave home. Leave one copy with someone at home for safe-keeping and keep another with you, separate from the originals.

It's also a good idea to store details of your vital travel documents in Lonely Planet's free online Travel Vault in case you lose the photocopies or can't be bothered with them. Your password-protected Travel Vault is accessible online anywhere in the world – create it at www.ekno.lonelyplanet.com.

Formalities for Yachts

In addition to presenting the certificate of ownership of the vessel, sailors are subject to the same passport and visa requirements as those travellers arriving by air or by cruise ship. Unless you have a return air ticket, you are required to provide a banking guarantee of repatriation equivalent to the price of an airline ticket to your country of origin.

Yachties must advise the Frontier Police at Papeete of their final departure and the police will then issue a release from the bond. This release document must be presented to the *gendarmerie* (police station) on the last island of call (generally Bora Bora for westbound yachts). Yachties may then have their bond released. It should be noted that each crew member must pay the bond.

It is compulsory that your first port of call, if it's not Papeete, be one of those with a gendarmerie: Afareaitu (Moorea), Uturoa (Raiatea), Fare (Huahine), Vaitape (Bora Bora), Taiohae (Nuku Hiva, Marquesas), Hakahau (Ua Pou, Marquesas), Atuona (Hiva Oa, Marquesas), Mataura (Tubuai, Australs), Moerai (Rurutu, Australs), Rairua (Raivavae, Australs), Avatoru (Rangiroa, Tuamotu) or Rikitea (Mangareva, Gambier). The gendarmerie must be advised of each arrival and departure, and of any change of crew.

Before arriving at the port of Papeete, notify your arrival on channel 12. Two anchorages are provided: the quay or the beach. There are no reserved places. Report to the *capitainerie* (harbour master's office) to complete an arrival declaration. To moor at the quay you have to pay a daily fee of 110 CFP per metre of boat length, plus 100 CFP per day for water, 288 CFP per day for electricity and 1000 CFP per month for garbage disposal, with a minimum of 5000 CFP. At the beach, but moored to shore, you pay a daily fee of 55 CFP per metre of boat length. Besides the Papeete harbour, there are anchorage points at the Yacht Club of Arue, the Taina Marina at Punaauia (often full) and the Vaiare Marina on Moorea.

Boats and equipment on board are considered duty-free for six months, which can be extended for a further six months upon application to the director of customs. Note that if the skipper works anywhere other than on the boat, he or she is no longer entitled to this exemption and must pay import duty on the boat.

The Papeete offices of the Frontier Police are open weekdays from 8 am to noon and from 2 to 4 pm; customs is open weekdays from 7 am to noon, and the capitainerie is open Monday to Thursday from 7 to 11.30 am and 1 to 4 pm, on Friday to 3 pm. They are all in the same building on the seafront, 50m from the tourist office. If you intend leaving Papeete on the weekend, report to these offices on Thursday to complete departure formalities.

On the other islands, the gendarmerie is the relevant authority, but in Papeete you must report to the three offices mentioned.

EMBASSIES & CONSULATES
French Embassies & Consulates

You will find diplomatic representation in :

Australia
Embassy
(☎ 02-6216 0100, fax 6273 3193)
6 Perth Ave, Yarralumla, ACT 2600
Consulate
(☎ 03-9820 0921, fax 9820 9363)
492 St Kilda Rd, Melbourne, VIC 3004
Consulate
(☎ 02-9261 5779, fax 9283 1210)
31 Market St, Sydney, NSW 2000
Belgium
Embassy
(☎ 02-548 8711, fax 513 6871)
65, rue Ducale, 1000 Brussels
Consulate
(☎ 02-229 8500, fax 229 8510)
12A, place de Louvain, BP 82, 1000 Brussels
Canada
Embassy
(☎ 613-789 1795, fax 789 0279)
42 Sussex Dr, Ottawa, ON K1M 2C9
Consulate
(☎ 416-925 8041, fax 925 3076)
130 Bloor St West, Suite 400, Toronto, ON M5S 1N5
Chile
Embassy
(☎ 02-225 10 30, fax 274 13 53)

Avenida Condell 65, Casilla 38-D, Providencia, Santiago

Fiji
Embassy
(☎ 312 233, fax 301 894)
Dominion House, Scott St, Suva

Germany
Embassy
(☎ 0228-955 6000, fax 955 6055)
An der Marienkapelle 3, D-53179 Bonn
Consulate
(☎ 030-885 90243, fax 885 5295)
Kurfürstendamm 211, D-10719 Berlin

Ireland
Embassy
(☎ 01- 260 16 66, fax 283 01 78)
36 Ailesbury Rd, Ballsbridge, Dublin 4

Israel
Embassy
(☎ 03-524 5371, fax 522 9294)
112 promenade Herbert Samuel, 63572 Tel Aviv

Japan
Embassy
(☎ 03-5420 8800, fax 5420 8847)
11-44 4-chome, Minami Azabu, Minato-ku, Tokyo 106
Consulate
(☎ 2-4790 1500, fax 4790 1511)
Crystal Tower 10F, 1-2-27 Shiromi, Cho-ku, Osaka 540-6010

New Zealand
Embassy
(☎ 04-384 2555, fax 384 2577)
Rural Bank Building, 13th floor, 34/42 Manners St, PO Box 1695, Wellington

Singapore
Embassy
(☎ 880 7800, fax 880 7801)
101 Cluny Park Rd, Singapore 1025

South Africa
Embassy
(☎ 021-21 2050, fax 26 1996)
807 George Ave, Arcadia, 0083 Pretoria
Consulate
(☎ 11-331 34 68, fax 331 34 97)
Carlton Center, 35th floor, Commissioner St, Johannesburg

Switzerland
Embassy
(☎ 031-359 2111, fax 352 2191)
Schosshaldenstrasse 46, 3006 Berne
Consulate
(☎ 022-319 0000, fax 319 0072/79)
11 Rue Imbert Galloix, 1205 Geneva

UK
Consulate
(☎ 020-7838 2000, fax 838 2001)

21 Cromwell Rd, London SW7 2DQ
Visa section is at 6A Cromwell Place, London SW7 2EW (☎ 020-7838 2051). Dial ☎ 0891-887733 for general visa information

USA
Embassy
(☎ 202-944 6000, fax 944 6166)
4101 Reservoir Rd NW, Washington DC 20007
Consulate
(☎ 310-235 3200, fax 312 0704)
10990 Wilshire Blvd, Suite 300, Los Angeles, CA 90024
Consulate
(☎ 212-606 3688, fax 606 3620)
934 Fifth Ave, New York, NY 10021
Consulate
(☎ 415-397 4330, fax 433 8357)
540 Bush St, San Francisco, CA 94108
Other consulates: Atlanta, Boston, Chicago, Honolulu, Houston, Los Angeles, Miami, New Orleans and San Juan (Puerto Rico)

Diplomatic Missions in French Polynesia

Since French Polynesia is not an independent country, there are no foreign embassies, only consulates, and many countries are represented in Papeete by honorary consuls, not by the regular diplomatic services. Curiously (if one considers the number of tourists that visit) neither Canada, the USA nor Japan have any diplomatic representation in French Polynesia. If you need an American visa the nearest place to inquire about it is Fiji. If you're a Canadian and you lose your passport the Australian consulate may be able to help.

Australia
(☎ 43 88 38, fax 41 05 19)
c/o Qantas Airways, Vaima Centre, Papeete
BP 1695, Papeete

Austria (also represents Switzerland and Liechtenstein residents)
(☎ 43 91 14, fax 43 21 22)
Rue de la Cannonière Zélée, Papeete
BP 4560, Papeete

Belgium
(☎ 82 54 44, 83 75 09, fax 83 55 34)
Ecole Notre-Dame des Anges, Faaa
BP 6003, Faaa

Your Own Embassy

It's important to realise what your own embassy – the embassy of the country of which you are a citizen – can and can't do to help you if you get into trouble. Generally speaking, it won't be much help in emergencies if the trouble you're in is remotely your own fault. Remember that you are bound by the laws of the country you are in. Your embassy will not be sympathetic if you end up in jail after committing a crime locally, even if such actions are legal in your own country.

In genuine emergencies you might get some assistance, but only if other channels have been exhausted. For example, if you need to get home urgently, a free ticket home is exceedingly unlikely – the embassy would expect you to have insurance. If you have all your money and documents stolen, it might assist with getting a new passport, but a loan for onward travel is out of the question.

Some embassies used to keep letters for travellers or have a small reading room with home newspapers, but these days the mail holding service has usually been stopped and even newspapers tend to be out of date.

Chile
   (☎ 43 89 19, 42 62 40, 82 90 23, fax 43 48 89)
   Ave du Général de Gaulle, Papeete
   BP 952, Papeete
Germany
   (☎ 42 99 94, 42 80 84, fax 42 96 89)
   Rue Gadiot, Pirae
   BP 452, Papeete
Italy
   (☎ 43 45 01, fax 43 45 07)
   Punaauia, Punaruu Valley
   BP 380 412, Tamanu
Netherlands
   (☎ 42 49 37, 43 06 86, fax 43 56 92)
   Mobil Building, Fare Ute, Papeete
   BP 2804, Papeete
New Zealand
   (☎ 54 07 47/40, fax 42 45 44)
   c/o Air New Zealand, Vaima Centre,
   Papeete BP 73, Papeete

CUSTOMS

The duty-free allowance for visitors entering French Polynesia includes 200 cigarettes or 50 cigars, two litres of spirits or wine, two cameras and 10 rolls of unexposed film, one video camera, 50g of perfume, and sporting equipment. Note that people arriving from Fiji or Pago Pago in American Samoa will have their baggage fumigated upon arrival at the airport because of concerns about introducing the destructive coconut fly. No live animals can be imported (if they're on a yacht

they must stay on board) and certification is required for plants. For information on customs regulations for yachts, see Formalities for Yachts earlier in this chapter.

MONEY
Currency

The unit of currency in French Polynesia is the franc Confédération Française du Pacifique (CFP), called the franc cours Pacifique. There are coins of 1, 2, 5, 10, 20, 50 and 100 CFP and notes of 500, 1000, 5000 and 10,000 CFP. French Polynesia has not accepted the introduction of the euro.

Exchange Rates

The CFP is at a fixed rate to the French franc (and thus to the euro) and therefore varies against other currencies with the franc.

country	unit		conversion
Australia	A$1	=	75 CFP
Canada	C$1	=	80 CFP
euro	€ 1	=	120 CFP
France	1FF	=	18 CFP
Germany	DM1	=	61 CFP
Japan	¥100	=	114 CFP
New Zealand	NZ$1	=	60 CFP
UK	UK£1	=	189 CFP
USA	US$1	=	118 CFP

An Expensive Place?

Tahiti has a reputation for being horribly expensive, rather snobbish and not as much fun as it should be. Well, it *is* pretty pricey, but if you can push thoughts of ticking meters to the back of your mind it can be an enormously enjoyable place to visit. Some prices you might encounter include US$50 per person per night for half-board in a local guesthouse; US$7 for *poisson cru* (raw fish), a popular snack; US$15 for a 36-exposure roll of slide film and US$500 for a return ticket to the Marquesas. On the other hand, a scuba dive costs US$50, not out of line with other dive locations, a litre of milk at the supermarket is US$1.50 and a 1.5-litre bottle of mineral water costs US$0.80.

Not everything in French Polynesia is priced through the ceiling. *Le truck*, as the truck-like local bus service is known, is definitely the way to get around the Papeete area. It's cheap (about US$1.30 along the hotel strip of the coast), very frequent and easy to use. And we may wish the French had left their nuclear bombs at home, but any visitor will be glad they brought their bread with them. Tahiti's terrific French-bread sandwiches *(casse-croûte)* have to be the best food bargain in the Pacific. There are even luxury bargains, like the cocktails in five-star hotels.

Some of those five-star over-water bungalows are truly superb, but the islands are still de-servedly popular with backpackers. You can rent bicycles or motor scooters to get around, there's a selection of small family-run *pensions* (guesthouses) on almost every inhabited is-land and, so long as you've got plenty of time, there are lots of inter-island boats to shuttle you around. It's no wonder backpacks are a common sight in the dockside bustle of Papeete.

Why are things so expensive? First of all, because it's a colonial economy with a heavy layer of French-style bureaucracy run at metropolitan-French costs – *plus* an overseas loading! – French Polynesia is weighed down with French civil servants pulling huge salaries. In turn, many other pay scales are linked to this inflated baseline. Secondly, income tax is minimal, but there are heavy import-duties on many products, and taxes on hotel rooms and tourist activities. Finally, a great many products are shipped all the way around the world from France rather than being bought from neighbouring Pacific nations. Of course there's one good thing about the high prices: French Polynesia is not plagued by mass tourism.

Exchanging Money

There are hefty bank charges for changing money (other than French francs) and trav-ellers cheques in French Polynesia. Banque Socredo charges 350 CFP for each transac-tion; Banque de Polynésie and Banque de Tahiti charge 400 CFP. This means on a US$100 exchange you lose around 4%. The answer, of course, is to spread the cost over a larger transaction – given the high cost of living, the money is soon going to disappear in any case! The exchange rates vary from bank to bank, so check before changing.

Banks There are three major banks oper-ating in French Polynesia: Banque de Tahiti, Banque de Polynésie and Banque Socredo. Socredo, with connections to Banque National de Paris (BNP) and Crédit Agricole, is the bank you find most commonly. In some places, like the islands of the Marquesas, it may be the only bank sign you see.

Apart from Banque Socredo most banks are concentrated in Papeete and the more populous islands of Moorea, Raiatea and Bora Bora. All the main islands in the So-ciety group, apart from Maupiti, have at least a banking agency. In the Tuamotus, only Rangiroa has a permanent banking ser-vice. In the Marquesas there are Socredo agencies on Ua Pou, Nuku Hiva and Hiva

Oa. In the Australs, Rurutu and Tubuai have some banking services.

Banking hours vary from branch to branch but are typically from 8 am to noon and 1 to 4 pm, perhaps only to 3 or 3.30 pm on Friday. Some branches in Papeete do not close for the traditional Polynesian lunch-break and a handful of Tahiti branches open on Saturday morning. The Banque de Polynésie has banking facilities open at Papeete's Faaa airport for flight arrivals.

ATMs Automated teller machines (DABs; *distributeurs automatiques de billets*) will give you cash advances on your Visa or MasterCard or, if linked to the international Cirrus or Maestro networks, they will let you withdraw money straight from your home bank account. The exchange rate on these transactions is usually better than you get with travellers cheques and, since the banks have such a hefty fixed rate on all exchange transactions, the charge your own bank makes on these withdrawals (typically about US$2 to US$5) doesn't hurt as much. Note that there's a limit of 35,000 CFP in withdrawals or advances per week from any one account.

ATMs can be found at numerous locations on Tahiti but they're less common on other islands. Moorea, Huahine, Raiatea and Bora Bora currently have ATMs, but just a few. On other islands you can forget it! It is, however, possible to get a cash advance in a bank with your credit card and passport.

Credit Cards Expensive and mid-range hotels, restaurants on the tourist islands, souvenir and jewellery shops, dive centres, the major supermarkets and Air Tahiti all accept credit cards, preferably Visa or MasterCard.

Tipping & Bargaining

Officially, tipping is not compatible with the Polynesian outlook on life and the tourist office discourages it. When it comes to bargaining, the Pacific is not like Asia: nowhere in the Pacific is bargaining the norm and the price listed is the price you're expected to pay. Throughout French Polynesia virtually the only exceptions are for black pearls or similar expensive jewellery, where some discounting can always be expected, and for craftwork sold directly by the artist (Marquesan sculptures for example).

POST & COMMUNICATIONS
Post

Mail to Europe, the USA and Australia takes about a week, and the postal system is generally quite efficient. There are modern post offices on all the main islands. French Polynesian stamps are often beautiful but even more often they're massive. Put stamps on your postcard first so you know how much space is left to squeeze the address in. If you're lucky there may still be room for your message.

Post offices are generally open weekdays from 7 am to around 3 pm. The main post office in Papeete has longer opening hours and the post office at Faaa airport is open from 6.30 to 11 am on weekends.

Aerograms cost 90 CFP. Postcards or letters up to 20g in weight cost 85 CFP to France, 120 CFP anywhere else.

Sending & Receiving Mail There is no door-to-door mail delivery in French Polynesia, so mail is usually addressed to a BP (*boîte postale* – post-office box) number. If you want to receive mail, ask for it to be addressed to you care of the poste restante at the appropriate place, eg John Doe, c/- Poste Restante, Vaitape, Bora Bora, French Polynesia.

American Express card or travellers-cheque holders can have mail addressed to them care of the American Express agent in French Polynesia: Tahiti Tours, BP 627, Papeete, Tahiti, French Polynesia.

Telephone

The telephone system is modern, easy to use, widespread and, when it comes to international calls, rather expensive. Public phone boxes are found even in surprisingly remote locations but most of them require phonecards rather than coins. Phonecards can be bought from post offices and from many retail shops. They're even available from vending machines at Faaa airport.

Phonecards are available in 1000, 2000 and 5000 CFP denominations. A 5000 CFP card will give you a more than a half-hour phone call from a public phone box to a US number. There's a mobile phone network in French Polynesia, but unless your phone will roam with the local Vini company, you're out of luck.

Local Calls There are no area codes in French Polynesia although the first two digits of the local number generally indicate its location. Tahiti numbers start with a 4, 5 or 8, Moorea is 56, Raiatea 66, Bora Bora and Maupiti 67, Huahine 68, Marquesas 92, Rurutu 94, Tubuai 95, Tuamotus 96 or 97, and the Gambier Archipelago 97. Local phone calls cost 32 CFP for four minutes at normal tariff rates. The rates for inter-island or inter-archipelago calls are much more expensive (40 CFP a minute inter-archipelago).

International Calls To call a number in French Polynesia from overseas, dial the international access number, then 689 (Tahiti's international dialling code), then the local number.

To call overseas from French Polynesia dial ☎ 00, then your country code, the area code (dropping any leading 0) and the local number. An information panel in the phone box explains, in French and English, how to make overseas calls. If you have any difficulty, call information on ☎ 3612. Contrary to what the panel says, the international operator (☎ 19) is not accessible from public phones boxes. If you want to make a reverse-charge call, ask for *un appel payable à l'arrivée*.

Although international call charges can still be astronomical from a hotel room, competition from American call-back companies has forced regular cuts in rates from French Polynesia. In 1999, the normal tariff (6 am to 12 midnight) and reduced tariff (12 midnight to 6 am) per-minute rates for overseas calls were: 135/100 CFP to France, Australia, New Zealand, USA and Canada; 200/100 CFP to other EU countries and Switzerland; and 175/100 CFP to Fiji and the Cook Islands.

Fax
You can send faxes from post offices but it costs 1250 CFP for the first page.

Email & Internet Access
The French Polynesian company Mana, aware that the region is rather backward when it comes to Internet access, is trying to rapidly catch up. At present it's only the big hotels and some of the pearl trade specialists who have email addresses or Web sites, but that is changing rapidly. There is a cybercafe in Papeete, a computer shop with Internet access on Raiatea and a café where you can send emails and surf the web on Bora Bora.

INTERNET RESOURCES
The World Wide Web is a rich resource for travellers. You can research your trip, hunt down bargain air fares, book hotels, check on weather conditions or chat with locals and other travellers about the best places to visit (or avoid!).

There's no better place to start your Web explorations than at the Lonely Planet Web site (www.lonelyplanet.com). Here you'll find succinct summaries on travelling to most places on earth, postcards from other travellers and the Thorn Tree bulletin board, where you can ask questions before you go or dispense advice when you get back. You can also find travel news and updates to many of our most popular guidebooks, and the subWWWay section links you to the most useful travel resources elsewhere on the Web.

Other practical Web sites for French Polynesia include: Tahiti Tourisme (www.tahiti-tourisme.com), Tahiti Nui Travel (www.tahiti-nui.com), Tahiti Communications (www.tahiti.com) and Tahiti Explorer (www.tahiti-explorer.com).

BOOKS
There is a surprisingly wide range of literature about French Polynesia and a number of excellent bookshops in Papeete. Some of the most interesting titles are readily available only in French Polynesia and there are some very interesting books that are available

only in French. Although the suggestions that follow are predominantly for books available in English, there are a few French titles that may be of interest even if your French is poor (or nonexistent).

Most books are published in different editions by different publishers in different countries. As a result, a book might be a hardcover rarity in one country while it's readily available in paperback in another. Fortunately, bookshops and libraries search by title or author, so your local bookshop or library is best placed to advise you on the availability of the following recommendations. See the relevant island chapters for information on bookshops.

Lonely Planet

If French Polynesia is just one stop on your Pacific travels, look for Lonely Planet's *South Pacific* guidebook, which is packed with information on exploring nations in Polynesia, Melanesia and Micronesia.

The extensively illustrated new Lonely Planet Pisces guide, *Diving & Snorkeling – French Polynesia*, covers 40 popular dive sites in the Society Islands, the Tuamotus and the Marquesas. To come to grips with Tahitian, look for Lonely Planet's *South Pacific phrasebook*, which also covers 12 other Pacific languages.

Guidebooks

In the 1960s and 70s, Nouvelles Éditions Latines in Paris and the Société des Océanistes produced a number of small guidebooks to French Polynesia, most of them available in French and English. Outdated but often interesting, they include the booklets *Moorea*, *Huahine*, *Wings over Tahiti* (the history of aviation in French Polynesia), *Sacred Stones & Rites* (about Polynesian temples), *Pomare – Queen of Tahiti* and *Bougainville in Tahiti*.

Mave Mai, The Marquesas Islands, by Chester, Baumgartner, Frechoso & Oetzel, was published in 1998. Two of the authors worked for several years as guides aboard the popular ship *Aranui*.

Even if you can't understand French, keen walkers may find *Randonnées en*

Montagne – Tahiti – Moorea, by Paule Laudon (1995, Les Éditions du Pacifique), invaluable. It grades by difficulty all the best walks on Tahiti and Moorea.

Visiting yachties will probably carry a copy of *Landfalls of Paradise: A Cruising Guide to the Pacific Islands* by Earl R Hinz. It gives a thorough coverage of Pacific cruising, including a number of islands in French Polynesia.

Travel

The congenitally acerbic Paul Theroux was at his sourest when he visited *The Happy Isles of Oceania* (1992). Crossing the whole South Pacific from Australia and New Zealand to Hawaii, he didn't find much of it, apart from Hawaii, very happy, but the insights are up to his usual high standards. In French Polynesia he visits Tahiti and Moorea but saves most of his energy for a trip on the *Aranui* to the Marquesas. As usual, his fellow passengers are prodded unmercifully with his sharpest pen and the beautiful yet gloomy, historic yet tragic, isolated yet spoilt Marquesas are the perfect site for a Theroux visit. The French don't come out of it very well but nor do the Polynesians, eagerly embracing their own decline.

Much more upbeat is Gavin Bell's award-winning *In Search of Tusitala* (1994), which traces the Pacific wanderings of Robert Louis Stevenson. Like a number of other writers, Bell finds the Marquesas fascinating, beautiful and deeply, almost frighteningly, depressing. 'How long has it been raining?' Bell asks the first Marquesan he meets, after a terrifying five approach landing. 'About one year,' comes the reply.

History

The European Arrival The contrast between the early explorers' accounts and the disillusionment of writers like Herman Melville and Robert Louis Stevenson just a century later is a measure of the Tahitian tragedy. For a concise and highly readable account of the collision of Europe and Polynesia, David Howarth's *Tahiti: a Paradise Lost* is hard to beat, although it's out of print.

Polynesia & the Pen

French Polynesia clearly has a magnetic effect on writers, who have flocked to the islands like bees to honey, gaining inspiration to launch careers, produce masterpieces or simply sit back and enjoy the scenery.

Herman Melville Melville (1819-91) was only a would-be writer when he turned up in Polynesia in 1842, but he arrived at a critical time, when the French were in the process of taking over. He deserted the whaler *Acushnet*, a real hell-ship (it became the *Dolly* in his novel), and escaped into an almost-forgotten valley on the island of Nuku Hiva. *Typee*, his first literary success, was inspired by his adventures there.

On the Australian whaleboat *Lucy Ann* (it became the American *Julia* in his second book, *Omoo*), Melville sailed on to Tahiti, where he was accused of attempting a mutiny. He arrived just as the French admiral Dupetit-Thouars was threatening Papeete. Melville was arrested and imprisoned, first on the French warship and then in the British prison in Papeete. With the government collapsing in the face of French threats, Melville simply wandered off and went to Moorea, where he briefly worked on a plantation, enjoyed a last look at the delights of Tahitian dance and sailed off, thoroughly disheartened by the French and the missionaries.

Victor Segalen A doctor in the French navy, Segalen (1878-1919) sailed round the world on the *Durance* and spent a year in Polynesia. He wrote a magnificent narrative about it, *Les Immémoriaux*, a vibrant homage to Polynesian civilisation that appeared in 1907. He also published *Journal des îles*, which grew out of his day-to-day impressions.

Following in the steps of Paul Gauguin, whom he passionately admired, Segalen examined Gauguin's attachment to the Polynesians, and used the artist's painting and writing to gain a better grasp of the cultural complexity of the region.

Robert Louis Stevenson Stevenson (1850-94) came to the Pacific seeking not inspiration, but good health. Chronically unhealthy from childhood, in 1888 he chartered the 74-ton *Casco* for a prolonged Pacific voyage from San Francisco. They paused first at Nuku Hiva, an island in the Marquesas that had suffered a catastrophic population decline since Melville's stay 40 years earlier. They then moved on to Hiva Oa, and to Fakarava in the Tuamotus.

Finally, they stopped in Papeete, which Stevenson did not like, but then continued on to a long and delightful stop at Tautira on Tahiti Iti. Stevenson enjoyed himself so much at Tautira that writing was pushed very much to one side, and his account of the voyage is not his best work. The trip inspired him to settle in the Pacific and he spent the rest of his life in Samoa.

Jack London A larger-than-life character, London (1876-1916) was born in San Francisco and grew up across the bay in Oakland. As a teenager, he began to build his legend, poaching oysters on San Francisco Bay, riding trains across the USA and joining the Klondike Gold Rush were all part of the story. The fortune he made from his many successful books never caught up with the even greater fortune he spent. His 1907-08 Pacific voyage, recounted in his 1911 book *Cruise of the Snark*, provided the background for *South Sea Tales* in the same year.

Pierre Loti There is a statue of him at Loti's Pool, on the outskirts of central Papeete, but Pierre Loti was in fact the pen name of Louis-Marie-Julian Viaud (1850-1923), a French naval

Polynesia & the Pen

officer whose life often imitated his art. Pierre Loti was the main character in *The Marriage of Loti*, based on the writer's experiences on Tahiti in 1872.

Rupert Brooke Rupert Brooke (1887-1915) was a patriotic soldier-poet at the beginning of WWI, before the idiocy of the war had really sunk in. His sonnets *1914*, with the lines about foreign fields which are forever England, are still remembered. His two-month stay on Tahiti in 1914 was highlighted by a passionate love affair with the beautiful Mamua, as he called his Tahitian lover, the inspiration for his poem *Tiare Tahiti*. Brooke returned to the USA but died a year later of food poisoning on a hospital ship in the Mediterranean en route to the madness in the Dardanelles.

Robert Keable Nobody much remembers Keable (1888-1928), whose religious novels *Simon Called Peter* and *Recompense* enjoyed huge sales in the early 20th century. He came to Tahiti in the 1920s hoping to find a cure for his tuberculosis, but lived only another five years. He did, however, write about Tahiti in two books, *Tahiti, Isle of Dreams* and *Numerous Treasures*. Despite his religious background, he was far from impressed by the missionaries on Tahiti.

W Somerset Maugham Novelist, short-story writer and playwright, Maugham (1874-1965) not only did well with his Gauguin-inspired novel, *The Moon & Sixpence*, but also, unlike other visitors intent on finding forgotten masterpieces, managed to find one of Gauguin's works. During his 1916 sojourn on the island, Maugham lived in Papeete and in Mataiea, Gauguin's old haunt between 1891 and 1893, and tracked down a glass-panelled door Gauguin had painted for his local landlord. Maugham bought it for 200 francs, and later installed it in his French Riviera villa. Shortly before he died, it sold for £13,000.

Nordhoff & Hall Charles Nordhoff (1887-1947) and James Norman Hall (1887-1951) went to Tahiti after WWI and eventually settled there, turning out a variety of articles, books and other works, both separately and as a team. Their big inspiration was to take the records of the *Bounty* mutiny and turn it into a three-part historic novel, based on facts but somewhat embroidered. They used Bligh's log, the British court martial proceedings, the account of James Morrison (the *Bounty*'s boatswain's mate) and accounts of the discovery of the mutineers' descendants to write three books, first published in 1934.

James Michener An American novelist (1907-97), whose name goes hand-in-hand with the word 'epic', was a foundling, adopted and brought up as a Quaker. He commenced his love affair with the Pacific as a WWII naval historian from 1944 to 1946; his first book, *Tales of the South Pacific*, was based on his experiences there and was an instant success, winning the Pulitzer Prize and appearing on Broadway as *South Pacific* a year later. Michener wrote two more South Pacific books.

Explorer James Cook's logbooks are the prime accounts of his pioneering visits to Polynesia. Originally they were published in heavily edited version that took considerable liberties with his observations. The most thorough version of the original logs, Professor John C Beaglehole's four volume, 3000 page *The Voyages of the Endeavour, 1768-1771*, by Captain James Cook, was published progressively between 1955 and

1967. It's recently been reprinted (Boydell & Brewer, US$1070). Beaglehole edited Sir Joseph Banks' account in the two volume *The 'Endeavour' Journal of Joseph Banks*, and has also written *The Exploration of the Pacific* and *The Life of Captain James Cook*.

Briefer accounts of Cook's voyages include *The Explorations of Captain James Cook in the Pacific*. These annotated extracts from his logs are fascinating even though they give you only a taste of the real thing. *The Voyage of the Endeavour: Captain Cook and the Discovery of the Pacific*, by Alan Frost, is a recent account of the epic voyage and is available in paperback. *The Fatal Impact*, by Alan Moorehead, is out of print but its account of Cook's voyages and the impact they had upon the untouched cultures of the Pacific and Australia are riveting.

Joseph Banks: A Life, by Patrick O'Brian, is a readable account of the life of the likeable young scientist on Cook's first expedition. Many other early visitors, including Wallis and Morrison, the boatswain's mate on the *Bounty*, wrote accounts of Tahiti, but you would have to use a major library to track them down. One of the few Polynesian accounts of pre-European Tahiti is Teuira Henry's book about her investigations into the ancient religion of the islands, *Ancient Tahiti*, published in 1928.

The American duo of Nordhoff & Hall wrote three books on the *Bounty* mutiny and its aftermath, published in 1934. *Mutiny on the Bounty* recounts the famous mutiny and provided the plotline for the first two cinematic versions of the story. *Men Against the Sea* follows Bligh's epic open-boat voyage, while *Pitcairn Island*, which makes use of much more imagination because so little is known about the facts, follows Fletcher Christian and his band of mutineers and Tahitians to their Pitcairn hideaway.

Natural History A variety of small books is available on the flora and fauna of Polynesia. Two worth looking at are *Birds of Tahiti*, by Jean-Claude Thibault & Claude Rivers (1988, Les Éditions du Pacifique), and *Sharks of Polynesia*, by RH Johnson (1990, Les Éditions du Pacifique).

General

A remarkable number of renowned writers have written books either using Polynesia as a setting or describing their own visits; see the boxed text 'Polynesia & the Pen' in this chapter for more information on some of these authors.

Melville was the first of the important literary visitors, deserting whalers in the Marquesas and then on Tahiti. His experiences in the 'cannibal' valley, where he made his Marquesan escape, resulted in his first novel, *Typee* (1846). Seductively subtitled in the British edition 'Narrative of a Four Months' Residence among the Natives of a Valley of the Marquesas Islands: or, a Peep at Polynesian Life', it was an instant success. He followed it up with *Omoo* (1847), based on his further Polynesian adventures.

French literature's primary addition to the Tahiti bookshelves was Pierre Loti's 1876 novel *The Marriage of Loti*, which made its own contribution to the romantic Tahitian myth.

Robert Louis Stevenson's cruise through Polynesia resulted in the book *In the South Seas*, published in 1900; although he was clearly falling in love with the region, the book is far from Stevenson at his best. Jack London also cruised the Pacific but, again, *South Sea Tales* (1911) is not the writer at his best. The greedy pearl buyer portrayed in 'The House of Mapuhi' successfully took London to court.

W Somerset Maugham managed rather better with Tahiti. He visited the island to research his 1919 novel *The Moon & Sixpence*, which is rather loosely based on Gauguin's life. See the boxed text 'Gauguin: the Wild & the Primitive' in the Marquesas chapter for information on Paul Gauguin.

James Michener launched his prodigious career in 1947 with *Tales of the South Pacific*, stories drawn from his experiences in the region during WWII. The most famous of those tales created the myth of Bali Ha (Bora Bora, of course, though it migrated many miles before becoming the setting of the stage play and film *South Pacific*). Michener returned to this happy hunting ground with *Return to Paradise* (1951) and *Rascals in Paradise* (1957).

Norwegian explorer Thor Heyerdahl's *Kon-Tiki: Across the Pacific by Raft* recounts the epic voyage that eventually ended in the Tuamotus (see the boxed text 'The Kon Tiki Voyage' in the Tuamotus chapter). Two other Heyerdahl books are out of print. He tried, unsuccessfully, to live in the Marquesas and wrote about it in *Fatu Hiva: Back to Nature*. His post-Kon Tiki archaeological exploits in Easter Island and on Rapa in the Australs are described in *Aku Aku*.

Art & Culture
The Art of Tahiti, by Terence Barrow, is a succinct and colourfully illustrated introduction to the art of the Society, Austral and Cook islands. Unfortunately, it does not extend to the Marquesas and it's out of print.

There are countless books on Gauguin and his works, but *Noa Noa: The Tahiti Journal of Paul Gauguin* is his own illustrated account of his life on Tahiti.

Tatau – Maohi Tattoo, by Dominique Morvan, with photographs by Claude Corault and Marie-Hélène Villierme (1993, Tupuna Productions), is a fascinating account of the resurgence of traditional tattooing in French Polynesia. See the following Coffee Table Books section as well.

Hiva Oa – Glimpses of an Oceanic Memory, by Pierre Ottino & Marie-Noëlle de Bergh-Ottino (1991, Département Archéologie, Papeete), is a locally produced book on the archaeology and art of the Marquesan island of Hiva Oa.

In 1999, publisher Le Motu launched a series on local artists with a short introductory text in English and French. The first three titles were *Dubois, Deloffre* and *Boullaire*.

Coffee-Table Books
French Polynesia is a region of amazing natural beauty, so it's hardly surprising that there are some excellent collections of high-quality photos.

Fabled Isles of the South Seas, by Winston Stuart Conrad, makes an erratic swing through the islands of Polynesia, dropping in on some rarely visited and photographed locations, including the Marquesas, the Tuamotus, the Gambier Archipelago and even remote Pitcairn Island, contrasting contemporary images with historical photos and old illustrations.

Photographer Marie-Helen Villierme's *Visages de Polynésie* (Faces of Polynesia) contains more than 100 black-and-white portraits of Polynesians of all ages and origins, from cargo-ship mechanics to village tradesmen, together with brief conversations in French and English. Also in black-and-white, *Tahiti Tattoos* by Italian fashion photographer Gian Paolo Barbieri, is a large-format photographic book featuring the human canvases of some of the island's best-known tattooists.

Tahiti from the Air, by Erwin Christian & Emmanuel Vigneron (1985, Les Éditions du Pacifique), has wonderful aerial photographs of French Polynesia. However, the construction of new hotels has already made some of the shots look out-of-date. Other books on the islands by the same photographer are *Marquesas, Images from the Land of Men* and, in French, *Bora Bora, Impressions d'une Île* and *Lumières du Lagon*.

Out of print, but worth a look if you can find a copy, are *Islands of Tahiti*, by Raymond Bagnis with photographs by Erwin Christian, a big coffee-table book with good photographs and some interesting text; and James Sears' *Tahiti – Romance & Reality*, which has some very interesting long excerpts from early visitors' journals.

The History of Aviation in French Polynesia/L'Aviation à Tahiti, by Jean-Louis Saquet, uses wonderful photographs and illustrations to tell the often colourful story of aviation in the region. It's just as well it's driven by the images, because the translation is appalling.

FILMS
Tahiti would seem to offer lots of cinematic possibilities, but nobody has made a movie about Wallis, Bougainville or Cook, the big names in early Polynesian exploration. James Michener's *South Pacific* may have been about Polynesia but it certainly wasn't filmed there. The great

Mutiny in the Cinema

Three times in 50 years the story of the famous uprising aboard the *Bounty* has been borrowed and embellished by big-budget film-makers.

Mutiny on the Bounty The original and most 'Hollywood' of the *Bounty* epics was made in 1935. It was directed by Frank Lloyd and starred Charles Laughton as Bligh at his worst. Fletcher Christian was played by Clark Gable at his clean-shaven (this was his last moustacheless film), all-American best. Although critics insist that this is the classic *Bounty* film, it certainly played fast and loose with history. Bligh flogs, keel-hauls, lies and cheats his way through the entire film. Life on the ship is unbearable and Fletcher Christian is a charming, brave, purposeful, rather American aristocrat. Furthermore, in this film, quite unlike history, it's Bligh himself who comes storming back to Tahiti to round up the mutineers. Christian and company even hang around on Tahiti waiting for British naval justice, when in reality they took off as quickly as possible. Very little of the film was made on Tahiti.

Mutiny on the Bounty The lavish three hour 1962 remake was directed by Lewis Milestone, and stars Trevor Howard as Bligh and Marlon Brando as Christian. This film is a much lusher and bigger budget affair than the black-and-white original. Filmed on Tahiti and Bora Bora, it makes the islands look just like the Polynesian myth, but Bligh remains a monster and Christian is a very strange creation – a sort of simpering fop who clearly would have driven any captain nuts. Making this film on Tahiti had a great effect on the local economy.

The Bounty This film is surprisingly respectable. Moorea, where most of the location filming was done, looks mouth-wateringly beautiful. And 1980s cinematic freedom meant that Polynesian nudity, and those goddess-like 'celestial forms' Bougainville so enthusiastically described, finally made it on to the screen.

Produced by Dino de Laurentis, directed by Roger Donaldson and released in 1984, Anthony Hopkins is the not-quite-so-bad-and-mad Bligh and Mel Gibson is the more-handsome-than-ever Christian. The scenery on Moorea looks fantastic, but better on the big screen than on video. This production abandoned the standard Nordhoff & Hall text and was based on *Captain Bligh & Mr Christian: The Men and the Mutiny* by Richard Hough, and thus seems to paint Bligh as more driven, stubborn and uncompromising than simply cruel and vindictive. It's not a bad film at all. If you want to re-enact your own *Bounty* adventure, the ship built for this version now operates cruises on Sydney Harbour in Australia.

Polynesian migration voyages have also been ignored, as has French colonialism and the world wars in the Pacific. In fact, Tahiti's role as a movie backdrop is almost exclusively tied up with the *Bounty* see the boxed text.

Tabu is the only quality film shot in Polynesia that has nothing to do with the *Bounty*. In 1931, American Robert Flaherty and German Friedrich Murnau filmed this 80 minute work of fiction, showing the inhabitants of Bora Bora in their natural environment. Reri, a young woman, becomes a priestess and, as such is *tapu* (taboo) to men. Her lover, Matahi takes her away. Their unfortunate liaison finishes with the death of the young man who has broken the law. Friedrich Murnau's accidental death just after completion of filming in March 1931 was a shock to the whole film crew, and some even thought that it may have been linked to the fact that he included certain taboo parts of the island in the film.

A 1979 big-budget remake of a 1937 classic (the original wasn't filmed on Tahiti), *Hurricane,* was based on a Nordhoff & Hall novel. It was filmed on Bora Bora and was a major flop, despite an all-star cast. For TV it was retitled *Forbidden Paradise.* Produced by Dino de Laurentis, it clearly didn't kill his passion for Tahiti, as he came back to make the third *Bounty* epic.

NEWSPAPERS & MAGAZINES

Le Kiosque in the Vaima Centre and the Polygraph bookshop in downtown Papeete have a wide selection of international newspapers and magazines. There are other well-equipped newsstands in Papeete, but elsewhere, local TV is probably the best way of keeping up to date with world events.

Even finding current editions of the two French-language Tahitian dailies, *Les Nouvelles de Tahiti* and *La Dépêche de Tahiti*, is not easy away from Tahiti and Moorea. Both papers are part of the local Hersant empire and are strong supporters of Tahoera Huiraatira, which is adamant that French Polynesia should remain part of France. *Tahiti Pacifique* is a monthly news magazine covering political, economic, social and cultural life in French Polynesia. It doesn't shirk controversial issues and could be considered a newspaper of the opposition.

Tahiti Beach Press is a free English-language weekly tourist paper with some local news coverage. *Pacific Islands Monthly,* also known as *PIM,* is the news magazine of the ex-English and Australian colonies of the Pacific. It's published in Fiji, which does raise some questions of political bias when it comes to reporting in that area.

RADIO & TV

There are about 15 independent radio stations broadcasting mainly musical programs, a few interviews, news flashes in French and Tahitian, and advertising. Broadcasting is mainly from Tahiti and Moorea, with some on the Leeward Islands. Among the best-known are Radio Tiare (the pioneer nongovernment radio station), Radio Tahiti

Api, Radio Bleue, Radio Maohi, Te Reo o Tefana (pro-independence), Radio 1, NRJ and RFO Radio. Radio Marquises is based on Nuku Hiva. RFO Radio is received everywhere and broadcasts many local programs in Tahitian as well as the news from France Inter live every hour.

Radio France Outremer has two television channels, Télépolynésie and Tempo. The first channel broadcasts from 5.30 am to midnight and the second from 9 am to midnight. The programs consist of a selection of the main films and broadcasts from the three national channels, particularly the TF1 news (live) and France 2 news (delayed broadcast). The local news (Vea Tahiti) is in Tahitian at 6.45 pm and in French at 7.15 pm. In addition to these, on Tahiti only, are Canal + and Téléfenua, a cable package including, among others, CNN, Canal J, Planète, Eurosport and Ciné Cinéma. The Australs, Tuamotus and Marquesas have to make do with Télépolynésie for the moment.

VIDEO SYSTEMS

The video format in French Polynesia is SEACAM, but videos made for tourists are generally also available in PAL or NTSC.

PHOTOGRAPHY

The tropical light is intense in French Polynesia, so it's better to take photographs in the early morning or late afternoon. Take slow film (100 or 50 ISO), and more sensitive film (200 or 400 ISO) and a flash for dance performances or archaeological sites hidden in the vegetation, particularly on the Marquesas. A 28-80mm lens, or even a 35-80mm lens will meet most of your needs, and don't forget a polarising filter or a sunshade. You'll need a macro lens if you want to photograph flowers.

The sand, heat, salinity and air humidity are very tough on camera equipment so bring desiccating sachets. Take a waterproof bag or even a bin liner, and clean your lenses regularly. The humidity can also be tough on video cameras.

No restrictions apply to photography, but as a courtesy you should always ask permission of any people you wish to photograph. Film is expensive in French Polynesia. In Papeete, for 36 exposure film, count on 1700 CFP for slide film, 1000 CFP for print film. Film gets more difficult to find and more expensive as you get farther from Papeete. Fast developing and printing is easy to find on Tahiti and other touristed islands, but developing print film is expensive – ridiculously so.

Underwater Photography

The lack of plankton guarantees maximum water clarity. For beginners, a disposable camera will basically do, but these are waterproof only to three or four metres.

Divers with high-performance equipment should check that the charger and pins are compatible before plugging in the flash.

TIME

French Polynesia is 10 hours behind GMT, and is just two hours east of the International Date Line. When it is noon on Tahiti it is 2 pm on the US West Coast, 5 pm on the US East Coast, 10 pm in London, 11 pm in Paris, 8 am the next day on the Australian east coast, and 10 am the next day in New Zealand. The Marquesas are a half-hour ahead of the rest of French Polynesia (noon on Tahiti is 12.30 pm in the Marquesas) but check flight schedules carefully: Air Tahiti departures and arrivals in the Marquesas may run on Tahiti time.

ELECTRICITY

Electric current is generally 220V, 60 MHz, as in most of the western world apart from Japan and North America. Sockets are generally French-style, requiring a plug with two round pins. Some deluxe hotels may have 110V supply for electric shavers.

WEIGHTS & MEASURES

French Polynesia uses the metric system; see the inside back cover for a conversion chart.

LAUNDRY

Laundry can be a real problem in French Polynesia. Big hotels will, of course, wash clothes at prices that make it feasible to simply throw things away and buy new ones. Otherwise, laundrettes are just about unknown outside of Papeete, and even there the prices are amazing. Can you picture US$8 to run a load of washing through the machine? And the same again to dry it? On the other hand you'll certainly need to wash some clothes if you're doing anything other than lazing back in air-conditioned comfort. A day's bike riding or mountain walking will work up a sweat that can cause your clothes to develop alien life forms within 24 hours if they're not washed.

HEALTH

French Polynesia is generally a healthy place for locals and visitors alike. Food, and water on Tahiti and Bora Bora, are usually good, fresh, clean and readily available, there are few endemic diseases, and the most serious health problem visitors are likely to experience is sunburn. Nevertheless, it never hurts to know some basic travel-health rules, anytime you travel.

Travel health depends on your predeparture preparations, your day-to-day health care while travelling and how you handle any medical problem or emergency that develops. If you do need medical care, the facilities in French Polynesia are generally of a high standard, although on the outer islands the number of medical practitioners may be limited. However, there will be hospitals or dispensaries even out there.

Predeparture Planning

Make sure you're healthy before you start travelling. If you are embarking on a long trip, make sure your teeth are OK; there are lots of places where a visit to the dentist would be the last thing you'd want. If you wear glasses take a spare pair and your prescription. Losing your glasses can be a real problem, although you can often get new spectacles made up quickly and competently.

If you require a particular medication, take an adequate supply, as it may not be available locally. Take the prescription, with the generic name rather than the brand name (which may not be locally available), as it will make replacements easier to get. It's a good idea to have a legible prescription with you to show you legally use the medication – it's surprising how often over-the-counter drugs from one country are illegal without a prescription or even banned in another.

Immunisations A yellow fever vaccination certificate is required from travellers over one year of age coming from infected areas. No other vaccinations are required for entry to French Polynesia. It's always a good idea to keep your tetanus shot up to date, no matter where you are (a booster is required every 10 years). A combined hepatitis/typhoid vaccine has recently been developed, although its availability is limited – check with your doctor to find out its status in your country.

Health Insurance Make sure that you have adequate health insurance. See Travel Insurance under Visas & Documents earlier in this chapter.

Travel-Health Guides There are a number of books on travel health.

CDC's Complete Guide to Healthy Travel, Open Road Publishing, 1997. The US Centers for Disease Control & Prevention (CDC) recommendations for international travel.
Healthy Travel: Australia, New Zealand & the Pacific, Lonely Planet Publications, 2000. A handy pocket-sized book packed with useful information including pretrip planning, emergency first aid, immunisation and disease information and what to do if you get sick on the road.
Travel with Children, Maureen Wheeler, Lonely Planet Publications, 1995. Includes basic advice on travel health for younger children and pregnant women.
Travellers' Health, Dr Richard Dawood, Oxford University Press, 1995. Comprehensive, easy to read, authoritative and highly recommended, although it's rather large to lug around.
Where There Is No Doctor, David Werner, Macmillan, 1994. A very detailed guide intended for someone, such as a Peace Corps worker, going to work in an underdeveloped country.

Medical Kit Check List

Following is a list of items you should consider including in your medical kit – consult your pharmacist for brands available in your country.

- ☐ **Aspirin or paracetamol (acetaminophen in the USA)** – for pain or fever
- ☐ **Antihistamine** – for allergies, eg, hay fever; to ease the itch from insect bites or stings; and to prevent motion sickness
- ☐ **Cold and flu tablets, throat lozenges and nasal decongestant**
- ☐ **Multivitamins** – consider for long trips, when dietary vitamin intake may be inadequate
- ☐ **Antibiotics** – consider including these if you're travelling well off the beaten track; see your doctor, as they must be prescribed, and carry the prescription with you
- ☐ **Loperamide or diphenoxylate** –'blockers' for diarrhoea
- ☐ **Prochlorperazine or metaclopramide** – for nausea and vomiting
- ☐ **Rehydration mixture** – to prevent dehydration, which may occur, for example, during bouts of diarrhoea; particularly important when travelling with children
- ☐ **Insect repellent, sunscreen, lip balm and eye drops**
- ☐ **Calamine lotion, sting relief spray or aloe vera** – to ease irritation from sunburn and insect bites or stings
- ☐ **Antifungal cream or powder** – for fungal skin infections and thrush
- ☐ **Antiseptic (such as povidone-iodine)** – for cuts and grazes
- ☐ **Bandages, Elastic plasters and other wound dressings**
- ☐ **Water purification tablets or iodine**
- ☐ **Scissors, tweezers and a thermometer** – note that mercury thermometers are prohibited by airlines

There are also a number of excellent travel health sites on the Internet. From the Lonely Planet homepage, there are links at www.lonelyplanet.com/weblinks/wlprep.ht m#heal to the World Health Organization (WHO) and the US Centers for Disease Control & Prevention (CDC).

Basic Health Rules

Care in what you eat and drink is the most important health rule; stomach upsets are the most common travel-health problem, but the majority of these upsets will be relatively minor and are not usual in French Polynesia. But trying the local food is part of the travel experience.

Water Tap water is only completely safe in Papeete and on Bora Bora. On some islands, particularly low-lying atolls, rainwater is collected and stored separately from well water, which can be tainted by sea water. Bottled spring water or mineral water is readily available in French Polynesia. If you are concerned about water purity, boil it for at least five minutes or use iodine water-purification tablets. Follow the directions carefully and remember that too much iodine can be harmful.

In hot climates you should always make sure you drink enough – don't rely on feeling thirsty to indicate when you should drink. Not needing to urinate or very dark yellow urine is a danger sign. Excessive sweating is another problem and can lead to loss of salt and therefore to muscle cramping.

Nutrition Good food is readily available in French Polynesia so enjoying a balanced diet presents no problems.

If your diet is poor or limited in variety, if you're travelling hard and fast and therefore missing meals or if you simply lose your appetite, you can soon start to lose weight and place your health at risk.

Make sure your diet is well balanced. Cooked eggs, tofu, beans, lentils and nuts are all safe ways to get protein. Fruit you can peel (eg bananas, oranges or mandarins) is usually safe (melons can harbour bacteria in their flesh and are best avoided) and a good source of vitamins. Try to eat plenty of grains (including rice) and bread. Remember that although food is generally safer if it is cooked well, overcooked food loses much of its nutritional value. If your diet isn't well balanced or if your food intake is insufficient, it's a good idea to take vitamin and iron pills.

Medical Problems & Treatment

Self-diagnosis and treatment can be risky, so whenever possible seek qualified help. Although we do give treatment dosages in this section, they are for emergency use only. Medical advice should be sought whenever possible before administering any drugs.

Note that antibiotics should ideally be administered only under medical supervision. Take only the recommended dose at the prescribed intervals and use the whole course, even if the illness seems to be cured earlier. Stop immediately if there are any serious reactions and don't use the antibiotic at all if you are unsure that you have the correct one. Some people are allergic to commonly prescribed antibiotics such as penicillin; carry this information (eg on a bracelet) when travelling.

French Polynesia has medical facilities equivalent to the west. Papeete has a public hospital and two private clinics as well as numerous pharmacies. On all tourist islands you will find at least a medical clinic with one or more physicians, and on Moorea, Raiatea, Bora Bora, Nuku Hiva and Hiva Oa there are small medical centres. Even the most remote islands have a clinic.

The price of a consultation with a doctor is about 3000 CFP. French visitors can get the fee refunded when they return home; citizens of the EU should obtain a form E 111 before leaving home.

Environmental Hazards

Although the northern islands in French Polynesia can get much hotter and more humid than the islands to the south, the climate does not suffer from major extremes.

External Ear Infections This condition can affect divers and swimmers in tropical waters. Warm water, micro-organisms in coral, and humidity in the external ear ducts can encourage the proliferation of germs, leading to a very painful ear some hours after swimming or diving. Consult a physician if you are affected. To prevent the condition, rinse your ears thoroughly with fresh water after each immersion and use drops of alcohol to disinfect the duct.

Fungal Infections Hot-weather fungal infections are most likely to occur on the scalp, between the toes or fingers (athlete's foot), in the groin (jock itch or crotch rot) and on the body (ringworm). You get ringworm (which is a fungal infection, not a worm) from infected animals or by walking on damp areas, like shower floors.

To prevent fungal infections wear loose, comfortable clothes, avoid artificial fibres, wash frequently and dry carefully. If you do get an infection, wash the infected area daily with a disinfectant or medicated soap and water, and rinse and dry well. Apply an anti-fungal powder like the widely available Tinaderm. Try to expose the infected area to air or sunlight as much as possible, wash all towels and underwear in hot water and change them frequently.

Heat Exhaustion Dehydration or salt deficiency can cause heat exhaustion. Take time to acclimatise to high temperatures and make sure you drink sufficient liquids. Salt deficiency is characterised by fatigue, lethargy, headaches, giddiness and muscle cramps, and in this case salt tablets may help. Vomiting or diarrhoea can deplete your liquid and salt levels. Anhydrotic heat exhaustion, caused by an inability to sweat, is quite rare. Unlike the other forms of heat exhaustion, it is likely to strike people who have been in a hot climate for some time, rather than newcomers.

Heatstroke This serious, sometimes fatal, condition can occur if the body's heat-regulating mechanism breaks down and the body temperature rises to dangerous levels. Long, continuous periods of exposure to high temperatures can leave you vulnerable to heatstroke. You should avoid excessive alcohol or strenuous activity when you first arrive in a hot climate.

The symptoms are feeling unwell, not sweating very much or at all and a high body temperature (39°C to 41°C). Where sweating has ceased, the skin becomes flushed and red. Severe, throbbing headaches and lack of coordination will also occur, and the sufferer may be confused or aggressive. Eventually the victim will become delirious or convulse. Hospitalisation is essential, but meanwhile get victims out of the sun, remove their clothing, cover them with a wet sheet or towel and then fan them continuously. If they are conscious, give them fluids.

Motion Sickness Eating lightly before and during a trip will reduce the chances of motion sickness. If you are prone to motion sickness try to find a place that minimises disturbance – near the wing on aircraft, close to midships on boats, near the centre on buses. Fresh air and looking off into the distance or at the horizon usually helps; stale air, cigarette smoke or reading will make it worse. Commercial anti-motion-sickness preparations, which can cause drowsiness, have to be taken before the trip commences; when you're feeling sick it's too late. Dramamine, sold over the counter at pharmacies, is usually the preferred medication. Sea Legs tablets or the Scopamine patch worn behind the ear are also good. Ginger is a natural preventative and is available in capsule form. Lots of people get seasick on the Inter Island ships in French Polynesia, so if you think you are a likely victim, a few precautions can help prevent a miserable experience.

Prickly Heat Prickly heat is an itchy rash caused by excessive perspiration trapped under the skin. It usually strikes people who have just arrived in a hot climate and whose pores have not yet opened sufficiently to cope with greater sweating. Keeping cool and bathing often, using a mild talcum powder or even resorting to air-con may help until you acclimatise.

Sunburn You can get sunburnt surprisingly quickly in the tropics, even through cloud. Use a sunscreen and take extra care to cover areas which don't normally see the sun, such as your feet. A hat provides added protection and you can also use zinc cream or some other barrier cream for your nose and lips. Take special care in situations where a cool breeze may disguise the power of the sun, such as when riding around in an open 4WD vehicle or travelling in an open boat. Calamine lotion is good for mild sunburn.

Infectious Diseases

Ciguatera Ciguatera is a rather mysterious form of food poisoning that comes from eating infected reef fish. Outbreaks of ciguatera have been reported in French Polynesia as well as in many other Pacific centres. Reefs that have been disturbed, such as by urban development, are particularly prone to develop the microorganism, which becomes present in fish and passes up the food chain until a human eats it. Diarrhoea, muscle and joint aches and pains, numbness and tingling around the mouth, hands and feet, nausea, vomiting, chills, headaches, sweating and dizziness can all be symptoms of ciguatera. Seek medical attention if you experience any of these after eating fish. It's always wise to seek local advice before eating reef fish as any ciguatera outbreak will be well known. It's also wise to avoid eating fish heads or organs.

Diarrhoea A change of water, food or climate can all cause the 'runs'; diarrhoea caused by contaminated food or water is more serious. Despite all your precautions you may still have a bout of mild travellers' diarrhoea, but a few rushed toilet trips with no other symptoms is not indicative of a serious problem. Moderate diarrhoea, involving half-a-dozen loose movements in a day, is more of a nuisance. Dehydration is the main danger with diarrhoea, particularly for children where dehydration can occur quite quickly. Fluid replenishment is the number-one treatment. Weak black tea with a little sugar; soda water; or soft drinks allowed to go flat and diluted with 50% water are all good. With severe diarrhoea a rehydrating solution is necessary to replace minerals and salts. You should stick to a bland diet as you recover.

Lomotil or Imodium can bring relief from the symptoms, although they do not cure the problem. Only use these drugs if absolutely necessary – if you *must* travel, for example. For children, Imodium is preferable, but do not use these drugs if the person has a high fever or is severely dehydrated.

Antibiotics can be very useful in treating severe diarrhoea, especially if it is accompanied by nausea, vomiting, stomach cramps, blood in the stools or mild fever. If severe diarrhoea persists, see a doctor.

Although French Polynesia is generally a safe and healthy place, some urban areas and small settlements have very rudimentary sanitation facilities. Avoid swimming or walking barefoot on beaches that may not be clean and be very suspicious about seafood caught near such communities.

Hepatitis A Hepatitis is a general term for inflammation of the liver. It is a common disease worldwide. There are several different viruses that cause hepatitis, and they differ in the way that they are transmitted. The symptoms are similar in all forms of the illness, and include fever, chills, headache, fatigue, feelings of weakness and aches and pains, followed by loss of appetite, nausea, vomiting, abdominal pain, dark urine, light-coloured faeces, jaundiced (yellow) skin and yellowing of the whites of the eyes. People who have had hepatitis should avoid alcohol for some time after the illness, as the liver needs time to recover.

Hepatitis A is transmitted by contaminated food and drinking water. You should seek medical advice, but there is not much you can do apart from resting, drinking lots of fluids, eating lightly and avoiding fatty foods.

Sexually Transmitted Infections Sexual contact with an infected partner spreads these infections. While abstinence is the only 100% preventative, using condoms is also effective. Gonorrhoea and syphilis are the most common of these infections; sores, blisters or rashes around the genitals, discharges or pain when urinating are common symptoms. These may be less marked or not observed at all in women. Syphilis symptoms eventually disappear completely but the infection continues and can cause severe problems in later years. Gonorrhoea and syphilis are treated with antibiotics. There are many other sexually transmitted infections, and while most can be treated effectively there is no cure for herpes and there is also currently no cure for AIDS.

HIV/AIDS & Hepatitis B There were 177 cases of AIDS (SIDA in French) reported in French Polynesia in 1997. Particularly in Papeete, which has an international mix of tourists, prostitution and a local bisexual population, it would be surprising if HIV/AIDS were not a problem at some level.

There are almost 300 million chronic carriers of hepatitis B in the world. Like AIDS, hepatitis B can be spread through contact with the body fluids of another person, primarily blood and semen, and can be spread through infected blood transfusions as well as by sexual contact. It can also be spread by dirty needles – vaccinations, acupuncture, body piercing and tattooing can potentially be as dangerous as intravenous drug use if the equipment is not properly clean. Using condoms is extremely wise for those engaging in sexual relations with anyone other than a regular partner. There is a hepatitis B vaccination available.

Tetanus This potentially fatal disease is difficult to treat but is preventable with immunisation. Tetanus is no more of a problem in French Polynesia than in any other part of the world, but it's still a good idea to keep your tetanus immunisation up to date.

Tetanus occurs when a wound becomes infected by a germ that lives in the faeces of animals or people – so clean all cuts, punctures and animal bites. Tetanus is also known as lockjaw, and the first symptom may be discomfort in swallowing, or a stiffening of the jaw and neck; this is followed by painful convulsions of the jaw and the whole body.

Typhoid Typhoid fever is a dangerous gut infection caused by contaminated water and food. Medical help must be sought.

In its early stages sufferers may feel they have a bad cold or flu on the way, as early symptoms are a headache, body aches and a fever that rises a little each day until it is around 40°C (104°F) or more. The victim's pulse is often slow relative to the degree of fever present - unlike a normal fever where the pulse increases. There may also be vomiting, abdominal pain, diarrhoea or constipation.

In the second week the high fever and slow pulse continue and a few pink spots may appear on the body; trembling, delirium, weakness, weight loss and dehydration may occur. Complications such as pneumonia, perforated bowel or meningitis may occur.

Insect-Borne Diseases

Malaria does not exist in French Polynesia but an antifilariasis campaign is in operation and there have been outbreaks of dengue fever. Filariasis affects the lymphatic system and is spread by mosquitoes and flies; treatment is available.

Dengue fever is also spread by mosquitoes and there is no prophylactic available. The main preventative measure is to avoid mosquito bites by covering up and using mosquito repellent. Dengue outbreaks generally occur during the rainy season (100 to 200 cases are reported annually in French Polynesia). A sudden onset of fever, headaches and severe joint and muscle pain are the first signs before a rash starts on the trunk of the body and spreads to the limbs and face. It is very important to rest. After a few more days, the fever will subside and recovery will begin. Serious complications are not common.

Cuts, Bites & Stings

Cuts & Scratches Any puncture of the skin can easily become infected in the tropics and may be difficult to heal. Treat any cut with an antiseptic solution and Mercurochrome or other protective antiseptic creams. Where possible avoid bandages and elastic plasters, which can keep wounds wet; if you have to keep a bandage on during the day to protect the wound from dirt or flies, take it off at night while you sleep to let it get air.

Coral cuts are notoriously problematic – they seem to be particularly susceptible to infection, can take a long time to heal and can be quite painful. If you do get cut by coral, be sure to clean the wound thoroughly, get all the coral out and keep the wound clean and disinfected until it heals. You can treat it with Mercurochrome or other protective antiseptic cream or try the local cure – fresh lime juice. Avoid coral cuts by trying not to touch coral when swimming.

Since any cut or puncture to the skin can turn septic in this climate, don't hesitate to visit a doctor if you notice any sign of infection.

Bites & Stings French Polynesia's mosquitoes can be bad but they have absolutely nothing on the *nono* (blackflies) of the Marquesas, which, at their worst, make life a misery. Unfortunately, nono are found on beaches as well. In his book *In Search of Tusitala*, Gavin Bell succinctly describes the problem with these creatures, for while mosquitoes are 'like flying hypodermic needles, inserting suckers and withdrawing blood with surgical precision, the latter chew and tear at flesh to drink the blood, leaving ragged wounds susceptible to infection'. Scratching at the itch only makes the problem worse.

There are a number of ways to fight insect problems. First of all, wear an insect repellent; the most effective will have 100% DEET. Carry it with you if you go walking or if you visit marae. Insect repellents are readily available in French Polynesia. Second, avoid using perfumes or after-shave when the insects are a problem. Wearing light-coloured clothing and covering as much skin as possible by wearing long-sleeved shirts and long trousers will also reduce the problem. Burning mosquito coils, readily available throughout French Polynesia, will also help. If a mosquito net is available, use it. They're usually provided because mosquitoes are a local problem. Check that window screens are insect proof.

Mosquitoes are usually worst during the wet season from November to March.

Other insect stings are usually painful rather than dangerous. Take care on some walking routes, where wasp nests sometimes overhang the path. Large centipedes can give a painful or irritating bite but it's no more dangerous than a bee or wasp sting, despite the strange dread Polynesians have of these creatures.

Finally, if you are bitten, using calamine lotion, ammonia, antihistamine skin cream or ice packs to reduce the pain, swelling and itching will help. Or you can try the local remedy: pick a frangipani leaf and rub the white liquid that oozes from the stem onto the bite. If you are allergic to bee or wasp stings, be sure to carry your medication with you.

Jellyfish & Other Sea Creatures Jellyfish are not a big problem in French Polynesia because people mostly swim in protected lagoons, and jellyfish are rarely washed in from the open sea. Stings from most jellyfish are simply rather painful. Dousing in vinegar will deactivate any stingers that have not 'fired'. Ammonia is also effective, but the folk remedy, used all over the world, is to apply fresh urine to the sting as soon as possible. This also neutralises the venom. Calamine lotion, antihistamines and analgesics may reduce the reaction and relieve the pain.

Poisonous stonefish are rare, but extremely painful for those unfortunate enough to step on one. These ugly and well disguised creatures lurk on the sea floor, and stepping on one forces poison up spines in the dorsal fin and into the victim's foot. Heeding local advice about areas that may harbour stonefish, and wearing shoes or thongs (flip-flops) when walking in the lagoon is the best protection. If you do step on a stonefish, bind the affected limb tightly to slow circulation and then seek medical attention, because there is an antidote available. Stingrays should also not be stepped upon, as their sharp tails can lash up, causing a nasty cut that is difficult to heal. Usually rays zip away as they sense your approach. Sea urchins are another bad thing to step upon. The spines break off in your foot and can be difficult to remove and become easily infected.

You'll sometimes encounter stinging coral or fire coral (usually brown or yellow and branched); the simple solution is to avoid touching it. If you are stung, it's bothersome rather than dangerous, and can be treated like a jellyfish sting. Some cone shells can fire a dangerous, potentially fatal, dart if picked up. Treat any cone shell with caution.

Shark bites are a very unlikely occurrence – the sharks regularly encountered around the reefs are impressive to look at but quite innocuous – and other sharp-toothed creatures, like moray eels, are feared more than they deserve.

Women's Health

Gynaecological Problems Poor diet, lowered resistance through the use of antibiotics for stomach upsets and even contraceptive pills can lead to vaginal infections when travelling in hot climates. Maintaining good personal hygiene, and wearing skirts or loose-fitting trousers and cotton underwear will help to prevent infections.

Thrush (yeast infection) is characterised by a rash, itch and discharge. Nystatin, miconazole or clotrimazole pessaries or vaginal cream are the usual treatment, but some people use a more traditional remedy involving vinegar or lemon juice douches, or yoghurt

Trichomonas is a more serious infection; symptoms are a discharge and a burning sensation when urinating. Male sexual partners must also be treated, and if a vinegar-water douche is not effective medical attention should be sought. Metronidazole (Flagyl) is the prescribed drug.

Pregnancy Most miscarriages occur during the first three months of pregnancy, so this is the riskiest time to travel. The last three months should also be spent within reasonable distance of good medical care as quite serious problems can develop at this time. Pregnant women should avoid all unnecessary medication, but vaccinations should still be obtained where necessary.

Additional care should be taken to prevent illness and particular attention should be paid to diet and nutrition.

Women travellers often find that their periods become irregular or even cease while they're on the road. A missed period doesn't necessarily indicate pregnancy.

WOMEN TRAVELLERS

French Polynesia is a relatively safe place for solo women travellers, although in the rougher quarters of Papeete, particularly late at night, care should be exercised. The majority of complaints received from women visitors are about cheaper hotels where some male staff have taken an unhealthy interest in the female guests. Peeping toms are also not unknown, so take special care in establishments that look run down and would seem to offer opportunities for spying on guests, particularly in the showers. Make sure your room can be securely locked. As anywhere in the world treat drunks with great caution.

GAY & LESBIAN TRAVELLERS

There are no networks or associations for gays in French Polynesia but French laws concerning homosexuality prevail and there is no legal discrimination against homosexual activity. Homophobia in French Polynesia is uncommon. You will meets lots of very camp *mahu* working in restaurants and hotels. *Rae rae* are transvestites, very visible as prostitutes (see the 'Mahu & Rae Rae' boxed text in the Facts about the Islands chapter). HIV testing is readily available at the Mamao Hospital and the Malardé Institute in Papeete and condoms are sold in all pharmacies.

The Scorpio disco behind the Vaima Centre in Papeete is a popular centre for *popaa* (western) gays as well as rae rae, but it's also frequented by heterosexuals.

DISABLED TRAVELLERS

Travellers with restricted mobility will unfortunately find very little in the way of infrastructure designed to make it easier for them to get around. With narrow flights of steps on boats, high steps on le trucks and difficult boarding on Air Tahiti aircraft, the disabled traveller's itinerary in French Polynesia resembles an obstacle course as special equipment is sadly lacking. What is more, hotels and guesthouses are not used to receiving disabled guests, and nautical and open-air activities are geared for the 'able-bodied'.

Those who are not put off by these obstacles can contact the Polynesian Association of War Invalids & Military Pensioners (☎ 43 17 89, 48 22 93), which can provide some advice and assistance.

SENIOR TRAVELLERS

Seniors will have no problems in French Polynesia, and Air Tahiti gives reductions to those over 60 once they have obtained a Troiseme Age (Third Age) card, which requires a photo and piece of identity, costs 1000 CFP and takes three days to obtain.

TRAVEL WITH CHILDREN

The climate, natural setting, aquatic games and lack of poisonous creatures make Polynesia a paradise for children.

You should, however, ensure that vaccinations are up-to-date, and that you have your health records with you. Take a baby carrier, light clothes that cover the whole body and total-block sunscreen. Do not leave your child unsupervised near beaches or reefs. Buy bottled mineral water and make your children drink frequently. Nappies (diapers) are very expensive, even in the Papeete supermarkets.

In the event of an emergency, you should be aware that there are medical facilities everywhere in Polynesia. Mamao hospital has a modern paediatric department. Make sure that your repatriation insurance also covers your child.

You will have priority when boarding Air Tahiti aircraft. A *carte famille* (family card), which costs 2000 CFP and requires identity photos of the mother and father, takes three to five days to obtain, and entitles you to significant reductions on some flights. At hotels and guesthouses, children under 12 generally pay only 50% of the adult rate. Lastly, Tahiti Plongée in

Papeete takes children aged eight and over on dives.

USEFUL ORGANISATIONS

Te Fare Tauhiti Nui (☎ 54 45 44, 54 45 40) is the new name of the Territorial Cultural Action Office (OTAC) and is at 646 Blvd Pomare, Papeete, at the western exit from the city. In addition to the traditional Heiva (see the Heiva entry in the 'Ori Tahiti – Tahitian Dance' special section), it organises concerts and craft exhibitions and stages plays in French and Tahitian. Cultural weeks or gatherings are held there regularly. Tahitian language courses at beginners and more advanced levels are also available. It's open weekdays from 8 am to noon and 1 to 5 pm (Friday to 4 pm).

DANGERS & ANNOYANCES

See Health earlier in this chapter for medical warnings and precautions.

Alcohol & Drugs

Polynesians like their beer, particularly at festivals and other local feasts, in which case there are two points to remember: first that some Polynesians are not good drunks and second that many Polynesians are very big and very strong. There is a locally grown marijuana known as *pakalolo*; the local police can be extremely unpleasant if they catch you using it.

Dogs & Roosters

Some guesthouses are very quiet until 3 am when you discover that they are completely surrounded by roosters who keep up a non-stop symphony until 4 am. The only solution is to change guesthouse. On some islands, particularly the atolls of the Tuamotus, dogs should be treated with caution. They often appear to have no interest in obeying their masters; if you go out for a sunset stroll carry a stick.

Mosquitoes & Nono

French Polynesia does not have malaria but the mosquitoes can still be an intolerable nuisance. They're usually not a problem around the coast, where sea breezes keep them away, but inland they can be a pest. For some reason, marae seem to attract them in swarms, and standing to read an explanatory noticeboard at an historic marae site can be a real test of any visitor's enthusiasm. If anything, the tiny nono of the Marquesas are an even worse annoyance.

Swimming

Swimming in French Polynesia usually means staying within the protected waters of a lagoon, but swimmers should still be aware of tides and currents, and particularly of the swift movement of water out of a lagoon and through a pass into the open sea. Around Papeete, beware of the dangers of untreated sewage contaminating the water.

Theft & Violence

Although early explorers all complained about the Polynesian propensity for theft, it is not a big problem today. Which is not to say that your camera won't disappear if you leave it lying around on the beach. Despite recent increases in theft and petty violence, even busy Papeete is relatively safe compared to cities in the USA and Europe. Nevertheless, there are occasional robberies and pickpocketings.

Theft is less of a problem on the islands, but take care in cheaper hotel rooms – leaving something on a table close to an open window is no different to leaving it on the beach. If you have real valuables, such as jewellery, and are staying in a more expensive hotel, it's probably wise to use the hotel safe. Don't leave anything of value in a rental car, either.

Violence is also rarely a problem in French Polynesia. Intoxicated youths are the most likely troublemakers and it rarely gets beyond shouting at tourists that they're *titoi* – wankers. Ignore them. The size of the bouncers outside Papeete's nightclubs indicates that it's a good idea to keep well clear of unfriendly drunks. The bars most likely to be trouble spots are the ones frequented by French military personnel.

Women should be vigilant in isolated places and should always make sure that their rooms can be locked securely.

Yacht Security

Yacht crews should take care in popular yachting centres like Bora Bora, and in the Marquesas, where theft from yachts has been a problem. See the Sailing section in the Activities chapter for more advice.

BUSINESS HOURS

Shops and offices are normally open weekdays from 7.30 or 8 am to 5 pm, although many places close at 4 pm on Friday. A long lunchbreak is still common, but many places tend to work straight through. Some food shops and supermarkets remain open late in the evening.

Shops generally open Saturday morning, but almost all are closed that afternoon, and most are closed on Sunday. Food shops and supermarkets are the exception; even on smaller islands they're usually open all week.

PUBLIC HOLIDAYS & SPECIAL EVENTS

Public holidays, when businesses and government offices shut down, are:

New Year	1 January
Arrival of the First Missionaries	5 March
Easter, Good Friday and Easter Monday	March/April
May Day	1 May
VE Day	8 May
Ascension	late May
Pentecost and Pentecost Monday	early June
Internal Autonomy Day	29 June
Bastille Day	14 July
Assumption	15 August
All Saints' Day	1 November
Armistace Day	11 November
Christmas Day	25 December

Popular holidays and festivals include:

January
New Year's Day
New Year's Eve and New Year's Day are celebrated with friends, family, singing and dancing.
Chinese New Year
Usually falling between late January and mid-February, the new year is ushered in with dancing, martial arts displays and fireworks.

February
International Marathon
If you're keen to run around most of the island, the Moorea Marathon is in late February.

March
Arrival of the First Missionaries
The arrival of the first London Missionary Society (LMS) missionaries on board the *Duff* is commemorated on 5 March. The landing is re-enacted at Point Venus and there are celebrations at Protestant churches on Tahiti and Moorea and in the stadiums in Tipaerui on Tahiti and Afareaitu on Moorea. (Actually, the missionaries arrived on 4 March but didn't know about the International Date Line.)

June
Beauty Contests
The Tahitians love beauty contests and there are lots of them held in April and May leading up to the Miss Tahiti and Miss Heiva i Tahiti contests in June. Just to show there is no sexism involved, there are also Mr Tahiti contests.
Tahiti International Golf Open
The four day championship takes place at the Olivier Breaud Golf Course on Tahiti in late June to early July.

July
Heiva i Tahiti
Heiva means 'festival'; this is the major French Polynesian festival, in Papeete each July. There are traditional demonstrations throughout the month. Mini-Heiva events take place on other islands in August. See the 'Ori Tahiti – Tahitian Dance' special section for details.

September
Annual Flower Show
This kicks off in September in the Bougainville Park in Papeete.
Surfing Contest
In September there is a major surfing competition at Punaauia on Tahiti.

October
Stone-Fishing Contest
Traditional stone-fishing takes place on Raiatea during the first half of October.
Carnival
At the end of October in Papeete there are parades of floats decked with flowers.
Hawaiki Nui Canoe Race
French Polynesia's major sporting event of the year is the three-day *pirogue* (outrigger canoe) race from Huahine to Raiatea, Tahaa and Bora Bora. See the boxed text 'Hawaiki Nui Canoe Race' in this chapter.

November
All Saints' Day
Graves are cleaned and decorated and hymns are sung in candle-lit cemeteries on 1 November.

December
Tiare Tahiti Days
The national flower is celebrated on 1 and 2 December.
The Marquesas Islands Festival
Held in December at least every four years, this arts festival is a celebration of Marquesan identity. See the boxed text 'The Marquesas Islands Festival' in the Marquesas chapter.
Christmas
Christmas Day, 25 December, is celebrated with enthusiasm.

ACTIVITIES
See the Outdoor Activities chapter for specific information on surfing, boating and walking, and the 'Diving' special section for information on dive operators and dive sites.

Diving & Snorkelling
Plongée (scuba diving) is very popular in French Polynesia. Apart from the French CMAS, all dive certifications are recognised, including PADI and NAUI. Bring your certification card and dive log. There are about 20 professional dive centres on Tahiti, Moorea, Raiatea, Huahine, Bora Bora, Rangiroa, Tikehau, Manihi, Nuku Hiva and, from July to September, Rurutu.

The coral reefs and the coral outcrops that dot the lagoons are perfect sites for snorkelling. You can join a lagoon tour by pirogue, or rent an outboard-powered boat to explore the lagoon yourself.

Surfing
Polynesia was the birthplace of surfing and in recent years there has been a major resurgence in local interest. Tahiti in particular has surf shops, board shapers and a local surfing scene. Tahiti, Moorea and Huahine are the three main islands for surfing.

Boating
Raiatea is the main yachting base in French Polynesia, and there are a number of yacht charter operations with a flotilla of modern monohulls and catamarans.

Hawaiki Nui Canoe Race

In French Polynesia, the Big Event – the sporting spectacular that has the entire nation glued to its TV sets and talking passionately about favourites and challengers – is a canoe race. The three day, four island, 116km Hawaiki Nui Va'a race pits 60-odd of the islands' best six-man pirogues against each other and against any paddlers who are brave enough to turn up from overseas.

The race, held in late October to mid-November, starts on Huahine and goes out of the lagoon and across 44.5km of open sea to Raiatea. The canoes are a superb sight, dramatically televised live for the four hour crossing. The brawny paddlers, often sporting vivid Tahitian tattoos, paddle three on each side for about 10 strokes then switch sides with precise timing and lightning speed.

Day two takes the canoes on a 20km sprint within the lagoon between the twin islands of Raiatea and Tahaa. Plan on completing this leg in under 1½ hours if you want to remain in contention.

Day three, a Saturday, is the big one: a 52km crossing of open sea to Bora Bora. Starting around 6.30 am, the leading canoe arrives at the Matira Beach finish line about four hours later. It's a fantastic sight – thousands of cheering spectators lining the beach and wading out to greet the arriving canoes. Drummers pound out an encouraging rhythm from a float by the finishing line, TV camera crews wade out into the water to film the excitement, and happy supporters wait with flower *lei* (necklaces) to garland their teams.

Faaa is one of the local favourites – the supermen from Papeete's airport suburb have won several times but there's always great interest in overseas competitors, particularly from Hawaii. So far the Polynesian paddlers have remained supreme, but there's increasing international interest in the race and more iron men turn up every year. There's also a women's Hawaiki Nui race, known as the Vaa Hine, a pun on *vaa*, Tahitian for canoe, and *vahine*, Tahitian for 'woman'. Other major pirogue marathons include a little jaunt from Papeete across the open sea to Moorea, and then right around Moorea and back to Tahiti! This 100-plus kilometre race takes place during the Heiva festival in July.

Walking

The high islands offer superb walks, but the tracks are often hard to follow and a guide may be needed. Tahiti and Moorea are the main islands for walking; there are also walks on Raiatea, Bora Bora and Maupiti. The Marquesas has huge untapped potential; the only popular walk is on Nuku Hiva.

Cycling

On many islands it is possible to rent bicycles, and the rough roads leading into the interior are perfect for mountain-biking.

Horse Riding

There are equestrian centres on Tahiti, Moorea, Raiatea, Huahine and Bora Bora in the Society Islands. They offer short jaunts, and longer excursions to explore the island interiors. Horses are an important part of life in the Marquesas, and there are various places to rent them, with or without a guide.

Other Activities

There are squash and tennis courts on Tahiti, and the tourist office can provide more information. On other islands, tennis courts can be found at the larger hotels. Tahiti has the only golf course in French Polynesia. Tahiti's soaring mountains promise interesting opportunities for *parapente* (parasailing) and, sure enough, there are facilities for this sport. There is also a centre on Nuku Hiva in the Marquesas.

Windsurfing is popular and many resorts offer instruction and use of equipment. Unfortunately, jetskis, those noisy and antisocial devices, are also popular on some islands. You can rent small boats for exploring the lagoons on a number of islands. Farther afield, game-fishing boats can be chartered.

COURSES

Tahitian language can be studied at, among other places, ASFOP (☎ 41 33 89), Immeuble Fara, Rue Nansouty, Papeete, Tahiti; the Chamber of Commerce (☎ 54 07 00) Rue du Dr Cassiau, BP 118, Papeete, Tahiti; and at Maison de la Culture (☎ 54 45 44).

WORK

French citizens are not required to complete any formalities but for everyone else, even other EU citizens (with the exception of those with very special skills), it is difficult to work in French Polynesia. Unless you are a Japanese pearl grafter, a tourist guide, Chinese chef or a banking executive, you stand little chance. Authorisation to take up paid employment is subject to the granting of a temporary-residence permit, issued by the French State, and a work permit, issued by the Territory.

You need an employer willing to employ you and draw up a work contract. Attach a copy of it to your temporary-residence permit application, which you must lodge with the French consular authorities in your own country. After about a month, the consulate will let you know whether the permit has been granted. The temporary-residence permit is granted for one year (renewable), or five years for citizens of the EU.

To obtain a work permit, the employer (or you) must send the Agence pour l'Emploi et la Formation Professionnelle (AEFP, Employment & Professional Training Agency, ☎ 54 31 31), BP 540, 98713 Papeete, the draft work contract, copies of your qualifications, a letter from you applying for a work permit, two passport-size photos and various other paperwork. The employer must advertise the position at the AEFP for four weeks. If equally qualified French Polynesians apply during that time, they will be given preference. The work permit is granted for one year, but it's renewable.

ACCOMMODATION

Tourist brochures may focus on the sumptuous over-water bungalows, but in fact French Polynesia has a very wide accommodation range, from camping and hostel dormitories right the way up to five star luxury. Whatever the category, the price-to-quality ratio may be discouraging. It's not that places are necessarily bad, it's just that at the prices charged visitors have a right to be super critical! Service, comfort and even the sites are often not what you'd expect for the price being asked.

Before choosing, check what's on offer. Is the beach nearby? Are there dive clubs, shops, restaurants or other facilities in the vicinity? Are airport or ferry wharf transfers included? How will you get around?

Always distrust the 'lagoonside' label. Sometimes it's technically true, but a long way from what you might hope. Being right by the lagoon certainly doesn't guarantee you're by a beach, and getting across a sharp-edged reef to the water may be impossible. The only establishments guaranteed to have a beach are the classy places on motu.

Many cheaper places do not supply towels or soap: come prepared if you're economising. Even some quite expensive places may not have air-con, but this is generally a pleasure rather than a discomfort. Even at the hottest times of year a cool breeze seems to blow at night and a fan is all that's needed.

Check if credit cards are accepted; they will be at the luxury resorts but a surprising number of mid-range places only want cash. There's generally an 8% government tax on the mid-range and top-end places.

Camping & Hostels

Camp sites don't really exist in French Polynesia, but some guesthouses have places where you can put up a tent and use the guesthouse facilities. They're found on Moorea, Huahine, Raiatea, Bora Bora, Maupiti and Rangiroa. Count on 800 CFP to 1800 CFP per person; be prepared to shift accommodation

Taxes

Introduced in 1998, a value-added tax (VAT; known as a Goods & Services Tax, or GST, in some countries) has been applied to hotels. In 1999 it stood at 2% for accommodation, and is scheduled to go up every year until it reaches 5%. VAT also applies to restaurants, but it's hidden in the prices so customers don't see it directly. Big hotels also charge a government tax of 8%. On some islands there's a tax on simply being there. Moorea, Bora Bora, Rangiroa and Tikehau charge 50 CFP to 150 CFP per adult per day, depending on whether you stay at a guesthouse or a hotel.

if the rain is too hard; and make sure your tent is mosquito-proof. There aren't any official youth hostels, but again there are guesthouses, with dormitory facilities for around 1500 CFP a bed on Tahiti, Moorea, Huahine, Raiatea, Tahaa and Bora Bora.

Guesthouses

Staying with a family in a guesthouse, or *pension*, is popular on nearly every island. It can mean a room in the family house, or an independent bungalow. The cheapest bungalows may be very rudimentary constructions with plywood walls in a vaguely traditional style, equipped at best with a shower, toilet, a bed perhaps decorated with a tifaifai, a screen or net to keep the mosquitoes at bay, and a ceiling fan. Hot water is rarely available but generally this is not a problem.

There are some more-attractive mid-range bungalows with more-solid construction and *niau* (traditional coconut-palm) roofs, sometimes with walls of plaited bamboo. Don't get your hopes too high: these are still simple places. Food varies from guesthouse to guesthouse, but some enjoy an excellent reputation.

Guesthouses often offer all sorts of enticements, including motu picnics, island tours, fishing trips and pearl-farm visits. If they don't organise their own they'll certainly put you in touch with local operators.

Guesthouses often include *demi-pension* (half-board), which means breakfast and dinner. It typically costs 5000 CFP to 6000 CFP per person per day in the cheaper places, and perhaps 9000 CFP in a mid-range place, although prices can vary widely from island to island. For *pension complète* (full board) add 1500 CFP to 2000 CFP per person. Children younger than 12 usually pay half-tariff, and credit cards are rarely accepted.

Tahiti Tourisme (☎ 50 57 00, fax 43 66 19) produces a booklet about guesthouses, but the information is very basic.

Small Inns & Resorts

The intermediate range can offer excellent lodging; generally these places are well situated and more comfortable than the guesthouses. The rooms are usually well equipped independent bungalows in the

What to Look for in a Guesthouse

Many visitors stay in family *pensions* or guesthouses, the most common form of accommodation on the less-touristed islands. Simplicity and authenticity, together with the opportunity to share the life of a Polynesian family, are attractions, but there are some downsides.

The level of comfort and friendliness can vary widely. Polynesian hospitality is not an assured thing, but you'll fit in better if you don't expect the services and professional standards of a hotel. A group of guesthouse owners have formed the association *Haere May* (welcome) to promote this form of lodging and to educate its members about tourist needs. They hold a yearly meeting in Papeete.

There's one simple solution if you really don't like your guesthouse: move to another one.

traditional Polynesian style with niau roofs and modern comforts. Tariffs are typically US$80 to US$150 per night for a bungalow. Meals are not included but there will often be a restaurant on the site. Most places in this category accept credit cards and some are subject to 8% value-added tax (VAT) and a nightly tourist tax.

Deluxe Hotels

Luxury hotels are what French Polynesia is all about – these sumptuous complexes often manage to blend their opulent bungalows into the natural setting. Four and five-star establishments are found on Tahiti, Moorea, Huahine, Raiatea, Rangiroa, Manihi, Hiva Oa, Nuku Hiva, and especially Bora Bora. They're usually found on the most beautiful parts of the island, some of them even on motu, where coconut palms and white-sand beaches are the order of the day. They generally have restaurants, bars (including a beach bar), a swimming pool, a boutique, a jewellery shop specialising in black pearls, and sporting facilities. They organise activities on land and water and usually put on a Polynesian dance performance with buffet meal two or three times a week.

Bungalows are typically classed as garden, beach or over-water, with room prices ranging from US$300 to US$800 a night. The over-water bungalows, standing on stilts and reached by walkways over the lagoon, are always the most expensive. You can add another US$50 to US$80 a day for meals. These prices are subject to 8% tax.

The architecture is usually in traditional style, with pandanus roofs and bamboo walls, while the artistic decorations will include wonderful woods, parquet floors, and tapa hangings on the walls. Glass-bottomed coffee tables, which look straight down into the lagoon like huge aquariums, have become standard features of the over-water bungalows. There will also be a private terrace with steps into the lagoon. You can even ask to have breakfast delivered by pirogue.

The good news is that these complexes are not isolated fortresses. If you buy a drink at the bar or a meal in the restaurant you will be welcome to use the beach or catch a dance performance.

FOOD

Good news: you will eat well in multi-ethnic French Polynesia. From a classic pizza to a snack like chow mein, to mahi mahi in coconut milk, the repertoire is varied. Nevertheless, the westernisation of eating habits is increasingly noticeable. Prices mentioned are indicative and apply to Papeete; transport costs can push prices up on other islands.

Snacks

Sandwiches can be great value in French Polynesia. They usually cost 100 CFP to 150 CFP in *snacks* (takeaways), 200 CFP to 300 CFP in places where you can sit down to eat them. The excellent bread and low prices make a *casse-croûte*, as one of these French-bread sandwiches is known, the best food bargain on Tahiti. Snack bars – small food shops-cum-eating places, usually with a handful of stools at a bar – are all around the island. Sometimes they may be more like a restaurant but they're always simple and cheap. Dishes like delicious poisson cru

---

Ahimaa & Tamaaraa

An *ahimaa* is the Polynesian oven in which food is baked. On the most touristy islands, it tends to be replaced by a barbecue. Branches and stones are arranged at the bottom of a hole dug in the ground. The branches are kindled and heat the stones. A layer of banana leaves is then placed on top and the food is placed on this (often a suckling pig, fish and vegetables). The whole thing is covered with leaves and canvas bags and then sand to make it perfectly airtight. Cooking takes several hours. When the oven is opened, the *tamaaraa* (meal or banquet), which is common at family parties and religious festivals, commences. Big hotels generally put on a tamaaraa once a week, usually on Sundays.

cost 800 CFP to 1000 CFP. The other bargain-priced dining possibility is *roulottes*, vans with a kitchen inside and a fold-down counter along each side for customers. The nightly gathering of roulottes wharfside in Papeete is a real institution.

Restaurants

Most restaurants are concentrated in the Papeete area and on the most touristy islands. They serve French, Polynesian and Chinese food, and prices vary considerably according to specialities and the type of restaurant. Count on about 1500 CFP for a typical main course.

Try to have at least one meal in the sumptuous setting of a luxury hotel. The room prices may be sky high but, contrary to what you might expect, the restaurant prices are not. Several times a week they put on superb buffets with seafood, Polynesian or international cuisines as a theme. Accompanied by a Polynesian dance performance, they cost 4000 CFP to 6500 CFP per person.

Self-Catering

The markets are laden with food – vegetables, fruit, meat and fish. Papeete's central market opens at 5 am and has products from all the archipelagos. The market in Pirae also deserves a detour.

Food shops are usually traditional grocery stores, run by Chinese, and can be expensive. Supermarkets on Moorea, Raiatea and particularly on Tahiti are bringing them increased competition. The biggest and best-supplied supermarkets on Tahiti are the Continent Hypermarket (Arue and Punaauia), Tropic Import (Papeete) and Cash & Carry (Faaa). If you're restocking a yacht, this is where to come. On other islands you're at the mercy of cargo-ship schedules.

Avoid European imports; cheese airfreighted from France can be incredibly expensive. Most islands have at least one bakery. A French baguette costs less than 50 CFP and a pain au chocolat costs about 120 CFP. Small food stalls along the road, particularly on Tahiti, sell fruit and vegetables.

Polynesian Cuisine

The traditional cuisine, based on fresh produce, is called *maaa tahiti* in the Society Islands and the Tuamotus, and *kaikai enana* on the Marquesas. Maaa tahiti is traditionally eaten with the fingers. See the 'Ahimaa & Tamaaraa' boxed text for more information.

Fish & Seafood Open-sea fish (tuna, bonito, *thazard* (wahoo), scad and mahi mahi) and lagoon fish (parrotfish, unicornfish, perch and mullet) feature prominently in traditional cuisine. Poisson cru, raw fish in coconut milk, is the most popular local

Recipe for Raw Fish in Coconut Milk

This dish appears on almost every menu. For four people, use garlic, limes, two carrots, grated coconut (or failing this, packaged coconut milk), two tomatoes, one capsicum (bell pepper), 1kg of red tuna, and some green onions.

Cut the fish into small cubes. Rinse it with sea (or salt) water, then leave it in the refrigerator to soak for half an hour in salt water and crushed garlic.

Grate the carrots, and chop the tomatoes, capsicum and green onions. Drain the fish and place it in a salad bowl. Squeeze the limes into the bowl and leave the fish to stand for at least four or five minutes before removing it.

Put the grated coconut in a cloth and wring it to extract the coconut milk (or open the packaged coconut milk). Add a dash of red-wine vinegar, some salt, pepper and Tabasco sauce. Pour this dressing over the fish, mix, add the vegetables and sprinkle with onions. You can also add parsley and crushed hard-boiled eggs.

dish (see the boxed text 'Recipe for Raw Fish in Coconut Milk' in this chapter); it is also eaten grilled or cooked (poached or wrapped in buttered paper) accompanied by lime, coconut milk or vanilla sauce. *Fafaru*, raw fish soaked in seawater, is renowned for its particularly strong smell. *Inaa* (young fish), mixed with fried dough, is enjoyed in various ways.

Lobster, crayfish, sea urchin and freshwater shrimp (*chevrettes* rather than *crevettes*) are highly prized, usually served in curry. As the seafood on offer is rather limited, there are no restaurants specialising only in seafood. Salmon and trout generally come from Australia or New Zealand and lobsters and prawns may also be imported.

Fruit & Vegetables Most tropical fruit can be found in French Polynesia, including mangoes, grapefruit, green lemons, watermelons and melons (grown on the motu of Maupiti and Huahine), pineapples (from Moorea) and bananas. *Pamplemousse* (grapefruit) are the large, thick-skinned South-East Asian variety rather than the grapefruit familiar in Europe and North America. The rambutan is another South-East Asian introduction, a red spiny-skinned close cousin to the lychee. Mangoes are so common they fall off the trees and rot on the ground.

Baked papaya is a succulent dish, as is *poe*, small pieces of crushed fruit (papaya or banana) mixed with starch, wrapped in a banana leaf and baked in the oven with a vanilla pod split down the middle. The whole thing is then sprinkled with coconut milk.

Local market-gardens produce European-style vegetables that are also grown on the cooler Austral Islands. Vegetables are eaten together with meat or fish. *Uru* or *maiore*, breadfruit, is quite unpleasant raw and is eaten cooked. On the Marquesas, the basic dish is *popoi*, a sweet-and-sour dish that looks like a yellow paste. It consists of cooked uru, crushed in a mortar, mixed with uru pulp and left to ferment; coconut milk is added. The whole thing is covered with a *purau* leaf. To

western tastes, taro and other local staples can be rather bland. They are usually boiled but additional flavouring can make them more palatable. *Fei*, a sort of plantain banana, is only eaten cooked and has a bittersweet taste. Taro root is eaten cooked, as are sweet potato and manioc (cassava). *Fafa* (taro leaves) are often served with chicken.

Meat *Pua* (suckling pig) is the preferred meat for a traditional underground oven known as an *ahimaa* (see the boxed text 'Ahimaa & Tamaaraa' in this chapter). New Zealand beef also often features in dishes, as does chicken. On the Marquesas, goat meat takes pride of place, and dog is still eaten on the remote atolls of the Tuamotus. Although it is protected, turtle is still eaten in French Polynesia. Categorically refuse to eat it to avoid supporting this practice.

The most common accompaniments are coconut milk (not to be confused with coconut juice), which is obtained by grating the white flesh inside the nut and wringing it in a cloth; *miti hue*, a fermented sauce based on coconut flesh mixed with shrimphead juice and salt water; and *taioro*, another variety of fermented sauce.

Breads *Faraoa coco* (coconut bread) is a tasty cake. *Firifiri*, sweet fritters, are generally shaped like a figure eight or a plait. *Ipo* is Tuamotuan bread and has a heavy consistency. The flour is mixed with coconut juice, sugar and grated coconut. *Pai* are turnovers filled with coconut or banana.

Other Cuisines

Among the Chinese specialities, *maa tiniot* is a mixture of pork pieces and red beans. *Chaomen*, or chow mein, is a mixture of rice, noodles, red beans, vermicelli, vegetables and fried pork. Rice is found everywhere, and pizza and pasta are very popular on the tourist islands.

French cuisine is especially common on Tahiti and on touristy islands. French bread, croissants and snacks are available everywhere.

DRINKS
Nonalcoholic Drinks
Fruit Juice Several delicious fruit juices are made locally, notably the Rotui brand of pineapple juice produced on Moorea, grapefruit juice and guava juice. Lime juice added to mineral water is very thirst quenching.

The big international softdrink brands are distributed in French Polynesia.

Coconut Juice *Pape haari* is the healthiest, cheapest, most natural and thirst-quenching drink around. It is totally free of microbes and bacteria. After the fibre surrounding the coconut is removed, the top of the nut is taken off with a machete. You can drink directly from the nut or through a straw. The juice has a slightly bitter taste.

Mineral Water Several brands are available, the main ones being French (Volvic, Vittel). The cheapest is the local spring water, Eau Royale or Vaimato. With the exception of Papeete and Bora Bora, it is not advisable to drink the tap water.

Coffee In most cases this is instant Nescafé. Allow 200 CFP to 300 CFP for a coffee in a Papeete bar.

Alcoholic Drinks
Beer The local brand of *pia* (beer), Hinano, is sold everywhere and is available in glass 500ml bottles, 330 and 500ml cans, and on tap. Foreign beers, notably Heineken, are also available. Allow at least 350 CFP in a bar or restaurant.

Wines & Spirits Papeete supermarket shelves have plenty of red and white French wines. The cheapest bottles cost around 800 CFP. Restaurants enjoy a tax reduction on alcohol sold at 'agreed prices', which makes it affordable (allow 1500 CFP to 3000 CFP for a bottle).

You must try the *maitai*, a local speciality. This cocktail is like a punch, and is made with brown and white rums, pineapple, grenadine and lime juices, coconut liqueur and, in some cases, Grand Marnier or Cointreau.

ENTERTAINMENT
Don't expect to party until all hours of the night in French Polynesia; this is a place to catch up on early nights.

Papeete, on the weekends, is the only place with a really active nightlife in its numerous discos, and it's also the only place with cinemas. On other islands, a drink in a bar and perhaps dinner and a dance performance in a big hotel is about as active as it gets. *Bringues* (family events with friends) are an interesting slice of life although too much beer can certainly make them degenerate. See the boxed text 'Bringues & Kaina Music' in the Facts about the Islands chapter.

SPECTATOR SPORTS
Polynesian kids are a sporting bunch and you may catch a volley ball or football event. The national sport is, without dispute, pirogue racing, especially on Tahiti (see the 'Hawaiki Nui Canoe Race' boxed text in this chapter). You will certainly have the opportunity to admire the pirogue teams training on the lagoon. Tahiti has hosted events in the world surfing championship, and French Polynesia participates in the annual South Pacific Games.

SHOPPING
There are plenty of souvenir shops and craft outlets waiting to lure you in. Beware of local souvenirs that aren't local at all – the colourful wood carvings, even with Bora Bora neatly painted on them, probably come from Bali or Colombia. Nevertheless, French Polynesia does have some excellent local crafts and many of them can be found on Tahiti, especially in Papeete Market. When shopping for craftwork remember that bargaining is not the norm anywhere in the Pacific.

There are duty-free shopping facilities in Papeete and at Faaa airport with the usual liquor, tobacco and perfume discounts, but the prices are not very exciting by international standards. Stamp collectors will find some interesting and very colourful stamps on sale. The Papeete post office has a section for philatelists.

For more information, see the 'Marquesan Handicrafts' boxed text in the Marquesas chapter, and the Arts section in the Facts about the Islands chapter.

Clothing & Decoration

Hats, bags and mats of woven pandanus are among the best examples of a true local craft. The best work is said to come from the Australs.

Tapa is a traditional nonwoven fabric made from the bark of the uru, banyan or paper mulberry trees. Nowadays the craft is almost disappearing, as it's fast being replaced by woven fabrics. Only the women on Fatu Hiva in the Marquesas still practise the ancient technique, but tapa can be bought in Papeete.

Tifaifai are large, brilliantly coloured patchwork cloths, usually decorated with stylised flower or fruit designs. Produced on a number of islands, including Rurutu, tifaifai are often sold as tablecloths, bedspreads and curtains.

The *pareu* is a single piece of cloth, colourfully decorated and usually worn by women – although it's equally appropriate for men. There are numerous ways to tie a pareu. They cost about 1500 CFP to 2500 CFP, but if you're buying one, beware! Many of them are imported from Asia.

Widely available as moisturising cream, soap, shampoo, sunscreen and perfume, *monoi* is a blend of coconut oil perfumed with flowers.

Painting & Sculpture

A number of interesting European and Polynesian artists work in French Polynesia and their work is on display in galleries on Tahiti and Moorea. Originals and high-quality prints and posters are available.

Sculpture and woodcarving, done in fine wood and in stone or bone, are particularly renowned in the Marquesas. Many settlements in that archipelago have craft centres where you can see local artists' work, although you can also approach them directly. Tiki, *umete* (traditional wooden bowls), trunks, spears, hair pins and other personal adornments are the most popular work; see the boxed text 'Marquesan Handicrafts' in the Marquesas chapter.

Specialist galleries in Papeete also sell sculptors' work but at higher prices. Twice a year Marquesan sculptors have an exhibition and sale in the Territorial Assembly building, usually in June and November.

Music

Polynesian song has become a sort of island form of country & western music – down home tales of lost love and day-to-day life to the accompaniment of guitar and ukelele. It's easy on the ear and very popular locally. More-traditional dance music has strong rhythms and lots of drumming. Both forms can be easily found on tapes and CDs in music shops and hypermarket music sections in Papeete and in other major centres.

Tattoos

Traditional Polynesian tattooing has enjoyed a major resurgence in recent years and like that pioneering collector, Sir Joseph Banks in 1769, you could come back with your very own example of Tahitian art. See the 'Tattooing' special section for more information.

Black Pearls

Black pearls, cultivated in the Tuamotus, have become a major factor in the French Polynesian economy. There are jewellery shops and black-pearl specialists in Papeete and on other islands. In Papeete, allow 5000 CFP to 200,000 CFP and more for single pearls, which are available both mounted and unmounted.

Getting There & Away

Occasionally a cruise ship calls in at Tahiti and there's a steady trickle of cruising yachts, but visitors to French Polynesia generally arrive by air. Tahiti is a long way from anywhere: 6500km south-west of the Californian coast, 5500km north-east of Australia, 8000km west of South America and 9500km south-east of Japan. It's practically the antipodes of Europe – 16,000km away.

AIR
Airports & Airlines
Faaa airport, on the outskirts of Papeete on the island of Tahiti, is French Polynesia's only international airport. International check-in desks are at the east end of the terminal. There is no departure tax in French Polynesia.

There are long runways on Hao and Moruroa in the Tuamotus, but these were used solely by the French military in connection with its nuclear-testing program. There has been talk about extending the runway on Nuku Hiva in the Marquesas to open up these remote islands to international tourism, but it's likely to be a long time before that happens.

The increasing use of long-range aircraft has considerably reduced the number of options for getting to Tahiti and other Pacific islands in recent years. Most air traffic across the South Pacific is between North America and Australia or New Zealand. Not so many years ago that long flight required a refuelling stop somewhere along the way, but the advent of the 400 series Boeing 747 changed all that. Los Angeles (LA)-Sydney and LA-Auckland flights have become nonstop affairs and nobody wants to stop on Tahiti in the middle of the night for no good reason, and so there are now fewer trans-Pacific flights stopping in French Polynesia.

Visitors to Tahiti come from a number of directions and on airlines that currently include:

Aircalin (Air Calédonie International)
www.aircalin.nc
Air France
www.airfrance.com
Air New Zealand
www.alrnz.com
Air Tahiti Nui
www.airtahiti-nui.com
AOM (Air Outre-Mer) French Airlines
www.aom.com
Corsair (Nouvelles Frontières)
www.corsair-int.com
Hawaiian Airlines
www.hawaiianair.com
LanChile
www.lanchile.com
Qantas
www.qantas.com

Airline schedules are always prone to change, so the details in this chapter are given as an indication of flight frequencies and the fares available.

If you want to organise your travels around French Polynesia and at the same time decipher the complexities of Air Tahiti ticketing, it would be wise to contact a good general travel agent rather than one of the low-price specialists recommended here. Local airline phone numbers and addresses are in the Getting There & Away section under Papeete in the Tahiti chapter.

Other Pacific Islands
There is remarkably little air traffic between the island nations of the Pacific. Connections to Pacific islands not mentioned here, such as Tonga or the Samoas, will require a change at one of the other islands. See the USA & Canada section for information on Hawaii-Papeete direct flights, and see the Special Fares section later for information on round-the-world (RTW) and Circle Pacific fares.

Easter Island With its Polynesian links, Easter Island is an important connection with Papeete. LanChile flies Papeete-Easter Island-Santiago three or four times weekly.

Air Travel Glossary

Cancellation Penalties If you have to cancel or change a discounted ticket, there are often heavy penalties involved; insurance can sometimes be taken out against these penalties. Some airlines impose penalties on regular tickets as well, particularly against 'no-show' passengers.

Courier Fares Businesses often need to send urgent documents or freight securely and quickly. Courier companies hire people to accompany the package through customs and, in return, offer a discount ticket which is sometimes a phenomenal bargain. However, you may have to surrender all your baggage allowance and take only carry-on luggage.

Full Fares Airlines traditionally offer 1st class (coded F), business class (coded J) and economy class (coded Y) tickets. These days there are so many promotional and discounted fares available that few passengers pay full economy fare.

Lost Tickets If you lose your airline ticket an airline will usually treat it like a travellers cheque and, after inquiries, issue you with another one. Legally, however, an airline is entitled to treat it like cash and if you lose it then it's gone forever. Take good care of your tickets.

Onward Tickets An entry requirement for many countries is that you have a ticket out of the country. If you're unsure of your next move, the easiest solution is to buy the cheapest onward ticket to a neighbouring country or a ticket from a reliable airline which can later be refunded if you do not use it.

Open-Jaw Tickets These are return tickets where you fly out to one place but return from another. If available, this can save you backtracking to your arrival point.

Overbooking Since every flight has some passengers who fail to show up, airlines often book more passengers than they have seats. Usually excess passengers make up for the no-shows, but occasionally somebody gets 'bumped' onto the next available flight. Guess who it is most likely to be? The passengers who check in late.

Promotional Fares These are officially discounted fares, available from travel agencies or direct from the airline.

Reconfirmation If you don't reconfirm your flight at least 72 hours prior to departure, the airline may delete your name from the passenger list. Ring to find out if your airline requires reconfirmation.

Restrictions Discounted tickets often have various restrictions on them – such as needing to be paid for in advance and incurring a penalty to be altered. Others are restrictions on the minimum and maximum period you must be away.

Round-the-World Tickets RTW tickets give you a limited period (usually a year) in which to circumnavigate the globe. You can go anywhere the carrying airlines go, as long as you don't backtrack. The number of stopovers or total number of separate flights is decided before you set off and they usually cost a bit more than a basic return flight.

Transferred Tickets Airline tickets cannot be transferred from one person to another. Travellers sometimes try to sell the return half of their ticket, but officials can ask you to prove that you are the person named on the ticket. On an international flight tickets are compared with passports.

Travel Periods Ticket prices vary with the time of year. There is a low (off-peak) season and a high (peak) season, and often a low-shoulder season and a high-shoulder season as well. Usually the fare depends on your outward flight – if you depart in the high season and return in the low season, you pay the high-season fare.

It has a low season promotional tariff of 39,900 CFP and a regular fare of 56,000/59,000 CFP in the low/high season.

Fiji The once-weekly Papeete-Nadi-Noumea Aircalin flight with a Nadi stopover costs 81,400/93,600 CFP return in the low/high season. Air New Zealand's LA-Papeete-Auckland flight continues once a week from Papeete via Rarotonga with a connection to Fiji. Papeete-Nadi return costs 59,000/69,000 CFP in the low/high season

New Caledonia The only flights to French Polynesia by the airline of another Pacific island are from the French colony of New Caledonia. Aircalin has two Papeete-Noumea flights per week, one via Wallis & Futuna, the other via Nadi. The flight takes about eight hours. There's a super-apex fare of 78,000 CFP return on certain low-season flights and a normal apex fare of 92,200 CFP year-round. If you want to stopover in Wallis or Nadi, the ticket will cost 111,400/124,000 CFP in the low/high season. From Noumea there are direct connections to Brisbane and (with a bit of a wait) to Sydney in Australia.

Rarotonga (Cook Islands) Twice a week, Air New Zealand's LA-Papeete-Auckland flight goes via Rarotonga. The Papeete-Rarotonga return fare is 39,000/59,000 CFP in low/high season.

Wallis A Papeete-Wallis return ticket aboard Aircalin's weekly Papeete-Noumea flight via Wallis costs 77,300/87,600 CFP in the low/high season.

The USA & Canada
Fares to Tahiti from North America are seasonal; late December to mid-June is the low season. From Canada you have to connect on the west coast or in Hawaii. See also the Special Fares section later in this chapter.

Honolulu Hawaiian Airlines flies Honolulu-Papeete (about five hours) twice weekly. It has connections to and from LA (direct), San Francisco, Seattle and Las Vegas. Honolulu-Papeete return fares are US$629/829 in the low/high season.

Los Angeles & Oakland There are no American airlines operating direct flights from the US mainland to Tahiti. Air France, Corsair and AOM all fly Paris-Papeete via LA (Corsair also via Oakland). Air New Zealand flies Frankfurt or London-Papeete via LA. The Tahitian airline Air Tahiti Nui also flies LA-Papeete.

The airlines' flight details and US phone numbers are:

Air France
(☎ 1800 237 2747) 747s, three or four times weekly
Air New Zealand
(☎ 310-662 1860) 747s, three times weekly
Air Tahiti Nui
(☎ 1877 TAHITIN or ☎ 310 662 1860) Airbus A340s, three times weekly
AOM
(☎ 310-338 9613) DC10s, three to five times weekly
Corsair
(☎ 1800 677 0720) 747s, twice weekly (once via LA, once via Oakland)

The LA-Papeete return fare is about US$700. It's possible to go via Hawaii with Hawaiian Air (☎ 1800 367 5320) at similar cost although the flight takes longer.

Sunday travel sections of major newspapers like the *New York Times, Los Angeles Times, San Francisco Examiner-Chronicle* and the *Chicago Tribune* are good sources of advertisements for competitively priced air fares. Council Travel and STA Travel have very competitive air fares and have offices across the country.

In Canada, the *Globe & Mail, Toronto Star, Montreal Gazette* and the *Vancouver Sun* carry travel agents' ads and are a good place to look for cheap fares. Travel CUTS, the Canadian student-travel network, has offices around the country offering competitively priced tickets.

Australia & New Zealand
There are six weekly connections between Auckland in New Zealand and Papeete. Air

Flying to Tahiti

Until the American forces built an air base on Bora Bora during WWII, nobody flew to French Polynesia. True, the French military had stationed a few small seaplanes on Tahiti prior to the war but there were no airports nor, for that matter, were there many aircraft capable of the long ocean crossings.

After the war some test flights were made across the Pacific via French Polynesia. In 1950 a French DC-4 island-hopped across the Pacific from Noumea via Vanuatu (the New Hebrides in those days), Fiji and Aitutaki in the Cook Islands to Bora Bora. In 1951 an Australian Catalina amphibious aircraft flew from Sydney via Papeete and the Gambier Islands to Chile.

In 1947, TRAPAS (Transports Aériens du Pacifique Sud), a locally established airline using war-surplus Catalinas, started a once-monthly Noumea-Tahiti service, which continued until 1950. Reinvented as Air Tahiti it began a service to Aitutaki, but in 1951 TEAL (Tasman Empire Airways Ltd), the predecessor of Air New Zealand, started a monthly and then twice-monthly Auckland-Suva (Fiji)-Apia (Western Samoa)-Aitutaki-Papeete service using a DC-6 on the first leg, then a four-engined Solent flying boat the rest of the way. With an overnight stop at Western Samoa the trip took at least two days. The Aitutaki stop was purely for refuelling and passengers could have a swim in the lagoon during the two-hour stop. The service continued until 1960.

The wartime airfield at Bora Bora was neglected after the war but it was still in good enough repair for Pan Am to fly to Bora Bora from the USA in 1951. In the late 1950s, a French connection was established using land aircraft (Constellations and then DC-4s) to fly Noumea-Fiji-Bora Bora, with an amphibious connection to Papeete. Finally, in 1960 the first stage of Faaa airport was opened on reclaimed land in the lagoon near Papeete and Tahiti entered the jet age.

New Zealand flies Auckland-Papeete-Los Angeles three times weekly, once direct, once via Rarotonga and once via Fiji and Rarotonga. Qantas flies Sydney-Auckland-Papeete three times weekly. Both airlines have connecting services from Melbourne, Sydney and Brisbane.

Auckland-Papeete direct takes about six hours and costs NZ$1211/1417 return in the low/high season. Discount agencies can offer the fare below NZ$900.

From Sydney, return fares to Papeete are A$1285/1429 in the low/high season. Discount tickets are available at around A$1000.

STA Travel and Flight Centres International are major specialists in low-priced air fares out of Australia and New Zealand. Weekend travel sections in major newspapers, such as the *Age*, *Australian* and *Sydney Morning Herald* in Australia, and the *Auckland Herald* in New Zealand, also carry advertisements from agents specialising in lower priced air fares. See the Special Fares section later for information on RTW and Circle Pacific fares.

Europe

There are French, German and British connections to Papeete from Europe. From any other European country you have to connect through Paris, Frankfurt, London or the USA. See the Special Fares section later in this chapter for information on RTW fares.

France Corsair, AOM and Air France operate between Papeete and Paris and have competed fiercely since the route has been opened up to competition. Travel agencies also offer Air New Zealand flights with reasonably priced connecting flights to Frankfurt or London and it's possible to extend trips as far as New Zealand. All airlines stop briefly at LA (and/or Oakland for Corsair).

Reckon on about a 21-hour flight to Papeete – longer if you have to transfer to Air New Zealand.

The lowest fares are quite similar. Take advantage of competition for the little 'extras' (type of aircraft, frequency, stopovers, discounts for children, ticket validity, alteration or cancellation fees, baggage allowance etc). The low season is from early January to late June, and September to mid-December. The high season (July-August and the Christmas period) is divided into two fare categories according to departure dates. The airlines have agencies or representatives in Switzerland and Belgium offering connecting flights to Paris at reduced fares. You can get information directly from the airlines or your travel agent.

Air France
  (☎ 0802 802 802, minitel 3615 or 3616 AFS) Flies Paris-Papeete three or four times weekly with Boeing 747s. Economy return fares vary seasonally from 6180 FF to 9985 FF. Tickets are valid for 90 days and stopovers in LA are possible subject to certain conditions. Contact the airline or your travel agency.
Air New Zealand
  (☎ 01 43 80 30 10, ☎ 40 53 82 23) Offers connecting flights from Paris, Lyons, Nice and Marseille to London or Frankfurt, from where their regular flights leave for New Zealand via Papeete. There are two or three flights per week from London and three from Frankfurt. Fares vary seasonally from 6320 FF to 8060 FF return from Paris (440 FF from other French cities). Stopovers in LA are free and the ticket is valid for six months. Belgian and Swiss travellers can connect in Frankfurt or London.
AOM
  (☎ 0803 00 12 34, minitel 3615 AOMS) Has three to five weekly Paris-LA-Papeete flights with DC 10s. There are four seasonal fares varying from 6180 FF to 9600 FF return. LA stopovers are available under certain conditions – contact AOM or your travel agency. For connections from Belgium contact Sabena (☎ 02-723 2323). In Switzerland, call ☎ 01-212 12 24.
Corsair
  (☎ 0803 33 33 33, minitel 3615 NFS) Flies Paris-Papeete twice weekly with Boeing 747s, once via Oakland (San Francisco) and once via LA. Return fares vary from 5000 FF (ticket cannot be modified or refunded and payment must be made at the time of booking) up to

9000 FF. An LA or San Francisco stopover is possible at additional cost. Contact the nearest Nouvelles Frontières agency or phone the airline.

The UK Flights from the UK to Tahiti are usually en route to Australasia. Only Air New Zealand's London-LA-Papeete-Auckland-Australia flight has straight-through connections. It's also possible to visit Rarotonga (Cook Islands) and Nadi (Fiji) between Papeete and Auckland. London-Auckland-London fares vary seasonally from £500 to £900.

UK travel agents offering competitive air fares can be tracked down through the travel pages of the Sunday newspapers, magazines like *Time Out* or in a host of giveaway papers in London. Good travel agents for low-priced air fares include STA Travel, Council Travel and Trailfinders.

Germany There is an Air New Zealand service flying Frankfurt-LA-Auckland via Papeete. Contact your travel agency.

Asia
Air Tahiti Nui has one or two weekly Papeete-Tokyo direct flights and a Papeete-Osaka service. Otherwise the simplest connection is via Australia or New Zealand with a Circle Pacific fare, which is also the best way of approaching Tahiti from other countries in Asia. See Special Fares later for more information.

South America
The Chilean airline LanChile has three or four weekly Papeete-Easter Island-Santiago

Air Tahiti Nui

Since late 1998 French Polynesia has had its own international airline. Air Tahiti Nui operates just three routes, Papeete-Los Angeles, Papeete-Tokyo and Papeete-Osaka, and has just one aircraft, an Airbus A340 in an unmistakable colour scheme of turquoise and ultramarine featuring a magnificent tiare flower.

flights. This is one of the most popular routes linking Australia and New Zealand with South America, and it's a common sight to see the Air New Zealand, Qantas and LanChile aircraft lined up at Faaa airport in the middle of the night, transferring passengers in both directions.

American travellers intending to visit South America and Easter Island may find a loop through Santiago, Easter Island and Papeete more attractive than a North America-Chile return ticket (around $US1000) with a Santiago-Easter Island return (US$800) tagged on (see Special Fares later in this chapter). Flying from Australia via Tahiti and Easter Island to Santiago costs around A$2200 return.

Special Fares

Round-The-World A RTW ticket that takes in French Polynesia costs about £1000 in the UK. It's value for money and you get to more places, such as Africa and Asia as well as the Pacific. RTW tickets cost around A$2400 in Australia and about US$2080 in the USA.

Circle Pacific Similar to RTW tickets but covering a more limited region, Circle Pacific uses a combination of airlines to connect Australia, New Zealand, North America and Asia, with a variety of stopover options in the Pacific islands. There are advance-purchase restrictions and limits on how many stopovers you can make. Travel agents are well informed about these tickets.

A Circle Pacific pass is likely to be about 15% cheaper than a RTW ticket but it's better value from the USA than from Australasia. For example: LA-Tahiti-Rarotonga-Fiji-Auckland-Sydney-Hong Kong-Taipei-Chicago costs US$1695, while LA-Hong Kong-Auckland-Fiji-Tahiti-LA is US$1539. Sydney-Tokyo-LA-Tahiti-Rarotonga-Auckland-Sydney costs A$1960.

An Air New Zealand-LanChile combination Circle Pacific fare flying LA-Sydney (or Melbourne or Auckland)-Papeete-Easter Island-LA costs around US$2090.

SEA
Cargo & Expedition Ships

There are no regular passenger shipping-services to French Polynesia and cruise ships stopping at Papeete are few and far between. Travel on cargo ships is, however, making a steady comeback on those that do occasionally call in to Papeete.

This is not, however, like deciding which day of the week you want to fly; it means contacting shipping companies and seeing which month something *might* be going by. In his book *In Search of Tusitala* (see Books in the Facts for the Visitor chapter) Gavin Bell manages to get to Tahiti by freighter but it isn't exactly easy.

There are two ships operating through French Polynesia with some regularity. The Canadian company Marine Expeditions specialises in Antarctic and Arctic trips. It repositions its ships via the Pacific on a trip that departs Valparaiso in Chile and then goes via Robinson Crusoe (Juan Fernandez), Alejandro Selkirk and Easter islands (all Chile), Ducie, Henderson, Pitcairn and Oeno islands (all part of the Pitcairn group) before entering French Polynesian waters. It stops at Mangareva, Rapa, Raivavae, Rurutu and Moorea before the voyage finishes in Papeete, Tahiti. The 27 day trip aboard the *Akademik Shuleykin* costs from US$5995, including LA-Santiago (Chile) and Papeete-LA flights, all meals and excursions from the ship. Marine Expeditions (☎ 416-964 9069, fax 964 2366, toll free ☎ 1800 263 9147) is at 890 Yonge St, 3rd floor, Toronto, Ontario, Canada M4W 3P4. Its Web site is at www.marineex.com.

Society Expeditions does somewhat similar trips on *World Discoverer*. Some of its voyages do a loop from Papeete through various islands of French Polynesia. Others go from Papeete to Easter Island, or vice versa, typically via a number of islands in the Tuamotus and Marquesas, Mangareva in the Gambier Archipelago and several islands in the Pitcairn group. A typical 17 to 20 day Papeete-Easter Island trip costs from US$7400, including LA-Papeete and Easter Island-Santiago-LA air fares. Society Expeditions (☎ 206-728 9400, fax 728 2301, ☎ toll free 1800 548 8669) is at 2001 Western Ave, Suite 300, Seattle, Washington 98121, USA. Its Web site is at www.societyexpeditions.com.

Yacht

Travelling to French Polynesia by yacht is eminently feasible, even if you don't own one! Cruising yachts heading across the Pacific from North America, Australia or New Zealand are often looking for crew and, if you're in the right place at the right time and have the right attitude, it's often possible to pick up a ride. Sailing experience will definitely score extra points but so will the ability to cook soup when the boat's heeled over and waves are crashing through the hatch. Being an easy-going person who can put up with anything and being always ready to lend a hand will count for a lot.

On the eastern side of the Pacific, try the yacht clubs in San Diego, LA, San Francisco or Honolulu. On the western side, Auckland, Sydney and Cairns will be good places to try. Look for notices pinned to bulletin boards in yacht clubs and yachting-equipment shops and post your own notice offering to crew. Simply asking around the yachts can often turn up possibilities.

The sooner you make contact the better, as it's better to do some sailing with the boat before you really set off. A month from the next landfall is not the time to find you don't get on with the crew (or vice versa) or that your immunity to seasickness was just wishful thinking.

It takes about a month to sail west from the US west coast to Hawaii and another month south from there to the Marquesas. With stops, a further month takes you west again to Tahiti and the Society Islands and then it's another long leg south and west to Australia or New Zealand.

There are distinct seasons for sailing across the Pacific, as yachties like to be out of the tropics during the cyclone season. Late September to October, and January to March are the usual departure times from

the USA. Yachts tend to set off from Australia and New Zealand after the cyclone season, around March and April.

It's also possible to pick up crewing positions in French Polynesia.

ORGANISED TOURS

There are a variety of tour packages available from travel agents in all western countries. If you want more than just a straightforward cheap fare, a general travel agent can be an excellent first stop. A good travel agent can negotiate better prices at the larger hotels, can handle Air Tahiti bookings and have your schedule finalised before you arrive. See the Getting Around chapter for more details.

In France, in addition to the traditional travel operators, there are agencies specialising in diving tours. Their packages typically include flights, accommodation, diving fees and diving tours on the main islands.

Warning

The information in this chapter is particularly vulnerable to change: Prices for international travel are volatile, routes are introduced and cancelled, schedules change, special deals come and go, and rules and visa requirements are amended. Airlines and governments seem to take a perverse pleasure in making price structures and regulations as complicated as possible. You should check directly with the airline or a travel agent to make sure you understand how a fare (and ticket you may buy) works. In addition, the travel industry is highly competitive and there are many lurks and perks.

The upshot of this is that you should get opinions, quotes and advice from as many airlines and travel agents as possible before you part with your hard-earned cash. The details given in this chapter should be regarded as pointers and are not a substitute for your own careful, up-to-date research.

Getting Around

Getting from island to island in French Polynesia involves flights or boats and, thanks to a great deal of financial support from the French government, travel to the larger, more populated islands is relatively easy and fairly reasonably priced. Getting to the remote islands can be time consuming or even difficult, but never boring.

On some islands there are paved roads, local *le truck* (public transport) services and ranks of rental cars; on others there are rough dirt tracks and very little local transport. Only around Papeete and its suburbs is there reasonably comprehensive public transport; for anywhere else renting a car or even a bicycle may be the best bet.

Island to Island

AIR

There are some charter operators with small aircraft and helicopters but essentially, flying within French Polynesia means Air Tahiti and its associate, Air Moorea. Air Tahiti flies to 38 islands in all five of the major island groups. Window seats on its modern fleet of high-wing twin-turboprop aircraft offer great views – perfect for flying over beautiful islands. Air Moorea is the secondary airline, operating smaller aircraft between Tahiti and Moorea and Tetiaroa.

The best bargains for travel in French Polynesia are the air passes that allow you to visit a number of islands for one fare. Note that Papeete is very much the centre for flights within French Polynesia and, with a few exceptions, you will generally have to pass through Papeete between island groups.

Domestic Air Services

All Air Tahiti flights are nonsmoking. Theoretically the free-baggage allowance is 10kg, except for international passengers on direct connecting flights, who get 20kg. There is an (expensive) left-luggage facility

at Faaa airport in Papeete. Although the airline is pretty reliable, plan to be back in Papeete a day or two before your departing international flight.

Flight frequencies vary seasonally and the indications that follow are generally a minimum. In July and August in particular, extra flights are scheduled. Air Tahiti publishes a very useful flight schedule booklet, which is essential reading for anyone planning a complex trip around the islands. See the individual island chapters for Air Tahiti phone numbers, or contact the head office on Tahiti (☎ 86 42 42, fax 86 40 69; on Saturday afternoon and Sunday ☎ 86 41 84, 86 41 95).

Following is an indication of the flight distances between Papeete and some of the other islands serviced by Air Tahiti:

destination	flight distance from Papeete
Moorea	17km
Huahine	170km
Raiatea	220km
Bora Bora	270km
Maupiti	320km
Rangiroa	350km
Nuku Hiva	1500km
Rurutu	570km
Mangareva	1700km

The Society Islands From Papeete, there are direct flights every half-hour or so to Moorea and several times a day to other major islands in the group, except for Maupiti, where connections are less frequent. There are daily connections on most routes between Moorea, Huahine, Raiatea and Bora Bora. On some routes, like the busy Papeete-Bora Bora connection, there may be up to eight flights a day in the high season. The Society Islands are quite close together, and the longest nonstop flight lasts 45 minutes, between Papeete and Bora Bora. Other flights may be as short as 10 minutes, even less between Papeete and Moorea.

JEAN-BERNARD CARILLET

JEAN-BERNARD CARILLET

JEAN-BERNARD CARILLET

JEAN-BERNARD CARILLET

JEAN-BERNARD CARILLET

French Polynesian handicrafts have an excellent reputation and include sculpture, vividly coloured *pareu* (sarongs), shell necklaces, basketwork and *tapa* (bark-cloth).

Goélettes (cargo ships) and the aircraft of Air Tahiti are the main forms of inter-island transport. On Tahiti, *le truck* is the favoured mode of local transport.

The Tuamotus Air Tahiti divides the Tuamotus into the busier and more touristed northern Tuamotus and the much less frequented eastern Tuamotus. The Gambier Archipelago is reached via the eastern Tuamotus.

Rangiroa is the main centre in the Tuamotus, with between one and five one-hour flights to/from Papeete daily. On most days, a flight continues on to Manihi. Other flights, either direct or via Rangiroa include Apataki, Arutua, Faaite, Fakarava, Kaukura, Mataiva, Takaroa and Takapoto and Tikehau.

Apart from Tahiti the only Society island with a direct connection to the Tuamotus is Bora Bora. There are three Bora Bora-Rangiroa-Manihi flights weekly and one in the opposite direction. Some flights continue from Rangiroa to Nuku Hiva in the Marquesas.

There are connections to Anaa, Takume, Fakahina, Fangatau, Napuka, Puka Puka, Hao, Makemo, Nukutavake, Pukarua, Reao, Tatakoto, Tureia and Vahitahi in the eastern Tuamotus. Some of these connections are very infrequent, so check a current Air Tahiti timetable.

The Marquesas Flights to the Marquesas are usually direct from Papeete (about three hours) but some are via Rangiroa. There are six or seven weekly connections to Nuku Hiva, some of which continue to Hiva Oa. From Nuku Hiva there are three weekly flights to Ua Pou, and one to Ua Huka.

The Australs Air Tahiti has three to six weekly flights from Papeete to Rurutu (about 1½ hours) and Tubuai. One flight goes Papeete-Rurutu-Tubuai-Papeete, the other one Papeete-Tubuai-Rurutu-Papeete.

The Gambier Archipelago There are three monthly flights to Mangareva from Papeete (about five hours with a half-hour stop at Hao).

Charter Flights Wan Air (☎ 85 55 54, fax 85 55 56) and Air Archipels (☎ 81 30 30, fax 86 42 99) are based at Faaa airport and arrange charter flights with small aircraft to any destination in French Polynesia. Héli Inter Polynésie (☎ 81 99 00, mobile 77 80 08, fax 81 99 99) and Héli Pacific (☎ 85 68 00, fax 85 68 08) are also at the airport and organise helicopter charters. Héli Inter Polynésie (☎/fax 67 52 59) offer the same service on Bora Bora. In the Marquesas, Héli Inter Marquises (☎/fax 92 02 17) operates regular shuttle services (see the Marquesas chapter for details).

Buying Tickets

You can pay for flights by credit card at most Air Tahiti offices or agencies.

Reservations If your travel agent tells you that Air Tahiti flights are fully booked, do not despair. French Polynesians are in the habit of reserving seats and changing their minds at the last moment. Seats may therefore become available right up to the last minute. Reapply frequently, even on the spot.

You can make reservations at a travel agency or by phone and be issued with a purchase date; if you haven't paid for it by that date the reservation is automatically cancelled. If, however, you buy the ticket and don't show up for the flight you'll be penalised 25% of the ticket price.

You are not officially required to reconfirm Air Tahiti flights except in certain cases. However, it's wise to do so, particularly on infrequent services such as those to the Marquesas and the Gambier. If you've not given Air Tahiti a contact phone-number then you should definitely reconfirm. Note that if you fail to fly on a confirmed flight, all your subsequent reservations may be cancelled. So if you decide to get from one island to another by some different means, make sure you reconfirm the rest of your flights.

Air Tahiti's central booking number in French Polynesia is ☎ 86 42 42, fax 86 40 69; on Saturday afternoon and Sunday ☎ 86 41 84 or 86 41 95 (email rtahitim@mail.pf).

Fares See the Domestic Air Fares map in this chapter for fares between the various islands of French Polynesia. Air fares are heavily subsidised, but since distances to the remote islands are great, some of the full

DOMESTIC AIR FARES

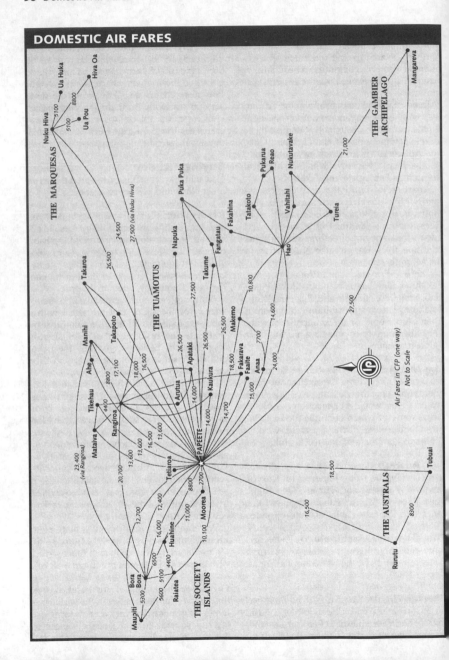

THE GAMBIER ARCHIPELAGO

THE MARQUESAS

Ua Huka
Hiva Oa
Nuku Hiva
5100
8800
5100
Ua Pou
Mangareva

Pukarua
Reao
Nukutavake
Vahitahi
Fakahina
Tatakoto
Puka Puka
21,000

Napuka
Fangatau
Takume
Hao
Tureia

Takaroa
27,500 (via Nuku Hiva)
24,500
26,500
10,800

THE TUAMOTUS

Manihi
Takapoto
27,500
Ahe
26,500
Makemo
14,600
27,500
8800
17,100
18,000
16,500
Apataki
26,500
7700
Tikehau
4400
Arutua
14,000
Fakarava
18,500
Kaukura
Faaite
24,000
Rangiroa
Anaa
15,000

23,400 (via Rangiroa)
13,600
16,500
13,600
14,000
14,700

Air Fares in CFP (one way)
Not to Scale

Mataiva
20,700
PAPEETE

13,600
Tetiaroa
12,700
Tubuai
18,500

Moorea
8800
2700
11,000
12,400
Huahine
Bora Bora
16,000
6500
5100
4400
10,100
16,500
8300

Maupiti
5300
5600
Raiatea

THE SOCIETY ISLANDS

Rurutu

THE AUSTRALS

fares are still quite high. However, Air Tahiti has been reviewing its prices and, in some cases, lowering them. There are a number of air passes that bring prices down to more acceptable levels and a system of reduced fare cards (see later in this section).

Other cost-saving options include flight and accommodation packages utilising hotels or guesthouses on most of the tourist islands. For some islands there are even weekend packages. Contact Séjours dans les Îles (Stay on the Islands) on ☎ 42 70 00.

Children from age two to 12 pay about 50% of the adult fare. Infants under two years of age pay 10%. If you buy tickets overseas they may work out about 5% more expensive due to travel agency commissions.

Flights are classified (in ascending order of demand) as blue, white or red. There may be restrictions on the flights you can use, particularly the popular peak-period red flights.

Reduced Fare Cards Air Tahiti has several cards available that let you buy tickets at reduced prices, depending on whether the flight is blue, white or red. If you're under 25, the Jeunes (Young) card gives you a 50% reduction on blue flights and 25% on white flights. If you're over 60, a Troiseme Age (Third Age) card gives you 50 and 40% reductions respectively. A Familles (Family) card gives family members a 50% (adults) and 75% (children) discount on blue flights, 25% and 50% on white flights and, for children only, 50% on red flights.

Jeunes and Troiseme Age cards cost 1000 CFP. You need a passport-type photo and your passport or other form of identification. For the 2000 CFP Familles card you need photos of the parents, and birth certificates or equivalent for the children – just having them in your passport isn't enough.

It takes three days to issue these cards and they are available only in French Polynesia, so if you want one apply as soon as you arrive in Papeete.

Air Passes

There are six island-hopping air passes offering inclusive fares to a number of islands.

Travel must commence in Papeete and there are restrictions on the number of transits through Papeete. You are only allowed one stopover on each island, but you can transit an island so long as the flight number does not change. If you stop at an island to change flights it counts as a stopover.

Passes are valid for a maximum of 28 days and all flights (except Papeete-Moorea or Moorea-Papeete) must be booked at the beginning. You can use either Air Tahiti or Air Moorea on the Papeete-Moorea sector. Once you have taken the first flight on the pass the routing cannot be changed, and the fare is nonrefundable.

Discovery Pass (Society Islands) This is the most basic pass and allows visits to Moorea, Huahine and Raiatea for 21,000/11,400 CFP for adults/children.

Blue Pass & Blue Discovery Pass The Blue Discovery Pass covers travel to Moorea, Huahine and Raiatea for 14,000 CFP, while the Blue Pass adds Bora Bora and costs 20,000 CFP. There is no children's fare. The conditions of this pass are that you must leave Papeete on a blue flight, you can only use blue or white flights on subsequent sectors, and Moorea must be your last visit.

Bora Bora Pass This more thorough pass lets you visit the six main islands in the Society group: Tahiti, Moorea, Huahine, Raiatea, Bora Bora and Maupiti. It's one of the two passes that include Maupiti and it costs 30,500/16,200 CFP for adults/children.

Bora Tuamotu Pass This pass includes air travel to Moorea, Huahine, Raiatea, Maupiti and Bora Bora in the Society group, as well as Rangiroa, Manihi and Tikehau in the Tuamotus. Since you cannot transit Papeete, you must use the Bora Bora-Rangiroa-Manihi flight, which operates three times a week from Bora Bora to the Tuamotus, but only weekly in the other direction. For this reason, you'll have more flexibility if you visit the Tuamotus after the Society Islands rather than before. This pass costs 45,500/23,700 CFP.

Lagoon Pass This pass combines Moorea with visits to Rangiroa, Manihi and Tikehau, with a transit through Papeete between Moorea and the Tuamotus. It costs 35,000/18,400 CFP.

Marquesas & Australs Extension You can extend a pass to include the Marquesas (Nuku Hiva and Hiva Oa) for 45,000/23,400 CFP. An extension to the Australs (Rurutu and Tubuai) costs 20,000/10,900 CFP. A Marquesas and Australs extension to cover all four islands costs 65,000/34,300 CFP. Note that this is an 'extension' – you have to buy one of the other passes first.

BOAT

It's no problem getting from one island to another in the Society group. Between Tahiti and Moorea, high speed and regular ferries shuttle back and forth. The ultra-quick *Ono-Ono* offers a reliable and speedy service between other Society islands, specifically aimed at tourists.

In the other archipelagos, the situation is more difficult. There are no ships specifically for passenger transport, and maritime links are relatively infrequent and uncertain. Cargo ships, known as *goélettes*, or schooners, are principally involved in freight transport. They do take passengers, however, and for those who want to get off the beaten trail such a voyage can, depending on the circumstances, be anything from a memorable experience to an outright nightmare. The level of comfort is rudimentary; some ships don't even have passenger cabins and you have to travel deck class, providing your own bedding to unroll on the deck. You will get wet and cold. And then there's seasickness.

A notice posted at Chez Guynette in Huahine sums up the cargo ship schedules: "The boats arrive when they are here and leave when they are ready..."

Ferry & Cargo Ship

The Society Islands It takes less than half an hour to travel between Tahiti and Moorea on the faster ferries. Slower car-ferries operate on this route, but motorcycles and bi-

cycles can be taken on the high-speed ones (cars too on the *Corsair*). See the Moorea chapter for more information.

Ono-Ono Since 1994 the high-speed *Ono-Ono* has been a very popular method of getting around the Society Islands, carrying up to 450 passengers and reaching speeds of 35 knots (65km/h).

The air-con *Ono-Ono* runs a daily schedule connecting various combinations of Tahiti, Huahine, Raiatea, Tahaa and Bora Bora. Turnaround times in port are more akin to those of aircraft than of regular ships – the *Ono-Ono* is usually in port for just 10 to 15 minutes. Note that when the weather is particularly bad the *Ono-Ono* does not sail, it's wise to allow adequate time to get back to Tahiti before your flight out. Journey times and prices are as follows:

from	to	one way (CFP)	hours
Papeete	Huahine	4895	3¾
Papeete	Raiatea	5445	5
Papeete	Tahaa	5995	5¼
Papeete	Bora Bora	6545	7
Huahine	Raiatea	1760	1
Huahine	Tahaa	2090	1¾
Huahine	Bora Bora	3080	3
Raiatea	Tahaa	660	½
Raiatea	Bora Bora	1760	1¾
Tahaa	Bora Bora	1320	1

Return tickets cost about 10% less than two one-ways. Children from two to 12 years of age pay half-fare. There is a 30kg baggage allowance and the *Ono-Ono* will also take bicycles (1200 CFP to/from Tahiti, 650 CFP between the other islands), surfboards (650 CFP) and freight. On board there's a snack bar and before departure you can order meals for a fairly steep 1600 CFP or 2350 CFP.

In Papeete, bookings can be made at its office (☎ 45 35 35, fax 43 83 45, email onoono@mail.pf) on the ferry quay in the centre of town. It's open Monday to Thursday from 6.30 am to 5 pm, Friday from 8 am to 5 pm, Saturday from 8 to 11 am and

Sunday from 10 am to noon and 2 to 3 pm. Credit cards are accepted. Representatives of the *Ono-Ono* on other islands are covered in the individual island chapters.

Raromatai Ferry Until the *Ono-Ono* arrived on the scene, the *Raromatai Ferry* was the fastest and most regular ship around the Society group. With a 362-passenger capacity (deck, lounge and cabin), it ran a once-weekly Papeete-Huahine-RaiateaTahaa-Bora Bora-Tahaa return route.

At the time of the writing, however, the ship has been sitting dockside in Papeete for many months, waiting for some serious mechanical repairs. Phone ☎ 43 19 88 or fax 43 19 99 to see if it is back in service.

Vaeanu This cargo ship can take about 100 passengers and departs Papeete for the Leeward Islands on Monday, Wednesday and Friday. Much slower and less comfortable than the *Ono-Ono,* it remains popular with shoestring travellers because it is cheaper. There are deck class, two triple cabins, 12 double cabins and one single cabin. Except for the Wednesday departure, travel is cabin-class only; reservations are advisable.

The *Vaeanu* operates Papeete-Huahine-Raiatea-Tahaa-Bora Bora return, but does not stop at Tahaa on Wednesday. It departs Papeete at 5 pm, arrives at the various Leeward islands the next morning and sets out from Bora Bora on Tuesday, Thursday and Sunday. The Huahine and Raiatea arrivals are in the middle of the night and guesthouse owners will not pick you up.

The deck-class fare from Papeete to any of the islands is 1751 CFP; inter-island fares range from 510 CFP to 1096 CFP. Cabin class from any island costs from 4080 CFP in a triple cabin with shared bathroom, to 5610 CFP in a double cabin with private bathroom.

In Papeete, the office (☎ 41 25 35, fax 41 24 34) is on the cargo ship quay at Motu Uta, near the *Arunui* office. Take le truck No 3 from the *mairie* (town hall).

Maupiti To'u Aia This small cargo ship goes to Maupiti from Papeete weekly, with a stop at Raiatea on every other trip. The departure is on Wednesday evening, the arrival at Maupiti the following morning and the return to Papeete two days later. The one-way fare is 2299 CFP. Contact the shipowner (☎ 42 44 92 extension 226, fax 43 32 69) for more information.

The Tuamotus The small cargo vessels that serve the Tuamotus, goélettes are true lifelines between Tahiti and the atolls of the archipelago. They can and do take passengers, but their main purpose is to transport freight and the standard of comfort is generally basic.

The routes and fares mentioned are purely an indication and are subject to change. Obtain information directly from the shipowners. Their offices are in the Motu Uta port area in Papeete (take le truck No 3 at the mairie) and are generally open Monday to Friday from 7.30 to 11 am and from 1.30 to 5 pm. Some also open on Saturday morning. For inter-island hops, contact the ship's master directly.

Dory This vessel does a Papeete-Tikehau-Rangiroa-Manihi-Arutua-Kaukura-Apataki-Papeete route, departing Papeete on Monday and returning on Friday. There are berths on board, but no meal service is provided for passengers, so you must buy food at each stop. A single trip costs 3570/5100 CFP deck/cabin class. Contact the office on ☎ 42 30 55.

Cobia I Departing from Papeete on Monday, this vessel travels Kaukura-Arutua-Apataki-Aratika-Toau and returns to Papeete on Thursday. There are no cabins. The fare is 3060 CFP; contact the office on ☎ 43 36 43.

Hotu Maru This ship does a Papeete-Faaite-Katiu-Makemo-Papeete circuit, departing on Monday and getting back on Friday. Fares are 3600 CFP to Faaite, 5856 CFP to Makemo and 10,700 CFP for the complete circuit. No meals are served but there are four berths. Contact the office on ☎ 41 07 11.

Saint Xavier Maris Stella This vessel travels Papeete-Makatea-Mataiva-Tikehau-Rangiroa-Ahe-Manihi-Takaroa-Takapoto-Aratika-Kauehi-Raraka-Fakarava-Toau-Apataki-Arutua-Kaukura-Niau twice a month. Departing from Papeete, allow 5050 CFP to Rangiroa, 6060 CFP to Manihi, 7575 CFP to Fakarava and 22,220 CFP for the complete trip (10 days) on the deck, meals included. To get to the office (☎ 42 23 58), which is in the warehouses, follow the road that goes along the cargo quay and, at the bend, take the right fork.

Mareva Nui Twice a month, the *Mareva Nui* follows the Papeete-Makatea-Tikehau-Mataiva-Rangiroa-Ahe-Manihi-Arutua-Apataki-Takaroa-Takapoto-Aratika-Raraka-Kauehi-Fakarava-Toau-Niau-Kaukura-Papeete route. Fares vary from 2400 CFP to 4450 CFP for a part-journey, 9900 CFP for the complete eight day circuit in deck class. Add 2000 CFP per day for meals. To get to the office (☎ 42 25 53), take the same road as for the *Saint Xavier Maris Stella* office.

Vai-Aito This vessel provides a Papeete-Rangiroa-Manihi-Ahe-Kauehi-Raraka-Fakarava-Toau-Aratika-Apataki-Papeete service three times a month. From Papeete allow 4040 CFP to Rangiroa, 8080 CFP to Manihi, 14,140 CFP to Fakarava and 21,210 CFP for the complete six to eight day trip (deck class) and 2500 CFP a day for food. Contact the office on ☎ 43 99 96.

Auura'Nui 3 Once a month this ship services 19 remote atolls of the central and eastern Tuamotus, including Anaa, Hao and Fakarava (Tetamanu). Prices range from 3120 CFP (Fakarava) to 7280 CFP on deck and 7080 CFP to 12,480 CFP in a berth, depending on the distance of the atoll. Add 2200 CFP a day for food. The complete circuit takes 18 days. To get to the office (☎ 43 92 40) take the same road as for the *Saint Xavier Maris Stella* office.

Kura Ora Once a month this ship visits 22 remote atolls of the central and eastern Tuamotus, including Anaa, Hao and Makemo.

Deck-class prices range from 6000 CFP to 7000 CFP depending on the distance, plus 1850 CFP a day for food. The complete trip takes three weeks. To get to the office (☎ 45 55 45), take the same road as for the *Saint Xavier Maris Stella* office.

Rairoa Nui This vessel does a weekly Papeete-Rangiroa-Arutua-Papeete circuit. Papeete-Rangiroa-Papeete costs 3000 CFP including meals. Contact the ship's master direct. The office (☎ 48 35 78) is on the 3rd floor in the same building as the head office of the Bank of Tahiti, near the market.

Other Ships The *Taporo IV* and *Aranui* serve certain atolls in the Tuamotus en route to the Marquesas. So does the *Nuku Hau* on its way to the Gambier Archipelago. See the following sections.

The Marquesas Two ships go to the Marquesas: the *Aranui,* which operates a regular and reliable service, and the *Taporo IV*.

Aranui A veritable institution in French Polynesia and very popular with tourists, this 104m-long cargo and passenger vessel takes freight and passengers on 15 annual trips from Papeete. It stops at Takapoto, the six inhabited islands in the Marquesas, and Rangiroa, taking 16 days (of which 10 are in the Marquesas) for the complete circuit. This very special boat and its voyage is described in detail in the Marquesas chapter.

Taporo IV This 75m cargo vessel sails the following route every 15 days, departing Thursday: Papeete-Takapoto-Fatu Hiva-Tahuata-Hiva Oa-Ua Huka-Nuku Hiva-Ua Pou-Papeete (11 days). Allow 11,000/15,000 CFP on deck/air-con cabin to Takapoto and 22,000/32,000 CFP to the Marquesas, meals included. The shipowner, Compagnie Française Maritime de Tahiti, has an office at Fare Ute (☎ 42 63 93) and on the cargo ship quay at the entrance to the Motu Uta port area (☎ 43 89 66).

Kahoa Nui This small ferry, normally based at Taiohae (Nuku Hiva), travels round the archipelago only on certain occasions (school transport, sports events, religious festivals etc). Information is available at Taiohae mairie (☎/fax 92 03 07).

The Australs Services between the Society Islands and the Australs are limited; make sure you plan ahead.

Tuhaa Pae II This 60m boat leaves Papeete for the Australs three times a month. It stops at Rurutu and Tubuai on every trip, Rimatara and Raivavae twice a month, Rapa once a month and Maria Island very occasionally.

There are deck class, berths and 13 air-con cabins. From Papeete to Rurutu, Rimatara or Tubuai costs 3817/5343/6680 CFP deck/berth/air-con cabin; 5502/9628/7702 CFP to Raivavae. Three meals adds another 2300 CFP a day. To find the office (☎ 43 15 88) take the same road as for the *Saint Xavier Maris Stella* office.

Vaeanu II This cargo ship goes to Rurutu, Tubuai and Raivavae twice a month and on to Rapa once a month. It can take 12 deck-class passengers; Papeete-Rurutu costs 3817 CFP. It belongs to the same shipowner as the *Vaeanu*, which operates in the Society Islands. The office (☎ 41 25 35, fax 41 24 34) is on Motu Uta, close to the *Aranui* offices.

The Gambier Archipelago Every three weeks, the *Nuku Hau* does a 15 day circuit to Rikitea in the Gambier Archipelago via several remote atolls in the eastern Tuamotus. Straightforward deck class costs 7670 CFP plus 1950 CFP per day for food. The office (☎ 45 23 24) is in the Motu Uta port area, close to the warehouses of the other ship operators.

Cruise Ship
The complete opposite of the often rudimentary cargo ships are the luxury cruise ships operating through the Society Islands. They provide maximum comfort, high style and shore excursions at each stop. These boats are a long way from the leaky copra boats of traditional inter-island travel.

Haumana Managed by Bora Bora Pearl Cruises (☎ 45 10 66, 43 43 03, fax 45 10 65), the *Haumana* is a magnificent 36m catamaran which can accommodate 40 to 60 people. It offers three, four and seven-day cruises between Bora Bora, Raiatea, Tahaa and Huahine, starting and finishing at either Bora Bora or Huahuine. Its Web site is at www.boraborapearlcruises.com

Paul Gauguin You may see this enormous 156m 320-passenger ship anchored in Papeete. It departs Papeete every week for a one week cruise which includes Huahine or Tahaa, Raiatea, Bora Bora and Moorea. In French Polynesia, contact SCAT (☎ 54 51 00, fax 45 52 66). In France, contact the Compagnie Maritime de Croisière (☎ 01 40 67 77 95, fax 01 40 67 77 71). In the United States, the cruise is marketed by Radisson Seven Seas Cruises (☎ 402-498 5072). In other countries, contact a good travel agent.

Renaissance Two cruise ships named *Renaissance*, the *R3* and *R4*, of the company American Renaissance Cruises, started operating in 1999. These two monsters can each accommodate 684 passengers. Departing Papeete, they do 10-day cruises in the Society group. At the time of the writing, the cruises were marketed only in the USA. Contact Renaissance Cruises (☎ 954-4630982, fax 463 9216, email renaissance_cruises@rcruises.com).

Archipels Croisières Operating four large 18m sailing catamarans, this Moorea-based company does a variety of interesting trips in the different island groups of French Polynesia. A seven day trip through the Society Islands, visiting Bora Bora, Tahaa, Raiatea and Huahine costs 160,000 CFP per person. An eight day trip through the Marquesas visiting Nuku Hiva, Ua Huka, Hiva Oa, Tahuata and Fatu Hiva costs 215,000 CFP, including a return flight from Papeete. A three day trip around the Rangiroa lagoon costs 60,300 CFP; four days costs 81,000 CFP. Eight-day diving trips with the Raie Manta Club cost 200,000 CFP and depart from either Fakarava, visiting Fakarava,

Toau and Kauei, or Rangiroa, visiting Rangiroa and Tikehau.

Archipels Croisières (☎ 56 36 39) can be contacted through BP 1160, Papetoai, Moorea. In France, its office (☎ 01 42 46 70 13) is at 36 Rue Dombasle, 75015 Paris.

Other Cruises See 'The *Aranui*' special section in the Marquesas chapter for more on this very popular vessel. Society Expeditions' *World Discoverer* and Marine Expeditions' Russian polar vessels make trips through remote islands of French Polynesia. See the Cargo & Expedition Ships section in the Getting There & Away chapter for more details.

Yacht

French Polynesia is an enormously popular yachting destination, as the international line-up of yachts along the Papeete waterfront testifies. It's also eminently possible to rent a yacht in French Polynesia (see the Outdoor Activities chapter for more details). See Formalities for Yachts in the Facts for the Visitor chapter for information about bringing your own boat into French Polynesian waters.

Around the Islands

Coast roads trace much of the outline of each of the major islands of the Society group. Tahiti (where there is even a stretch of freeway), Moorea and Bora Bora have paved and well-maintained roads. On Raiatea and Huahine the coast roads are partly sealed, formed partly of ground coral, but are generally in good condition. On Tahaa and Maupiti there are only limited stretches of paved or sealed road, although even here they present no problems for a regular car. On all of these islands the roads leading inland into the mountains are often rough-and-ready tracks requiring a 4WD vehicle.

Sealed roads encircle Tubuai and Raivavae in the Australs, and there are reasonable stretches of sealed road on Rurutu. Otherwise, roads in this archipelago are

---

Le Truck

Le truck is the public bus service of French Polynesia; the vehicles are just what the name indicates: trucks. Down each side of the back is a bench seat for passengers. Riding le truck is something every visitor to French Polynesia should do. You'll enjoy natural air-conditioning (the breeze blows straight through) and convivial fellow passengers.

Unfortunately, only Tahiti has a reasonably comprehensive and regular le truck service. See the Tahiti chapter for more details on using le trucks on that island. Note that you pay at the end of the trip and that for many routes there is a set fare, irrespective of distance, typically 120 to 200 CFP.

Moorea has a fairly regular le truck route around the island plus services for ferry arrivals and departures. Bora Bora has le trucks connecting the major hotel enclave with boat and flight arrival and departure points. On some other islands there are even more-limited services. On Raiatea and Huahine there are just a couple of services a day between outlying villages and the main town. Tahaa and Maupiti have no regular le truck service (although there are le trucks on both islands, they're usually for school transport).

There are hardly any roads in the Tuamotus and in the Marquesas, and the only le trucks in Taiohae (Nuku Hiva) and Atuona (Hiva Oa) are those reserved for school transport. There is virtually no public transport in the Australs.

---

fairly limited and little transport is available. There are far more boats than land vehicles in the Tuamotus, although there is a sealed road running the length of Rangiroa's major island – all 10km of it!

Except in towns, there are hardly any sealed roads in the Marquesas. Tracks, suitable for 4WD vehicles only, connect the villages.

TAXI

Tahiti has metered taxis and Moorea, Huahine, Raiatea and Bora Bora also have taxi services. Unfortunately, all these taxis have one thing in common: they are very expensive. The US$20 to US$25 taxi fare for the 6km trip between Faaa airport and downtown Papeete is a pretty clear indicator of the problem.

Hotels, from cheap backpacker hostels to expensive luxury resorts, will generally collect pre-booked guests from the airport or ferry quay and this is a service well worth taking advantage of (although you may be charged for it).

On other islands, taxis do not exist as such, but if there's a car and a customer, arrangements can usually be made. As there are no taxis on the Marquesas, you have to hire a 4WD vehicle and a driver to get around.

CAR & SCOOTER

Island tours are generally available but, if you want to explore the larger islands of the Society group on your own, it's generally worth renting a car. Taxi fares are exorbitant and, apart from locations reasonably close to Papeete, public transport is infrequent and inconvenient.

Road Rules

Driving is on the right, the standards are not too bad and traffic is light almost everywhere apart from the busy coastal strip around Papeete on Tahiti, where you can experience rush hour traffic jams. Beware of drunk drivers at night and pedestrians and children who may not be used to traffic, particularly in more remote locations.

Rental

Rental rates are not cheap; a small car, which is all you need, typically costs US$60 to US$80 per day including insurance and unlimited kilometres. Fuel is extra, and at 113 CFP a litre (about US$5 a gallon), it is decidedly pricey. Fortunately, the cars available are pretty economical and you won't cover too many kilometres, no matter how hard you try. Off-road excur-

---

BPs & PKs

Most mail in French Polynesia is delivered to post boxes (BP or *boîte postale*) so there is rarely any need for a street address. Since most buildings are found around the narrow coastal strip and most islands have a single coast road running right around the island, locations on high islands are often referred to as 'coast, lagoon or oceanside' or 'mountainside'. In French this would be *côté mer* or *côté montagne*. This doesn't mean a mountainside house is halfway up a mountain, it simply means that it's on the inland side of the road.

On many islands there is also a *pointe kilométrique* (PK) system of distance markers around the coast road. These usually start in the main town and run around the island in both directions. On Moorea, for example, the PK markers start at the airport and run anticlockwise to PK35 and clockwise to PK24, meeting at Haapiti, the major village on the west side of the island. On other islands, locations may be referred to on a PK basis even though there are no PK-marker stones.

Finally, locations may also be referred to by a district name rather than a village name. A hotel in the popular tourist enclave of Hauru Point on Moorea, for example, may fall in the Haapiti district. So a location may be referred to as PK30, coast side, Haapiti, even though it's some distance from the village of Haapiti.

---

sions into the interior are usually off-limits to anything other than a 4WD.

Agencies usually offer four, eight and 24-hour rates, as well as two and three-day rentals, and cars can be delivered to the airport. At certain times of year –July, August and New Year's Eve – it's wise to book vehicles a few days in advance. An international driving permit is useful but your national driving licence is often enough. You'll need a credit card, of course.

On Tahiti you will find the major international car-rental names like Avis, Budget, Europcar and Hertz. On other islands like Moorea, Huahine, Raiatea and Bora Bora, as well as on Rangiroa in the Tuamotus, the market is divided up between Avis and Europcar. Smaller local agencies exist on some islands, but the rates are almost as high.

There are a handful of rental cars on Tahaa in the Society group and on Tubuai in the Australs. On the Marquesas, rental vehicles are mainly 4WDs, with a driver. Rental without a driver is possible only at Atuona (Hiva Oa) and Taiohae (Nuku Hiva).

Avis and Europcar rent scooters on a number of islands. It's a good way of getting around the small islands ... when it doesn't rain. Tariffs are around 5000 CFP to 6000 CFP a day. After numerous accidents there are no rental scooters on Tahiti.

BICYCLE

French Polynesia is an ideal region to explore by bicycle. Traffic is rarely a problem away from Tahiti, and on most islands the distances are relatively short. You can ride a complete circuit of many of the islands in a morning or afternoon and the coast roads are generally flat.

The more remote islands, and the more-remote parts of the major islands, cry out for a good mountain bike. It's even worth bringing your own with you – they're accepted on all the inter-island ships.

Bicycles can be rented on many of the islands for around 1000 CFP to 1500 CFP per day. On the touristy islands, many guesthouses have bicycles for guests, usually at comparable rates.

HITCHING

Hitching (*auto-stop* in French) is never entirely safe in any country in the world and we don't recommend it. Travellers who decide to hitch should understand that they are taking a potentially serious risk. French Polynesia is generally a safe location but the usual worldwide rules for hitchhiking still apply: do not accept a ride with someone you do not have confidence in and

women should never hitch alone. People who do choose to hitch will be safer if they travel in pairs and let someone know where they are planning to go.

On the less touristed islands, and on islands where public transport is limited, hitching is a widely accepted way of getting around (although the very light traffic can be a problem). On tourist-saturated Tahiti, Moorea and Bora Bora the situation may not be quite so straightforward, although in more remote locations you may not even need to stick your thumb out.

BOAT

In several places it's possible to rent small outboard-powered boats. No permit is necessary and it's a great way to explore the Bora Bora and Raiatea lagoons. Lagoon tours by *pirogue* (local outrigger canoe) are good value for two or more people. Anywhere in French Polynesia, if you need to get across a lagoon, there will be somebody available with the appropriate boat. Just ask.

ORGANISED TOURS

Many of the more touristed islands have regularly scheduled tours, which can be excellent value, particularly if you're on your own. There are straightforward round-the-island minibus tours on Tahiti, Moorea and other islands, and increasingly popular 4WD trips across the centre of Tahiti and into the highlands of Moorea, Bora Bora and other islands in the Society group.

It's more than just a mode of transport! Riding le truck is an experience no visitor to French Polynesia should miss.

Mountain-bike and hiking trips are growing in popularity. Boat trips can range from sunset cruises to round-the-lagoon expeditions with motu picnics or a spot of shark feeding. Lagoon tours by pirogue are an activity no visitor should miss. See the individual chapters for details. Sometimes the trips are organised by your guesthouse but it's always worth reserving – a minimum number of participants may be required and some tours may be fully booked in high season.

Outdoor Activities

French Polynesia's exceptional natural heritage lends itself to a range of leisure activities. Scuba diving is the main activity but sailing is also very popular. Increasing numbers of surfers are sampling the islands' excellent reef breaks and the jagged relief of the high islands makes for some superb hiking.

Walking

A single glance at the mountains of Tahiti and Moorea hints at the hiking opportunities available for walking enthusiasts (or anyone keen to find an alternative to the lagoons). Unfortunately the trails are rarely well kept and are badly marked, if marked at all. A local guide is often essential. April to October is the ideal season for walking, as the trails can be dangerous, if not impassable, during the wet season.

Tahiti and Moorea are the only islands with serious hiking possibilities, although Raiatea and Bora Bora offer more-limited opportunities. Walks on the other islands are usually simple, short jaunts and are covered in the relevant island chapters. The walks described here are only a selection; local guides will probably have other suggestions. See Guides later in this section for contact information.

EQUIPMENT

Sunglasses, sunscreen, a hat, mosquito repellent, something to keep the rain off and something to keep you warm if you're climbing the high peaks are all essentials. You'll need good walking shoes and plastic sandals for crossing rivers. Bring plenty of drinking water and a plastic bag or something similar to keep your camera dry.

GUIDES
Tahiti & Moorea

Tiare Mato (☎ 43 92 76, 77 48 11, fax 42 21 03) offers walking guides for all the Tahiti and Moorea hikes. Count on 6000 CFP per person for a day climb to the top of Mt Aorai, including picnic lunch; 12,500 CFP for the two day walk to the Te Pari cliffs; and 8000 CFP to the Hitiaa Lava Tubes.

Polynesian Adventure (☎ 77 24 37, ☎/fax 43 25 95) charges 8700 CFP for a Mt Mouaputa or Mt Rotui ascent on Moorea, 7600 CFP for a one day walk to Mt Marau and 10,200 CFP for the two day ascent of Mt Aorai on Moorea.

Presqu'Île Loisirs (☎ 57 00 57) is directed by Mata, a pleasant Polynesian from Tautira and specialises in walks on Tahiti Iti. An all-inclusive two day walk to Te Pari costs 10,000 CFP per person. A two day walk following the coastline to the Vaipoiri Cave, with a bivouac at the refuge on Faaroa Bay, costs 12,500 CFP per person.

Le Circuit Vert (☎ 57 22 67) is run by Zéna Angélien and specialises in Tahiti Iti.

Chez Tefaarahi Safari Tours (☎/fax 56 41 24) is on Moorea. Derek Grell, of American origin, will guide you to the Three Coconut Trees for 3500 CFP per person, or up Mt Rotui for 1000 CFP per hour.

Raiatea

Raiatea Pearl Resort Hawaiki Nui's reception desk (☎ 66- 20- 23, fax 66- 20- 20, email h.raiateapearl@mail.pf) will put you in contact with a guide, which is highly desirable for Temehani Plateau hikes.

Bora Bora

Ato of Chez Ato (☎ 67 77 27) will take you up Mt Pahia for 3000 CFP per person (minimum five people). Otemanu Tours (☎ 67 70 49) offers an all-inclusive price of 15,000 CFP, including transport and food.

TAHITI
Fautaua Valley

It's only 2.5km from the centre of Papeete to Bain Loti (Loti's Bath), featured in the 1880 novel *The Marriage of Loti* (see Books in the Facts for the Visitor chapter). From there a three or four hour walk climbs up the river valley towards the spiky profile of the Diadème.

To walk further up the valley, you need permission from either Service de l'Hydralique (☎ 43 02 15), just beyond the pool, or Service des Régies des Recettes in the *mairie* (town hall). It takes about an hour for the easy 4km walk to the Fachoda (Tearape) Bridge. The first waterfall on Fautaua River is an hour from here. Another hour takes walkers past the *belvédère* (lookout) to Fort Fachoda where, in 1846, French soldiers climbed ropes up a cliff face to overpower a Tahitian position. The Governor's Garden is a little beyond the fort.

Mt Aorai

Mt Aorai (2066m) is the third-highest peak on the island and only about a dozen kilometres as the crow flies from Papeete. The ascent is one of Tahiti's classic climbs The path is regularly maintained by the Centre d'Instruction Militaire (CIM) and is clearly visible, so a guide is quite superfluous. There are signposts at trail junctions to prevent confusion. Count on at least 4½ hours of steady walking to reach the top.

Two refuges break up the route. They can accommodate about 20 walkers, have electricity and are equipped with aluminium containers usually filled with drinkable rainwater.

The climb is feasible for anyone in good physical condition with experience of walking in the mountains. There are, however, several difficult sections at about the midpoint and near the summit, so people who suffer from vertigo should stop at the first refuge. Hardier walkers can make the return trip in a day, but start at dawn because the summit tends to be covered in cloud after 11 am. All in all, it makes more sense to allow a day and a half. By spending a night in the second shelter you can be on the summit for an unobstructed dawn across the neighbouring valleys.

Before starting an assault on Aorai, make sure you have warm clothing and a change of clothes, at least two litres of water (in the dry season the water cisterns may be empty) and good walking shoes. Never go alone.

The starting point is at Le Belvédère Restaurant, at 600m altitude and accessible by car. From central Papeete take Ave Georges Clémenceau and turn right 200m after the Total petrol station. Turn right again at the sign for Le Belvédère, which is 7km from the coast road. Fill in the CIM's safety book.

From the restaurant count on an hour's walk to get to Hamuta Pass (900m), the easiest part of the walk. From the CIM, you reach the ridge via a reasonably wide track that winds up the flank of the mountain. From the pass you can see all the Fautaua Valley, the ghostly and disjointed silhouette of the Diadème, Mt Marau (preceded by its TV-transmission aerial to the south) and the walls of the ravines of the Pic Vert massif to the west.

It's then 1¼ hours walk to the first refuge, Fare Mato, perched on a rocky promontory at 1400m. The route this far isn't difficult except for a steep section before the refuge. Moorea stands on the horizon to the north-west, while to the east the Pirae Valley forms a breach in the massif.

The path continues to the crest and about 10 minutes later reaches a difficult passage, the Devil's Rock (Mato Mati), which is probably the toughest part of the climb. The path passes along a flank of the crest and you'll have to keep a tight grip on the judiciously placed cables and cords. It's about an hour's climb to the second refuge, which you'll see high up on the crest.

At 1800m, Fare Ata, the second refuge, has two units. An open-sided *fare potee* on the promontory functions as the open-air 'dining room'. The water in the cistern is not drinkable, but there are two cisterns of drinking water outside the actual refuge, 50m away and slightly below. From the promontory it's possible to see the first refuge, small as a pinhead and far below.

The summit is less than an hour from here. The path continues along a jagged ridge, like a flight of steps, very narrow on this section and bearing off to the south. The vegetation is more sparse as this is the upper limit for the *puarata* bushes. The view from the top is definitely worth the effort: to the east is Orohena,

Pito Hiti and the Pirae Valley. To the north-west lies Moorea, Papeete is to the north and beyond that the line of the reef.

Don't relax on the way down, as the rock can easily crumble and don't forget to sign off in the safety book at the CIM.

The Thousand Springs

At around PK11 at Mahina two roads turn off inland and climb for about 3km before they meet. The road continues for about another kilometre from where the walking track commences. This easy 1½ hour walk up the east side of the Tuauru Valley climbs to an altitude of 650m, from where there are superb views. This is the starting point of the difficult Mt Orohena climb. The walk goes through a water-catchment area and you must seek permission from Sotagri (☎ 48 11 84) before setting out.

Mt Orohena

The ascent of Mt Orohena (2241m) is a tough two day mission plagued by dense undergrowth, a crumbling ridgeline and often-fierce winds. Despite numerous earlier attempts, the first European ascent of the mountain did not take place until 1953. This walk definitely requires the assistance of local experts.

From the Thousand Springs, the route climbs to the ridgeline at Moto Fefe (1142m) in about 1½ hours and follows the ridge from there to the summit. It's a further 1½ hours to Pihaaiateta (1742m), two hours more to Pito Iti (2110m) and another two hours to the summit. There are some extremely narrow ridgelines on the ascent but fixed cables on certain tricky sections make the climb a little easier.

Hitiaa Lava Tubes

The Arahoho Blowhole, at PK22, is a small lava tube that incoming waves can rush through to produce a dramatic waterspout. It's possible to walk through the much larger Hitiaa Lava Tubes, but this fascinating walk can only be attempted when there is no danger of a sudden downpour.

From the turn-off at PK39.9, a 4WD track runs 6km inland past a dam at 500m altitude and up to another one, at the start of the walk at 630m. A powerful and (most importantly) reliable torch (flashlight) is essential for investigating the lava tubes. A walk through all three takes about three hours.

It's less than 15 minutes walk to the first tube, at 750m. It's about 100m long and only about 200m from the second tube (300m long), with two waterfalls just before the entry. Between the second and third tube, the trail goes under a stone bridge, the remains of a collapsed lava tube. The third tube is longer, darker and more complex. About 100m in, it divides. The left fork continues about 300m to an exit and the right fork leads to a large cavern, complete with lake and waterfall.

Te Pari

Te Pari means 'The Cliffs' in Tahitian and it's the name applied to the stretch of the Tahiti Iti coast from Tautira in the north to Vaipoiri Cave in the south. It's practically uninhabited, a wild and desolate area light years from the noise and confusion of Papeete. It is strongly recommended not to visit this coastal region alone; certain parts can be dangerous and the some of the many archaeological sites scattered in the vegetation along the route are difficult to locate. You can call on the competence and experience of the peninsula guides to recount the legends and your imagination can wander. Since you will often have to wade through water, bring a change of clothes, plastic shoes and a waterproof bag to protect your camera equipment. If your guide doesn't provide a mask and fins, bring your own.

From Tautira you usually go directly to the mouth of the Vaiote River by speedboat (about 25 minutes). This saves three hours of dull walking along the coast. The boat is moored over the coral near a small *motu* (islet) in the lagoon and you'll find petroglyphs facing the motu, 30m back from the beach, to the right of a banyan tree. One of these petroglyphs is of a solar disk with its rays surmounting a pirogue. The second illustrates the same motif but with hands around it. Apparently the chiefs of neighbouring tribes met here to hold councils of war and to plan attacks on the rival tribes of Teahupoo. A god answered their incantations and left his imprints on the stones.

A 15 minute walk inland, after crossing the Vaiote River, are The Honoura Drums (Te Pahu O Honoura). The rocks have cavities about 20cm in diameter and resonate when struck with a coconut-tree branch. According to legend, the hero Honoura tapped on the first rock (the one with two holes) to warn the inhabitants of Tautira of an attack by their enemies from Teahupoo.

Back on the track, follow the Vaiote for about fifteen minutes; on the left is a *pae pae* (traditional meeting platform) hidden in a tangle of ferns and *mape* (chestnut) and *purau* (hibiscus) trees. This valley's rich archaeological remains speak of a significant pre-European population.

Continuing south along the coast, 10 minutes by boat brings you to Vaitomoana Cave, partially invaded by the sea. The guide will lend you a mask and snorkel to collect sea urchins, which cling to the bottom of the cliff, 5m below.

A further five minutes by boat, or 1½ hours on foot along a ledge overhanging the ocean, brings you to the Devil's Passage (Vahi Hororaa, literally, 'Place Where One Must Run'). It's a narrow passage on the side of the rock that you must cross over quickly as the waves retreat. You're helped by the ropes attached to the cliff.

Anaihe Cave is 20 minutes walk from there. Well known to fishers from the Tahiti Iti peninsula, it serves as a shelter during bad weather. It is fitted out with a basic table and benches of coconut wood and is a popular place for visitors to picnic. The coral formations a few metres from the shore make a great snorkelling site.

There's a waterfall not far from here. You emerge in a narrow and slippery horseshoe-shaped passage about 20m long, which brings you out 5m above the waves. There are good handholds on the rocks and ropes attached to the sides with pitons help you. Your efforts are rewarded by the view of the Queen's Cave, about 10 minutes from here. If you believe the legend, the queen who lived in the Taapeha Valley was accustomed to bathing in

the small water hole in the interior of the cave and sitting on the nearby rock to be prepared by her servants. If the sea is calm you can dive in the turquoise water a few metres below. Watch for the returning waves.

The very deep Taapeha Valley is 10 minutes walk from here. About 100m back, where the stream threads its way through the huge stone blocks, you'll find on the right the 'giant *umete* of Taapeha'. An umete is a Tahitian wooden dish or bowl and erosion has given this rock that characteristic shape. This rock makes multiple appearances in legends: it was used to make traditional medications and was a traditional birthing site – its shape follows the body's contours perfectly and new-born children were washed in the stream and coated with *monoi* (scented oil).

The Faaroa refuge is the next stopping point. It's on the banks of the river of the same name, which marks the Tautira-Teahupoo district boundary. If you are on a two day walk, this is where you spend the night. The walk can continue the next day to Vaipoiri Cave, where you can go swimming. The return to Tautira is by boat, with a possible picnic stop on Motu Fenua Ino.

It's also possible to follow the trail from Teahupoo to the Vaipoiri Cave.

MOOREA
Vaiare to Paopao

This interesting and reasonably easy walk takes about two hours, starting from Vaiare and climbing to the ridge between Mt Tearai (770m) and Mt Mouaputa (830m) before dropping down into the valley and emerging at Paopao on Cook's Bay. There are great views and dense vegetation cloaking the steep mountains.

From the ferry terminal at the centre of Vaiare, walk south across the first bridge and turn inland along the road beside the Chez Méno store. The road forks twice; take the right fork on both occasions. There may be a sign pointing to Paopao at the second fork. Don't take the next turn right but keep following the road, which deteriorates to a muddy track as it passes through plantations of pineapples, taro, papaya and bananas and climbs up above the south bank of the river. Do not follow the track right to the end; it follows the river to an eventual dead end. Look for a walking track, which turns sharply off the vehicle track just before it becomes too narrow for a 4WD.

Finding the start of the track is the most difficult part of this walk. There may be a red arrow painted on a pole on the opposite (river) side of the vehicle track, or you may just have to cast around until you find the trail markers (splashes of red paint on trees).

The walking track climbs steeply uphill and can be slippery after rain; once you've found it it's easy to follow. Eventually the track emerges on the ridge between the two peaks. Follow the ridge uphill (south) a short way to a rock with a wonderful view of Tahiti and of the pineapple plantations in the valley below. Towering above is the spectacular peak of Mt Mouaputa, the mountain with the 'hole' through it (see the boxed text 'Hiro & the Hole Through Mt Mouaputa' in the Moorea chapter).

The track drops very steeply but handy vines and creepers make the descent fairly simple. The track passes through a thicket of bamboo and crosses a river before emerging on the flat valley floor. It's much easier to make this walk in the direction Vaiare-Paopao.

Three Coconut Trees Pass

This is an exhilarating climb. It's hard, sweaty work but the pay-off is superb views from the ridge separating Mt Mouaroa (880m) from Mt Tohiea (1207m). There are not, however, three coconut trees – two were blown down in an early 1980s cyclone.

Start by taking the inland road from the top of Opunohu Bay towards the Opunohu Valley *marae* (traditional temples) and the *belvédère* (lookout). Shortly after the Cook's Bay road joins the route and before the agricultural college, another road turns to the right. There's a sign pointing the way to the 'Vue de Roto Nui et du Marae' and a much smaller and rather obscure pictogram of three coconut trees. Follow the turn-off road a couple of hundred metres to its end and park just before the pig farm.

The walking path, with its red trail-markers, continues straight on from the road and drops down to a small stream then climbs up the other side, through ferns, with the ridge and the coconut tree clearly visible to the right.

The route takes a sharp turn and drops steeply down to a wider river. Cross this river but don't go straight up the other side. The path now follows the river, crossing it half-a-dozen times as it tumbles down through a dark and magnificent mape forest. Eventually the walking trail diverges from the river and heads up the hill. If you're uncertain whether you're still on the correct route, search for the red markers. If you go far without them, you're lost.

Higher up the hill the markers seem to fade but bits of plastic tied to branches help. Clearings are the easiest places to get lost; each time you exit one, make sure you're on the right trail. A clearing closer to the top can cause confusion but there's a marker on a big, mossy rock off to the right of the clearing.

The final climb to the top of the knife-edge ridge is a real root-hanger but you emerge from the undergrowth to the first unobstructed views on the way up.

Trodden-down barbed wire along the ridge line shows where a fence once ran. Follow the ridge to the right (west) for the best views over the bays – and all the way to Tetiaroa on a clear day.

Keep an eye out for the route markers on your way down. It's even easier to lose them when you're walking faster and possibly paying less attention.

Mt Rotui by the North Ridge

More than a mere walk, this ascent is akin to a real mountain-climb. Mt Rotui (899m) is oriented north-south, parallel to Opunohu and Cook's bays, which lie on either side. The height isn't that spectacular but the panoramic view over the two bays makes the effort worthwhile. Count on a minimum of four hours to make the exhausting climb and about two hours to come down.

It is definitely not a good idea to attempt this walk without a local guide. The route is used infrequently and a machete is often necessary to cut through the dense vegetation. There are dangerous drops where you need to hang on to the bushes and on both sides of the ridge there are vertical drops. In case of an injury, a simple sprain for example, you would not be able to descend to get help. Don't start if there has been rain in the past few days and this is not a good walk for anyone who suffers from vertigo. You need to be in good physical condition and, at the risk of being repetitive, there are many passages that are more like rock climbing than walking.

It's vitally important to take plenty of drinking water because, once you're on the ridge, there is no shade. A hat or cap, sunscreen and sunglasses are also necessary. Wear walking shoes with good grip and trousers to protect your legs from scratches.

The departure point is near Faimano village, beside the Outrigger Hotel. The first part of the climb, to the *aito* (flame tree) massif, which you can see from the road, is the most testing. If you're forced to leave the path due to wasps' nests you will have to hack a way through the bushes and guava trees. There are particularly steep rocky boulders just before the aito trees. From this rocky spur the route continues along the crest, unprotected from the sun, through puarata and ferns. Take great care on this stretch because the path is narrow and there are sheer drops on each side. It's like walking up a series of stairways, with relatively flat passages followed by steep slopes where you will need to hang on with your hands. The views of Cook's Bay to the left and Opunohu Bay to the right defy all superlatives and if it's clear you can see the foothills of Tahiti to the south-east.

At the summit you can see the volcano crater and, to the south, Mt Tohiea (1207m) and Mt Mouaputa (830m). The descent should be made with the maximum of care, particularly at the aito-massif level, where it is necessary to go round to the right. It's easy to miss the trail among the piles of rocks and there are cliff faces in the vicinity.

After this little jaunt you'll better understand why, according to Maohi legend, Mt Rotui is the place of purgatory for the dead before they ascend to paradise.

Afareaitu Waterfalls

Afareaitu has a couple of short waterfall walks. The Putoa and Vaioro rivers both reach the sea at Afareaitu, where a low ridge divides the wider valley behind the village into two smaller river-valleys.

From right in the middle of town, opposite the church and between the Ah Sing store and the Putoa River bridge, a road runs back up the valley. It starts sealed, soon becomes dirt, then gets rougher and narrower until even a 4WD can't proceed further. Depending on how far you want to push your wheels, it's a 20 to 30 minute walk to the falls. There's a confusing maze of tracks and footpaths but if you basically head north along the valley and follow the footprints, you'll get there. The falls fan out as they tumble down a wide rock face, dropping into a pool edged by a wide arc of boulders and stones.

The other waterfall on the Vaioro River is quite well known and is reached by a very short walk. If you look up the valley you can see the falls from the coast road. The dirt road is just north of the hospital (just south of the Vaioro River bridge). After a few hundred metres there's a sign reporting that the road and the falls are on private property, care of the Atna Association and that you should pay a 200 CFP entry charge. After that the road deteriorates, although your rent-a-car will manage it with care. When the road ends it's only 10 minutes along a well tended path to the falls. Obviously the flow varies with the amount of rain but the waterfall can be a beautiful thin wisp, feathering down the rock face to a ferny pool at the bottom.

RAIATEA
Mt Tapioi

Take the road inland towards Mt Tapioi (294m) from between the post office and *gendarmerie* (police station) in Uturoa. A short distance along this road a sign indicates 'Mt Tapioi' off to the right, followed by another sign proclaiming (in French):

'private road, bad dogs, no entry' – but hey, we can't read French can we?

There are several more Tapioi signs as the slightly rough road switchbacks up, but it's nothing a Citroën or Renault won't manage. Unhappily, the next 'no' sign means it; a chain across the track, backed up by several padlocks, underlines the negatives. From here it's a half-hour uphill stroll past some surprised cows to the TV masts and superb views of the Raiatea-Tahaa reef, the lagoon, Uturoa and the airport and, if the visibility is reasonable, all the high islands of the Leeward group.

Temehani Plateau

Tracks suitable for 4WD vehicles climb to the 750m Temehani Plateau at the northern end of the island. There are also some interesting walks. The plateau is home to the *tiare apetahi*, a white gardenia endemic to Raiatea (see the boxed text 'Raiatea's Emblem – the Tiare Apetahi' in the Raiatea and Tahaa chapter). Further south, Mt Tefatua (1017m) is the highest point on the island.

BORA BORA
Mt Pahia

A track beside the Banque Socredo in the centre of Vaitape leads straight back towards the mountain. There's a trail to the left, but it soon peters out; another trail leads off slightly to the right (south), eventually heading resolutely east and up. It's often very steep (but not as steep as it looks from sea level) and involves hauling yourself from one tree root to another. The trail is not marked but it's pretty easy to see where it goes.

The climb reaches the rocky band around the top of the peak and then traverses the mountain northwards. It sticks closely to the rock face at first, but eventually diverges from the face and climbs steeply up the narrow, rocky course of a stream (dangerously slippery when wet).

This difficult climb takes you back to the rock face where there there's another clamber up a rocky course, although not so steep or difficult. That brings you out to a point overlooking Faanui and the track across the island. Another steep and rather loose climb

brings you to the bushy top of the peak, from where it's a short and easy climb to the summit of Mt Hue (619m). The top is marked by a flagpole and there are superb views right the way around the motu encircling Bora Bora.

A short descent and another climb along the knife-edge ridge takes you from Mt Hue to the summit of Mt Pahia (661m) and more superb views. There may even be a length of rope to make the final ascent easier.

The views from these peaks are superb but it's no easy climb; allow five hours for the return trip – if you're fit.

Surfing

French Polynesia is a paradise for surfing and body (boogie) boarding; some of the breaks are internationally known. Expert or beginner, there's a site to suit. The main islands for surfing are Tahiti, Moorea and Huahine.

In general, the north and east coasts work from November to April and the west and south coasts work for the other half of the year – but these distinctions are really just theoretical. In practise it is the direction of the swells that makes a spot work at any given time.

Access to the shorebreaks is generally easy from the coast roads. You may need to find a boat to take you out to the reefbreaks, or resign yourself to a lot of paddling. There's no problem taking a surfboard on le trucks.

Always check the weather reports and ask the locals what they feel about the conditions. Like surfers in many other places in the world, French Polynesians can be very possessive of *their* waves. If you want to enjoy the surf, observe all the usual surfing etiquette and give way to local surfers.

The sites in this section are marked on the relevant island maps.

EQUIPMENT

There are several surf shops in Papeete. You certainly don't need a wetsuit in the warm waters of French Polynesia but a T-shirt or Lycra vest will protect you from the sun. The local surf shops all have boogie-board equipment as well as shortboards and traditional surfboards.

LESSONS

Tura'i Mataare's surfing and boogieboarding school on Tahiti offers courses by the day (4500 CFP per person) or a program of 10 half-day lessons for 26,500 CFP. The courses are run by an instructor with a state diploma and include equipment, transport to the different surfing spots and insurance. Contact Kelly Surf (☎ 45 44 00) in Fare Tony in Papeete.

TAHITI
East Coast
Lafayette Beach
PK7. Shorebreak – November to April. Easy access from the coast road. A fairly radical shorebreak with powerful waves and a shallow bottom. The best spot is towards the river mouth.

Matavai Bay & Point Venus
PK10 (access from coast road). Shorebreak – November to April. Reefbreak – all year after the swell. Depending on the swell direction, there's a choice between the shorebreak or the reefbreak. The right-hand reefbreak at Point Venus reef is one of the most spectacular on the island.

Ahonu – Orofara
PK12.5-13. Shorebreak – November to April. These spots work on a northern swell and the waves are rather easy. There's access from the coast road.

The Right Line at Papenoo: The Source-Les Sapins (The Firs) – Rocky Point
PK13-14. Shorebreak – November to April. The waves here are more hollow and more powerful. Beware of occasional strong currents. Easy access.

Papenoo: The Bay
PK14.5. Shorebreak – November to April. An ideal spot for beginners, with long and not very hollow waves.

Papenoo: The Mouth
PK15.5. Shorebreak – November to April. The waves are difficult and are best in the early morning.

Faaone: Mouth of the Mahaena & Mouth of the Vaiiha
PK33.5 & PK44.5. Shorebreak – November to April. Fairly difficult waves at the mouth of the river.

West Coast
Papara
PK38.7. Shorebreak – May-October. A very popular spot with easy access from the coast road and moderately challenging waves. Beware of strong currents if there's heavy swell. A minor plus is you can swim in the Taharuu River.

Paea
PK21.5. Shorebreak – May-October. In front of the Paea mairie, this spot rarely works – when it does, the waves are powerful.

Sapinus – Pointe des Pêcheurs (Fisherman's Point)
PK15. Shorebreak – May-October. A fairly radical shorebreak with fast hollow waves. It's possible to park in the Museum of Tahiti's car park.

Taapuna
PK12. Reefbreak – all year. A classic – a very beautiful left that attracts lots of surfers.

Tahiti Iti
Big & Small Vairao Passes
Reefbreak – all year. Magnificent lefts and rights for experienced surfers. Ask the locals for the best way to get to these breaks.

Teahupoo
Reefbreak – April-October. At the end of the coast road, where the world professional-surfing round, the Tahiti Gotcha Pro, takes place around May each year. The prime spot is the tremendous left, reserved strictly for the best surfers. A guaranteed rush.

MOOREA
Temae
Reefbreak – all year, depending on the winds. Not far from the airport, this spot is unusual in that it isn't at a pass. The break is a right and appears where a recess and the curvature of the reef combine perfectly. A very technical wave.

Paopao (Cook's Bay & Opunohu Bay)
Reefbreak – mainly from November to April. A magnificent setting. Look for the left at Paopao and the right and left at Opunohu.

Beachcomber Parkroyal
Reefbreak – June to October. Not far from the hotel's beach. A difficult left which can be dangerous if there is a big swell because of the narrowness of the pass and the strong currents that run through it.

Haapiti
PK30. Reefbreak – May to October. A must. The left at Haapiti is allied with the regularity and strength of the reef waves and the security of the beach waves. There's a reasonable depth at the take-off point.

HUAHINE
Fare

Reefbreak – all year. The left attracts the big names of surfing. The right is also pretty good.

Fitii

Reefbreak – all year. As with the left at Fare, this one works when a south-west swell is running.

Parea

Reefbreak – all year. Beautiful waves so long as the trade winds aren't blowing.

PLACES TO STAY
Tahiti
Moana Surfing Tours (☎/fax 43 70 70), on the inland side of the road at PK8.3 in Punaauia, is run by Moana David, the brother of Vetea David, a Tahitian surfer of world standard. There is a variety of accommodation to choose from, including dorm beds, half-board, airport transfers and transfers (if necessary by boat) to the best surfing spots, for 10,000 CFP per day per person.

Te Miti (☎/fax 58 46 61) in Paea is another good address, and *Pension Bonjour* (☎ 57 02 15, ☎/fax 43 69 10) looks straight out on to the famous and fabulous break at Teahupoo.

Moorea
Fare Tatta'u (☎/fax 56 35 83) is close to the Haapiti Pass and there's a boat to take surfers out to the break.

Huahine
Surfers usually head for *Hotel Huahine (☎ 68 82 69)*, *Chez Lovina (☎/fax 68 88 06)* or *Vaihonu Ocean Camping (☎ 68 87 33, fax 68 77 57)* in Fare. In the south of the island, *Ariiura Ocean Camping (☎ 68 85 20, 68 83 78)* is also a good place for the surfing spots.

Sailing

See Formalities for Yachts in the Facts for the Visitor chapter for important information on the legalities and procedures of entering French Polynesian waters.

SEASONS & CONDITIONS
The dominant winds are the easterly trade winds. In the dry season (May-October) the south-easterly *maraamu* sometimes blows. It's best to avoid the November to March cyclone season.

Anchorages are described later in this section. Crews should take precautions against theft at popular tourist centres such as Bora Bora and in the Marquesas. Never leave cash, travellers cheques, passports or other documents on board. Always lock up the boat when you go ashore and take special care of any outboards and tenders. A runabout tied up beside a yacht at night can quite easily sail away before dawn.

CREWING POSITIONS
It's often possible to pick up crewing positions on yachts, particularly if you have had some relevant sailing experience. Check noticeboards in popular restaurants and at the yacht clubs on Tahiti, Bora Bora, Raiatea and other popular yachting stops. Yacht owners have to put up with some complex paperwork when making crew changes so make sure your own papers are in order.

The yacht owner will want to vet potential crew members but it's equally important to check the boat and crew you are considering joining. Make sure the boat is safe and the crew are compatible. Readers have suggested that the Marquesas is probably not the ideal place to join a boat. As the first arrival point for yachts from North America it makes little sense for a crew member to leave his or her boat there – unless there is something seriously wrong with it!

ANCHORAGES
The Society Islands
Only enter lagoons through passes with navigation markers. Navigation inside the lagoon is relatively simple but beware of coral outcrops and avoid shallow water; if the water looks clear, it's shallow.

On Tahiti you can anchor at the yachting quay along the Papeete waterfront and at the marinas at Taina and the Arue Yacht Club.

On Moorea the most beautiful anchorages are in Cook's and Opunohu bays, each accessible by a pass. There is a marina at Vaiare.

Huahine has Maroe, Bourayne, Haapu and Avea bays. The area around Fare, the main town, is not ideal because it's simply too busy.

Raiatea is an ideal stopover, with all the services a visiting crew could ask for. The Apooiti Marina has mooring buoys, as does the Stardust Marina. It's also possible to tie up at the Uturoa wharf, although there is a lot of traffic. There's also a magnificent anchorage at Motu Naonao, to the south.

At Tahaa you can stop at Haapu or Haamene bays, off Tuvahine Motu (where the Vahine Island resort is) and in Tapuamu Bay. Hotel Hibiscus (☎ 65 61 06, fax 65 65 65), Hotel Marina Iti (☎ 65 61 01) and Vahine Island Resort (☎ 65 67 38, fax 65 67 70) all have mooring buoys and offer an excellent welcome to yachties.

At Bora Bora, you can anchor in front of the yacht club, north of Vaitape. It's not possible to moor at Vaitape itself but many boats anchor at Raititi Point, near the Hotel Bora Bora.

The Tuamotus

Yachts crossing the Pacific from east to west appreciate the lagoons of Manihi, Ahe, Takaroa, Rangiroa and, to a lesser extent, Fakarava, Toau, Arutua, Apataki and Aratika.

The most direct route to Papeete makes a stop at Takaroa then runs slightly south-east via the channel separating Rangiroa and Arutua. It's also possible to leave Takaroa to the north and cross the channel between Fakarava and Toau.

Caution is required in these low-lying islands because they do not come into view until you are very close. Also, most of the lagoons are sprinkled with coral outcrops that are rarely marked; these areas can be real labyrinths. If possible, take along a fisherman who knows the lagoon.

Restrictions apply to atolls where there are pearl farms, where the lagoons will be dotted with numerous platforms imperfectly marked by buoys. At Takaroa, a sign beside the pass states that you are not allowed to anchor in the lagoon. Ask a local to guide you to a safe anchorage spot.

Getting in and out of the passes can also be dangerous, so it's wise to avoid the countervailing currents on entry and departure.

The Marquesas

The Marquesas is an important stop for yachts crossing the Pacific, and is usually the first point of entry for those westbound.

At Nuku Hiva, besides the Taiohae port, you will find excellent anchorages in the Hakatea and Hakaui bays to the south-west, the Hatiheu and Anaho bays to the north-east and Taipivai Bay to the east. At Taiohae, contact Rose Corser at the Keikahanui Nuku Hiva Pearl Lodge (☎ 92 03 82, fax 92 00 74) for laundry and poste-restante services.

A Beginner's Guide to Yacht Hire

There are four basic ways of renting a yacht.

Bareboat Hire You charter the yacht without crew or skipper and it's up to you to organise supplies and sail it. The chartering operations can often arrange to provision the boat for you.

Hire with a Skipper You rent the yacht with a skipper, a good way to go if you're uncertain of your own abilities or have limited knowledge of the islands. A host can also be provided.

Charter You rent the yacht with skipper, host and crew so you don't have to do a thing, unless you want to, of course.

Cabin Charter Similar to a charter except you only rent one cabin, ideal if you do not have a big enough group for a whole boat.

At Ua Huka, you can stop in the Haavei, Vaipaee or Hane bays.

Hakahau Bay at Ua Pou has a marina. Pukuéé Restaurant-Pension (☎/fax 92 50 83) offers laundry and poste-restante services. Other anchorages are found on the west coast at Hakamaii, Hakahetau and Vaiehu. At Hakahetau, ask for Étienne Hokaupoko, the multilingual *tavana* (mayor).

At Hiva Oa, the serrated coastline near Tahauku is well sheltered and has a marina with moorings close to the yacht club. On the north coast of the island it is possible to make stops at Hanapaaoa or Hanamenu.

Tahuata has several idyllic creeks, especially at Hanahevane and Hanamoenoa; Hapatoni is also beautiful. At Fatu Hiva, the mythical Bay of Virgins (Hanavave) is a stopover well-known in the yachting world.

BAREBOAT CHARTERS & CRUISES

Renting a yacht is a fine way to explore French Polynesia, whether it's a bareboat charter (you sail it yourself) or a cabin on a crewed yacht. It's not even necessary to be an experienced sailor as there are options for a variety of experience levels – see the boxed text 'A Beginner's Guide to Yacht Hire' in this section.

Raiatea, centrally positioned in the Society Islands and with a fine lagoon, has become the yacht-charter centre of French Polynesia. Most operations will offer whatever a customer demands and prepare fully stocked and equipped boats. Bareboat charter rates vary seasonally (July-August is the high season).

Cruises on a crewed yacht will usually include tour programs at the stops en route. Dive cruises are also possible. From Raiatea, count on eight to 10 days to explore the Leeward Islands.

Aqua Polynésie (☎/fax 85 00 00) Luxurious 14m catamarans with crewed cruises around the Leeward Islands, the Tuamotus and Marquesas and boats specially equipped for dive cruises. Departures are from Bora Bora or Huahine, Fakarava (Tuamotus) or Nuku Hiva (Marquesas).

Archipels Croisières (☎ 56 36 39, fax 56 35 87, email archimoo@mail.pf) Luxurious 18m catamarans with crewed cruises to the Leeward Islands, Tuamotus and Marquesas and dive cruises. Departures are from Bora Bora, Rangiroa (Tuamotus) and the Marquesas. It also has day cruises aboard a 32m schooner departing from Moorea or Papeete.

Bisou Futé (☎ 65 64 97, fax 65 69 08) The Crafty Kiss operation on Tahaa charters boats by the day for individually planned cruises.

Cruise Danae (☎ 66 12 50, fax 66 39 37, email claudine.danae@mail.pf) A variety of one to seven-day crewed cruises departing from Raiatea.

Faimanu (☎ 65 62 52, fax 65 69 08) Based on Raiatea, this operation organises cruises by the day.

Pacific Dream Charter (☎ 77 87 05, fax 45 46 02) Catamarans based at the Taina Marina at Punaauia on Tahiti.

Stardust Marine (☎ 66 23 18, fax 66 23 19, email stardustraiatea@mail.pf) About 20 boats of a variety of types. At the Stardust Marina at Raiatea, it rents bareboat, with skipper and/or hostess, and crewed cruises.

Tahiti Yacht Charter (☎ 45 04 00, fax 42 76 00, email tyc@mail.pf) Catamarans and monohulls rented from Raiatea, bareboat or with skipper and hostess.

The Moorings (☎ 66 35 93, 66 26 26, fax 66 20 94) About 20 boats of a variety of types – chartered bareboat, with skipper and hostess and by the cabin with crew. It's based at Apooiti Marina at Raiatea.

VPM Dufour Yachting (☎ 56 40 50, fax 56 40 60) Groupe Nouvelles Frontières has 25m Nemo catamarans rented bareboat or by the cabin, with cruises to the Leeward Islands, the Tuamotus and the Marquesas. Dive cruises are also possible.

DIVING

Translucent lagoons, deep blue ocean, warm water year-round and exceptional marine life make French Polynesia a dream destination for scuba divers.

If you're interested in snorkelling rather than scuba diving check the Swimming or Snorkelling sections in the individual island chapters. There are also a variety of dive cruises covering a number of islands, see Bareboat Charters & Cruises in the Outdoor Activities chapter.

Dive Centres

There are about 25 professional dive centres in French Polynesia. They're open year-round, most of them every day. They typically offer two to four dives a day, generally at 8 or 9 am and around 2 pm. Most centres don't have a definite schedule for dives but decide each day which sites are most suitable for the weather conditions and the divers who have signed up. It's a good idea to reserve at least a day in advance.

Many of the centres' offices close during dives, so contact them before or after the morning or afternoon dives. The centres are affiliated with a number of diving associations. Some are attached to the FFESSM, others are also PADI or SSI centres. All are at least Level 1 on the French CMAS scale. At all the tourist-oriented dive operations there are personnel who speak English.

Costs & Services

The dive centres in French Polynesia offer beginner's dives for children and adults, exploration dives, night dives, multi-dive packages and dive courses. Dive courses are generally only offered for the most frequently requested French Level 1 and the basic PADI course (Open Water, or OW) and typically cost 30,000 CFP to as much as 50,000 CFP.

A single dive typically costs 5000 CFP to 6000 CFP (more for beginners), usually including equipment rental but not necessarily the 8% VAT. At some centres you get a reduction after five dives, or five and 10-dive packages are offered. International visitors get a 20kg baggage allowance on Air Tahiti flights but officially the limit is just 10kg, so don't bring more equipment than necessary, although some dive operators' equipment may be rather old and worn.

Many centres have arrangements with hotels offering reduced-price accommodation for divers, or accommodation and dive packages. The dive centres (see later in this section) can tell you about these packages and most (except for those on Tahiti) offer free pick-ups within a certain area.

Almost all dive centres accept credit cards and many video-record dives; cassettes typically cost 8000 CFP to 12,000 CFP.

Documents

If you are already a certified diver you will need your dive card and it's a good idea to have your dive logbook with you. Centres accept any dive-association accreditation (PADI, CMAS etc) but may ask you to do a preliminary dive to check your expertise and make sure you're not too rusty. A medical certificate is necessary if you're doing a dive course and some operators may require one for general dives. No certification is required for beginner's dives – baptisms, as they're known – although parental authorisation is required for minors.

All operators have professional insurance for their local liabilities but it's a good idea to hold supplementary insurance from your own country. Check that your travel insurance covers scuba diving and that you're covered for repatriation in case of an accident. The Diver Alert Network (DAN) is a popular worldwide association for divers and membership covers air evacuation for dive-related illness or injury. A couple of the Tahiti operators, which principally cater to local French residents, require divers to have a FFESSM licence that includes insurance.

Choosing a Centre

Like a hotel or restaurant, each dive centre has its own personality and style. There are small family centres at one extreme and highly professional, highly technical centres at the other. On islands with several centres, it's worth paying a visit to each one to check the welcome, the divemasters, the organisation, the equipment and the general feel and ambience. Talk to other divers, although almost every centre has critics and fans.

The Society Islands

Tahiti Scuba Tek Tahiti (☎/fax 42 23 55) is at the Arue Marina, at the Yacht Club of Tahiti at PK4. This centre covers dive sites along the coast, including the Falls and the Dolphin Bank. It's closed on Sunday afternoon and Monday.

Dolphin Sub (☎/fax 45 21 98, email dolphin.sub@usa.net) is based at Fare Ute, close to the Nautisports store. It's a PADI centre and dives on the main sites along the east and west coasts, as well as beginner's sites in the lagoon. Snorkelling trips in the lagoon at Punaauia are also possible for a minimum of four people at 2500 CFP each.

Aquatica Dive Center (☎ 53 34 96, mobile ☎ 77 60 01, fax 43 10 65, email aquatica_dive@hotmail.com) has two bases, one in the Beachcomber Parkroyal, the other in the Paea Marina at PK27. This allows it to cover a large area of dive sites.

Eleuthera Plongée (☎ 42 49 29, fax 41 04 09) is at the Taina Marina in Punaauia, 400m after the Continent Hypermarket. Monthly trips are made to Moorea, a 55 minute boat-trip away, and sometimes to Tetiaroa.

Tahiti Plongée (☎ 41 00 62, 43 62 51, fax 42 26 06, email plongee .tahiti@mail.pf), beside the lagoon at PK7.5, is a local institution. Its director, Henri Pouliquen, pioneered scuba diving in French Polynesia

A Beginner's Dive in the Lagoon

French Polynesia is a great place to make a first scuba dive. The water is warm and clear and the lagoon is like a giant swimming pool, secure and not too deep. All the main dive centres cater to first timers and offer beginner's dives. A baptism – *baptême* – in French scuba-diving jargon typically takes place in relatively shallow (3 to 4m) and calm water and lasts about 30 minutes. As in any new activity, confidence is important for a first timer; if there are several centres on an island you may want to check them out to find the one you prefer. No formalities are required unless there are serious medical contra-indications, and parental permission for minors. The cost of a first dive is usually about US$50.

The divemaster takes only one or two pupils and, before entering the water briefly explains the elementary rules and the equipment (mask, fins, regulator, air tank, buoyancy compensator, weight belt), which at first seems constraining – but underwater, the ease of movement is astonishing.

The big moment comes with that first immersion in the lagoon. On the surface, with your divemaster, you test the regulator and then descend, with the divemaster keeping an eye on you all the way. All you have to do is breathe and experience that first sensation of weightlessness! If it appeals, you can sign up for a course to obtain a dive card that will let you dive anywhere in the world. See Dive Centres in this section for details.

and is very well known in the Francophone scuba-diving world. He's particularly renowned for teaching very young children to dive. There are several dive boats and sites from Arue to Paea are regularly visited. Local residents are its main clientele and they come to Tahiti Plongée for the relaxed family atmosphere. It's closed on Monday.

Iti Diving International (☎/fax 57 77 93, email itidiving@hotmail .com) is the only centre on Tahiti Iti. It's at the Puunui Marina in Vairao at PK6. Gilles Jugel offers some little-known dives to drop-offs rich with gorgonia corals and with a more-varied marine life than at Tahiti Nui sites, including the Marado, the Hole in the Lagoon, the Ietopa Cave and the Gorgonias. The atmosphere is friendly and family oriented.

Moorea Bathy's Club (☎ 56 31 44, 56 38 10, email bathys@mail.pf) is in the Beachcomber Parkroyal complex and is a very professional PADI centre, the showcase of diving in French Polynesia. The centre puts on shark-feeding dives and is the only centre to dive with the rays at Stingray World.

Moorea Fun Dive (☎ 56 40 38, ☎/fax 56 40 74, email fundive@mail.pf) is a pleasant centre in the Moorea Beach Club complex at Hauru Point.

Scubapiti (☎ 56 12 67, ☎/fax 56 20 38), a small and friendly centre in Les Tipaniers' compound, is one centre that doesn't believe

Diving with Children

Children from the age of eight can make a beginner's dive. Several centres have child-size scuba equipment, and Tahiti Plongée specialises in teaching small children.

in fish-feeding. It covers the same sites as other centres but also, for experienced divers, some less well-known sites on the western side of the island, like the Taota Canyons.

MUST (☎ 56 17 32, ☎/fax 56 15 83, email mustdive@mail.pf) is run by Philippe Molle, author of numerous dive books and a pioneer of scuba diving in France. The centre is beside the lagoon on Cook's Bay, next to the defunct Cook's Bay Resort. Shark-feeding is on the menu at the morning dive. The centre is closed on Monday.

Huahine Pacific Blue Adventure (☎ 68 87 21, fax 68 80 71), right on the quay at Fare, is a convivial centre that makes dives at the Avapeihi Pass, Faa Miti, the Coral City and the Yellow Valley.

Centre Nautique Oiri (☎ 68 81 46, 68 76 84, fax 68 85 86) is in the Huahine Beach Club compound on the south of the island. The young divemasters are a pleasant couple who offer a personalised service and day trips by zodiac involving two dives, a motu picnic, a pearl-farm visit and snorkelling stops at some of the most beautiful places in the lagoon for 11,400 CFP. The sites are different from those offered by Pacific Blue at the north of the island; they go from Parea to Tiare Pass at the east of the island.

Raiatea & Tahaa Hémisphère Sub (☎ 66 12 49, fax 66 28 63) is at Marina Apooiti and offers dives on the east and west coasts as well as around Tahaa. Snorkelling trips to the Teavapiti Pass are also possible for 2800 CFP per person.

Raiatea Plongée (☎ 66 37 10, fax 66 26 25) is at the Hotel Tepua, to the south of Uturoa and makes trips to sites along the east coast and at Tahaa.

Bora Bora Bora Diving Center (☎ 67 71 84, ☎/fax 67 74 83), managed by Anne and Michel Condesse, is right next to Hotel Bora Bora at Matira Point. Apart from dives inside and outside the Bora Bora lagoon, trips can be organised to Tupai, north of Bora Bora, and the centre also offers Aqua Safari outings, strolling along the lagoon bottom wearing a weighted helmet.

Nemo Worlds Diving Center (☎/fax 67 63 33, email divebora@ mail.pf) is across from Hotel Beach Club and Sofitel Marara.

Topdive (☎ 60 50 50, fax 60 50 51, email topdive@mail.pf) is a luxurious and very high-tech centre in the complex of rooms and restaurant of the same name, on the northern edge of Vaitape. There's a swimming pool for dive training and it offers a beginner's Discover Scuba Diving package.

The Tuamotus

Rangiroa Paradive (☎ 96 05 55, fax 96 05 50) is operated by Bernard White and is at the eastern end of the string of islets, next to Chez Glorine guesthouse.

Raie Manta Club (☎ 96 84 80, fax 96 85 60) is beside the lagoon at the entrance to Avatoru village, between Pension Herenui and Rangiroa Lodge. The centre has a second office near the Tiputa Pass, next to Pension Teina & Marie. The director Yves Lefèvre played a major part in the growth of diving on Rangiroa and the centre has a strong reputation.

The Six Passengers (☎/fax 96 02 60) is a small, simple and relaxed operation in an airy *fare* beside the lagoon, about 500m east of Kia Ora Village. It specialises in small groups and the dives are videoed by Ciao Rangiroa (☎ 96 04 14). You can see the film on return and purchase it for 7000 CFP.

Manihi Manihi Blue Nui (☎ 96 42 17, fax 96 42 72) is in Manihi Pearl Beach Resort and, like the hotel, is luxurious and immaculate.

Tikehau Raie Manta Club of Rangiroa has a small operation at the Tikehau Village (☎ 96 22 86).

Fakarava Te Ava Nui (☎ 82 08 05) started operating in November 1999 and offers dives in the Garuae Pass.

The Marquesas

Centre Plongée Marquises (☎/fax 92 00 88) is a pleasant and well-run operation on the Taiohae marina embankment on Nuku Hiva. Dive cruises are offered with Archipels Croisières as well as regular day-excursions to Anaho for 10,000 CFP per person, with the possibility of a dive for 5000 CFP.

The Australs

Raie Manta Club (☎ 96 84 80, fax 96 85 60) of Rangiroa sends a dive-master to Rurutu for the July to October whale-watching season. The cost is 25,000 CFP per person per day including whale-watching trips, other activities and accommodation with all meals at Rurutu Village.

Dive Sites
Diving Conditions

Diving conditions in French Polynesia are exceptional. The water temperature varies from 26 to 29°C, reaching a peak during summer (November to March). Each location and season has its particular attraction, and visibility is excellent (except in the Marquesas, where it rarely exceeds 20m); often reaching 40m, apart from during rainy periods, when sediments are carried into the lagoon.

Polynesia – Spectacular Dives

Shark feeding, diving with rays, whale watching, drift diving – French Polynesia provides superb dive sites and close encounters that will seduce even the most blasé diver. Furthermore all these dives are accessible to divers with a simple Level 1 or PADI OW dive card.

Shark feeding – a popular activity at Moorea, Raiatea and sometimes at Bora Bora and Manihi – is guaranteed to speed up your heart rate. The divemaster drops down to the bottom at around 15 to 20m, signals to the divers to form a semi-circle, and produces a large hunk of fish from a feedbag. Hundreds of fish hurl themselves on this offering and the orgy begins. The divemaster is enveloped in a cloud of fish, but soon black-tip reef sharks, grey sharks and even lemon sharks appear. After 15 minutes of intense activity, the remains are tossed aside and the dive continues at a calmer pace.

Of course feeding any fish, let alone sharks, is a controversial practice and even on Moorea, the shark-feeding centre, not all dive centres approve. It clearly disrupts natural behaviour patterns, and encouraging sharks to associate divers with a free feed is not a good idea.

Diving with rays is less thrilling than mingling with sharks, but just as spectacular. You may see manta and leopard rays at a number of sites, but Moorea and Bora Bora have shallow waters where you'll encounter stingrays so accustomed to divers – and to being fed by them – that they will dance around divers and gently brush against them.

A drift-dive through a pass is the major speciality in the Tuamotus. On the rising tide, as ocean water flows into the lagoon, the narrow passes create powerful currents surging through at 3 to 6 knots. Outside the pass, divers simply drop into the flow and are swept through into the calm waters of the lagoon, accompanied by a busy escort of fish. It's an indescribable sensation.

Diving with whales takes place at Rurutu in the Austral Islands when the humpback whales stage their annual July to October migration. Having found the whales it's simply a matter of donning snorkelling equipment and jumping in with them – they're unconcerned about being approached.

Diving with electra dolphins is the speciality of the Marquesas. On the east side of Nuku Hiva, hundreds of these white-lipped dolphins assemble daily; again, a mask, snorkel and fins are all that's necessary to join in.

The dive sites are wonderfully situated. On most islands the sites are very accessible, typically just a five to 15 minute boat ride, except for the Marquesas, where it is sometimes necessary to travel for 30 to 40 minutes by boat, in which case a trip will usually include two dives. Only Tahiti and Raiatea have shipwreck dives. See the boxed text

'Polynesia – Spectacular Dives' in this section for more information on the types of dives available.

The site reports that follow are only a sample. For more information look for Lonely Planet's new *Diving & Snorkeling Tahiti & French Polynesia*, which fully describes around 45 dive sites.

The region's marine life is varied, and although sharks and rays are the main attraction there are other interesting species as well. Corals and invertebrates are not the region's strong point and do not rival those found in the Indian Ocean. See the Flora & Fauna section in the Facts about the Islands chapter for more information.

The positions of the dive sites in this section are shown on the relevant island maps in each chapter.

The Society Islands

Tahiti There are about 20 lagoon and ocean sites between Arue and Punaauia.

The **Cliffs of Arue** in Matavai Bay is the best-known site on the east coast. On the outside of the reef a plateau of coral emerges at 5m depth – ideal for beginners – and is sited above a steep drop-off. Less than 100m from here, at between 10 and 30m depth, two narrow rifts shelter an abundance of marine life, including a variety of corals, nudibranchs (sea slugs), alcyonaires, coral polyps, anemones and crabs.

The **Aquarium** is a delight for beginners. With dozens of fish species, it is indeed an aquarium, part-natural, part-artificial, created by Henri Pouliquen and his divemasters from Tahiti Plongée, who used air bags to assemble hundred of tons of coral in the lagoon not far west from Faaa airport's runway. They also tossed in an old Cessna aircraft and the wreckage of a cargo boat at about 7m depth.

It's easy to find **the Spring**, in front of Fisherman's Point at Punaauia on the west coast, because this fresh-water spring looks like frosted glass as it merges with the salt. There are several coral pinnacles sheltering a dense marine life at 15 to 20m depth.

The south coast of Tahiti Iti offers several excellent dives sites, far from Papeete. The **Hole in the Lagoon** is a vast depression in the lagoon bottom where numerous rays are found at around 25m depth. Beside the Tetopa Pass, on the ocean side, lobsters and shellfish abound in the **Tetopa Cave**, a cavity hollowed out of the coral reef in barely 8m of water.

Moorea Moorea's sites are mainly along the north coast near the four dive centres.

The water clarity is usually superb at **the Tiki**, off the extreme northwestern corner of the island, close to Motu Fareone and in front of Club Med. The exceptional density of marine life includes perch, surgeon fish, triggerfish, snapper, butterfly fish, groupers and wrasse. This is a popular site for shark-feeding and black-tip reef sharks and grey sharks usually join the divers while large lemon sharks sometimes make a fleeting appearance.

MICHAEL AW

Squadrons of leopard rays regularly keep an appointment in the 20m-deep **Ray Passage**, on the west side of Tareu Pass. Currents often limit the visibility but on those occasions there are greater numbers of rays. The drop-off, in just 6m of water, shelters all sorts of reef life and the shallow upper part of the drop-off is ideal for beginners.

Between the Tareu and Teavarua passes, the **Garden of Roses** is reserved for experienced divers because the descent is made through open water to a depth of 50m. The coral 'roses' open out to 3m across to catch the maximum amount of light on the ocean side of the reef.

Stingray World is just a stone's throw from the Beachcomber Parkroyal and is an exclusive for Bathy's Club. The stingrays are almost tame and it's a great sensation to gently stroke them as they brush past.

Huahine The **Avapeihi Pass** (Fitii Pass) is by the lighthouse to the north of the island, near Fare. Divers encounter many barracudas, jackfish and grey sharks that don't even expect to be fed! There are also rays, but the current can be strong. Other popular sites include Faa Miti, north-west of the island near the airport, where moray eels, stingrays and a wide variety of small fish will be seen around the coral outcrops.

South of the island is **Parea Pass**, close to the village of the same name, and **The Canyon**, which forms a large rift in the Tiare Pass.

Raiatea & Tahaa Close to Hotel Hawaiki Nui on the east coast of Raiatea is one of French Polynesia's rare shipwrecks, the relatively well preserved *Nordby*, which lies in 18 to 29m of water. Launched in 1900,

Top Left: A pair of white-eyed Moray eel peer from crevasses in the coral.

the 50m-long three-master lies on its side. Further to the south, the superb **Teavapiti Pass** has many fish and beautiful coral massifs. The local club feeds grey sharks at this site.

On the other side of the island is **Miri Miri Pass**, where purple coral can be seen on the drop-off. **The Roses**, a little further north, has a vast field of coral roses at 40m depth.

At Tahaa, peaks vary the relief in the **Céran Pass**, a superb untouched site with yellow coral, barracudas, grey sharks and white-tip reef sharks at about 35m.

Bora Bora Bora Bora has magnificent lagoon dives, such as **Toopua** and Toopua Iti to the south-west. The drop-off, at 3 to 34m, is frequented by leopard rays, moray eels and abundant reef life. **Toopua Iti** has an interesting relief with many small canyons and tunnels.

Anau, in front of the Méridien resort, inside the lagoon on the eastern side of the island, is a popular spot for manta rays and black-tip reef sharks. The visibility can be limited because of the sandy bottom, but that's what rays like.

North of the island, outside the reef but close to the airport, **Muri Muri** (also known as the White Valley) is a magnificent site, where sharks are the main attraction. Accustomed to being fed, they converge on the site as soon as the boat stops. **Tapu**, to the west of the island by the large motu of the same name, is a site for more experienced divers. Canyons and crevasses vary the relief and lemon sharks are encountered at 15 to 40m depth.

Tupitipiti is a magnificent site but infrequently dived, as it's a long way to go – out the Teavanui Pass and right round the island to the southern tip of Motu Piti Aau.

The Tuamotus

Rangiroa Rangiroa is one of the best-known dive areas in the Pacific, but in fact just five or six sites are regularly dived and the coral is relatively poor. It's the powerful currents running through the passes and the density of sharks that those currents attract which accounts for Rangiroa's fame. Divers enter on the ocean side with the current flowing in to the lagoon and a zodiac follows the divers and recovers them at the end of the dive. This type of dive is strictly for the experienced.

The **Tiputa Pass** is the most famous site and the dive usually starts outside the pass with a visit to the **Shark Cave** at 35m, where there are usually about a dozen grey sharks. From November to February enormous hammerhead sharks can be seen sticking discreetly close to the bottom. Napoleon wrasses, barracudas, manta and leopard rays are also encountered. The dive ends at **Motu Nuhi Nuhi**, a calm and sheltered reserve popular with beginners and snorkellers, where there is a great density of small marine life around the coral and the depth doesn't exceed 10m.

The **Avatoru Pass**, 10km to the west, also offers plenty of interest. Manta rays appear in the pass and the Raie Manta Club feeds the white-tip reef sharks, which approach divers as soon as they appear.

Inside the lagoon, **Mahuta** is a magnificent and calm site with channels of sand between pretty coral massifs that attract an abundant reef life. On the axis of the Avatoru Pass, it also attracts larger pelagic species.

Manihi At **Le Tombant** (the Drop-off), on the ocean side of Tairapa Pass, a dizzy wall topples toward the abyss. Grey sharks, napoleons, jackfish, banks of perch and barracudas appear regularly. Every year in July, impressive formations of marbled groupers hang out there.

The **Tairapa Pass** forms a passageway about 70m wide and 20m deep; you simply let yourself get sucked into the lagoon by the current and observe the amazing density of marine life as you slip past. There are banks of barracudas and unicornfish, sharks sleeping in cavities in the pass wall, and white-tip reef sharks and triggerfish. This dive ends at **The Circus**, inside the lagoon, where there's an entanglement of pinnacles from 20m right up to the surface, peppered with coral fish. Eagle rays often hunt around this area but the visibility may not be the best.

The Cliffs is another ocean dive at a fracture in the reef, where divemasters feed grey sharks and black-tip reef sharks.

Tikehau Dives generally take place in **Tuheiava Pass**, 30 minutes by boat from the village of Tuherahera. A rather wild and unfrequented dive site somewhat like the passes at Rangiroa, it can offer magnificent surprises. Manta rays, grey sharks, jackfish, barracudas and white-tip reef sharks all make regular appearances.

Fakarava There are a dozen untouched sites on this atoll. The huge **Garuae Pass** measures nearly 800m across and offers divers a fantastic spectacle of sharks, dolphins, rays, barracudas and enormous banks of fish. It makes the Avatoru and Tiputa passes in Rangiroa seem like timid little playgrounds in comparison.

The Marquesas

The diving conditions in the Marquesas are completely different from the other archipelagos. The dives take place in water saturated with plankton and close to cliffs battered by surge. As a result, visibility is generally only 10 to 20m, but these waters support a most unusual abundance of pelagic, open-sea, species. The cliffs are honeycombed with cavities and there are some superb cave dives. Diving trips here

Snorkelling

Snorkelling is diving with just a mask, snorkel and fins. Some of the most beautiful sites are in the coral gardens, just inside a lagoon's barrier reef. Lagoon tours will generally include a snorkelling stop at one of the prime spots. See the snorkelling sections in the relevant chapters for more information.

Scuba-diver briefing, Cook's Bay (Moorea)

Snorkelling at Huahine

A variety of fish congregate around the coral just a few metres beneath the surface.

Anemones

A moray eel checks out a diver from its coral hideaway.

Grey shark

Playing with rays in Moorea's lagoon

Gorgonian coral, Tahiti Iti

Don't touch! A lionfish

Shark feeding always increases the heart rate (Raiatea).

Diving Terms

You'll find that most dive centres are used to dealing with English speakers but the following French terms may be useful.

a dive	*une plongée*
a beginner's dive or first dive	*un baptême*
dive centre	*un centre de plongée*
diving licence	*un brevet de plongée*
drift dive	*une plongée à la dérive*
air tanks	*des bouteilles de plongée*
fins	*des palmes*
mask	*un masque*
regulator	*un détendeur*
snorkel	*un tuba*
wetsuit	*une combinaison de plongée*
weight belt	*une ceinture de plomb*

KATE NOLAN

are very dependent upon weather conditions, since surge can make manoeuvring and anchoring very difficult.

There are about 10 sites regularly dived on the south and west coasts of Nuku Hiva. On the eastern side of the island, **Pygmy Orcas** is an exceptional site where you can simply snorkel amongst the group of electra dolphins (*Peponocephala electra*, also known as pygmy orcas or melon-headed whales) that assembles there every morning.

At the entrance to Taiohae Bay is the **Sentry of the Hammers** where, at between 10 and 40m depth, there are hammerhead sharks with curious wavy protuberances, known as festoons, close to their mouths, as well as manta and leopard rays, moray eels, sea urchins and beautiful shells.

Ekamako Cave, to the east of Taiohae Bay, is a submarine cavity about 10m in diameter, penetrating more than 100m into the cliff at a depth of about 15m. The main attraction is the stingrays that bury themselves in the sand and enormous lobsters that crouch in the rocky debris.

Tikapo is the name of the headland at the south-eastern corner of Nuku Hiva. Facing this point, surrounded by the sea, a rock emerges from the ocean; circling around it is an abundant fauna including sharks, jackfish, leopard rays, barracudas and perch. This dive can only be made in calm sea conditions.

The rocky **Motumano Point** advances onto a sandy plateau to the south-west of the island. It's a good site for manta rays and sharks. At the other end of the island, on the west coast, **Matateiko Point** is a rocky pinnacle frequented by manta and leopard rays, jackfish and sharks.

The Australs
The Raie Manta Club of Rangiroa stations a divemaster on **Rurutu** from July to October to organise whale watching and even swimming with the whales that congregate around the island at that time.

MANOLO MYLONAS

THE SOCIETY ISLANDS

TIARE

MANOLO MYLONAS

The Society Islands

The Society Islands form the main archipelago of French Polynesia. They include the largest islands and are home to the vast majority of the population. Most of the group are high islands, as opposed to the low-lying coral atolls of the Tuamotus.

The Society Islands are subdivided into the eastward Windward Islands (Îles du Vent) and the westward Leeward Islands (Îles sous le Vent). The Windward group comprises two major islands, Tahiti and Moorea, and three smaller islands: Tetiaroa, Maiao and the unpopulated Mehetia.

Tahiti is the largest and best-known island in French Polynesia, the site of both the capital, Papeete, and the only international airport. Moorea is smaller and quieter, visually spectacular and very popular with visitors.

The Leeward group includes five very varied high islands. Huahine is popular for its relaxed atmosphere and has the most extensive pre-European marae site in French

Polynesia. The twin islands of Raiatea and Tahaa share a lagoon. Raiatea, the 'sacred island' of Polynesia, is the site of legend and has the most important ancient marae in French Polynesia. Bora Bora is one of the most beautiful islands on earth and sees a steady flow of visitors keen to pay homage to that beauty! Remote Maupiti is beautiful, smaller and far less developed for tourism. The Leeward group also includes four smaller islands: Tupai, Mopelia, Scilly and Bellingshausen. All are atolls and, apart from Tupai, far to the west.

Almost every early European visitor took the opportunity to rename Tahiti – and any other island they chanced upon. Captain Cook dreamed up the Society name in 1769. He originally attached the Society tag solely to the Leeward group because they were close to each other, or 'in close society'. The name was later applied to the Windward group as well.

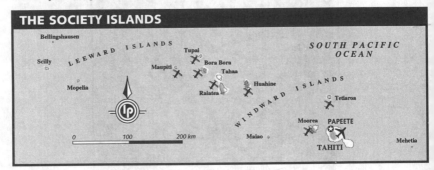

THE SOCIETY ISLANDS

Tahiti

It's common to speak of Tahiti as if it were the whole of French Polynesia, when in fact it is merely the largest island, the site of the capital, Papeete.

Despite its alluring name and image, Tahiti does not match the standard perception of French Polynesia. The beautiful beaches on postcards are on motu on other islands, the glamorous over-water bungalows on brochures are at hotels on Bora Bora, the underwater glimpses of sharks cruising past colourful reefs are in the Tuamotus. Even the paintings by Gauguin are probably of the Marquesas, not Tahiti.

Most visitors soon head to other islands but Tahiti deserves more than a cursory glance. It may not inspire love at first sight but it has plenty to offer. After all, this is the economic centre of French Polynesia and it has a historic dimension no other island can match. Tahiti boasts remains of ancient marae and it was here that Cook and Bougainville first anchored and from here that they carried back the first enticing reports of Polynesia's exotic wonders.

The downside is that there are crowds, traffic jams, very few beaches, often-mediocre accommodation and it's expensive. In compensation, there are the joys of the lagoon and a wild and uninhabited interior with secret valleys and impressive peaks waiting to be explored on foot or by 4WD. A circuit of Tahiti reveals its historic places, its small museums and the untouched wilderness of Tahiti Iti. Finally there's Papeete, with its always active and intriguing waterfront, a good place to sip a sunset cocktail, dine in a fine restaurant, do some shopping or catch a great dance performance.

History

Like other islands in the Society group, Tahiti is the creation of volcanic eruptions. The larger circle of Tahiti Nui probably came into existence around 2½ to three million years ago, while smaller Tahiti Iti was created perhaps less than a million years ago.

HIGHLIGHTS

pop: 150,000
area: 1045 sq km
reef passes: 33
highest point: Mt Orohena (2241m)

- Dine at a quayside *roulotte* or in one of Papeete's classy restaurants
- Stroll along the Papeete waterfront
- Shop in Papeete's boutiques or in the colourful market
- Catch a Polynesian dance performance in one of the big hotels
- Investigate the mountainous centre
- Explore the mysteries of Tahiti Iti and its little-visited attractions

---

Tahiti was not the first of the Society group to be populated in the great Polynesian migrations. Legends relate that the first settlers came to Tahiti from Raiatea; their landing place, on the south-east coast of Tahiti Nui, is painstakingly pinpointed. Despite its size, Tahiti was not the most important of the Society islands – that honour went to 'sacred' Raiatea.

Tahiti's rise to central importance began in 1767, when Samuel Wallis 'discovered' the island. He was soon followed by Bougainville and Cook, who made Tahiti the favoured base for European visitors. Prior to European arrival no kingdom exercised more than local power; it was a considerable feat for an *arii* (chief) even to control a whole island.

European arms and, for a time, European mercenaries, soon changed that equation and the Pomare dynasty eventually controlled not only all Tahiti but various other Society and Austral islands. It was a fleeting moment. Tahiti soon became a minor pawn

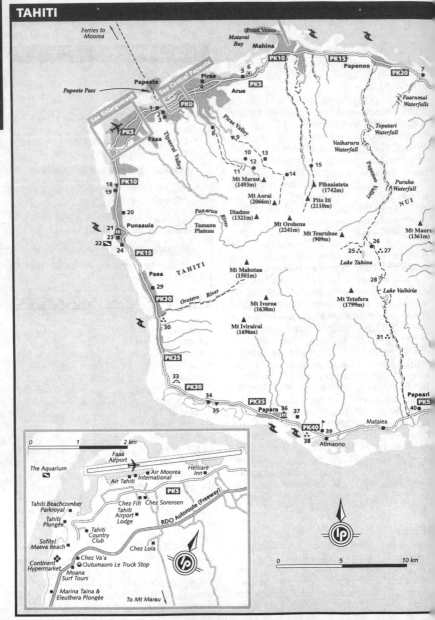

TAHITI

TAHITI

Ferries to
Moorea

Point Venus

Matavai
Bay

Mahina

PK10

PK15

Papenoo

PK20   7

Papeete Pass

Papeete

Papeete

See Central Papeete

Pirae

5 6

PK5

Arue

Faarumai
Waterfalls

PK0

See Enlargement

Pirae Valley

1

2
3

8

9

Topatari
Waterfall

PK5

Faaa

Tipaerui Valley

10   13

Vaiharuru
Waterfall

Papenoo Valley

Puraha
Waterfall

12

11   Mt Marau
(1493m)

14   15

Pihaaiateta
(1742m)

NUI

18   PK10

19

Mt Aorai
(2066m)

Pito Iti
(2110m)

20

Panaruu

Diadme
(1321m)

River

Mt Orohena
(2241m)

Mt Teuruhue
(909m)

Mt Mauru
(1361m)

21

Punaauia

Tamanu
Plateau

26

23

25   27

22

24

TAHITI

Lake Tahinu

PK15

Paea

Mt Mahutaa
(1501m)

28   Lake Vaihiria

29

PK20   Orotero   River

Mt Ivoroa
(1638m)

Mt Tetufera
(1799m)

30

Mt Ivirairai
(1696m)

31

PK25

33

PK30

34

Papeari

35

PK35   Papara   36

37

PK5

40

PK40   39

Mataiea

38   Atimaono

Inset (bottom left)

0   1   2 km

Faaa
Airport

The Aquarium

Air Moorea
International

Heitiare
Inn

Air Tahiti

PK5

Tahiti Beachcomber
Parkroyal

Chez Fifi   Chez Sorensen

RDO Autoroute (Freeway)

Tahiti
Plongée

Tahiti
Airport
Lodge

Sofitel
Maeva Beach

Tahiti
Country
Club

Chez Lola

Continent
Hypermarket

Chez Va'a

Outumaoro Le Truck Stop

Moana
Surf Tours

Marina Taina &
Eleuthera Plongée

To Mt Marau

0   5   10 km

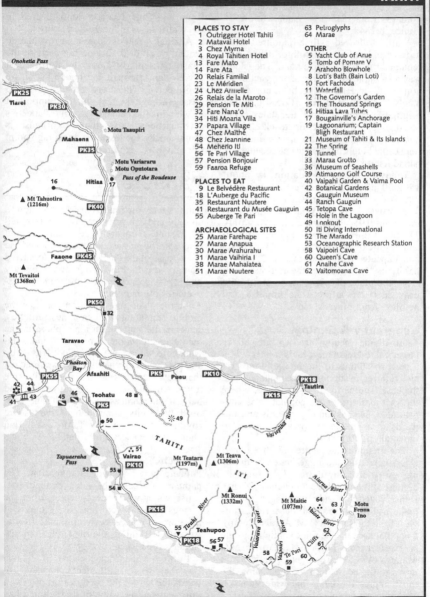

PLACES TO STAY
1 Outrigger Hotel Tahiti
2 Matavai Hotel
3 Chez Myrna
4 Royal Tahitien Hotel
13 Fare Mato
14 Fare Ata
20 Relais Familial
23 Le Méridien
24 Chez Armelle
26 Relais de la Maroto
29 Pension Te Miti
32 Fare Nana'o
34 Hiti Moana Villa
37 Papara Village
47 Chez Malthé
48 Chez Jeannine
54 Meherio Iti
56 Te Pari Village
57 Pension Bonjouir
59 Faaroa Refuge

PLACES TO EAT
9 Le Belvédère Restaurant
18 L'Auberge du Pacific
35 Restaurant Nuutere
41 Restaurant du Musée Gauguin
55 Auberge Te Pari

ARCHAEOLOGICAL SITES
25 Marae Farehape
27 Marae Anapua
30 Marae Arahurahu
31 Marae Vaihiria I
38 Marae Mahaiatea
51 Marae Nuutere

63 Petroglyphs
64 Marae

OTHER
5 Yacht Club of Arue
6 Tomb of Pomare V
7 Arahoho Blowhole
8 Loti's Bath (Bain Loti)
10 Fort Fachoda
11 Waterfall
12 The Governor's Garden
15 The Thousand Springs
16 Hitiaa Lava Tubes
17 Bougainville's Anchorage
19 Lagoonarium; Captain
   Bligh Restaurant
21 Museum of Tahiti & Its Islands
22 The Spring
28 Tunnel
33 Marae Grotto
36 Museum of Seashells
39 Atimaono Golf Course
40 Vaipahi Garden & Vaima Pool
42 Botanical Gardens
43 Gauguin Museum
44 Ranch Gauguin
45 Tetopa Cave
46 Hole in the Lagoon
49 Lookout
50 Iti Diving International
52 The Marado
53 Oceanographic Research Station
58 Vaipoiri Cave
60 Queen's Cave
61 Anaihe Cave
62 Vaitomoana Cave

in the European colonial quest and it was only a generation from Tahiti's takeover by Pomare II in 1815 to its annexation by France in 1842.

Wallis followed a time-honoured tradition when he claimed Tahiti for Britain and renamed it King George's Land. The island was also claimed for France and Spain but none of those early claims held; nor, fortunately, did the island's new title. Tahiti, the original Polynesian name, translates along the lines of 'to remove' or 'to take to the border', perhaps because the original settlers came here from Raiatea or because the island itself shifted here.

Today, Tahiti's population is about 150,000 people, which represents about 70% of French Polynesia's population. The growth in recent years has been dramatic: in 1956 the population was only 37,000. Tahiti is the economic, cultural and political centre of French Polynesia and Papeete, with more than 100,000 inhabitants, has become the region's 'big city', the place of bright lights and fragile prospects that attracts the hopeful and helpless from other islands.

Geography & Geology

Tahiti divides neatly into two circles: the larger Tahiti Nui to the west is connected by a narrow isthmus to the smaller Tahiti Iti, also referred to simply as 'the peninsula', to the east. The narrow coastal fringe, where the vast majority of the population is concentrated, sweeps rapidly inwards and upwards to a jumble of soaring, green-clad mountain peaks.

The mountainous centre of Tahiti Nui is effectively a single huge crater, with the highest peaks arrayed around the rim. The highest of them all is Mt Orohena (2241m). Dense vegetation and crumbling ridgelines make it difficult to climb but a ridge runs west from the summit to Mt Aorai (2066m), a popular ascent. The ridge continues to the spectacular rocky Diadème (1321m) and Mt Marau (1493m). A number of valleys run down to the coast from the mountains, the most impressive being the wide Papenoo Valley to the north.

Tahiti Iti is geologically younger than the bigger Tahiti Nui; its highest point is Mt Ronui (1332m). Eastern Tahiti Iti ends in steep cliff faces in the Te Pari district.

A fringing reef encloses a narrow lagoon around much of the island but parts of the coast, particularly along the north coast from Mahina through Papenoo to Tiarei, are unprotected. There are no less than 33 passes through the reef, the most important of which is the Papeete Pass into Papeete's fine harbour. Less than 10km east is Matavai Bay, the favourite anchorage point of many early explorers.

Papeete

Tahiti's busy metropolis has a reputation as an ugly and overpriced port town, blighted by tasteless concrete development and heavy traffic. It has even been labelled the 'Las Vegas of the Pacific'. Try to cross Blvd Pomare during rush hour and the ugly image may seem to have some truth, but Papeete is not really that bad.

Amble along the waterfront, sample the mobile restaurants known as les roulottes, soak up the Polynesian atmosphere in the busy Papeete Market, sip a coffee in a sidewalk café while you watch the world go by and plan visits to other islands – approached that way Papeete can be a very enjoyable town. All roads in French Polynesia lead here so you might as well enjoy it. Throughout July the city jumps to the Heiva festival rhythms – see the 'Ori Tahiti – Tahitian Dance' special section for details.

HISTORY

Papeete was a European invention. The name means 'basket of water', probably because water was once collected from the springs in what were once the grounds of the Pomare palace, between the Territorial Assembly Building and the High Commissioner's Residence.

In 1769, when Cook anchored in Matavai Bay, there was no settlement in Papeete. Towards the end of the century European visitors realised the value of its sheltered bay

CENTRAL PAPEETE

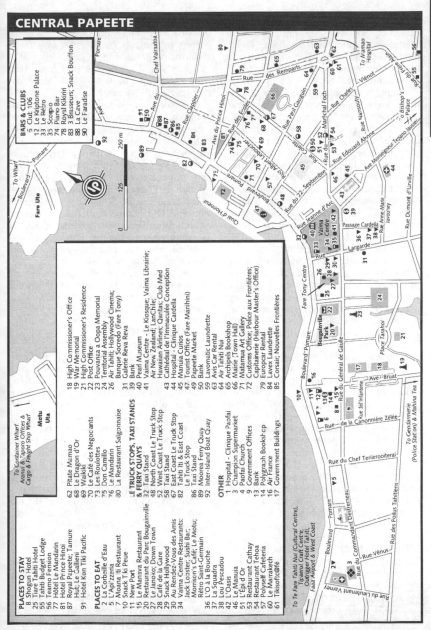

PLACES TO STAY
8 Shogun Hotel
25 Tiare Tahiti Hotel
55 Tahiti Budget Lodge
56 Teamo Pension
77 Hôtel Le Mandarin
81 Hôtel Prince Hinoi
87 Royal Papeete; Tamure
   Hut; Le Gallieni
91 Hotel Kon Tiki Pacific

PLACES TO EAT
2 La Corbeille d'Eau
5 L'Api'zzeria
7 Moana 'ti Restaurant
10 Snack T'ki Peue
11 New Port
15 Le Manuia Restaurant
20 Restaurant du Parc Bougainville
27 Le Janoxo; Down Town
28 Café de la Gare
29 Snack Hollywood
30 Au Rendez-Vous des Amis
34 Vaima Centre Restaurants;
   Jack Looster; Sushi Bar;
   Morrison's Café; Le Motu;
   Rétro Saint-Germain
36 L'O à la Bouche
37 La Squadra
38 Lou Pescadou
42 L'Oasis
46 Le Manuia
51 L'Epi d'Or
53 Restaurant Cathay
54 Restaurant Tehoa
57 Polyself Cafeteria
60 Le Marrakech
61 Tikisofc@fé

62 Pitate Mamao
68 Le Dragon d'Or
69 Waikiki
73 Le Café des Negociants
75 Les Roulottes
76 Le Mandarin
80 La Restaurant Saïgonnaise

18 High Commissioner's Office
19 War Memorial
21 High Commissioner's Residence
22 Post Office
23 Poivana a Oopa Memorial
24 Territorial Assembly
26 Air Tahiti; Hollywood Cinema;
   Banque Socredo (Fare Tony)
31 Galerie Reva Reva
39 Bank
40 Pearl Museum
41 Vaima Centre - Le Kiosque; Vaima Librairie;
   Air New Zealand; LanChile;
   Hawaiian Airlines; Qantas; Club Med
43 Cathédral de l'Immaculée Conception
44 Hospital - Clinique Cardella
45 Manuia Curios
47 Tourist Office (Fare Manihini)
49 Papeete Market
50 Bank
59 Lavomatic Laundrette
63 Avis Car Rental
64 Air Tahiti Nui
65 Archipels Bookshop
66 Mairie (Town Hall)
71 Matamua Art Gallery
72 Customs Office; Police aux Frontières;
   Capitainerie (Harbour Master's Office)
79 Europcar Rental
84 Lavex Laundrette
85 Corsair; Nouvelles Frontières

LE TRUCK STOPS, TAXI STANDS & FERRY QUAYS
32 Taxi Stand
48 North Coast Le Truck Stop
52 West Coast Le Truck Stop
58 Taxi Stand
67 East Coast Le Truck Stop
82 Tahiti Iti & East Coast
   Le Truck Stop
86 Taxi Stand
89 Moorea Ferry Quay
92 Inter-Island Boat Quay

OTHER
1 Hospital - Clinique Paofai
3 Champion Supermarket
4 Paofai Church
9 Government Offices
13 Bank
14 Polygraph Bookshop
16 Air France
17 Government Buildings

BARS & CLUBS
5 Club 106
12 Le Kriptone Palace
33 Le Rétro
35 Scorpio
74 Piano Bar
78 Royal Kikiriri
83 3 Brasseurs; Snack Bouffon
88 La Cave
90 Le Paradise

and easy access through the reef. London Missionary Society (LMS) missionaries arrived in Papeete in 1824, the young Queen Pomare became a regular visitor to the growing town and the city became a religious and political centre.

Visiting whaling ships made Papeete an increasingly important port and Governor Bruat selected the town as the administrative headquarters for the new French protectorate in 1843. By 1860 the town had taken its present form, with a straggling European settlement between the waterfront and the street known as 'the Broom' (now Rue du Commandant Destremeau, Rue du Général de Gaulle and Rue du Maréchal Foch). Already development was extending back from the narrow coastal strip into the Sainte Amélie Valley and the district known as The Mission.

Chinese merchants and shopkeepers started to trickle in to Papeete, but at the beginning of the 20th century the population was still less than 5000. A disastrous cyclone in 1906 and a German naval bombardment in 1914 that destroyed the central market took a toll, but during WWII the population reached 10,000 and by the early 1960s it was past 20,000.

The city's growth and change accelerated in the 1960s. The opening of Faaa airport kicked off the tourist industry and the first beachside hotels saw the light of day. Nuclear testing operations brought in massive flows of money while a huge expansion of administrative and government jobs brought a flood of people from remote islands.

Today Papeete and its suburbs are home to more than 100,000 people. Unfortunately, this rapid expansion has had its costs and the almost total destruction of the charming old colonial heart of Papeete is one of them.

ORIENTATION

Central Papeete curves around an almost enclosed bay and the central district is a compact area, easily covered on foot. Blvd Pomare follows the waterfront and most of the central businesses, banks, hotels and restaurants are concentrated along this busy

street or in the few blocks back from the water's edge. The Vaima Centre marks the centre of the city but it's the waterfront, with its constant shipping activity, that is the city's true heart. The port zone, Fare Ute and Motu Uta, is easily visible across the harbour to the north.

Greater Papeete forms a vast conurbation, squeezed between the mountains and the lagoon along the north coast of Tahiti. The westward sprawl of Papeete extends beyond the airport in the unattractive suburb of Faaa (yes it *is* three consecutive vowels although it is also spelt Fa'aa) and on to Punaauia. The coast road westwards is complemented by the Route de Dégagement Ouest (RDO), French Polynesia's freeway, which runs slightly inland, starting on the western edge of central Papeete and extending to just beyond Faaa airport before rejoining the coastal road.

On the other side of Papeete, Ave du Prince Hinoi and Ave Georges Clémenceau run eastwards through the suburb of Pirae before joining at Arue.

INFORMATION
Tourist Offices

The Tahiti Tourist Board (GIE) has its office (☎ 50 57 00, fax 43 66 19, email tahititourisme@mail.pf) in Fare Manihini on Blvd Pomare in the centre of Papeete. It has a large collection of information sheets detailing cheaper accommodation, island by island, and also distributes tourist brochures and leaflets. It covers the whole of French Polynesia and is much better than any local office you'll find on other islands, so make the most of it. It's open weekdays from 7.30 am to 5 pm, Saturday from 8 am to noon.

There is an information desk at the airport, in the enclosure with the car rental agencies, but it's often unstaffed.

Money

Banques Socredo, de Tahiti and de Polynésie are all found in Papeete and its suburbs. Banques Socredo and de Polynésie have branches at Faaa airport. See Money in the Facts for the Visitor chapter for general information on banks and changing money.

Most Papeete branches will change money or travellers cheques and most have automated teller machines (ATMs) that accept Visa and MasterCard for cash advances and let you withdraw money from your home account. Outside the Papeete area, the only ATMs are in Taravao. Note that there is a weekly limit of 35,000 CFP for ATM withdrawals or advances from any one account.

On the Quai d'Honneur, in the same building as the *capitainerie* (harbour master's office), there's a foreign exchange bureau called MG Finances, which is open weekdays from 7.30 am to noon and 2 to 4.30 pm, as well as Saturday from 7.30 am to 4.30 pm. It doesn't charge commission except for currencies belonging to the Euro zone.

The Banque Socredo branch in the Fare Tony Centre on Blvd Pomare has a machine that changes foreign bills.

Post & Communications
Papeete's main post office is on Blvd Pomare, next to Bougainville Park. For stamps and general postal services go upstairs from the Blvd Pomare entrance. The poste restante is downstairs. The post office also offers phone, fax and telegram services and has an excellent philatelic department. It's open weekdays 7 am to 6 pm and Saturday 8 to 11 am. There are post office branches in Papeete suburbs and at Faaa airport.

Tahiti Tours (☎ 54 02 50), BP 627, Papeete, Tahiti, is the American Express agent and will hold clients' mail. Its office is at 15 Rue Jeanne d'Arc, next to the Vaima Centre.

Email & Internet Access
The only real cybercafé in French Polynesia is on the Pont de l'Est roundabout, close to the *mairie* (town hall). Tikisoftc@fe (☎ 77 44 34, 88 93 98, email tikisoft@mail.pf) is a place where you can surf the web or check your emails. Its Website is at www.tikisoft.pf. Count on 1000 CFP per half-hour.

Bookshops & Newsagencies
Papeete has several excellent bookshops with special sections for Polynesia and the Pacific. They're open Monday to Saturday. There will usually be some books in English

as well as the wider French selection. Archipels (☎ 42 47 30) is at 68 Rue des Remparts, to the east of the centre. Prince Hinoi Centre (☎ 54 05 04) is on Ave du Prince Hinoi and Vaima Librairie (☎ 45 57 44) is in the Vaima Centre.

The Prince Hinoi Centre and the small Klima bookshop (☎ 42 00 63), 13 Place Notre Dame, beside the cathedral, have marine charts and maps. For French and foreign newspapers and magazines, go to Polygraph on Ave Bruat, Vaima Librairie, or Le Kiosque at the front of the Vaima Centre.

Photo Developing
There are lots of photo-developing centres around Papeete but the costs are fairly astronomical. See Photography in the Facts for the Visitor chapter for more information. Then take your undeveloped films home with you! At Chez Photo Te Pari, 25 Rue Paul Gauguin, or at one of the many QSS outlets, you'll pay about 3900 CFP (US$35!) for developing and printing a 36 exposure film.

Laundry
Getting clothes washed on Tahiti is ridiculously expensive although after returning from the outer islands you may appreciate being able to find a laundrette. Lavomatic on Rue Paul Gauguin, across from the mairie, is open Monday to Saturday from 6.30 am to noon and 1.30 to 5.30 pm. It costs 1600 CFP for a load, washed and dried. Lavex, next to the Taina bar on Blvd Pomare, is open weekdays from 7 am to 6 pm and Saturday from 7 am to 3 pm. It costs 825 CFP to wash, 825 CFP to dry.

Toilets
There are public toilets by the green le truck terminus, which is beside the mairie. There are more on the wharf, close to the Tourist Office.

Left Luggage
There's a left-luggage department next to the domestic flights area in Faaa airport. It's open weekdays from 6 am to 7 pm, weekends from 6 am to noon and 1.30 to

6.30 pm, as well as from two hours before the arrival of international flights. It's expensive – 395 CFP a day for a suitcase or backpack, 620 CFP for a bicycle, 1030 CFP for a sailboard or surfboard. It's better to try and leave your baggage with a hotel. Tahiti Budget Lodge keeps bags for 1000 CFP per week; the expensive hotels, and the Te Miti guesthouse in Paea, will do it for free.

Medical Services & Emergency

For police phone ☎ 17; in a medical emergency, phone ☎ 15. You can also call SOS Médecins on ☎ 42 34 56.

The Mamao Hospital (☎ 46 62 62 or for emergencies 24 hours ☎ 42 01 01), on Ave Georges Clémenceau, is the biggest hospital in French Polynesia and covers all the medical specialities.

There are two 24-hour private clinics: Cardella (☎ 42 81 90) on Rue Anne-Marie Javouhey, behind the cathedral and Paofai (☎ 46 18 18) at the corner of Blvd Pomare and Rue du Lieutenant Varney. They're more expensive than the public hospital; day/night or Sunday consultations cost 3000/7000 CFP.

Your hotel desk can recommend a doctor or other medical assistance. There are a number of pharmacies open on Sunday morning as well as during the week.

WALKING TOUR

Papeete would be rather charmless and dull were it not for the waterfront. Rows of visiting yachts, cargo ships loading and unloading from the furthest reaches of French Polynesia and the arrivals and departures of the inter-island ferries make it a colourful and ever-interesting strip by day and it's just as interesting after dark.

Start a waterfront stroll from the west along the four-lane Blvd Pomare, shaded by overhanging trees and brightened by hibiscus. Close to the metal footbridge on the lagoon side of the road is the imposing **Te Fare Tauhiti Nui**, the Polynesian-style centre. Various exhibitions and events are regularly staged here.

The imposing pink and white Protestant **Paofai Church** marks Papeete's birthplace,

as the first Protestant church, built on this site in 1818, effectively signalled the beginning of the town. Across the road is a memorial to the great double-canoe *Hokule'a*, which emulated the feats of the legendary Polynesian navigators by sailing from Hawaii to Tahiti in 1967. As you walk east there are racing *pirogues* (local outrigger canoes) stacked up under trees on the quayside. Local teams can be seen practising some afternoons and every Saturday morning. Past Ave Bruat, local boats and cruising yachts from both sides of the Pacific give Papeete an international flavour. On the inland side of the road is **Bougainville Park** and the adjacent post office.

Next up on the island side is the glossy **Vaima Centre**, with shops, restaurants and airline offices. On the harbour side, Fare Manihini is the home of the Tahiti Tourist Board, perched on the **Quai d'Honneur**. There's usually something interesting tied up at this quay, and in the late afternoon local fishing boats land the day's catch here.

At night les roulottes line up in the car park from here to the Moorea Ferry Quay, the busy shipping centre of the port, where a variety of ferries regularly arrive from and depart for Moorea.

On the inland side of Blvd Pomare, the sometimes seedy but always noisy and energetic **entertainment district** starts just south of Ave du Prince Hinoi and extends north past Ave du Chef Vairaatoa.

Tourism and entertainment fades out farther along the waterfront as the road continues through the docks and industrial zone of **Fare Ute** (which becomes Motu Uta after the bridge). This is the sweaty working part of the harbour where the copra boats unload their cargoes from the islands and the sweetish smell of coconuts hangs in the air. Pallets of everything, from building materials to crates of Hinano beer, drums and shiny new Taiwanese bicycles, are loaded on the ships to transport to the outer islands.

PAPEETE MARKET

Papeete Market (Marché du Papeete) makes an excellent starting point for an exploration of Papeete. It's colourful, appetising and very Polynesian. Although the market is a fine place to visit any day, early Sunday morning, when local residents flock in from all around Papeete, is the prime occasion.

The market covers the whole block between Rue du 22 Septembre and Rue Cardella, just one block back from the waterfront Blvd Pomare. In its 250 years, Papeete Market has been variously replaced and upgraded, damaged by a cyclone and even destroyed by German cruisers in WWII. Today's airy structure was built in 1987.

The market covers two floors; fruit, vegetables, meat and fish are downstairs and clothes, materials and tourist crafts can be found upstairs. It's a wonderful place to wander through and see traditional Polynesian produce. Fish from other islands is on sale early in the day but the Tahitian catch does not appear until late afternoon. Vibrantly coloured flowers add to the market's appeal.

CHURCHES & TEMPLES
Cathédrale de l'Immaculée Conception
Also known as the Cathedral of Notre Dame, the cathedral's story started in 1856, with plans for it to be built of stone imported from Australia and with a doorway carved out of granite from Mangareva in the Gambier Archipelago. Construction got underway using stonemasons from Mangareva, trained by Catholic missionaries. Money ran out just a year later and the original edifice was demolished in 1867. A new, smaller cathedral was commenced in 1869 and completed in 1875.

Mission Quarter
From the cathedral, Ave Monseigneur Tepano Jaussen leads into the Mission district, the site of Catholic colleges and Protestant schools. Jaussen, the Catholic bishop of Tahiti from 1848, acquired the mission lands in 1855 and turned them into a local **botanical garden**. He is buried in the mission's cemetery, beside Father Honoré Laval, the controversial apostle of the Gambier Archipelago. The road from the cathedral crosses the Papeava River on a small stone bridge and leads into the gardens of the fine

bishop's palace (1875). The gardens also contain a pretty Gothic-style chapel.

Paofai Church
Although the Catholic cathedral stands squarely in the town centre, Tahiti remains predominantly Protestant, an enduring reminder of the lasting effects of the LMS missionaries. The large pink, green and white bayside Paofai Church on Blvd Pomare makes a colourful scene at Sunday services with a congregation arriving and departing beneath a flotilla of wide-brimmed white hats and belting out rousing *himene* (hymns) in the interim.

Other Churches & Temples
Papeete's principal Chinese temple, the 1987 Kanti de Mamao, is on Ave Georges Clémenceau and Ave du Commandant Chessé. It replaced a century-old Chinese temple. There's a synagogue just off Ave du Prince Hinoi and an imposing Seventh-Day Adventist church just south of Ave Georges Clémenceau on the Route du Fautaua.

PEARL MUSEUM
In the Vaima Centre on the Rue Jeanne d'Arc side, the Pearl Museum (☎ 45 21 22) was created by pearl magnate Robert Wan and is open daily from 8 am to 7 pm (from 9 am on Sunday). This small, modern and well-presented museum covers all facets of the pearl cultivating business including its history, techniques, economics and art. Entry is 600 CFP and there are explanations in English. Of course, at the end of the visit you find yourself in one of Monsieur Wan's pearl boutiques.

BOUGAINVILLE PARK
Bougainville Park stretches from Blvd Pomare to Rue du Général de Gaulle and is fronted, on the waterfront side, by a 1909 bust of the great French navigator. Two naval guns flank the plinth. On the eastern side is a cannon salvaged from Count Felix von Luckner's WWI raider the *Seeadler* (Sea Eagle), which was wrecked on Mopelia in 1917 (see the Other Leeward Islands chapter for more details). On the

western side is a gun from the French vessel *La Zélée*, sunk at the harbour mouth during the German raid in September 1914.

ADMINISTRATIVE BUILDINGS

Named Place Tarahoi after Marae Tarahoi, the royal marae of the Pomare family, the **Territorial Assembly** and other government buildings occupy the former site of the Pomare palace. The termite-riddled 1883 palace was razed in 1960, but you can get an idea of what it looked like from the modern mairie, which is built in a similar style. On Rue du Général de Gaulle the assembly building is fronted by a **statue** of Pouvanaa a Oopa, a Tahitian patriot and WWI volunteer (see the boxed text 'Pouvanaa a Oopa – A Tahitian Leader' in the Huahine chapter).

The **High Commissioner's Residence** stands to one side of the assembly building replaced the 1843 Palace of the Governor (termites again). The earlier building arrived on Tahiti in pieces and was intended to be assembled on Nuku Hiva in the Marquesas, but was sidetracked to become the governor's residence! Behind and between the two buildings is the freshwater spring whose gushing waters gave Papeete its name. The pool is still known as the 'queen's bathing place', as the young Queen Pomare used to visit it. A more recent addition is the **Presidential Palace**, an imposing building used by the president.

Papeete's **mairie**, is two blocks back from Blvd Pomare and a block north of Papeete Market. It was completed in 1990, in vague imitation of the old Queen's Palace.

LOTI'S BATH

From east of the centre, the Route de Fautaua runs inland through lower-income dormitory suburbs to Loti's Bath (Bain Loti), 2.5km inland. It was here in Pierre Loti's 1880 novel *The Marriage of Loti* that the beautiful Rarahu met the novel's hero. This pool once supplied the town with drinking water, but now it's led through a concrete channel and surrounded by development. Nevertheless, it remains a favourite meeting place and swimming hole for local youngsters and a bust of Pierre Loti still overlooks the scene.

From Loti's Bath a walking path leads inland to the Fautaua River waterfalls, the **Fachoda Fort** and the **Garden of the Governor**. To go on this walk you'll need to ask permission from the Service de l'Hydraulique (see the Outdoor Activities chapter for more information).

MT MARAU

Directly across from the Faaa airport terminal, a road signposted as Saint-Hilaire runs inland, under the RDO and up towards the summit of Mt Marau (1493m). It's possible to drive up as far as the TV relay station at 1441m, although the rough road really requires a 4WD for the 10km climb. The route passes through varied vegetation before emerging among the damp ferns above 800m. It reaches a *belvédère* (lookout) at 1241m.

From the end of the road it is only a half-hour walk to the top of Mt Marau, from where there are superb views of the peaks around Tahiti Nui's central crater, the Tamanu Plateau immediately to the south and the ridgeline running east from Mt Marau to the Diadème (1321m), Mt Aorai (2066m) and Mt Orohena (2241m). The Fautaua River and its waterfalls, reached by the walk from Loti's Bath, can be seen to the north. There are also walking paths up Mt Marau from Punaauia that take about 3½ hours.

You can descend from Mt Marau in three hours via the Pic Vert (1159m) and the Pic Rouge. The track down starts from just before the TV-transmitter site and there are good views over the upper Fautaua Valley.

BEACHES

The splendid Polynesian beaches of tourist brochures are not on Tahiti, but if you just want to get into the water there are a few places within reasonable distance of Papeete. Eight kilometres west of the centre, just beyond Faaa airport, there's a bit of beach by the Sofitel Maeva Beach Hotel. The Outumaoro le truck terminus is just across the main road from the hotel, so getting here is very easy.

On the other side of town, 3km east in Pirae, there's a stretch of black-sand beach by the Royal Tahitien Hotel. It's not exactly inspiring, but things get better at the fine black-sand stretch at PK *(pointe kilométrique)* 7. Farther along again there's a popular beach at Point Venus at PK10. Unhappily, beaches within Papeete's urban sprawl can be subject to the same problems as city beaches in many modern countries: pollution from badly treated (or even untreated) sewage and industrial waste.

ACTIVITIES
Walking, Diving & Surfing
Walking and surfing are the principal activities of interest for residents and tourists and, along with sailing, they're covered in detail in the Outdoor Activities chapter. See the 'Diving' special section for information on diving opportunities.

Horse Riding
Ranch Gauguin (☎ 57 51 00), half a kilometre inland from the coast road at PK53, organises horse rides in the Papeari area. The hourly cost is 2500 CFP and a half-day outing with lunch costs 11,000 CFP. It's open daily and also has accommodation – dorm beds/doubles cost 2500/6000 CFP.

Golf
If you've come all the way to Tahiti to play golf, then the Olivier Bréaud Golf Course (☎ 57 40 32, 57 43 41) is the only place to do it. The 18-hole, 5950m, par-72 course is at PK42 on the site of Tahiti's former cotton plantation at Atimaono. A round costs 4786 CFP and there's a clubhouse, swimming pool and restaurant. Transfers can be arranged from Papeete and it's open weekdays from 8 am to 6 pm, weekends from 7 am to 6 pm.

Other Activities
Contact the tourist office about deep-sea fishing. There are tennis courts at several hotels and a number of private tennis clubs. If you want a gym, try the Gymnase Garden Club (☎ 53 49 50) at 95 Ave Georges Clémenceau in Mamao. Tahiti's dramatic

mountains provide superb hang-gliding opportunities; contact Tahiti Parapente Excursions (☎ 58 26 12, 46 60 12).

PLACES TO STAY
Papeete's places to stay can be neatly divided into two zones: the places in the central city area and the places on the edge of town. They're covered in the following Central Papeete and Outer Papeete sections.

There's a range of accommodation but bargains are rare and the price to quality ratio is not good. Don't expect to find stylish places with that mythical Polynesian feel either. Note that public transport farther afield is often not very convenient.

It's wise to reserve ahead during the Heiva festivities in July, when many hotels are completely booked out. There is an 8% VAT added to prices at the more expensive establishments.

Central Papeete
Budget There are not many options here and if Papeete is the first place you stay in French Polynesia you're likely to be very disillusioned. Places in this category are spartan and basic – they'll do for a night or two but location is their sole attraction.

Tahiti Budget Lodge (☎ 42 66 82, fax 43 06 79) is on Rue du Frère Alain, about 10 minutes walk from the waterfront in a quiet district. This family establishment is very simple, with 13 fan-cooled rooms in a big *fare*. A dorm bed costs 2000 CFP, rooms for one or two people are 4000 CFP or 5000 CFP with toilet and shower. It's very pricey considering its rustic nature but there's a shared kitchen, you can leave luggage for 1000 CFP per week and credit cards are accepted.

Teamo Pension (☎ 42 00 35, 42 47 26, fax 43 56 95) is only a couple of minutes walk from the Tahiti Budget Lodge. It has basic/better dorms with beds for 1300/1600 CFP. Rooms with shared bathroom cost 3700 CFP for one or two people, 4200 CFP with bathroom. They're pretty basic and the walls are paper thin. Hot water is available from 6 to 9 pm and there's a shared kitchen at the rear. Credit cards are accepted.

Shogun Hotel (☎ *43 13 93, fax 43 27 28, 10 Rue du Commandant Destremeau)*, just west of Ave Bruat, is strictly a last resort. Its reputation isn't good, but a 2000 CFP dorm-bed might be better than sleeping in the street.

Mahina Tea (☎ *42 00 97)*, BP 17, Papeete, Tahiti, is more like a cheaper hotel or motel than the two backpacker favourites. Walk up Ave Bruat and from the gendarmerie take the road on the right-hand side, Route de Sainte Amélie. It's in a quiet location only 10 or 15 minutes walk from the centre, although Old Macdonald's entire farm seems to break into song around dawn.

Its very plain rooms have bare concrete walls and tiled bathrooms. Prices for a basic single or double start at 4000 CFP and drop to 3200/3500 CFP for stays of three days or longer. Other rooms are in the 4700 CFP to 6000 CFP bracket; studio apartments with kitchen facilities cost 10,000 CFP (8000 CFP from three days). Monthly rates are from 65,000 CFP to 75,000 CFP. Credit cards are not accepted.

Mid-Range Prices quoted here include the 8% VAT. All these hotels accept credit cards.

Hôtel Le Mandarin (☎ *42 16 33, fax 42 16 32, email mandarin@chris.pf)* is centrally located on Rue Colette, right beside the mairie. Singles/doubles with air-con, attached bathroom and TV cost from 12,960/15,120 CFP. It's relatively modern, well kept and has a small cafeteria offering continental breakfast for 900 CFP and an adjacent Chinese restaurant with excellent food.

Overlooking the Moorea ferry wharf from Blvd Pomare, **Kon Tiki Pacific** (☎ *43 72 82, fax 42 11 66)* has a colourful setting and terrific views from the rooms at the front. At 7540/10,260 CFP for singles/doubles with bathroom and TV, this unremarkable business-style hotel is not bad value.

Royal Papeete (☎ *42 01 29, fax 43 79 09)* is slightly closer to the centre on Blvd Pomare. It's an old tourist hotel past its use-by date, although it's clear to see it once had real South Pacific charm. It still has one of the town's busiest nightclubs. Singles/doubles cost 9000/10,700 CFP,

deluxe rooms 10,500/12,000 CFP. Breakfast costs 980 CFP.

Hotel Prince Hinoi (☎ *42 32 77, fax 42 33 66)* is at the corner of Blvd Pomare and Ave du Prince Hinoi, right in the heart of the nightlife quarter. This modern business hotel is featureless but efficient and reasonable value for Papeete. Singles and doubles with air-con and private bathroom cost 12,545 CFP. The hotel puts on a popular 1000 CFP buffet lunch.

Tiare Tahiti Hotel (☎ *43 68 48, fax 43 68 47)* is a relatively new place facing the seafront on Blvd Pomare, beside the post office. The comfortable seafront rooms (12,000 CFP to 15,500 CFP) have balconies and great views of the port – the downside is they can be noisy if Papeete is having a late night, and rush hour is underway by 6 am. Continental breakfast costs 1100 CFP.

Outer Papeete

Most places on the city periphery, including the luxury hotels, are on the west coast between Faaa (the airport district) and Punaauia. There are frequent Papeete-Faaa-Outumaora le trucks during the day and even at night. There are several budget-priced places very close to the airport and easily reached by le truck. Except for the big hotels, nowhere on this stretch has a beach or swimming place. The following places are within 8km of central Papeete.

Budget **Heitiare Inn** (☎ *83 33 52, 82 77 53)* is at PK4.3, just a kilometre or so from the airport towards the city. Free transfers are provided from the airport; you can walk there in 15 minutes, but this is not a particularly attractive area. Singles/doubles around a tiled patio cost 4500/5000 CFP with shared bathroom, 6000/7000 CFP with air-con and attached bathroom. Rooms are mainly occupied by the month or even year. The busy little snack bar may disturb your sleep but there is a shared kitchen.

Chez Fifi (☎ *82 63 30)* is good value. Take the small road beside the Mea Ma laundry across from the airport car park. There's a sign and the guesthouse is 150m on the left. Beds in the impeccably clean dorm cost 2000 CFP including breakfast. The two rooms with shared hot-water bathroom cost 3500/6000 CFP including breakfast. Other meals cost 2000 CFP. There's a kitchen and the airport and Moorea are on view from the lounge room.

Chez Sorensen *(☎ 81 93 25)* is 50m from Chez Fifi and owned by the same people. Simple singles/doubles with shared bathroom cost 3500/5500 CFP. The rates drop 500 CFP after three days. There's a basic but acceptable dorm with beds at 2500 CFP. These tariffs include breakfast and airport transfers. There's a small terrace overlooking the airport with Moorea as a backdrop.

Chez Lola *(☎/fax 81 91 75)* is also near the airport but on the inland side of the RDO, high up in the Saint-Hilaire district. Singles/doubles in an airy *fare* with fan and shared bathroom cost 4000/5500 CFP including breakfast and airport transfers. It's quiet and one of the two rooms has a view of Moorea. The Saint-Hilaire le truck passes close by about every hour during the week but it's easier to ask the owners to take you down to the main road, about 1.5km away.

Tahiti Airport Lodge *(☎ 82 23 68, fax 82 25 00)* overlooks the airport, about 100m from the coast road. Rooms cost 3500/5500 CFP with shared bathroom; doubles with attached bathroom cost 7500 CFP. Airport transfers and breakfast are included and dinner costs 1000 CFP. This is a pleasant place, providing the owner is in a good mood.

Vaimana Fare *(☎/fax 48 07 17, fax 43 87 27)* is east of the city, at PK10.5 in Mahina. It has two self-contained units at 6500 CFP per day, dropping to 6000 CFP after one week. By the month they cost 90,000 CFP.

Chez Myrna *(☎/fax 42 64 11)*, 500m from Matavai Hotel in the Tipaerui Valley, is the only budget place with really acceptable standards. In the German owner's house there are two well kept rooms for 3500/4500 CFP a single/double including breakfast. There's a two night minimum stay and weekly rates of 23,400/28,500 CFP. Airport transfers cost 1000 CFP each way and credit cards are not accepted. There's no sign for the guesthouse.

Mid-Range *Tahiti Country Club (☎ 42 60 40, 43 08 29, fax 41 09 28)* is about 6km west of Papeete, just beyond the Beachcomber Parkroyal Hotel. It's on the slopes of Punaauia Hill, away from the water, but offers superb views of Moorea. The 40 aircon rooms with bathroom and TV cost 8640 CFP single or double. The rooms are very straightforward, lined up in two-storey motel-style blocks. The recently renovated rooms are more attractive. There's a bar, swimming pool and tennis courts.

Matavai Hotel *(☎ 42 67 67, fax 42 36 90)* is towards the western edge of the city, on Route de Tipaerui. It's nondescript, functional and modern and rooms cost 12,000/16,000 CFP. Reductions are available for longer stays. There's a restaurant, bar, swimming pool and tennis courts.

Royal Tahitien Hotel *(☎ 42 81 13, fax 41 05 35)* is about 3km east of the centre in Pirae. Nicely situated on a reasonable stretch of black-sand beach, this modern hotel has 40 very motel-like rooms and a pleasantly grassy garden setting. There's a waterfront restaurant with a deck looking out over the beach. The nightly cost is 10,800 CFP. Local musicians perform on Friday and Saturday evenings and le trucks stop less than 100m from the hotel.

Top End The luxury hotels are west of Papeete and they have all the amenities you'd expect. Sited directly beside the lagoon, their small beaches are artificial but quite authentic-looking and there are beautiful views of Moorea. Several times a week these hotels offer Polynesian dance performances by the best dance groups on the island, as well as *tamaaraa* (feasts from a traditional Tahitian oven) on the weekends. Naturally these establishments accept every credit card you'd care to think of.

Outrigger Hotel Tahiti *(☎ 86 48 48, fax 86 48 40, email reservation@outrigger.pf)* is beside the lagoon at PK2. Opened in late 1999, it combines traditional and modern elements and has 200 rooms from 29,700 CFP to 70,200 CFP. The restaurant is built out over the lagoon.

Tahiti Beachcomber Parkroyal Hotel (☎ 86 51 10, fax 86 51 30, email tahiti@ parkroyal.pf) is a stone's throw from the end of Faaa airport's runway. Right on the waterfront, it has 269 rooms including 17 motu bungalows (built around an islet) and 15 lagoon bungalows (over-water). One of the swimming pools has a sand beach and swim-up bar, part of the superb Lotus Restaurant, where you can sip a cocktail in the water. The other restaurants are the relaxed Tiare Restaurant and the intimate Hibiscus Restaurant. Rates vary from 31,664 CFP for the cheapest garden-view rooms to 52,380 CFP for the lagoon bungalows. Half-board (breakfast and dinner) adds 5900 CFP. There are washing machines and driers for guests' use.

Sofitel Maeva Beach Hotel (☎ 42 80 42, fax 43 84 70) is on Maeva Beach, one of the best beaches close to Papeete. It's beside the roundabout where the RDO from the city meets the coast road. The Outumaoro le truck terminus is immediately beyond the roundabout, on the inland side of the road. This hotel is older and more traditionally hotel-like and doesn't have over-water bungalows or other more-recent innovations. Some of the 224 rooms are definitely looking a little worn. Tariffs range from 21,600 CFP to 43,200 CFP, breakfast costs 1900 CFP, half-board adds 5800 CFP. The hotel has Restaurant Bougainville and the Sakura.

Le Méridien (☎ 47 07 07, fax 47 07 28, email sales@lemeridien-tahiti.com) is Tahiti's most luxurious hotel. Opened in 1998, it's beside the lagoon at PK15 in Punaauia, not far from the Museum of Tahiti. Its 138 rooms and suites occupy several buildings around a magnificent sand-bottomed swimming pool facing the lagoon. Costs range from 34,020 CFP, via 52,164 CFP for the very sumptuous over-water bungalows, right up to 112,266 CFP for the largest suite. Half-board adds 7000 CFP. There's a large room for conferences and the gastronomic La Plantation and beachside Fare Te Moana restaurants.

PLACES TO EAT
Papeete has many quality restaurants serving a wide variety of cuisines. French, Chinese,

Polynesian, Italian and Vietnamese are all represented. You can try anything from *mahi mahi* (dolphin fish - nothing to do with dolphins) with Tahaa vanilla sauce, to chow mein or a pizza from a wood-fired oven, complemented by reasonably priced French wines. After a stay on the outer islands you'll definitely appreciate the comfort and quality to be found in Papeete.

Establishments range from classic restaurants and snack bars to Tahiti's famed roulottes and the luxury-hotel restaurants. Sometimes the price difference between a snack bar and a restaurant is minimal.

Sunday is the closing day for most places and finding a meal can be difficult. For breakfast go to one of the numerous snack bars where, from 5.30 am, you can get coffee, baguettes and croissants.

Restaurants
Italian *Lou Pescadou* (☎ 43 74 26), on Rue Anne-Marie Javouhey, is a real Papeete institution. It's exuberant owner Mario, usually presiding over the pizza oven at the front, is certainly part of its fame. It's a block back from Rue du Général de Gaulle, near the cathedral. Pizzas cost from 600 CFP to 980 CFP, pasta dishes from 750 CFP to 950 CFP, other meals around 1700 CFP and the dish of the day costs 1600 CFP. It's open Monday to Saturday until 11 pm and credit cards are accepted.

La Squadra (☎ 41 32 14) is right behind Lou Pescadou on Passage Cardella and offers standard Italian dishes such as pasta from 950 CFP to 1400 CFP, salads around 1100 CFP and main courses from 1000 CFP to 1600 CFP. It's closed Monday and Tuesday evenings and all day Sunday. Credit cards are accepted.

At *L'Api'zzeria* (☎ 42 98 30) the apostrophes seem to have gone walkabout. It's just west of the Paofai Church and you can approach it from either Rue du Commandant Destremeau or from Blvd Pomare. This is a popular pizzeria with a pleasant open-air dining area just across the road from the waterfront. Pizzas cost from 700 CFP to 1300 CFP, pasta dishes from 950 CFP to 1950 CFP, salads from 790 CFP to

1930 CFP, main courses from 1900 CFP to 2180 CFP and the dish of the day from 1780 CFP to 1850 CFP. The winelist starts from 1870 CFP. It's open Monday to Saturday. Takeaway pizzas are available and credit cards are accepted.

Don Camillo (☎ *42 80 96)* on Rue des Écoles is simple and opens out on to the street. It's open daily except for Sunday lunch.

Asian *Le Mandarin* (☎ *42 16 33)* on Rue des Écoles, just round the corner from the hotel of the same name, offers guaranteed disorientation. Wood panelling, hanging tapestries and lacquerwork lend a Far-Eastern air to this venerable institution, which has hardly acquired a wrinkle (well, very few) since its opening in 1964. The chef is from Hong Kong and manages all the flavours of China in no less than 180 dishes (some vegetarian). There are also set meals for at least two people from 2300 CFP to 3350 CFP and a comprehensive winelist; Bordeaux start at 1470 CFP and go all the way up to Château Pétrus. There's live music on Friday and Saturday evenings, it's open daily for lunch and dinner and credit cards are accepted.

Le Dragon d'Or (☎ *42 96 12)*, next to Hôtel Le Mandarin on Rue Colette, is another classic Chinese restaurant. With bamboo and pandanus panelling, it looks less like a Chinese establishment than a big, traditional Polynesian *fare*. It's pleasantly intimate, almost romantic. Dishes cost from 1080 CFP to 1420 CFP and there are specials like Chinese-style *poisson cru* (raw fish) for 1080 CFP and salted shrimps sauteed in garlic for 2180 CFP. It's open Tuesday to Sunday and credit cards are accepted.

Restaurant Cathay (☎ *42 99 67)* and *Restaurant Tehoa* (☎ *42 99 27)*, almost side by side on Rue du Maréchal Foch near the market, turn out basic, cheap Chinese dishes. The Tehoa is as bare and spartan as a canteen but the serves are large, the prices (700 CFP to 900 CFP) are low and you can eat there or take away. Neither takes credit cards and both are open Monday to Saturday.

Pitate Mamao (☎ *42 86 94)* is at the start of Ave Georges Clémenceau, just after the Pont de l'Est traffic roundabout. The menu

is predominantly Chinese but has French and Polynesian specialities. Soups cost 810 CFP to 1060 CFP, main courses 1100 CFP to 2000 CFP. The Friday lunchtime special is piglet in coconut milk (1920 CFP). It's open Monday to Saturday and credit cards are accepted.

Restaurant Saïgonnaise (☎ *42 05 35)*, on Ave du Prince Hinoi, is the only Vietnamese restaurant in Papeete, which is a pity, as it's excellent. Spring rolls cost 1350 CFP, pork with caramel is 2450 CFP and Vietnamese omelette costs 1370 CFP. It's open Monday to Saturday and credit cards are accepted.

Other Cuisines Papeete has an excellent range of restaurants.

Budget *Le Marrakech* (☎ *42 80 00)* is a Moroccan restaurant on the Pont de l'Est. It has a variety of couscous and tajine dishes for 1325 CFP to 1960 CFP, plus other North African specialities. It's open Monday to Saturday. Credit cards are accepted.

On the Blvd Pomare side of the Vaima Centre, *Jack Lobster* (☎ *42 50 58)* is American-style, with red-and-white check tablecloths, background music and, of course, its predominantly Tex-Mex-and-grilles menu. Fajitas cost from 1600 CFP to 1990 CFP, the American sandwich 1300 CFP, T-bone steak 2400 CFP, chicken *chimichangas* (tortillas, chicken and sausage with rice) 1700 CFP. It's open weekdays for lunch and dinner, Saturday for dinner only. Credit cards are accepted.

Sushi Bar is directly above Jack Lobster. This rather chic Japanese place is a 'rotating sushi bar', where you sit at a bar and small dishes of sushi float by on little pirogues, under the eye of traditionally-clad servers. Each small plate costs 250 CFP to 450 CFP. It's open Monday to Thursday for lunch, Friday and Saturday for lunch and dinner.

Le Gallieni (☎ *42 01 29)* is in the seafront Royal Papeete on Blvd Pomare. It's got a delightfully antiquated setting and dishes from 1400 CFP to 2280 CFP. The house speciality is prime rib from 2000 CFP. It's open daily.

Café des Negociants (☎ 48 08 48) is on Rue du Commandant Jean Gilbert, a narrow street leading back from Blvd Pomare to Rue Leboucher. It's a charming place with a bar/restaurant and a mezzanine level for those seeking a little privacy. Dishes cost from around 2000 CFP and can vary from couscous to moussaka. A light breakfast costs 680 CFP. It's open weekdays from breakfast to 10.30 pm, Sunday just for dinner. Credit cards are accepted.

Restaurant-École du Lycée Hôtelier du Taaone (☎ 45 23 71) is a hotel and restaurant training-school where you can try dishes prepared and served by the students, under the eye of their teachers. There's a set tourist meal at 1800 CFP or you can order from the menu for 1000 CFP to 1500 CFP. It's in Pirae (take a Pirae le truck) and is open only during school term; weekdays for lunch, Tuesday, Thursday and Friday for dinner. Bookings are essential and payment must be cash.

Mid-Range & Top End *L'O à la Bouche* (☎ 45 29 76), right in the centre of town on Passage Cardella, very stylish (and very yellow and very blue) and not exceptionally expensive. The menu has a modern French flavour with dishes like a pan-fried fillet of *carangue* (trevally) at 2200 CFP, magret of duck with honey for 2500 CFP, salmon of the gods (*salmon de dieu*; a salmon-like ocean fish) with a melon-and-citrus coulis for 2300 CFP (delicious!) and sashimi at 1550 CFP. The desserts are inventive (around 800 CFP) and the extensive winelist starts at 1750 CFP a bottle. It's closed Saturday lunchtime and Sunday evening. Credit cards are accepted.

Morrison's Café (☎ 42 78 61), atop the Vaima Centre, takes its name from Jim (not Van) as is abundantly clear as soon as you step inside the restaurant. Featuring rooftop and open-air sections, Morrison's anonymous entrance and discreet signs all go to prove it's one of Papeete's trendier spots and *branché* ('connected', as the French say). The boss, Pascha, is very 60s and keeps things lively with rock or blues performers several times a week, and various

theme evenings. There's a view of the harbour from the open section. Main courses cost 1900 CFP to 2800 CFP and there's a good winelist (from 2100 CFP). It's closed Saturday lunchtime and all day Sunday but open until midnight on Friday and Saturday. Credit cards are accepted.

L'Excuse (☎ 53 13 25) is a small establishment on Rue du Maréchal Foch, near the junction with Rue Cardella. The menu is principally French (2000 CFP to 2500 CFP) with specialities at 1500 CFP to 2000 CFP. Sometimes there are more-daring dishes, such as ostrich or kangaroo, at 2700 CFP to 3000 CFP. It's open Monday to Saturday and credit cards are accepted.

Close to the Pont de l'Est roundabout, *La Petit Auberge* (☎ 42 86 13) welcomes French-cuisine enthusiasts in a small room of classic decor. The specialities are from southwestern France and include confit of duck (2700 CFP) but also couscous on Tuesday (1850 CFP) and *choucroute* (cabbage with pork, potatoes and sauerkraut) on Thursday (2350 CFP). Seafood dishes start at 1650 CFP. It's closed Saturday lunchtime and all day Sunday. Credit cards are accepted.

Le Manuia (☎ 43 94 92) is on Rue Edouard Ahnne, close to Rue du Maréchal Foch. It's a well respected place with an intimate and sober setting and a gracious welcome to customers. The cuisine is traditional French with specialities from the south-west. Main courses cost from 2000 CFP to 2500 CFP and there's a good winelist (from 2000 CFP). It's open for lunch and dinner Tuesday to Saturday. Credit cards are accepted.

Around Ave Bruat, west of the town centre, there are two more expensive and very French-influenced restaurants aimed at business expense-accounts and officials from the nearby government offices. *Le Manava Restaurant* (☎ 42 02 91) is on Ave Bruat on the corner of Rue du Commandant Destremeau and offers poisson cru with coconut milk for 1000 CFP, escalope of mahi mahi for 1545 CFP and various French specialities from 900 CFP to 2200 CFP. With its patio and open latticework, it's pleasant but there's lots of traffic noise. It's closed

Saturday evenings and all day Sunday. Credit cards are accepted.

Moana Iti Restaurant (☎ 42 65 24), on Blvd Pomare just west of Ave Bruat, is a long-term survivor with classic French dishes at 1500 CFP to 2500 CFP. It's also closed on Sunday.

La Corbeille d'Eau (☎ 43 77 14) is a small, anonymous and modern restaurant a little farther west on waterfront Blvd Pomare. It regularly wins accolades as the home of fine French dining in Papeete. Rugs, carpets and paintings by local artists all add to the intimate setting. Starters cost from 1600 CFP to 2800 CFP, main courses from 2200 CFP to 3200 CFP and there are excellent desserts. There are some excellent bottles on the winelist. It's open weekdays for lunch and dinner, Saturday for dinner only. The restaurant's name translates as 'the basket of water', which is what 'Papeete' means in Tahitian. Credit cards are accepted.

Le Lion d'Or (☎ 42 66 50) is by the post office just back from Ave du Prince Hinoi at the corner with Rue Bernière-in Pirae to the east of the centre. Its relatively isolated location makes this strictly a restaurant for people with wheels. Seafood is the speciality. It's closed on Sunday and credit cards are accepted.

Le Belvédère (☎ 42 73 44) is perched 600m above the city, at the start of the walking track to the top of Mt Aorai (see the Outdoor Activities chapter for details of this walk). The views over Papeete are fantastic, particularly at sunset. Fondues are the speciality – seafood (4200 CFP), Savoyarde (2300 CFP) and Bourguignon (2300 CFP). Le Belvédère provides free transport from Papeete hotels at 11.45 am, 4.30 and 7 pm. If you drive, take the first right turn after the Hamuta Total fuel station. The 7km road to the restaurant is steep, winding and rugged towards the top. It's open for lunch and dinner Wednesday to Sunday.

Cafés & Snack Bars

Central Papeete There are several basic snack bars in Papeete Market; those on the ground floor serve sandwiches and take-away meals (600 CFP). There is nowhere to sit down.

Close to the post office, **Restaurant du Parc Bougainville** is in the pleasant, shady Bougainville Park. It's open daily from about 5 am to 10 pm and serves various local, Chinese and Polynesian specialties. The cool tuna sashimi costs 1020 CFP, an omelette 670 CFP to 815 CFP, chow mein 820 CFP and tuna with coconut-milk curry 930 CFP. Friday lunchtime there's a *maa Tahiti* (Tahitian buffet) for 1700 CFP. Various snacks are served at all hours and credit cards are accepted.

Le Janoko in the Fare Tony Centre offers a variety of dishes from 1300 CFP to 1800 CFP and snacks for about 900 CFP. Hinano beer on tap *(pression)* costs 290 CFP, fresh fruit juices from 450 CFP. **Down Town** is a low-priced snack bar in the same centre.

Right in the centre of town (in fact it defines the town centre), the Vaima Centre has a number of excellent cheap-eats and more-expensive restaurants. The ever-popular **Le Rétro** (☎ 42 86 83) is Papeete's number one place to see and be seen. Looking out on busy Blvd Pomare, Le Rétro plays multiple parts – see Pubs & Bars under Entertainment later in this chapter. The open-air part on Blvd Pomare serves reasonably priced snacks and ice creams as well as beer (750 CFP for a half-litre jug of Hinano) and cocktails (900 CFP for a maitai).

Rétro Saint-Germain is the restaurant part, serving classic French dishes. It's closed on Sunday afternoon. Adjoining it is Le Rétro's piano-bar/discotheque, a very 'with it' place offering everything from techno to zouk.

L'Oasis (☎ 45 45 01) is on the Rue du Général de Gaulle side of the Vaima Centre, facing the cathedral. A very popular spot for breakfast and lunch, it has excellent croissants and *pain aux raisins* to start the day and terrific French-bread sandwiches from 300 CFP at lunchtime. You can get salads, burgers from 470 CFP, a dish of the day for 1250 CFP and fresh fruit juices for 420 CFP. There's an air-con room upstairs. L'Oasis is open daily until about 6 pm but is closed every Sunday.

TAHITI

Le Motu has a great selection of Tahiti's major meal-time bargains, French-bread sandwiches *(casses-croûtes)*. It's on the Rue du Général de Gaulle side of the Vaima Centre, on the corner of Rue Lagarde. There are tables you can stand at to eat a 200 CFP to 450 CFP sandwich, a 150 CFP or 220 CFP ice-cream cone, a 200 CFP to 500 CFP crêpe or a 400 CFP fruit juice. L'Oasis also closes around 6 pm.

Across Rue Lagarde from Le Motu is *Au Rendez-Vous des Amis*. Always jumping, it's ideal for a 650 CFP breakfast or a quick, cheap meal. There are salads (500 CFP to 900 CFP), omelettes and burgers (600 CFP to 900 CFP) and grills (900 CFP to 1700 CFP), which you can wash down with a Hinano (350 CFP) or fresh orange juice (450 CFP). Credit cards are accepted.

Café de la Gare (☎ 42 75 95) is on Rue du Général de Gaulle, across the road from McDonalds. It looks authentically Parisian, unusual in the tropics, and is open Monday to Saturday, 7 am to 1 am. It's a little pricey, with salads from 1290 CFP to 1600 CFP, steak tartare at 1520 CFP, pastas from 1270 CFP to 1570 CFP, beer at 400 CFP and wine by the glass from 500 CFP.

On pedestrianised Rue Lagarde, beside the Vaima Centre, *Snack Hollywood* is open daily and serves simple snacks and light meals at reasonable prices, such as chicken and French fries for 750 CFP.

Cross Blvd Pomare from the Vaima Centre to *Aux Delices Chez Louisette*, a genteel little patisserie and ice-cream place on Passage Cardella. It's good for an early morning pain au raisin and coffee.

Other snack-bars are aimed at office workers. The self-service *Polyself Cafeteria*, on Rue Paul Gauguin, is excellent value. You pay only 690 CFP for a generous chow mein, 860 CFP for sashimi. It's open weekdays for lunch only.

Waikiki is a Chinese restaurant on Rue Albert Leboucher with a varied menu and low prices (800 CFP to 1000 CFP per dish). It's closed Monday evening and Sunday lunchtime.

L'Épi d'Or is in front of the station for le trucks to the west coast. Pizzas cost 850 CFP to 1000 CFP, salads 800 CFP to 1300 CFP, burgers 750 CFP to 950 CFP and panini about 500 CFP. Weekdays it's open until 5.30 pm, Saturday until 2 pm.

On Blvd Pomare, shortly after the Hotel Prince Hinoi, *3 Brasseurs* is always crowded. This restaurant-style establishment brews its own beer, a major contribution to its success. The house choucroute costs 1900 CFP, the tarte flambé 850 CFP. There's a set meal of starter, dish of the day and a beer for 1600 CFP. It's open daily from 9 am to midnight and credit cards are accepted. Next door is the minuscule *Snack Buffoon*, ideal for a takeaway meal and open daily until midnight.

Right on the Pont de l'Est roundabout is *Tikisoftc@fé*, which has various reasonably priced snacks and a young and trendy setting. Panini costs 550 CFP, the dish of the day about 1200 CFP and salad 900 CFP. A fenced-in area spills on to the sidewalk. It's open from 7 am to 11 pm weekdays, until 1 am on the weekend.

Outer Papeete *Hilaire – pâtissier, confisseur, glacier* (☎ 43 65 85) is a *salon de thé* on the corner of Ave du Commandant Chessé and Ave Georges Clémenceau, next to the Chinese temple. It's frequented by people who work locally because hot chocolate costs 260 CFP, an almond croissant 210 CFP and a pain au chocolat 130 CFP. A cheese omelette costs 640 CFP, fruit juices (pineapple, grapefruit or watermelon) are 530 CFP and ice cream is 480 CFP a cup. The pastries are excellent but the characterless décor is not so special. It's open Monday to Saturday from 5 am to 5.30 pm (Saturday it closes from noon to 3 pm) and Sunday from 5 to 10 am.

Nearby, at the intersection of Ave du Prince-Hinoi and Ave du Commandant Chessé, *Pâtisserie-Salon de thé Moutet* is an invitation to gluttony. A variety of simple lunch plates cost less than 1000 CFP. Ice creams, pastries and sandwiches are sold at moderate prices and it's open Monday to Saturday to 6 pm.

Despite the arrival of McDonalds in the city centre, *Snack Lagon Bleu*, on the bypass road to Patutoa, 100m from the crossroads with Ave du Commandant Chessé, still cuts it. Tourists are rare; it's usually port zone employees who turn up here for lunch or dinner, sitting at the counter consuming great burgers or a surprisingly good chicken and pineapple for 422 CFP, all of it turned out by several bustling *mamas*. Small/large fruit juices cost from 248/618 CFP.

At the corner of Blvd Pomare and Ave Bruat, *New Port* offers simple Polynesian and French food at reasonable prices under a shady terrace. It's open Monday to Saturday until 6 pm.

Snack Tiki Peue (☎ *43 23 57)*, on the seafront side of Blvd Pomare near New Port, is rather discreet but is panelled like a luxury train compartment. Not many people can squeeze inside to enjoy poisson cru in coconut milk for 1040 CFP, sashimi for 1500 CFP or a cheeseburger with the trimmings for 1350 CFP. A half-litre of Hinano costs 500

CFP. Its unusual opening hours are Wednesday to Sunday from 7.30 pm until 1 am.

Self-Catering

Papeete has several large, well stocked supermarkets. They're generally open Monday to Saturday from 7 am to 7.30 or 8 pm, and Sunday morning. If you're restocking a yacht for the next leg of a Pacific cruise, these are the places to go. They include *Supermarket Champion*, Rue du Commandant Destremeau, close to the Paofai Church; *Hypermarkets Continent*, at PK4.5 in Arue (Arue le truck) and in the Moana Nui Commercial Centre at PK8.3 in Punaauia (Outumaoro le truck); *Tropic Import*, next to the Pater Stadium, Pirae; and *Cash & Carry*, PK3 in Faaa.

ENTERTAINMENT
Pubs & Bars

On a balmy tropical evening the first question is where to go for a cold Hinano or a

---

Les Roulottes

Good food, good fun and the best prices in town – that's *les roulottes*, quayside in central Papeete every evening until around 1 am. Roulottes are vans-turned mobile-diners. Flaps lowered on each side become the counters, stools are set up for the customers and staff inside the vans prepare the food. They're arrayed all around the car park area by the waterfront and people come here to eat or just grab some late-night sustenance. They're a colourful Polynesian institution and something every visitor should try.

MANOLO MYLONAS

What do the roulottes turn out? Well, pretty much everything you'll find at regular restaurants around town but at lower prices. Typically, a roulotte meal will be in the 800 CFP to 1000 CFP bracket. Roulottes' names tell what they're all about; the cast may change from night to night but you may come across mobile pizzerias (would you believe a wood-fired pizza-oven on wheels?) like *Vesuvio Pizza, Pizza Napoli* and even *Pizza Hut* (should that be Pizza Van?). There's steak and chips at *Chez Roger*, and steak and pizza at *Le Romain*, complete with Roman columns to support the van's side-flaps and a cut-out figure of a centurion. Of course there are plenty of Chinese roulottes *(spécialités chinoises)* like *Chez Michou, Chez Lili, Pacifique Sud Roulotte* and *Hong Kong* (a specialist in chow mein).

You can finish up with a crêpe or *gaufre* (waffle) for 250 CFP to 600 CFP at mobile crêperies like *Crêperie du Port, Crêperie Tiki, La Boule Rouge* and *Suzy Gaufre*. A fresh-fruit roulotte would be a nice idea, but otherwise the only thing the roulottes can't provide is alcohol. But the Blvd Pomare bars are just across the road.

well poured maitai. For further information on the following suggestions, see Central Papeete under Cafés & Snacks in the Places to Eat section earlier in this chapter. *Le Rétro* (☎ 42 86 83) fits the bill for most things and it'll do for a watch-the-world-go-by cold beer as well. It's on the waterfront side of the Vaima Centre and a 250ml draught Hinano will set you back 430 CFP, the perfect complement to a Tahitian sunset. Imported beers are 600 CFP to 1200 CFP, cocktails 750 CFP to 1000 CFP (900 CFP for that maitai).

For a real French-bar experience go back a block from the waterfront to *Café de la Gare* (☎ 42 75 95) on Rue du Général de Gaulle. It looks like it was beamed down straight from the centre of Paris, complete with a full contingent of chain Gauloise-smokers (if you're unlucky). There's beer for 380 CFP. *Tikisoftc@fe* (☎ 77 44 34, 88 93 88) is Papeete's only cybercafé, run by a friendly young team of *popaa* (westerners) who substitute rock and blues for the usual Polynesian background music. Try a fresh fruit juice for 450 CFP, a Hinano for 400 CFP, a maitai for 750 CFP and check your email at the same time.

Several places along the busy and noisy nightlife strip of Blvd Pomare are also good spots for a contemplative beer at any time, particularly the popular *3 Brasseurs* with its excellent boutique-brewery beer on tap for 400 CFP and cocktails at 850 CFP.

Café des Negociants, just off Blvd Pomare, is an ideal place to start the evening and has about 50 beers from 385 CFP and a cocktail list at 850 CFP. Jazz groups play from time to time. See Restaurants in the Places to Eat section earlier in this chapter for more information on this venue and on *Morrison's Café*, upstairs in the Vaima Centre, a popular and trendy spot to drink, with rock and blues groups playing several times a week.

The bar/discos on Rue des Écoles (see Nightclubs & Discos later in this section for details) can be interesting although most of them are rather charmless hangouts for the local military. For some local ambience try *Royal Kikiriri*, on Rue Colette, which becomes a disco later in the evening.

Of course, *Outrigger Tahiti*, *Beach-comber Parkroyal*, *Sofitel Maeva Beach* and *Méridien* all have a variety of bars – wonderful places to enjoy the ocean breezes and nibble the free peanuts.

Nightclubs & Discos

After a stay on other islands, where nightlife is frankly non-existent, Papeete could almost pass for a city of wild abandon ... although actually it only really gets busy on the weekend. The waterfront Blvd Pomare is the main centre, with international-style discos and more-local dancing and nightclub activity. From the Tahitian waltz to techno, it's all here.

Some establishments open only at the weekend, when you will need your elbows to force an entrance and they typically close around 3 or 4 am.

To the rear of the Vaima Centre, next to the Concorde Cinema, *Scorpio* probably has the most eclectic clientele – popaa gays, neat-as-a-pin *rae rae* (transvestite prostitutes) and heteros who come to dance to music ranging from techno to house. There's a cabaret show on Thursday; entry is 1500 CFP including a drink.

Piano Bar, a few steps back from the waterfront, is one of Papeete's most famous institutions. Rue des Écoles (Street of the Schools) is certainly a place to get an education. At night any woman along this street who looks like far too much of a woman to really be one probably isn't and the Piano Bar isn't a place for prudes. Although the rae rae officiate in this quarter and it's popular with gays, the clientele ranges from lovelorn sailors to passing tourists – the whole world seems to come and go from the Piano Bar. The music (techno, dance, local) isn't so important as the general atmosphere. The rae rae do a show on Friday and Saturday nights towards 1 am. It's open Monday to Saturday; entry is 1500 CFP on weekends including a drink.

Manhattan, in the Hotel Kon Tiki Pacific, is open nightly and is a favourite with local military, who come to dance to disco and techno. On Friday and Saturday nights entry for men is 1500 CFP including a drink. *Zizou* is on the adjacent street corner and offers the same type of music for the same style of clientele. It's also open every night, and on Friday and Saturday entry for men is 1000 CFP, including a drink.

Le Paradise, on Blvd Pomare next to Kon Tiki Pacific, is the centre for traditional and tropical dancing. The Tahitian-style waltz, fox trot, zouk, reggae, Caribbean-African soukouss and the twist are what's done here. It attracts a slightly older crowd, predominantly popaa but there are also Tahitians, *demis* (Tahitian-Europeans) and Chinese. There's even a room for karaoke. Fruit juices are 1000 CFP, cocktails 2000 CFP. It's open daily from 10 pm to 3 am and entry is free.

If you want a more *kaina* (local) atmosphere head to *La Cave*, beside the Hotel Royal Papeete on Blvd Pomare. The attraction is the music – the Royal Band plays a local repertoire including the Tahitian waltz, zouk and fox trot. It really gets going after midnight and the plain decor is there to remind tourists that dancing is the pleasure, the setting secondary. It's open Friday and Saturday night and entry, for men only, is 1500 CFP including a drink.

Next door, *Tamure Hut* offers the same music and style from Thursday to Saturday night; entry is 500 CFP. *Royal Kikiriri* on Rue Colette, between Rue des Écoles and Ave du Prince Hinoi is in similar style. It's the main centre for Tahitian dancing, it's often crowded on the weekends and the Trio Royal Kikiriri make this their home. It's open Wednesday to Sunday and on Friday and Saturday nights there's a 1000 CFP entry charge, including a drink.

Le Kriptone Palace, on Ave Bruat next to the New Port, is the favourite hangout of the town's wealthy youngsters, especially demis and Chinese. House and techno are the music of choice and it's open Thursday to Saturday; entry for men is 2000 CFP, with a drink. *Club 106* is on the waterfront to the east of the centre, shortly after Ave Bruat and mingles music styles from disco to rock and techno. The clientele is older than at the Kriptone Palace and is mainly popaa. It's open

Thursday to Saturday and entry for men is 1500 CFP, including a drink.

Cinemas

Papeete has a number of cinemas where films are shown either dubbed in French or with subtitles. The letters VO (*version originale*) indicate that if the film started life in English it will still be in English, with subtitles rather than dubbed audio. Admission is usually 830 CFP. Cinemas include *Concorde (☎ 42 63 60)*, on Rue du Général de Gaulle in the Vaima Centre; *Hollywood (☎ 42 65 79)*, in the Fare Tony Centre on Rue Lagarde; *Liberty (☎ 42 08 20)*, on Rue du Maréchal Foch; and *Mamao Palace (☎ 42 54 69)*, on Ave du Commandant Chessé.

Dance Performances

Tahiti offers the opportunity to see the best Polynesian dance performances, with dance groups like O Tahiti E, Ballets de Tahiti, Heikura Nui and Te Maeva, which appear several times a week in the big hotels and at certain restaurants. Don't miss the opportunity to see these excellent performers in their extravagant costumes perform the *otea* and the furious and sensual *aparima* (see the 'Ori Tahiti – Tahitian Dance' special section for more information). The performances generally take place around 8 pm and last about 45 minutes. They're accompanied by a 5000 CFP to 6500 CFP dinner buffet in the big hotels, although a drink at the bar will sometimes get you in. Check with the hotel reception desks at *Tahiti Outrigger*, *Beachcomber Parkroyal*, *Sofitel Maeva Beach* or *Méridien* about their programs and entrance policies.

Captain Bligh Restaurant (☎ 43 62 90) at the Lagoonarium at PK11 in Punaauia also has an island-night performance on Friday and Saturday nights for only 4200 CFP. The decor is simple but local and the terrace is right on the lagoon.

SHOPPING

Although Tahiti is not the centre for any particular crafts, you can buy products from all over French Polynesia.

Handicrafts

Te Fare Tauhiti Nui (Territorial Cultural Centre), at the western end of Blvd Pomare, has regular exhibitions of traditional and contemporary Polynesian art. Just beyond the centre, before the footbridge, the Tipaerui Craft Centre displays local crafts including cloths, sculptures, basketwork and mother-of-pearl work. They're produced by craft workers from all over Polynesia who now live on Tahiti. It's open daily from 7 am to 5 pm.

A variety of handicrafts are on sale at Papeete Market, particularly upstairs, where you will find sculptures, *monoi* (fragrant oil) products, pareu, clothes, shells, engraved mother-of-pearl, jewellery and basketwork.

There are numerous craft and souvenir shops along Blvd Pomare and Rue du Général de Gaulle and in the Vaima and Fare Tony centres. Manuia Curios (☎ 42 04 94), at Place Notre Dame, right beside the cathedral and Ganesha (☎ 43 04 18), in the Vaima Centre, have craftwork from French Polynesia and from other Pacific centres.

Art Galleries

Papeete has a number of art galleries showing the work of locally resident and Polynesian artists, including Galerie des Tropiques (☎ 41 05 00), at the corner of Blvd Pomare and Rue Cook; Gallery Matamua (☎ 41 34 95), in front of the Quai d'Honneur on Blvd Pomare; Galerie Reva Reva (☎ 43 32 67), 36 Rue Lagarde, near the Vaima Centre; and Gallery Winkler (☎ 42 81 77), 17 Rue Jeanne-d'Arc, close to the cathedral.

Pearls

There are so many jewellery shops and pearl specialists in Papeete that you have to be careful not to trip over them.

GETTING THERE & AWAY

The overwhelming majority of visitors to French Polynesia arrive at Papeete, the colony's flight and shipping hub.

Air

Faaa airport (correctly Fa'aa and pronounced 'fa-ha-ha') is the aviation centre for all of French Polynesia. International flights all come here and most of the Air Tahiti domestic flights fan out from Faaa. Inter-island flights in each group hop from one island to the next but many connections between island groups are via Papeete.

International check-in desks are at the east end of the terminal. Air Tahiti's domestic check-in is at the west end, but Air Moorea is in a separate small terminal slightly to the east of the main terminal.

For international flights to/from Tahiti, see the Getting There & Away chapter. For general information about air travel within French Polynesia see the Getting Around chapter; for connections to/from an island group or an individual island, see the relevant chapter or section. For flight information, call ☎ 82 60 61.

Airlines In Papeete, the main Air Tahiti office (☎ 86 40 00, 86 42 42, or on weekends ☎ 86 41 84, 86 41 95) is upstairs in the Fare Tony Centre. It's open weekdays from 7.30 am to noon and 1 to 4.30 pm. There's also an Air Tahiti office in the domestic area of the airport, open daily from 5 am to 5.30 pm.

Other airline offices in Papeete include:

Aircalin (Air Calédonie International)
(☎ 85 09 04) Faaa airport
Air France
(☎ 42 22 22) Blvd Pomare near Ave Bruat
Air New Zealand
(☎ 54 07 47) Vaima Centre, Blvd Pomare
Air Moorea
(☎ 86 41 41) Faaa airport
Air Tahiti Nui
(☎ 45 55 55) Immeuble Dexter, Pont de l'Est
AOM (Air Outre Mer)
(☎ 54 25 25) Rue des Remparts
Corsair
(☎ 42 28 28) junction of Blvd Pomare and Rue Clappier
Hawaiian Airlines
(☎ 42 15 00) Vaima Centre, Blvd Pomare
LanChile
(☎ 42 64 55, or at the airport prior to flights ☎ 82 64 57) Vaima Centre, Blvd Pomare
Qantas
(☎ 43 06 65, or at the airport prior to flights ☎ 83 90 90) Vaima Centre, Blvd Pomare

Charter Operators Charter operators and helicopter services on Tahiti include:

Air Archipels
  (☎ 81 30 30) Faaa airport
Héli Pacific
  (☎ 85 68 00) Faaa airport
Héli-Inter Polynésie
  (☎ 81 99 00) Faaa airport
Wan Air
  (☎ 83 57 36) Faaa airport

Sea

Moorea ferries and the *Ono-Ono* moor at the ferry quay at the north-east end of Blvd Pomare. Cruise ships and other interesting visitors moor at the Quai d'Honneur close to the tourist office and capitainerie. The numerous cargo ships to the different archipelagos work from the Motu Uta port zone, to the north of the city (le truck route 3 from the mairie).

See the Getting Around chapter for general information on inter-island shipping and the individual island chapters or sections for specific information on travel to/from those destinations.

GETTING AROUND
To/From the Airport

Le Truck Any le truck going towards town from the airport (east bound, or to your left as you leave the airport terminal) will take you straight into the centre of Papeete in about 15 minutes for a flat fare of 120 CFP during the day or 200 CFP at night (and an extra 100 CFP for your baggage). Unfortunately, le trucks tend to disappear after 10 pm and, although you should be able to find one until about 1 am, catching one after then is not easy even though (in principle) they run 24 hours a day.

At more reasonable times of the day simply walk straight across the open car park outside the airport terminal, up the steps to street level and across the road to hail a city-bound le truck.

From Papeete, take a le truck heading for Faaa and Outumaoro – the destination will be clearly posted on the front.

Taxi Taxis are expensive everywhere in French Polynesia and Faaa airport is no exception. If your hotel offers to collect you from the airport, jump at the chance. Otherwise the short drive to central Papeete will set you back 1600 CFP during the day or 2500 CFP at night (8 pm to 6 am). That's US$15 to US$20! They charge an extra 100 CFP for baggage but at least they don't expect to be tipped.

Other fares include the short run west (away from town) to the Beachcomber or Sofitel for 1000 CFP (1500 CFP at night) and to Hotel Outrigger Tahiti and other places on the way into town for 1300 CFP (2300 CFP at night).

Le Truck

Le truck, the standard public transport of French Polynesia, is comprehensive and well organised on Tahiti.

On weekdays le truck operates from dawn until about 5.30 pm except for the Papeete-Faaa-Outumaoro line, which operates 24 hours but gets very quiet after 10 pm. On weekends, particularly on Sunday, services are less frequent. Fares for the shortest trips, from Papeete to a little beyond the airport for example, start from 120 CFP (60 CFP for children). Out to about 20km from Papeete the fare will go up in stages to around 200 CFP; getting to the other side of the island might cost 400 CFP.

Le Truck Stands Tahiti le trucks have their route number and the final destination posted on the front. Although there are no official le truck stops, complete with blue 'Le Truck' signs (and sometimes canopies and seats), le trucks will generally stop anywhere for anybody who hails them. In Papeete there are several le truck stations for the various directions.

Arrêt Central du Marché – red stop Outside Papeete Market, it covers Faaa airport and the dormitory suburbs to the west, including Faaa, Punaauia and Paea, plus destinations farther out like Papara and Taravao. The very popular Outumaoro le truck goes to Faaa airport and to the west-coast hotels just beyond the airport. Le truck numbers from Papeete Market include 30 Outumaoro, 31 Punaauia/Punaruu, 32 Punaauia/Taapuna, 33 Pamatai, 34 Puurai/

Oremu, 35 Taravao, 36 St Hilaire, 37 Teroma/ Heiri, 38 Paea/Maraa and 39 Papara.

Arrêt Central du Front de Mer – blue stop On the waterfront Blvd Pomare, opposite the Tahiti Tourist Board in Fare Manihini, it covers the north coast as far as Papenoo, about 17km west of Papeete. Le truck numbers from the seafront terminus include 60 Mahina, 61 Arue, 62 Erima, 63 Papenoo, 64 Tenaho, 65 Nahoata, 66 Hamuta, 67 Princesse Heiata and 68 CPI.

Embarquements Longues Distances – yellow stop On Blvd Pomare near the Moorea Ferry Terminal, this stop is for le trucks heading farther east along the north coast and to Tahiti Iti. Le truck numbers from this long-distance stop include 40 Tevaiuta, 41 Teahupoo, 42 Tautira and 70 Hitiaa/Mahaena.

Gare de l'Hôtel de Ville – green stop On one side of the imposing mairie, it handles le trucks heading out along the east coast as well as commuter routes to a variety of Papeete dormitory suburbs. The route most likely to be used by overseas visitors is the No 7, which heads east to the tomb of Pomare V. Le truck numbers from the mairie stop include 1 Titioro, 2 Mission, 3 Motu Uta, 4 Tipaerui, 5 CPS/Mamao, 6 Vairaatoa, 7 Pomare V and 8 Taupeahotu.

Taxi

Taxis are expensive. Apart from the official government-established flat fares from the airport to most hotels, taxis are metered. The flag fall is 800 CFP (1200 CFP at night – from 8 pm to 6 am) plus 120 CFP (24υ CFP at night) per kilometre and additional charges for baggage. That's a pretty clear indication of the scale of taxi fares – more than US$10 just to turn on the meter at night! Any trip of a reasonable length will approximate a day's car rental, so if you want wheels you may as well rent them – it's expensive but cheaper than taking taxis. See the Car entry later in this section.

Within the city of Papeete a fare shouldn't be over 1000 CFP. Problems with taxi drivers are rare on Tahiti (with the level of fares it's hardly necessary to cheat you), but any complaints should be brought to the Tahiti Tourist Board (☎ 50 57 00).

Tahiti's taxi ranks, which you can phone to order a taxi, include those at Faaa airport (☎ 86 60 66); the Vaima Centre (☎ 42 33 60); Papeete Market (☎ 43 19 62); and Jasmin Station, Hotel Prince Hinoi (☎ 42 35 98).

Car

Driving on Tahiti is quite straightforward and, although accident statistics are not encouraging, the traffic is fairly light once you get away from Papeete and its horrific rush-hours. Apart from on the RDO out of Papeete to the west, the traffic doesn't go too fast. Beware of children on the road, a sometimes casual attitude towards overtaking and weekend drunks. Don't leave anything on view in your car; in fact make it clear there's nothing to steal – leave the glovebox open, for example.

Although there are many rental agencies in Papeete, their rates are very similar and there's no great gain in shopping around. By American, Australian and even European standards the rates are high. At Avis or Europcar, small cars (and on Tahiti distances are not great, so for most people a small car is quite sufficient) cost around 1800 CFP a day, plus 35 CFP to 40 CFP per kilometre and 1200 CFP a day for collision-damage waiver. Although there are eight-hour rates, the 24-hour rates aren't much more and, if you're going to do a circuit of the island, a daily rate with unlimited distance and insurance will work out better; count on 7500 CFP to 8000 CFP per day. Rates drop slightly from the third day onwards but 10% reductions are often offered simply for the asking.

Many agencies will bring the car to you at the start of the rental period, but check the car over carefully for damage before accepting it. Fuel costs 119 CFP a litre (about US$5 a gallon).

Car-rental companies on Tahiti include:

Avis
   (☎ 41 93 93, fax 42 19 11), Rue des Remparts and Ave Georges Clémenceau, Papeete; (☎ 43 88 99), Quai des Ferries, Papeete; (☎ 57 70 70), Taravao; (☎ 85 02 84), Faaa airport
Centre Auto Paea
   (☎ 53 33 33, fax 53 33 46), PK20.2 at Paea
Daniel Rent-a-Car
   (☎ 82 30 04, 81 96 32, fax 85 62 64), Faaa airport
Europcar
   (☎ 45 24 24, fax 41 93 41), Ave Prince Hinoi and Rue des Remparts, Papeete; (☎ 86 60 61), Faaa airport; (☎ 45 24 24), Quai des Ferries, Papeete; (☎ 57 01 11), Taravao

Hertz

(☎ 42 04 71)Tipaerui, Papeete; (☎ 82 55 86), Faaa airport

Robert Rent-a-Car

(☎ 42 97 20), opposite Vaimi Hospital, Rue du Commandant Destremeau, Papeete; (☎ 42 97 20), Blvd Pomare east of Ave Bruat, Papeete

Tahiti Rent-a-Car

(☎ 42 74 49, 81 07 77), Chez Pierrot & Jacqueline, Fare Ute, Papeete; (☎ 81 94 00), Faaa airport

Hitching

Hitchhiking (*auto-stop* in French) is not as easy as it used to be on Tahiti but it's still possible, particularly when you get to the far end of the island from Papeete, where le truck services are infrequent. The world-wide rules for hitching apply: it's not the safest means of travel and women should never hitch alone. We don't recommend it.

Around Tahiti Nui

COAST ROAD

The coast road runs right around Tahiti Nui, the larger of Tahiti's double circles. The 114km circuit is marked by PK markers that start at 0 in Papeete and increase in both a clockwise and anticlockwise direction. They meet at Taravao, the town and military base at the narrow isthmus that connects Tahiti Nui with Tahiti Iti. Taravao is 54km from Papeete clockwise (via the north coast) and 60km anticlockwise (via the south coast).

It's relatively easy to circle the island in a day by car but the trip can easily be extended to last longer. There are only a few places to stay around the island. Tahiti's accommodation is mostly close to Papeete.

The circuit that follows goes around Tahiti Nui from Papeete in a clockwise direction and lists the appropriate PK-marker numbers followed by the distance from the starting point. See the Tahiti Iti section for excursions beyond Taravao on to the smaller part of Tahiti.

Tomb of Pomare V (PK4.7, 4.7km)

On Point Outuaiai in Arue, on the water's edge, signposted and just a short detour off

the coast road, is the tomb of the last of the Pomare family. Prior to the Pomares, power on Tahiti had been predominantly local, but when Pomare I enlisted *Bounty* mutineers as mercenaries the picture soon changed. See History in the earlier Facts about the Islands chapter for details.

The Tomb of Pomare V looks like a stubby lighthouse made of coral boulders. It was actually built in 1879 for Queen Pomare, who died in 1877 after 50 years in power. Pomare V, her ungrateful son, had her remains evicted a few years later and when he died in 1891 it became his tomb. It's said that he drank himself to death and that the Grecian urn replica atop the structure should be a liquor bottle. Gauguin witnessed the funeral and described it in his book *Noa-Noa*.

Other Pomares are buried (or may be buried – their tombs are unmarked) in the Cimetière Pomare opposite the artisanat building at PK5.4. There's a board at the cemetery indicating where Pomare I, II, III and IV are supposed to be interred.

On the mountain side of the road at PK5.4, just past the turn-off to the Pomare Tomb, is the former home of James Norman Hall, co-author of the *Bounty* saga that the first two Hollywood films were based on (see Books and the 'Mutiny in the Cinema' boxed text in the Facts for the Visitor chapter). Unfortunately, the house is not open to the public.

Taharaa Point & One Tree Hill (PK8.1, 8.1km)

Taharaa Point is the western boundary of Matavai Bay, the favourite locale of early European explorers who seemed enormously keen on renaming the point. Samuel Wallis named the point 'Skirmish Hill', but when Cook came along two years later he noted a solitary *atae* tree on the point and renamed it 'One Tree Hill'.

There are fine views back towards Papeete from the viewpoint just at the entrance to the old Hyatt Regency Hotel, currently indefinitely closed. Don't look straight down towards the beach – the viewpoint is also an unofficial garbage dump.

Point Venus & Matavai Bay (PK10, 10km)

Mahina marks the eastern end of Papeete's coastal sprawl and the site of Tahiti's first real contact with Europe. Wallis and Bougainville had come to Tahiti two years earlier and Wallis had actually anchored in Matavai Bay, but their visits had been fleeting affairs; part of Cook's mission on his three-month sojourn in 1769 was to record the transit of Venus across the face of the sun in an attempt to calculate the distance between the sun and the earth. Point Venus, the promontory which marks the eastern end of Matavai Bay, was the site of Cook's observatory. Until Papeete began to develop around the 1820s, Matavai remained the principal anchorage for visiting European ships. See History in the Facts about the Islands chapter for more information on early European visits to Tahiti.

Of course there is no trace left today of those early visits; nevertheless Point Venus retains a, historic resonance and some more-recent memorials add to the interest.

Today Point Venus is a popular beach excursion from Papeete with shady trees, a stretch of lawn, some black-sand beach, a couple of souvenir shops and an impressive lighthouse (1867) to overlook the whole show. This place is a popular centre for local outrigger-canoe racing clubs and the speedy pirogues are stacked up outside the clubhouse, just to the west of the point. There is no sign to Point Venus from the main road; just turn off when you see shops and activity at the PK10 point. It's about a kilometre from the road to the car park near the end of the point.

There is a memorial to the first LMS Protestant missionaries, who also made their Tahitian landfall at Point Venus, on 4 March 1797.

Papenoo (PK17, 17km)

There's a popular surf break just before the headland that signals the start of the small village of Papenoo. A long bridge crosses the Papenoo River at the far end of the village and the 4WD route up the Papenoo Valley, cutting through the ancient crater rim to Relais de la Maroto, starts up the west side of the river. See the Inland section later in this chapter for more information about this interesting route.

Arahoho Blowhole (PK22, 22km)

Appropriate swell conditions produce a geyser-like fountain of water from the blowhole (le trou du souffleur) by the road just before Tiarei. The blowhole is right on the corner and there's a car park just beyond, if you're coming from Papeete. Take care walking back to the blowhole, as traffic rounding the blind corner may be unaware of pedestrians wandering on to the road. And then take even more care at the blowhole: it may be a very low-key attraction most of the time but when the waves are right, the blow can be very dramatic – so dramatic that people have been swept right off the rock and into the sea!

Just beyond the blowhole there's a fine sliver of black-sand beach, ideal for a picnic pause. There may be vendors here, waiting to sell coconuts or fruit.

Faarumai Waterfalls (PK22.1, 22.1km)

Only about 100m past the blowhole, a signposted road leads just over a kilometre inland to the car park for the three Faarumai waterfalls. Bring a swimsuit if you want to stand under the cooling shower and mosquito repellent if you simply want to stand still and enjoy the view! It's a couple of hundred metres walk through a forest of mape (native chestnut trees) to Vaimahutu, the first of the waterfalls. Another 20 minute stroll leads to the other two falls, the Haamarere Iti and Haamarere Rahi, which stand almost side by side.

Through Tiarei & Mahaena

At PK25 there's a picture-postcard copra plantation beside the road with neat rows of coconut palms aligned across a uniform green lawn.

The French takeover of Tahiti in 1843 was not accepted happily by the Tahitians and in 1844 a pitched battle took place at

Mahaena (PK32.5). There is nothing to see of the battle site and the struggle ended disastrously for the Tahitian defenders.

If the weather had been cloudy over Point Venus at the critical moment on 3 June 1769, Captain Cook's long voyage to Tahiti to observe the transit of Venus would have been in vain. So he established a second observation post on tiny **Motu Taaupiri**, 1km off shore around PK34. As further insurance, a third post, commanded by Joseph Banks, was set up on a motu close to Hauru Point on Moorea.

Hitiaa & Bougainville's Anchorage (PK38, 38km)

A plaque on the river bridge at the village of Hitiaa commemorates the visit to Tahiti in April 1768 by the French explorer Louis-Antoine de Bougainville.

The small village of Hitiaa has a new **church** and a charming but abandoned and fast-decaying old one, topped by a tower made of coral blocks.

Taravao (PK54, 54km)

Strategically situated at the narrow isthmus connecting Tahiti Nui with Tahiti Iti, the town of Taravao has been a military base on and off since 1844, when the first French fort was established. The original fort was intended to forestall Tahitian guerrilla forces, opposed to the French takeover, from mounting operations onto Tahiti Nui from Tahiti Iti.

From Taravao, roads run along the north and south coasts of Tahiti Iti. The central road into the Tahiti Iti highlands commences a short distance along the north-coast road. Although there is little of interest in the town, it does have shops, banks, fuel stations and a number of small restaurants, so this is a good place for a lunch stop on a round-the-island circuit.

Arrival Point of the First Tahitians (PK52, 62km)

Tahitian legends relate that the great migration canoes that carried their ancestors across the Pacific made their Tahitian landfall at this point. As a result, the chiefs of this district were much more important than those from other parts of the island. Tales of the great migrations, phenomenal feats of ocean navigation, are treated with enormous respect in Polynesia. Their departure and arrival points are pinpointed with equal exactitude on Rarotonga in the Cook Islands and at Taipa on the far north of New Zealand.

Botanical Gardens & Gauguin Museum (PK51.2, 62.8km)

Tahiti's fine Botanical Gardens and the interesting Gauguin Museum share an entrance road and car park. There is a café at the entrance building to the gardens; although it is cheaper than the Restaurant du Musée Gauguin, which is 500m farther west, it is definitely not a place for an economical snack. It is possible to get to the gardens and museum from Papeete by le truck but the last return trip usually departs early in the afternoon. Check the departure times or risk being stranded. Mosquitoes in the gardens can be fierce.

Botanical Gardens The gardens are open daily from 9 am to 5 pm and entry is 400 CFP. Interestingly, the gardens concentrate more on exotic vegetation than on Tahiti's own lush plant-life. Walking paths wend through the 137-hectare garden past ponds, palms and a superb thicket of bamboo. Look for the huge Galapagos tortoise.

The Botanical Gardens were founded in 1919 by Harrison Smith, a Massachusetts Institute of Technology professor who retired at the age of 37 and devoted the rest of his life to developing these gardens. He introduced many plants to Tahiti including the large, thick-skinned South-East Asian citrus fruit known on Tahiti as *pamplemousse*, the French word for grapefruit, although it is rather different and known in other locales as the *pomelo*. Unfortunately, Smith also introduced one or two botanical disasters that Tahiti could well have done without. He died in 1947 and the garden eventually became public property.

Gauguin Museum The museum is open daily from 9 am to 5 pm and entry is 600 CFP.

Don't expect an art gallery – this is a museum of Gauguin's life rather than a gallery of his work. Although the museum is often dimly lit and wastes the opportunity to bring Gauguin's work vividly to life in its natural setting, it is still definitely worth a visit. See the 'Gauguin: the Wild and the Primitive' boxed text in the Marquesas chapter.

There are exhibits on his earlier painting in Europe and the Caribbean, the family he abandoned, his clashes with French bureaucracy in French Polynesia and his work on Tahiti and the Marquesas. There are reproductions of many of his works but they are not of any quality.

A gallery within the complex shows temporary exhibits and works by local artists and Europeans who have worked in Polynesia.

The Gauguin Museum gardens are home to three superb tiki from Raivavae in the Australs. Tiki do not like to be moved so it's probable that these three have stored up a lot of trouble for some foolish individuals. The huge figure beside the walkway stands 2.2m high and weighs in at 900kg. It's a baby compared to the figure towards the waterfront, which stands 2.7m high and weighs 2110kg. A third, smaller figure stands beside the giant. These tiki are endowed with strong *mana*, supernatural power and are treated with great veneration. See the 'Civilisation & Archaeology' special section for more information on tiki.

Vaipahi Garden & Vaima Pool (PK49, 65km)

Beyond the Botanical Gardens there are more well-tended gardens along the mountain side of the road. Just past these gardens is Vaima Pool (Bain de Vaima). The Vaipahi Waterfall is a few minutes walk inland, dropping from pool to pool through a stand of stately mape trees. There are great views from a small plateau beyond the falls and there are a number of short walks you can take from here. A one hour walk brings you back to the road at PK50.2.

Mataiea

At PK47.5 is the turn-off for the rough track up to Lake Vaihiria, the Relais de la Maroto

and on across the island to the north coast. See the Inland section later in this chapter for details.

During his first visit to Tahiti Gauguin lived in Mataiea, near PK46, between 1891 and 1893. Although he was sick and impoverished, this was a happy period in his so often depressed life and he produced works including *Two Women on the Beach, Woman with a Mango* and *Ia orana Maria – Hail Mary*.

The **church of St John the Baptist** (1857) is just outside the town. The curious Protestant **chapel** by the road in the village looks vaguely like a Hindu temple.

The Mataiea district ends with the golf course at Atimaono at PK42, the site of the abortive Terre Eugénie cotton plantation in the 1860s. Descendants of some of the Chinese workers, imported to supplant the unwilling Polynesian labour force, are still around. The cotton plantation and other land devoted to coffee and sugar production played an enormously important role in the Tahitian economy for some years.

Marae Mahaiatea (PK39.2, 74.8km)

Just east of the village of Papara, the Marae Mahaiatea was the most magnificent marae on Tahiti at the time of Cook's first visit. The great navigator measured it at 80m by 27m at its base, rising in 11 great steps to a height of 13m. It was the marae of Obarea, the 'queen' of Tahiti who befriended both Wallis and Cook and was an ancestor of the Pomare dynasty.

Today the crumbling remains of the marae are still impressive for their sheer size – only as you clamber up the tree-covered 'hill' does it become clear that this is no natural feature.

Coming from Papeete, take the first turn towards the sea past the 39km sign. The turn is between the roadside Beach Burger restaurant and the PK39 sign if you're heading towards Papeete. Follow the road all the way towards the coast, about half a kilometre. In the middle of the car park area what looks like a densely vegetated hill is, on closer inspection, the massive remains of the stone marae.

Church on Sunday morning is an occasion to dress up.

Papeete Market is always bustling.

Fishing with a net on Tahiti Iti

Bourayne Bay, Huahine

The lagoon and the barrier reef at Tahaa

Small traditional-style bungalow, Moorea

Tahaa has many small villages.

Over-water bungalows at a five star resort on Bora Bora

Papara

Museum of Seashells (PK36, 78km)

In the village of Papara, the Musée du Co-quillage is open daily from 8 am to 5 pm and admission is 300/200 CFP for adults/children. The associated shop sells shells, something which doesn't sit well when their rarity and importance is emphasised in the museum.

Mataoa Garden (PK34.5, 79km) A variety of flowers and tropical plants are assembled in this botanical garden. Entry is 400 CFP and includes a glass of fruit juice. It's open weekdays from 10 am to 4 pm, weekends from 1.30 to 4 pm.

Paea

Maraa Grotto (PK28.5, 85.5km) Along-side the road a manicured path runs through a garden past a series of overhung caverns, with crystal-clear pools and ferny grottoes. It's a popular stop on round-the-island circuits.

Paea Marae In the Paea district, **Marae Arahurahu** at PK22.5 is the best-looking marae on the island, although it was in fact only a secondary marae. Not only has it been restored, it has also been embellished with impressive tiki and a variety of bamboo and cane huts, all of which make it an interesting site, perhaps approximating what a marae might have looked like in its prime. The lushly photogenic site is used for performances, particularly during the July Heiva festivities. See the 'Ori Tahiti – Tahitian Dance' special section for details on Heiva.

Marae Tataa at PK19 may have been much more important, as it was restored in 1973 but it's on private land and hard to get to. The **Orofero River** at PK20 is a popular surfing site. This was also the spot where, in 1815, Pomare II fought the battle that brought him back to power over Tahiti.

Museum of Tahiti & Its Islands (PK15.1, 98.9km)

Only 15km from Papeete in the anticlockwise direction, the Musée de Tahiti et des Îles (☎ 58 34 76) is in Punaauia and has one of the best collections in the Pacific. The museum is right on the coast, several hundred metres from the coast road after the Punaruu bridge. From Papeete, a Punaauia le truck will drop you at the road junction for 160 CFP. In the afternoon check the time of the last return trip, which is generally about 4.30 pm

The museum is open Tuesday to Sunday from 9.30 am to 5.30 pm and entry is 500 CFP. It's in a large garden and if you get tired of history, culture and art you can wander out to the water's edge to watch the surfers at one of Tahiti's most popular breaks.

The museum is divided into four distinct sections – geography and natural history, pre-European culture, the European era and outdoor exhibits. The museum's highlights include:

Polynesian Environment The geography of Polynesia is shown, with some rather fascinating views of the picture below the water as well as above. Volcanoes, reefs and the formation of atolls are explained and theories on the great Pacific migration voyages are detailed.

Agriculture, Animal Husbandry & Hunting When the first Europeans arrived the Polynesian economy was predominantly a subsistence one, although fertile soil and the abundant waters around the island meant that survival was easy. Horticulture consisted chiefly of growing taro in swampy places and irrigated terraces and growing sweet potatoes on small sunny terraces where the plants were covered with humus. Digging sticks were virtually the only farming implements, although in the Tuamotus shovels of pearl or turtle shell were used. Growing breadfruit was no problem at all and animal husbandry consisted of letting the pigs, dogs and chickens (the only domesticated animals prior to Cook's arrival) run free. Birds were the only wildlife hunted, both for their flesh and feathers. The *Journal of James Morrison* reported that: 'They catch birds by putting breadfruit sap on lengths of bamboo on which the birds alight.'

Polynesian Culture The exhibits on pre-European Polynesian culture feature a wonderful display of tiki and petroglyphs, many of them from the Australs and Marquesas. They include a huge wooden tiki and a very expressive large stone one, both from the Marquesas.

Displays about Polynesian games and sports include archery equipment, surfboards (surfing originated in the Society Islands and was carried from there to Hawaii before being discovered by the west) and even some of the enormously heavy stones used in stone-lifting contests. Also on display are drums, split drums and the xylophones that were once used in the Marquesas.

Warfare & Weapons Until Europeans arrived, bringing with them more sophisticated weapons, no rulers exercised more than purely local power. The exhibits include clubs, daggers and spears. Weapons were often used in an unusual fashion: spears, for instance, were mainly used as hitting weapons rather than to throw or pierce. Archery was almost only used in ceremonial or sporting events. Only Mangareva were bows and arrows used in warfare.

European Exploration The early explorers – Wallis, Bougainville, Cook and the rest – are all featured. The displays relating to early European contact also include cannons off the *Mathilda*, an English whaling ship (but French built), which was wrecked on Moruroa Atoll in 1792. They were recovered by divers from the nuclear-testing operations on the atoll in 1968.

The Nobility & Priests Symbols of the power of chiefs and the nobility include the belts of red feathers that were worn only for a single day at the time of investiture of a future great chief. Plaited fans with carved handles were another symbol of power and the collection of chiefs' wooden stools, in-

cluding the one Omai carried to Europe when he was taken to Britain on Cook's second voyage, are also featured. This is the same stool Omai was holding when his portrait was painted by Nathaniel Dance in 1775. It recently came up for auction in London, sold for US\$128,000 and was returned to Tahiti. There are some fine headdresses and necklaces of dolphins' teeth.

Religion Pre-European religious exhibits include funeral-house posts and wooden figures of gods. The explorers were a passing wave but the European missionaries had a lasting effect on the islands. The missionary exhibits include an interesting panel on the first abortive Mormon missions between 1844 and 1852. They were back in action later in the century and are probably the most active current missionaries. John Williams, the pioneering LMS missionary, is featured, as is Father Honoré Laval, whose work on Mangareva still raises so many questions.

Colonial Polynesia The museum features exhibits on the Tahitian royal family, the Pomares, who briefly extended their control farther than any previous Polynesian rulers. They were then subsumed by the growing European power. There's an interesting photo collection on turn-of-the-century Tahiti and some fascinating displays about the Chinese community who first turned up to work on Tahiti's short-lived cotton plantations and later as shopkeepers and merchants. Of course the numerous writers who sought inspiration on Tahiti are also well covered.

Tourism's influence on modern Tahiti is so widespread it's enlightening to realise that there was indeed a pre-tourism Tahitian economy in which copra and fishing played an important part. For a time the mainstay of the French Polynesian economy was, however, the phosphate on the tiny island of Makatea (see that section in the Tuamotus chapter).

Outside the Museum The displays conclude outside with canoes, pirogues and tiki. The museum gardens extend right to the lagoonside.

Punaauia

There are good **beaches** between PK15 and PK10 through Punaauia. See the South Coast entry under Places To Eat later for information on Punaauia's excellent restaurant scene. The most expensive homes on Tahiti are found along this stretch of coast, often high above the coast where they enjoy fresh breezes and fine views across the strait to Moorea.

On the hillside above the bridge at PK14.8 in Punaruu Valley is the site of a French fortification from the 1842-46 conflict when France took control of Tahiti. It's now used as a TV relay station. A walking trail leads farther up the valley to the Tamanu Plateau at around 600m, an area known for its wild **orange trees**, escapees from the citrus plantations that once grew here.

Site of Gauguin's Home (PK12.6, 101.4km)

Gauguin lived here in 1897-98 during his second Tahitian visit, but there is no trace of his wooden colonial-style home, built by a river on the lagoonside. Here he painted 60-odd pictures, including some of his masterpieces: *Nevermore, The White Horse* and the evocatively named *Where Do We Come From? What Are We? Where Are We Going?* Of this picture Gauguin wrote: 'Before dying, I painted this with such a painful passion, in horrible circumstances and with a bright vision, without any corrections, that the hurry vanishes and life arises.' See the 'Gauguin: the Wild & the Primitive' boxed text in the Marquesas chapter for more information on this artist.

His house stood just south of the 2+2 = 4 Primary School at PK12.5. The school was named by the landowner who donated the site. Dubious about the usefulness of the French school system in the tropics, he reasoned that at least the children would learn to add!

Lagoonarium (PK11, 103km)

In Punaauia, well into the Papeete urban sprawl, the Lagoonarium is a pleasant little tourist trap, a meshed-in area of lagoon with a very modest underwater viewing room you reach by climbing down steps through a giant concrete shark's mouth. You can watch the small sharks and other creatures at their own level but making a snorkelling trip on one of the outer islands is far more interesting. The Lagoonarium is open daily from 9 am to 6 pm and entry is 500 CFP, 300 CFP for children. The entrance to the Lagoonarium is part of the Captain Bligh Restaurant, a popular stop for tourist trips. Diners can visit the Lagoonarium without charge.

Organised Tours

Hotel activity desks, numerous Papeete travel agencies and a number of independent operators offer island circuit tours by minibus, generally for about 4500 CFP, although you should check if entry and/or lunch are included.

Trips into the interior of the island require a 4WD; see Organised Tours under Inland later in this section for details. For hikes in the interior see the Outdoor Activities chapter. For helicopter flightseeing trips contact Héli-Inter (☎ 81 99 00) or Héli Pacific (☎ 85 68 00).

Places to Stay

North Coast *Fare Nana'o* (☎ 57 18 14, fax 57 76 10) is right on the water on the north coast at PK52, only a few kilometres before Taravao. It has six individualistic bungalows ranging from a tree house to Polynesian-style interpretations of an over-water bungalow. Some have separate bathroom facilities but not all of them are attached. Several have kitchen facilities. Prices for two people range from 5500 CFP to 7500 CFP. Additional people, in the rooms for three or four, are 1000 CFP. Breakfast adds 800 CFP, other meals 2000 CFP.

The natural construction is attractive and the lush setting is a delight, although the beach is nothing special. The doors can't be locked by key which can be a negative factor for women travelling alone. Transfers from the airport cost 3000 CFP and there's a pirogue for guests to use.

TAHITI

South Coast There are a number of places in the Punaauia-Paea-Papara sector. Compared to Papeete they're quiet, and are close to some unexceptional black-sand beaches. During the day there are regular le truck services but they dry up towards 4 or 5 pm. If you need to go into Papeete with any frequency this could be a problem.

Chez Va'a (☎/fax 42 94 32) is at PK8 in Punaauia, but well back up the mountainside from the Sofitel. It has two rooms with shared bathroom for 3500/5000 CFP, including breakfast and airport transfers.

Moana Surf Tours (☎/fax 43 70 70) is run by Moana David, the brother of the famous local surfer Vetea David and is clearly aimed at visiting surfies. It's on the mountain side of the road at PK8.3 and has dorm beds from 6000 CFP including transport to the surf breaks on Tahiti and Moorea.

Relais Familial (☎/fax 45 01 98) is at PK12.5 in Punaauia, 200m inland from the coast road. It has two rooms with shared hot-water bathroom for 3500/4500 CFP. Breakfast/other meals cost 500/1200 CFP but there are shared kitchen facilities. Airport transfers cost 1000 CFP per person.

Chez Armelle (☎ 58 42 43, fax 58 42 81) is on the lagoon side of the road at PK15.5 in Punaauia, just beyond the Tahiti Museum and the Hotel Méridien. It's a family-style place with a small beach and seaside snack bar. Functional singles/doubles with attached bathroom cost 4500/6000 CFP including breakfast. If you stay seven nights, one night is knocked off and you can rent by the month for 70,000/85,000 CFP. There's also a dorm, often occupied by locals, at 2000 CFP a night. Credit cards are accepted (minimum charge of 5000 CFP).

Le Bellevue (☎/fax 58 47 04), at PK16, is a possibility if you're staying at least one week. An equipped studio costs 23,000 CFP for two people, including airport transfers.

Pension Te Miti (☎/fax 58 46 61, mobile ☎ 78 60 80) is on the mountain side of the main road at PK18.5 in Paea, about 200m from the shore. It has a friendly backpacker-hostel atmosphere is very popular with young travellers. It's run by a young popaa couple (he's a surfer), who offer a wide

range of services and assistance. A bed in a four-mattress dorm costs 1800 CFP (1500 CFP after one week) including breakfast. There are five double rooms with screen, fan and bathroom for 4500 CFP to 6000 CFP including breakfast; knock off 500 CFP a night after the first week. There's an equipped kitchen but meals are available for 1200 CFP. There are two bicycles for guests' use, laundry service (500 CFP) and airport transfers anytime of the day or night for 1000 CFP per person. The owners can also arrange reasonably priced car rentals in Paea and they'll store baggage for free while you visit other islands. There are shops and a small park nearby and a beach at PK17. Credit cards are accepted.

Fare Opuhi Roti (☎ 53 20 26) is just off the coast road on the inland side at PK21.2. It has a simple but neat *fare* with all equipment on a green and lush property. It costs 6500 CFP per day for one or two people, including breakfast but it's usually rented by the month. The owners may also have a room in their own *fare* for 2500/5000 CFP single/double, including breakfast. Transfers to the airport are free.

Hiti Moana Villa (☎ 57 93 33, fax 57 94 44) is on the lagoonside at PK32 in Papara. Its four solidly built and impeccably kept bungalows with hot-water bathroom, kitchen and fan cost 8160 CFP for one or two, 10,200 CFP for three or four. In principle there's a three day minimum stay and prices drop 10% after a week. There is no beach but there is a pontoon for swimming and a small swimming pool. Bicycles, pirogues and kayaks can be rented (all 1000 CFP) and lagoon tours by motorboat (from 5000 CFP) and island tours by minibus are offered. There's a supermarket and the Nuutere restaurant nearby. Airport transfers are 2060 CFP per person return. Travellers cheques are accepted.

Papara Village (☎ 57 41 41, fax 57 79 00) is at PK38.1, perched on the hillside on a garden-like site 800m off the coast road. The small Marae Tetaumatai is on the site, which has fantastic views of the lagoon and the mountains. There are two bungalows with hot-water bathroom, TV and refrigerator for

7000/10,000 CFP. There's an equipped kitchen, a superb traditional-style dining room and a swimming pool. A much larger bungalow is generally rented by the month; it can accommodate two or three couples and costs 15,000 CFP a night (12,000 CFP after the first week). Airport transfers cost 5000 CFP for a couple, return.

Places to Eat

Finding a place to eat around the island is much simpler than finding a place to stay. There are small shops, some of them selling sandwiches, dotted round the coast and a number of small restaurants at Taravao, the mid-point on the island circuit.

North Coast Once you've left Papeete's urban sprawl, east of Mahina, there are not many places to eat before Taravao, although there are a number of excellent snack bars. *Fare Nana'o* (☎ 57 18 14) (see North Coast under Places to Stay earlier in this section), at PK52 just before Taravao, has meals for 2000 CFP if you make reservations.

Taravao has quite a collection of snack bars and restaurants.

Ahki Vairua (☎ 57 20 38), on the Papeari road, is a modest, long-running Chinese place. It's bare but it's certainly authentic and you can enjoy a filling chow mein for 850 CFP. It's open for lunch daily and dinner except Tuesday and the third Sunday of the month.

L'Escale Restaurant (☎ 57 07 16), also on the Papeari road, does fine French cuisine in a classic setting. It also has Moroccan specialities like couscous and, on some days, tajine. It's closed Sunday evening and all day Monday. Credit cards are accepted.

Te Honu (☎ 57 21 84) is in the centre of the town, next to the Continent supermarket. The rotunda-shaped tiled room is antiseptic but the Chinese specialities include chow mein with curry at 1000 CFP and fish dishes at 990 CFP to 1750 CFP. There may even be live music on weekends. It's closed Sunday evening and all day Monday. Credit cards are accepted.

Snack Restaurant Chez Myriam (☎ 57 71 01) is across the road and has an indoor restaurant section and outdoor tables for snacks. The Chinese, French and Polynesian dishes are reasonably priced and it also has ice creams. In principle it's open Monday to Saturday from 7 am to 10 pm.

South Coast Continuing on from Taravao, there is a rather larger choice of restaurants along the south coast. You will find also various small snack bars along the road.

Restaurant Baie Phaéton (☎ 57 08 96), at PK58.8, has a superb view across Phaéton Bay from its terrace built out over the lagoon. The menu is varied but predominantly Chinese and the prices are moderate. Glazed duck costs 930 CFP, raw freshwater shrimp Chinese-style 1340 CFP and poisson cru in coconut milk just 770 CFP. There's a set meal at lunch and on weekend evenings (1600 CFP to 2500 CFP). It's open everyday for lunch, Thursday to Saturday for dinner. Credit cards are accepted.

Restaurant du Musée Gauguin (☎ 57 13 80), at PK50.5, is firmly targeted at tourist groups visiting the museum and is only open for lunch. The Sunday maa Tahiti costs 2750 CFP. *Atimaono Golf Club House* (☎ 57 40 32), at PK40.2, is open daily for lunch. There's a menu and a dish of the day for 1500 CFP. Credit cards are accepted.

Nuutere Restaurant (☎ 57 41 15), at PK32.5 in Papara, has an extravagantly painted façade and a good reputation. French specialities using local ingredients are served in an intimate and refined dining room and bar. Salmon of the gods in papaya sauce costs 1950 CFP, *maoa* (sea snails) 1500 CFP, poisson cru in coconut milk only 1000 CFP. There's a set meal for 2500 CFP and a good winelist. Outside there's a garden with play equipment for children. It's open Wednesday to Monday and credit cards are accepted.

The chic suburbs around Punaauia, on the western edge of the Papeete coastal strip, is the main restaurant centre after Papeete itself.

Coco's Restaurant (☎ 58 21 08) is beside the sea at PK13 and has a magnificent setting, with a room decorated with paintings by Marere opening on to the lagoon and an interior garden. The cuisine is gastronomic French with local flavours – foie gras, terrine of mahi mahi, ravioli with lobster. Main courses cost 2000 CFP to 4000 CFP and from 5.30 pm you can enjoy the happy-hour chariot of desserts with champagne for 2600 CFP. It's open for lunch and dinner daily and credit cards are accepted.

There are two Chinese restaurants in this sector. At PK15, *L'Impérial* (☎ 45 18 19) has a restaurant and an outside counter for snacks and takeaways. The menu is extremely comprehensive – nothing is missing – and there's hardly a dish for more than 1500 CFP. It's open daily for lunch and dinner and credit cards are accepted. On the lagoon side of the road at PK13, *Le Fleur de Lotus* (☎ 41 97 20) has a games area for children. There are numerous dishes between 800 CFP and 1200 CFP and live music on Saturday. It's closed Sunday.

Venezia (☎ 41 30 56) is nearby at PK12.7 and serves pizzas from 990 CFP to 1250 CFP, pastas from 1250 CFP to 1400 CFP and other dishes at higher prices.

Captain Bligh Lagoonarium (☎ 43 62 90), at the Lagoonarium at PK11.4, is a very tourist-oriented restaurant where the main attraction is the Friday and Saturday evening buffet and dance performance (4200 CFP) by one of the best island dance groups. Otherwise the 3500 CFP seafood plate is the house speciality. The dining area opens out on to the lagoon and it's open Tuesday to Sunday lunchtime. Credit cards are accepted from 2000 CFP.

L'Auberge du Pacifique (☎ 43 98 30), beside the lagoon at PK11.2, has been a Tahiti institution since it's opening in 1974. The chef, Jean Galopin, is the author of several works on the cuisine of Tahiti and its islands. The gastronomic menu is French-Polynesian with prices from 2000 CFP for main courses. You could be tempted by a mahi mahi soufflé for 2100 CFP or *cigalles du mer* (a small lobster) sautéed in ginger for 3200 CFP, or try the set tourist menu meal for 4650 CFP. There's a children's at 2450 CFP. The wine cellar (from 2350 CFP) is excellent and there's even a small tasting lounge for wine enthusiasts. The dining

room, decorated with paintings by local artists, opens on to a terrace on the lagoon. It's open Monday to Saturday.

Casablanca (☎ 43 91 35), at the Taina Marina at PK9, offers a variety of dishes at 1950 CFP to 2550 CFP, as well as couscous on some days. There are superb views from the terrace. Live music is offered several times a week. It's open daily for lunch and dinner.

INLAND

Although roads and tracks climb some distance into the central highlands of Tahiti at several points around the island, the only route that extends right across the island is a wonderful, but quite rugged, trip. The 39km route runs from Papenoo in the north to Mahaiatea in the south, via the Relais de la Maroto and Lake Vaihiria in the middle of the island. The crossing makes a great excursion and several 4WD operators offer this completely different look at Tahiti – not lagoons, but mountain landscapes, waterfalls, a lake and mysterious archaeological sites.

Although unpopulated today, these central valleys once sheltered a dense population and it was here that the *Bounty* mutineers took refuge. When the missionary influence began to spread along the coastal regions, the Papenoo Valley became a last refuge of the ancient Polynesian religion and was also a shelter for the Tahitian rebel forces that opposed the French takeover until 1846. Archaeologist Kenneth Emory started the first systematic study of the valley's historic sites 1925.

Some parts of the track are quite perilous but the specialised operators do this route regularly and safely. From the Relais de la Maroto, which was originally built to house hydro-electricity workers, in the centre of the island, there are many fine walking tracks and the cross-island route can make a fine two day walk.

Papenoo to the Relais de la Maroto

The 18km route from Papenoo to the Relais de la Maroto follows the wide Papenoo

Valley, the only valley to cut right through the ancient crater. The Papenoo River is the largest on Tahiti and at one time the route crossed the river 10 times. Now a new track runs higher up one side of the valley and cuts out all the river fordings.

The turn-off is just past PK17 in Papenoo. The track has its own PK markers and after an ugly garbage dump and signs warning of the dangers of the track, the **Topatari Waterfall** cascades down to the river at PK5. A little farther up the valley the **Vaiharuru Waterfall** comes down from the west side and the **Puraha Waterfall** from the east. At PK16 the track passes the **Vaituoru Pool** (Bassin Vaituoru) and reaches the Relais de la Maroto just past PK18. Remarkably, the climb up the Papenoo Valley only reaches 230m at the Relais de la Maroto.

Otiaroa to the Relais de la Maroto

Coming from Papeete the turn-off on the south coast is at PK47.5, just beyond the Seventh-Day Adventist church and just before the Tahiria River bridge and a settlement of modern, prefab-like buildings. At one time this road was officially closed to private vehicles, but now it has become a popular route. Close to the ancient crater rim the rough track goes through a tunnel to emerge inside the crater.

From the turn-off the road runs straight inland, about 200m before taking a signposted sharp-left turn. From there it follows the Tahiria River upstream to a small catchment lake (6.7km, 145m) and **Marae Vaihiria I** (7.5km). The extensive remains of the marae include an artificial canal, which carried water through the site and stretches up the hillside on both sides of a small stream that runs down and under the road to the Tahiria River. The marae was in use from the 16th to the 19th century and there are several informative noticeboards by the roadside and up the hill. Another marae is being restored farther down the valley, about 4km from the start of the cross-island road.

Continuing uphill, there is a second small catchment lake (10km, 270m) before the road makes a very steep and winding (but paved) climb to Lake Vaihiria (11.3km, 450m), the 200m-long tunnel (14.9km, 770m), a road junction (17km) and finally the Relais de la Maroto (20.7km). The 4WD track runs up the west side of Lake Vaihiria to the tunnel, but there is a walking track that runs around the east shore of the lake and then climbs up to meet the vehicle track at the tunnel, just below the Urufau Pass (Col Urufau).

Around the Relais de la Maroto

The Relais de la Maroto was originally built as accommodation quarters for workers on the hydro-electricity project. Exploitation of the island's hydro-power potential commenced in 1980 and now supplies 40% of the island's electricity. It is intended to increase that to 50% by 2000. Marama Nui, the power company, claims to have been as environmentally conscious as possible during the construction. Power cables and water conduits have been routed underground and workers have also been involved in the restoration of marae around the project.

From the Relais de la Maroto, tracks fan out to the various hydropower dams. The extensive **Marae Farehape** site is almost directly below the ridgeline on which the Relais de la Maroto perches. There has been a great deal of restoration of this site, which includes an archery platform from where contestants shot up the valley.

From the marae, a track climbs up to the Tahinu dam. A walking track skirts around the edge of the lake behind the dam to the **Marae Tahinu** archaeological sites on both sides of the river. Another 4WD track starts from the dam and climbs up the Maroto Valley to the small Maroto Barrage. A rough track turns off this route and leads to the top of the spectacular **Maroto Waterfall**. There are great swimming pools above and below the falls but getting to the bottom of the falls entails an hour or so of rock-hopping up the river, starting from Marae Farehape.

The beautifully restored **Marae Anapua** perches up above the Vainavenave Dam reservoir. The **Anapua Caves** are directly below the marae site, which can be reached on foot around the side of the reservoir or by the track around the valley side. Vaitamanu and Vaitapaa are two smaller dams, but both with nice natural swimming pools directly behind them.

Organised Tours

Two companies specialise in 4WD island crossings that include swimming stops, explanations on geology and botany and visits to the archaeological sites. Contact Tahiti Safari Expedition (☎ 42 14 15, fax 42 10 07) or Freddy Adventure (☎ 41 97 99, fax 53 21 22) to check departures. In the high season it's wise to book several days in advance. Count on 6000 CFP to 7000 CFP per person, not including meals.

Places to Stay & Eat

Relais de la Maroto (☎ 43 97 99, fax 57 90 30, email maroto@mail.pf) is smack in the middle of the island. Its growing popularity has resulted in the original construction-workers quarters being upgraded and expanded. There are 28 comfortable rooms for up to three people, with attached bathroom. Per-person costs are 4400 CFP for the room, 5650 CFP for the return transfer from Papenoo and 9700 CFP for three meals. Alternatively there are set lunches for 2500 CFP and dinners for 3500 CFP. The wine cellar is exceptional – probably the most extensive in the South Pacific; the Relais even has a sommelier. You can also reach the Relais by helicopter.

Various walks are possible from the Relais; ask for its walking booklet or check the Web site at www.maroto.com.

Getting There & Away

Two companies organise trips across the island (see Organised Tours earlier in this section) but you can also walk it in a couple of days or ride across on a mountain bike if you've brought one with you. You can also rent a 4WD but check out the conditions of the track and the dangers before you start out. In the rainy season this route can be truly perilous.

Tahiti Iti

The smaller loop of Tahiti's figure eight is Tahiti Iti (Little Tahiti) as opposed to the larger loop, which is Tahiti Nui (Big Tahiti). There are three roads into Tahiti Iti: a road 18km along the north coast to Tautira, another 18km along the south coast to Teahupoo and a third up the centre to a lookout. The PK markers start at 0 at Taravao for both the north and south coast roads, which do not meet. Although walking trails extend around the coast from both road ends, the sheer Te Pari cliff-faces cut the trails off and walking right around the coast is very difficult – but it can be done! There are, however, some superb walks on Tahiti Iti including a fine walk from Tautira to a series of marae and petroglyphs in the Vaiote River valley. See the Outdoor Activities chapter for details.

NORTH COAST ROAD

The coast road from Taravao runs through Pueu, past steep hills with numerous waterfalls, to Tautira. This stretch of coast has the highest rainfall on Tahiti. It's easy to walk beyond Tautira for a further 12km.

The north coast of Tahiti Iti has had some interesting European visitors. In 1772 the Spanish captain Boenechea anchored his ship *Aguilla* off the Aiurua River, about 10km beyond Tautira and then closer to the village. Cook followed suit in 1774; the Aguilla returned later that same year and Boenechea established a very brief and very unsuccessful Spanish mission. Subsequent landings of Catholic missionaries at Tautira eventually led to the French takeover of Tahiti and the end of the Protestant monopoly. See the History section in the Facts about the Islands chapter for more about this interesting series of European visitors.

In 1886 the unhealthy, but very successful, Robert Louis Stevenson came by Tautira in his ship the *Casco*. Stevenson and his party stayed in the village for nearly two months. See the 'Polynesia & the Pen' boxed text in the Facts for the Visitor chapter for more details.

The Forgotten Island

Tourists, quickly losing interest in Papeete, rush off to other islands in French Polynesia; the tourist office ignores it, preferring to sell the classic Pacific images of Moorea or Bora Bora; and even the residents of Papeete snub it, judging it to be unsophisticated and uninteresting.

In fact, Tahiti Iti (Little Tahiti), the *presqu'île* or 'nearby island' to the French, and also known as Fenua Aihere, is the unrecognised jewel of French Polynesia. This wild appendage to Tahiti Nui (Big Tahiti) begins about 60km from Papeete and is like the Tahiti of 30 years ago, before urban sprawl and consumerism were even heard of.

Tahiti Iti is a place for people who can look after themselves and offers activities far from the usual clichés of French Polynesia. Unusual and original places to stay and eat, the Te Pari Cliffs, the Teahupoo-Tautira crossing, the black-sand beaches beside the lagoon, the unexplored dive sites and the traditional Polynesian village life are all waiting to be discovered. And surfers already know this is the hottest spot in French Polynesia.

The sealed road ends at Tautira but you can bump along the lagoonside for another kilometre or two before the road becomes impassable to vehicles. A good walking track leads round the coast for another 12km or so before reaching the **Te Pari Cliffs**, which make walking all the way to Teahupoo so difficult.

Boenechea anchored for a time off the Aiurua River, about 10km around the coast from Tautira. Two kilometres farther along is the Vaiote River, with some noted **petroglyphs** inscribed on boulders near the coast and a series of **marae** inland in the valley. See the Outdoor Activities chapter for information about walking in the Vaiote Valley.

Offshore at this point are two **motu**; Fenua Ino is the larger of the two and is a popular picnic spot.

CENTRAL ROAD

From Taravao two routes climb to a **lookout** less than 10km east. Both start from the north coast road and can be combined to make a loop. In Afaahiti, at PK0.6, the first turn is signposted shortly before a school. The 7km road climbs through green fields, some home to most un-Tahitian-looking herds of cows, to the car park just before the lookout. The alternative route turns off the north coast road at PK2.5 and is rather rougher and more potholed. It meets the first route just before the car park, from where it's a short walk to the viewpoint with superb vistas across the isthmus of Taravao to the towering bulk of Tahiti Nui. It's possible to walk for about an hour towards **Mt Teatara** (1197m).

SOUTH COAST ROAD

The south coast road runs by beaches and bays to Vairao and the small settlement of Teahupoo before abruptly stopping at the Tirahi River at PK18. Two guesthouses are situated a little farther on; they can be reached by boat and sometimes on foot. From the end of the road it is possible to walk about another 10km before the steep Te Pari Cliffs cut off the path.

Author of American westerns, Zane Grey was a keen fisherman. During his longest Tahitian sojourn in 1929 he was based at about PK7.3. He recounts the visit in *Tales of Tahitian Waters*. The Tapuaeraha Pass through the reef is the widest and deepest around Tahiti, suitable for ships that are too large to enter Papeete's harbour. Due to its remote position it's rarely used.

A turn-off at PK9.5 leads a short distance inland to the scant remains of **Marae Nuutere**, restored in 1994. The name of this large marae translates as 'armies on the move' and it belonged to the female chief of the district, who was married to a member of the royal family of Huahine. There are three *tohua* (paved yards) with *ahu* (places for the gods) at the end of them and large *turui* (seats) for priests or *arii* (chiefs, or kings). See the 'Civilisation & Archaeology' special section for more information on marae and traditional culture.

At PK10.4 there's an **oceanographic research station** operated by Centre National pour l'Exploitation des Océans (CNEXO).

The south-coast road ends very decisively at Teahupoo, where the Tirahi River is crossed only by a footbridge. From here it is an easy 2½ hour walk to **Vaipoiri Cave**. See the Outdoor Activities chapter for a description of this walk.

PLACES TO STAY & EAT

Fare Nana'o is only a couple of kilometres north of Taravao, so it's an option if you want to explore Tahiti Iti. The only camping possibility on Tahiti is on Tahiti Iti.

Chez Maïthé (*☎/fax 57 18 24*) is on the north coast, facing the Nono Islet from the lagoonside at PK4.5 en route to Tautira. There are two rooms for 6500 CFP for two people, 7500 CFP with breakfast. There's a kitchen for guests' use and bicycles.

Chez Jeannine (*☎/fax 57 07 49*) is at PK4 on the plateau road and has beautiful views of the isthmus. There's a well kept main building, with *Eurasienne Restaurant*, which serves Vietnamese specialities and has four rooms for 4000 CFP. Beside it are four large, separate bungalows with hot-water bathroom for 6000/30,000 CFP per day/week. There's a small swimming pool and the setting is green and pleasant but this part of the island doesn't feel very exotic – with cows in the field you could be somewhere in Europe! Airport transfers cost 1000 CFP per person and credit cards are accepted.

Meherio Iti (*☎ 57 73 56*), on the south coast beside the lagoon at PK11.9, has three well equipped bungalows with hot-water bathroom for 6000/8000 CFP single/double. Full board (three meals) is an extra 4500 CFP per person. Various activities can be

organised and airport transfers cost 1000 CFP per person.

Te Pari Village (*☎/fax 42 59 12*), 10 minutes by boat from the Teahupoo pier, is in the middle of a magnificent coconut grove and beside the lagoon. It's a place for a complete escape; traditional-style bungalows with attached hot-water bathroom cost 8500 CFP per person per day with all meals and transfers from the Teahupoo pier. Various expeditions to the end of the island can be organised and daily excursions are included in the tariff.

Pension Bonjouir (*☎ 57 02 15, ☎/fax 43 69 10*) is a little beyond Te Pari Village and also has that Robinson Crusoe feeling. It's only accessible by boat, a 10 minute trip from the Teahupoo pier. Isolated though it is, it's well known to surfers who come here for the nearby reef break. You can put your tent up for 500 CFP (the only campsite on Tahiti) or sleep in one of the three rudimentary dorms for 2500 CFP. Simple bungalows with attached toilets (for three of the four) cost 4500 CFP for two; the family bungalow costs 14,500 CFP. The comfort and the fittings are limited but the setting and ambience more than makes up for it. There's a kitchen for guests' use, but you can also get half-board for 4000 CFP. Airport transfers cost 3000 CFP per person return, or it's 1200 CFP from the Teahupoo pier. Kayaks and pirogues are there for your use and surfers can be ferried out to the waves for 600 CFP to 800 CFP. Various excursions are offered.

The collection of restaurants and snack bars in Taravao is easily reached from the north or south coasts of Tahiti Iti. On the south coast, *Auberge Te Pari* (*☎ 57 13 44*) is in Teahupoo, right at the end of the road and right beside the beach. There's a pleasant seaside terrace and crustaceans are the house speciality. Count on 8100 CFP for a seafood platter for two. It's open for lunch Saturday to Thursday and for dinner on demand. Credit cards are accepted.

Moorea

Mountains that leap almost vertically out of the lagoon, terrific scuba diving, interesting marae, a number of excellent walks, some fine beaches, a pleasantly unhurried pace of life and absurdly easy access from Tahiti combine to make Moorea the second most popular destination in French Polynesia. Subtract the Tahiti visitors who are simply passing through the major island, en route to somewhere else, and Moorea could well be the most popular. One-third of all hotel rooms in French Polynesia are on Moorea.

The outer reef at Moorea is not dotted with idyllic motu; instead the island's seduction comes from the successful alchemy of mountains and volcanic peaks contrasting with the turquoise lagoon, the perfectly cut bays, the lush vegetation and the relaxed atmosphere. It's hardly surprising that it's so popular with artists. It's also popular with residents of Papeete, just 20km away from Moorea. Papeetians often make weekend escapes to enjoy an island that has not been overbuilt, where the traditional Polynesian charm reasserts itself as soon as you leave the tourist sectors. Moorea's tourist infrastructure fits all budgets – it has its share of deluxe hotels but also caters very well for shoestring travellers.

Moorea is, however, becoming a victim of its own success and 'no trespassing' signs have been popping up around the lagoon edge, letting visitors know that paradise can be a jealously protected territory.

History

The island was once known as Aimeho or Eimeo, but Moorea means 'yellow lizard' and it's speculated that this was the name of one of the ruling families of the island. The Opunohu Valley has the greatest number of marae in French Polynesia and in the pre-European era was heavily populated.

Samuel Wallis, on HMS *Dolphin*, was the first European to sight the island, in 1767, followed soon after by Louis-Antoine de Bougainville in 1768 and James

HIGHLIGHTS

pop: 11,965
area: 132 sq km
reef passes: 12
highest point: Mt Toheia (1207m)

- Explore the Cook and Opunohu Bays, with a motu-stop for a picnic and snorkelling
- Scuba dive for a shark-feeding session or make a first dive in the lagoon
- Hike into the inner valleys, follow the trail from Vaiare to Paopao or climb Mt Rotui
- Visit the archaeological sites of the Opunohu Valley
- Sample fine dining Polynesian-style in one of the island's restaurants

Cook in 1769. When Cook returned on his second voyage in 1774, Tahiti was preparing for a war with Moorea and it was not until his third voyage in 1777 that Cook visited Moorea. Curiously, he anchored not in Cook's Bay but in Opunohu Bay, which he belatedly discovered looked even better than his old favourite anchorage at Matavai on Tahiti. The bay certainly looks achingly attractive in the Mel Gibson 1984 remake of *The Bounty* (see the 'Mutiny in the Cinema' boxed text in the Facts for the Visitor chapter).

Despite being bypassed by the early European visitors, Moorea was the springboard from which the London Missionary Society (LMS) took Christianity to the other islands of French Polynesia. Missionaries arrived at Papetoai, just west of Opunohu Bay, in 1808 and it was established as the site for their Pacific headquarters in 1811. William Ellis, a pioneering missionary, wrote *Polynesian Researches – The Recollections of a Protestant Missionary in*

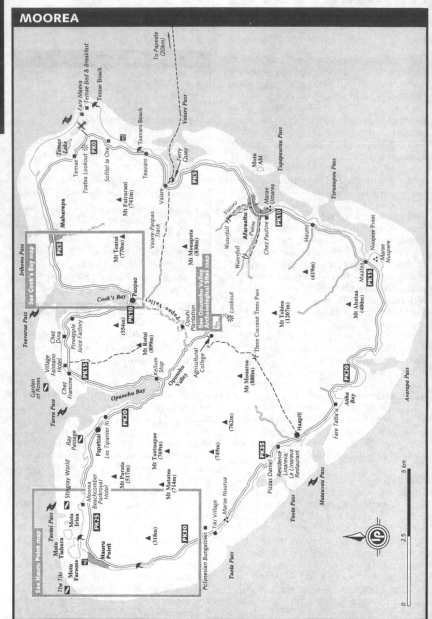

MOOREA

the Leeward Islands from 1817 to 1823 about his time on Moorea and Huahine.

Moorea had long been a refuge to which Tahitians on the losing side of power struggles could flee. Pomare I conquered the island in 1790, leaving his son Pomare II in control of Tahiti. In 1808, however, Pomare II had to retreat to Moorea. He settled at Papetoai and befriended the missionaries. When he returned to power in 1815, he took Christianity with him, and it quickly became dominant. From then on Moorea was subservient to Tahiti. European diseases, weaponry and alcohol had a disastrous effect on the population during the mid-19th century, reducing it to less than 1000 in 1860. A French protectorate was first established in 1843.

Copra and vanilla have been important crops in the past and today Moorea is the pineapple-growing centre of French Polynesia. Although tourism is the island's other major business and continues to grow rapidly, it's a very new industry; in 1960 Moorea had a mere 13 hotel beds!

Orientation

Moorea is the remains of a massive volcano, the northern half of which has eroded away. Cook's Bay and Opunohu Bay mark the floor of the ancient crater, and if you follow the trail from the Opunohu Valley up to the Three Coconut Trees Pass you stand very clearly on the knife-edge of the old crater rim. The island and its mountains feature in ancient Polynesian legends.

Moorea is shaped like an equilateral triangle, its point downwards, with two bites taken out of the top side. The bites are the two magnificent bays, Cook's Bay and Opunohu Bay. A reef encircles the island with a narrow and generally shallow lagoon. There are a number of passes through the reef, particularly at Vaiare on the east coast, where ferries dock from Papeete. Two beautiful motu lie just offshore from the Hauru Point tourist strip; Moorea has only two other motu, tiny Motu Irioa just to the east of the two Hauru Point motu, and Motu Ahi off the east coast.

Moorea is magnificently mountainous and the peaks rise with dramatic abruptness from the coast. Mt Rotui (899m) is a good example of this roller-coaster topography because it tumbles into Opunohu Bay on one side and Cook's Bay on the other, only 3km apart. Mt Mouaputa (830m), which is known as the 'pierced mountain', is famed for the hole through its top (see the boxed text). Other mountains are Mt Mouaroa (880m), also known as The Cathedral, and Mt Toheia (1207m), the highest mountain on the island. The untouched interior is covered in dense forests of *mape*, the gigantic chestnut trees of Polynesia. Two roads, beginning from the two bays, run into the interior and meet and climb up to the *belvédère* (lookout).

The population is concentrated in a number of villages around the coast, including Paopao, Papetoai, Haapiti, Afareaitu, Vaiare and Maharepa. With its frenetic ferry quay, Vaiare is the busiest centre but Afareaitu is the administrative headquarters. Tourist development is concentrated in two strips, one from Maharepa down the eastern side of Cook's Bay to Paopao, the other around

Hiro & the Hole through Mt Mouaputa

One dark night, Hiro, the Polynesian God of Thieves, tried to steal Mt Rotui and tow it behind his mighty canoe to Raiatea. It was probably the same canoe that he carelessly rammed into Huahine, splitting the island into two parts. Unfortunately for Hiro, he was spotted by Pai, a legendary Polynesian hero. Climbing Tataa Hill on Tahiti, Pai hurled his mighty spear at Hiro but missed, and created the hole you can still see in Mt Mouaputa today. The spear carried on all the way to Raiatea, where it knocked off part of a peak. Hiro still managed to grab a small hill and carry it back to Raiatea, where he plonked it down near Marae Taputapuatea. The hill's vegetation is similar to that on Mt Rotui, and is quite unlike the surrounding growth on Raiatea.

MOOREA

Hauru Point on the north-western corner of the island. The airport is at the north-eastern corner of the island.

As on most French Polynesian islands, beaches are rare; the only ones worthy of the name are at Hauru Point, the main tourist centre, and at Temae, near the airport. The PK *(pointe kilométrique)* markers start at 0 at the airport and go round the coast clockwise to Haapiti at PK24 and anticlockwise to Haapiti at PK35.

Information

Tourist Offices The Moorea Tourist Bureau (☎ 56 29 09) is in Le Petit Village shopping centre, opposite Club Med at Hauru Point. It's officially open Tuesday to Thursday from 8 am to 4 pm, Friday 8 am to 3 pm and Saturday 8 am to noon. On Monday you can call ☎ 56 38 53 for information. There is a counter at the airport (☎ 56 26 48) open Monday to Wednesday and Friday from 6 am to 7 pm. A ticket window (☎ 56 38 53) at the Vaiare ferry quay is open Monday and Wednesday to Friday from 7 am to 3 pm, Saturday 7 to 11 am.

Money The Banque Socredo across from the wharf at Vaiare has an automatic teller machine (ATM). Another Banque Socredo branch with ATM can be found at PK6.3 in the small shopping centre in Maharepa; a Banque de Tahiti and a Banque de Polynésie branch are right across the road. In Le Petit Village (the Hauru Point shopping centre) there's a Banque de Polynésie with ATM. The banks are closed on weekends.

Post & Communications A post office at the Maharepa shopping centre is open weekdays from 7.30 am to noon (to 3pm on Friday) and 1.30 to 4 pm, Saturday 7.30 to 9.30 am. The island's other post office is in Papetoai, just before Hauru Point, and it's open weekdays from 8 am to noon and 1.30 to 3.30 pm and Saturday 8 to 10 am. Phone boxes can be found all around the island and phonecards are on sale at many outlets.

Medical Services Your hotel can advise if you need medical assistance. The Moorea

Hospital (☎ 56 23 23, 56 24 24) is in Afareaitu. There's a pharmacy (☎ 56 10 51) at PK6.5 in Maharepa, open daily but only in the mornings on weekends. There's another pharmacy shortly after Tiki Village at PK31 heading north. Both pharmacies are open Monday to Saturday and Sunday morning.

Coast Road

It's 60km right around the island and the circuit can easily be made in a day by bicycle. The following circuit starts at the airport and proceeds in an anticlockwise direction. As you progress round the island it's worth noting that one reason for Moorea's enduring attractiveness is the absence of electrical power poles, the work of former mayor John Teariki.

Temae (PK1, 1km) This village has long been famed for its dancers. They performed for Tahitian royalty when the Pomares held court at Papetoai, put on a hot version of the sexually charged *lori-lori* for Herman Melville and still appear at tourist dance performances today. See the 'Ori Tahiti – Tahitian Dance' section for information on traditional dance. The village is well inland from the coast, which is unusual not just for Moorea but almost anywhere in Polynesia.

Maharepa (PK4 to 5, 4 to 5km) The technicolour *pareu* (sarong-like attire), floating in the breeze like an artist's washing line, announce the beginning of Maharepa village at the Lili Shop. Opposite the lagoonside Jehovah's Witness church, a road runs directly inland towards the mountains, getting rougher the farther it goes. It doesn't lead anywhere in particular.

At PK5, the early 20th-century **Maison Blanche** is a fine example of a *fare vanira*, a plantation house from Moorea's vanilla-boom era. Around the island, particularly from the airport to Cook's Bay and around Papetoai, there are a number of these elegant, single-storey houses with verandas, reminders of the fortunes made from vanilla production. From 1860 to 1960 vanilla, backed up by copra, dominated the economy, but a vanilla-crop disease and the growth of tourism finished off the business. Today, hardly any vanilla is produced on Moorea. See the boxed text 'Tahaa – the Vanilla Island' in the Raiatea & Tahaa chapter for information on vanilla production. Maison Blanche, just beyond the Bali Hai hotel, is now a souvenir shop with a typical selection of pareu and Balinese wood carvings.

Cook's Bay to Paopao (PK6 to 9, 6 to 9km) Cook's Bay is somewhat of a misnomer since Cook actually anchored in Opunohu Bay, but that's unimportant; backdropped by Mt Rotui, it's simply a spectacular stretch of water, especially when there's an interesting ship anchored in the middle. Cook's Bay is also one of the two tourist centres of Moorea. The tourist activity starts at PK5 with Maharepa and continues round to PK9 with the belvédère turn-off in Paopao. The Cook's Bay shops, restaurants and hotels are not lined up side by side, however. There's simply a handful of them dotted along the lagoonside road.

The road passes the **van der Heyde Gallery** with a collection of oceanic art. Farther along there's the **Cook's Bay Gallery**, across from the Club Bali Hai. The gallery has a small museum with items from all over the Polynesian world including Tahiti, Easter Island and New Zealand.

At the base of Cook's Bay is the village of Paopao, with a shipping dock, a popular **market** and a variety of shops. The market has a wall mural painted by Moorea-based artist François Ravello. A road turns inland from Paopao, leading to the marae of the Opunohu Valley, the belvédère and walking tracks across the ridge to Vaiare and up to the Three Coconut Trees Pass (see Walking in the Outdoor Activities chapter for details).

Catholic Churches (PK10, 10km) Two Catholic churches stand side by side on the western side of Cook's Bay. The dull, modern St Joseph's Church dates from 1979 and has mother-of-pearl inlays in the altar. The adjacent abandoned old church has a fine **mural** painted by Peter Haymann (1908-82) above the altar, depicting Polynesian-featured Joseph, Mary, the Archangel Gabriel and the infant Jesus with the lush and mountainous profile of Moorea as a background.

Pineapple Juice Factory (PK11, 11km) A short distance inland from the coast road, Distilleries Tahiti-Moorea or Jus de Fruits de Moorea (☎ 56 11 33) has a pineapple juice factory. It's open weekdays from 7 am to around 3 pm, but get there early, when it's most active. Entrance is free and you can buy mineral water, rum liqueurs and various fruit juices.

Opunohu Bay (PK14 to 18, 14 to 18km) The coast road rounds Mt Rotui and at about PK14 turns inland along the eastern side of Opunohu Bay. There is less development than around Cook's Bay and if anything Opunohu Bay is even more spectacularly beautiful. Most of the Polynesian scenes in the 1984 *Bounty* movie were shot on Opunohu Bay.

Kellum Stop (☎ 56 18 52) is at PK17.5, almost at the top of the bay. This fine old house has an interesting history. In 1925 the wealthy Medford Kellum visited Tahiti on his 55m four-mast *Kaimiloa* along with six scientists from the Bishop Museum in Hawaii, including Kenneth Emory. Emory spent the next 15 months on the islands making pioneering studies of ancient Polynesian marae.

Kellum fell in love with Moorea, bought 1500 hectares of the Opunohu Valley and spent most of the rest of his life on the island. His ownership of the valley facilitated Emory's early archaeological investigations on Moorea. Roger Green's more extensive studies of the valley in the 1960s also owed a debt to the Kellums.

The Kellums' daughter Marimari also became an archaeologist and conducts personal tours around the gardens of her house, a sweep of land running down to the bay that is dense with local plants and flowers. A small sign on the mountain side of the road announces 'Kellum Stop'. Cross the road, ring the cowbell hanging by the gate and wander in. Kellum Stop welcomes visitors weekdays, preferably in the mornings, and a stroll round the garden costs just 300 CFP.

At PK18, right at the top of the bay, a road turns off inland along the Opunohu Valley to the valley marae, the belvédère and the walking route to Three Coconut Trees Pass (see Walking in the Outdoor Activities chapter for more information).

Papetoai (PK22, 22km) Established as the Pacific headquarters of the LMS in 1811, it was to Papetoai that Pomare II retreated from Tahiti in 1808. Between 1822 and 1827 the missionaries constructed an octagonal **church** at Papetoai; today this is the oldest European building in the South Pacific, although it was rebuilt in the late 19th century. As at many other locations around Polynesia, the missionaries deliberately built their church atop an old marae. A single spike-like stone is the sole reminder of the ancient **Marae Taputapuatea**, dedicated to the god Oro.

Papetoai is a busy little village with a post office and a number of restaurants.

Hauru Point (PK25 to 30, 25 to 30km) The coast road rounds Hauru Point, the north-western corner of the island, between PK25 and PK30. This is one of the island's major tourist enclaves but addresses and locations can be a little confusing here as the area is often referred to as Haapiti, since it's in the Haapiti district, even though the village of Haapiti is well to the south. The tourist strip starts with the big Moorea Beachcomber Parkroyal Hotel at about PK25; Tiki Village at PK31 marks the end of the strip.

Tiki Village is open Tuesday to Sunday from 10.30 am to 3 pm, and presents various facets of traditional Polynesian culture for tourists. You can see pearl farm demonstrations, learn the techniques of plaiting and of dyeing pareu, go lagoon fishing, meet craftworkers and even get a tattoo from one of the three tattooists (see the 'Tattooing' special section for information). Entrance costs 2000 CFP and a small dance performance is put on around 3 pm. Le Papayer restaurant welcomes visitors. Friday and Sunday at 11 am historical events are replayed for 3000 CFP, and 50 comedians and dancers in stunning costumes perform a ceremony enthroning a prince, and a marriage.

Hauru Point has one of the best **beaches** on the island, a narrow but sandy stretch that extends for about 5km. Finding your way to the beach is not easy because of the continuous nature of beachside developments. All beaches, however, are public property in French Polynesia and the hotel proprietors along this popular strip do not seem to mind if you walk through their grounds.

Immediately offshore from the point are **Motu Tiahura** and **Motu Fareone**, attractive little islets so close to the shore you can easily swim out to them, and enjoy fine snorkelling on the way. A little farther east is the tiny **Motu Irioa**.

Marae Nuurua (PK31.5, 31.5km) Marae Nuurua is easy to find. Continue past the Tiki Village Theatre on the lagoon side and then the combined ambulance and fire station on the mountain side. On the lagoon side there's a football field and the marae is right on the water's edge, just past the end of the field.

An impressive wall of coral boulders stands at the water's edge with a trail of tumbled boulders leading back to another cairn of boulders and then a restored three level structure. This is flanked by twin spike-like upright stones, one of them broken off but with clear petroglyphs, including one of a turtle. Despite neglect and its relatively populated setting, it's a very evocative ruin, overgrown with vegetation and surrounded by coconut trees. Marae Nuurua was dedicated to the god Taaroa, popular before the Oro cult developed (see the 'Civilisation & Archaeology' special section).

This is the start of the less developed coast of Moorea, but the road is sealed and although the traffic is lighter and the population sparser it doesn't feel that different from other parts of the island.

Haapiti to Atiha Bay (PK24 to 18, 35 to 41km) The largest village on the less populated west coast, Haapiti boasts two **churches**. The small grey-trimmed church in the centre of the village is dwarfed by the huge twin-towered Catholic Église de la

View of Moorea's lagoon from the summit ridge of Mt Rotui

Mt Aorai, Tahiti

Tahiti (pictured here on the west coast), Moorea and Huahine have many surf-breaks.

Yachts at Raiatea

The Marquesas offers interesting horse-riding opportunities.

Hibiscus

A tropical fruit salad

Hibiscus

Baskets of fruit (Gambier Archipelago)

Bird of Paradise

Custard apple (soursop)

Frangipani

Sainte Famille on the mountain side of the road. Built of coral and lime, the church was once the centre of the island's Catholic mission. Haapiti's Matauvau Pass has a popular surf break (see Surfing in the Outdoor Activities chapter).

Moorea's lazy west-coast atmosphere continues round to **Atiha Bay**, a sleepy fishing village that also attracts some surfers.

Marae Nuupere (PK14, 45km) Nuupere Point is immediately south of **Maatea** village and the marae stands just 100m or so south of the point. All that remains is a massive coastal cairn of coral boulders, and it stands on private property. The property owner is not enthusiastic about visitors so permission must be obtained before entering the property.

Back on the coast road the route continues through Maatea village and, 2km farther along, don't blink or you will miss tiny **Haumi** village (PK12, 47km).

Afareaitu (PK10, 49km) The administrative centre of the island, Afareaitu has shops, a hospital, a small hotel, walks to two beautiful waterfalls, a church dating from 1912 and the oldest marae on the island. Chez Pauline is the village's hotel, with a fine collection of ancient stone tiki and other pre-European artefacts. Only about 100m south of Chez Pauline is **Marae Umarea**, thought to date from about 900 AD and the oldest marae on the island. Take the road that goes straight to the coast to see the marae, which is a long wall of coral boulders right along the waterfront. **Marae Matairea** stands inland, up the valley.

Afareaitu's two **waterfalls** are a major island attraction; roads turn inland to these waterfalls on the rivers that enter the sea here. See Walking in the Outdoor Activities chapter for details.

Vaiare Ferry Dock (PK4, 55km) The constant arrival and departure of ferry boats and high speed catamarans coming from and going to Papeete, the busy market scene on the wharf and the cars, taxis and le trucks shuttling visitors to and from their hotels combine to make the 100m or so around the dock area the busiest patch of real estate on Moorea. Vaiare is also the starting point for the interesting walk across the ridge to Paopao and Cook's Bay (see under Walking in the Outdoor Activities chapter).

Teavaro & Temae Beaches (PK1 to 0, 58 to 59km) The best beaches on the east coast stretch from Teavaro round to the airport. The expensive Sofitel Ia Ora Hotel occupies **Teavaro Beach**, where there's good snorkelling in the shallow water. The island road climbs away from the coast to the **Toatea Lookout**, high above Teavaro Beach and with great views over to Tahiti. Temae Beach is close to the end of the airport runway, a pleasant stretch of sand with an unfortunate accumulation of garbage. When the swells run from the south, the reef at **Faaupo Point**, at the southern end of the runway, can have the most powerful waves in French Polynesia (see Surfing in the Outdoor Activities chapter).

A road on the lagoon side of the runway extends around **Temae Lake**, almost to Aroa Point, but the route is cut off by the swampy inlet so it is not possible to rejoin the main coastal road. The lake has lost almost half of its area and two-thirds of its depth over the past century, a process accelerated by the construction of the airport. Salty and semi-stagnant, the isolated lake is one of the rare breeding grounds for the only species of duck found in French Polynesia.

Paopao & Opunohu Valleys

From Moorea's two great bays, valleys sweep inland, meeting south of the coastal bulk of Mt Rotui. Settlements are creeping up the Paopao Valley but the principal activity is still agriculture, with many hectares of pineapple plantations. In the pre-European era the valleys were densely populated and the Opunohu Valley was dotted with marae, some of which have been restored and maintained. The great marae sites of Titiroa and Afareaito were extensively reconstructed by Dr Yoshihiko Shinoto in 1967.

All marae seem to attract mosquitoes and these ones are no exception. Bring insect

MOOREA

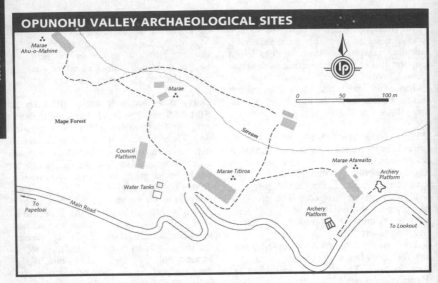

OPUNOHU VALLEY ARCHAEOLOGICAL SITES

repellent or expect to have difficulty withstanding their onslaughts while you read the information boards!

The road leading inland from Paopao and Cook's Bay meets the Opunohu Valley road, just before the agricultural college. From here the road continues inland and up to the marae sites and finally to the **belvédère**, on the slopes of Mt Toheia (1207m).

Archaeological Sites The archaeological sites of the Opunohu Valley are among the most important in French Polynesia. Unusually, you can walk to them along marked tracks and there are explanatory panels in French and in English. The complex includes a range of partially restored remains including family and communal marae as well as dwellings, archery platforms and other structures. See the 'Civilisation & Archaeology' special section for more information on marae.

It's believed the valley was continuously inhabited for six centuries, and the oldest structures date from the 13th century. This agricultural community reached its apogee in the 17th and 18th centuries. The first excavations date from 1925. It was Roger Green, in 1960, who did the most complete research and 500 structures have been inventoried.

Marae Titiroa & Marae Ahu-o-Mahine
Past the agricultural college, the valley road comes to a parking area beside the huge Marae Titiroa, on the edge of a dense forest of magnificent mape trees. From the marae a walking track leads to the council platform, or *tohua*, and two smaller marae. From there it continues to the Marae Ahu-o-Mahine, a more recent marae of individually hewn round stones with an imposing three-stepped *ahu* (altar), which may have been added towards the end of the 18th century. You can cross the small water course running down the valley to discover other more modest marae.

Marae Afareaito & Archery Platforms A short distance farther up the road from Marae Titiroa is Marae Afareaito. Although there is a walking path between the two, it is not easy to follow; the main road is an easier route. The large marae has a small raised-terrace ahu and backrests used by the priests.

Archery in Ancient Times

Archery, as it existed before the arrival of Europeans, was not a wartime activity but a sacred game, reserved exclusively for the male elite of *arii* (chiefs) and *raatira* (middle rank). It involved complex religious rituals and very strict rules. Precision played no part in contest; it was strictly a test of strength – from the archery platform the archers simply had to shoot an arrow the longest possible distance towards a deforested hill. Several referees validated shots and announced results by waving flags. Archery was only practised in the Society Islands and on Mangareva (Gambier Archipelago). The best archery platforms are found on Moorea, in the Opunohu Valley.

The marae is flanked by two crescent-shaped archery platforms from which competing archers would shoot their arrows down a cleared range. Archery was strictly a pastime of the nobility and purely a ritual sport; bows and arrows were not used in battle. See the boxed text for more information.

The Belvédère Beyond Marae Afareaito the road continues to climb steeply, winding up to its conclusion at the belvédère. This lookout offers superb views of Mt Rotui, which splits the two bays, and back to the towering mountains that rise in the centre of the island and once formed the southern rim of the ancient crater. There's a van here that offers snacks and drinks.

Activities

It is wise to book activities as soon as you arrive on the island; contact organisers directly or check with your hotel or guesthouse.

Diving There are some magnificent dive sites for beginners and more experienced divers both inside and outside the reef at the north of the island. The island has four dive centres (see the 'Diving' special section in the Outdoor Activities chapter for details)

and it's a good place to watch shark-feeding or to swim with rays in just 1.5m of water.

Swimming, Snorkelling & Diving Helmets There are several beaches ideal for swimming; you can even swim across to the two motu. For the best snorkelling, join an organised lagoon tour. *Pirogue* (outrigger canoe) trips usually make a snorkelling stop.

Aqua Blue (☎ 56 53 53, fax 56 42 51) in the Beachcomber Parkroyal has an unusual activity. In relatively shallow water at Papetoai's lagoon, you walk along the bottom wearing a *scaphandre* (weighted helmet) into which air is pumped. A diving monitor accompanies you and, since you actually walk on the bottom, you don't even need to be able to swim. You can even communicate with the boat via an intercom. The half-hour stroll costs 10,000 CFP; snorkellers can come along to watch for 1500 CFP.

Walking & Surfing Mt Rotui and Mt Mouaputa, the Afareaitu waterfalls, the Three Coconut Trees Pass and the Vaiare-Paopao route are exhilarating hikes, of varied difficulty, that let your discover the heart of the island. Some of the trails are not often used and are poorly marked so it's wise to use a guide. See the Outdoor Activities chapter for information on walking and on Moorea's important surfing spots.

Dolphin Encounters Dolphin Quest (☎ 55 19 48) in the Beachcomber Parkroyal has dolphins in an enclosed basin and lets you stand in the water and observe them for 30 minutes (9500/6500 CFP adults/children) or snorkel with them for 30 minutes for 10,500 CFP.

Dr Michael Poole is an American working with the Centre Océanographique du Moorea and his Moorea Dolphin Watch (☎ 56 14 70, 56 13 45) has a different approach from Dolphin Quest. Several times a week he takes people on a morning or afternoon boat trip to observe and research dolphins or whales around Moorea. It costs 5000 CFP to 6000 CFP per person and the money goes to finance scientific research.

Horse Riding Tiahura Ranch (☎ 56 28 55) at Hauru Point in front of the Moorea Village offers various two-hour guided rides into the island interior for 3500 CFP. The well mannered horses are from the Marquesas and there are also ponies for children. You can take rides from Tuesday afternoon through to Sunday morning.

Other Activities For game fishing aboard the *Tea Nui*, contact the activities desk at the Beachcomber Parkroyal (☎ 55 19 19). A half-day trip costs 13,780 CFP per person (minimum of four participants). Go to the same activities desk for parasailing, which costs 5830 CFP per person for 10 to 15-minute flights. Jetski tours with guide cost 10,000 CFP an hour and are organised by the Sofitel Ia Ora, Beachcomber Parkroyal and Moorea Village. These three hotels, plus Les Tipaniers, offer water-skiing for 2000 CFP per 15 minutes. Helicopter flights over Moorea are made by Héli Pacific (☎ 85 68 00) in Papeete.

Organised Tours

4WD Tours Several operators organise island tours, called Safari 4x4, aboard open Land Rovers. There are complete tours of the island with visits to the Opunohu Valley archaeological sites, stops at the belvédère and the Afareaitu waterfalls and visits to pineapple and vanilla plantations and the fruit juice factory. The half-day tours cost 3500 CFP to 4000 CFP per person and are good value if you're by yourself or don't want to rent a car. Check that the guide speaks English.

Operators include Inner Island Safari Tours (☎ 56 20 09), Ron's Tours (☎ 56 42 43), Tefaarahi Safari Tours (☎ 56 41 24), Torea Nui Safari (☎ 56 12 48, 56 15 05) and Albert Transports (☎ 56 13 53, 56 19 28). Tefaarahi Safari Tours is operated by an American who also offers visits to petroglyphs on his property.

Lagoon Tours The best way to discover the magnificent lagoon of Moorea is by joining a lagoon excursion in a pirogue with outboard. Tours typically visit the two bays,

stop to feed the sharks, swim with the rays and picnic and snorkel on Motu Fareone. The costs vary from operator to operator, so check the competition and ask what they offer (length of trip, itinerary, whether picnic and drinks are included, transfers and so on). A 9 am to 3 pm day-trip typically costs 4000 CFP to 7000 CFP. Shark feeding and a visit to the rays only will cost about 2500 CFP.

Shark Tour at Moorea Camping is the cheapest operator at 1000 CFP, for which you get the sharks, the rays and a motu snorkelling stop. Other operators include Albert Tours (☎ 56 13 53, 56 19 28), What to do on Moorea Tours (☎ 56 57 64), Moorea Boat Tours (☎ 56 28 44) and Te Aho Nui (☎ 56 31 42). The activities desks at the Sofitel Ia Ora, the Moorea Beachcomber Parkroyal Hotel, Les Tipaniers, the Moorea Village Hotel and the Hotel Hibiscus offer similar trips. If you wish to visit the lagoon aboard the *Manu* catamaran for 5300 CFP for a half-day, check with the Beachcomber Parkroyal activities desk.

Each operator organises two or three trips a week; contact them as soon as you arrive since a minimum number of participants may be required.

Places to Stay

Although there is accommodation scattered around the island, most is concentrated on the eastern side of Cook's Bay and around Hauru Point. Both these centres are very spread out; if you're staying at one end and want to eat at the other it's not a case of just wandering a few steps along the road.

Moorea has superb over-water bungalows but it also has the best selection of economical (by local standards, of course!) accommodation in French Polynesia. There are backpacker centres with camping sites and dorm facilities, some cheaper hotels and a host of local bungalow complexes that generally include kitchen equipment so you can cook your own food. Note that while most places will supply sheets and other bedding, towels are often not provided in the cheapest places. The top-end places and most of the mid-range places accept credit cards. Most budget places don't; any exceptions are noted in each budget section in this chapter. There's an 8% VAT and daily 50 CFP or 150 CFP tourist tax on top of most prices. Unless otherwise stated, the following prices for accommodation are for one night only.

Cook's Bay The bay looks magnificent but there is no beach.

Budget *Motel Albert (☎ 56 12 76, fax 56 58 58)*, on the mountain side of the road at PK7 at Cook's Bay, has 19 *fare*. A two room *fare* costs 7000 CFP for up to four people. A one room *fare* costs 4000 CFP for one or two people; 5000 CFP for three. The rooms have kitchen facilities and hot-water bathroom. There's an extra charge of 1000 CFP if you stay just one night. In spite of the number of *fare*, the site doesn't feel too congested. There's free fruit on offer and if you're preparing your own food there are several places to shop nearby.

Mid-Range *Bali Hai Moorea (☎ 56 13 59, fax 56 19 22)* is just past PK5, at the start of the hotel and restaurant strip around Cook's Bay. The hotel has a well stocked boutique, a pool, tennis court, a very popular bar, restaurants and a tiny patch of beach. The island-night dance performance is one of the best on Moorea. The cheapest rooms, at 12,960 CFP, are depressing little boxes that are best avoided. The bungalows are much brighter and more cheerful, starting at 15,120 CFP for the garden and poolside bungalows up to 27,000 CFP for the over-water ones. Prices include VAT.

Club Bali Hai (☎ 56 13 68, fax 56 13 27) is farther round the bay at about PK8 and has rooms and bungalows classified as bayview, beachfront or over-water and ranging in price from 7560 CFP to 16,200 CFP. There's a swimming pool, tennis court, restaurant, a very popular bar (particularly on Friday night) and a nice setting right on

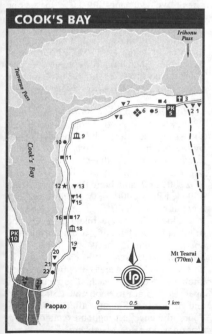

COOK'S BAY

PLACES TO STAY
- 4 Bali Hai Moorea
- 11 Kaveka Hotel; Fisherman's Wharf Restaurant
- 16 Club Bali Hai
- 17 Motel Albert

PLACES TO EAT
- 1 Le Mahogany
- 2 Le Cocotier
- 7 La Case
- 8 Le Pêcheur
- 13 Allo Pizza
- 14 Caprice des Îles
- 15 L'Ananas Bleu
- 19 Alfredo's
- 20 Snack Te Honu Iti
- 21 Chez Jean-Pierre
- 23 Snack Chez Michèle
- 24 Snack Rotui

OTHER
- 3 Jehovah's Witness Church
- 5 Maison Blanche
- 6 Maharepa Shopping Centre; Crêperie-Snack Sylésie; Post Office
- 9 van der Heyde Gallery
- 10 MUST Dive Centre
- 12 Gendarmerie (Police Station)
- 18 Cook's Bay Gallery
- 22 Fish Market

the bay with great views of Mt Rotui. These bungalows are usually rented by the week.

Also on the lagoon side on Cook's Bay, *Kaveka Hotel* (☎ 56 50 50, fax 56 52 63, email kaveka@mail.pf) is managed by an American. The units are fairly ordinary but functional and well equipped, with hot-water bathroom. Prices vary from 10,260 CFP to 15,120 CFP including VAT. Half-board (bed, breakfast and lunch or evening meal) at the hotel's Fisherman's Wharf restaurant adds 3800 CFP per person and return transfers to the airport or ferry quay are 1200 CFP.

Cook's Bay to Hauru Point *Chez Dina* (☎ 56 10 39) at PK12.5 is on the mountain side of the road and has three *fare* with kitchenette and shared cold-water bathroom for 5000 CFP for up to three people. There's a pirogue available for free, a pedal boat and bicycles for rent, and fishing trips and motu excursions can be organised.

A new *Hotel Moorea Lagoon* was under construction at PK14 at the time of writing.

Village Faimano Hotel (☎ 56 10 20, fax 56 36 47) is at PK14; its three garden bungalows cost 7500 CFP to 8500 CFP, the two by the water are 9000 CFP and the two family *fare* (with two rooms) are 11,500 CFP. All have kitchen facilities and attached hot-water bathroom. There's a 5% reduction after a week; pirogues are provided free and there are bicycles for 1000 CFP a day. Credit cards are accepted.

Chez Francine (☎ 56 13 24), BP 659 Maharepa, Moorea, is close to PK14 and has a big garden right by the lagoon. There are two simple adjoining rooms for one or two people with hot-water bathroom; one is 6500 CFP, the other has a kitchenette and terrace and costs 8500 CFP. The whole building rents for 12,500 CFP. Rates drop after a week, there's a barbecue (BBQ) and a pirogue available for guests' use and the owner will drive guests to the shops to stock up every other day.

Les Tipaniers Iti (☎ 56 12 67, fax 56 29 25) is associated with the popular Les Tipaniers at Hauru Point and has five very pleasant bungalows with kitchen, sitting area and veranda for 8424 CFP. Special

prices are available for longer stays. A free shuttle to Hauru Point departs at 10 am and returns at 2 pm and also runs to the Les Tipaniers restaurant at night. There's no beach but the lagoonside setting at PK21 at the entrance to Opunohu Bay is very attractive and there are terrific views.

Hauru Point Unlike Cook's Bay this sector has a pleasant beach, although it's rather narrow and access is not easy. This strip can feel quite crowded but there's a wide variety of accommodation. The two motu directly offshore are very easy to reach.

Budget Chez Nelson & Josiane (☎ 56 15 18) at PK27 has a spacious site by the beach and is very popular with backpackers. There's a wide accommodation range starting with tent sites for 700 CFP per person and dorm beds for 1020 CFP each. Five beach cabins are pretty basic, although they have mosquito nets, and cost 2244 CFP for one or two occupants (3060 CFP for the one beside the sea). Garden *fare* cost 2550 CFP for one or two people. There are two good bungalows by the sea with hot-water bathroom and kitchen for 5100 CFP for one or two people (including free use of a pirogue). All these costs are for stays of two nights or more; add 20% if you're staying one night only.

Moorea Camping (☎ 56 14 47, fax 56 30 22) at PK27.5 is another popular place with shoestring travellers. The huge site is right by the beach and offers a variety of accommodation starting with tent sites at 800 CFP per person. Dorm beds cost from 1000 CFP to 2200 CFP and bungalows range from 4500 CFP to 6000 CFP. There have been complaints about the cleanliness of the sanitary blocks; costs are hiked 20% for one night stays and there's a daily 200 CFP charge for renting sheets and towels. A big *fare potee* (originally the chief's house – now an open dining area) with two equipped kitchens faces the beach. The reception is open from 8 am to noon and 1.30 to 5 pm and is closed Sunday afternoon. Shark Tours, the cheapest lagoon-excursion operator on Moorea, is based here.

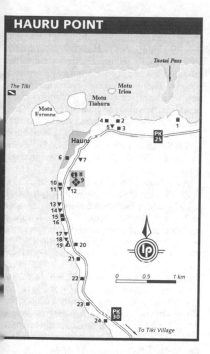

HAURU POINT

The Tiki

Taotai Pass

Motu
Irioa

Motu
Tiahura

Motu
Fareone

Hauru

PK
25

PK
30

To Tiki Village

0   0.5   1 km

HAURU POINT

PLACES TO STAY
1   Moorea Beachcomber Parkroyal Hotel
2   Moorea Beach Club
3   Fare Condominium
4   Hotel Les Tipaniers
6   Club Méditerraneanée Moorea (Club Med)
10 Hotel Hibiscus
15 Chez Nelson & Iosiane
16 Hotel Fare Vaimoana
19 Moorea Camping
20 Fare Auti Rua
21 Moorea Village Hotel; Tiahura Ranch
22 Chez Billy Ruta
23 Fare Mato Iea
24 Fare Manula

PLACES TO EAT
5   Les Tipaniers Restaurant
7   Le Motu
11 Sunset Restaurant
12 La Plantation
13 Pâtisserie Sylésie
14 Restaurant Tumoana
17 Coco d'Îsle
18 Pitcairn

OTHER
8   Tourist Office
9   Le Petit Village (Shopping Centre & Restaurants)

At either of these locations do not expect any luxury, or even a friendly welcome. Setting and the competitive prices are the only assets. Don't leave objects of value in your room or tent either.

Fare Auti Rua (☎ 56 14 47) is across from and connected with Moorea Camping and has six comfortable and spacious bungalows with mezzanine, hot-water bathroom and equipped kitchen. Rates range from 000 CFP for two people up to 11,000 CFP or four although a two night minimum stay is required. Guests can access the beach via Moorea Camping. Credit cards are accepted.

Chez Billy Ruta (☎ 56 12 54) at PK28 has 2 basic *fare* side by side along the beach. These cabin-like places have two single beds and cold-water bathroom and cost 000 CFP, 6000 CFP with kitchenette. Cell-ke rooms with two beds cost 3000 CFP.

Mid-Range Moorea Beach Club (☎ 56 15 3, fax 41 09 28) is the first place along the

Hauru Point strip after the big Beachcomber Parkroyal Hotel. It's an unexciting beachfront place with a pool, tennis courts and a beachfront restaurant. The cost is 9720 CFP for two people and credit cards are accepted. There's musical entertainment on Friday and Sunday evenings.

Fare Condominium (☎ 56 26 69, fax 56 26 22) is at the same location. It's a funny name for a bunch of bungalows – standard, spacious and functional units with kitchenette, air-con and TV, costing 13,500 CFP to 15,800 CFP according to their garden or beach location. The bungalows accommodate up to five or six people, and the prices jump to 16,000 CFP or 18,000 CFP. They especially suit families and credit cards are accepted.

Hotel Les Tipaniers (☎ 56 12 67, fax 56 29 25) is also at the beginning of the Hauru Point hotel and restaurant strip. Its *fare* are in a garden leading down to the beach where there's a restaurant/bar and fine views of the motu. The thatched-roof bungalows have a veranda, small lounge area, slightly elevated sleeping area, fan and hot-water bathroom. They range in price from 9450 CFP to 15,660 CFP. These rates include VAT and credit cards are accepted.

Les Tipaniers' restaurant has an excellent reputation (see Hauru Point under Places to Eat later). Breakfast is 900 CFP, half-board 3750 CFP, and there's a bar and a variety of sporting facilities. It's an easy swim out to the motu and pirogue trips and the use of bicycles are free for guests. Activities include lagoon tours and motu drop-offs and the Scubapiti dive centre is on the site (see the 'Diving' special section for details). Thursday evening there's musical entertainment at the beach bar.

Hotel Hibiscus (☎ 56 12 20, fax 56 20 69, email hibiscus@tahiti.net), at PK27, next to Club Med, has 29 very functional and slightly spartan thatched-roof bungalows, in a pleasant garden. They all have three beds, attached hot-water bathroom, veranda and kitchenette. They cost 12,960 CFP (garden) or 15,120 CFP (beach). The Sunset Restaurant on the beach is quite good and there's a swimming pool. Half/full board adds 4300/7500 CFP per person. Credit cards are accepted.

Hotel Fare Vaimoana (☎/fax 56 17 14), at PK27.5, is straddled by Chez Nelson & Josiane and has 13 very comfortable bungalows with mosquito nets, fan, refrigerator, mezzanine and hot-water bathroom. They accommodate up to four people and cost from 9720 CFP to 14,040 CFP for beachfront units. There's a good and pleasantly situated restaurant, and half-board adds 3500 CFP per person. Canoes at 2500 CFP a half-day and kayaks at 3500 CFP can be rented to go to the motu. Credit cards are accepted.

Moorea Village Hotel (☎ 56 10 02, fax 56 22 11), on the beach side of the road at PK28, beyond Moorea Camping, is also known as Fare Gendron. Ideal for families, it has 80 functional bungalows with hot-water bathroom, fan and refrigerator (some have kitchenettes). Depending on their garden or beach location and facilities, the bungalows range in price from 8640/9720 CFP

a single/double up to 27,000 CFP for the largest beachside bungalows for three or four, including VAT. Half/full board adds 3900/5400 CFP per person. The site is rather crowded but hedges and trees break the monotony. There's a tennis court, swimming pool, bar and restaurant; bicycles, pedal boats and kayaks are available to rent and motu excursions are organised. On Saturday evening there's a Tahitian BBQ (3600 CFP) and at Sunday lunchtime there's a dance performance (3900 CFP). The hotel accepts credit cards.

Fare Mato Tea (☎ 54 14 36, fax 56 32 54) at PK28.7 has nine simple motel-style beach cabins with a big kitchen and dining area and lots of sleeping space. Dotted around a wide expanse of lawn, sweeping down to the beach, the cabins cost from 8500 CFP to 10,000 CFP per day. A minimum stay of two nights is required.

Fare Manuia (☎ 56 26 17, fax 56 10 30) has a pleasant stretch of beach at PK30, towards the end of the Hauru Point strip. There are six bungalows spaced out around the grassy grounds of this family-oriented place. All have hot-water bathroom, kitchen facilities, TV and large veranda. They accommodate four to six and rent for 8000 CFP to 12,000 CFP. There's a washing machine at the site, a pirogue for free use and a kayak that can be rented. There's a two night minimum stay.

Polynesian Bungalows (☎ 56 30 20, 56 30 77, fax 56 32 15) are just before Tiki Village at PK31, marking the extreme end of the Hauru Point tourist strip. The thatched-roof bungalows have bathroom, a kitchenette and a mezzanine area but are rather jammed together and unlikely to be of interest to short-term visitors since they're mainly rented by the week or month. Count on 51,840 CFP per week for two people including VAT; credit cards are accepted.

Top End The start of the Hauru Point tourist strip is demarcated by the large **Moorea Beachcomber Parkroyal Hotel** (☎ 56 19 19, fax 56 18 88, email moorea@parkroyal.pf) one of the most luxurious and expensive, not to mention biggest, hotels on the island.

The Beachcomber has a lavish reception, restaurant and bar area stepping down to a swimming pool and waterfront activities area, while the 147 rooms wind around the artificial lagoon, where the hotel's resident dolphins live. Nightly costs range from 29,160 CFP for basic rooms to 44,280 CFP for over-water bungalows. Half/full board adds 6936/9996 CFP. There are many sporting facilities, and a thrice-weekly evening dance performance with an excellent reputation.

Club Méditerranée Moorea (☎ 55 00 00, fax 55 00 10) at Hauru Point opened in 1963 and is still the largest resort in French Polynesia. It's a typical Club Med facility with activities intended to keep you running until you drop. On Moorea, that includes the usual gamut of island activities including boat trips, diving, horse riding, fishing, island tours and trips to Tetiaroa (Marlon Brando's island). Club Med visitors almost always book their holiday prior to arrival in Tahiti, typically at around US$220 to US$260 per day. There's usually a three-day minimum stay and a Club Med 'joining fee'. There is a Club Med office in the Vaima Centre in Papeete (☎ 42 96 99, 42 16 83).

Haapiti *Fare Tatta'u* (☎/fax 56 35 83), at PK21.3, is an excellent address well away from the tourist crush. There's a friendly, family atmosphere in a quiet and green location with four miniature cabins with two beds and cold-water bathroom for 4000 CFP; 5000 CFP if it's for just one night. There's also a dorm *fare* with two small rooms with two beds at 1500 CFP each and a larger one with four at 1200 CFP each. In the middle of the property is a superb *fare potee*, which is used as a kitchen. Purotu, one of the best tattooists on Moorea, did much of the decoration. Transfers from the airport or ferry wharf are 500 CFP. This place is popular with surfers because of its proximity to Haapiti's Matauvau Pass, and a boat ride out to the break costs 500 CFP per person.

Residence Linareva (☎/fax 56 15 35) is just north of Haapiti village, at PK34.5 just past where the PK24 clockwise markers meet the PK35 anticlockwise ones. It has very pleasant bungalows in a well kept garden by the beach, and a respected restaurant. The bungalows are attractively furnished and garden rooms cost 7776/8856 CFP for singles/doubles. The beachfront rooms cost 10,260/11,340 CFP while the beachfront bungalows cost 12,096/13,176 CFP. All prices include VAT and reduced rates are available for longer stays. Bicycles, pirogues and snorkelling equipment are all provided free of charge. So long as you don't mind the somewhat isolated location it's a great place to stay.

Afarealtu *Chez Pauline* (☎ 56 11 26) is all by itself in the village of Afareaitu, 5km south of the Vaiare ferry quay and a long way from the tourist activity at Cook's Bay and Hauru Point. This is one of the most interesting places on the island. Opened by Pauline Teariki's mother in 1918, for many years it was the only hotel on the island. Although it most definitely lacks the comforts of a modern hotel it has a historic but spartan charm and offers a real opportunity to sample local life. There are seven rooms, sharing two cold water bathrooms. Costs are 2500/4000 CFP for one/two people, 6000 CFP for four to six. The restaurant specialises in Tahitian cuisine. Credit cards are not accepted.

Temae *Sofitel Ia Ora* (☎ 56 12 90, fax 56 12 91) looks across to Tahiti from Temae Beach, just 2km south of Moorea's airport. It vies with the Beachcomber Parkroyal for the title of Moorea's most luxurious hotel. Beautifully situated on one of the island's best beaches, the hotel has two restaurants, bars, swimming pool and tennis courts. The room costs range from garden bungalows for 25,812 CFP up to over-water bungalows for 54,000 CFP. Prices include VAT and half-board adds 5916 CFP. A wide range of activities is offered on land and sea and bicycles are available for 2000 CFP a day. Two or three times weekly there's a buffet dinner with Polynesian dance performance.

Temae Bed & Breakfast (☎/fax 56 42 92) offers a simple but charming room in a *fare* for 6000 CFP a double, including a big breakfast. The shower is outside. The *fare* is by the sea, next to the owner's house and in an isolated and luxuriant setting. There is a small snack bar nearby.

Fare Maeva (☎/fax 56 18 10) has three attractive bungalows with hot-water bathroom and kitchenette for 6500 CFP for two. The setting is dominated by bushes, coconut trees and coral debris, giving it an atoll flavour. The owners will take you to shops for food supplies and they sell their handpainted pareu and cushions.

Places to Eat

There are plenty of restaurants around Moorea including hotel restaurants and independent outlets. Cook's Bay and Hauru Point are the main dining centres and although there are more hotel beds at Hauru Point, there are probably more restaurant tables at Cook's Bay. You'll find crêperies, snack bars, seafood specialists, pizzerias, Polynesian restaurants and many others.

Most places close towards 9 pm and on Sunday the choice can be surprisingly restricted. Menus are generally translated into English and some establishments will collect you from your accommodation and return you after your meal. If you're fixing your own food there are plenty of food shops.

Cook's Bay & Maharepa In addition to the places listed here, there are restaurants at the three main hotels in this sector – the Bali Hai, the Kaveka and the Club Bali Hai. *Fisherman's Wharf* in the Kaveka is built out over the lagoon with tables arranged around a hole in the floor.

Restaurants Le Mahogany (☎ 56 39 73) is at the eastern or airport end of Cook's Bay, past PK4 in Maharepa. The menu is essentially French but with some Chinese dishes to add variety. Starters are 600 CFP to 1200 CFP, meat dishes cost from 1250 CFP, sashimi is 950 CFP and chow mein is 1150 CFP. At lunchtime the snack menu has dishes from 650 CFP to 1350 CFP. The mahogany panelled restaurant features paintings by local artists, transport is offered between the Bali Hai and Club Bali Hai and credit cards are accepted.

Le Cocotier (☎ 56 12 10), in Maharepa village just before PK5 and the Bali Hai, is a popular and well run restaurant specialising in French cuisine. You could try *mahi mahi* (dolphin fish – a type of fish, not a dolphin!) in ginger butter for 1650 CFP or andouillete sausages in mustard for 1550 CFP. There are dishes of the day at 1000 CFP to 1500 CFP and a fairly good wine list. There's a communal table reserved for people who turn up alone. Transport is offered anywhere between the Sofitel Ia Ora and Cook's Bay. It's open for lunch and dinner daily and credit cards are accepted.

At *Le Pêcheur* (The Fisherman; ☎ 56 36 12) it's seafood, hardly surprisingly, that is the speciality. The menu features *cigalle de mer* (a type of small lobster) for 700 CFP for 100g, a fisher's plate for 2200 CFP, mahi mahi with vanilla for 1950 CFP, and the dish of the day for 950 CFP weekday lunchtimes. The restaurant is on the inland side of the road between the Bali Hai and the Kaveka Hotel. Transport is offered between the Bali Hai and the Faimano Village and it's open for lunch and dinner daily.

La Case (☎ 56 42 95), across the road and a little farther along from Le Pêcheur, used to be Caribbean but has been taken over by Swiss management who offer raclettes, fondues, *pierrades* (food cooked on a heated stone) including a pierrade of mahi mahi in coconut milk for 2000 CFP, pastas and some local specialities like *poisson cru* (a raw fish dish) for 1250 CFP. The decor – colourful chairs and posters – remains Caribbean! Transport is offered from between the Sofitel Ia Ora and Cook's Bay. It's closed Wednesday and credit cards are accepted.

Caprice des Îles (☎ 56 44 24), in Cook's Bay, shortly after the Club Bali Hai and on the mountain side of the road, looks like an enormous Polynesian *fare*. Everything is made of coconut including the tables, chairs and flooring. The food is French, Chinese (chow mein for 1000 CFP) and Tahitian (chicken curry with coconut for 1450 CFP). Transport is provided within a 2km radius. It's open Wednesday to Monday for lunch and dinner and credit cards are accepted.

Alfredo's (☎ *56 17 71)*, on the mountain side of the road nearly at the end of the bay, is a popular Italian restaurant with a pleasant open-air dining area. Pizzas at about 1300 CFP are the house speciality although some diners say the pizza standards have slipped of late. Starters are 800 CFP to 1400 CFP, pasta dishes 1250 CFP to 1750 CFP, main courses – salmon, shrimp, mahi mahi, tuna – are 1700 CFP to 2100 CFP. Transport is offered as far back as the Bali Hai. It's closed Sunday and credit cards are accepted.

Snack Te Honu Iti (☎ *56 19 84)*, almost at the top of Cook's Bay, was a popular restaurant, but it's currently closed.

Chez Jean-Pierre (☎ *56 18 51)* is at the very top of the bay, just 50m from the fish market in a featureless building, and offers Chinese food. It looks out on the lagoon, and six different shrimp dishes are the house speciality (1350 CFP to 1850 CFP). On Saturday evening piglet in coconut milk is the featured dish at 2100 CFP. It's closed Wednesday, Saturday lunchtime and Monday evening. Credit cards are accepted.

Cafés & Snack Bars *Crêperie-Snack Sylésie*, in the Maharepa shopping centre, is an ideal place for breakfast (880 CFP), a crêpe or a modestly priced snack. It's open from 6 am to 6 pm. *Allo Pizza* (☎ 56 18 22) is just in front of the gendarmerie and is open for lunch and dinner (except for Monday and Tuesday lunchtimes), offering about 30 different pizzas from 900 CFP to 1500 CFP. It will even deliver them in this area. *L'Ananas Bleu* (The Blue Pineapple) is on the inland side of the road and is recommended for breakfast or lunch, served at tables on its pleasant veranda.

In Paopao, at the head of Cook's Bay where the Opunohu Valley road turns off the coast road and where the river from the valley enters the bay, there are several small snack bars including *Snack Chez Michèle* and *Snack Rotui*.

Opunohu Valley En route to the belvédère or the archaeological sites, stop at the agricultural college, where a small *fare* sells delicious ice creams in local flavours including guava, passionfruit and even *uru* (breadfruit) and *tiare* (the flower!). They cost 500 CFP; excellent cool fruit juices cost 300 CFP. It also offers dried bananas and homemade jams.

Papetoai *Chez Serge* (☎ *56 13 17)* is on the inland side of the road, right by the turn-off to the octagonal church and is one of the most interesting places on the island. Polynesian food is served in a traditional-style *fare* with two small rooms, a sandy floor, wooden tables and walls and roof in *niau* (woven coconut-palm leaves). Bananas are suspended from the ceiling and you can feast on local specialities including a variety of fish, shrimp, lobster, chicken and piglet dishes accompanied by *fei* (a type of banana), French-fried taro or uru. This is one of the rare establishments where you can try the famous *fafaru* or a delicious dessert of poe bananas in coconut milk for 500 CFP. Prices are reasonable: fish and crustaceans for 980 CFP to 1500 CFP, poisson cru at only 850 CFP. Don't miss the *ahimaa* (traditional Tahitian oven) for 2000 CFP on Wednesday evening and Sunday lunchtime. Bookings are necessary. Chez Serge is open for lunch and dinner daily and credit cards are accepted.

At the time of writing it was possible that Chez Serge might move closer to the Beachcomber Parkroyal, to a more comfortable but still traditional setting.

Hauru Point Hauru Point offers a variety of dining options.

Restaurants *Beachcomber Parkroyal* (☎ *56 51 10)* has three restaurants. *Fare Nui* is the gastronomic restaurant on the open terrace looking out at the lagoon. *Fare Hana* is beside the swimming pool with a lighter menu, such as grills from 1700 CFP. *Motu Iti* is decorated by local artists. Each week a dance performance is put on with two or three buffets with BBQs, grills and seafood for 4500 CFP to 6100 CFP.

Les Tipaniers Restaurant (☎ *56 12 67)*, at the hotel of the same name, combines French-Italian food with a Tahitian flavour

MOOREA

and has a great reputation. It's a moveable feast, with breakfast and lunch at the beach, while at dinnertime it shifts up to the main road. At lunchtime there are pasta dishes from 950 CFP to 1050 CFP and an excellent hamburger for 850 CFP. Dinner features entrees like poisson cru at 950 CFP and tartar of tuna for 1500 CFP. Main courses include a luscious fillet of mahi mahi with Tahaa vanilla for 1600 CFP. Desserts are 450 CFP to 650 CFP and the house vanilla ice cream is recommended. Transport from the Beachcomber zone can be arranged for 400 CFP and credit cards are accepted.

La Plantation (☎ 56 45 10), immediately south of Le Petit Village, has an air of refinement with a tropical atmosphere, exuberant greenery and a large interior room and outside terrace in local style. Fish dishes are about 1950 CFP, meat dishes are 1850 CFP to 2650 CFP and pizzas are 1100 CFP to 1450 CFP. You can finish with an 800 CFP ice cream. It's open Wednesday to Monday for lunch and dinner. Credit cards are accepted.

The beachfront *Sunset Restaurant (☎ 56 12 20)* at the Hotel Hibiscus looks out over the lagoon to the two motu; ideal to catch the sunset. It turns out pizzas for 1100 CFP, a variety of main courses for 1100 CFP to 2800 CFP, a set meal for 2400 CFP and some simple snacks and drinks at the bar. It's open daily for lunch and dinner. Credit cards are accepted.

Restaurant Tumoana (☎ 56 37 60) is next to the Hotel Fare Vaimoana, back from the road, and serves attractively priced Chinese dishes like chow mein for 750 CFP and other dishes for around 1000 CFP. The decor is dull but there are beautiful views from the terrace. It's open Monday to Saturday for lunch and dinner. Credit cards are accepted.

The restaurant at *Fare Vaimoana (☎ 56 17 14)* has a pleasant beachside setting. The interior is elegantly stylish using local wood, sculptured posts and a terrace over the beach, with front-row seats for the sunset. Fish dishes are 1600 CFP to 2200 CFP, meat dishes 1500 CFP to 2300 CFP and desserts about 800 CFP. Live music is sometimes provided. Credit cards are accepted.

Moorea Village Hotel (☎ 56 10 02) has a restaurant next to the swimming pool, in a beautiful room in local style, facing the motu. Prices are very reasonable and there's often music with dinner. Saturday evening features a BBQ with a pareu show and fire dance for 3600 CFP. Sunday lunchtime you can try a Tahitian *tamaaraa* (feast from a traditional Tahitian oven) with entertainment by a dance group for 3900 CFP.

Cafés & Snack Bars Le Motu is in a small shopping centre across from Club Med, and has light meals, salads, pizzas, crêpes and a big choice of hamburgers from 470 CFP to 800 CFP. The setting is ordinary and the air-con room rather sterile. It's open Tuesday to Saturday from 9 am to 9 pm, and Sunday morning.

There are two snack bars in Le Petit Village centre. *Lagoon Café* is open from Monday to Saturday for lunch and dinner. *Garden* is open Tuesday through to Sunday morning. These places serve meals, ice cream and snacks including salads, sandwiches, omelettes and burgers. Main meals cost from 1300 CFP, pizzas 800 CFP to 1200 CFP.

Pâtisserie Sylésie has a dull roadside setting but you can get light lunches from 950 CFP; crêpes, ice creams, very fancy sandwiches for 400 CFP; milkshakes for 500 CFP and cold fruit juices (mango, pineapple, grapefruit depending on the season) for 500 CFP a half-litre. It's open daily from 6 am to 5 pm.

Coco d'Îsle has a good balance of quality and price and is open daily from 6.30 am to 10 pm. Breakfast costs 400 CFP; the dish of the day is 950 CFP as are poisson cru, chow mein, spaghetti and chicken dishes. Prices drop 50% if you take away. Burgers and other snacks are 400 CFP, crêpes between 200 CFP and 450 CFP. Although it's beside the road it's got a pleasant setting in a small glade of passion fruit trees.

Pitcairn is open daily for breakfast and lunch. A continental breakfast costs 500 CFP, chow mein 900 CFP, a fish fillet is around 1500 CFP and hamburgers are around 500 CFP. There are set menus at

1000 CFP and 1200 CFP including a salad, dessert, drink and coffee.

Haapiti *Le Linareva* (☎ 56 15 35), at the hotel of the same name at PK34.5, is a floating restaurant installed at the end of the wharf. The food is essentially French but with a local flavour and enjoys an excellent reputation. In this very maritime setting of portholes and nautical pictures, you can try a starter of gratin of crab for 1450 CFP, followed by mahi mahi fillets seasoned with ginger for 2180 CFP, beef fillet seasoned with morels for 3650 CFP, or shark sauteed with garlic for 2150 CFP. Cocktails at the bar are 950 CFP and a half-litre of Hinano is 500 CFP. Transport from Hauru Point hotels costs 400 CFP. It's open daily for lunch and dinner and reservations are recommended because it's quite small. Credit cards are accepted.

Pizzas Daniel, a little beyond the Linareva restaurant to the north, is a straightforward place with pizzas to take away or eat there for 1000 CFP. It's closed on Thursday, open other days from 11 am to 9 pm.

Afareaitu *Chez Pauline* (☎ 56 11 26) requires advance reservations and offers Polynesian specialities such as poisson cru, shrimp curry with coconut milk and desserts like papaya with coconut milk. The simple family setting is typically Polynesian and meals cost around 1300 CFP and a complete *maa tahiti* (Tahitian buffet) 3500 CFP.

Vaiare You won't starve while you wait for your ferry to depart. *Roulottes* set up by the wharf to feed hungry voyagers when boats are coming and going.

Temae *La Pérouse* at Sofitel Ia Ora, in the garden looking across a pretty pool of lilies, has dishes from around 1700 CFP. *Molokai* is next to the Sofitel's swimming pool and has a terrace over the beach and a bar.

Self-Catering There are quite a few supermarkets and smaller shops around the island. Most are open on Sunday morning and accept credit cards. The TOA supermarket,

just over 500m south of the quay in Vaiare, is the largest on the island and is open Monday to Saturday from 8 am to 8 pm and Sunday morning. There are fish markets in Maharepa and at the municipal market in Paopao, where the night's catch goes on sale at dawn. The Municipal market is open daily from 5 to 8 am.

Entertainment

Bars Although Moorea is a fairly 'early-to-bed' sort of place, there are some good places for a sunset drink. *Club Bali Hai's* bar offers a magnificent panorama of Cook's Bay. It's one of the most popular places on the island on Friday night for both visitors and locals. Towards Maharepa, *Bali Hai* is another good place for a cold beer and *Le Cocotier* restaurant has a well equipped bar.

At Hauru Point, *Les Tipaniers* and *Sunset Restaurant* have popular beachside bars. The Residencial Linareva's floating *Le Linareva* at PK34.5 is a great place to watch the sunset with a cocktail in hand and it's also right out over the water.

Discos Better head back to Papeete if you want real nightlife; only *Club Med* has any on Moorea. There's a disco every night from 9.45 pm; it's particularly busy on Friday and Saturday nights. Entrance, which includes a string of beads to buy drinks, costs 2000 CFP on the weekend and 1000 CFP during the week.

Dance Performances *Tiki Theatre Village* (☎ 56 18 97, fax 56 10 86, email tikivillage@mail.pf), just south of Hauru Point at PK31, has an excellent dance performance by a troupe of 60 professional dancers on Tuesday, Wednesday, Friday and Saturday at 8.45 pm. The performance alone costs 3000 CFP. Dining at 6 pm before the dance adds 3500 CFP and return transport from your hotel (in a canoe from Hauru Point) another 1000 CFP. The terminally romantic can try a Tahitian wedding – including a tattooing ceremony for the man – before sailing off in a royal canoe for a sunset cruise. Well, Dustin Hoffman did it.

MOOREA

There are also Polynesian music and dance performances by local groups at *Moorea Village*, *Moorea Beach Club*, *Sofitel Ia Ora*, *Beachcomber Parkroyal*, *Club Med* and *Bali Hai* a couple of times a week (see Places to Stay earlier in this chapter for hotel details). In principle the performances come with a buffet dinner and cost 4000 CFP to 6000 CFP but in practise a drink at the bar will get you in. Entrance at the Bali Hai is free. Call the hotels for dates and times.

Shopping

There are two small shopping centres. The Commercial Centre in Maharepa has a bookshop/newsagency, a variety of other shops and a crêperie-snack bar. Le Petit Village, across from Club Med at Hauru, has various shops and souvenir outlets, a bank, supermarket and bookshop/newsagency. Boutiques and jewellery shops are not always open on Sunday.

Souvenirs & Crafts Lots of places sell pareu (some of them hand-painted), T-shirts, the Balinese wood carvings that have become worldwide tropical souvenirs, and other curios. At the eastern end of the Cook's Bay strip, Maison Blanche, easily recognised by its colonial architecture, has a fairly typical selection including shells, mother-of-pearl and wood sculptures. Look for the colourful roadside display of hand-painted pareu at the Lili Shop, between the airport and Cook's Bay.

At Hauru Point, Te Anuanua is a T-shirt and pareu emporium. Leilani, Carole Boutique and Sable Blanc are other pareu and T-shirt specialists. In Le Petit Village, the Maison du Tiki offers sculptures and Polynesian art including *tapa* (nonwoven barkcloth), mother-of-pearl work, Marquesan sculptures, prints and watercolours. Next to the Hotel Hibiscus, Bowser's has various original sculptures in wood and bone as well as some tapa.

Vaimiti, at the entrance to Maharepa at PK6, specialises in pareu, as does Cathy Paréos at PK35. At Cook's Bay, stop at Honu Iti and L'Atelier du Santal (The Shop of Sandalwood) behind L'Ananas Bleu snack bar. At PK28.2, Tihoti Soleil sells an exclusive line of clothes and T-shirts inspired by traditional motifs. Tihoti is also a stone sculptor and some of his works are immersed in the lagoon as a sort of underwater sculpture park. You will find vanilla at Vanilla Products, on the mountain side of the road at PK6.7 in Afareaitu.

Art Galleries In Maharepa, at PK5.5, the painter Christian Deloffre (☎ 56 21 56) displays and sells his work. At Cook's Bay, Gallery van der Hyde displays the Dutch owner's art around the inside wall of the compound. As well, there are Papua New Guinean wood sculptures on the veranda and a shop with jewellery and wood carvings. The Cook's Bay Gallery (☎ 56 25 67) is in part a museum, with an ancient pirogue, sculptures, paintings by local artists and musical instruments. Close to the Kaveka Hotel, the Teva Yrondy Gallery displays Teva's pottery.

Woody's Sculpture (☎ 56 17 73) at PK24, just before the Hauru Point enclave, has interesting wood carvings. The Stanley Haumani Gallery (☎ 56 21 57), on the mountain side of the road at Papetoai, shows Stanley's paintings. Jean and Mireille Campistron (☎ 56 19 16) show their works, canvases and paintings on cloth, close to the Tiahura market and not far from the Beachcomber Parkroyal.

Black Pearls A number of places around Moorea specialise in Tahitian black pearls. They include the major Tahitian pearl specialists whose pearls come from the Leeward Islands and the Tuamotus. Some of them will even provide free transport to their shops.

At Hauru Point, in Le Petit Village and around, there are several jewellery shops like World of Pearls (part of the Sibani group), Pai Moana Pearls (also found next to the Linareva), Herman Perles, Tahiti Perles and the Black Pearl Gem Company (which specialises in unmounted pearls). At Cook's Bay there's Heiva Black Pearl, in front of the Club Bali Hai, and Island Fashion Black

Pearls, next to the van der Heyde Gallery. Maherepa has Tikitea Pearls and the Golden Nugget, where creations by the artist Alain Kerebel are on show. The boutiques of the Sofitel Ia Ora and Beachcomber Parkroyal also display pearls.

Getting There & Away

There's less than 20km of blue Pacific between Tahiti and Moorea and getting from one island to the other is simplicity itself. You can stroll down to the quay in Papeete, hop on one of the high-speed ferries and be in Moorea in less than half an hour. Or you can go out to the airport, hop on an Air Moorea aircraft and be there in less than 10 minutes. There's so much transport between the two islands that simple arithmetic proves you could totally evacuate Moorea in a couple of days!

Air Air Moorea (☎ 86 41 41 on Tahiti, ☎ 56 10 34 on Moorea) flies from Faaa airport on Tahiti to Moorea about every half-hour or less during the busiest times, from 6 am to 6 pm. There's no need to book – just turn up and if there's an oversupply of passengers they'll just put on more flights. The advertised flight time of 10 minutes is really being conservative. Seven or eight minutes is more like it! The one-way fare is 2700 CFP. At Faaa airport, Air Moorea is in a separate small terminal, a short stroll to the east of the main terminal.

Air Tahiti (☎ 86 42 42 on Tahiti, ☎ 56 10 34 on Moorea) also flies to Moorea but is chiefly for passengers making onward connections to other islands in the Society group. There are usually only one to three flights a day. Onward fares are: Moorea-Huahine or Moorea-Raiatea for 11,000 CFP and Moorea-Bora Bora for 16,000 CFP.

Boat Competition is fierce between Tahiti and Moorea across the 'Sea of the Moon', with two high-speed services and two slower car-ferries. First departures in the morning are usually around 6 am; last trips are in the afternoon around 4.30 or 5.30 pm.

Le Prado (☎ 43 76 50 in Papeete, ☎ 56 13 92 on Moorea) has the fast ferry *Tamarii*

Moorea VIII, better known as the Corsair 6000, and the ferry *Tamarii Moorea VIII H*. The *Corsair 6000* does the crossing five times daily (four times on Sunday) in about 30 minutes. The one-way fare is 1020/510 CFP for adults/children. You can take a two-wheeler for 1020 CFP or a car for 3060 CFP. The ferry *Tamarii Moorea VIII H* does the crossing four times daily on weekdays, once or twice on weekends and takes 1¼ hours. Passenger fares are identical but a car only costs 2040 CFP one way.

Degage (☎ 42 88 88 in Papeete, ☎ 56 31 10 on Moorea) operates the *Aremiti* catamaran and the *Aremiti Ferry*. The *Aremiti* does six to seven daily shuttles on weekdays, four to five on weekends and takes 30 minutes. Fares are identical to the *Corsair 6000*, but the *Aremiti* doesn't take vehicles, apart from bicycles, which are free, and scooters or mopeds, which are 1020 CFP one way. On the *Aremiti Ferry* passengers cost the same but cars are 2550 CFP one way. It does four to five daily crossings weekdays, two to three on weekends and takes about 45 minutes.

From Papeete, departures take place from the ferry wharf, about 300m north-east of the tourist office and the Vaima Centre.

Because the ferries are so frequent and have so much capacity it's not necessary to reserve, except perhaps for cars at rush hours. You can buy tickets at the ticket counter on the wharf just a few minutes before departure.

Getting Around

To/From the Airport & the Wharf The Cook's Bay hotels are 5 to 9km from the airport while the Hauru Point establishments are 25 to 30km away. It's a further 5km from the Vaiare wharf. Moorea's taxis are notoriously expensive; from the airport to the Beachcomber Parkroyal, at the very start of Hauru Point, will be about 3400 CFP, more if you want to go to somewhere farther around the point.

A shuttle bus theoretically meets all the boat arrivals and departures and costs just 200/100 CFP for adults/children to or from any of the Cook's Bay or Hauru Point hotels.

Departures from Club Med are one hour 15 minutes before the boat departure.

Air Moorea offers a 100 CFP minibus service to any of the island hotels after each flight. This recent introduction is such a bargain it seems unlikely it will last! Otherwise you could walk about 500m to the road and wait for the shuttle to come by from the wharf.

Car Although there's a little public transport it's not very reliable or convenient. If you're not doing a tour this is an island where having your own wheels is very useful. Car-rental operators can be found at the Vaiare boat quay, at the airport, at some of the major hotels and dotted around the Cook's Bay and Hauru Point tourist centres. Four, eight and 24-hour rates are quoted as well as cheaper rates after two or three days. There are petrol stations near the Vaiare ferry wharf, close to the airport, beside Cook's Bay and at Le Petit Village near Club Med on Hauru Point.

Europcar (☎ 56 34 00, fax 56 35 05) has its main office at Le Petit Village close to Club Med. You can also find it at the ferry wharf at Vaiare, at the Sofitel Ia Ora, in front of Club Bali Hai and at the Beachcomber Parkroyal, and it can be contacted by phone from the airport. A Fiat costs 7900 CFP for one day with unlimited distance.

Avis (☎ 56 32 61, 56 32 68, fax 56 32 62) is at the ferry wharf at Vaiare, at the airport, at the Bali Hai and in front of Club Med. It has small cars with unlimited mileage for 8639 CFP per day.

Albert Rent-a-Car (☎ 56 19 28, 56 33 75) is a local operator found in front of Club Bali Hai and facing Club Med. Cars cost 7500 CFP for one day with unlimited mileage.

Taxi Taxis are horribly expensive in Moorea, even by French Polynesian standards. The meters start at 600 CFP. It's not much more expensive to rent a car than to take a taxi from the airport or ferry wharf to a hotel at Hauru Point. If you have to take a taxi they can be found at the airport (☎ 56 10 18) from 6 am to 6 pm and at the taxi rank in front of Club Med at Hauru Point (☎ 56 33 10).

Scooter & Bicycle Tehotu Renting (☎ 56 52 96, 56 37 24) at the Vaiare ferry wharf rents scooters for 4700 CFP a day.

Albert Rent-a-Car has bicycles for 1000 CFP to 1500 CFP a day. Rando Cycles (☎ 56 35 02) at Club Med rents mountain bikes for 1500 CFP a day and organises guided rides for 5000 CFP per person (minimum of five participants). It also has bicycles at Hotel Hibiscus and the Moorea Beach Club. Some other hotels, including Les Tipaniers, the Moorea Village and the Beachcomber Parkroyal, also have bicycles to rent.

Boat Loca Boat (☎ 78 13 39), on the beach at the Moorea Beach Club, has boats to rent – an ideal way to explore the lagoon and the small motu by yourself. They cost 5000/7000/9000 CFP for two/four/eight hours, including fuel.

TATTOOING

Since the early 1980s, tattooing has enjoyed quite a strong revival in Polynesia. Like dance, singing and handicrafts, it has become one of the most expressive and vibrant vehicles of traditional Polynesian culture.

With encouragement from the great Samoan masters, young Tahitians and Marquesans have delved deeply into their ancient traditions and have brought this ancestral form of bodily adornment, with its undisputed artistic qualities, completely up-to-date. Today there are many Polynesians, both men and women, sporting magnificent tattoos as symbols of their identity.

History

The word 'tattoo' comes from the Tahitian *tatau*, which refers to the practice of carving indelible marks onto the skin. This practice is well known in a number of different cultures but it is within the Polynesian triangle (Hawaii-Marquesas-New Zealand) that it developed its most consummate and spectacular form. Throughout their lifetimes, individuals were gradually tattooed with more and more complex geometrical patterns.

Eighteenth-century European navigators were the first westerners to give an account of the practice, which was unknown at the time in Europe. The scientists who accompanied them designed geometrical patterns and some sailors even got themselves tattooed. When the missionaries settled in Polynesia, tattooing suffered the same fate as the rest of Polynesian culture. Considered pagan, it was simply banned.

In the traditional culture, tattooing was associated with many different meanings. First and foremost it was a symbol of community or clan membership, a form of social recognition. It was also an initiation rite: in the Marquesas, reaching adulthood was marked by a ceremony on the *tohua* (ceremonial platform) during which young men would display their tattoos as symbols of their bravery.

Tattooing was an expression of an individual's social status: as they progressed through different stages of life, people expressed their identities by covering their bodies with more tattoos. It was also an aesthetic adornment that had its part to play in the seduction process. Finally, tattooing served to intimidate: In the Marquesas, warriors tattooed their faces with thick horizontal stripes to make themselves look terrifying to enemies. Both women and men were tattooed, although women tended to have fewer tattoos.

The techniques and designs used followed strict conventions. The art of tattooing was the prerogative of a highly respected profession, the guild of master-tattooists, who underwent a long apprenticeship before they could practise their art. They used pieces of bone that were sharpened to a point and joined together in the shape of a sort of comb. The comb was then fixed onto a wooden stem.

The tattooist soaked the comb in a black pigment made from a mixture of soot and water or vegetable matter, and stuck the stem with a small mallet to cause the pigment to penetrate the skin. Designs consisted mainly of abstract geometrical shapes (triangles, solid colours, checks and blocks) or of highly stylised animal or plant motifs (trees, turtles, lizards, fish, and human figures).

The Renaissance
Polynesians of the present day are going back to their roots and are rediscovering this form of bodily decoration. Women wear discreet motifs around the ears or navel, and around the wrists or ankles. Men are distinguished by magnificent adornments covering the shoulders, torso, thighs or calves.

Many tattooists draw their inspiration from the motifs collected by the German ethnologist Karl von den Steinen in the late 19th century, which are included in his work *Die Marquesaner und Ihre Kunst* (1928).

If you wish to go into greater detail, the highly graphical work *Polynesian Tattoos*, by ex-fashion photographer Gian Paolo Barbieri, displays the tattoos and physiques of beautiful young Polynesian men.

Getting a Tattoo
Choosing a Tattoo Artist
In Polynesia the number of professional and semi-professional tattooists is thought to be between 20 and 30. Some regularly take part in conventions abroad, and are rapidly reaching the international status of the Samoan and Japanese masters.

All of the professional tattooists have equipment such as tattooing machines and sterile needles, satisfying the required hygiene standards. There are also dozens of amateurs working with electric razors that they have adapted, in a makeshift way, to hold a needle, but the reliability of this technique is strictly limited and the results can be disappointing. It is far better to pay more to deal with a tattoo artist who has a solid reputation and uses professional equipment and procedures.

Choosing a tattooist is not an everyday occurrence, and is worth taking time over. First of all make an appointment to see the artist. Ask to see a portfolio to get an idea of the style and work. Talk to the artist: is the level of communication good? Is he listening to your wishes? A minimal

MANOLO MYLONAS

Left: Traditional motifs symbolise the vibrant Maohi culture.

amount of tacit understanding between you both is essential. Also, get a feel for the atmosphere in the studio: is the place congenial and does it inspire confidence? How clean is everything? Take plenty of time, and go and see a number of artists before making your final choice.

The following list of tattooists is by no means exhaustive.

Papeete

Efraima Huuti (☎ 41 01 22, 82 17 38) Studio upstairs in Papeete Market, next to a shop selling pareu. Marquesan tattooist; good reputation. Marquesan designs. Good prices.

Polynesian Tattoo Above the Taina bar, Blvd Pomare. Three Tahitian tattooists. All styles (local, Celtic, tribal, colour). Tracings, custom-created pieces and freehand.

Jordi's Tattoo Shop (☎ 42 45 00), 43 Rue Albert Leboucher (behind the Prince Hinoi Hotel). Run by a Spaniard. All styles (tribal, modern, colour). Very commercialised American-style studio. Works with tracings from catalogues. Reckoned to be expensive. An ordinary bracelet is advertised at 30,000 CFP.

Moorea

The finest grand masters practise their art on Moorea. They work freehand and only do traditional designs. Considering their skill and reputation, prices are very reasonable (about 10,000 CFP to 15,000 CFP for a bracelet).

Chimé Tattoo (☎ 56 58 33) At his house at PK14 between Opunohu and Cook's Bays. Half Marquesan. One of the pioneers of the revival of this art form. Practised several years in Spain, and posed for photographer Gian Paolo Barbieri for the book *Polynesian Tattoo*.

Roonui Tattoo (☎ 56 37 53) Studio opposite Club Med, at Hauru Point. Roonui, who is almost completely tattooed, was also a model for *Polynesian Tattoo*.

Purotu Tattoo (☎ 77 57 59) At Maharepa, opposite the art gallery.

Tiki Village (☎ 56 18 97) At PK31. Three tattooists including Tavita, the most well known.

The Marquesas

Teiki Barsinas (☎ 92 92 67) and his brother **Fii** (☎ 92 93 04). On Tahuata. Excellent reputation.

Rafaël Ah-Scha or **Kina** (no ☎). At Taiohae (Nuku Hiva).

Tuarae Peterano (☎ 92 72 16). At Atuona (Hiva Oa).

Choosing a Tattoo

Choosing a tattoo is an equally difficult task and will commit you for the rest of your life. In Polynesia it is preferable to select a traditional motif design, since it is the type of image that is executed best and is the most authentic. Study the tattooist's portfolio and be clear about what you want. Any self-respecting tattooist will not reproduce an exact copy of a pre-existing design but will display creative ability in tailoring the design you have chosen to suit your own requirements.

The portfolio is no more than a starting point. The tattoo is a unique work of art, not simply a transfer. Going beyond aesthetic considerations, you should take into account the symbolism and meaning of the design; the tattoo artist will take pains to explain it to you. Think about where you wish to be tattooed and the size of the design. If you care for something both aesthetically pleasing and discreet, Marquesan bracelets around the ankles and arms are particularly well liked. Or you might prefer a complex tattoo covering the shoulder, pectorals, thigh or calf.

You should also agree on a price, without beating about the bush. There is no official price list. Different parameters should be taken into account: the size, intricacy and originality of the design, as well as the reputation of the artist, and the facilities. Some artists work for a flat fee, and others at an hourly rate. For a small bracelet around the ankle or arm you should count on paying between 10,000 CFP and 15,000 CFP.

A Tattoo Session

Once you've agreed on a design with the tattoo artist, the work can start. You sit down comfortably on a mattress or armchair and your skin is cleaned and disinfected. Some artists work freehand, which means they draw the design directly onto the skin. Others create the design on paper and trace it onto the skin. With a tattooing machine, the artist inks in the outlines, and uses a set of several needles to fill in the design.

Now comes the question of pain. It all depends on where you want the tattoo. The most sensitive areas are those where the skin is the most delicate (eg the inside of the thigh) and those directly next to a bone (such as the shin or spine). According to people who have been tattooed, the pain is definitely bearable. It is unwise to take aspirin, since it has the effect of thinning the blood and so preventing scarring.

The length of time a session takes can vary considerably. A small design might be completed in half an hour but some require three hours or even a whole day, including breaks.

Once the tattoo is finished, you have to apply a coating of oily cream for several days. A scab will form and scarring will not be complete for a week or two. During that time you must not go swimming in the sea or expose the tattooed area to sunlight – so it's wise to leave your tattooing until the end of your stay.

MANOLO MYLONAS

Other Windward Islands

Tahiti and Moorea are the only major islands in the Windward group. However, the group also includes two small high islands and a single atoll. Tetiaroa, north of Tahiti, is the atoll; Maiao, to the west of Moorea, and uninhabited Mehetia, well to the east of Tahiti, are the high islands.

TETIAROA

pop 50 • area 6 sq km • reef passes 1

A dozen or so sandy motu dotted around the 7km diameter of a 30m-deep lagoon of 55km circumference – that's Tetiaroa. It's the postcard-perfect atoll: beautiful beaches, water as clear as fine vodka, a population mainly comprising migratory birds, and the whole show is owned by actor Marlon Brando. Nowhere does Tetiaroa rise more than 3m above sea level. In the pre-European period the atoll was known as Teturoa.

The first European known to have visited the atoll was none other than William Bligh, who went there in search of three deserters in January 1789. Later he probably wished he hadn't found them, as, embittered by their treatment, they all joined the initial mutineers on the *Bounty*.

The island was once a Pomare family playground, an escape from its kingdom on Tahiti. In 1904 the Pomare family presented Dr Williams, Tahiti's only dentist, with the atoll, perhaps as payment for its dental bills. Williams was the British consul for French Polynesia from 1916 to 1935. He turned Tetiaroa into a copra plantation and died on the atoll in 1937. Tetiaroa made its next significant change of ownership in 1965 when Brando, fresh from making *Mutiny on the Bounty* (see the 'Mutiny in the Cinema' boxed text in the Facts for the Visitor chapter), acquired the island on a 99-year lease and added the airstrip and the low-key hotel on Motu Onetahi.

Motu Rimatuu was the Pomare family residence. There are **marae** ruins on the island and a number of gigantic *tuu* trees (their dark, hard, grained wood is greatly

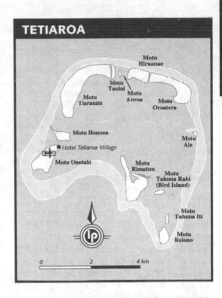

valued by sculptors). Motu Tahuna Rahi is the **nesting island**, a reserve used by countless migratory sea birds to lay their eggs and hatch their young. Frigates, gannets, petrels, black terns, brown and red-footed boobies and long-tailed tropical birds all nest on Tetiaroa.

Bring along a mask and snorkel, and plastic sandals or thongs to protect your feet. It's also advisable to bring a hat and good sunscreen.

Places to Stay

Tetiaroa's hotel, indeed the only habitation, is on Motu Onetahi, where the airstrip is located. *Hotel Tetiaroa Village (☎ 82 63 02, 82 63 03, fax 85 00 51)* has just nine beach *fare*, which are very low-key and not in prime condition. Tetiaroa is simply a rather expensive back-to-nature experience. A two day and one night excursion to the island costs 37,400 CFP for one person or 58,600 CFP for two. Bookings can be made through BP 2418, Papeete, Tahiti or by going to the

Tetiaroa hotel counter at the Air Moorea terminal at Faaa airport.

Getting There & Away

Tetiaroa is 40km north of Tahiti and is accessible by air and sea.

Air Air Moorea operates regular 20-minute flights. The return fare, including lunch at the Hotel Tetiaroa Village and an excursion to Motu Tahuna Rahi, is 24,300 CFP; you leave at 8.15 am and return at 4 pm. Contact the Tetiaroa hotel counter at the Air Moorea terminal for details. Departing from Moorea costs an additional 4000 CFP.

Boat There are quite a few day-trips from Papeete and Moorea to Tetiaroa. The Nouvelles Frontières (☎ 77 64 46, 56 40 50, fax 56 40 60) catamaran *Va'a Rahi* does two or three day-trips weekly, leaving at 7.30 am and returning towards 5 pm. Departures are possible from Papeete or Moorea, the trip takes 2½ hours each way and the per-person fare is 12,500 CFP including lunch. America Excursions (☎ 42 88 88) asks 14,000 CFP for a similar trip.

Jet France (☎/fax 56 15 62) has a catamaran crossing three times weekly. Departures are from Papeete and possibly from Moorea. The fare is 9500 CFP but you have to bring your own lunch.

Pacific Charter (☎ 77 39 77, fax 56 44 38) has a high-speed boat that makes the crossing in 1½ hours. There are usually two trips weekly, mainly departing from Moorea. The 15,500 CFP fare includes a meal and drinks.

Boats don't enter the lagoon; a Zodiac inflatable takes visitors in across the reef. Bring something warm to wear on the boat and if you're prone to seasickness you may want to consider taking medication. During the high season it's wise to book some days in advance but note that trips are sometimes cancelled if the seas or weather forecasts are bad.

MAIAO

pop 250 • area 9 sq km • reef passes 2

Maiao comes under the administration of Moorea, 75km to the east. It consists of a high island, rising to 154m at its highest

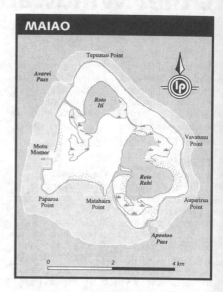

point, and a low-lying motu that wraps itself around the high island, almost totally enclosing two brackish lakes, Roto Iti and Roto Rahi.

The island was sighted by Samuel Wallis in 1767, a postscript to his 'discovery' of Tahiti, but until 1809, when a pair of London Missionary Society (LMS) missionaries were forced to stop, no Europeans are known to have visited the island. During the late 1920s and early 30s, an Englishman named Eric Trower tried to take over the island so that he could exploit the guano deposits he thought were there. His actions resulted in the islanders developing a strong mistrust of foreign influence, and for many years Europeans and Chinese were forbidden to live on the island. Even today the small population prizes its isolation and has vigorously resisted the construction of an airstrip.

Some copra is produced on Maiao but the island is famed for the exceptional quality of its leaves, used for traditional Tahitian roof thatching. Today houses on Maiao are roofed with more prosaic tin. This is not traditional and is less picturesque, but it's infinitely better for collecting rainwater on an island where freshwater supplies are scarce.

Nouvelles Frontières (☎ 77 64 46, 56 40 50, fax 56 40 60) organises two-day trips on its catamaran *Va'a Rahi* for 25,500 CFP to 29,500 CFP per person. You can also get there by chartered yacht – see Bareboat Charters & Cruises in the Outdoor Activities chapter for more information. Avarei Pass on the north-west side has been widened to allow small boats to enter, and Apootoo Pass to the south-east is the only other pass.

MEHETIA
pop 0 • area 3 sq km • reef passes 0
Geologically the youngest island in the Society group, Mehetia is situated 100km east of Tahiti, is 1.5km across and rises steeply from the sea to its highest point of 435m. The island is totally uninhabited and has no lagoon; landing on the uninviting shoreline is, to say the very least, difficult. Only in one place does the rocky shoreline form a small pebbly beach. Yet when Wallis chanced upon Mehetia in June 1767, the population is said to have been 1500. It seems scarcely possible that the population could have been that large, but the **marae** ruins on the island confirm that it certainly was populated. The fierce piratical warriors of Anaa Atoll (Tuamotus) drove the population off Mehetia in 1806, and it was used briefly in 1835 as a penal colony. The island has freshwater springs, and coconut and *uru* (breadfruit) trees. The surrounding waters are rich with fish and other marine life. The island is now privately owned, and Tahitians occasionally visit to gather copra.

Huahine

Huahine is actually two islands: Huahine Nui (Big Huahine) to the north and Huahine Iti (Little Huahine) to the south. They're actually of fairly similar size. The islands are only barely separated and at low tide you can wade from one to the other; a road bridge spans the narrow gap. A Polynesian legend relates that the split came about when the god Hiro ploughed his mighty canoe into the island, creating deep and majestic Bourayne Bay to the west and Maroe Bay to the east. Huahine Nui is more developed and is home to the main tourist and administrative facilities, while Huahine Iti is wilder in character. Agriculture – vanilla, melons and citrus fruit – and fishing are the mainstays of the island economy.

Huahine is green, lush and beautiful, just like other Society islands, and has an easy-going atmosphere that entices visitors to kick back and watch the world go by. It has some fine beaches to the south, excellent and easily accessible motu, fantastic snorkelling and scuba diving, popular surf breaks and, in the village of Maeva, the most extensive complex of pre-European marae in French Polynesia. Each year in October or November, Huahine is the starting point for the annual Hawaiki Nui *pirogue* (outrigger canoe) race. See the boxed text 'Hawaiki Nui Canoe Race' in the Facts for the Visitor chapter.

History

Just north of Fare, archaeological excavations have revealed some of the earliest traces of settlement in the Society Islands. Research has revealed that Huahine managed to maintain a degree of independence during the era when powerful chiefs of Bora Bora were extending their power to the east and west.

In 1769, Cook was the first European to visit Huahine and, although he did not receive a warm welcome, he returned in 1774. In 1777 he visited again, bringing with him Omai, the young Tahitian he had taken back

HIGHLIGHTS

pop: 5411
area: 75 sq km
reef passes: 5
highest point: Mt Turi (669m)

- Study the extensive archaeological remains of the Maeva marae
- Discover the lagoon and the motu in a pirogue
- Laze on the beaches of Huahine Iti
- Dive in the Fitii or Parea passes
- Snorkel in the Coral Garden or the Safari Aquarium

to Britain following his second expedition. A group of London Missionary Society (LMS) missionaries moved to Huahine in 1808 to escape the turmoil on Tahiti, but remained for only a year. The group returned in 1818.

Huahine supported Pomare in the struggle against the French, which resulted in a number of clashes between 1846 and 1888, when French rule was eventually, and reluctantly, accepted. A monument on the ocean side of the Maeva bridge marks the site of a skirmish in 1846. Although the French kicked the Protestant English missionaries out, the island remains predominantly Protestant.

Orientation

A road follows the coast most of the way around both islands, but between Faie and the Hotel Bellevue on Huahine Nui, and on the brief Parea-Tefarerii section on the less densely populated Huahine Iti, the road is unsealed. The circumference of Huahine is about 60km.

A series of motu stretches along the east coast of the two islands, while around the north coast is Lake Fauna Nui, which is actually an inlet from the sea. It almost cuts off the motu-like northern peninsula, with

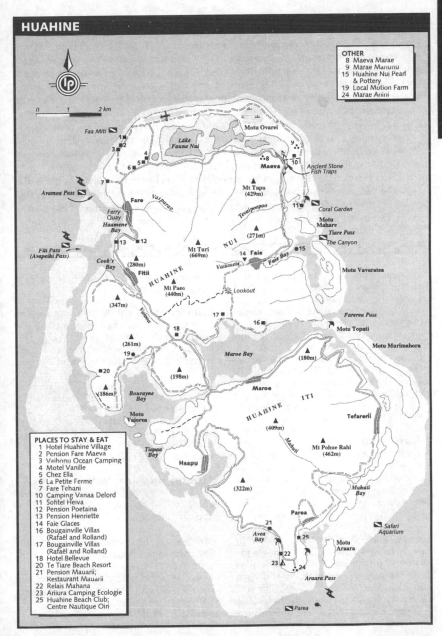

HUAHINE

OTHER
8 Maeva Marae
9 Marae Manunu
15 Huahine Nui Pearl
& Pottery
19 Local Motion Farm
24 Marae Anini

0   1   2 km

Faa Miti

Motu Ovarei

Lake
Fauna Nui

Maeva

Ancient Stone
Fish Traps

Avamoa Pass

Coral Garden

Fare

Vaiparao

Mt Tapu
(429m)

Tevaipoopoo

Motu
Mahare

Ferry
Quay
Haamene
Bay

Tiare Pass

The Canyon

Fiti Pass
(Avapeihi Pass)

(271m)

Motu Vavaratea

13   12

(280m)

Fitii

Cook's
Bay

HUAHINE

Mt Turi
(669m)

NUI

Faie

Vaiumete   Faie Bay

Motu
Topati

(347m)

Mt Paeo
(440m)

Vaiona

Lookout

17

16

Farerea Puss

18

(261m)

Motu Murimahora

19

(198m)

Maroe Bay

(180m)

20

(186m)

Bourayne
Bay

Maroe

ITI

HUAHINE

Motu
Vaiorea

Tiapaa
Bay

Haapu

(409m)

Mahuti

Tefarerii

Mt Pohue Rahi
(462m)

(322m)

Mahuti
Bay

Parea

21   Avea Bay

25   Safari
Aquarium

22

23   24   Motu
Araara

Araara Pass

Parea

PLACES TO STAY & EAT
1 Hotel Huahine Village
2 Pension Fare Maeva
3 Vaihonu Ocean Camping
4 Motel Vanille
5 Chez Ella
6 La Petite Ferme
7 Fare Tehani
10 Camping Vanaa Delord
11 Sofitel Heiva
12 Pension Poetaina
13 Pension Henriette
14 Faie Glaces
16 Bougainville Villas
(Rafaël and Rolland)
17 Bougainville Villas
(Rafaël and Rolland)
18 Hotel Bellevue
20 Te Tiare Beach Resort
21 Pension Mauarii;
Restaurant Mauarii
22 Relais Mahana
23 Ariiura Camping Ecologie
25 Huahine Beach Club;
Centre Nautique Oiri

Pouvanaa a Oopa – a Tahitian Leader

French Polynesia's most famous politician came from Huahine. Born in 1895, and a WWI volunteer in the Pacific Battalion, Pouvanaa a Oopa founded the Rassemblement Démocratique des Populations Tahitiennes (RDPT) in 1949. For nearly 10 years he was at the front of the local political stage, opposing French colonial rule, denouncing capitalism and pushing for local employment in government and administrative posts. A man of the people and a strong Protestant, the charismatic leader was strongly supported by Polynesians who considered him a *metua* (father) figure, able to restore their dignity against the cynicism of the 'métropole'.

It all fell apart in 1958 when a 'yes' vote in the referendum to remain in the French community destabilised the party. Pouvanaa a Oopa was blamed for the riots that shook Papeete on 10 and 11 October 1958 and he was exiled to France. Split by internal dissension, the RDPT was not able to mobilise itself against the nuclear testing program in 1963, and was dissolved. De Gaulle had won. Pouvanaa a Oopa was allowed to return to the Pacific in 1968 and until his death in 1977 he struggled tirelessly, but unsuccessfully, for his rehabilitation. Today he remains the pre-eminent Polynesian father-figure, a man who made the all-powerful colonial structure tremble.

the airport, from the rest of Huahine Nui. The reef fringes the north coast and there are only a few beaches.

Fare, the port, principal town and administrative centre, is on the west coast of Huahine Nui, just 2.5km south of the airport. Faie and Maeva, on the east coast, and Fitii, on the west, are the other main settlements on Huahine Nui. There are four villages on Huahine Iti: Haapu, Parea, Tefarerii and Maroe. Mt Turi (669m) is the highest peak on Huahine Nui, and Mt Pohuerahi (462m) is the highest on Huahine Iti.

Information

Tourist Offices Your hotel or guesthouse will be the best information source. Chez Guynette's noticeboard in Fare is one of the best information sources on the island (see Fare under Places to Stay later). Some tourist information may be available at the airport.

Money, Post & Communications In Fare, there's a Banque de Tahiti opposite the wharf and a Banque Socredo on the bypass road. Both are open weekdays and have automatic teller machines (ATMs). The post office, in a brand-new but colonial-looking building, is a little to the north towards the airport and on the edge of the town. It's open on weekdays from 7 am to 3 pm (it closes at 2 pm on Friday).

Laundry, Medical & Other Services Chez Guynette has a laundrette and charges guests 750 CFP for a 6kg load. You can get print film developed and printed in 24 hours at Studio Jojo, next door to Chez Guynette. Visiting yachties can obtain water from Pacific Blue Adventure, on the quay. The *capitainerie* (harbour master's office) is also on the quay.

There are two private medical centres in Fare on the bypass road; phone ☎ 68 82 20 or 68 84 93. There's also a clinic and a pharmacy across from the quay.

Around Huahine Nui

This 60km circuit of the larger island starts with Fare and goes around the island in a clockwise direction.

Fare Fare is the image of a sleepy South Seas port, where people sit on the wharf waiting for boats to arrive while children tumble into the water and splash around. There's a colourful little waterside **market**, roulottes, shops, nice restaurants and a selection of hotels and *pensions* (guesthouses). Throw in banks, a post office, car and bike-rental facilities and a dive shop and it's easy to see why many visitors find Fare the ideal place to relax for a few days.

Fare looks out on **Haamene Bay**, which has two passes out to the sea. The northern Avamoa Pass is the main entry point for inter-island shipping, while the Avapeihi Pass is to the south. The town only really came into existence with the arrival of the missionaries in 1818, but within a few years it was already a bustling little port. Whalers started to call in at Fare from the 1830s and the French protectorate brought an influx of island merchants and traders. The wooden shops and buildings along the main street came with the Chinese shopkeepers who settled here in the 1920s.

Old Hotel Bali Hai Archaeological Site

The site of the old Hotel Bali Hai, damaged in a cyclone in 1998, is only a few minutes walk along the beach north of Fare. The ponds winding around the site were a swamp until they were dredged out during the hotel's construction in 1972. When pre-European artefacts were found, archaeologists were notified and Dr Yoshihiko Shinoto started work on the site in 1973.

It is believed that there was a village here over 1000 years ago. The swampy ground preserved wooden objects including house foundations and constructions, canoe planks and water bailers, and a wide variety of tools, tool handles and weapons. It is estimated that the area was inhabited from around 850 to 1100 AD. For the archaeologists, the most interesting find was *patu*, flattened club-like weapons made of wood or whalebone and used by New Zealand Maoris for striking and thrusting under the ribs. Such weapons had never been found outside New Zealand and their discovery here supported theories of migration from Tahiti to New Zealand.

Lake Fauna Nui & Fish Traps The shallow expanse of Lake Fauna Nui (also known as Lake Maeva) is referred to as a lake or sometimes as a lagoon, but in fact it is an inlet from the sea. The land to the north is in every way – except for its firm

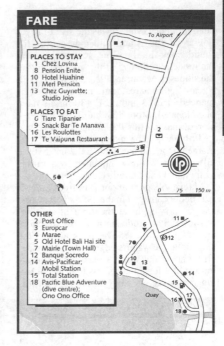

FARE

To Airport

PLACES TO STAY
1 Chez Lovina
8 Pension Enite
10 Hotel Huahine
11 Meri Pension
13 Chez Guynette;
   Studio Jojo

PLACES TO EAT
6 Tiare Tipanier
9 Snack Bar Te Manava
16 Les Roulottes
17 Te Vaipuna Restaurant

OTHER
2 Post Office
3 Europcar
4 Marae
5 Old Hotel Bali Hai site
7 Mairie (Town Hall)
12 Banque Socredo
14 Avis-Pacificar;
   Mobil Station
15 Total Station
18 Pacific Blue Adventure
   (dive centre);
   Ono Ono Office

0   75   150 m

Quay

connection to the main island – like the motu off the east coast, and indeed is known as Motu Ovarei.

About 2km north of Fare, the main sealed road runs along the inland side of Lake Fauna Nui, but it's also possible to turn off to the airport and take the unsealed road on the ocean side of the lake and return to the main part of the island by the bridge at Maeva village. At this end the lake narrows down to a channel, extending for 3km to Faie Bay.

Beside the bridge are a number of V-shaped fish traps, made from coral blocks. These traps have been here for centuries and some are still in use today. The tips of the Vs point towards the ocean so that fish, as they are pulled towards the sea by an ebb tide, are trapped in the Vs as the long stone arms emerge above the water level. Once they are in the circular basin at the point of the trap the fish are easily caught, usually by net or harpoon.

Maeva Village & Marae Prior to European influence, Maeva was the seat of royal power on the island and marae are still found along the shoreline, scattered among the modern buildings of the village, and up the slopes of Matairea (Pleasant Wind) Hill. Excavations and restoration of the site commenced in 1923 and nearly 30 marae have been located. More than half have been restored, making this the most extensive site in Polynesia. The exceptional density of marae on the hill has led to a theory that the hillside was entirely inhabited by families of the chiefs and nobility.

Maeva village is about 7km from Fare. It was badly damaged in the 1998 cyclone and was a sorry sight at the time of writing. Sofitel Heiva produces a useful brochure and map to the site. The walk around the site, along the water's edge and up Matairea Hill, can be hot work, so take some drinking water. Mosquitoes show their usual liking for marae, so carry insect repellent as

well. And if you've come in a car, park in the shade under the trees across from the school, on the Fare side of the church.

See the 'Civilisation & Archaeology' special section for more information on marae in French Polynesia.

Fare Potee On the water's edge on the Fare side of Maeva, the *fare potee* (chief's house or community meeting place) was a small site museum until the April 1998 cyclone destroyed it. The *fare potee* explanation panel is about all that's left but there are plans to rebuild it. Around the site are 10 or more marae, some of which may date back to the 16th century. Flagstones cover a wide expanse of land along the shoreline.

Te Ana (Matairea Huiarii) It is easiest to start the walk at the defence wall on the Fare side of Maeva. It's thought that the wall was constructed in 1846, when French marines mounted an assault on resistance forces.

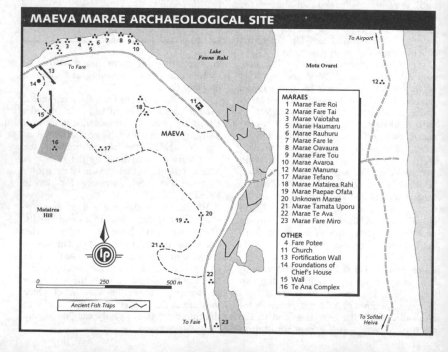

MAEVA MARAE ARCHAEOLOGICAL SITE

MARAES
1 Marae Fare Roi
2 Marae Fare Tai
3 Marae Vaiotaha
5 Marae Haumaru
6 Marae Rauhuru
7 Marae Fare Ie
8 Marae Oavaura
9 Marae Fare Tou
10 Marae Avaroa
12 Marae Manunu
17 Marae Tefano
18 Marae Matairea Rahi
19 Marae Paepae Ofata
20 Unknown Marae
21 Marae Tamata Uporu
22 Marae Te Ava
23 Marae Fare Miro

OTHER
4 Fare Potee
11 Church
13 Fortification Wall
14 Foundations of Chief's House
15 Wall
16 Te Ana Complex

Lake Fauna Rahi

To Fare

Motu Ovarei

To Airport

MAEVA

Matairea Hill

Ancient Fish Traps

To Faie

To Sofitel Heiva

0   250   500 m

Look for the trail going uphill; it soon enters dense forest and passes through patches of **vanilla plantations**, then crosses through another fortification wall. This second, older wall was built during the pre-European era, probably as protection against the warlike Bora Bora tribes.

A side path leads off to the big multitiered complex of Te Ana, or Matairea Huiarii, draped up the hillside. This area included marae, houses, agricultural terraces and other signs of habitation from around 1300 to 1800 AD, plus indications of an early settlement around 900 AD, contemporaneous with the discoveries at the site of the old Hotel Bali Hai near Fare.

Marae Tefano The side path winds prettily on through the forest to Marae Tefano, a real Indiana Jones complex with a massive banyan tree overwhelming one end of the *ahu* (altar).

Marae Matairea Rahi Farther on, a trail branches off and runs slightly downhill to Marae Matairea Rahi. This was the principal marae at Maeva, where the most important island chief sat on his throne at major ceremonies. It was superseded by Marae Manunu, on the motu below. Also surviving are the foundations of a *fare atua* or 'god house', where images of gods were protected by a 24 hour watch.

A few steps farther along is the small Marae Matairea. You can continue down this way, as the trail eventually emerges behind a house in the middle of the village.

Marae Paepae Ofata Retrace your steps to the main trail and continue to the turn-off to Marae Paepae Ofata, a steep climb above the main trail. It's worth the effort: the marae is like a large platform perched on the edge of the hill with fine views down the hillside and across Motu Papiti to the outer lagoon, and down to the mouth of Lake Fauna Nui.

Marae Tamata Uporu Retrace the route to the main path that continues over a second part of Marae Paepae Ofata. The path winds on around the hillside to Marae Tamata Uporu, before dropping steeply down to the road, past fruit trees.

Marae Te Ava & Marae Fare Miro The path emerges just south of the lagoonside Marae Te Ava. A short walk east leads to the lagoonside Marae Fare Miro, which has some particularly neat stonework and a fine setting.

Marae Manunu A final marae stands on the motu, across the bridge from the main Maeva complex. The 'Eye of the North' marae is a massive structure measuring 40m long by nearly 7m wide and standing 2m high. Manunu replaced Marae Matairea Rahi as the community marae of Huahine Nui; Marae Anini was the community marae of Huahine Iti. The two-stepped ahu platforms at these two marae are unique in the Leeward Islands. While Marae Anini was dedicated to Oro (the god of war) and Hiro (the god of thieves and sailors), who were worshipped on other Polynesian islands, Manunu was dedicated first and foremost to Huahine's own god of war and fish.

Faie & Route Traversière The coast road turns inland beside narrow Faie Bay to the village of Faie. You pass the pier for the pearl firm Huahine Nui Pearls & Pottery, then the boutique of Denise Jamet (see Shopping later). Huahine's famous **blue-eyed eels** can be seen in the river immediately downstream of the bridge. They are quite used to visitors and are happy to be handfed, and even have an official feeding time of 9.15 am for Sofitel Heiva's guests.

Just inland from Faie you can pause for an ice cream at Faie Glaces before making the steep climb to the *belvédère* (lookout) on the slopes of Mt Turi. From the high point, the Route Traversière drops even more steeply to the shores of Maroe Bay. A heavily loaded small rental car can have real difficulty getting up this road and if it's wet it may be impossible.

Local Motion Near the Bellevue Hotel, this farm (☎ 68 86 58) is about 1.5km off the main coast road. It's open Monday to Saturday from 9 am to 4 pm, and produces a wide variety of organically grown tropical fruit and coffee as well as jams, preserves and dried fruit. The 300 CFP entry charge is waived if you buy something, such as a 400 CFP glass of its excellent fruit juice.

It's possible to visit the farm and its orchards, have lunch in the and climb up to the panoramic viewpoint, although the 800m walk is not very interesting. See Places to Eat later in this chapter.

Fitii Just before completing the Huahine Nui circuit, the road passes through the Fitii district. This is an important agricultural area in the shadow of Mt Paeo (440m), where taro, vanilla and other crops are grown.

Around Huahine Iti

The smaller southern island is reached by the bridge that separates the two bays, Maroe and Bourayne. This route circles the island in a clockwise direction.

Island Agriculture

Huahine has a busy agricultural workforce with plantations of vanilla, grapefruit, *uru* (breadfruit), taro and pineapples on local *faapu* (agricultural allotments). On the motu, melons and *pastèque* (watermelons) are grown, many of which are sold in Papeete's market. This market-gardening technique originated on Maupiti but has been taken up successfully on Huahine. Some village plantations look remarkably wild and neglected, but don't think for a moment that somebody doesn't own every single plant. Casually gathering fruit, in particular the much-prized pineapples, may result in an enraged villager emerging from the undergrowth with a sharp machete. Mangoes are one of the few exceptions: they fall from the trees, rot on the ground and, delicious though they may be, are treated like trash.

East Coast The village of **Maroe** stands on the southern side of Maroe Bay, an area dotted with reminders of the god Hiro's splitting of the island in two with his canoe. You can spot the marks left by his paddle, the imprint of his finger (and even his rocky phallus). The coast road skirts across the mouth of a number of shallow inlets, looking across to Motu Murimahora before coming to **Tefarerii** (The House of the Kings). This small village was the centre of Huahine's most powerful family a century ago, but today the inhabitants devote their time to fishing and growing watermelons and other produce on the nearby motu.

Marae Anini Right at the southern tip of Huahine Iti is the important Marae Anini, a community marae echoing the role of Marae Manunu on the larger island. Constructed of massive coral blocks, this large marae is a comparatively recent construction, dedicated to Oro and Hiro. The Oro cult, with its human sacrifices, was almost a last gasp for the old religion, but it soon collapsed before the growing influence of Christianity.

Despite its beautiful lagoonside setting and its historical importance, the area is liberally sprinkled with garbage and many of the marae stones have been disfigured with feeble graffiti. One almost wishes for some modern human sacrifices. There's no signpost from the coast road but the site is about 600m after the Huahine Beach Club, at the exit from a wide bend and on the left when coming from Tefarerii. Don't cross private property.

West Coast Some of the best **beaches** around Huahine are found on the southern peninsula and along its western shore around Avea Bay. The road comes to a junction where a left turn leads to the village of **Haapu**. Turning right, the route soon brings you back to the bridge and the completion of the island circuit.

Activities

Diving Huahine has two dive centres, both offering magnificent dives at all experience

Huahine's sleepy South Seas pace makes it the ideal place to relax.

MANOLO MYLONAS

levels. See the 'Diving' special section following the Outdoor Activities chapter.

Swimming & Snorkelling Fare has a pretty, sandy beach by the site of the old Hotel Bali Hai, just north of the town. The lagoon here is very wide, but farther north the fringing reef means there is no beach or place to swim until you get right around to Sofitel Heiva. Near the visitor's car park at the Sofitel there's a **coral garden** with superb snorkelling among coral pinnacles, with rich marine life just a few metres from the shore.

Motu Topati, at the entrance to Maroe Bay, is a magnificent site accessible by boat.

There's a beautiful white-sand **beach** around the hotel and guesthouse area of south-western Huahine Iti. The lagoon here is again very wide and Relais Mahana and Ariiura Camping Ecologie have fine beaches. Unfortunately, the same cannot be said about rubbish-strewn Anini Beach, right at the southern tip and next to the marae of the same name.

Surfing Huahine has some of the best and most consistent surf in French Polynesia. Local surfers, however, can be very possessive and visitors should make a serious effort to fit in. There are reef breaks, both left

and rights, best tackled by experienced surfers. See Surfing in the Outdoor Activities chapter for details.

Walking Walking possibilities on the island are very limited; there are no clearly marked trails and the occasional paths in the interior grow over quickly if they're not maintained. The **marae walk** at Maeva will work up a sweat for most people, but another interesting walk is the 3km trail from midway along the road between Fitii and the Hotel Bellevue across to the mountainous Route Traversière, joining that road close to the belvédère. This pretty trail is shown as a track on the maps but is best for walkers or riders; the Petite Ferme (☎ 68 82 98) two day horseback trek takes this route. It's possible to climb Mt Turi (669m) from Fare but you certainly need a guide.

On Huahine Iti, a short **circuit walk**, easily done in an hour, goes from Parea, taking the fork towards the interior just before the bridge. There are fragrances of fruit and flowers as it crosses a number of *faapu* (small cultivated fields) before coming back to Parea near the bridge.

Lagoon Excursions The lagoon around Huahine is superb and includes many untouched motu accessible only by boat. You can rent a boat with outboard motor to explore the lagoon and visit the motu by yourself. Huahine Lagoon (☎ 68 70 00), at the end of the main street in Fare, charges 3000/5000/8000 CFP for two/four/eight hours. Nautical maps and scuba equipment are provided but you have to pay for fuel.

On Huahine Iti, contact the Centre Nautique Oiri (☎ 68 76 84, 68 81 46) at the Huahine Beach Club, where a boat costs 6000/8500 CFP for two/three hours.

Organised Tours
Island Tours There are numerous tours by 4WD or minibus; they're good for people who want a quick view of the island without renting a car. The tours typically start in the morning or early afternoon and take three hours. Reserve ahead because a minimum number of participants, usually two,

HUAHINE

may be required. The tours cover the principle places of interest including villages, archaeological sites, viewpoints, plantations, pearl farms, fish parks and handicraft outlets.

Tours with Huahine Land (☎ 68 89 21) cost 4120 CFP per person; Huahine Discovery Tours (☎ 68 75 18) is close to the quay in Fare and charges 2500 CFP; Huahine Local Tour (☎ 68 89 14) costs 3500 CFP and Huahine Explorer (contact Étienne, the manager of Vaihonu Ocean Camping on ☎ 68 87 33) charges 3600 CFP. Félix Tours (☎ 68 81 69), operated by a Tahitian from Huahine, charges 3500 CFP. In principle, guides speak English but check when you book.

La Petite Ferme (☎ 68 82 98), on the main road between Fare and the airport, offers an interesting variety of guided horse-riding trips using 15 Marquesan horses that are suitable for beginners, children and more-experienced riders. For 3800 CFP you can take a two hour ride along the beach and through the coconut plantations and along Lake Fauna Nui. Longer excursions include an all-day ride with a picnic lunch for 8800 CFP. This ride includes a visit to a vanilla plantation and a stop at the Sofitel Heiva before returning to Fare by the motu. Or you can go on a two day miniexpedition, which combines riding on the beach, around Lake Fauna Nui and up into the mountains for a cost of 18,550 CFP, including meals and camping equipment.

Lagoon Tours A variety of lagoon tours are offered, with stops for snorkelling, swimming, fish-feeding and a picnic on a motu. Departures are around 9 or 10 am, returning towards 4 pm. A minimum number of participants is required so book ahead.

Centre Nautique Oiri (☎ 68 76 84, 68 81 46) at the Huahine Beach Club organises guided snorkelling trips to the Safari Aquarium, a fine site in the lagoon close to the outer reef. The 1½-hour excursions cost 2500 CFP.

Vaipua Cruises (☎ 68 86 42) in the Arts Polynésiens shop in Fare has day tours for 3600 CFP, 5600 CFP with picnic lunch. The

Sofitel also organises this type of excursion for 5350 CFP with picnic.

Guided jetski trips (☎ 68 83 15) cost 10,000 CFP per hour for two or three people.

Places to Stay

Most of Huahine's accommodation is concentrated in and around Fare but there are a few places further afield on Huahine Nui and four places on the southern point of Huahine Iti. Tariffs quoted are per-person per night, including airport transfers but not including VAT, unless otherwise noted.

Fare There are three places to stay right in Fare: a couple just south of the town and several north of Fare towards the airport. Although some are by the lagoon, the reef is fringing so there isn't a good beach.

Chez Guynette (☎/fax 68 83 75), mischievously dubbed 'Club Bed', is one of the most popular backpackers' centres in French Polynesia. It's right on the colourful main street of Fare, about a minute's walk from the wharf and right across from the beach. Seven simple but reasonably comfortable rooms, each named after a French Polynesian island and with a fan, cost 3400/4000/4600 CFP for one/two/three people. There's also an eight bed dorm for 1400 CFP per person, bedding included (but not towels). All of them share cold-water bathrooms. If you only stay one night there's an extra charge of 200/300 CFP per person/room. Airport transfers are 500 CFP.

There is a large kitchen and laundry area (750 CFP for a load). Breakfast (500 CFP), lunch and refreshments through late evening are served on the shady open terrace at the front. There's an excellent noticeboard at the entrance, where shoes are left because Chez Guynette is shoe-free. Book ahead; it's often full. Credit cards are accepted.

Hotel Huahine (☎ 68 82 69) is on the corner where Fare's main street turns away from the beach. It's a large building with a definite 'old South Seas hotel' feel. However, a renovation is long overdue so it's difficult to find much to recommend about the eight dilapidated rooms, even though some look out on the sea. With toilet and shower they cost 3500 CFP for one or two people, 4500 CFP for three. There are two rather basic dorms at 1000 CFP. The place is popular with surfers, who know they can ask advice of Doumé, the manager and a former surfer. There's a snack bar and airport transfers are 500 CFP.

Pension Enite (π/fax 68 82 37), set back across the road from Hotel Huahine, has eight well-kept rooms with fan and communal hot-water bathrooms. There's also a small TV lounge for guests. Per-person it costs 6000 CFP with half-board (bed, breakfast and lunch or evening meal) and a two-night minimum stay. Meals are taken in the restaurant in a traditional *fare* by the water and the food has an excellent reputation. Airport transfers are 1000 CFP return.

Taahitini Supermarket (π 68 89 42), immediately south of the town on the coast, 100m from the main street, has six rooms above the store. They're intended for visiting sales reps but if the rooms are vacant, tourists can rent them for 5000 CFP. Equipped with large cold-water bathrooms, they're spacious and functional but lack style.

Meri Pension (π 68 82 44, fax 68 85 96, email pension_meri@unforgettable.com) is five minutes from the centre of Fare. It's actually a furnished flat, not a pension. There are three units that can accommodate up to seven people and two bungalows for up to four. They're well equipped, have hot water and cost 6500 CFP for the units and 7000 CFP for the bungalows for up to four people. Additional people cost 1000 CFP each. There's a three day minimum and you have to find your own way to and from the airport.

North of Fare There are half a dozen places between Fare and the airport, 2km to the north. Several are on the beach, although there is not much of a beach, while others are set slightly back.

Chez Lovina (π/fax 68 88 06) has a small-village ambience. The clientele includes many surfers, who appreciate the nearby breaks. Camping costs 1000 CFP per person, dorm beds 1200 CFP (1500 CFP for just one night). Five small garden *fare* in local style with tattoo motifs, fan, screened windows and small terrace cost 3000/5000 CFP a single/double. Bathroom facilities are shared and there's a big and well-equipped kitchen. Three family bungalows with private bathroom cost 5000 CFP to 15,000 CFP. In the small restaurant you can get breakfast for 1000 CFP, half-board for 3700 CFP or full board (accommodation and all meals) for 5600 CFP. Return transfers to the airport are 1000 CFP, to the wharf in Fare 500 CFP. Credit cards are accepted from 10,000 CFP with a 3% charge.

Fare Tehani (π/fax 68 71 00) is about 50m beyond the Chez Lovina, on the track that goes down to the coast. The accommodation here is good for somebody looking for independence, quiet and comfort. The three stylish local-style bungalows have fully equipped kitchen, lounge area, hot-water bathroom and mezzanine. A minimum of two nights is required at 10,000 CFP for two people, up to 16,000 CFP for seven or eight. Tariffs for longer stays are possible. Make your own way from the airport.

La Petite Ferme (π 68 82 98) is a popular horse-riding centre by the road that also offers accommodation in a verdant setting, somewhat like a mini-ranch. There's a simple but quite acceptable six bed dorm for 1650 CFP and a small double room at 1950 CFP per person. A small equipped bungalow with cold-water bathroom costs 5000/7500/9000 CFP for one/two/three occupants; 1000 CFP for children younger than eight. Lunch/dinner costs 1200/1650 CFP and transfers to the airport or the quay in Fare are free.

Pension Fare Maeva (π 68 75 53, fax 68 77 51) is on the beach, or would be if there was a beach on this stretch, and is accessible by the track that leaves the road at right angles by La Petite Ferme. There are 10 well-kept and well-equipped bungalows with kitchen, hot-water bathroom and screened windows. They accommodate one or two people, cost 6000 CFP and airport transfers are included. In association with Europcar it does a room-plus-car deal at 12,900 CFP per day for two people.

Vaihonu Ocean Camping (π/fax 68 87 33, email vaihonu@mail.pf) is 150m farther along from Pension Fare Maeva, by the water and in a wild setting. Étienne, the friendly owner, speaks perfect English. Camping costs 1000 CFP per person, dropping to 800 CFP from day three. You can rent a tent for 500 CFP a night. The eight bed dorm is tiled, has mosquito screens and costs 1200 CFP. Cabins with fan and shared bathroom cost 2000/3000 CFP a single/double. A large, fully equipped *fare* costs 6000 CFP to 10,000 CFP. A duplex chalet, also fully equipped, costs 5200 CFP for two or three people. There are bicycles available free for guests' use, airport transfers are included and 4WD island-tours are organised. Good standards, a warm welcome and Étienne's professionalism make this a good blend of price and quality.

Chez Ella (☎ 68 73 07 or ☎ 83 75 29 in *Papeete*), BP 71, Fare, at the intersection of the coast road and the turn-off to the airport, has two houses with two bedrooms each and a chalet with mezzanine. They're comfortable and have a lounge area, TV, washing machine, refrigerator, kitchen area and hot-water bathroom. Costs are 5500 CFP for one or two people; 7000 CFP for three or four.

Motel Vanille (☎/fax 68 71 77) is hidden in vegetation across from Chez Ella; access is by the airport road, 50m from the cross-roads. It's actually not a motel but a pretty guesthouse with five local-style bungalows with hot-water bathroom and small veranda around a swimming pool. They cost 7200 CFP for one or two people. There are also four ordinary and rather small rooms with fan and shared cold-water bathroom for 4800 CFP. Half-board adds 2900 CFP per person and includes three hours of bicycle rental (normally 200 CFP an hour). Meals are taken in a pleasant *fare* beside the swimming pool. Credit cards are accepted.

Hotel Huahine Village (☎ 68 87 00, fax 68 86 99) is right by the sea and close to the airport but at the time of writing was closed for renovations.

The old *Hotel Bali Hai*, a well known and long-running establishment with a pleasant beach just north of Fare, was badly damaged in the 1998 cyclone and is also closed. There are plans to build a new luxury hotel on the site.

Pension Poetaina (☎/fax 68 89 49) is a huge place, about 1km south of town, on the inland side of the road at the turn-off just past the bridge. Despite appearances, it's immaculately kept and has a big, well-equipped kitchen, a lounge and small swimming pool. Rooms with shared bathroom facilities are 7500 CFP for two people, and two family rooms with hot-water bathroom are 9500 CFP for two. Breakfast and airport transfers are included and there's a two-night minimum.

Chez Henriette (☎ 68 83 71), BP 288, Fare, is only 500m away from Pension Poetaina, beside the lagoon. The three big bungalows are 6000 CFP for up to four people, the three smaller ones are 4000 CFP or 5000 CFP for one or two people. They all have small kitchen areas, refrigerator, mosquito screens, fan, and cold-water bathroom. The tariffs drop after three days.

Maeva Area *Camping Vanaa Delord* (☎ 68 89 51), on the track to the Sofitel and shortly after the bridge to Maeva near the fish traps, is beside a pleasant beach about 50m from the reef. In the middle of a grove of coconut and pandanus trees are 13 tiny bungalows constructed of local materials – basic little huts known as *paillottes*. They're minimally equipped – just a bed, table and light – for 2500 CFP per person including breakfast. Camping costs 1000 CFP per person. There are shared bathroom and kitchen facilities. In the rather interesting local-style restaurant *fare* you can get Chinese dishes or grilled fish for 1300 CFP, accompanied by a large jug of fruit juice for 500 CFP. Airport transfers cost 1000 CFP return. This place will suit shoestring travellers and those searching for local ambience.

Sofitel Heiva (☎ 68 86 86, fax 68 25 25) is 8km from Fare, at the southern tip of Motu Papiti. It's the biggest hotel on the island and is beautifully situated with a sandy beach and shallow water separating it from Motu Mahare. There's magnificent snorkelling among the coral pinnacles at the Coral Garden site, and there's a popular surf-break just off the reef edge.

The 61 well-equipped units start with garden rooms among the coconut palms for 24,300 CFP. and move up through garden/beach/over-water bungalows for 34,560/51,840/64,800 CFP. Add another 5600/8100 CFP per person for half/full board. Return airport transfers are 1900 CFP. There's a swimming pool, the Manuia Bar, the poolside Omai Restaurant and twice-weekly island-night performances with a buffet. The hotel is conveniently close to the Maeva marae sites and offers a range of activities on land and sea.

South of Fare *Hotel Bellevue (☎ 68 82 76, 68 81 70, fax 68 85 35)* is rather a long way from anywhere: 5km south of Fare, 7km from the airport and close to the junction where the road down to the Huahine Iti bridge splits off from the road that encircles Huahine Nui. The main building has eight rooms with cold-water bathroom at 3780/4860 CFP a single/double and 12 bungalows with hot-water bathroom, mosquito screens and veranda from 6480 CFP to 7560 CFP. It's a place with few pretensions and the bungalows are certainly faded but the quiet setting and views over Maroe Bay are superb.

There's a restaurant with fine views and a swimming pool that was being renovated at the time of writing. Half-board adds 3200 CFP, Chinese and Polynesian dishes cost 1700 CFP. The manager is a fisher and will organise various excursions and motu trips. Airport transfers are 500 CFP per person each way and credit cards are accepted.

Te Tiare Beach Resort (☎ 60 60 50, fax 60 60 51, email tetiarebeach@mail.pf) is at the south-western corner of Huahine Nui, a good location for a complete getaway. Along the lagoon and accessible only by sea, this appealing complex has 41 traditional-style but luxurious bungalows, 16 of them over-water. Prices range from 32,400 CFP to 60,480 CFP. The restaurant has fine food at reasonable prices and there's a full range of activities. Airport transfers cost 4000 CFP return.

Chez Bougainville, Oiseau de Paradis (Bird of Paradise), Chaouia and *Saint Mandrianus* are four furnished, fully equipped, comfortable villas in a superb garden setting to the north of Maroe Bay, close to the coast road. They accommodate up to six people and cost 16,500 CFP (two or three people) to 23,500 CFP (five or six people) including the use of a car and a boat, ideal for getting out to idyllic Motu Topati. The car and boat are guaranteed to be in good condition but it's a good idea to check this as soon as you arrive. The villas are also known collectively as Rafaël and Rolland. For Bougainville and Bird of Paradise, phone ☎/fax 68 81 59 and ask for Rafaël. For Chaouia and Saint Mandrianus phone ☎ 82 49 65 and fax 85 47 69 in Papeete.

Huahine Iti The (marginally) smaller island has several ideally situated places, the most beautiful beaches and the widest lagoon. If you're fixing your own food, however, it's a long way to any shops, and there's no public transport to speak of.

Budget Ariiura Camping Ecologie (☎ 68 85 20, 68 83 78) is right on the beach, shortly after Relais Mahana to the south. It's a good place, but is strictly for people on a low budget looking for a relaxed atmosphere and Polynesian setting. It's also close to a prime surfing location. The owners, Cecele and Hubert, the latter a Polynesian English teacher who knows all the island legends, offer camp sites and several 'camping *fare*'. A camp site costs 1200 CFP per person (1000 CFP from the third day). The 'camping *fare*' are simple small cabins on the sand with a bed and mosquito net (3500 CFP for two people, 3000 CFP from the third day). The cabins don't lock and even the toilet facilities are local style! A small thatched *fare* beside the beach offers meals if you don't intend to use the kitchen.

Hubert may be able to drive you to Fare (300 CFP) or to the airport. Le trucks leave for Fare around 7.30 am, return at 11 am and cost 300 CFP. It's also possible to rent pirogues/bicycles/snorkelling equipment for 250/1000/200 CFP per day. Hubert is an environmentalist and will certainly suggest you visit his botanical garden, beside Maroe

Bay, where he cultivates Polynesian medicinal plants.

Mid-Range *Pension Mauarii* (☎/fax 68 86 49) is about 3km from Parea in a beautiful seafront garden. It's full of style and character, with two impeccable garden bungalows with hot-water bathroom, mosquito screens and bamboo bed for 9500/10,000 CFP a single/double. There's a comfortable local-style beach bungalow for 15,000 CFP for two and another for 17,000 CFP.

Close to the beach, an immense traditional Polynesian *fare* has two rooms on the ground floor for 6500/7500 CFP a single/double, while the mezzanine rooms cost 12,000 CFP for two. The adjoining lagoonside restaurant is very well known for local specialities: see Around Huahine under Places to Eat later. Half/full board costs 3000/5000 CFP per person. Return airport transfers are 1800 CFP.

Huahine Beach Club (☎ 68 81 46, fax 41 09 28) is at the southerly entrance to the village of Parea, right on the beach and looking across to Motu Araara. Bungalows cost from 15,120 CFP to 17,280 CFP. There's a bar, restaurant, small boutique and bicycles and scooters to rent. Pirogues and kayaks, ideal for exploring the nearby motu, are free. Transfers cost 900 CFP per person each way and credit cards are accepted.

Top End *Relais Mahana* (☎ 68 81 54, fax 68 85 08) is about 1km south of Pension Mauarii, almost at the southern point of Huahine Iti, and has beach and garden bungalows for 18,360 CFP to 24,624 CFP. It's on a beautiful shady beach with coconut palms and is owned by *popaa* (westerners). Breakfast costs 1300 CFP, other meals are à la carte and are taken in a lagoonside restaurant *fare*. There's a small laundrette (1060 CFP a load), a swimming pool and a variety of sporting equipment, including kayaks, pedal boats, bicycles, snorkelling and tennis gear, all available free for guests' use. The hotel is run with almost military precision, however, which some visitors find off-putting. Airport transfers are 1050 CFP each way and credit cards are accepted. It's closed mid-November to mid-December.

Places to Eat

Fare For cheap eats and late eats, the wharfside *roulottes* are Huahine's best bargain. Otherwise plan to eat early, as after 9 pm most places start to close their doors. Fish, chicken, burgers, steaks and chips are the order of the day from roulottes, and a meal typically costs around 800 CFP. Your meal could be followed by crêpes and *gaufres* (waffles) or a slice of *pastèque* (watermelon). The roulottes operate from early morning until late at night and if a ship is due in the early hours they'll open up to feed the passengers.

There are a number of places to eat along the main street of Fare. In the pleasant open-air area at the front of *Chez Guynette* you can get breakfast for 550 CFP or a light lunch for 1000 CFP to 1500 CFP.

Snack Bar Te Manava (☎ 68 76 02), at the end of the main street, is more restaurant than snack bar. Pleasantly situated right on the beach, it has an interesting and reasonably priced menu offering chicken *fafa* (taro leaves) in coconut milk for 1500 CFP, chow mein for 1000 CFP. It's open Saturday to Thursday evening for lunch and dinner.

Pension Enite (☎ 68 82 37) has a restaurant with an excellent reputation and a charming setting beside the lagoon. Bookings are essential and a complete meal costs 2500 CFP, or 3500 CFP with crustaceans.

Hotel Huahine's ground-floor snack bar does some moderately priced simple dishes such as *poisson cru* (a raw fish dish) for 950 CFP and sashimi rice for 1150 CFP. It's closed on Sunday.

Te Vaipuna Restaurant (☎ 68 70 45) is opposite the wharf and has a strong local reputation for its excellent and reasonably priced Chinese food. Most dishes are in the 900 CFP to 1500 CFP range, though crab and lobster can cost 2500 CFP to 5000 CFP. Te Vaipuna is open weekdays for lunch and dinner, Saturday for dinner only. Credit cards are accepted.

Tiare Tipanier (☎ 68 80 52) is very popular, offering an excellent blend of price and quality. At lunchtime there are burgers for 480 CFP, pizzas for 950 CFP and omelettes from 500 CFP. In the evening there's a complete meal for 2000 CFP, which might start with salad followed by tuna either grilled or with green-pepper sauce. Other dishes are 950 CFP to 1500 CFP and a half-litre of red wine is 480 CFP. It's closed all day Sunday and Monday lunchtime. Credit cards are accepted.

Fare Pizza (☎ 60 60 01) is next to the Taahitini store and prepares very straightforward pizzas for 950 CFP to 1500 CFP. Deliveries are possible Monday to Saturday, from Fitii to Maeva. It's open daily from 11 am to 8 pm but on Sunday only in the evening.

If you're preparing your own meals, fresh supplies such as fruit, vegetables and fish are available from the impromptu quayside **marketplace**. Fare has several shops that open daily (mornings only on Sunday). There's **Super Fare Nui**, across from the waterfront, and *Taahitini* immediately south of the town centre. They accept credit cards.

Around Huahine Once you've left Fare there aren't too many places to eat, apart from at the hotels. You can try the pleasant *Omai Restaurant* at the Sofitel Heiva, where there's a varied menu including an evening buffet.

In the south-western corner of Huahine Nui, *Local Motion* (☎ 68 86 58) is a local fruit farm and orchard with delicious cool fruit-juices from 200 CFP and set meals for 1000 CFP to 2950 CFP. It's closed on Sunday.

Faie Glaces (☎ 68 87 95), on the exit from Faie, at the start of the Route Traversière and to the right of the road, has great home-made coconut, pineapple, banana, vanilla, melon, papaya and other flavours of ice cream for 250 CFP. It's closed on Sunday.

Restaurant Mauarii (☎ 68 86 49), in the pension of the same name on Huahine Iti, has some of the best food on the island, perhaps in all the Leeward Islands. The hostess prepares fine Polynesian cuisine including many specialities such as an *ahimaa* (Tahitian oven) for 3500 CFP per person. Or there's the traditional Polynesian meal, served every day, which includes chicken fafa, hot pork, poisson cru, taro, *fei* (a type

of banana), *uru* (breadfruit) and *poe* (plantain-like banana) for dessert for 2000 CFP. Or try shark curry (2100 CFP), crab in ginger coconut-milk (3200 CFP), oven-baked papaya (550 CFP) and the house punch (850 CFP). It is right by the lagoon and is open for lunch and dinner every day.

Huahine Beach Club restaurant occupies a vast but impersonal room where some light meals are offered at lunchtime. The menu is more elaborate for dinner.

Relais Mahana also has a restaurant, facing the lagoon.

There are small shops with rather variable opening hours around the island at Maeva and Fitii on Huahine Nui, and at Haapu and Parea on Huahine Iti.

Entertainment

Entertainment on Huahine is very limited. *Sofitel Heiva* has twice-weekly buffet dinners with good-quality traditional dance performances for 5000 CFP to 6000 CFP.

Shopping

Plenty of places sell souvenirs and local crafts in and around Fare. Right across from the wharf on the single main street, Rima'i Te Niu Taue is a friendly, small boutique with pottery, jewellery and colourful *pareu* (sarong-like attire). Souvenirs des Îles is right beside it and also has a good selection. A few steps along the street brings you to the bright and energetic Studio Jojo, where you can buy postcards and other souvenirs, and get your film processed in 24 hours. At the end of Fare's main street, next to the Snack Bar Te Marava, is Faahotu Arts Creation, with good-quality local crafts including paintings and pottery.

In Faie, at the entrance to the village when coming from Maeva, Denise Jamet (☎ 68 81 97) offers pareu. Also in Faie, don't miss a visit to Huahine Nui Pearl & Pottery. Peter Owen, the owner, specialises in pearl farming and pottery and his work is shown in Papeete galleries. His studio is on a farm on the lagoon. From the Faie exit there's a ferry that operates at 10 am and 3 pm daily except Sunday and costs 1000 CFP. Credit cards are accepted.

In Maeva, ask for Piera, who sells vanilla pods. Next to the Marae Manunu is Atiho Peinture, a small studio where you can find pareu and engraved pearl shells.

Getting There & Away

Westbound from Tahiti it's 170km to Huahine, the first of the Leeward islands. The twin islands of Raiatea and Tahaa lie a farther 35km to the west.

Air The airport is 2.5km from Fare. Air Tahiti connects with Papeete two to four times daily, taking 35 minutes (slightly longer on connections via Moorea). Onward flights continue to Raiatea and/or Bora Bora. The short hop to Raiatea can take less than 15 minutes. Connections to Maupiti are more complex, usually requiring a change of aircraft at Raiatea or Bora Bora. One-way adult fares to or from Huahine are: Bora Bora 6500 CFP, Maupiti 7700 CFP, Moorea 11,000 CFP, Papeete 8800 CFP and Raiatea 4400 CFP. The Air Tahiti office (☎ 68 82 65, 68 82 89) is at the airport.

Boat The high-speed *Ono-Ono* and the cargo ship *Taporo IV* operate to Huahine. See the Ferry & Cargo Ship section in the Getting Around chapter for more information. The *Ono-Ono* can be booked through the office (☎ 68 85 85) on the quay in the centre of Fare. It takes just 3½ hours to get to Papeete (4895 CFP), 45 minutes to Raiatea (1676 CFP) with continuations to Tahaa and Bora Bora.

Getting Around

To/From the Airport You could walk into town from the airport if you were really intent on saving CFP, but pensions and hotels in Fare will arrange taxi transfers that are sometimes included in their tariffs.

Le Truck & Taxi The extreme shortage of public transport is Huahine's biggest drawback. A le truck belonging to each district shuttles in to Fare early each morning and returns to the various villages late in the morning for 300 CFP. Pension Enite (☎ 68 82 37) and Felix Tours (☎ 68 81 69) can organise taxis.

Car Avis-Pacificar and Europcar are the two car-rental operators in Huahine. They are open daily from 7 am to 6 pm. They will deliver directly to the airport or to your hotel but it's wise to book ahead for long weekends, school vacations, Christmas and peak tourist seasons. Both agencies offer four, eight, 24 and 48-hour rental periods with or without unlimited mileage. If you're intending to drive all around the island, unlimited mileage will probably work out cheaper. Discounts of 10% are easy to get and credit cards are accepted.

The main agency of Europcar (☎ 68 82 59, 68 88 03, fax 68 80 59) is north of the centre of Fare, near the post office. It also has a counter at the airport for arriving flights, and counters at Sofitel Heiva, Relais Mahana and Huahine Beach Club. A Fiat Panda costs 7900 CFP for 24 hours with unlimited mileage. See the Pension Fare Maeva entry under North of Fare in the Places to Stay section, earlier, for information about its room and a rent-a-car package.

The main agency of Avis-Pacificar (☎ 68 73 34, fax 68 73 35) is next to the Mobil station in Fare and also has a counter at the airport, for arriving flights. A Ford Fiesta costs 7900 CFP for 24 hours with unlimited mileage.

There are two service stations in Fare; one or the other will be open Sunday and early mornings.

Scooter & Bicycle Europcar rents out bicycles for 1900 CFP a day, Avis for 1800 CFP. Chez Huahine Lagoon (☎ 68 70 00, 68 87 57), on the waterfront at the northern end of the main street in Fare, charges 1200 CFP a day for a mountain bike in excellent shape. Across the road, Chez Jojo (☎ 68 89 16) asks 1500 CFP. Some guesthouses and hotels have bicycles for guests either free or at pleasantly low rates. This is the case with Huahine Beach Club, Motel Vanille, Vaihonu Ocean Camping, Relais Mahana, Ariiura Camping Ecologie and Sofitel Heiva.

For scooters, check with Europcar or Avis, which both charge 5900 CFP for 24 hours.

Raiatea & Tahaa

Between Huahine and Bora Bora, the twin islands of Raiatea and Tahaa share a common lagoon. Less touristy than their neighbours, the islands offer an opportunity to enjoy a more old-fashioned and relaxed Polynesian lifestyle. A narrow 3km channel separates the two islands, but the airport is on Raiatea and most inter-island ships dock at Uturoa, so visitors to either island will usually come to Raiatea first.

The Hawaiki Nui canoe race starts each October or November on Huahine and continues to Raiatea and Tahaa before finishing on Bora Bora (see the 'Hawaiki Nui Canoe Race' boxed text in the Facts for the Visitor chapter).

Raiatea

Largest of the Leeward islands and outranked in the whole Society group only by Tahiti, Raiatea's main island has no beaches. This may account for its comparatively untouristed flavour, although there are fine beaches on its many motu and its yachting marinas make this the sailing centre of French Polynesia. See the Outdoor Activities chapter for details. The large lagoon is ideal for diving courses and pirogue tours while the mountainous interior is the place for walks and horse rides.

Uturoa, the principal town on Raiatea, is the administrative centre of the Leeward Islands of the Society group but the rest of the island is wild and lightly populated. Often referred to as 'sacred Raiatea', it had a central role in ancient Polynesian religious beliefs; Marae Taputapuatea is the largest in French Polynesia and one of the most important. It's said that any new marae on another island had to incorporate a stone from Marae Taputapuatea.

Raiatea's Faaroa River, which runs into Faaroa Bay, is the only navigable river in French Polynesia. Polynesian oral history relates that it was from this river that the

great migration voyages to Hawaii and New Zealand commenced.

History

Raiatea, known as Havai'i in ancient times, is the cultural, religious and historic centre of the Society Islands. Polynesian legends relate that Raiatea and Tahaa were the first islands to be settled, probably by people from Samoa, far to the north-west. It is said that Raiatea's first king was the legendary Hiro and that it was Hiro and his companions who built the great canoes that sailed to Rarotonga and New Zealand.

Later, Raiatea was a centre for the Oro (God of War) cult, which was in the process of replacing the earlier Taaroa (God of Creation) cult when Europeans turned up and disrupted the entire Polynesian religious pattern. At the time of Cook's first Polynesian visit, Raiatea was probably under Bora Bora's control and the Raiatean chiefs were scattered far and wide. Tupaia, who sailed with Cook from Tahiti on the *Endeavour*, but died in the Dutch East Indies (now Indonesia), was one of these exiled Raiateans.

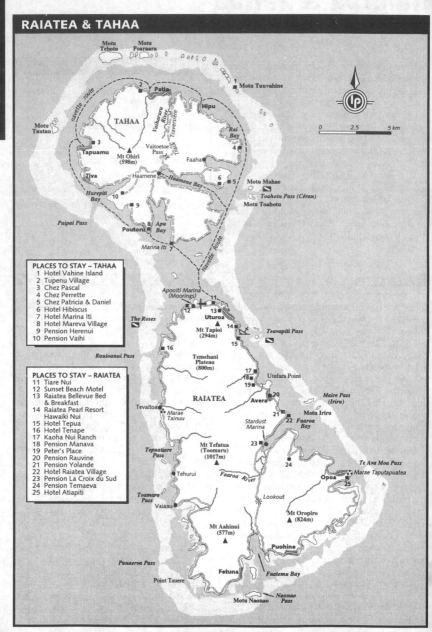

RAIATEA & TAHAA

Motu Tehotu
Motu Poaraara

Motu Tuuvahine

navette route

Patie

Hipu

TAHAA

Rai
Bay

Motu
Tautau

Tapuamu

Mt Ohiri
(598m)

Vaitoetoe
Pass

Vaiharuru River
Traversière
Traversière River

Faaha

Tiva

Haamene

Haamene Bay

Motu Mahae

Toahotu Pass (Céran)

Motu Toahotu

Hurepiti
Bay

Paipai Pass

Poutoru

Apu
Bay

Marina Iti

Navette Route

PLACES TO STAY – TAHAA
1 Hotel Vahine Island
2 Tupenu Village
3 Chez Pascal
4 Chez Perrette
5 Chez Patricia & Daniel
6 Hotel Hibiscus
7 Hotel Marina Iti
8 Hotel Mareva Village
9 Pension Herenui
10 Pension Vaihi

Apooiti Marina
(Moorings)

The Roses

Uturoa

Mt Tapioi
(294m)

Teavapiti Pass

Rautoanui Pass

Temehani
Plateau
(800m)

Utufara Point

PLACES TO STAY – RAIATEA
11 Tiare Nui
12 Sunset Beach Motel
13 Raiatea Bellevue Bed
   & Breakfast
14 Raiatea Pearl Resort
   Hawaiki Nui
15 Hotel Tepua
16 Hotel Tenape
17 Kaoha Nui Ranch
18 Pension Manava
19 Peter's Place
20 Pension Rauvine
21 Pension Yolande
22 Hotel Raiatea Village
23 Pension La Croix du Sud
24 Pension Temaeva
25 Hotel Atiapiti

RAIATEA

Avera

Maire Pass
(Iriru)

Tevaitoa

Marae
Tainuu

Motu Iriru

Faaroa
Bay

Stardust
Marina

Tepuatiare
Pass

Mt Tefatua
(Toomaru)
(1017m)

Faaroa River

Te Ava Moa Pass

Tehurui

Opoa

Marae Taputapuatea

Toamaro
Pass

Vaiaau

Lookout

Mt Oropiro
(824m)

Mt Aahinui
(577m)

Punaeroa Pass

Puohine

Point Tauere

Fetuna

Faatemu Bay

Motu Naonao

Naonao
Pass

0   2.5   5 km

Raiatea today is the most popular yachting base in French Polynesia. This is a fitting role given that it was a centre for the great Polynesian-migration voyages and that James Cook, the greatest European Pacific navigator, visited Raiatea so often and at such length. He first came to the island on the *Endeavour* in 1769, when he anchored off Opoa. He returned in 1774 during his second great Pacific voyage and on this occasion took Omai back to Europe. In 1777 he made a prolonged visit before sailing to Hawaii and to his death.

The pioneering English missionary John Williams turned up on Raiatea in 1818 and the island remained under British missionary influence long after Tahiti came under French control. It was from Raiatea that missionaries continued to Rarotonga in the Cook Islands in 1823 and to Samoa in 1830. The French takeover of Tahiti in 1842 led to a long period of instability and fierce Raiatean resistance. It was not until 1888 that the French attempted a real takeover and not until 1897 that troops were sent to put down the final Polynesian rebellion. Teraupoo, the last Raiatean chief, was exiled to New Caledonia, where he remained until 1906.

Orientation

Raiatea is vaguely triangular in shape with an encircling road that hugs the coast all the way around. It's not all sealed but it's suitable for cars. *Pointe kilométrique* (PK) distances are not signposted, but start in Uturoa near the *gendarmerie* (police station) and run south and north to Faatemu Bay. Although the interior is mountainous and includes the 800m-high Temehani Plateau, the mountains don't have the close-up immediacy that they do on Moorea or Tahiti. The island's highest point is Mt Tefatua (1017m), right in the centre of the island. The main range runs north-south for most of the length of the island with smaller ranges in the south, separated by a valley through which a cross-island road runs from Faaroa Bay to Faatemu Bay. Faaroa Bay is unique in French Polynesia, fed by the only navigable river on the islands.

The Raiatea airport, which also serves Tahaa, is right at the northern tip of the island. The town of Uturoa is just south-east of the airport and extends almost to the entrance to Faaroa Bay. The rest of the way around the island there are only small, scattered villages. Although there are no beaches worthy of note on the main island, there are many small motu, with good beaches, flanking the eight passes through the outer reef.

Information

Tourist Offices There is a small tourist office (☎ 66 23 33) near the wharf with an adjacent crafts market. It's essentially a ticket window but the rebuilding of the port area includes plans to move it to the docks terminal. Official opening hours are Monday, Tuesday and Thursday from 7.30 to 11 am and 1.30 to 3.30 pm, Wednesday from 8 to 11.30 am and 1.30 to 3.30 pm and Friday from 8 to 11.30 am. There's also a desk at the airport (☎ 66 23 34) for flight arrivals.

Money The three French Polynesian banks have branches in Uturoa that are open weekdays. Banque Socredo and the Banque de Tahiti have automatic teller machines (ATMs).

Post & Communications The post office, just north of the centre towards the airport, is open Monday to Thursday from 7 am to 3 pm, Friday from 7 am to 2 pm and Saturday

Raiatea's Emblem – the Tiare Apetahi

Raiatea has one of the world's rarest flowers, the *tiare apetahi*. This endemic species is found only on Mt Temehani. White in colour, it is shaped like a half-corolla and opens dramatically at dawn. You should be able to see it while hiking on the mountain – but note that it is strictly protected, so no picking.

from 8 to 10 am. Eloy Informatique (☎ 66 35 85, fax 66 14 05, email eloyinfo@ tahiti.net), between the marina in Uturoa and the airport, is in the building on the lagoon side of the road with the parrot on the shop window. It offers various services for travellers and yachties including Internet access, faxes at 450 CFP a page, email at 250 CFP a message, express mail and poste restante. It will also forward messages for yachts and can help English-speaking yachties with their paperwork. It's open weekdays from 8 am to noon and 2 to 5 pm.

Medical Services & Emergency Raiatea has good health facilities including a hospital (☎ 66 35 03) in front of the post office and several doctors. The pharmacy (☎ 66 34 44) is on the main street and is open every day.

The gendarmerie is to the north of the town, after the post office.

Laundry The Bleu des Îles laundry in the Tahina Commercial Centre, on the inland side of the airport road (behind the Afo store) charges 1450 CFP a load for washing and drying. It's open weekdays from 7.30 to 11.30 am and 2 to 6.30 pm. The Jacqueline Laundrette (☎ 66 28 36) is 200m before the Apooiti Marina clubhouse when coming from Uturoa and charges 150 CFP per kilogram, washed and dried.

Photo Developing For films and photo developing go to Photo Gauguin next to the Hotel Hinano.

Around the Island

There are not many specific 'sights' along the 98km circuit of Raiatea – it's more an opportunity to enjoy the island's relaxed atmosphere and splendid views of mountains and motu. Just over half of the circuit is on roads of crushed coral – *soupe de corail* (coral soup) as they're known locally.

In the south of the island, a short stretch of fine mountain road between Faaroa and Faatemu bays takes you away from the coast and past an excellent lookout. Adding this road into the itinerary, adding it twice in fact by making the circuit into a figure

eight, extends the drive to just 111km. The following drive starts with Uturoa and goes clockwise, but the bottom half of the figure eight goes anticlockwise. Apart from places on the outskirts of Uturoa there is virtually nowhere along the way to get lunch. You'd be better to bring a picnic if you want to make a day of it.

Uturoa Uturoa, Raiatea's busy port town, is the largest town in French Polynesia after Papeete and is the administrative centre of the Leeward Islands. Its jumble of varied buildings is not terribly attractive, but the main street, with its colourful shops and busy central **marketplace**, is certainly active. A project was launched in 1999 to re-build and renovate the town centre and port district. The modernisation of the dock area will allow it to handle larger fishing ships and cruise liners.

The wharf is often busy with the arrival and departure of inter-island boats and the regular *navette* (shuttle) service to nearby Tahaa. The strength of the town's Chinese community is evident in the many shops and restaurants and the Kuo Min Tang Association building. The Protestant church on the northern side of the town centre has a memorial stone to pioneer missionary John Williams. Queen Pomare, exiled from Tahiti in 1844 by the French takeover, took refuge in Vairahi, now swallowed up by the southward expansion of Uturoa. She remained there for three years before returning to Tahiti.

Uturoa is overlooked by **Mt Tapioi** (294m), topped by TV-relay masts and offering fine views over the lagoon.

Uturoa to Faatemu Bay (16 to 22.5km) From the centre of bustling Uturoa the town blends seamlessly into **Avera**, site of the final battle between the French and local rebels, before turning away from the coast up the long narrow Faaroa Bay. At 12.5km the road passes Stardust Marina, one of the island's two major yacht-charter operations. Soon after, you reach the turn-off to the south coast. The **Faaroa River**, the only navigable (albeit

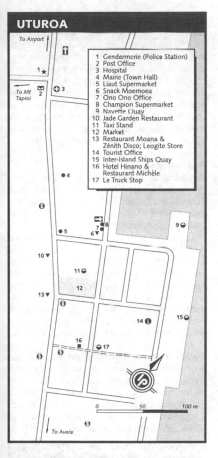

UTUROA

To Airport

1 Gendarmerie (Police Station)
2 Post Office
3 Hospital
4 Mairie (Town Hall)
5 Liaut Supermarket
6 Snack Moemoea
7 Ono Ono Office
8 Champion Supermarket
9 Navette Quay
10 Jade Garden Restaurant
11 Taxi Stand
12 Market
13 Restaurant Moana &
   Zénith Disco; Leogite Store
14 Tourist Office
15 Inter-Island Ships Quay
16 Hotel Hinano &
   Restaurant Michèle
17 Le Truck Stop

To Mt
Tapioi

0   50   100 m

To Avera

barely!) river in French Polynesia, leads inland from the end of the bay.

From the turn-off the road runs smoothly to the *belvédère* (lookout; 26.5km) with great views down along Faaroa Bay towards the coast and of the surrounding mountains. The road drops down to the south coast road.

Faatemu Bay to Marae Taputapuatea (22.5 to 42km) Turn left at the coast so that the bottom half of the figure-eight circuit will take you round the coast anticlockwise. The crushed-coral road winds

along the coast, crossing narrow bridges over many crystal-clear little streams.

In places near the village of **Puohine** (25km) the road runs on embankments, cutting off shallow ponds used to farm oysters and mussels. There's a long stretch past the village where the steep green mountainsides, falling down towards the coast, are streaked with innumerable **waterfalls** during the wetter months of the year. Along this part of the road there are many king-size **crabs** scuttling across the road and not all of them make it, although traffic is light along this stretch. Just before reaching Raiatea's sacred marae you come to the outskirts of the village of **Opoa** (41km).

The most important marae in Polynesia, Marae Taputapuatea looks out to the Te Ava Moa Pass. Dedicated to Oro, the god of war who dominated 18th century Polynesian religious beliefs, the marae sprawls extensively across Cape Matahira. The marae only dates from the 17th century, when it replaced Marae Vaearai, which was dedicated to Taaroa, the god of creation, and located farther inland.

Despite its relatively short history, the marae had clearly assumed central importance in the Polynesian religion, as any marae constructed on another island had to incorporate one of Taputapuatea's stones as a symbol of allegiance and spiritual lineage. When the first Europeans arrived, this was the centre of spiritual and temporal power in Polynesia. In fact its influence was international; *arii* (chiefs) from throughout the Maohi world including the Australs, the Cooks and even New Zealand came to this marae for important ceremonies.

The site encompasses an international, a district and a domestic marae. The main part of the marae is a large flag-stoned platform with a long *ahu* (the equivalent of an altar) stretching down one side. At the very end of the cape is the smaller **Marae Tauraa**, a *tapu* (taboo) enclosure with the tall 'stone of investiture', where young arii were enthroned. The lagoonside **Marae Hauviri** also had an upright stone. The whole site is made of pieces of coral. The huge double canoes of royal pilgrims used to sail through the Te Ava Moa (Sacred) Pass en route to the marae.

Well restored and on a cleared, land-scaped site, the marae makes an imposing impression but unfortunately there is little explanation to help independent visitors understand this historic place. It's well worth visiting with a guide who can explain the cultural significance of the site – see Island Tours under Organised Tours later in this chapter and refer to the 'Civilisation & Archaeology' special section for more information on marae.

Marae Taputapuatea to Tevaitoa (42 to 95km) The road winds around bays and inlets for 10km of unsealed road before the surface improves along the southern side of Faaroa Bay. At 57.5km you again turn off the coast road and repeat the short mountain stretch back to the south coast.

The road follows the coast, sometimes running over causeways cutting off shallow, stagnant inlets, through the village of **Fetuna** (68km). Motu Naonao, just across from the Fetuna village, has a pleasant **beach**. During WWII, when the US military occupied Bora Bora, a landing strip was constructed here. Just before **Vaiaau** (85.5km), where the sealed road recommences, there may be a small stall by the roadside selling nicely crafted models of paddle and sailing pirogues for 3000 CFP to 3500 CFP. The road continues through **Tehurui** (88.5km).

Marae Tainuu (95km) In the middle of the village of **Tevaitoa** stands the island's oldest Protestant church, an architecturally curious-looking creation but not of great interest were it not built, in one of those examples of Christian respect for other beliefs that warms the heart, smack on top of a magnificent marae. Behind the church the walls of the marae stretch for just over 50m, some of the massive upright stones standing over 4m high. Unusually, there's an explanation panel at the site entrance.

Apooiti Marina (107km) From Marae Tainuu to the Apooiti Marina, the road continues around the convoluted coast line with more superb views, more waterfalls visible on the hillsides and turn-offs leading to the Temehani Plateau. **Apooiti** was the last centre for fire-walking on Raiatea.

The mega-bucks Apooiti Marina, also known as Marina Moorings, features shops, a restaurant and bar, a diving centre and, of course, lots of yachts. From the marina the road passes by the airport and returns to Uturoa, 111km from the starting point.

Activities
Walking & Diving Walking opportunities are rather limited on Raiatea. Apart from Temehani Plateau walks with a guide, the short climb up Mt Tapioi, dominating Uturoa, is the only real interest.

Diving is a major activity on the island and there are two centres for beginners and experienced divers. One is at the Hotel Tepua, the other at the Apooiti Marina. There are about 10 dive sites along the east and west coasts and around Tahaa. See the Outdoor Activities chapter for more information on walking, and the 'Diving' special section for information on diving opportunities.

Swimming & Snorkelling Raiatea has no beaches – a hotel or guesthouse pontoon is the most you can expect – but some of the reef motu are splendid and perfect for swimming or snorkelling. **Motu Iriru** to the west of the island and **Motu Naonao** to the south are good examples. Ask at your

---

Stone-Fishing Festival

The annual stone-fishing festival takes place in the last week of October. Events include singing and dancing, agricultural and craft displays, local sporting events (including fruit-carrying races!), fishing contests and canoe races. A fire-walking ceremony is a highlight of the festivities before the final event, when flower-bedecked pirogues fan out across the lagoon and the surface of the water is beaten with stones to herd the fish into an enclosure.

accommodation about renting a boat or joining a lagoon tour.

Sailing & Jetskiing Raiatea is the principal nautical centre in the Leeward Islands and the point of numerous cruise departures. See Sailing in the Outdoor Activities chapter for more information, and Lagoon Tours later in this chapter.

Horse Riding The well respected Kaoha Nui Ranch (☎/fax 66 25 46) is 6km south of Uturoa and has 10 Marquesan horses. For a minimum of four people it does 1½-hour guided excursions for 3200 CFP per person, half-day trips for 4800 CFP and one day trips including picnic lunch for 8500 CFP. The routes generally follow the ridgelines or valley bottoms. Lessons for beginners or more experienced riders are offered on the property for 2000 CFP an hour. The ranch also offers several packages including accommodation and food.

Game Fishing Game-fishing trips can be organised with the *Sakario* (☎ 66 35 54) or the *Tevaite* (☎ 66 32 69). Count on 70,000 CFP to 90,000 CFP per day for up to four people.

Organised Tours

Lagoon Tours Several companies do pirogue lagoon-tours with motu picnics and snorkelling and swimming stops. Reserve ahead because a minimum number of participants is required. Manava Tours at the Pension Manava (☎ 66 28 26) does tours to Tahaa for 4000 CFP and Faaroa River excursions with a visit to Marae Taputapuatea for 2700 CFP. Raiatea Safari Tours (☎ 66 37 10) is based at the Hotel Tepua and does similar trips. Raiatea Jet Cruising (☎ 66 32 33) does guided tours of the Raiatea-Tahaa lagoon for 8500/12,000 CFP for one/two hours. The Raiatea Pearl Resort Hawaiki Nui (☎ 66 20 23) organises daily glass-bottom boat excursions for 2800 CFP.

Island Tours 4WD island tours to Marae Taputapuatea, fruit plantations, Faaroa Bay and other sites last three to four hours and

More than just a means of travel, sailing across Raiatea and Tahaa's beautiful lagoon is an activity in itself.

can be a good alternative if you're alone or don't want to rent a car. Contact Raiatea 4x4 (☎ 66 24 16), Raiatea Safari Tour (☎ 66 37 10) at Hotel Tepua, Anapa (☎ 66 20 50) and Jeep Safari Raiatea (☎ 66 15 73). Tariffs vary between 4000 CFP and 5000 CFP per person and you should reserve as soon as you arrive.

Almost Paradise Tours (☎ 66 23 64) rather proudly announces on its leaflet that tours are 'in English only'. Operated by a long-term American resident, the three-hour minibus trip to Marae Taputapuatea and island plantations costs 3500 CFP per person.

Places to Stay

Places to stay on Raiatea are, with a few exceptions, in or close to Uturoa. None are on a beach, although some have pontoons anchored in the lagoon. There are three places where you can camp.

Uturoa *Hotel Hinano* (☎ 66 13 13, fax 66 14 14) is the only place right in the centre of Uturoa. It's only 100m from the docks and has modern, spacious, functional and rather dull motel-style rooms around a patio. Tiled and equipped with hot-water bathrooms, the six fan-cooled rooms cost 4600/5700 CFP a single/double, the four air-con ones 5700/6800 CFP. The Restaurant Michèle is on the ground floor, airport transfers are included and credit cards are accepted.

Right on the lagoon edge, at PK2, just south of the centre of Uturoa, the old Hawaiki Nui Hotel has been beautifully renovated and rebaptised *Raiatea Pearl Resort Hawaiki Nui (☎ 66 20 23, fax 66 20 20, email h.raiateapearl@mail.pf)*. There are 32 bungalows and rooms: nine overwater/lagoon-side/garden bungalows cost 34,560/24,000/19,440 CFP. Ordinary studios opening onto a superb floral floor cost 15,120 CFP. The bungalows are particularly spacious and comfortable and come with hot-water bathroom, telephone, TV, refrigerator, fan and terrace. There's a restaurant and bar by the swimming pool and lagoon, as well as a boutique. Various activities can be organised, including transfers to a motu across the lagoon for 500 CFP return. Credit cards are accepted.

Half a kilometre farther along the road, at about PK2.5, the old Chez Marie-France is being rebuilt and renamed *Hotel Tepua (☎ 66 37 10, fax 66 26 25)*. This small lagoon-side hotel is owned by *popaa* (westerners) and will offer budget accommodation, bar and restaurant, activities centre and dive centre. Bungalows with bamboo façade, hot-water bathroom, mezzanine and fan cost 8000/9000 CFP a single/double. Ask for one looking onto the pool or lagoon. In another building, simple rooms with fans and shared hot-water bathroom cost 4500 CFP for one or two people. A rather drab six-bed dorm costs 1300 CFP for a bed. These rates are for a minimum of two nights stay.

There's a shared kitchen, small swimming pool, washing machine and restaurant. Raiatea Safari Tour and Pacific Dive Adventure are based here. You can be dropped on a motu for the day for 800 CFP return or rent a bicycle for 1000/1500 CFP a half/full day. Yachts can be moored just off the hotel but contact the reception on VHF 71. Return ferry wharf/airport transfers are 700/1000 CFP per person. Credit cards are accepted.

Perched high above the northern side of Uturoa, the quiet and relaxing *Raiatea*

Bellevue Bed & Breakfast (☎/fax 66 15 15) has extraordinary views of the city, lagoon and Tahaa. Its five small but tidy rooms with hot-water bathroom, TV, refrigerator and fan open onto a terrace beside a small swimming pool and cost 5500/6500 CFP a single/double with breakfast. Transfers cost 1250 CFP per person return, or take the first sealed road on the left after PK1 and follow it for 800m.

Shortly before the airport on the sea side of the coast road, *Tiare Nui (☎ 66 34 06, fax 66 16 06)* is in the Europcar compound. Small, neat bungalows with hot-water bathroom, fan, TV and refrigerator cost 5100/6100 CFP a single/double. The location is rather noisy and not particularly charming but the owner, who also manages Europcar, offers a very competitive package including a car, or boat with outboard motor, for 9500/11,000 CFP a single/double. Transfers are included and credit cards are accepted.

East Coast South of Uturoa, between the PK6 and PK10 markers, you have the choice of six establishments.

Kaoha Nui Ranch (☎/fax 66 25 46) is a well kept and charming equestrian centre on a large, green property. One of the buildings has four simple, impeccably neat rooms, decorated with *pareu* (sarong-like garments) with two single beds and shared hot-water bathroom for 1900 CFP per person, 2200 CFP if you only stay one night. The dividing walls don't reach the ceiling so privacy is lacking. There's also a separate double with hot-water bathroom and fan for 5800 CFP single or double, 6800 CFP for a one night stay. At the same price there's a separate bungalow. There's a fully equipped kitchen for anybody to use. Bicycles are available for 700/1000 CFP a half/full day. Airport and dock transfers are free and meals are available.

The Brotherson's very friendly *Pension Manava (☎ 66 28 26, fax 66 16 66)* has two rooms in a *fare* with hot-water bathroom and equipped kitchen for 4000 CFP for two people. Tidy, spacious bungalows in the leafy garden all have hot-water bathrooms. Two of them cost 5000 CFP for two; the two with equipped kitchens cost 6000 CFP. There's an additional 500 CFP charge for one-night stops and breakfast is available for an additional 600 CFP or 900 CFP. Free transfers are provided from the airport or ferry quay at any hour of the day or night. Andrew Brotherson offers trips to Marae Taputapuatea, various lagoon pirogue trips and he'll leave you on a motu for the day for 1000 CFP per person (minimum four). Roselyne Brotherson hand paints pareu. Bicycles are available for 1000 CFP per day.

Peter's Place (☎ 66 20 01), just beyond Pension Manava, at PK6.5, offers camping space for 800 CFP per person. There's also a single row of eight spartan rooms, each with two single beds for 1200 CFP per person or 1400 CFP for a one-night stand. There's a shared kitchen area, showers and toilets, all fairly rustic. The grassy grounds are on the mountain side of the road and although the whole set-up is as simple as it comes, economy-minded backpackers may find the Polynesian ambience hits the spot. There are two pirogues for free use and various tours are offered. Return transfers are 500 CFP per person.

The three options around the PK10 mark, just before the road turns away from the coast to follow the northern side of Faaroa Bay inland, are all on the lagoon side of the road.

Pension Rauvine (☎/fax 66 25 50) is a new arrival at PK8.5 with eight bungalows with kitchenette and cold-water bathrooms at 5500 CFP for one or two people, or two rooms with shared bathroom at 4000/4500 CFP a single/double, all including transfers. There are various activities including half-day 4WD island tours for 4000 CFP, pirogue tours to Tahaa and motu drop-offs.

Pension Yolande (☎/fax 66 35 28), right on the water near PK10, has four functional rooms with kitchen facilities and hot-water bathroom. Each room sleeps up to three people, two with a double bed and a single, two with three singles. Although the walls are a bit thin, the pension is clean and well kept. It's run by the cheery Yolande Roopina, nightly cost is 5000 CFP for one or two people and meals are available in a

small diningroom *fare* facing the sea. Transfers cost 1500 CFP for the car per journey.

Hotel Raiatea Village (☎ 66 31 62, fax 66 10 65) is a small resort right on the water's edge. Bungalows with attached hot-water bathroom and kitchen cost 5940/7020 CFP. Ask for one looking out on the lagoon. Airport and ferry-quay transfers cost 1080 CFP per person return. Credit cards are accepted.

Right opposite the entry to the Stardust Marina on the northern side of Faaroa Bay, 12km from the centre of Uturoa, is *Pension La Croix du Sud* (The Southern Cross) (☎/fax 66 27 55). The hillside setting is luxuriantly vegetated and offers fantastic views over Faaroa Bay. The French-Tahitian owners have three rooms, two in the same *fare*, decorated with pareu and with hot-water bathrooms. Costs are 6000/6500 CFP including breakfast and transfers. Other meals cost 2000 CFP; the food has a good reputation and meals are taken on the pleasant terrace by the small swimming pool, looking out over the bay. Eric, the host, is a dive master and boat skipper and organises pirogue tours. In compensation for the rather isolated location, bicycles are offered free.

Pension Temaeva (☎/fax 66 37 28, email temaeva@mail.pf) is at PK24, 7km before Marae Taputapuatea. Quiet and tranquillity are guaranteed in this tropically luxuriant haven of flowers. Perched on the mountain flank, two comfortable bungalows with hot-water bathroom, fan and terrace cost 5500/6000 CFP including breakfast and transfers. Slightly below is a small swimming pool next to the owner's house. It's also possible to camp here for 1500/2000 CFP for one/two people including breakfast. A shower and toilet are reserved for campers. There are no kitchen facilities but you can get fresh supplies from the vans that pass twice daily and meals can be provided for 2000 CFP. There are two bicycles available for guests and the owner will take you with him when he drives to work in Uturoa.

Hotel Atiapiti (☎/fax 66 16 65), right next to Marae Taputapuatea, is a very relaxing place with a flower-bedecked garden beside the lagoon and a small beach. Spacious, comfortable beach bungalows with

RAIATEA & TAHAA

hot-water bathroom, fan, lounge area and terrace cost 9180 CFP for two people. There's also a garden bungalow for 12,960 CFP. Breakfast costs 1000 CFP, half-board (two meals) adds 3500 CFP, full board (three meals) 6000 CFP per person. Motu drop-offs cost 2000 CFP per person including a picnic. Airport transfers are 2000 CFP per person return. Credit cards are accepted.

West Coast *Sunset Beach Motel* (☎ *66 33 47, fax 66 33 08)*, at PK5, is right on the waterfront. The extensive coconut-plantation grounds contain 22 large and comfortable bungalows, all with hot-water bathroom, kitchen and TV. Rates are 7000/8000 CFP for one/two people, but the units will sleep up to five. There's a 1000 CFP extra charge per bungalow for one-night stays. Camping space is also available at 1100 CFP per person per night and there are excellent kitchen facilities and bathrooms. The warm welcome includes tropical fruits. Pirogues and pedal boats are available, the lounge area has a library and credit cards are accepted. There are free transfers to/from the airport or the ferry quay and the owners will take you along on their daily shopping trip to town.

The new *Hotel Tenape* (☎ *60 01 00, fax 60 01 01, email raiatea@spmr.com)*, 4km from the airport, is built on two levels in colonial style. From its mountain-side location there are great views of the lagoon and across to Bora Bora. Comfortable air-con rooms with terrace cost 15,120 CFP, suites 25,920 CFP. There's a good restaurant, a bar and a swimming pool. Add 5000/5780 CFP for half/full board and 1500 CFP for return transfers. Credit cards are accepted.

Places to Eat
Uturoa On the waterfront, *Snack Moe-moea* is a pleasant, busy little café with an open terrace and straightforward dishes at modest prices. It's open from 6 am to 5 pm. *Restaurant Michèle* (☎ *66 14 66)* is in the Hotel Hinano (enter from the quay side) and offers Chinese, Tahitian and standard French dishes for 1000 CFP to 1200 CFP. It's open weekdays, only until lunch on Saturday.

Uturoa has two popular Chinese restaurants. *Restaurant Moana* (☎ *66 27 49)*, above the Leogite store and at the same location as the Zénith Disco, is closed at lunchtime Sunday and all day Monday. The setting is dull but the food is surprisingly good, with dishes such as piglet in coconut milk for 1800 CFP, shrimps at 1800 CFP and salted calamari at 1500 CFP. It has a good winelist. *Jade Garden Restaurant* (☎ *66 34 40)* is also on the main street and is closed Sunday and Monday.

Uturoa has several well stocked supermarkets that accept credit cards. They are open Monday to Saturday, some of them on Sunday morning as well. They include the *Champion Supermarket* on the seafront and the *Leogite* store on the main street. The *Liaut Supermarket,* also on the main street, offers free delivery to yachts for all purchases over 15,000 CFP.

East Coast Bring a picnic if you're travelling round the island as there are not many places to get a meal, although some places to stay offer food.

Raiatea Pearl Resort Hawaiki Nui does very reasonably priced meals right beside the swimming pool and the lagoon. A set lunch costs 1400 CFP, there are fish dishes from 1000 CFP and the bar serves good cocktails for less than 800 CFP.

At the *Kaoha Nui Ranch* at PK6, meals in a pleasant small *fare* on the lush property cost 900 CFP to 1700 CFP. It's open for lunch and dinner and reservations are not necessary, in principle. At PK9.5, *Snack Iriru* faces the pass of the same name from the mountain side and offers sashimi with a bowl of rice for 950 CFP, *mahi mahi* (dolphin fish, which is a type of fish, not a dolphin) or a steak for 1100 CFP. It's open Monday to Saturday for lunch and dinner.

Pension La Croix du Sud (☎ *66 27 55)* has very good food and you take your meals on the terrace with an unbeatable view over Faaroa Bay. A complete set meal costs 2000 CFP but you must make reservations. If you're a little peckish after visiting Marae Taputapuatea you can take some refreshment at the restaurant of *Hotel*

Atiapiti. The setting is calm and pleasant, facing the lagoon.

West Coast Between Europcar and the airport, on the sea side of the road, *Havai'i Snack* offers a varied menu with fish and meat dishes for 1000 CFP to 1500 CFP. There's a small curio shop and a pool of eels nearby. It's closed Sunday evening and Monday.

Club House (☎ 66 11 66), at the Apooiti Marina, is a huge place with lots of plants, views over the marina and a pirogue suspended from above. The French-Polynesian menu offers fish dishes from 1500 CFP and meat dishes from 2050 CFP. There are five different mahi mahi dishes – try the one with vanilla sauce for 1900 CFP. Light meals cost about 900 CFP. Bars inside and on the terrace complete the picture. The restaurant is open for breakfast, lunch and dinner every day and will collect and return diners between the Sunset Beach Motel and Pension Manava. Credit cards are accepted.

At the end of the Apooiti Marina, facing Tahaa, the snack-restaurant *Tamaa Maitai* enjoys a pleasant lagoon side site and offers very reasonable prices. The usual fish dishes cost from 800 CFP to 1650 CFP, meat dishes from 850 CFP to 1300 CFP, *poisson cru* (raw fish) from 600 CFP to 800 CFP, depending on the portion. More originally, different couscous dishes are offered on Saturday and Sunday, notably a royal couscous for 1700 CFP and a vegetarian one for 950 CFP. There's a double pirogue hung from the ceiling and a local band plays on Saturday evening. It's open Wednesday to Sunday, and Monday for lunch only.

Tenape Hotel, towards Tevaitoa, is a tablecloths-and-starched-napkins sort of place offering classic French specialties at reasonable prices. You can get foie gras and other pâtés from 950 CFP to 2100 CFP, fish dishes such as parrotfish fillets with cream of garlic for 1500 CFP and meat dishes from 1450 CFP. There's a good winelist.

Two kilometres south of Tevaitoa, *Chez Fifi* snack bar is an excellent French-Tahitian place looking across the road to the lagoon. Large serves of poisson cru cost

700 CFP, chow mein 850 CFP, green-pepper steak 1000 CFP, soft drinks 120 CFP and milkshakes with surprising flavours (taro for example) 300 CFP. It's open Tuesday to Sunday for lunch and dinner.

Entertainment

It's difficult to find a reason for a late night on Raiatea. But it is mandatory to sip a sunset drink at the Apooiti Marina *Club House*. On weekends Restaurant Moana, above the Leogite store, metamorphoses into *Le Zénith*, where you can check out the local young people on the dance floor; entry costs 500 CFP for girls, 1000 CFP for boys.

Shopping

Uturoa has several well stocked souvenir outlets. Arii Boutique (☎ 66 33 53), on the main street facing the market, specialises in Polynesian *tapa* (nonwoven bark cloth). For Tahitian black pearls head for La Palme d'Or (☎ 66 23 79), on the main street. Next to it is the Anuanua Gallery with works by craftspeople of different islands, including sculptures, ceramic work, pictures and objects in mother-of-pearl. The Te Fare boutique (☎ 66 17 17) is in the quayside Banque Socredo building and sells cloths, pictures, jewellery, basketwork and sculptures.

At the Apooiti Marina, the Art-Expo Gallery (☎ 66 11 83) has jewellery, clothes, decorative trinkets and handicrafts. The owner of Pension Manava (☎ 66 28 26) sells pretty hand-painted pareu. Local women sell their crafts, particularly shellwork and pareu, in the airport building.

Getting There & Away

Raiatea is 220km north-west of Tahiti and 40km south-east of Bora Bora.

Air Air Tahiti flies to Raiatea two to seven times daily from Tahiti, directly (40 minutes) or via Moorea and/or Huahine. There are also daily connections with Bora Bora and Huahine and three times weekly with Maupiti (directly or via Bora Bora). One-way fares to/from Raiatea include: Bora Bora 5100 CFP; Huahine 4400 CFP;

Maupiti 5600 CFP; and Papeete 10,100 CFP. The Air Tahiti office (☎ 66 32 50, 66 30 51) is at the airport and is open weekdays from 7 am to noon and 2 to 5.30 pm, Saturday from 6.30 to 10.30 am and 3 to 6 pm and Sunday from 7 to 10 am and 3 to 6 pm. Credit cards are accepted.

Boat Raiatea is separated from Tahaa by a 3km-wide channel.

Tahaa Tahaa Transport Services (☎ 65 67 10, 66 13 33) operates two navette services between Uturoa on Raiatea and various stops on Tahaa – Marina Iti, Poutoru, Tapuamu, Patio, Hipu and Haamene. You can buy tickets on board or at the company office in the Blue Lagoon real estate agency on the waterfront, across from the Champion store. The services operate weekdays; there is no service on Saturday afternoon or Sunday. It takes less than 15 minutes from Uturoa to Iti Marina, the closest stop on Tahaa. The one-way fare is 850 CFP and there are two to four services a day, depending on the destination on Tahaa.

The same company offers a charter service, a 'taxi-boat', between the two islands and can transfer customers directly from the airport quay to the marinas, the Uturoa quay or any of the accessible quays on Tahaa. Charter rates start from 2000 CFP and, with at least two passengers, it costs 1530 CFP per person to south Tahaa, up to 3570 CFP to Patio on north Tahaa. Prices jump 50% on Sunday and 24-hour advance booking is required.

The *Tamarii Tahaa* (☎ 65 65 29, 65 60 18) goes to the west coast of Tahaa twice daily from the Uturoa navette quay, at around 10.45 am and 4.45 pm. It operates weekdays and Saturday morning. Fares are 500 CFP to Marina Iti and 700 CFP for the one-hour trip to Patio.

Other Islands The cargo ships *Vaeanu, Taporo* and *Maupiti Tou Ai'a* serve Raiatea from Tahiti. See the Getting Around chapter for details.

Specifically aimed at tourists, the fast *Ono-Ono* sails from Papeete through to Bora Bora.

Huahine-Raiatea takes barely an hour and costs 1795 CFP; it's 1¼ hours to Bora Bora, also for 1795 CFP. Papeete-Raiatea costs 5554 CFP. The office (☎ 66 24 25) is on the waterfront next to the Champion store.

The smaller 50-passenger *Maupiti Express* (☎ 67 66 69) is based on Tahaa and circulates between Bora Bora, Tahaa and Raiatea. On Wednesday and Friday, it leaves Vaitape (Bora Bora) at 7 am, Tahaa at 8.15 am and arrives at Uturoa at 8.30 am. The same day it leaves Uturoa at 4 pm and goes directly back to Bora Bora where it arrives at 5.30 pm. The one-way/return fare is 2000/3000 CFP.

Getting Around

Rent a car or hitchhike – hitchhiking appears to be fairly accepted on Raiatea as a result of the low-key tourism and lack of public transport. Remember, however, that there are always dangers associated with hitching.

To/From the Airport There are taxis at the airport – count on 1000 CFP for the 3km into Uturoa – but most island accommodation will pick you up (although you may be charged).

Le Truck Don't count on le trucks. They're so infrequent they're useless for visitors. They operate mainly in the morning, between outlying districts and Uturoa then return in the early afternoon. The colour-coded le trucks run from Uturoa to Opoa near Marae Taputapuatea (blue), Fetuna on the south coast of the island (turquoise) and Vaiaau on the west coast (red). The le truck terminus is centrally located in Uturoa. Check that there will be a return trip if you don't want to get stuck at your destination.

Car Europcar (☎ 66 34 06, fax 66 16 06) has its head office on the edge of Uturoa towards the airport and other desks at the airport, in Uturoa and in the Raiatea Pearl Beach Resort. A Fiat Panda costs 8056 CFP for a day. Avis (☎ 66 34 35, 66 15 59, fax 66 15 59) is represented at the airport and charges 7500 CFP. Garage Motu Tapu (☎ 66 33 09, fax 66 29 11) is 200m before the airport and rents small cars for 6500 CFP a day. Cars can always be delivered to the airport.

Bicycle & Scooter Europcar has scooters for 5300 CFP and bicycles for 2120 CFP. Some hotels and guesthouses have bicycles for their guests and sometimes for outsiders; that's the case at Pension Manava, Hotel Tepua, Raiatea Pearl Resort Hawaiki Nui and Kaoha Nui Ranch. Pension La Croix du Sud and Pension Temaeva provide bicycles for their guests for free.

Taxi There's a taxi stand by the market (☎ 66 20 60, 66 23 33) and taxis can also be found at the airport but, as usual in French Polynesia, they're very expensive.

Boat Europcar rents boats with outboards for 8480/9540 CFP for eight/24 hours; they're the perfect way to explore the lagoon on your own.

Tahaa

Raiatea may be quiet but Tahaa is even quieter. The island is an undiscovered jewel, little known by tourist operators, accessible only by boat, with a village atmosphere but also equipped with some good places to stay. Like its southern sister, there are no beaches to speak of on the main island and the tourist facilities are even more basic. A coast road encircles most of the island but traffic is very light and there is no public transport. Vanilla cultivation and, recently, pearl farming, are important activities but the main tourist attraction is the string of beautiful motu along the northern reef edge. Tahaa's easily navigable lagoon and safe yacht anchorages make it a favourite for visiting yachties.

History

Tahaa was once known as Kuporu (or Uporu), a name which pops up in other

Polynesian centres, perhaps indicating some great migratory connection. Tahaa lived in the shadow of Raiatea, its larger, stronger and more important neighbour and was at times a pawn in struggles between Raiatea and the fierce rulers of Bora Bora.

The first missionaries arrived from neighbouring Raiatea in 1822 and the island came under French control at the same time as Raiatea. Tahaa was once a centre for firewalking ceremonies, but they have died out.

Orientation

The northern coastline is fairly continuous but the south of the island is punctuated by deep and impressive bays. Tahaa is a quiet little place with a 70km crushed-coral road winding around most of the coast. The road is in reasonable condition and there are sealed sections through the main towns and where the road leaves the coast and climbs over the hills, particularly the nicely sweeping road up and over the centre from Haamene to Tiva.

The population is concentrated in eight main villages on the coast. Tapuamu has the main wharf, Patio is the main town and Haamene is where the roads round the southern and northern parts of the island meet, forming a figure eight. Mt Ohiri (598m) is the highest point on the island. Apu Bay to the south, Haamene Bay to the east and Hurepiti Bay to the west are deep inlets offering sheltered anchorages for yachts.

Information

Tahaa's only bank branch, the Banque Socredo in Patio, is open weekdays. Bring credit cards and enough cash.

Around the Island

The 70km circuit of the island is quite possible as a bicycle day-trip although most of the route is unsealed crushed coral and there are some steep up-and-down sections. PK markers start at Haamene and go up clockwise and anticlockwise around the northern half of the island, terminating at Patio around PK25.

Starting from the Marina Iti (the first navette stop if you're coming from Raiatea and the best place to rent bicycles) the road sticks to the coast around Apu Bay. At the top of the bay there's a turn-off south to the Hotel Mareva Village and the village of Poutoru, where the road ends. The round-the-island route leaves the coast and climbs up and over to the larger village of **Haamene**.

On the right of the road into Haamene is the **Maison de la Vanille** (☎ 65 67 27), a small operation where, for 100 CFP, you can see the drying and preparation processes and buy vanilla pods. A little farther along, just before arriving in Haamene, a right turn leads to **Alfred** (☎ 65 61 16), a German former Foreign Legionnaire and another vanilla producer. He sells vanilla pods and vanilla powder from his red and green house. See the boxed text 'Tahaa – the Vanilla Island' for information about vanilla cultivation.

At Haamene the road barely reaches sea level before climbing again, a long sweeping ascent and descent down to pretty Hurepiti Bay and the village of **Tiva** where there are several **pearl farms** by the coast. Bora Bora comes into view as you round the end of the bay, looking surprisingly close beyond the lagoon edge.

Tapuamu is the site of the island's main wharf, where the *Ono-Ono* docks. From here the chain of motu that fringe the northern coast of the island come into view. **Patio** is the administrative centre of the island, with offices, a post office, a bank,

shops and a small artisans' centre. Beyond Patio more of the 60-odd motu around the north of the island are visible as the road winds along the coast. They include the luxurious resort motu of Vahine Island. The road continues around the coast, past copra plantations, to **Faaha** and Faaha Bay. On the northern side of the bay are two **pearl farms**: Ofaifea (☎ 65 69 77), which sells pearls (mounted and unmounted), *keshi* (pure mother-of-pearl) and vanilla pods, and Motu Pearl Farm (☎ 65 69 18), which has a small shop.

From the bay the road climbs over a headland and drops down to Haamene Bay. Alternatively, a rougher track, the **track traversière**, turns off the coast road just beyond Patio and takes a direct route over the hills and down to Haamene. This track starts shortly after the village but although the first part is driveable, the second section needs a 4WD. It's really better as a walk or mountain-bike ride.

From the coast road, where it meets Haamene Bay, turn east to Hotel Hibiscus, where the **Foundation Hibiscus** is dedicated to saving turtles that have become entangled in local fishers' nets. They're transferred to remote Scilly Island (see the Other Leeward Islands chapter), a favourite nesting ground for sea turtles. Smaller turtles, bought from the fishers by the hotel owner Léo, are kept in pens beside the hotel's pier and fed every morning until they've grown large enough to be released. By early 1999 they had saved around 700 endangered turtles.

From the Hotel Hibiscus the coast road goes around the northern side of the bay to Haamene, passing the pearl farms of **Patricia & Daniel** (☎ 65 60 83) and Rooverta Ebbs' **Poerani** (☎ 65 60 25), where you can watch pearl grafting and other operations for 100 CFP. Mounted and unmounted pearls and mother-of-pearl are sold, as well as vanilla pods. The road then continues along the southern side of the bay and, on the final long stretch back to the starting point, winds in and out of seemingly endless small bays before coming back to the Marina Iti.

Tahaa – the Vanilla Island

Tahaa is accurately nicknamed 'the vanilla island', since three-quarters of French Polynesian production (about 25 tons annually) comes from here. This is a long way from the 150 to 200 tons a century ago, when vanilla cultivation flourished in the Society Islands.

Several vanilla farms are open to the public and at these small family firms you can buy vanilla pods at reasonable prices, about 1000 CFP a dozen. They will explain the technique of 'marrying' the vanilla, a delicate operation of fertilising the flowers by hand because the insects which do the job in other regions are not found in French Polynesia. Nine months later the pods are put out to dry, and turn brown over four to five months. They are then sorted and boxed in sachets or bamboo tubes before being sold to Papeete or exported.

Activities

Diving There's no dive centre on Tahaa although the Hotel Marina Iti has plans for one. The dive centres on Raiatea regularly dive sites to the east of the island by the Toahotu Pass and will collect you from hotels at the south of the island. See the 'Diving' special section for more details.

Swimming & Snorkelling Like Raiatea, there are no beaches on Tahaa and you have to go to the motu for swimming and snorkelling. Some guesthouses will drop you on a motu for the day or you can join an organised pirogue tour.

Walking You can take the little-used 7km route across the centre of the island from Patio to Haamene, but otherwise there are very few trails into the Tahaa interior. There are dazzling views of Haamene Bay from the **Vaitoetoe Pass** on this partially shady walk.

Fishing The Hotel Marina Iti (☎ 65 61 01) and the Hotel Hibiscus (☎ 65 61 06) organise fishing trips.

Organised Tours

Island Tours There are half-day island tours by 4WD or minibus, visiting pearl farms, craft shops, plantations and possibly the track traversière for 3500 CFP to 5000 CFP per person. A minimum of four people is usually required, so reserve ahead.

Alain and Cristina Plantier's Vanilla Tours (☎ 65 62 46) charges 4500 CFP per person and has a good reputation. Pearl-farm visits cost an extra 500 CFP. Alain explains the island's flora and its traditional and medicinal uses and takes the track traversière. The office is on Hurepiti Bay, after the Sophie Boutique. Yachts can contact them on VHF 9 and can anchor in front of the house. Tahaa Safari Tours (☎ 65 61 01), in the Hotel Marina Iti, has similar rates.

Lolita Tours (☎ 65 61 06), at the Hotel Hibiscus, is slightly more expensive. Poerani Tours (☎ 65 60 25) and Hainanui Tours (☎ 65 61 90) ask 3500 CFP and need at least two people. Hanalei Tours (☎ 65 67 60) has the lowest charges, 2500 CFP, but needs at least eight people.

Lagoon Tours Tahaa Pearl Tours (☎ 65 67 80), at Haamene Bay, takes day tours on Tahaa Lagoon with swimming stops on a motu, a meal at Haamene Bay and visits to a pearl and vanilla-farm for 8000 CFP. On Raiatea transfers to the Uturoa quay are free. The Hotel Marina Iti (☎ 65 61 01) offers similar tours for 3500 CFP to 8000 CFP per person depending on the program and the length of the excursion.

Places to Stay

Tahaa's places to stay are dotted around the coast – there's no concentration in a single area. It's wise to make reservations, so you'll be collected from the appropriate village quay, or even the airport on Raiatea.

The Island Going round the island from the first regular navette stop, *Hotel Marina Iti* (☎ *65 61 01, fax 65 63 87, VHF 68*) on Toamaro Point has its own navette stop, the pier to the hotel. This is the busiest place on the island, with a popular restaurant and a regular yachtie clientele. The pleasant coconut-grove site is right on the waterfront looking across to Raiatea and the forests of yacht masts at its north-coast marinas. There's a tiny beach at the hotel and lots of fish off the end of the pier, which is a good place for a swim.

Accommodation is in five lagoon bungalows and two garden ones, which are pleasant, with very necessary mosquito nets over the beds, attached hot-water bathrooms and handy little veranda areas. The nightly cost is 13,260 CFP for two people, 3750 CFP to 5100 CFP extra for half-board. Stroll along the sea wall at night, when a good torch (flashlight) will illuminate all sorts of creatures, from eels and crabs to colourful scorpion fish.

Meals are served in the well respected restaurant and bar by the pier and visiting yachties using the restaurant get free moorings. See Places to Eat later for more details. The Marina Iti has cars and bicycles to rent. It offers a variety of tours and credit cards are accepted. Return transfers from the airport on Raiatea cost 3060 CFP per person and take just 10 minutes.

Right across the bay from the Marina Iti, near the next navette stop at Poutoru, *Hotel Mareva Village* (☎/fax 65 61 61) has spacious and sturdily built bungalows with kitchen, hot-water bathroom, TV and terrace overlooking Apu Bay. They cost 7560 CFP a double, 8640 CFP for a family or 10,800 CFP for two couples. You have to fix your own meals but transfers to the Poutoru quay are free.

At the north exit from Poutoru, on the inland side of the road, *Pension Herenui* (☎ 65 62 60) rents two charming bungalows with hot-water bathroom for 8000 CFP a double, plus 3500 CFP per person for half-board. The site is lush, the rooms are around a swimming pool and the lagoon is right across the road.

Attractively sited on the southern side of Hurepiti Bay, *Pension Vaihi* (☎ 65 62 02) is a new place with a family atmosphere that will appeal to those searching for isolation and tranquillity. There are three bungalows with bathrooms beside the lagoon at 6000 CFP double. Half/full

board adds 3800/5800CFP per person. The Uturoa-Tahaa ferry will drop you at this pension's pontoon.

If you are really penniless, *Restaurant Louise* (see Places to Eat later in this chapter) might have a dorm bed available for just 1500 CFP with breakfast.

Shortly after Tapuamu, heading north, after the sealed road ends and you cross a bridge, the turn-off towards the island interior brings you to *Chez Pascal* (☎ 65 60 42), the cheapest place on the island. It's spartan but clean and there's a typically Polynesian family atmosphere. Small bungalows with shared toilet and shower cost 2500 per person, or 3000/4500 CFP with breakfast/half board. Bicycles cost 1000 CFP and Pascal offers Motu Tautau excursions for 4000 CFP.

The only place on the north shore of the island is *Tupenu Village* (☎ 65 62 01), by the lagoon about 1.5km west of Patio. There's a big two-level *fare* with five rooms sharing two hot-water bathrooms for 6000 CFP a double. Breakfast is 600 CFP, lunch or dinner 1800 CFP, but cheaper meals are available. The charges fall after the third day. Motu drop-offs cost 1000 CFP per person and there's a scooter available for 2000 CFP per day. Transfers to/from Patio are free; to the airport costs 2000 CFP per person each way.

On the eastern side of the island at PK10, *Chez Perrette* (☎ 65 65 78) is a huge white house beside the road on the coast side and in the middle of a coconut plantation. Its two *fare* are prohibitively expensive at 14,000 CFP plus 3500 CFP per person for half-board. Return transfers from the Tahaa quay are included.

There are two places on the north shore of Haamene Bay. *Hotel Hibiscus* (☎ 65 61 06, fax 65 65 65, VHF 68) has bungalows with hot-water bathroom, terrace, mezzanine, fan and refrigerator for 5000 CFP per person (up to three people). Bungalows with shared cold-water bathroom cost 8250 CFP for two people. Add 3750 CFP per person for half-board. The setting is lush and green, on the inland side of the road but just across from the water. Transfers from

Raiatea depart from Snack Moemoea and cost 1350 CFP per person each way. Credit cards are accepted.

This is a popular place for yachties, with 14 moorings, as well as the busy nautical-themed restaurant and bar by the lagoon. Island tours by 4WD, traditional fishing trips, motu picnics and even a motu wedding can be organised. Bicycles are rented for 1000 CFP per day. Léo, the all-singing, all-dancing patron, also runs the turtle-rescue operation Foundation Hibiscus (see Around the Island earlier).

Chez Patricia & Daniel (☎/fax 65 60 83) is a popular place just after the Hibiscus towards the east. On the inland side of the road, with access to the lagoon, bungalows with hot-water bathroom, kitchenette and terrace cost 6000 CFP for two people plus 2500 CFP for half-board. The owners have a pearl farm you can visit. Activities offered include a motu picnic and swimming stop for 3000 CFP, island tours for 3000 CFP and game fishing. Airport transfers cost 1500 CFP per person return.

The Motu *Vahine Island* (☎ 65 67 38, fax 65 67 70, email vahine.island@usa.net, VHF 70) occupies a motu on the outer reef to the north of Tahaa. This small resort has just nine rooms, three of them over-water bungalows and is the only real beach-type resort on Raiatea or Tahaa. There's a white-sand beach and clear water and, on a much smaller scale, it manages to compete very effectively with the luxury resorts on other islands. Beach bungalows are 32,400 CFP for one or two people, while the larger over-water bungalows (with glass lagoon-viewing table, of course) are 48,600 CFP. You can quickly add another 10,000 CFP per person per day for meals, but the owners ran a renowned restaurant in the south-west of France, so the food should be excellent. Pirogues and snorkelling equipment are available for free, lagoon tours and mountain-bike trips are organised, pedal boats and outboard-motor boats are there for lagoon exploration. Transfers from the airport on Raiatea cost 5000 CFP per person return. Of course, credit cards are accepted.

Places to Eat

There are shops in each village but the dining possibilities are very limited.

At the *Marina Iti's* well known restaurant the à la carte lunch-menu features French specialities such as steak for 1800 CFP, fish dishes for about 2000 CFP and sandwiches for 500 CFP. In the evening there's a menu and a set meal for 3650 CFP or a fish and seafood fondue for 3450 CFP. The *Hotel Hibiscus* restaurant has a good reputation, with a complete menu for 3250 CFP and specialities such as crab with green lemon and grilled lobster. There's musical entertainment on Saturday night.

If you want something more local, try *Restaurant Louise* (☎ 65 66 68) at Tiva. This small domestic establishment has *niau* (woven palm) walls and a lagoon-side terrace facing Bora Bora and enjoys an excellent word-of-mouth reputation. It's open from 8 am to 10 pm. Breakfast is 500 CFP and the marina menu for 2500 CFP is a true feast, with a half-lobster, curried shrimps, poisson cru and rice. There are simpler dishes such as steak and French fries for 800 CFP and mahi mahi with vanilla for 1200 CFP. At Wednesday lunch there's an *ahimaa* (Tahitian oven) organised for customers of the *Haumana* catamaran cruise for 3000 CFP with musical entertainment; you must book.

Entertainment

Tahaa is not the island for night owls. There's really just the bars at the *Marina Iti* and the *Hibiscus*, popular with yachties and decorated with hundred of their pennants and flags. There's a group of dancers and musicians on Saturday night at the Hibiscus.

Shopping

There are some interesting shopping possibilities, including vanilla, black pearls and local handicrafts.

Luc Izquierdo of Coco Vanille (☎ 65 64 01) and his companion have a studio-shop in the Hotel Marina Iti compound. They make superb pieces, including painted tablecloths and pareu at reasonable prices. The Sophie Boutique (☎ 65 62 56), on the southern side of Hurepiti Bay, has paintings, pottery, pareu and jewellery fantasies.

Shortly before Haamene, coming from Poutoru, Kaheilany (☎ 65 63 77) is a family craft-shop where you can find dance costumes, *purau* (hibiscus) bark sandals, shells and mother-of-pearl. Patricia, of the Chez Patricia & Daniel guesthouse, has a small boutique where you'll find pearls and mother-of-pearl engraved by an island craftsman. In Tapuamu, Mama Naumi also sells necklaces and shells.

Tahiti pearls and the famous Tahaa vanilla, sold in pods, are directly available from some producers. See the Island Tours entry under Organised Tours earlier in this section for details.

Getting There & Away

There is no airport on Tahaa but the airport on Raiatea is only 15 minutes away across the lagoon and some hotels will pick up guests from the airport or from the ferry quay at Uturoa on Raiatea.

See the Getting There & Away section under Raiatea earlier in this chapter for information on the navette service between Raiatea and Tahaa. This local ferry service shuttles back and forth between Uturoa and a number of stops on Tahaa and costs 850 CFP one way.

Inter-island ships stop at Tapuamu on Tahaa en route from Raiatea to Bora Bora, but not on every voyage. If your trip doesn't stop at Tahaa it's easy enough to debark at Uturoa and take the navette across. The high-speed *Ono-Ono* stops at Tahaa on some

of its passages between Raiatea and Bora Bora. Fares are: Papeete-Tahaa 6115 CFP; Tahaa-Bora Bora 1346 CFP; Huahine-Tahaa 2132 CFP; and Raiatea-Tahaa 673 CFP.

Getting Around

There is no public transport on Tahaa and if you're contemplating hitching remember that traffic is very light. Renting a car or a mountain bike are the only ways to see the island by yourself. The coast road, not all of it sealed, is quite OK. If you decide to tackle it by bicycle there are some steep stretches on the south of the island that you may find pretty trying.

Car & Bicycle The Marina Iti (☎ 65 61 01) rents small Renault Kangoos for 8480/9540 CFP for eight/24 hours including insurance, fuel and 100km – enough to do the island circuit. Bicycles are 1000/1500 CFP for a half/full day.

Monique Location (☎/fax 65 62 48), close to the church in Haamene, has reasonable tariffs, like a Ford Fiesta at the same rates as the Marina Iti and bicycles for 1060 CFP for 24 hours. Europcar (☎ 65 67 00, fax 65 68 08) at the Total de Tapuamu petrol station asks 7828 CFP for 24 hours with a Fiat Panda, unlimited mileage and insurance included, but not fuel. Hotel Hibiscus has bicycles for its customers only for 1000 CFP per day.

If you want a scooter you can rent one on Raiatea and bring it across on the navette. There are petrol stations in Patio and Tapuamu.

ORI TAHITI – TAHITIAN DANCE

Tahitian dance has enormous cultural and symbolic significance. Much more than a tourist attraction, it is one of the most vibrant forms of expression underlying Maohi (Polynesian) culture and plays a major part in spreading the influence of Tahitian culture abroad. Behind every performance lies months of rehearsals, a rigorously standardised choreography and an important piece of legend that is consummately acted out with its own hierarchical structure and meaning. In this land of oral traditions, dance is in effect not merely an aesthetic medium but also a way to preserve the memory of the past.

History
Traditional Culture
Little is known about Polynesian dance before the arrival of the Europeans. What we do know, from the accounts of the first explorers and missionaries, is that entertainment, and especially dancing, held an important place in the society of that period. Dancing accompanied ceremonies on the *marae* (traditional temples) and group rituals. It even had sacred overtones that were embodied by the *arioi*, the actor-dancer-troubadours who performed in various clans. Many different *heiva* (celebrations) in the life of the community incorporated dancing, singing and mime. Dancing was accompanied by *pahu* (drums) and *vivo* (nasal flute).

The Missionaries
After the arrival of the missionaries, dancing suffered the same fate as tattooing and the traditional places of worship. Deemed to be both pagan and lewd, dancing was forbidden by the Pomare laws of 1819. The practice carried on in secret. From 1895, a number of tightly controlled dance performances were allowed to take place to celebrate the republican festival of 14 July, known as Tiurai.

The Renaissance
From 1956 onwards, traditional dancing was modernised by a former primary school teacher by the name of Madeleine Moua and was given a new image free of demonic overtones. She created the first professional dance group, Heiva; perfected the costume; and made choreography more straightforward, but still connected to the rich Maohi cultural heritage. Since then other dance companies have appeared on the scene, and Tahitian dance has become vibrant once again, even though the dancing we see today probably has little to do with the spectacles of former times.

Types of Dance
There are five types of dance. They are seldom performed on their own but are usually integrated into a program where each is performed in

turn. But beware the *tamure*, a term of recent origin referring to a popularised form of Tahitian dance that has no traditional cultural basis.

The Otea

Impressive and highly physical, the *otea* is a very distinctive group dance: the accompanying music is provided entirely by percussion instruments that produce the rhythmic sequences the dancers perform to. Originally this was a male-only war dance. Nowadays it is more likely to be both male and female, but the 'manly' character is still preserved in the body language, the rhythm and the sudden loud cries of the dancers.

The men's steps are radically different from the women's. The men mainly use their legs to perform a very specific and highly spectacular movement known as *paoti*: with knees bent and heels together but slightly raised, they alternately open and close their knees with a scissor-like movement that can be fast or slow depending on the tempo set by the percussion. The basic female movement is a swaying of the hips caused by intensive bending and straightening of the knees with the feet level on the ground. The men must not move their hips and the women must keep their chests and shoulders completely still.

There is an extensive repertoire of steps in the otea, especially for the men. The *tu'e* (forward kick), the *ui* (a movement towards the side or the front while at the same time performing a chassé with one leg), the *patia* (a piston-like movement with the leg) and the *horo* (another, lesser movement) are the most frequent steps after the paoti.

The movements in which arms and hands are directed in a rather sharp and angular fashion towards the upper part of the body are equally common to men and women. On stage the dancers are placed in a geometric formation, in men-only or women-only rows.

The otea occasionally includes a solo performance: the group sits or kneels while a single performer or a couple stands up and dances, each in turn.

The choreography is governed by a number of underlying themes, such as volcanoes, sharks, historical events or legends, all of which may be suggested by the use of props. Since it is so gruelling, an otea sequence lasts only a few minutes.

The Aparima

The *aparima* is free-flowing and graceful, and beguiles and soothes the spectator. In very rough terms, the aparima is a mixed-gender dance that tells a story using hand movement and song. The story may be a legend, a love song or a scene from everyday life. In contrast to the otea, the hand and arm movements are predominant. Although the movements are not codified, there is a great deal of expressiveness and realism: the dancers mime each scene very effectively (eg paddling, opening a coconut), using props where necessary.

The musical accompaniment is provided by guitar and ukulele. Percussion is less important and simply there to set the tempo. The dancers follow every hand movement with their eyes and faces.

There are two variants of the aparima: the *aparima himene*, which is sung by the orchestra and the dancers, and the *aparima vava*, which is instrumental, the story told entirely by means of gesture. An aparima sequence lasts only a few minutes.

The Hivinau

The *hivinau* mimics the body language of English sailors hoisting the anchor to the shouts of 'heave now'.

Men and women form a double circle surrounding the orchestra (drums only) and a male vocal soloist, known as the *raatira hivinau*. The soloist recites a few words and the dancers, playing the part of the choir, reply with a typical chorus. The two groups of dancers cross and turn in opposite directions or both groups go in a clockwise direction. During the chorus, the dancers in each circle turn and face a partner and dance as a couple. Then they resume dancing the *ronde* (round dance). The steps are the same as those of the otea but less complicated. The percussion merely beats out time.

The hivinau's predominant aspect is the interplay between the vocal parts of the soloist and the responses from the choir. Performance of the hivinau is becoming something of a rare occurrence since it requires such a large number of participants.

The Paoa

The *paoa* is said to have its origins in the manufacture of *tapa* (non-woven bark-cloth). The women, sitting in a circle, would sing for motivation as they pounded the bark. One of them would get the group going by singing the words and the others would respond. Every so often a woman would get up to dance a few steps.

A male and female choir seated on the ground forms a semicircle, in the centre of which a male vocal soloist recites a few words, often based on legend. The members of the choir respond and keep time by slapping their thighs with both hands. The orchestra (drums only) maintains a position next to the soloist. One couple then comes into the centre and improvises a dance using the simplified steps of the otea, interspersed with shouts of 'hi' and 'ha' that have strong erotic overtones. As in the hivinau, it is the dialogue between the leader and the choir that is the key element of the paoa.

The Fire Dance

This dance, which is thought to have originateed in Samoa, is frequently put on as part of shows in hotels because it is both impressive and highly aesthetic. The performer, always a man, juggles a flaming torch alight at both ends, against a background of drums.

Instruments

Dancers and musicians must display perfect harmony and synchronisation. The musicians usually stand at the front of the stage and to one side so as to maintain visual contact with the group.

Percussion is used for the otea, hivinau, aparima vava, paoa and fire dance. Stringed instruments accompany the aparima himene. The orchestra is considered a male preserve, and this is true particularly of percussion. Very much all-rounders, the musicians play both percussions and strings as well as sing.

Percussion

Drums are the Maohi instruments *par excellence*. Three types are used. The *toere* is a drum with no membrane that is carved out of a piece of wood. It is cylindrical in shape, and hollowed out with a narrow slit down the whole of its length, and it is this that produces resonance. The orchestra comprises different sizes of toere, each of which produces a distinct sound. Toere are played in two ways: when placed vertically, the drummer holds the upper end with one hand and with the other hits the split side with a stick; when supported horizontally on trestles, two sticks are used to hit it. The drummers may be either seated or kneeling. Usually an orchestra comprises between one and five toere.

The *faatete* is a drum with a single membrane. It is played with two sticks, and rests on a support aimed at raising the height of the resonance chamber.

The *pahu*, or *tari parau*, is a two-membraned drum rather like a bass drum. The musician plays from a seated position and strikes his side-held drum with a special beater to produce a more muffled sound.

Strings

String instruments represent the influence of western civilisation. The ukulele, a mini-guitar with four strings, comes from Hawaii. Guitars-proper are also now an integral part of the orchestra.

Costumes

Costume is a key component of Tahitian dance and the glamour surrounding it. It is made from plant matter. A distinction is made between two types of costume, one for the otea and the other for the aparima.

For the otea, the outfit covers the dancers' bodies from head to foot. Dancers wear a crown of fresh flowers (frangipani, tiare, bougainvillea) or a huge and elaborate headdress, as well as garlands of flowers and seashells. Women wear a bra made of two halves of a coconut, polished and dyed black, and held together with a piece of string. Dancers of both sexes wear a *more* (skirt) made of *purau* (hibiscus) bark cut into very thin strips, sewn together and dyed red or yellow. Men's *more* hang down slightly below the knees and are attached to the waist; women's are knotted around the hips and hang down as far as the ankles.

A decorative belt of flowers, mother-of-pearl, pieces of polished coconut and seashells is worn over the *more*. The inner part of the belt is fitted with pendants made of vegetable fibres and seashells, which emphasise the swaying movements of the hips as the women dance. Men wear purau fibres around their calves, and dancers of both sexes sport plumes that they wave in their hands to emphasise movement of the upper limbs

The outfit for the aparima is simpler and usually consists of a *pareu* (sarong-type garment) worn as a loincloth for the men, or tied like a skirt or dress for the women. Garlands of flowers or seashells are used as hats.

These descriptions are a rough guide only, and every variation is possible. In the 1998 Heiva, the women in one group even performed in evening dress and the men in dinner jackets!

The costumes are designed by the group leader to suit the theme, which is reinforced by frequent use of props (eg paddles). Usually the dancers themselves have to produce their own outfits.

Masks have no place in Tahitian dance: facial expressions, which reflect hand movements, and smiling are integral parts of the overall staging.

Marquesan Dance

Very particular about their own cultural identity, the Marquesans have developed types of dance that are very different from the ori tahiti. These dances are performed on the Marquesas for specifically Marquesan festivals. The most famous of these is the Haku Manu, modelled on the movements of a bird. The Dance of the Pig, very impressive on account of its physicality, mimics the symbolic phases of the animal's life. The design of the set is highly suggestive due to the loud husky shouts of 'hi' and 'ha'. Percussion instruments alone are used, and the great size of the drums can go up to 1.5m. Usually Marquesan costumes are plainer than Tahitian ones, being simply loincloths made out of vegetable matter.

Dance Groups

A dance company might well perform with as many as 150 participants on important occasions but, as a rule, there is a core of about 20 dancers for any year.

There is no truly professional group. The best-known are semi professional. Their members perform in hotels two or three times a week but the group fees are not sufficient to allow the performers to make a living out of their activities.

Usually between 15 and 35 years of age, the dancers are from very different social and ethnic backgrounds. The *demis* (mixed-race Polynesian-Europeans) are in the majority, but you also find Maohi, Chinese and even *popaa* (westerners). The criteria for employment are motivation and a love of bodily expression rather than a beautiful physique but, given the sheer physical energy required and the bodily exposure, dancers' bodies tend to be very impressive. Three to five months' rehearsing is necessary before a dancer can hope to perform in public.

On Tahiti the most frequently performing groups that you will find in hotels are O Tahiti E, Les Ballets de Tahiti, Te Maeva and Heikura Nui. Every company has its own style and personality, depending largely upon the choreographer, as well as on the group's charisma.

Where the Performances Are

The Heiva I Tahiti

It is, without any doubt, on the occasion of the Heiva i Tahiti, which takes place in June and July in Papeete, that you will see the finest dance spectacles. The best groups in Polynesia turn out in full strength to compete with each other in competitions where every type of dance and song is performed in front of a jury. There are a number of mini-Heiva in July and August on other Society islands. See Heiva I Tahiti in this section for details on the Papeete festivities.

Hotel Shows

The luxury hotels offer top-quality dance shows twice a week, on average. On Tahiti and Moorea they are performed by the very best semi-professional groups (O Tahiti E, Te Maeva and Heikura Nui), represented by their core of about fifteen performers. On other islands, the companies are rather more amateur but, in any event, it will not be a typically touristy show, and you will see actual rehearsals or full-scale 'coaching sessions'. These shows come with a buffet (reckon on between 4000 CFP and 6500 CFP) that is available to the public. If you only wish to attend the show, inquire about the hotel's policy. Some ask for an entrance fee or insist you have the buffet, while others require you to buy a drink at the bar (about 1000 CFP). On Moorea, you can go to Tiki Village. The performances last about 45 minutes, and comprise several sequences of otea and aparima and, sometimes, a fire dance.

Other Shows

Shows take place following the arrival of cruise liners, at official festivals and at various events held by parishes, schools and other organisations.

Companies are highly structured. The *raatira* (leader) is choreographer and conductor, directing rehearsals, choosing costumes, selecting themes and deciding on the exact positions of performers on stage. During major performances the raatira announces the theme to the public and encourages the dancers by circulating among the spectators, shouting out recommendations. The *orero* (orator) announces the theme to the public. The most experienced dancers, male and female, are called *pupahu*, and are placed at the front of the stage.

The musicians are an integral part of the group. They are highly versatile, singing, playing percussion and strings. They are always men.

The Heiva I Tahiti

The Heiva (Festival) is the high point in the celebration of Maohi culture. Every year for a month, from late June to late July, islanders from all the archipelagos join together for a full program of festivities in Papeete and on some of the other islands. The emphasis is on traditional dance contests and singing competitions but there are numerous other activities on offer, from craft demonstrations to Maohi sports and events such as walking over fire. For the tourist, this is a unique opportunity to discover first-hand the rich Maohi cultural heritage.

Prior to 1985, the Heiva was known as Tiurai (July). The first Heiva took place in 1882, when the object of the event was to celebrate the highly republican 14 July. Dancing was at first banned but was slowly introduced. Gradually the festival's republican overtones disappeared and the Tiurai became a festival of Polynesian culture.

The Heiva is organised by Te Fare Tauhiti Nui (Territorial Cultural Centre) (☎ 54 45 44, 54 45 40). Reservations for the evening dance contests can be made from May onwards. The evening will set you back between 1800 CFP and 2500 CFP. Dance performances take place next to the cultural centre.

Events

Dancing Dance contests are the star events of the Heiva. Over a period of several evenings about twenty groups from different islands compete with each other before a jury for a number of different prizes including Best Group, Best Orchestra, Best Costume, Best Couple, and Best Piece of Music. A strict set of rules governs the performances. The jury pays great attention to synchronisation, thematic interpretation, costumes and choreography.

There are two categories: freestyle and traditional. In the traditional category, each group must perform a classical dance based on a theme inspired by Polynesian history or legend. In the freestyle category, innovations in choreography and body language are the order of the day.

Singing Although singing competitions are less prestigious than dancing, they are part of the Heiva, and various competing choirs are held in high esteem. Unfortunately, they are more or less impenetrable to the novice, owing to the complexity of the polyphonic structures of songs such as the *himene ruau*, *himene tarava tahiti*, *himene tarava raromatai* and *ute paripari*. The choirs are mixed, both male and female, and comprise up to ten voices. The themes are suggestive of Maohi legend.

Orero Contest In ancient times, the orero acted as the 'memory' of Maohi culture. His role was to recite ancestries and to pass on cultural heritage. This new competitive category, launched at the 1998 Heiva, aims to revive and preserve the tradition. Each orero recites a text lasting five to 10 minutes, either based on legend or on a theme particular to the group he belongs to.

Vaa (Canoe) Racing The national sport of canoeing is in great favour at every Heiva. The finest rowers in Polynesia, in crews of one, three, six or 16 men and women, compete in several races over a distance of

2600 or 3500m in the Tahiti lagoon or out at sea. One race goes all the way round Moorea (84km) but changes of crew are allowed.

Amoraa Ofae (Rock Lifting) This event, from the Australs, is truly spectacular and calls for great strength and skill. Competitors are dressed in pareu and are required to lift a smooth rock weighing between 90 and 145 kilos, which they must hoist on to their shoulders. See the 'Stone Lifting' boxed text in the Australs chapter for more information.

Patia Fa (Javelin Throwing) This ancestral sport from the Tuamotus truly comes to life at the Heiva. The object is to reach a coconut tied to the top of a 7.5m pole from a distance of 22m. Individuals or two-person teams can compete in this event.

Coconut Shelling This traditional activity, which is still widespread on the Tuamotus and the Marquesas, has been turned into a competition. Each team of three competitors has to split open and scoop out the insides of between 150 and 200 coconuts in the shortest possible time and place the meat in a hessian sack. The tools used are an axe and a *pana* (curved knife).

Fruit-Bearers' Race In ancient times, Polynesians would hang the fruit they had picked from both ends of a stick, which they carried on their shoulders. There are two races involving this over a distance of about 2km. The first is run with a burden of 30kg and the second with a load of 50kg.

Historical Reconstructions The marae come back to life in a number of historical reconstructions. Actors in ceremonial dress take you back to an earlier period of Tahitian history. The most usual scenes you will encounter are of ceremonies investing kings with royal powers, and princely marriages. The sites selected for these events are usually the marae at Paea (Arahurahu) or those in the Papenoo Valley.

Other Events Other features of the Heiva include *niau* (woven coconut-palm leaves) *tifaifai* (appliqué) and tapa-making demonstrations, as well as a stone-carving competition, a procession of floral floats, voting for Miss Heiva and Mr Heiva, a funfair, firework displays, walking on fire, and tattoo displays.

Top: *More* (dancers' skirts) in different colours.

Middle: Dance has played a role in the Marquesas' cultural renewal.

Bottom Left: A decorative belt of shells and mother-of-pearl is worn over the *more*.

Bottom Right: *Pahu* (drums) play a major part in Polynesian dance. In the Marquesas they stand up to 1.5m high.

Top: Spectacular leg-movements are the main feature of the highly energetic *otea*.

Bottom Left: Flowers and shells are used to make collars and to decorate the performers' hair in Tahitian dances.

Bottom Right: The dancers' eyes always follow the hands.

Top Left: Children learn the basics of dancing at an early age.

Top Right: The fire dance is performed by a man who juggles a flaming torch to a background drum beat.

Bottom: The very expressive movements of the hands are crucial in the *aparima*.

Energetic and expressive, rhythm and costumes combine to make Tahitian dance the best ambassador for Polynesian culture.

Bora Bora

Bora Bora is the most difficult Polynesian island to describe realistically. Few people have actually visited the island but the name has become synonymous with a view of paradise. The standard postcards of five-star over-water bungalows are the embodiment of the tropical dream, and aerial views of volcanic peaks, lush vegetation and white-sand beaches fringing the immense turquoise lagoon fully justify this world-wide notoriety.

The reality can be less enchanting: the islanders are not always welcoming, the stretches of beach are actually fairly limited, parts of the island are far from well looked-after and the recent spate of new hotel developments leaves little of the island untouched. Other islands of French Polynesia, less well known and less developed, may seem much more attractive.

Despite everything, Bora Bora remains a fascinating place. The lagoon is simply superb and waiting to be explored by *pirogue* (outrigger canoe), sailboat or by snorkelling or scuba diving. There are a number of small archaeological sites and some faint reminders of WWII, but watching a Polynesian dance performance at a five star hotel while sipping a cocktail is equally part of the Bora Bora experience.

History

The huge volcano that created Bora Bora came into existence three to four million years ago. In the pre-European era the island was known as Vavau, perhaps indicating that it was colonised from the Tongan island of the same name. The name Bora Bora means something like 'first born', indicating that this may have been the most important island after 'sacred' Raiatea. The legendary Hiro, said to have been the first king of Raiatea, is said to have sent his son Ohatatama to rule Bora Bora.

Land pressures, due to the shortage of level ground, helped to create a warlike population that not only squabbled with

HIGHLIGHTS

pop: 5767
area: 38 sq km
reef passes: 1
highest point: Mt Otemanu (727m)

- Tour the lagoon by motorised pirogue, stopping for a picnic on a *motu* and for a shark and ray-feeding session
- Go snorkelling and scuba diving
- Enjoy dinner (or at least a cocktail) and a Polynesian dance performance at a five star hotel
- Ascend Mt Pahia with a guide

each other, but also campaigned against other islands. Only Huahine managed to resist the warriors of Bora Bora at their most expansive.

Cook sighted Bora Bora in 1769, on his first voyage. He paused briefly on the island in 1777 on his last voyage. A London Missionary Society (LMS) station was established on the island in 1820 and, to this day, Bora Bora remains chiefly Protestant. Bora Bora supported Pomare in his push for supreme power over Tahiti, but the French protectorate over Tahiti in 1842 was not extended to Bora Bora, which resisted until it was annexed in 1888. Bora Bora was the setting for the classic silent movie *Tabu* (see Films in the Facts for the Visitor chapter), shot on Motu Tapu (now the property of Club Med) in 1929-30.

Although WWII never got as far south as French Polynesia, it had a major effect on Bora Bora. Soon after the Pearl Harbor bombing on 7 December 1941, the decision was made to establish a US supply base on the island. From early 1942 to mid-1946 Operation Bobcat transformed the island and, at its peak, up to 6000 men were stationed on

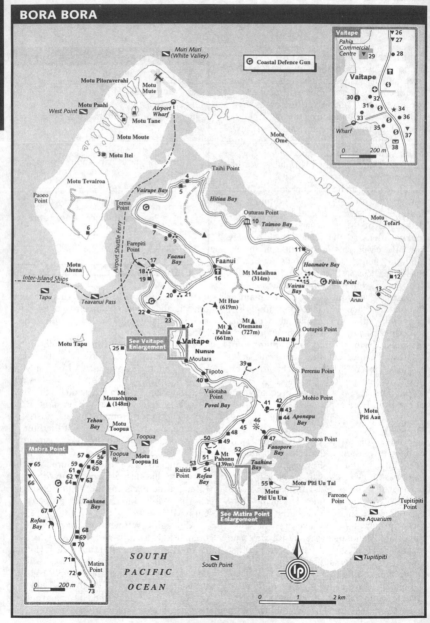

BORA BORA

BORA BORA

Muri Muri
(White Valley)

Coastal Defence Gun

Vaitape

Pahia
Commercial
Centre

Vaitape

Wharf

0   200 m

Motu Pitoraverahi

Motu Mute

Motu Paahi

West Point

Motu Tane

Airport
Wharf

Motu Moute

Motu Itel

Motu Ome

Motu Tevairoa

Paoeo
Point

Taihi Point

Vairupe Bay

Hitiaa Bay

Motu Tofari

Tereia
Point

Outurau Point

Taimoo Bay

Farepiti
Point

Faanui
Bay

Faanui

Haamaire Bay

Mt Mataihua
(314m)

Fitiiu Point

Motu
Ahuna

Vairau
Bay

Anau

Tapu

Teavanui Pass

Mt Hue
(619m)

Outupiti Point

Inter-Island Ships

Motu Tapu

See Vaitape
Enlargement

Mt
Pahia
(661m)

Mt
Otemanu
(727m)

Vaitape

Anau

Nunue
Moutara

Tiipoto

Pererau Point

Mt
Mauaohunoa
(148m)

Vaiotaha
Point

Povai Bay

Mohio Point

Aponapu
Bay

Motu
Piti Aau

Tehou
Bay

Motu
Toopua

Toopua

Paoaoa Point

Matira Point

Mt
Pahonu
(139m)

Faaopore
Bay

Toopua
Iti

Motu
Toopua Iti

Taahina
Bay

Raititi
Point

Rofau
Bay

Taahana
Bay

Motu Piti Uu Tai

Motu
Piti Uu Uta

Fareone
Point

Rofau
Bay

The Aquarium

Tupitipiti
Point

Matira
Point

SOUTH

PACIFIC

OCEAN

South Point

Tupitipiti

0   200 m

0   1   2 km

BORA BORA

PLACES TO STAY
1 Motu Tane Dream Island
2 Le Paradis
3 Mai Moana Island
5 Bora Bora Condos
6 Bora Bora Pearl Beach Resort
11 Revatua Club; L'Espadon Restaurant
12 Méridien Bora Bora; Tipanie Restaurant
19 Bora Bora Yacht Club
23 Topdive (hotel & dive centre)
24 Au Lait de Coco
25 Bora Bora Lagoon Resort; Otemanu Restaurant
39 Chez Ato
40 Blue Lagoon
42 Bora Bora Lagoonarium
43 Chez Stellio & Henriette
44 Chez Téipo
47 Club Med
48 Chez Rosina
49 Village Pauline
53 Hotel Bora Bora; Matira Terrace Restaurant
55 Sofitel Motu
56 Sofitel Marara; La Pérouse Restaurant
58 Beach Club Bora Bora
60 Bora Bora Motel

64 Maitai Polynesia Bora Bora; Haere Mai Restaurant
67 Hotel Matira & Restaurant
68 Pension Maeva – Chez Rosine Masson
69 Pension Temanuata (Accommodation & Restaurant)
70 Moana Beach Parkroyal; Noa Noa Restaurant
71 Chez Nono; Teremoana Tours
73 Chez Robert & Tina

PLACES TO EAT
26 Le Cocotier
27 Snack Michèle
29 L'Appetisserie
37 Brasserie Manuia
45 Bamboo House Restaurant; Camera Shop
50 Bloody Mary's
52 Snack Patoti
62 La Bounty Restaurant
63 Snack de la Plage
65 Ben's Place
66 Snack Matira

OTHER
4 Hyatt Remains
7 Seaplane Ramp
8 Submarine Dock

9 Marae Fare-Opu
10 Musée de la Marine
13 Lagoonarium
14 Marae Taharuu
15 Marae Aehua-tai
16 Faanui Church
17 Farepiti Wharf
18 Marae Marotetini
20 Faanui Power Station
21 Marae Tianapa
22 Old Club Med
28 Chin Lee Supermarket
30 Tourist Office
31 Alain Gerbault Memorial
32 Centre Artisanal de Bora Bora
33 Air Tahiti Office
34 Gendarmerie (Police Station)
35 Town Hall (Mairie)
36 Europcar
38 Post Office
41 Telephone Tower
46 Belvédère (Viewpoint)
51 Television Tower
54 Bora Diving Center
57 Nemo Worlds Diving Center
59 Tiare Market
61 René & Maguy (Taxi-Boat)
72 Matira Jet Tours

Bora Bora. The huge runway on Motu Mute is the clearest (and most useful) reminder of those frenetic days. It was completed in 1943 and after a period out of use after the war it was put back into operation in 1951. Until Faaa airport on Tahiti opened in 1961 this was the international airport for French Polynesia, and passengers were transferred from Bora Bora to Tahiti by seaplane. Eight massive seven-inch naval cannons were installed around the island during the war and all except one are still in place.

The island has always been a pioneer in tourist development; the first hotels appeared in the 60s and today it's the centre for Polynesia's trademark over-water bungalows.

Geography & Orientation

Like the other high islands, Bora Bora was created by volcanic action and it's easy to trace the rim of the ancient volcano. The sea has broken into the crater to form Povai Bay, and Motu Toopua and Motu Toopua Iti are fragments of the old crater rim, not low-lying sand motu like those on the northern and eastern edges of the lagoon.

Bora Bora is spectacularly mountainous, rising to Mt Hue (619m), Mt Pahia (661m) and Mt Otemanu (727m). The main island stretches about 9km from north to south and is about 4km in width at the widest point. A 32km road runs around the coast.

A wide, sheltered and navigable lagoon encircles the island, with sandy motu edging most of the outer reef. There is only one pass into the lagoon: the Teavanui Pass on the western side. Vaitape on the western side of the island is the main town. Faanui and Anau are other smaller settlements while Matira Point is the anchor for tourists. The wharf for inter-island ships is at Farepiti, between Vaitape and Faanui. The airport is on Motu Mute at the northern extremity of the outer-reef edge.

Information

Tourist Offices The Bora Bora Visitors Bureau (☎/fax 67 76 36) has an office on the wharf at Vaitape, open weekdays from 7.30 am to noon and 1.30 to 4 pm. Some Saturdays it's open 8 to 11.30 am.

Money There are branches of Banque de Tahiti, Banque de Polynésie and Banque Socredo in Vaitape. They all seem to keep slightly different hours but the approximate opening hours are 7.30 am to 4 or 4.30 pm, with one or 1½ hours off for lunch. Banque de Tahiti and Banque Socredo branches have automatic teller machines (ATMs) that accept Visa and MasterCard.

Post & Communications The post office is on the Matira side of the wharf in the middle of Vaitape. It's open Monday from 8 am to 3 pm, Tuesday to Friday 7.30 am to 3 pm and Saturday 7 to 9 am. There are telephones all around the island and phonecards can be bought at a number of shops, hotels and restaurants. L'Appetisserie (see Vaitape & Around in Places to Eat later in this chapter) offers Internet and email services, usually in the morning. Count on 500 CFP for 15 minutes of web surfing or sending emails, 300 CFP for receiving messages.

Photo Developing For film and processing head for the Camera Shop, next to the Bamboo House Restaurant. It's open Monday to Saturday.

Laundry In Vaitape, Cathina (☎ 67 65 27) will do a load of laundry for 1800 CFP.

Medical Services If you need medical assistance, inquire at your hotel. There's a medical centre in Vaitape (☎ 67 70 77) or contact Dr Juen (☎ 67 70 62), Dr Roussanaly or Dr Boutry (☎ 67 77 95), or the small medical centre (☎ 67 66 66, 67 78 44) behind the Herman Perles shop. There's a pharmacy in Vaitape open every day although only briefly on Sunday.

Yacht Facilities & Warnings Visiting yachts are warned to take care while moored on Bora Bora. Always take all valuables and documents with you when leaving the boat. Don't leave things outside: lock clothes, diving equipment and other stealable items away. Lock away dinghies and outboards, which have a tendency to sail away at night. If you eat at the Bora Bora Yacht Club, the 17 moorings and the showers are free.

Around the Island

Bora Bora's 32km coast road hugs the shoreline almost all the way around the island. Curiously, the road is not sealed all the way, and only at Fitiiu Point and just east of Club Med at Paoaoa Point does the road rise slightly above sea level. Since it's so level, doing the circuit by bicycle is easy, although motor scooters and cars can also be rented. The tour that follows starts with Vaitape and goes anticlockwise around the island.

Along the route there are a number of ancient marae and four WWII gun emplacements.

Vaitape Passengers arriving by air are transferred by catamaran from the Motu Mute airport to Vaitape, the island's main settlement. It's not the most attractive place but there are some cheaper places to stay

---

The Trashing of Bora Bora

Flattened crabs along the road may be an unhappy sight but even worse is the rubbish that disfigures stretches of the coast. The shoreline around Anau village sports a particularly dense scum of soft-drink cans and plastic packaging. It's a shame that an island frequently rated the most beautiful in the Pacific fades so badly when examined close up. The local government hardly sets an example, with eyesores like the garbage dump at the end of Fitiiu Point, set up right beside the magical lagoon. Nor do some international businesses operating in the Pacific set a very good example. When Club Med built a new resort on the island it left its predecessor to rot, and Hyatt had its name attached to a decaying slum for years.

and most of the tourist services are here. Vaitape is busy during the day but apart from *pétanque* (boules) players it becomes very quiet by late afternoon.

At Vaitape wharf stands a **monument** to Alain Gerbault, the pioneering French yachtsman who made the first nonstop solo crossing of the Atlantic in 1923. Between 1923 and 1929 he circumnavigated the world in his yacht *Firecrest*, visiting Bora Bora in 1926. From 1934 to 1940 he lived on Bora Bora but he died on the island of Timor, just north of Australia, in 1941. His remains were returned to Bora Bora in 1947 and the monument was erected in 1951.

The Overland Road (3km) Past the last houses south of Vaitape, the road curves around Povai Bay. One hundred metres past the Alain & Linda art gallery, opposite the soccer field and the gymnasium, take the small road that shortcuts across the island. You can only go partway by car. A decorative miniature wooden powerhouse marks the turn-off. The road turns into a steep paved track following the power lines up the hill past the water chlorination plant. At the top, turn left towards the telephone tower or right towards a private house. Just before the house, an overgrown footpath turns left down to the village of **Anau**, just beyond Club Med. Right across the island it's only 10 minutes up and 10 minutes down. Starting from the Anau side, the path commences behind the truck workshop – directly across the road from Chez Stellio.

The top of the hill offers fine views in both directions. To the west you can look out over Vaitape and the lagoon, while far to the east, across the lagoon and beyond the long sand-and-palm line of Motu Piti Aau, rise the profiles of Tahaa and Raiatea.

Lookout & Bloody Mary's (5km) Beyond the shortcut across the island via the telephone tower, the coast road passes the Bamboo House Restaurant and some shops. Just before Village Pauline is the turn-off to the TV tower. Bora Bora's TV-relay station makes a good lookout over the lagoon. Almost immediately beyond the turn-off is

Bloody Mary's, the best-known restaurant on the island. A large pirogue marks the site and a sign details the varied list of 'celebrities' who have dined here.

Matira Beach & Coastal Defence Guns (6 to 7.5km) The luxurious and expensive Hotel Bora Bora at Raititi Point marks the start of this pleasant stretch of public and easily accessible beach, which sweeps out to Matira Point. Along the road are several boutiques, snack bars and restaurants. From the eastern edge of the Hotel Matira property, a walking trail runs up the hill to a battery of coastal defence guns. It's only a 10 minute hike up to the emplacement.

Matira Point (7.5km) On the eastern side is the classy Moana Beach Parkroyal Hotel with its collection of over-water bungalows branching out over the lagoon. The hotel has a sign that points the way to the small road that runs out to Matira Point. The public **beach** of the same name extends out along the western side of the point where there are several popular guesthouses. The annual Hawaiki Nui canoe race in October or November finishes the final leg, from Tahaa to Bora Bora, right on the beach. See the boxed text 'Hawaiki Nui Canoe Race' in the Facts for the Visitors chapter for more information on French Polynesia's favourite sporting event.

The point takes its name from the 490-tonne British ship *Mathilda*, wrecked on Moruroa Atoll in the Tuamotus in 1792. The crew managed to get back to Tahiti where they were robbed, but Pomare I offered his protection and punished the thieves. Three of the survivors decided to remain on Tahiti and one of them, a James O'Connor, married Pomare's cousin. The cannons from the ship were salvaged at Moruroa in 1968 and are now on display at the Museum of Tahiti & Its Islands on Tahiti.

Matira Point to Club Med (7.5 to 9km) From Matira Point, the coast road passes a busy little collection of shops, restaurants and hotels including Maitai Polynesia and Sofitel Marara. The road rounds the point and passes Club Med (9km) on its own bay and with its own *belvédère* (lookout) atop the ridge above the bay. The path to the lookout is accessed by Club Med's private tunnel under the road; you can see the steps where they emerge from under the road. The road climbs the hill as it passes Club Med and then drops back down to the coast, past the Club Med tennis courts, just before the village of Anau.

Anau (10 to 12km) The scenery changes with the fishing village of Anau, a rather strung-out affair on a rather dismal stretch of shoreline. The Chez Stellio camping ground (10.5km) is at the start of the village, across the road from a truck workshop. The short, steep pathway to the telephone tower and down to the other side of the island starts from beside the workshop. Just past Chez Stellio is the office for the Lagoonarium, where motu excursions and island tours are organised.

Fitiiu Point Marae & Guns (15km) Fitiiu Point is also known as Tuivahora Point. On this finger-like peninsula, extending out into the lagoon, the road climbs briefly away from the coast. There are several interesting sites along the point but none of them is signposted, maintained or even easy to find. The authorities almost appear to have gone out of their way to make access difficult.

Just as the road starts to climb, a track peels off and runs down to **Marae Aehua-tai** at the water's edge. There are good views across the bay from the marae site, with Mt Otemanu in the background.

Farther along the point there's a natural 'marae' and two more WWII coastal guns. The walking trail along the ridge starts right behind the first house, at the sharp bend in the road, at the top of the ridge. If there's anybody around you should ask permission to take the trail but there is an alternative route. Simply continue on the road back down to sea level and take the track that turns off to the right and runs along the northern side of Fitiiu Point. The track terminates at, of all things, a scenic lagoonside garbage dump! Just before the dump a steep

path runs uphill and emerges on the top of the ridge just before the gun site. From the site there are fine views out over the lagoon to the motu.

Backtrack along the ridge-top footpath to **Marae Taharuu**, a natural rock pinnacle locally revered as a marae.

Haamaire & Taimoo Bays (16 to 21km) The road beyond Fitiiu Point traverses the most lightly populated stretch of coast around the island as it rounds Haamaire and Taimoo bays. The middle-of-nowhere Revatua Club at 16.5km on Taimoo Bay is a good place for a lunch or drink stop on a circuit of the island.

Marine Museum (21km) The small, private Musée de la Marine (☎ 67 75 24) has an interesting collection of model ships made by architect Bertrand Darasse. They include a variety of Polynesian pirogues and other island boats and models of the ships of the early European explorers including Cook's *Endeavour* and Dumont d'Urville's *L'Astrolabe* of 1811. Of course there's also a model of Bligh's *Bounty* and Alain Gerbault's *Firecrest*.

Entry to the museum is free but a donation is appreciated. The museum is generally open on weekends or during the week if the proprietor is at home.

Taihi Point (22km) Another lightly populated stretch of coastline continues to Taihi Point. Just before the point, a steep and often very muddy track climbs up to an old WWII radar station atop Popotei Ridge and on to a lookout above the village of Faanui.

A major Hyatt hotel project was started at this site but the money ran out close to completion and the whole thing was left to rot. Recently some of the mess has been cleaned up. Just beyond the ruins is Bora Bora Condos, on stilts above the lagoonside road.

More Wartime Reminders (23 to 26km) After the Hyatt remains, a seaplane ramp and an old ferry jetty pop up at around 24km. At the end of Tereia Point, a rectangular concrete water tank marks the position of another coastal gun. There's no path; just clamber for a couple of minutes straight up the hill behind the tank. Finally, there's a small **harbour**, originally built for submarines but now more likely to shelter visiting yachts.

Marae Fare-Opu (26km) Right after the former submarine base and immediately before Faanui village and speed-limit signs, the Marae Fare-Opu is squeezed between the roadside and water's edge. Two of the slabs are clearly marked with turtle **petroglyphs**. Turtles were sacred to the ancient Polynesians and a very similar design can be seen incised into stones at numerous other sites in the Society Islands.

Faanui Bay & Village (27km) Faanui Bay was the site of the main US military base during WWII. From the picturesque church at the head of the bay a road runs directly inland. Where the sealed road bends to the right, take the unsealed fork to the left. The road climbs up towards the ridge; continue to bear left at each fork. The track often deteriorates into a muddy morass more suitable for mountain bikes than the single-speed bikes generally rented out on Bora Bora. Eventually the track comes to the ridgetop and drops down the other side to Vairau Bay just south of Fitiiu Point.

Marae Taianapa (28km) Set well back off the mountain side of the road on private property, this fairly large marae overlooks a small field from the edge of a coconut plantation. It was restored in 1963. You've overshot the access to the temple by about 100m if you get as far as the Hinano Beer and Coca Cola depot.

Marae Marotetini & Farepiti Wharf (29km) Inter-island ships dock at Farepiti wharf, at the western end of Faanui Bay. The wharf was built during WWII and is often crowded with travellers.

Walk 100m south-west along the shoreline to Marae Marotetini. This second royal marae on the island is a fine, 50m-long shore marae and was restored by Dr Yoshihiko Shinoto in 1968. Bora Bora Yacht Club

is just beyond the marae so there are often yachts moored offshore from the point.

Club Med Ruins & Coastal Guns (30km) Along the road from Farepiti Point to Pahua Point, one of the WWII defence guns can be seen silhouetted against the skyline. The road rounds the point and arrives at the remains of the old Club Med. When one cyclone too many devastated its original Bora Bora resort, Club Med upped and moved to a better site on the southern side of the island, leaving the old resort to rot in the tropical air.

Two coastal defence guns overlook the point. They're a short walk up from the road although, as usual, the route is not indicated in any way. A very circuitous and rather poor 4WD track leads to the gun site from a turn-off just on the Faanui village side of Farepiti wharf. These guns were placed here to overlook the Teavanui Pass, the shipping route into the lagoon.

Activities

Bora Bora's activities are centred on the wonderful lagoon, although there are also plenty of opportunities in the mountainous interior. Operators will come to the place you're staying to scout for business.

Diving Diving is one of Bora Bora's prime activities. Sharks, rays and other marine life abound and can be seen in quite shallow waters in the lagoon or outside the reef. There are three dive centres, which welcome both beginners and more experienced divers. Check the 'Diving' special section in the Outdoor Activities chapter for details.

Swimming & Snorkelling Bora Bora, like most islands of Polynesia, doesn't have endless stretches of white-sand beach. In fact the only really superb beach on the main island is at **Matira Point**, to the south of the island. The snorkelling in this area is excellent, particularly close to Hotel Bora Bora, where fishing is banned and the currents are ideal.

The **motu**, on the other hand, are generally untouched and idyllic. Some are private

BORA BORA

Feeding Sharks & Stroking Rays

The *repas des requins* (meal time for the sharks) is a popular activity on a number of French Polynesian islands, and Bora Bora is no exception. Shark-feeding trips are organised by all and sundry. At certain established spots in the lagoon, the sharks have got used to having a free meal and while visitors snorkel around the action, the island's sharks (generally the smaller black-tip variety) are hand-fed by shark experts. Ecologically this is probably not a very sensible activity. Petting the stingrays has become an equally popular part of a number of island tours.

property and others are occupied by luxury hotels, although visitors are usually welcome if they buy a drink at the bar or a meal at the restaurant, and there are free shuttle boats that will take you back and forth. Island tours by pirogue with motu stops along the way are organised by many hotels and guesthouses. The **Coral Garden**, at the Aquarium in the south-east of the lagoon, is a popular stop. René & Maguy (☎ 67 60 61, fax 67 61 01), next to La Bounty Restaurant, will take you there for 1696 CFP per person. It also rents out small outboard-powered boats and even pedal boats, which let you make your own lagoon tour. Aqua Safari (☎ 67 74 83, 67 71 16) at Beach Club Bora Bora has diving helmets, as on Moorea. You stroll along the bottom, accompanied by a divemaster.

Walking There are beautiful walks on Bora Bora, including the Mt Pahia ascent; a guide is recommended. The Walking section in the Outdoor Activities chapter has details.

Horse Riding Ranch Reva Reva (☎ 60 44 61) offers horse-riding excursions on Motu Piti Aau for all levels. A 1½ hour ride costs 6500 CFP, 2½ hours 8500 CFP, including transfers from your accommodation.

Parasailing Société Parasail (☎ 67 70 34, fax 67 61 73), between Matira Point and the Méridien Hotel, offers solo or two-person parasails for 6000/10,000 CFP for a 15/30 minute flight.

Organised Tours

Pirogue Tours Tours by pirogue have become a standard part of the Bora Bora experience. There are half-day and all-day tours to some of the most beautiful spots around the lagoon, often stopping to hand-feed sharks, pausing for a barbecue lunch on a motu, a swimming and snorkelling stop at the Coral Garden, a swim with the rays and a walk on the outer reef. Of course there's no chance of playing Robinson Crusoe when your motu has 10 or 20 other tourists on it, but this a pleasant and easy way to see the marine life and get to otherwise inaccessible sites. Bring thongs or plastic sandals, a hat and sunscreen.

Costs vary from 3500 CFP to 5000 CFP for half-day trips and 5000 CFP to 7500 CFP for day trips, which typically go from 9 am to 4 pm and include lunch. Many hotels and guesthouses offer these lagoon tours, as well as the regular operators. Usually a minimum of four people is required. Try Matira Tours Excursions (☎ 67 70 97), Lagoonarium (☎ 67 71 34), Teremoana Tours at Chez Nono (☎ 67 71 38), Robert at Chez Robert & Tina (☎ 67 72 92), Bora Bora Poe Iti Tours (☎ 67 78 21), Raanui Tours (☎ 67 61 79) or Moana Adventure Tours (☎ 67 61 21, 67 75 97). Moana Adventure Tours also does 1½-hour glass-bottom-boat trips three times a week for 2400 CFP.

Catamaran & Game Fishing Trips
Richard Postma (☎/fax 67 77 79, email taravana@mail.pf) offers trips on the *Taravana*, a 15m catamaran with four double cabins. It makes half-day and day trips, inside and outside the lagoon, game-fishing trips and excursions to neighbouring Tupai. Daily cost is 95,000 CFP and sunset cruises are also organised for 5500 CFP per person, with a minimum of six participants.

The *Taravana*, the *Jessie L* (☎/fax 67 70 59) and Moana Adventure Tours (☎ 67 61 21, 67 75 97) organise game-fishing trips; count on at least 100,000 CFP for a day.

Taaroa (☎/fax 67 61 55), a 12m catamaran, does lagoon trips with swimming and snorkelling stops for 5400 CFP and sunset cruises for at least four people for 3600 CFP.

4WD Tours Tupuna Mountain Safari (☎/fax 67 75 06) runs popular guided tours by 4WD including visits to the American WWII sites and the archaeological sites, with some explanation of the island flora, and fruit-tasting in season. Half-day trips cost 6000 CFP per person. Otemanu Tours (☎ 67 70 49) also does tours by minibus or truck for 2200 CFP per person.

Helicopter Tours Héli-Inter Polynésie (☎ 67 62 59), adjacent to Air Tahiti in Vaitape, offers 15-minute flights for 13,500 CFP per person. Starting from Povai, that gives you long enough to complete a loop of the lagoon and fly over Matira Point, the Coral Garden, Mt Otemanu, Faanui Bay, the airport on Motu Mute, Teavanui Pass, Motu Tapu and Motu Toopua. There are commentaries in English and credit cards are accepted. The office is open weekdays from 7.30 am to noon and 1.30 to 4 pm, Saturday 8 am to noon.

Places to Stay

Bora Bora's deluxe hotels and over-water bungalows are symbols of a tropical Eden that appear on innumerable tourist brochures. In reality Bora Bora also has interesting possibilities for much smaller budgets including two camp sites, something fairly rare in French Polynesia. In fact the range of accommodation is vast, stretching from five-star establishments with astronomical tariffs down to guesthouses and mid-range hotels.

Although places to stay can be found all around the island and on the motu, the majority are concentrated along the southern side of the island, from Hotel Bora Bora at Raititi Point (6km from Vaitape) to Club Med on Faaopore Bay (9km from Vaitape).

All the top-end and mid-range places accept credit cards unless otherwise noted, but most of the budget places do not. Unless mentioned, the tariffs that follow include

the 8% VAT (value-added tax) but not the tourist taxes that are currently 50 CFP per person per night in guesthouses, 150 CFP in the classified hotels. Unless otherwise stated, the following prices for accommodation are for one night only.

Vaitape & Nearby Vaitape doesn't have many tourist attractions – there's no beach or place to swim – but does have all the tourist services like shops, offices and banks.

Au lait de Coco (☎ 67 67 66) is on the inland side of the road, 100m after the Nunue shop to the north of the town centre. Possibilities include dorm beds for 2000 CFP and rooms from 5000 CFP to 6000 CFP. There's an equipped kitchen for guests' use, or breakfast/dinner costs 500/1000 CFP. There's nothing luxurious about this guesthouse but it does have personality. Motu excursions cost 1000 CFP, or 2000 CFP with a picnic lunch; boat tours of the island are 2000 CFP (minimum six people) and mountain climbing trips are 4000 CFP (minimum two people). Transfers from the wharf are 300 CFP.

Topdive (☎ 60 50 50, fax 60 50 51, email topdive@mail.pf) is to the north of Vaitape, just after the Total petrol station, and features everything to do with diving. There's no beach even though it's right by the lagoon, but there is a swimming pool. It's a great location for divers, with some very high-tech equipment avaible. Expect to pay 14,580/36, 180/56,160 CFP for village/garden/over-water bungalows for two people. Breakfast is included in the two more-expensive categories. Transfers to the Vaitape wharf are free as are the resort's sailboards and kayaks. Credit cards are accepted.

Blue Lagoon (☎/fax 67 65 64), about 20 minutes on foot south of the Vaitape centre, is great value. The lagoonside building is very straightforward but the five fan-cooled rooms are just 2000 CFP per person. The shared bathroom has hot water, and halfboard (breakfast and dinner) adds another 2000 CFP. Breakfast alone at 1000 CFP isn't such good value. The owners offer free transfers to Matira Point's beach or to Vaitape itself. They'll also arrange to drop you on a motu. Transfers to the Vaitape

BORA BORA

wharf are free but credit cards are not accepted. There's a restaurant with a terrace on to the lagoon.

Turn off the main island coast road just over 2km from Vaitape and go inland about 500m to *Chez Ato* (☎ *67 77 27)*, on the slope running up to the central mountains. The five rooms arranged around a central open area share shower and toilet facilities and cost 5000 CFP for one or two people. There are also six bungalows at 60,000 CFP a month and a big fully equipped *fare* for 15,000 CFP a night. The quiet setting in a garden full of fruit trees is a major attraction and Ato leads hikes up Mt Pahia and organises canoe trips on the lagoon. Transfers to the Vaitape wharf are free.

There's a warm and friendly atmosphere at *Chez Rosina* (☎/fax 67 70 91*), on the mountain side of the road, 4.5km from Vaitape. *Fare* rooms cost 5000/6000 CFP to 5500/7000 CFP a single/double. Lounge, dining room and kitchen facilities are shared. Add 600 CFP for breakfast or 3500 CFP for half-board.

Village Pauline (☎ *67 72 16, fax 67 78 14)* is right after Chez Rosina towards Matira Point and also on the inland side of the road. This is undoubtedly the number one spot for budget travellers. The well kept minivillage starts with an eight bed dorm for 2500 CFP per person. Bungalows cost 6000 CFP to 9000 CFP, or you can pitch a tent for 1800 CFP per person. The Polynesian-style village is in a tropical garden. Matira Beach is about half an hour away on foot. Transfers from the ferry wharf are 500 CFP, 300 CFP from the Vaitape wharf. It has bicycles, scooters and kayaks to rent, the staff speak English and credit cards are accepted.

It's possible that the Outrigger chain may take over the old Club Med site to the north of Vaitape and convert it into a 60 bungalow complex.

Around Matira Point The 3km from Hotel Bora Bora to Club Med is packed with places to stay in all price ranges. Beautiful Matira Beach is a prime reason for all this activity. The accommodation possibilities in this area are arranged by price bracket, moving along the road from west to east.

Budget Matira Point, the eastern end of the best sweep of beach on the main island, has several budget-priced guesthouses. The very top-end Moana Beach Parkroyal Hotel occupies the other side of the point.

Chez Nono (☎ *67 71 38, fax 67 74 27)*, at the start of Matira Point and right on the beach, is a two storey house with six rooms for 5500/6500 CFP a single/double. There are shared bathroom facilities and a large kitchen and lounge area downstairs. The rooms are quite comfortable; some have verandas and a couple even have lagoon views, although the walls are paper thin. Two small bungalows with double bed cost 8500 CFP for one or two people and two larger family bungalows cost 11,000 CFP. The bungalows have attached hot-water bathrooms. Breakfast costs 800 CFP, bicycles 1200 CFP for a day and credit cards are accepted.

Chez Robert & Tina (☎ *67 72 92)*, right at the end of the point, has two simple fan-cooled houses with shared bathroom and kitchen facilities. The first night costs 4000 CFP per person, dropping to 3000 CFP on subsequent nights. Canoe tours of the island cost just 4500 CFP per person (minimum three people), including picnic lunch, or you can be dropped off on a motu for the day for 1500 CFP. Transfers from the Vaitape wharf are included and credit cards are accepted.

Pension Maeva – Chez Rosine Masson (☎/fax 67 72 04*), right on the water's edge just beyond the Matira Point turn-off, has loads of charm and character. The house is full of the late Jean Masson's exuberant paintings and the lagoonside setting is a delight. There are two rooms downstairs for 6000 CFP for one or two people, and three upstairs (two with sea views) at 5500 CFP. A dorm-style room with four single beds for 2500 CFP unfortunately doesn't offer much privacy. There's an additional charge of 1000 CFP per person for a one night stay. There's a shared lounge room, kitchen and cold-water bathroom. Transfers are included and credit cards are accepted.

Mid-Range Right on Matira Beach, shortly before the Matira Point turn-off, *Hotel Matira* (☎ *67 78 58, 67 70 51, fax 67 77 02)* has a restaurant on the lagoon side of the road and 20 simple, thatched-roof bungalows. The bungalows have attached bathroom and outside terrace, and some also have kitchenettes. Bungalows cost 22,203 CFP to 37,387 CFP. Half-board adds 4102 CFP per person, full board (all meals) 6201 CFP. Return transfers from Vaitape cost 1020 CFP.

Just after the Matira Point turn-off and the Moana Beach Parkroyal, *Pension Temanuata* (☎ *67 75 61, fax 67 62 48)* is behind the restaurant of the same name. There are five comfortable bungalows in local style in a pretty garden setting. They all accommodate up to three people, have fan, attached hot-water bathroom and cost 8500 CFP, or 9500 CFP for the one bungalow that is right on the beach.

Bora Bora Motel (☎ *67 78 21, fax 67 77 57)* is a smaller, beachfront place right across the road from the Tiare Market. A large *fare* is divided into four studios, each with double bedroom, hot-water bathroom, kitchen, living-and-dining area and outside terrace. Studios are 13,000 CFP and apartments and a Polynesian-style beach bungalow are 17,000 CFP. The site is a little cramped but there's a good stretch of beach and credit cards are accepted.

Beach Club Bora Bora (☎ *67 71 16, fax 67 71 30)* is between Bora Bora Motel and Sofitel Marara. There are 36 simple rooms in buildings of four rooms each. They start at 19,440 CFP (garden, no air-con) and go up to 24,300 CFP (beach, air-con). There's a bar and the Toopiti restaurant. The Beach Club does island tours by pirogue for 5300 CFP and picks up from Vaitape wharf for 1750 CFP return.

Top End On Raititi Point, about 7km from Vaitape, *Hotel Bora Bora* (☎ *67 44 60, 60 44 11, fax 60 44 66, 60 44 22)* has the best location on the island, with terrific views and a good beach.

Built right out on the point, the hotel has a restaurant overlooking the lagoon and a bar and restaurant down towards the beach. This is one of the best places to eat on the island. Prices start at 48,600 CFP for the standard garden bungalows but even these are very pleasantly designed. Prices climb through superior bungalows and private villas (some with their own small swimming pools) to the top over-water bungalows for 81,000 CFP. Half/full board adds 8000/11,000 CFP. There's a weekly dance-performance night.

Because the hotel owners have made efforts to protect the fish around the point, this is one of the island's better snorkelling sites. The hotel has a boutique and tour desk, and hires out cars, scooters and bicycles.

On the eastern side of Matira Point, the *Moana Beach Parkroyal Hotel* (☎ *60 49 00, fax 60 49 99, email borabora@parkroyal.pf)* is relatively small, with 51 rooms, but is very classy. Beach/over-water bungalows cost 50,898/74,052 CFP. The latter come complete with the famous glass coffee-tables for lagoon viewing that have become a French Polynesian trademark. Half/full board costs 7344/10,302 CFP per person. There's a charge for guests to be picked up from the airport by private speedboat. There is a bar, two restaurants, a swimming pool and regular dance performances for 6000 CFP.

Maitai Polynesia Bora Bora (☎ *60 30 00, fax 67 66 03, email maitaibo@mail.pf)* is one of the island's newest hotels. It sprawls across both sides of the road, just beyond the Matira Point turn-off. It offers a good balance of luxury and price, with aircon rooms on the inland side for 22,680 CFP, spacious villa-style units for 30,618 CFP and beach/over-water bungalows for 32,886/40,824 CFP. Although it's not as isolated or prestigious as its more luxurious competitors, the prices are certainly lower and it's nicely designed. The pleasant bar and restaurant are not, unfortunately, right on the lagoon. There's a Polynesian dance performance once a week.

Sofitel Marara (☎ *67 70 46, fax 67 74 03)* is at the end of Taahina Bay, before the road rounds the next point to Club Med. Bungalows cost 33,480 CFP to 54,000 CFP, plus an extra 1500 CFP in the high season. Half/full board is 6200/9000 CFP. Although the over-water bungalows are not of the same standard as other luxury hotels on the island, they are about 30% cheaper. There's a beachfront restaurant and bar, a swimming pool, a tennis court and the usual sporting and shopping facilities. Polynesian evenings are organised three times a week. Originally built by film-maker Dino de Laurentis, the hotel still has a certain style and today there's a delightful offshoot, Sofitel Motu on Motu Piti Uu Uta (see The Motu later in this section).

Around the next point from the Sofitel is *Club Med* (☎ 60 46 04 or ☎ 42 96 99, 42 16 83 in Papeete; fax 60 46 10, email cmbora@mail.pf), on Faaopore Bay, just before Paoaoa Point. It's big, with 72 garden rooms and 78 beach rooms. The blocks, painted in a variety of pastel shades, are straightforward two-storey affairs but the rooms are simply yet very tastefully designed and furnished. There's a swimming pool, two tennis courts, a wide range of other sporting facilities and a private stretch of beach on Motu Piti Aau. The Club Med pirogue shuttles back and forth to the motu beach all day.

Club Med stays are all-inclusive apart from pre-dinner and after-dinner drinks, and activities such as scuba diving. Meals are all-you-can-eat, usually buffet-style, and at lunch and dinner wine and beer are included.

Club Med visitors generally book through a travel agent. Typical per-person daily costs are in the US$220 to US$260 range, including all meals. There's usually a three day minimum stay requirement. If, however, you've always wanted to try Club Med and you just happen to be on Bora Bora, give it a call. If there's space, casual visitors are taken at 16,924/30,830 CFP to 23,961/31,052 CFP for singles/doubles, including all meals, depending on the season.

The Rest of the Island Continue right around the island beyond Club Med back to Vaitape and there are five more accommodation possibilities on this less developed side of the island.

Shortly after Club Med, *Chez Téipo* (☎ 67 78 17, fax 67 73 24, email teipo@tahiti.net), also known as Pension Anau, is very popular for its good quality/price trade-off. Close to the road beside the lagoon, bungalows cost 6500 CFP to 10,500 CFP. Taxes, free transfers from the Vaitape wharf and a light breakfast are included. There's no beach here but there are bicycles available free for guests' use. Credit cards are accepted.

At the entrance to Anau village, *Chez Stellio & Henriette* (☎ 67 71 32) is the cheapest place on the island. There's camping space for 1000 CFP, dorm beds for 1500 CFP and rooms for 4000 CFP to 5000 CFP, all sharing the communal kitchen area. It's right on the water and although there is no beach along this stretch of coast, Stellio takes

The Battle of the Luxury Hotels

Bora Bora has made a name for itself when it comes to some of the most spectacular hotels on earth. Here five star luxury means magnificent over-water bungalows or garden bungalows in beautifully luxuriant tropical settings, all equipped with the latest and most extravagant furniture and fittings.

There's fierce competition between operators and architects for the title of Most Beautiful Luxury Hotel in the Pacific. The battle rages between older hotels around the island and a spate of new constructions on the surrounding motu. Recent French taxation changes that permit wealthy investors to postpone tax payments by investing in overseas French territories have encouraged Bora Bora's building boom in top hotels. Even if you can't afford to stay at one of these escapist havens, a drink at the bar or an evening dance performance can still be a pleasant introduction to the gold-card lifestyle.

guests to Matira Point Beach twice a day or will drop you on a motu for the day for 1200 CFP. Island tours by canoe cost 6500 CFP. Free transport is offered from the Vaitape wharf on arrival but the return trip costs 300 CFP. There's a very pleasant family atmosphere at this relatively remote location.

Just after Chez Stellio, **Bora Bora Lagoonarium** (☎ 67 71 34, fax 67 60 29) has four rooms with shared bathroom for 6000 CFP for one or two people, and a small *fare* with bathroom right by the lagoon for 8000 CFP. There's a communal kitchen, bicycles can be rented and boat trips are made across to the Lagoonarium.

The pink and white **Revatua Club** (☎ 67 71 67, fax 67 76 59) is the most isolated outpost on the island and usually picks up guests directly from the airport. This vaguely colonial-looking establishment has a pleasant bar and restaurant by the lagoon with a long wharf reaching out over the water to a saltwater swimming pool. The 16 fan-cooled rooms are across the road on the mountain side and have attached bathrooms. There's also one villa on the lagoon side that has a separate lounge-and-kitchen area. Half/full board is 3800/5600 CFP per person. L'Espadon Restaurant is built out over the lagoon, and there are two small, artificial beaches and some good coral for snorkelling. Snorkelling equipment is provided free as are bicycles. Island tours by canoe cost 6000 CFP per person including lunch, or you can be left on a motu for the day for 1000 CFP. Credit cards are accepted.

Bora Bora Condos (☎ 67 71 33) is 10km from Vaitape, at the northern end of the island. Bring your own food as there aren't any places to eat here. The hillside bungalows on stilts cost 15,000/150,000 CFP a day/month; the over-water ones are 20,000/200,000 CFP a day/month. Costs go up in July and August. The bungalows have two bedrooms, living room, dining room, kitchen, bathroom and outside terrace. Airport transfers can be arranged and bicycles are available to borrow but credit cards are not accepted.

Only 3km from Vaitape, almost completing the island circuit, **Bora Bora Yacht Club** (☎ 67 70 69, 67 71 50) has two fan-cooled

garden bungalows with attached bathrooms and room for up to four people for 10,000 CFP, and three over-water bungalows for 11,000 CFP. While far from luxurious, the rooms are quite comfortable and the club's waterfront restaurant and bar is justifiably popular and a good place for a meal and for watching the sunset. Of course the yacht club also has moorings, a laundry and washing facilities for visiting yachties.

The Motu Staying on a motu ensures tranquillity, a complete escape and great views.

Motu Tane Dream Island (☎/fax 67 74 50) is on tiny four-hectare Motu Tane, very close to the airport motu at the northern end of the lagoon. There's a fine beach and good swimming. The house was built by French polar explorer Paul-Émile Victor and, since his death in 1995, has been run by his widow Teva and their sons. The two *fare* each have a double bedroom, living-and-dining room, equipped kitchen and hot-water bathroom. The cost for one or two people is 20,500 CFP; there is a minimum three night stay and credit cards are accepted. Airport transfers are included and snorkelling equipment, pedal boats, kayaks and bicycles are provided. The first shopping trip to Vaitape is free; after that it's 2000 CFP return.

Le Paradis (☎/fax 67 75 53), on Motu Paahi, the next island to the south, is probably the most affordable motu resort. There are five local-style *fare* in a lagoonside coconut plantation. Bathroom facilities are shared and rooms cost 5000 CFP per person. Two *fare* with private bathroom cost 15,000 CFP for up to three people. Half-board adds 2900 CFP per person. Airport transfers are included, transport to Vaitape costs 1000 CFP per person and island tours are offered for 4000 CFP (half-day) or 6000 CFP (all day including picnic lunch). Credit cards are accepted.

Mai Moana Island (☎ 67 62 45, fax 67 62 39) on Motu Ite, a few islands south, also has a dreamlike setting. Run by a retired Polish film-maker (relax, he speaks French and English), its three big bungalows have hot water and TV. Costs for two people are

28,000/32,000 CFP in the low/high season, including breakfast and airport transfers. Lunch costs 1500 CFP to 3000 CFP, dinner 3500 CFP. Twice daily there's a free boat-transfer to Vaitape. Credit cards are accepted.

Bora Bora Lagoon Resort (☎ 60 40 02, fax 60 40 03, email bblr@mail.pf) is on Motu Toopua, looking across the lagoon to Vaitape and across the Teavanui Pass, the only real entry into the lagoon. The resort, one of the most luxurious on the island, has garden/beach units for 52,000/55,000 CFP and over-water units (with glass-top tables that you can retract to feed the fish) for 82,000 CFP. For this price you get almost every luxury in the book and the resort has a swimming pool, tennis courts, gymnasium, boutiques and canoes and pedal boats for guests' use. There are restaurants and bars, and traditional dance performances twice a week. Three meals adds 11,000 CFP per person per day. Between the resort and the main island a shuttle boat operates every half-hour from 8 am to midnight, from the base just north of the centre of Vaitape.

On Motu Tevairoa, on the other side of the Teavanui Pass, **Bora Bora Pearl Beach Resort** (☎ 43 16 10, fax 43 17 86, email info@SPMhotels.pf) has luxurious bungalows constructed of natural materials. Expect to pay 49,680/56,160/64,800 CFP for beach/over-water/premium bungalows. Add 10,000 CFP for all meals. There's a magnificent swimming pool with a cascade and an over-water restaurant. Traditional dance performances are held three times weekly and there's a shuttle every 45 minutes between 8.15 am and 10 pm, operating from the yacht club.

Sofitel Marara has a brand-new offspring, **Sofitel Motu** (☎ 67 70 46, fax 67 74 03) on Motu Piti Uu Uta, five minutes by dugout from the Marara. The 30 bungalows on the tiny island are perched on a hillside, scattered among the coconut trees, on the beach or over water, enjoying fine views of Mt Otemanu or of the lagoon. Polynesian architecture hides air-con, satellite TV and computer modems. There's a restaurant with a panoramic view, a sunset bar and regular shuttle boats from Sofitel Marara.

On Motu Tofari, the long motu on the eastern side of the lagoon, **Méridien Bora Bora** (☎ 60 51 51, fax 60 51 52, email sales@lemeridien-tahiti.com) combines a novel style with a unique site offering an unaccustomed view of Mt Otemanu. Beach bungalows are 62,400 CFP, while over-water bungalows (distributed like an amphitheatre around the lagoon, with vast glass floors) cost 76,680 CFP. Half/full board adds 7000/10,800 CFP per person. The design draws elements from all over the Pacific and the fish-shaped swimming pool is a particular success. There's a huge lobby with a pool of water lilies, two restaurants – Tipanié and Te Ava – as well as the overwater Miki Miki bar. Traditional dance performances take place three times a week. There's a shuttle boat to and from Anau on the main island from 8 am to midnight.

Places to Eat

It may be a popular tourist spot but Bora Bora still goes to bed early – most restaurants (and the choice isn't particularly varied) firmly shut the door at 9 pm. A number of restaurants, including Bloody Mary's, Bamboo House, La Bounty and L'Espadon at the Revatua Club, offer a free transfer service, collecting you from and returning you to your hotel. The buffet dinners and Polynesian dance performances in the luxury hotels are well worth the expense of 4000 CFP to 6000 CFP per person and these hotels also welcome visitors to their bars and restaurants. There are several small supermarkets for those who prefer to prepare their own food.

Vaitape & Around There are no real restaurant possibilities in Vaitape but there are a number of good places for breakfast, a snack or a cheap meal. **L'Appetisserie** (☎ 67 78 88) is a very pleasant little open-air snack bar and pâtisserie in the Commercial Centre near the wharf. It's certainly the most sophisticated place in town for breakfast or a snack. You can start the day with a 110 CFP croissant or a 150 CFP pain aux raisins, and at lunchtime quiche, a pizza slice or a croque-monsieur costs 380 CFP to

420 CFP and the *plat du jour* (dish of the day) is 1250 CFP. The ice creams are great at any time of the day for 140 CFP to 240 CFP. L'Appetisserie is open Monday to Saturday from 6 am to 5.30 pm (to 2 pm Wednesday) and Sunday 5.30 am to noon. This is also the Bora Bora Internet centre and you can send or receive email messages most mornings.

Near the Banque de Polynésie, a little farther south, *Brasserie Manuia* (π 67 67 43) offers breakfast for 1050 CFP, sandwiches for 400 CFP to 700 CFP, grilles for 800 CFP to 1300 CFP and salads for around 900 CFP. A beer costs 350 CFP. It's closed on Monday. Facing it is the *Snack Bora Bora Burger*, which is very busy at lunchtime because the burgers are cheap.

On the inland side of the road, facing the hospital, the simple *Snack Richard* specialises in Chinese takeaways like lemon chicken for 800 CFP, fried wontons for 1000 CFP and Chinese *poisson cru* (raw fish) for 750 CFP. It's open from Tuesday to Saturday for lunch or in the evening. Next to the pharmacy, *Pizza Bora* (π 67 68 00) does pizzas for 1000 CFP to 1450 CFP and waffles for 250 CFP to 450 CFP. It's open Tuesday to Saturday from 10 am to 1 pm and 5 to 8 pm. On the northern side of the town, *Le Cocotier* snack bar is another Chinese specialist, with dishes such as chow mein for 1200 CFP. In the evenings several *roulottes* take up positions across from the artist market and serve simple dishes for less than 1000 CFP.

Blue Lagoon (π 67 65 64), about 1km south of Vaitape, has a great setting and the lowest prices on the island. There's a pleasant terrace beside the lagoon, perfect for catching the sunset, and it's one of the few places open really late, until 2 am. For a hearty dish of well prepared shark or peppered ray, the bill won't top 2000 CFP. Crayfish is 1500 CFP and poisson cru in coconut milk is just 500 CFP, probably the cheapest in all of French Polynesia. Pizzas and *flammeküche* (a speciality from the Alsace region: a thin layer of pastry topped with cream, onion and bacon) are just 1000 CFP and beer is pleasantly cheap. Free

transfers are offered at any time and delivery to your accommodation is possible but credit cards are not accepted.

North of Vaitape, after the Total petrol station, *Topdive* (π 60 50 50) resort has a restaurant open for breakfast, lunch and dinner. The lagoonside restaurant has an open terrace but the setting is bland and the prices are rather high. Pastas cost from 1860 CFP and main courses are 2580 CFP to 3300 CFP.

Vaitape has several well supplied supermarkets. On the northern side of town there's *Cash Api* and 50m farther there's *Nunue*. *Chin Lee* is across from the Pahia Commercial Centre. The supermarkets are generally open Monday to Saturday from 6 am to 6.30 pm, and for a few hours on Sunday morning. Credit cards are accepted.

Vaitape to Hotel Bora Bora This stretch includes the two best-known restaurants on Bora Bora if not the whole of French Polynesia, both on the inland side of the coast road.

Bamboo House Restaurant (π 67 76 24) is about 3.5km from Vaitape towards Matira Point. It's a pleasant and well run restaurant noted for its service and bamboo-dominated architecture and furniture. Seafood dishes include freshwater shrimp in green pepper with ravioli for 2800 CFP, and fettuccini and other pasta dishes from 1500 CFP. There's a good tourist menu for 3800 CFP and wines priced from 1900 CFP. The restaurant provides free transport, accepts credit cards and is open for lunch and dinner daily.

Bloody Mary's (π 67 72 86), 5km from Vaitape (or 1km before Hotel Bora Bora), is the island's best-known restaurant and one of the best-known in the Pacific. It's very pricey and inordinately proud of its list of celebrities who have dined here. The décor is planned to look island-like, with a sandy floor, coconut-tree-stump chairs and a thatched roof.

Set lunch menus will cost you 900 CFP to 1400 CFP, or there's sashimi and poisson cru in coconut milk for 800 CFP or 900 CFP. At dinner you choose your seafood, very fresh and on ice, and the chef grills it for you; one variety of fish costs 2400 CFP and the price steps up to 4000 CFP for lobster. Wines start from 2000 CFP. Dinner for two can easily cost 12,000 CFP to 15,000 CFP. Free transport is provided from anywhere between Vaitape and Club Med. It's closed on Sunday and credit cards are accepted.

Matira Point There are places to eat on both sides of the point. If you want to prepare your own food, the well stocked *Tiare Market*, across from the Bora Bora Motel, is the only supermarket on this side of the island. It's open Monday to Saturday from 6.30 am to 1.30 pm and 3 to 7 pm, as well as Sunday from 6.30 am to 1 pm and 3 to 6.30 pm.

Restaurants Restaurant Matira (☎ 67 70 51), between Hotel Bora Bora and Matira Point, has a magnificent location, right on the beach with superb views over the lagoon. The cuisine is Chinese with very reasonable prices such as duck tamarind for 1500 CFP, fish wontons for 1000 CFP and salads from 400 CFP to 1000 CFP. Snacks cost about 950 CFP and free transport is offered anywhere between Hotel Bora Bora and Anau.

Immediately beyond the turn-off and the Moana Beach Parkroyal is *Temanuata* *(☎ 67 62 47)*, in a garden setting at the guesthouse of the same name. It is bright and cheerful and features bamboo furnishings and glimpses of the nearby lagoon. Salad dishes are 600 CFP to 1150 CFP, meat or pasta dishes cost from 1300 CFP and there are no less than 18 different fish dishes for 1500 CFP to 2090 CFP. There are also Chinese dishes and you can get breakfast for 850 CFP. Credit cards are accepted but with an extra 2.5% charge. It's open Monday to Saturday and free transport is offered anywhere between Vaitape and Anau.

Between Maitai Polynesia and Bora Bora Motel is *La Bounty Restaurant (☎ 67 70 43)*, a popular place with fish specialities such as delicious *mahi mahi* (dolphin fish - nothing to do with dolphins!) with vanilla sauce and raspberry vinegar for 1450 CFP, meat dishes from 1150 CFP, pizzas from 1050 CFP to 1450 CFP and pasta dishes from 900 CFP to 1200 CFP. The restaurant

is a pleasant open *fare* although the furniture is rather unattractive plastic. It's open Monday to Saturday for snacks at lunchtime and for dinner. Credit cards are accepted.

All the luxury hotels have dance performances with buffet dinners several times a week. Expect to spend 4000 CFP to 6500 CFP. Hotel Bora Bora's *Matira Terrace (☎ 60 44 60)* offers excellent food in a romantic open-air setting looking out over the point. The prices are fairly reasonable. Lunch dishes cost 1400 CFP to 2400 CFP. Dinner could be seafood on a nest of tagliatelle for 2100 CFP or other fish dishes from 2500 CFP. Desserts start timidly at 900 CFP. The grand gourmet dinner menu costs 5300 CFP and the once-weekly buffet and dance performance costs 5850 CFP.

Noa Noa (☎ 60 49 00) at the Moana Beach Parkroyal has an especially attractive setting right on the lagoon. Among the various fish dishes is mahi mahi cooked in papaya butter for 2700 CFP. There's a lighter lunchtime menu. Moana Beach Parkroyal's three-times-weekly buffet and dance performance has a fine reputation, particularly the 'soirée merveilleuse'. It costs 5100 CFP to 6250 CFP.

Haere Mai (☎ 60 30 00) restaurant at the Maitai Polynesia Bora Bora is on the inland side of the coast road. There's a daily set menu for 500 CFP and á la carte dishes for 2500 CFP to 4700 CFP. At lunchtime there's a buffet for 2200 CFP. The once-weekly buffet and dance performance is 5200 CFP.

La Pérouse (☎ 67 70 46) restaurant at Sofitel Marara has a lunchtime snack menu with sandwiches, burgers and several hot dishes. In the evening the menu is more elaborate, with fish dishes from 1600 CFP and meat dishes from 1700 CFP. The three-times-weekly buffet and dance performance is 4200 CFP.

Cafés & Snack Bars Between Hotel Bora Bora and Matira Point, *Ben's Place* is a popular little vegetation-fringed open-air café with a straightforward menu. Poisson cru in coconut milk is 950 CFP, sashimi is 1800 CFP and burgers are 500 CFP to 700 CFP. There are Mexican dishes like fajitas for 1000 CFP to 1300 CFP, quesadillas for 650 CFP and tacos at 680 CFP. Count on 1700 CFP for a steak. Opening hours are variable although it should be open from 9 am to 8 pm daily except Tuesday, Thursday and Sunday, when it closes mid-afternoon. Credit cards are accepted.

Beside the lagoon, just after Ben's Place, *Snack Matira*, also known as *Chez Julie*, is a simple place just a few steps from the beach. The prices are pleasantly low: only 500 CFP for a mahi mahi burger, 1000 CFP for a steak and French fries and 160 CFP for soft drink. Takeaways are available and it's open daily, except Monday, from 10 am to 6 pm.

Right on the beach, the modest *Snack de la Plage* enjoys a remarkable site with views of the Sofitel motu and Raiatea and Tahaa. You can enjoy the setting for a modest price: poisson cru is 950 CFP, a hamburger 450 CFP and soft drinks are 150 CFP. It's open daily for lunch and dinner.

Across the road, inland from the Snack de la Plage, *La Rôtisserie* is a minuscule *fare* where you can get takeaway chicken dishes from 1200 CFP and sandwiches for 350 CFP to 400 CFP. It's open Monday to Saturday from 9 am to 6 pm.

Near the Sofitel bungalows but on the inland side of the road, *Snack Patoti* has a small but interesting menu with dishes such as grilled tuna for 1300 CFP, lemon chicken for 1200 CFP, chow mein for 1200 CFP and fishburgers for 800 CFP. In the morning breakfast is available from 780 CFP. It's open Monday to Saturday from 7.30 am to 2 pm and 6 to 9 pm.

Matira Point to Vaitape From Matira Point right round to Vaitape, moving in an anticlockwise direction, there are only a couple of places to eat, apart from local shops and snack bars. Either makes a good dinner excursion, if you have transport, or a good place for a lunch stop during a circuit of the island.

On the north-eastern side of the island, Revatua Club (☎ 67 71 67) is 16km from Vaitape in either direction and 9km from Matira Point. *L'Espadon Restaurant* is on the lagoonside and has a good reputation for

fish and seafood dishes. A seafood selection for two costs 8500 CFP. At lunchtime there are light snacks from 1000 CFP. Credit cards are accepted and transport can be arranged.

The final alternative is *Bora Bora Yacht Club* (☎ 67 70 69, 67 71 50), with a pleasant waterfront setting and a cool and breezy bar with nautical decorations. The food has a good reputation and includes fish with Tahaa vanilla for 2700 CFP, mahi mahi and mussels with saffron sauce for 3100 CFP and prawns in coconut-milk curry for 2500 CFP. Or you could simply enjoy a sunset drink on the open-air deck. Credit cards are accepted.

The Motu Free shuttles, which generally operate until midnight, allow you to enjoy the restaurants at the luxury hotels on the motu. Like their competitors on the main island, they offer evening performances with dinner buffets several times a week. Reservations are advisable.

On the eastern side of the island, Méridien has the superb surfboard-shaped *Tipanié* (☎ 60 51 51) restaurant right by the lagoon. Every evening there's a different set menu for 5100 CFP to 6100 CFP or you can order à la carte. There's a smaller restaurant beside the swimming pool. The shuttle operates from the Anau wharf.

Otemanu (☎ 60 40 02) restaurant at the Bora Bora Lagoon Resort challenges the superlatives; this is probably the most chic spot on the island. Perched over the lagoon, you can enjoy a wonderful candlelit dinner as you watch the sun set. The prices match the romance: meat dishes are 3000 CFP to 3650 CFP, fish dishes 2200 CFP to 3950 CFP and desserts start from 1250 CFP. Shuttles operate from the Vaitape wharf.

Bora Bora Pearl Beach Resort has two lagoonside restaurants with Mt Otemanu as a backdrop. The one beside the magnificent swimming pool offers a light menu until mid-afternoon, with dishes such as a mahi mahi burger for 1250 CFP and desserts for 950 CFP. The main restaurant, on stilts over the lagoon, has a fancier menu starting from 1700 CFP for meat dishes, from 2350 CFP for fish dishes. Its shuttle leaves from the yacht club, to the north of Vaitape.

Entertainment

Apart from dance performances at the big hotels, Bora Bora does not have a lot of night life.

Bars Any of the island's luxury hotels will provide a good cold beer or a reasonably priced cocktail (1000 CFP to 1300 CFP) in an attractive lagoonside setting. Some even have happy hours and the motu hotels offer free shuttle services, usually until about midnight.

Probably the most evocatively Pacific place on the island would be the waterside bar of *Bora Bora Yacht Club*, just past the Farepiti dock towards Vaitape. Sitting and watching the yachts at anchor and the motu on the lagoon edge is just perfect. On the opposite side of the island, the bar at the *Revatua Club* also has a great waterside setting. The famous *Bloody Mary's* is a good late-night hangout.

On the edge of Vaitape heading towards Matira Point, *Blue Lagoon* has an unexciting setting but there's a pleasant terrace and beer is just 600 CFP for a half-litre. Several of the roadside snack bars cater to a local clientele and come sunset will often have someone strumming on a guitar as another round of cans or bottles is passed out.

Dance Performances & Discos Don't miss a traditional dance performance by a local group in one of the luxury hotels. You can usually get in for the price of a drink at the bar, or for around 6000 CFP you can also enjoy the evening with a buffet dinner. Performances are two or three times weekly; ask at the reception desks about the schedule and their entry policy. *Sofitel Marara* and *Moana Beach Parkroyal* are the most costly, but there are also performances at *Hotel Bora Bora*, *Maitai Polynesia*, *Méridien*, *Bora Bora Pearl Beach Resort* and *Bora Bora Lagoon Resort*.

Otherwise prepare yourself for some very quiet evenings after dinner. The only other night-time entertainment worthy of the name is the Club Med disco, which is open to all for 2300 CFP. Entry includes one drink and it operates until the heady hour of 11.30 pm! Club Med's evening show, part Club Med staff and part Club Med guests, can be side-splitting. The large Japanese contingent on Bora Bora can make for an over-the-top evening – they really let their hair down.

Shopping

Art, Crafts & Pareu Centre Artisanal de Bora Bora in the tourist office by the Vaitape wharf has *pareu* (sarong-like garments), basketwork and other crafts produced by island women. Above Snack Bora Bora Burger, Pakalola Boutique sells pareu, crafts and pearls. In the Pahia Commercial Centre, Pacific Sud Boutique is a good place to find T-shirts and other clothing. Patine, in front of the Nunue store, to the north of Vaitape, has some interesting local clothing designs.

Boutique Gauguin (☎ 67 76 67), next to Bamboo House Restaurant, sells pareu, clothes, crafts and sculptures. Arts of the Pacific, just after the Bamboo House Restaurant, sells local artwork, hand-painted clothes, sculptures from the Marquesas, bronze and coral sculptures and ceramic work. Honeymoon Boutique (☎ 67 78 19), 100m before Village Pauline, offers a variety of Pacific crafts including clothes, perfumed *monoi* oils, engraved mother-of-pearl work, sculptures from the Marquesas and pearls. The Chez Alain & Linda Galerie d'Art (☎ 67 70 32) is on the lagoonside, close to the turn-off to the cross-island road via the telephone tower. It has clothes and original art including paintings, sculptures and ceramics. Moana Arts (☎ 67 75 06), just before Hotel Bora Bora, sells souvenirs and curios. Just after Club Med, Boutique Hibiscus (☎ 67 72 43) has everything from craft work and wood sculptures to hair oil, pareu and T-shirts.

Pearls The Sibani black pearl specialists have jewellery shops in the Pahia Commercial Centre in Vaitape and several hotels. Herman Perles also has a Vaitape outlet. The Office Polynésien d'Expertise et de Commercialisation (OPEC) has a showroom next to the Bamboo House

Restaurant. Matira Pearls, just after the Matira Point turn-off, has a vast assortment of mounted and unmounted black pearls and the owner speaks English.

Getting There & Away
Bora Bora is 270km north-west of Tahiti, only 15km north-west of Tahaa.

Air Air Tahiti (☎ 67 70 35, ☎ 67 70 85) connects Bora Bora five to nine times daily with Papeete, sometimes direct in about 45 minutes, other times via Moorea, Huahine, Raiatea or some combination of those islands. There are twice-weekly connections with Maupiti. One-way adult fares to or from Bora Bora are: Huahine 6500 CFP, Maupiti 5300 CFP, Moorea 16,000 CFP, Papeete 12,400 CFP and Raiatea 5100 CFP. Flying into Bora Bora, the left side of the aircraft usually offers the best views of the spectacular scenery.

Bora Bora has the only connections to the Tuamotus apart from via Papeete, with flights to Rangiroa (one hour and 20 minutes, 20,700 CFP) with an onward connection to Manihi (23,400 CFP). Flights operate to Rangiroa three times a week but in the reverse direction only once a week.

The Air Tahiti office is on the wharf at Vaitape and is open weekdays from 7.30 to 11.30 am and 1.30 to 4.30 pm, and Saturday from 8 to 11 am.

Boat Inter-island boats dock at the Farepiti wharf, 3km from Vaitape.

The high-speed *Ono-Ono* (☎ 67 78 00 or ☎ 45 35 35 on Tahiti) zips out to Bora Bora three times a week from Tahiti, taking as little as seven hours for the trip with stops en route at Huahine, Raiatea and Tahaa. The fares to Bora Bora are: 6676 CFP from Tahiti, 3142 CFP from Huahine, 1795 CFP from Raiatea and 1346 CFP from Tahaa. The cargo ship *Vaeanu* is cheaper but much less luxurious and makes three trips a week between Papeete and the Leeward Islands. See the Getting Around chapter for more details on the *Ono-Ono* and *Vaeanu*.

The *Maupiti Express* (☎ 67 66 69) makes regular trips between Bora Bora and Maupiti,

departing the Vaitape wharf at 8.30 am on Thursday and Saturday and arriving at Maupiti at 10 am. The return departure is at 4 pm the same day. The fare is 2000/3000 CFP one way/return and it's possible to spend a day on Maupiti.

Getting Around
To/From the Airport The airport is on Motu Mute at the northern edge of the lagoon and free transfers are made to and from the Vaitape wharf on two large catamaran ferries. You need to be at the wharf at least 1¼ hours before the flight departure. Some hotels transfer their visitors directly to and from the airport; others pick them up at the wharf.

Le Truck Although there's no really regular le truck service there often seems to be one going somewhere at the appropriate times, particularly for flight and boat departures. There's a regular service for Village Pauline (300 CFP) and the Matira Point guesthouses (500 CFP).

Car, Scooter & Bicycle Europcar (☎ 67 70 15, 67 70 03, fax 67 79 95) has a main agency (open 8 am to 6 pm) opposite the wharf in the centre of Vaitape, and desks in several of the main hotels. Vehicles can be rented for two, four, eight and 24-hour periods. A tiny Fiat Panda costs 7200 CFP for 24 hours. Fredo Rent-a-Car (☎ 67 70 31, fax 67 62 07) is also in Vaitape and at several hotels and charges 8000 CFP for 24 hours. Fare Piti Rent-a-Car (☎ 67 65 28, fax 67 65 29), in Faanui and across from Sofitel Marara, is open Monday to Saturday and has cars for 6700 CFP.

Scooters and bicycles are also available: Fredo has scooters for 6000 CFP a day, Fare Piti for 5200 CFP and Village Pauline for 4500 CFP. Bora Bora's back roads cry out for a mountain bike but many of the bicycles available are either French village single-speeders or American-style cruisers. You will find bikes for rent at Europcar for 1800 CFP, Fredo for 1500 CFP and Fare Piti for 1580 CFP. Village Pauline rents out bicycles for 1000 CFP for eight hours but they're not very good. There's a Total petrol station north of Vaitape, just before the Top-dive resort, but it's not open on weekends.

Boat, Kayak & Jetski Renting a boat is a good way to explore the lagoon. René & Maguy (☎ 67 60 61, fax 67 61 01), next to La Bounty restaurant, rents out outboard-powered boats for 6360 CFP for three hours, 7420/10,600 CFP for a half/full day including fuel. They seat up to four passengers

and snorkelling equipment is included as well as an icebox with water.

Village Pauline has kayaks for 1000 CFP per hour.

Miki Miki Jet Ski (☎ 67 76 44) is shortly before the Maitai Polynesia, coming from Vaitape, and rents out jetskis for 15,000 CFP for two-hour excursions, while Matira Jet Tours (☎ 67 62 73), on Matira Point be-tween Chez Nono and Chez Robert & Tina, charges 13,000 CFP for a similar trip.

Maupiti

The smallest and most isolated of the Society high islands, Maupiti is a miniature version of Bora Bora. Like its beautiful big sister, just 40km to the east, Maupiti has impressive soaring rocky peaks with slopes tumbling down to the lagoon, cloaked in the waving green of coconut plantations. Like Bora Bora it has a shimmering, shallow lagoon edged by a string of motu flaunting luxuriously white sand beaches. The difference is size: it's 32km around Bora Bora's coastal road, just 10km around Maupiti's.

Maupiti is like Bora Bora once was – it's more authentically Polynesian and much more low key, perhaps too low key for some tastes. Apart from guesthouses, Maupiti has hardly any tourist infrastructure – cars have yet to supplant scooters and bicycles. Visit Maupiti for quiet, tranquillity and isolation. Agricultural work on the motu, fishing on the lagoon, working on the pearl farms and church services set the pace of life. Although TV has taken its toll on village life, the homes still have a traditional touch, often with the family tombs right in the front yard.

Easily accessible from Bora Bora, Raiatea and Tahiti, Maupiti offers a different facet of Polynesia, well off the beaten track.

History

Like Raiatea, Maupiti has enjoyed great cultural importance and chiefs from other islands used to come here for ceremonial purposes. Archaeological investigations on Motu Paeao, at the northern end of the lagoon, revealed fish hooks and other items dating back to around 850 AD. Their similarity to objects discovered in New Zealand has played a part in the theories on Polynesian migration. This is one of the oldest archaeological sites in the Society Islands.

The European 'discovery' of Maupiti is credited to the Dutch explorer Roggeveen in 1722, nearly 50 years before Wallis, Bougainville and Cook made their important landfalls on Tahiti. Early in the 19th century the island came under the influence

pop: 1271
area: 11 sq km
reef passes: 1
highest point: Mt Teurafaatiu (380m)

- Tour the magnificent lagoon by boat
- Laze on Teria Beach
- Escape to a motu – get dropped off for a day
- Climb Mt Teurafaatiu for the view over the lagoon

of Bora Bora, but European missionaries brought another power struggle, eventually installing Protestantism as the major religion. Later in the century another struggle blew up with Bora Bora over control of the remote Scilly Atoll. French influence first touched the island during this period but missionaries and local chiefs continued to wield power until after WWII.

Maupiti has managed to remain remarkably untouched by mass tourism. The tricky Onoiau Pass, site of a number of shipwrecks over the years, is frequently suggested as one of the reasons for Maupiti's lack of tourist development, but it's just as likely to be because the islanders simply aren't too keen on being overrun.

Growing watermelons on the motu is a major source of income for the islanders. Copra production, heavily subsidised by the government, remains important but recently much energy has gone into producing pearl oysters on the atoll of Mopelia, which is treated as an extension of Maupiti. These are sold to Tuamotuans to be transported back for pearl production on those islands.

The devastating cyclone Oséa ravaged the island in late 1997 and many houses have been replaced by dull new Maison Territoriale de Reconstruction (MTR) buildings,

MAUPITI

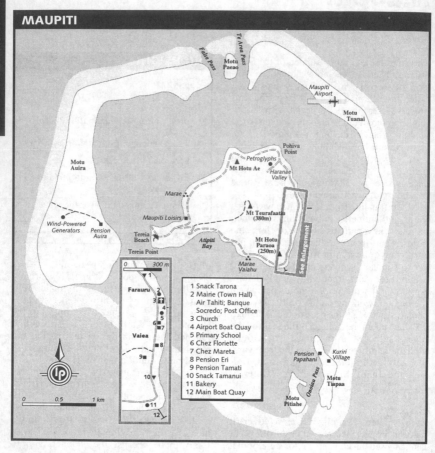

MAUPITI

1 Snack Tarona
2 Mairie (Town Hall)
   Air Tahiti; Banque
   Socredo; Post Office
3 Church
4 Airport Boat Quay
5 Primary School
6 Chez Floriette
7 Chez Mareta
8 Pension Eri
9 Pension Tamati
10 Snack Tamanui
11 Bakery
12 Main Boat Quay

which do have the virtue of being built to withstand winds of 200km/h.

Orientation

Maupiti is very easy to come to terms with. There's one road that encircles the island, only deviating from the coastline for a short stretch, where it climbs over the ridgeline running down to Tereia Point. On the east coast of the island the string of houses along the road technically constitutes two villages, Farauru to the north and Vaiea to the south but in practise the island's single real village is just one long main street, the only bit of

paved road on the island. The main shipping quay is at the south-eastern corner of the island, directly across from Onoiau Pass. The small airport quay is halfway up the eastern side of the island, just south of the church.

Inland the terrain climbs steeply to the summit of Mt Teurafaatiu (380m), also known as Mt Nuupure, but the most conspicuous feature is the sharp ridgeline running north-south, overlooking the village. The high island mass is encircled by a wide but very shallow lagoon. The motu that fringe the lagoon equal the main island's area. Villagers grow watermelons on Motu

Auira and on Motu Tuanai, which is where the airport is. At the southern end of the lagoon, two smaller motu, Motu Tiapaa and Motu Pitiahe, flank Maupiti's single accessible pass. There's only one beach on the island, at Tereia Point, but the motu have fine white-sand beaches.

Information

Just to the north of the village centre is the *mairie* (town hall) and the post, Air Tahiti and Banque Socredo offices, all together in one neat little group. The post office is open from 7.30 am to 12.30 pm on weekdays (to 3 pm on Tuesday). The bank is open only when a representative comes to the island, so don't plan to change money.

Around the Island

It's just under 10km right around the island, including the little side trip to Tereia Beach, so it's easy to walk it in a couple of hours. The road is paved only for a kilometre or so through the village. The neat village houses, brightened with hibiscus, are strung along the road and often have *uru* (breadfruit) trees shading the family tombs that front many of the houses. The following tour starts in the village and proceeds around the island in an anticlockwise direction.

Petroglyphs Leave the village towards the north, round the point and pass the church basketball court. You're now in the Haranae Valley and just before the sign for Tahiti Yacht Charter, on the mountain side and just after a green house, is a track heading inland. Follow it to a small pumping station about 200m inland. From here follow the rocky riverbed, which may have water in it during the wet season. After only 100m, on the left, you'll find boulders in the stream cut with petroglyphs. The biggest and most impressive is a turtle image on a flat boulder just to the right of the stream. If you follow the rocky riverbed farther inland for a few hundred metres it leads to a ruined **marae**.

Tereia Beach Lying between Tereia and Puoroo points, at the western end of the is-

land, Tereia Beach is the finest on the island. It's easy to walk right across the lagoon to **Motu Auira**, particularly at low tide. Beware of **rays** lying in the sand, although they usually shoot away when they sense your approach.

Continuing around the island, the coast road climbs up over the low ridgeline running down to the point, then drops down to Atipiti Bay on the south side of the island.

Marae Vaiahu Just north-west of the main quay is the area known as **Tefarearii** (The House of the Kings). The island's nobility once lived here and Maupiti's most important marae is a large coastal site with a wide expanse of paving-like stones and a rectangular 'fish box' used for ceremonial purposes to ensure successful fishing.

Made of coral blocks, the box has four stones representing four different kinds of fish. Traditionally, the marae guards would put a stone fish in the box to invoke the god of fishing before the canoes set out on fishing expeditions.

Just beyond the marae a sheer rockface rises up beside the road, overlooking the shipping quay at the south-eastern corner of the island. There are traces of a *pa* (fortification) atop this imposing outcrop.

Motu

The island guesthouses will organise picnic trips to Maupiti's untouched and idyllic motu. Motu Paeao, at the northern end of the lagoon, was the site for the important archaeological discovery of a series of 1000 year old burial sites.

Motu Paeao has False Pass to its west and the Te Area (Hiro's) Pass to its east, both of which are unnavigable. An island legend relates that Hiro tried to create this pass under the cover of night, using his mighty canoe to plough through the reef. He had already neatly chopped the island of Huahine in two by exactly the same method. Unfortunately for Hiro, an island warrior discovered his plan and hid nearby with his well-trained rooster. At a signal from the warrior the cock crowed and Hiro, thinking dawn was about to break, sailed away.

Walking

Above the Village Although it doesn't take you to the highest point on the island, the short climb to the ridge above Vaiea and Farauru gives excellent views over the lagoon and straight down to the village, right beneath your feet.

A spectacularly rocky ridge parallels the village road. From the village look up to the final rocky pillar, ending right at the southeastern corner of the island, directly above the main dock. At the north end of the pillar is a clump of coconut palms. Just north of the clump is a single palm, then a small saddle, then another clump of palms marking the southern end of the next rocky pillar. In less than an hour (30 minutes if you're fit and in a hurry) you can be up there. The trail is not always clear; it may be a good idea to get one of the village children to show you the way.

Head south past Pension Eri and you'll see a very clear track heading inland. After about 100m veer right and start climbing straight up the hillside. The trail can be faint at times but it's generally quite easy to follow. About halfway up, about 100m above sea level, there's a small rock strip to clamber over, but apart from this it's almost all walk rather than climb. You're soon rewarded with the first views back over the village – the church already toy-like below. The trail, now much clearer, bends off south and ascends the slope to arrive at the saddle between the two rocky outcrops.

You can follow the trail north or south. The southern extension takes you to the clump of palms, from where there are views of the dock and the southern end of the village. The northern extension and a bit of clambering will take you to the northern end of the rocky outcrop towering over the main part of the village. Going farther in either direction will involve real climbing. From the top there are views of Bora Bora and beyond to Raiatea and Tahaa. If it's clear you may be able to spot low-lying Tupai to the north of Bora Bora.

Mt Teurafaatiu It's a superb climb to the 380m summit of Mt Teurafaatiu. Allow three hours for the return trip and bring plenty of drinking water, or a good knife for opening coconuts. It's wise to take a guide as the trail is often indistinct.

The walk starts from where the road crosses the ridge above Tereia Point. From the apex of the corner the track starts straight up the ridge, which it follows most of the way to the peak.

At first there are views over the northern lagoon and higher up a short detour offers views to the south. Eventually the track hits the steep outcrop of the peak and traverses around to the south side, with some short stretches requiring real climbing. As you approach the top there are wonderful views over the three motu at the northern edge of the lagoon and the airport runway, jutting out into the lagoon. This is a fine spot to watch an Air Tahiti flight arrive.

The rocky summit offers a 360° perspective but you can drop down into the saddle and climb up again to the actual high point, with even better views to the north and of the long, rocky ridge running down to the main island's south-eastern corner. A final small summit stands directly above the village.

Swimming & Snorkelling

Maupiti has a magnificent lagoon with many coral pinnacles and dense fish populations, particularly around the Onoiau Pass. There are superb snorkelling sites and beautiful beaches for picnics. The island guesthouses will arrange excursions and organise lagoon tours with snorkelling stops for around 2000 CFP. The picnics are extra. Alternatively contact Richard (☎ 67 80 62) at Tahiti Yacht Charter, to the north of the village, who organises half-day lagoon tours including snorkelling stops for 2000 CFP or 3000 CFP with lunch. A Mt Teurafaatiu climb costs 1000 CFP per person.

Places to Stay

There are fewer places to stay on Maupiti after cyclone Oséa. There are no 'hotels' on Maupiti – everything is family-style although the motu resorts are a little more sophisticated. Most visitors opt for *demi-pension* (half-board – a room plus breakfast and dinner), or *pension* (full board – all meals). There's only one place with hot water and credit cards haven't arrived at Maupiti either – make sure you have enough cash.

The Island None of the village guesthouses has any sort of identifying sign, but anybody from the village will point them out. They're all either right on the lagoon or very close to it. All prices quoted in this section are per person.

Just south of the primary school, *Chez Mareta (☎ 67 80 25)* has a peaked blue roof and is the cheapest place on the island. Three very basic rooms sharing a bathroom cost 1000 CFP; 1500/3000 CFP with breakfast/half-board.

Next door, *Chez Floriette (☎ 67 80 85)* is the most popular of the village guesthouses, although part of it was destroyed in the cyclone. At the moment there's a bungalow costing 4500/5500 CFP with half/full board, including airport transfers. Motu excursions with a picnic lunch are organised for 1000 CFP.

Pension Eri (☎ 67 81 29), 200m south and also on the lagoon side of the road, is a well-run place with four rooms sharing bathrooms, kitchen and living room. Half/full board costs 4500/5000 CFP. Kayaks are available for 500 CFP for a half day, bicycles for 1000 CFP for a day and island tours by boat are regularly organised.

Pension Tamati (☎ 67 80 10), another 100m south and on the mountain side of the road, is a dismal-looking two-storey building with a veranda. Treat this nine room 'grande maison' as an emergency backup if everything else is full. The rooms at the front, looking towards Bora Bora, are best. Half/full board costs 4000/5000 CFP.

Simone Chan's pleasant *Maupiti Loisirs (☎ 67 80 95)* is close to Tereia Beach and has two rooms with shared bathroom for 2000 CFP. Add another 1000 CFP to use the kitchen facilities. Half/full board is 4000/5000 CFP. You can camp here but the

cost is the same. Airport transfers cost 1000 CFP return, an island tour by boat is 2000 CFP (3500 CFP with lunch) and an ascent of Mt Teurafaatiu is 1000 CFP.

The Motu The three places to stay on the motu exchange the low-key bustle of village life for the pleasures of isolated whitesand beaches on the lagoonside. If you want to return to 'civilisation', transfers to the main island are easily arranged, but the range of facilities and activities is very limited. Don't expect swimming pools, water-sports equipment or diving trips. Perperson prices are quoted here.

Pension Auira (☎/fax 67 80 26), on the eastern side of Motu Auira, is also known as Chez Edna. At low tide you can wade across to the mainland, as the deepest water is about waist high. There is a 'beach' bungalow at 8000 CFP half-board per person and very basic 'garden' bungalows at 7000 CFP; all the bungalows have attached toilet and shower. Lunch and airport transfers each cost 2000 CFP. There are plans to build more bungalows. Lagoon excursions with snorkelling and a picnic lunch are organised.

At the northern end of Motu Tiapaa, *Pension Papahani (☎ 67 81 58)*, BP 1, Vaiea, Maupiti, is right on the beach beside the pass. It's also known as Pension Vilna. There are two bungalows with bathroom for 6500/7500 CFP half/full board. Return transfers from the airport and island tours by boat cost 2000 CFP; mountain walks cost 1000 CFP.

Farther south and on the ocean side of the motu is Gérard and Evy Bede's *Kuriri Village (☎/fax 67 82 23, email hcc@tahiti.com)*, which is the only place on Maupiti aiming much above the budget-accommodation bracket. Traditionally styled bungalows with bathroom cost 9500/12,000 CFP half/full board. The bathrooms all feature internal gardens and open-air showers (one of them even has hot water!). The food at Kuriri Village has an excellent reputation and airport transfers are included in the accommodation price. The views across the reef-edge to Bora Bora are superb.

Places to Eat

The village has several small and simple snack bars, which are open irregular hours and carry uncertain provisions. Try **Snack Tarona** or **Chez Chanel** at the north end of the village or **Snack Tamanui** to the south. There are several small shops that sell basic supplies and soft drinks.

Getting There & Away

Maupiti is 320km west of Tahiti and just 40km west of Bora Bora.

Air Air Tahiti has about three flights a week between Papeete and Maupiti via Raiatea and/or Bora Bora. One-way adult fares from Maupiti are: Bora Bora 5300 CFP; Raiatea 5600 CFP; and Papeete 12,700 CFP. The Air Tahiti office (☎ 67 80 20, 67 81 24) is in the village beside the mairie and post office.

Boat Onoiau Pass, at the southern end of the lagoon, is the only entry point to the Maupiti lagoon and strong currents and a tricky sand-bar mean the narrow pass can be navigated only by smaller ships. Great care is required when attempting to enter the lagoon and ships are often forced to wait for the appropriate tidal conditions before it is safe to do so.

Maupiti Express (☎ 67 66 69), which is based on Bora Bora, travels to Maupiti on Thursday and Saturday for 2000/3000 CFP one way/return. Departing Vaitape (Bora Bora) at 8.30 am, the ship arrives at Maupiti at 10 am, then departs for the return trip at 4 pm and arrives at Bora Bora at 5.30 pm. The schedule allows enough time to have a good look around Maupiti and return to Bora Bora on the same day, although the crossing can be quite rough at times.

The rustic little *Maupiti To'u Aia* makes a once-weekly Papeete-Maupiti trip, via Raiatea on alternate weeks. See the Getting Around chapter earlier for more details.

There are semi-regular trips to Mopelia Atoll, far to the west. See the Other Leeward Islands chapter for more information on visiting Mopelia.

A Ship in Port

The arrival of a ship at Maupiti is a major event. Late one afternoon the small *Maupiti To'u Aia* zipped in through the pass, bustled importantly up to the quay and was fallen upon by what looked like half the population of the island. The other half sat down to watch the frenetic activity. Is there a Polynesian dockers' union? If so they were on holiday – everybody seemed to pitch in and most goods appeared to go straight into the hands of their owners. Bicycles were handed down off the stern while 3000-odd bottles of beer in cases of 20 went from hand to hand and into the back of a pick-up. An equal or even greater supply of soft drink followed a parallel route. Drums of fuel were rolled off the ship, across the dock and straight into waiting dinghies. Furniture was carried off on strong shoulders.

The working party was about equally divided between male and female. In between this confusing melee children ran back and forth while overhead the ship's crane nonchalantly swung bags of cement, bundles of water pipes, stacks of roofing iron and pallets of cement blocks. An hour or two later the activity was over and the docks were deserted once again.

Getting Around

To/From the Airport If you've booked accommodation you'll probably be met at the airport on Motu Tuanai – a necessity if you're staying on one of the motu. Motu transfers typically cost 1000 CFP to 2000 CFP return. The village guesthouses will usually meet their guests as well; nearly every household has a dinghy with an outboard motor. If there's no-one there to meet you, there's a boat that takes Air Tahiti staff and any hangers-on to the main island after the flight has departed. The one-way fare for the 15 minute trip is 400 CFP (children 200 CFP). The Air Tahiti boat also goes out to the airport motu for departing flights. Boat departure times are posted at the Air Tahiti office.

Bicycle Village guesthouses and Snack Tamanui rent bicycles for 500 CFP a half-day. Alternatively, you can count on about three hours to walk right around the island.

Boat It's a relatively simple operation to arrange a boat out to the motu from the village. Many of the village guesthouses organise a weekly motu picnic trip for a minimal cost. It's equally simple to get across to the main island from the motu. Count on 500 CFP to 1000 CFP between a motu and the main island or 2000 CFP for a lagoon excursion.

Other Leeward Islands

There are four other Leeward islands in the Society group, all of them atolls and three of them far to the west of the high islands of the Leeward group. All are important breeding grounds for green turtles, which lay eggs on the beaches from November each year.

Immediately north of Bora Bora is Tupai, very much under Bora Bora's influence. The other three islands come under Maupiti's aegis. Wallis, the first European to come upon Tahiti, sighted Mopelia and Scilly in 1767 as he continued west, but did not pause to investigate them further. Mopelia is the only one of these Leeward atolls with a pass for ships to enter its lagoon.

TUPAI

Ancient Polynesian beliefs held that the souls of the dead had to pass through Tupai on their way to the afterlife. Also known as Motu Iti, the 11 sq km atoll is only 16km north of Bora Bora and has a double lagoon. An outer reef encompasses a narrow lagoon, inside which is the circular atoll. Cloaked in coconut palms, the atoll's motu are used as Bora Bora copra plantations. There is an airstrip on the island but no pass big enough to allow ships to enter the lagoon.

MOPELIA

Mopelia (also known as Maupihaa) is an atoll treated very much as a possession of Maupiti, 160km to the south-east. The atoll is roughly circular, with a diameter of about 8km and an area of about 4 sq km.

In 1917 the German raider *Seeadler* (Sea Eagle) was wrecked on Mopelia when it paused for repairs. The ship's commander, Count Felix von Luckner, wrote an account of his Pacific adventure, *The Sea Devil*, which became a postwar best seller. One of the *Seeadler*'s cannons can be seen in Bougainville Park in the centre of Papeete.

Mopelia has a population of almost 100 people, stationed there purely to harvest pearl oysters, which are taken to Maupiti and then sold to pearl farmers. They, in turn, fly them to the Tuamotus, where they are implanted with seed pearls. The isolated island is home to many bird species and abundant turtles.

The atoll's tricky pass is just wide enough for small ships to enter. The *Maupiti To'u Aia* sails from Maupiti to Mopelia every two weeks. The overnight trip is followed by two days on the island. See the Getting Around chapter for details.

There is no formal accommodation on Mopelia so potential visitors must arrange to stay with one of the residents. This is usually organised through a friend or relation on Maupiti. The options are to stay two days, while the ship is in port, or two weeks, until the next visit. Yachts occasionally call into Mopelia – the only atoll in the Society Islands with a navigable pass.

SCILLY

Like Mopelia, the even more remote Scilly Atoll (also known as Manuae) is home to green turtles and oysters. Scilly is about 60km north-west of Mopelia and is covered in coconut palms. Although the atoll is about 15km in diameter, it has a land area of only about 4 sq km. In 1855 the three-mast *Julie Ann* was wrecked here and the crew and passengers, including 24 women and children, were marooned for two months before they managed to build a small boat and sail to Raiatea.

BELLINGSHAUSEN

Bellingshausen (also known as Motu One) was 'discovered' in 1824 by the Russian explorer of that name. Four low-lying islands, with a total area of about 3 sq km, encircle the reef but there is no entrance to the lagoon.

THE TUAMOTUS

TIARE

MANOLO MYLONAS

The Tuamotus

In the heart of French Polynesia, the Tuamotus are a world apart. The 77 atolls stretch 1500km north-west to south-east and 500km east to west. The closest islands are about 300km from Tahiti. These rings of coral are the posthumous witnesses to intense volcanic eruptions, scattered confetti on an ocean of ink.

Everything separates these atolls from the Society Islands and the Marquesas. The atolls are a continuous coral crown not reaching more than a few metres above the water and surrounding a central lagoon but each atoll has its own distinct features. For 30 islands, the outer ring is cut by passes or channels, as at Fakarava and Rangiroa, while others are completely enclosed, like Takapoto and Anaa. Some are huge; Rangiroa is 75km in length, others minute; Nukutepipi is no more than 4km across. Their shapes are equally variable: circular, square or rectangular. In some cases the lagoons have become so shallow they are almost filled in while Makatea is a high island, not an atoll at all.

The total land area of the Tuamotus is only about 700 sq km but the narrow chains of low-lying motu that make up the islands encircle about 6000 sq km of sheltered lagoons, more than 1000 sq km in the vast Rangiroa lagoon alone.

The atolls are fragile and vulnerable places. Their lack of height offers no protection against cyclones and the poor soil and freshwater make agriculture difficult. The Paumotu, the inhabitants of the archipelago, have had to use great ingenuity to cope with this hostile environment.

The Tuamotus has always been a dangerous place for navigators; Bougainville tagged it with the 'dangerous' epithet in 1768 and it's long remained in the shadow of the Society Islands. Today, however, the context has changed. Pearl cultivation has become a central pillar of the Polynesian economy. In fact, black pearls have reversed the outward migration of the population, which has grown from 12,500 to 15,500

people over the last two censuses. There are 45 inhabited islands, ranging from those with a mere handful of often transient occupants to Rangiroa, with its two large villages and total population of 1900. At the same time as the population explosion, infrastructure has been dramatically improved.

This modernisation is not evenly spread, however. The big winners are the north and the west of the archipelago; places like Rangiroa, Arutua and Manihi, which placed their bets on pearls and tourism. Others, like Hereheretue and Tematangi, remain connected to the outside world only by infrequent cargo ships.

Whatever the level of development, the Tuamotus embody absolute disorientation in an idyllic and wild setting. Life is simple, distractions are rare. The rhythm of life encompasses fishing and pearl culture, work in the coconut groves, the arrival and departures of planes and ships, and weekly church services.

History

The history of the Tuamotus is a mystery; stories from the early European navigators, archaeological vestiges and fragments of ancient traditions are the only historical sources.

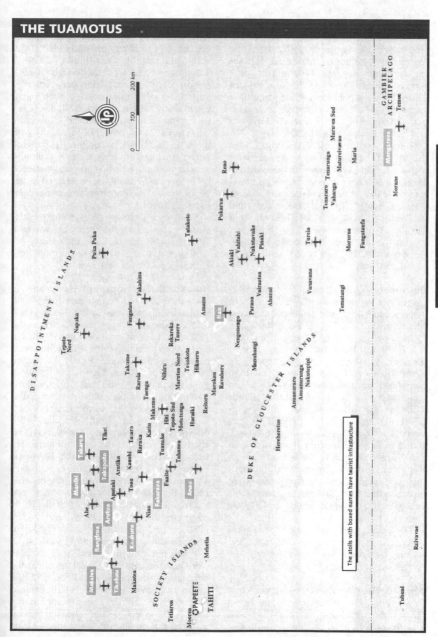

THE TUAMOTUS

The atolls with boxed names have tourist infrastructure

Early Settlers The origin of the Paumotu, the people of the archipelago, is unclear. One hypothesis is that they fled from the Leeward Islands and the Marquesas following conflicts from the 14th to 16th centuries. Another theory is that the eastern Tuamotus were populated at the same time as the major Polynesian diaspora moved on to the Marquesas, the Gambier Archipelago and Easter Island, around 1000 AD.

A survey of Tuamotu dialects in use at the start of the 20th century, together with archaeological excavations, divided the region into seven socio-political and linguistic areas: the Mihiroa (Makatea, Mataiva, Tikehau, Arutua, Apataki and Kaukura) and the Vahitu (Manihi, Ahe, Takaroa and Takapoto) to the north-west, the Parata and the Tapuhoe in the centre, the Manrangai to the south-east, the Napuka and the Fangatau to the north-east.

European Exploration European explorers first chanced upon the Tuamotus in 1521, when Portuguese explorer Ferdinand Magellan happened upon Puka Puka. An isolated outlier, well to the east of the central Tuamotus, Puka Puka gives no hint of the sheer number of islands in the chain. Later European explorers were less than complimentary about the group – Le Maire and Schouten in 1616 spoke of the 'Islands of Dogs', the 'Islands without End' or simply the 'Islands of Flies'. In 1722 Roggeveen, the 'discoverer' of Easter Island, called them the 'Pernicious Islands' and in 1768 French explorer Louis-Antoine de Bougainville was all too aware of the peril they presented to unwary navigators when he dubbed the islands the 'Dangerous Archipelago', an opinion confirmed in 1838 by Dupetit-Thouars.

These early explorers sealed the reputation of the group as an uninviting place and European attention was turned towards the more welcoming Society Islands.

Anaa & the Missionaries At the same time as the first explorers touched on the islands, the central and western Tuamotus were being torn apart by intense wars. The ferocious warriors of the Anaa Atoll spread terror across the whole region towards the end of the 18th century. Islanders from many other atolls were forced to flee to Tahiti, where they were sheltered by the Pomares. Many of these islanders were converted by the missionaries who were establishing themselves on Tahiti and when they returned to the Vahitu and Mihiroa islands in 1817 they brought Christianity with them. In 1821, under Pomare III, war between Anaa and its adversaries was finally concluded and, when Tahiti was annexed by France, the Tuamotus, considered as dependencies of the Pomares, also came under French control.

Souls were fiercely contested-for by missionaries and as a result there are numerous fine churches in the Tuamotus today including Catholic, Protestant, Mormon, Seventh Day Adventist and Sanito.

Industrial Development European rule over the scattered settlements came with Christian missionaries in the 1850s. They established copra production from the 1870s and planted vast coconut plantations. In 1900 copra represented 40% of the total exports of the colony. Pearl diving and mother-of-pearl production enjoyed a golden age from 1850 and Chilean, Australian and American traders were regular visitors to the lagoons of the Tuamotus.

For over 50 years, from 1911 until 1966, phosphate mining on the island of Makatea, south-west of Rangiroa, was the principal export activity not only for the Tuamotus but for all of French Polynesia, but this was an unusual exception to the slow pace of life in the island group. The population of the islands began to decline dramatically as copra production fell away and, in the 1960s, when plastic buttons finally killed off the mother-of-pearl button business.

It was not until the 1970s, when airstrips were built on many of the islands, that the population decline was slowed and the group's economic prospects began to brighten. Regular flights from Tahiti brought tourists to the archipelago. The flights back to Tahiti carried not only suntanned tourists but loads of fresh reef fish for the busy markets of Papeete. At the same time new techniques of pearl grafting led to pearl farms and the black pearls that have become synonymous with French Polynesia.

The 1970s brought another far less congenial employment prospect to the Tuamotus when the Centre d'Expérimentation du Pacifique (CEP) took over the central atoll of Hao and began to test French nuclear weapons on the western atolls of Moruroa and Fangataufa. The early 1980s brought a series of disastrous cyclones that wreaked havoc on a number of the atolls, particularly during the short period from December 1982 to April 1983. Nevertheless, tourism and pearl production have together reversed the population outflow, although areas of the archipelago are still economically depressed.

Population & People

The traditional local culture varies only slightly from Tahitian culture. In the east of the archipelago, the people still speak a Paumotu dialect that is a variant of Tahitian. Because of the relative rarity of natural resources, crafts and artwork have not developed as much as on other archipelagos.

The islanders' use of their limited land has been quite exceptional. To overcome the lack of water, the Paumotu dug pits down to the water table. These pits sometimes stretched for hundreds of metres and were up to 40m wide and up to 2m deep. They were then filled in with vegetable matter. This improvised compost enabled the cultivation of taro, which guaranteed regular nutrition. The development of coconut plantations and direct supplies from Tahiti by schooners eventually made these ingenious systems obsolete. Fish traps made of coral blocks provided animal protein and have survived to the present day.

The Paumotu had the same beliefs as other Polynesians but their marae were constructed with huge slabs of coral.

Accommodation

Only Manihi and Rangiroa have international-class hotels and camping possibilities are all but nonexistent in the Tuamotus.

From Coconut to Copra

Copra is found everywhere in the Tuamotus and Marquesas, and you can recognise it by the unmistakable, rancid smell it gives off in the coconut plantations, on the rack dryers or in the warehouses near the wharves.

Copra (from the Tamil word *kopparah*) is the dry residue of the white substance lining the inside of the coconut. Rich in vegetable fat (palmitin), it is regularly collected by schooners and taken to Papeete. Crushed, heated, pressed and refined in oil, it is then sold to the food and cosmetics industries.

Copra production is relatively recent. Introduced by the missionaries towards the end of the 1860s, it has continued to develop and is still an essential economic activity on numerous islands and atolls in Polynesia.

The copra producers go outside the village to the coconut plantations, and gather the fallen coconuts. Their basic tools include a machete and a *pana*, an implement with a short handle and a curved, narrow metal blade. The coconuts are split with a blow from the machete. The half-nuts are then turned over and left in the sun for a few days.

The second procedure consists of scooping out the coconut: using a pana, the copra producer separates the dried kernel from the shell with a quick, vigorous twisting action. The shavings collected are then placed on copra dryers (like raised racks topped with a movable roof to protect them from rain) until completely desiccated.

They are then packed in hessian bags, weighed and put in a hangar until a schooner arrives to collect them. The copra producer is paid directly by the inspector at the time of weighing, or by the supercargo when loading the ship, at a rate of 60 CFP to 80 CFP per kilogram, depending on the quality.

THE TUAMOTUS

The most widely used accommodation in the archipelago is undoubtedly the *pension* (guesthouse). Most islands only have a few places but there are great variations in the comfort and the facilities available, so trust word-of-mouth recommendations. Some guesthouses only offer the bare essentials, while others compete with good hotels (private bath, towels, good food and cleanliness). As there are very few places to eat out, a room with half-board (*demi-pension*; bed, breakfast and dinner) or full board (*pension*; bed and all meals) is the usual choice. Half-board typically costs 5500 CFP to 6000 CFP per person.

With the exception of a few hotels and guesthouses on Rangiroa and Manihi, credit cards are not accepted and Rangiroa is the only island with permanent banking services, so you should carry sufficient cash. Staff at the hotels will speak English but in the guesthouses it is not likely that the staff will know more than a few words.

Activities

You don't go to the Tuamotus for monuments, museums or food – activities in the lagoons are the attraction. Scuba diving, which opened up the atolls to tourism in the 1980s, is the number one activity. Rangiroa, Manihi and Fakarava have dive centres (see the 'Diving' special section in the Outdoor Activities chapter). Dive cruises are another way to dive the Tuamotus – see Bareboat Charters & Cruises in the Outdoor Activities chapter.

Pearl farming is a major economic activity and you can visit pearl farms and, with a little luck, observe the grafting operation. Many accommodation operators also have pearl farms.

Fishing is also important, both spear and line-fishing. You can also see fish parks, snorkel, explore archaeological sites and visit bird reserves on remote islets. Definitely bring a mask and snorkel.

There are many tourist operators on the islands although hotels and guesthouses often organise trips for guests. The best beaches are often on remote motu, far from the accommodation centres. Operators will take you on picnic trips to these motu, or arrange to leave you there and collect you later. Try not to leave yourself at the mercy of one hotel, guesthouse or operator. If you ask around you'll find many other possibilities, so there's no need to spend days in your guesthouse waiting for a trip to eventuate.

Getting There & Away

Air The archipelago is accessible by plane. Today, 27 atolls have airstrips and are served by Air Tahiti. Most of the traffic is to/from Papeete, but there are also connections with Bora Bora, the Marquesas and the Gambier Archipelago. Within the archipelago, Rangiroa and Hao are the principal flight centres. If you're visiting an island, always give the Air Tahiti representative a contact address or phone number, as schedules are subject to change.

Boat The *Dory, Cobia I, Mareva Nui, Taporo IV, Saint Xavier Maris Stella, Rairoa Nui, Auura'Nui 3, Kura Ora, Hotu Maru, Vai-Aito,* and *Aranui* all serve the archipelago from Papeete and most take passengers. See the Getting Around chapter for details. On those islands without wharves, loading and unloading of cargo and passengers is done by *bonitier* (whaleboat).

Yacht Information on cruising yachts can be found under Sailing in the Outdoor Activities chapter.

Getting Around

The road networks on the Tuamotu islands are often just crushed-coral or sand tracks, perhaps a few kilometres long, linking the village to the airport or to the areas where copra is produced. Sometimes there are school bus services but public transport usually does not exist. Ask at your accommodation about transport.

Airport are sometimes near the villages, sometimes on remote motu on the other side of the lagoon. If you have booked accommodation, your hosts will come and meet you but transfers are not necessarily free. If there is a charge it will depend on the distance travelled and the means of transport.

Hitching (by car or boat) is possible as many islanders go to the airports for arrivals and departures, although there may not be room for you by the time all the freight and merchandise is loaded on board!

It's usually easy to get across the lagoons by local outboard-powered boats. On atolls with relatively long tracks there may be a handful of cars but traffic is usually nonexistent. Bicycles and scooters are often used in the villages and some guesthouses rent them out or they can be hired from islanders.

Rangiroa

**pop 1913 • lagoon area 1640 sq km
reef passes 3**

Rangiroa (from 'Rairoa', literally 'Long Sky') is the second-biggest atoll in the world, outranked only by Kwajalein Atoll in Micronesia. Rangi, as it is usually called, measures 75km from east to west and 25km from north to south. From the edge of the lagoon, it is impossible to see the opposite bank. In fact, 'lagoon' seems a rather feeble word to describe the immense marine spread, encircled in the reef crown – 'internal sea' would be more appropriate.

Rangiroa, 350km north-east of Tahiti, is the most populated atoll in the Tuamotus and, in two decades, has established itself as the archipelago's most famous tourist destination. Its reputation is based on diving and excursions on the idyllic lagoon. Apart from tourism, fishing and pearl production have provided additional employment for the atolls's inhabitants.

Rangiroa is an important link for air and sea communication, located at the midpoint between Tahiti, in the Society Islands, and the Marquesas.

History

Rangiroa Atoll has more than 10% of the total population of the Tuamotus. It must have been even more populated in the past; marae and some cultivation pits are evidence of many population centres at Tereia, Fenuaroa, Otepipi, Tevaro, Avatoru and Tiputa.

Historically, Rangiroa has had to contend with two types of threat: pirates from Anaa Atoll in the south-east and devastating cyclones. Faced with the extortions of the pirates, the Rangiroa inhabitants sought refuge

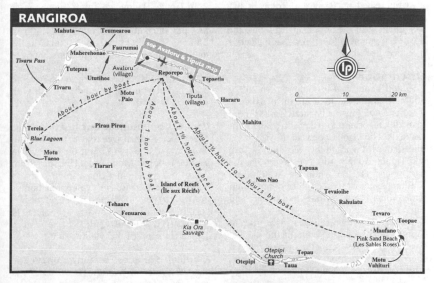

RANGIROA

close to Motu Taeoo (now the Blue Lagoon) on the south-western side of the atoll. A cataclysm, probably a tsunami, is said to have destroyed the human settlements on the west of the atoll in 1560.

Two centuries later, the population was settled mainly in the vicinity of the three passes, Tivaru, Avatoru and Tiputa. Rangiroa established strong relations with the other atolls of the northern Tuamotus. This good fortune did not last long, for the Anaa warriors pillaged the atoll again and destroyed the public buildings at the end of the 1770s. The survivors were forced into exile on Tikehau or Tahiti, where the Pomares gave them protection. They were able to return to Rangiroa in 1821, and repopulated the atoll.

Although 'discovered' by the Dutchman Le Maire on 18 April 1616, Rangiroa saw the first Europeans settlers only in 1851. These were Christian missionaries, who introduced coconut cultivation. Copra production enjoyed constant development until overtaken by fishing. Refrigeration facilities have been built, but direct dispatch by plane to the markets in Papeete is still a significant practice. Before plastic buttons replaced mother-of-pearl, pearl-oyster cultivation also flourished on Rangiroa. Today it has been replaced by cultured-pearl production. The opening of the airport in 1965 boosted the development of tourism, a leading activity since the 1980s.

Orientation

The atoll's coral belt is no more than 200 to 300m wide but the long circuit of islands, motu and *hoa* (channels) stretches for more than 200km, oriented on a north-west/southeast axis. The lagoon opens to the ocean via three passes: Tivaru to the west and Avatoru and Tiputa to the north. The Tivaru Pass is narrow and shallow while the Avatoru and Tiputa passes are each more than 200m wide. About 10km separates the Avatoru and Tiputa passes.

Rangiroa has two villages, Avatoru and Tiputa, situated on the edge of the passes. Avatoru is to the west of a string of islets, separated by a number of hoa that are usually dry, except when inundated by high tides. At the eastern end, the Tiputa Pass opens, beyond which is the village of the same name. Water moving through these passes creates strong currents and attracts abundant marine life.

Hotels and other essential tourist facilities are scattered along the 10km-long Avatoru string of islets. A few people live on a motu south of the lagoon, in the vicinity of the Kia Ora Sauvage, an annexe of the Kia Ora Village Hotel.

Information

Money Banque de Tahiti and Banque Socredo each have an agency in Avatoru and Tiputa, but take turns serving the two villages on designated days.

In Avatoru, Banque de Tahiti (☎ 96 85 52) is situated between the small supermarket, close to the Catholic church and the *mairie* (town hall). It is open Monday, Wednesday and Friday from 8 to 11 am and 2 to 4 pm. Banque Socredo (☎ 96 85 63) is in the mairie and operates weekdays from 8 to 10.30 am (on Wednesday also from 1.30 to 4 pm). You can exchange currency and travellers cheques or withdraw cash with your credit card at either bank.

In Tiputa, Banque de Tahiti (no phone) is in the mairie and opens Tuesday from 1.30 to 4 pm and Thursday from 8 to 11.30 am. Banque Socredo (☎ 96 75 57), also in the mairie, is open Monday and Thursday from 1.30 to 4 pm. At Tiputa you can change currency, with advance warning to the Avatoru branch, but you can't withdraw cash with your credit card.

Post & Communications In Avatoru, the post office is open weekdays from 7 am to noon and 1 to 3 pm (2 pm on Friday). In Tiputa, it opens Monday to Thursday from 7 am to 1 pm, and Friday from 7 am to noon. There are card-only telephone booths in Avatoru (next to the post office, at the airport, in front of the secondary school and at the wharf in front of Chez Glorine) and in Tiputa (in front of the Maihiti shop).

Medical Services & Emergency The medical centre in Avatoru (☎ 96 03 75) is

2km east of the village. The Rairoa medical centre, just east of Paréo Carole, has a private clinic operated by Dr Thirouard (☎ 96 04 44 or ☎ 96 04 43 at home). There is no pharmacy but the doctor has medicinal supplies. Paréo Carole has some medicine too. There is an infirmary in Tiputa.

The *gendarmerie* (police station; ☎ 96 73 61) is towards the eastern end of the Avatoru islet, not far from Kia Ora Village.

Avatoru

This village on the western end of the string of islets, on the edge of the pass and beside the lagoon, is organised around the mairie annexe. The Catholic church, 100m away, seems a precarious sentinel on the edge of the pass, while the Latter Day Saints (Mormon) church is a little farther off. There are a few small businesses and shops in the village.

L'Établissement pour la Valorisation des Activités Aquacoles et Maritimes (EVAAM), a fishing and research centre, has a sub-branch in Avatoru, a few kilometres east of the village and just a stone's throw from the Chez Béatrice snack bar. Its staff of 12 conducts cultured-pearl production research and manages the coldroom for the fishers. Le Centre des Métiers de la Nacre et de la Perliculture, on the ocean side of the island, just over 2km east of the village, trains young Polynesians in the art of pearl-grafting.

Rangiroa College is about 3.5km east of the village and has more than 400 students from the northern Tuamotu islands.

Tiputa

Tiputa is a striking contrast to Avatoru. On the edge of the pass and the lagoon, it's quieter and more secluded than relatively touristy Avatoru. There are fewer *popaa* (westerners) here and it is easier to meet the locals. Tiputa is the administrative centre and is effectively the main town for Rangiroa, Makatea, Tikehau and Mataiva. It has a gendarmerie with authority over several atolls. The village has the Centre d'Études des Techniques Adaptées au Développement (CETAD), which trains young people for catering and hotel jobs.

In the middle of the village there is a white Catholic church. In the same street, set back slightly, you can make out a discreet Marian altar (a shrine to the Virgin Mary), decorated with mother-of-pearl. After leaving the village the track continues through coconut plantations until you're halted by the next pass.

The Blue Lagoon

One of Rangiroa's most popular tourist spots, the Blue Lagoon is one hour away by boat on the western edge of the atoll, close to Motu Taeoo. A string of motu and coral reefs have formed a natural pool on the edge of the main reef, thereby creating a lagoon within a lagoon. Its sparkling white sand, ruffled coconut trees and water the colour of lapis-lazuli show why it received its name. The lagoon is not deep and offers safe **diving** among the myriad of little fish. Eating freshly barbecued fish and **shark feeding** are usual activities at the Blue Lagoon.

Les Sables Roses

The magnificent 'Pink Sand Beach', on the south-eastern edge of the lagoon near Motu Vahituri, is 1½ to two hours from Avatoru by boat. The sands contain Foraminifera deposits and various coral residues that glow with reflected pink light when the sun is shining. The crystalline water invites **swimming** and **snorkelling**. It's rarely visited due to its remote location.

L'Île aux Récifs

South of the atoll, an hour by boat from Avatoru, 'The Island of Reefs', also known as Motu Ai Ai, lies in water dotted with raised **coral outcrops** called *feo*, weathered shapes chiselled by erosion into strange petrified silhouettes. Because they're on the ocean side you don't immediately see them when arriving by boat. They stretch for several hundred metres, with basins and channels that make superb natural swimming pools. There's also a good hoa for swimming, some final coral stands for snorkelling and a pleasant coconut grove by the beach, ideal for a picnic.

THE TUAMOTUS

THE TUAMOTUS

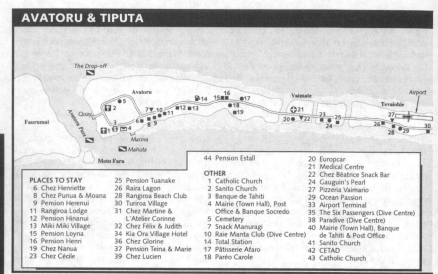

AVATORU & TIPUTA

PLACES TO STAY		OTHER			20 Europcar
6 Chez Henriette	25 Pension Tuanake	1 Catholic Church			21 Medical Centre
8 Chez Punua & Moana	26 Raira Lagon	2 Sanito Church			22 Chez Béatrice Snack Bar
9 Pension Herenui	28 Rangiroa Beach Club	3 Banque de Tahiti			24 Gauguin's Pearl
11 Rangiroa Lodge	30 Turiroa Village	4 Mairie (Town Hall), Post			27 Pizzeria Vaimario
12 Pension Hinanui	31 Chez Martine &	Office & Banque Socredo			29 Ocean Passion
13 Miki Miki Village	L'Atelier Corinne	5 Cemetery			33 Airport Terminal
15 Pension Loyna	32 Chez Félix & Judith	7 Snack Manuragi			35 The Six Passengers (Dive Centre)
16 Pension Henri	34 Kia Ora Village Hotel	10 Raie Manta Club (Dive Centre)			38 Paradive (Dive Centre)
19 Chez Nanua	36 Chez Glorine	14 Total Station			40 Mairie (Town Hall), Banque
23 Chez Cécile	37 Pension Teina & Marie	17 Pâtisserie Afaro			de Tahiti & Post Office
	39 Chez Lucien	18 Paréo Carole			41 Sanito Church
44 Pension Estall					42 CETAD
					43 Catholic Church

Otepipi

Otepipi is a motu on the south-eastern side of the atoll, about 1½ hours by boat, that once had a village. Some people say a contagious illness forced the inhabitants to leave but others maintain that cyclones and the demands of copra production caused the inhabitants to abandon the area and regroup closer to Avatoru and Tiputa. Only a **church** remains but religious retreats and pilgrimages are still made to the church periodically.

Motu in the Lagoon

There are a few motu scattered in the lagoon, rather than around the edge. They include Motu Paio and are **bird sanctuaries** that shelter nesting species including *oio* (noddies), *tara* (sea-swallows) and frigate birds.

Pearl Farms

Rangiroa has several pearl farms that you can visit and even buy pearls from.

Gauguin's Pearl (☎/fax 96 05 39), 800m east of the airport and on the lagoonside, is a medium-sized operator. There are tours, in English or French, up to three times daily that include a demonstration of grafting. Direct purchases can be made and credit cards

are accepted. Visits are made daily at 8.30 am and 2 pm and the shop is open Monday to Saturday from 8.30 am to 5.30 pm and on Sunday morning.

A smaller farm belongs to the family who owns the Chez Martine guesthouse. Mr Tetua looks after the grafting while Corinne, who is French and in charge of marketing, will take you around the farm and answer your questions. Direct sales take place at the small shop L'Atelier Corinne (☎ 96 03 13), opposite the guesthouse on the ocean side. Pearls are available mounted and unmounted. It's open daily from 10.15 am to 6 pm and credit cards are accepted.

Heipoe Ura (☎ 96 04 35) is another family business, to the east of the Rochette store on the lagoonside. The Tehahes sell mounted and unmounted pearls, *keshi* (pure mother-of-pearl) and mabe. The owners of the Turiroa Village guesthouse also have a small pearl farm and make direct sales.

Activities

Diving Diving is the main activity on Rangiroa and it has become world famous. The main sites are at the two passes and sharks

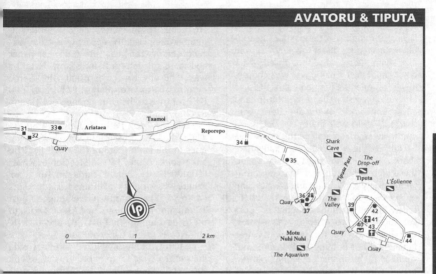

are the big attraction. There are three dive-centres, which welcome beginners and experienced divers. See the 'Diving' special section for details.

Snorkelling Snorkelling through the Tiputa Pass, accompanied by a guide who knows it and its currents, has become a popular activity. A boat follows the group and this is a perfect way for beginners to experience 'le grand bleu'. Starting outside the pass snorkellers are swept into the lagoon by the incoming tide, finishing with an exploration of Motu Nuhi Nuhi. The guide explains the marine life and if dolphins are around (they like to surf the incoming tide with boats) the boat will go to meet them.

Pascal and Cosetta, of Rangiroa Activities (☎ 96 03 31), charge 4000 CFP per person for a two hour trip, including equipment. Pascal is an experienced divemaster. Prices are similar at Oviri (☎ 96 05 87), which makes trips to both passes with a minimum two people.

Cruises There are several yacht and cruise charter operations on Rangiroa. See Bareboat Charters & Cruises in the Outdoor Activities chapter for details.

Parasailing & Game Fishing Société Parasail (☎ 96 04 96) offers 15-minute parasails over the lagoon for 5000 CFP (minimum of two people). Game fishing is also possible. Contact Hiria Arnoux of Atoll Excursion (☎ 96 02 88) and count on 10,000 CFP per hour (maximum of four people).

Organised Tours

The huge Rangiroa atoll contains sights well worth a day's excursion by boat. Most are on the opposite side of the lagoon from Avatoru, which takes at least an hour to cross. If the sea is rough it can be uncomfortable. Usually a minimum of four to six people is required, but in July-August there may be so many that you're either in an uncomfortably large group or have trouble getting a place at all. The opposite situation can apply in the off-season, when it may be difficult to organise a large enough party.

These tours rely on the state of the lagoon and weather conditions. In the event of *maraamu* (south-easterly wind), they may be cancelled. Bring some plastic sandals, sunscreen, sunglasses, a swimsuit and a change of clothes. Tour operators usually provide some snorkelling gear; you can deal

Shark Mealtime?

Diving at Rangiroa is famous for encounters with sharks. Lots of them. My second dive there started at a spot called Shark Point and if ever a name was well chosen, it was this one. We jumped out of the dive boat, dropped straight to the bottom and all around us, in every direction, were sharks. Wall-to-wall sharks. In fact, symmetrically arranged against the deep-blue backdrop, they looked remarkably like shark wallpaper. Nothing to worry about: these were white-tip reef sharks, a non-biting variety (so it's said) and after getting our wide-eyeful of sharks we set off to drift with the current through the Tiputa Pass between two of Rangiroa's islands. Our instructor led the way with three Japanese divers and myself following, but we hadn't left the shark meeting point far behind when we heard the instructor yell (not an easy task underwater) and turned around to find one much larger shark following us intently.

Was this to be a new variation of the *repas des requins* (shark feeding) that seems to be so popular in French Polynesia? When we all turned to face it, the monster shyly turned away, but as soon as we resumed our drift it swung back to have another look at us. This little dance was repeated several times before it eventually decided to look for something more bite-sized.

Tony Wheeler

with them directly or through your accommodation. Tours generally depart at 8.30 am and return at 4 pm, include a picnic or barbecue and are priced per person.

Hiria Arnoux of Atoll Excursion (☎ 96 02 88) does boat trips to the Blue Lagoon (7500 CFP), l'Île aux Récifs (7500 CFP) and, less frequently, Les Sables Roses (9000 CFP). A short snorkelling stop is usually made on the return trip at Motu Nuhi Nuhi in the lagoon or at the Tiputa Pass.

Tane Tamaehu, the husband of Henriette, of the guesthouse of the same name, is the owner of Tetiare Excursion (☎ 96 85 85). He specialises in excursions to the Blue Lagoon, which usually depart every day except Sunday. Tane is a line and spear-fisher and there's usually a fishing stop along the way. The day trip costs 6000 CFP. Serge Giroux of Rangiroa Parasail charges 7000 CFP for trips to the Blue Lagoon or l'Île aux Récifs.

Félix, of Chez Félix & Judith (☎ 96 04 41), is the head of Ariitini Excursions which goes to the Blue Lagoon (6000 CFP), l'Île aux Récifs (7000 CFP) and les Sables Roses (10,000 CFP). Punua Tamaehu (of Chez Punua & Moana) at Punua Excursions (☎ 96 84 73) goes to the Green Lagoon, just 10 minutes from the village (3000 CFP), to the Blue Lagoon (6500 CFP) and to l'Île aux Récifs (7500 CFP).

Gatien Guitteny (☎ 96 72 14), in Tiputa goes to the Blue Lagoon or l'Île aux Récifs (both 6500 CFP) and les Sables Roses (9500 CFP). To get to the church at Otepipi contact Alban, the husband of Cécile (of Chez Cécile, ☎ 96 05 06). He knows the atoll and its history well. Count on paying 6000 CFP.

Matahi Tepa (☎ 96 84 48) has a glass-bottom boat and does 1½-hour trips to Motu Nuhi Nuhi, to the south of the Tiputa Pass, for 2200 CFP including a snorkelling stop.

Places to Stay

Whether you'd like to spend the night in a tent, a guesthouse or a luxurious over-water bungalow, the choice on Rangiroa is vast. Guesthouses and hotels are dotted over a distance of 10km from the village of Avatoru in the west to the village of Tiputa, beyond the Tiputa Pass, in the east. On the other hand, the prices do not vary much: apart from the luxury hotels, most guesthouses charge relatively similar prices. To be on the safe side, it's wise to book in advance but once you are there you can move if you prefer. Prices quoted are per person per day and transfers to and from the airport are included, unless otherwise indicated. VAT is usually included but there's also a daily tax of 50 CFP per person.

Budget Hotels and guesthouses are on the edge of the lagoon, on the Avatoru string of islets. Bungalows usually accommodate two people, but a mattress or single bed can be added.

Avatoru *Chez Henriette* (☎ 96 84 68, fax 96 82 85), in Avatoru village next to the Daniel shop and close to the marina, has three rudimentary bungalows with cold-water bathroom for 5150/6170 CFP half/full board. This place is popular with people who appreciate simplicity, authenticity and homemade coconut bread.

Chez Punua & Moana (☎/fax 96 84 73), on the lagoonside, is run by the Tamaehus, who also own Snack Manuragi. There are two simple local-style bungalows with shared bathrooms for 3500 CFP per person including breakfast, 4500/5500 CFP half/full board. Airport transfers are 500 CFP per person and Punua organises lagoon excursions.

Pension Herenui (☎ 96 84 71), BP 31 Avatoru, Rangiroa, is next to the Raie Manta Club. There are three straightforward bungalows with cold-water bathroom and small veranda for 3500 CFP including breakfast, 5000/6000 CFP half/full board.

Rangiroa Lodge (☎ 96 82 13), next to the Raie Manta Club, is another place that's good for tight budgets. Jacques and Rofina Ly have a dorm with five or six mosquitonetted beds at 1500 CFP, two small rooms with bathroom for 5000 CFP for one or two people and two other rooms with shared bathroom facilities for 2000 CFP per person. Add 250 CFP for a fan. This is all squeezed into one *fare* so space is tight. Meals are not provided but there is a shared kitchen.

Pension Hinanui (☎ 96 84 61), BP 16, Avatoru, Rangiroa, is 200m farther on from Rangiroa Lodge and has three comfortable and well designed bungalows with mezzanine, small veranda and cold-water bathroom for 4000/7000 CFP single/double. Add 2000/3500 CFP per person for half/full board. A restaurant *fare* is being built. Mme Bizien prides herself on serving French, Spanish and Chinese meals. Credit cards are accepted. For snorkellers there's some pretty coral reef situated right in front of the bungalows.

The two pensions that follow are side by side and, unusually, are on the ocean side of the island. At *Pension Loyna* (☎/fax 96 82 09), you can stay in the owner's home, where there are two fan-cooled rooms on a mezzanine in a big, very well-kept house close to the road. The shared bathroom is in a separate building and has a hot-water shower. Behind the house is a separate *fare* with two rooms, a TV and cold-water bathroom. The cost is 5500/6500 CFP half/full board. The ocean is 300m away but the warm welcome and high standards make up for this.

Pension Henri (☎/fax 96 82 67) is owned by a French-Tahitian couple and has three local-style bungalows with attached cold-water bathroom and small veranda. They're airy, spacious, comfortable and have ocean views. The cost is 8000/10,000 CFP half/full board for one person, 6000/7000 CFP per person if there are two of you and 5000/6000 CFP if there are three. You take your meals in a large *fare*.

Chez Nanua (☎ 96 83 88), BP 54, Avatoru, Rangiroa, is set back from the Paréo Carole shop and is the cheapest place on Rangiroa. Nanua and Marie Tamaehu have five rustic bungalows, two of them with bathrooms for 4000 CFP per person halfboard; the others share a bathroom and cost 3000 CFP. Don't expect any luxuries, but the atmosphere is typical of the islands. You can also camp here for 1000 CFP per person or 2500 CFP half-board. Simple meals are taken with the family.

The popular *Chez Cécile* (☎ 96 05 06), BP 98, Avatoru, Rangiroa, is halfway between the airport and the village and is famous for Cécile's cooking. The varied and copious meals feature local specialities and are taken in a *fare potee* (open fare) in a garden setting. Three small, simple A-frame bungalows face the lagoon and sleep two or three people and there's a bungalow with mezzanine for four people, with cold-water bathroom, fan and mosquito nets for 6000/7000 CFP half/full board. Three new bungalows are rented at the same price, although preference is given to those who book in advance or stay for

THE TUAMOTUS

longer. Prices drop 5% if you stay for five days, 10% if you stay even longer. Credit cards are accepted.

Turiroa Village *(☎/fax 96 04 27)* is about 1km west of the airport near the Ocean Passion boutique. The four bungalows sleeping four people all have fan, mezzanine, cold-water bathroom, screened windows and equipped kitchen and cost 8000 CFP for up to four people. There's free transport to the shops for food, although meals are available. Half/full board costs 2000/3500 CFP. The owners have a pearl farm and the *fare* where the transplants are made is right next to the dining *fare*, beside the lagoon. On weekends trips to a private motu close to les Sables Roses can be organised.

Chez Martine *(☎/fax 96 02 51, 96 02 53)*, about 600m west of the airport, has four bungalows for two to four people with cold-water bathrooms for 6000/7000 CFP half/full board per person. The dining room is not very stylish but it is right on the lagoon and the garden setting is very pleasant. The Tetua family also has a pearl farm. Credit cards are accepted.

Next door, ***Chez Félix & Judith*** *(☎ 96 04 41)*, BP 18, Avatoru, Rangiroa, has six comfortable, tiled bungalows with thatched roofs and cold-water bathroom in a pleasant setting. They cost 7000/7500 CFP half/full board and there are two older bungalows at 6000/6500 CFP.

Pension Teina & Marie *(☎ 96 03 94, fax 96 84 44)*, at the end of the Avatoru string of islets, on the edge of the Tiputa Pass, is very popular with divers. It is only a short walk to the Paradive dive centre or to the Raie Manta Club annexe. Meals are delicious and generous and are taken in a large *fare*, opposite the lagoon. There are two bungalows with bathrooms for two people facing the lagoon which cost 6500/7500 CFP half/full board. Four other units, farther back from the lagoon, have two rooms and shared bathrooms and are priced at 5500/6500 CFP.

Lovers of fine food will enjoy the cooking at ***Chez Glorine*** *(☎ 96 04 05, 96 03 58, fax 96 03 58 – call first)* on the end of the Avatoru string of islets, next to the wharf and

Paradive. Glorine has made a name as a fine cordon bleu-chef and her *mahi-mahi* (dolphin fish – not a dolphin) and parrotfish, prepared in a host of ways, are always superb. Fried taro and *uru* (breadfruit) chips are other favourites and her pancakes and banana cake have long tempted visitors. The meals are taken in a *fare potee*, on the edge of the lagoon. She has three two-person bungalows and three family bungalows with cold-water bathroom. They're well looked-after and cost 6500/7500 CFP half/full board. Glorine charges 800 CFP per family for transfers to the airport.

Tiputa Chez Lucien *(☎ 96 73 55)*, BP 69, Tiputa, Rangiroa, on the edge of the pass, on the lagoonside, is a well maintained guesthouse that is sure to please. For 5000/6000 CFP half/full board, there are three spacious bungalows, one accommodating as many as seven people, with mezzanine and cold-water bathroom. Transfers to the airport are 500 CFP return per person. The generous meals are served in a covered dining room on the edge of the lagoon. If you stay for a minimum of three nights, Lucien will take you for a free picnic on a motu.

At the village exit, in a coconut plantation next to the ocean, ***Pension Estall*** *(☎ 96 73 16, 96 74 16)*, BP 15, Tiputa, Rangiroa, belongs to the mayor, Ronald Estall. The four oceanside bungalows with bathroom cost 4500/6000 CFP half/full board plus 500 CFP per person return for airport transfers. At the time of writing this pension seemed to be only partially operating.

Mid-Range *Miki Miki Village* *(☎ 96 83 83, fax 96 82 90)* has five charming bungalows for two or three people, with hot-water bathroom and ceiling fan or small veranda for 6000 CFP including breakfast, for one or two people. Half-board costs 9000/16,000 CFP a single/double. There's a bar/restaurant over the lagoon. Prices drop by 10% after three nights, 15% after six nights and credit cards are accepted.

Pension Tuanake *(☎ 96 04 45, fax 96 03 29)*, right by Gauguin's Pearl, about halfway between the airport and the village, has two small bungalows with room for three people and two large enough for six people, with cold-water bathroom and fan. It's extremely clean and set in a coconut plantation near the lagoon. There's a separate shower *fare* with hot water. Half-board costs from 8000 CFP for one person, dropping to 5000 CFP per person for a group of five. Full board costs from 10,000 CFP and drops to 7000 CFP. The food has a good reputation. Credit cards are accepted.

Raira Lagoon (☎ 96 04 23, fax 96 05 86, email rairalag@mail.pf), 4.5km east of the village and 1.5km west of the airport, has 10 fan-cooled bungalows with hot-water bathrooms. Two of them are larger family bungalows. All are comfortable, well maintained and clean. Singles/doubles are available for 11,000/14,000 CFP half-board, or for 13,000/18,000 CFP full board. The restaurant balcony faces the lagoon and the chef serves fine fish-dishes. Raira Lagoon accepts credit cards.

Rangiroa Beach Club (☎ 96 03 34, fax 96 02 90; or ☎ 43 08 29, fax 41 09 28 in Papeete) is 150m from the Raira Lagoon. The 11 bungalows are attractive and have hot-water bathroom and fan and cost 10,260 CFP to 12,960 CFP. Tour operators and travel agencies tend to dominate this hotel but you may find a bungalow vacant. Airport transfers cost 600 CFP return per person and credit cards are accepted.

Top End The supreme symbol of luxury hotels in the Tuamotus, *Kia Ora Village Hotel* (☎ 96 03 84, fax 96 04 93) has 60 dream bungalows dotted in a magnificent coconut plantation on the edge of the lagoon, 2.5km east of the airport. Everything is beautifully set-out in this tropical Eden. The 10 magnificent over-water bungalows are reached by a wooden walkway over the lagoon. The 50 other units are scattered along the beach and through the garden. Some beach bungalows have mezzanines, the over-water bungalows have glass-bottomed fish-viewing bays. All the ingredients of luxury are provided: meticulous décor, a white-sand beach, the restaurant-bar on stilts (see Places to Eat

later) and activities ranging from scuba diving to excursions on the lagoon as well as tennis and windsurfing.

Of course, extravagance comes at a price: 21,600/55,080 CFP for a beach/over-water bungalow. Half/full board adds 5300/7800 CFP per person. Credit cards are accepted and there are money-changing facilities for hotel patrons.

The Kia Ora Village Hotel has an annexe on Motu Avearahi, on the southern side of the lagoon, about an hour away by boat, called *Kia Ora Sauvage*. The setting of this motu will delight you. The five *fare* are traditional-style and cost 36,720 CFP for two people plus 7000 CFP per person for compulsory full board. The price includes return boat-transfers and it's suggested you stay for at least two nights.

Places to Eat

Most people choose half or full board with their accommodation, which can become monotonous. There are, however, dining possibilities for all tastes and budgets.

Restaurants The full-board formula can be constrictive on Rangiroa. You can enjoy more variety by choosing demi-pension and having lunch or dinner in different places. Some guesthouses are renowned for their excellent cooking and accept casual diners, provided there is space and you have booked in advance. This is true for *Chez Glorine*, *Teina & Marie*, *Raira Lagon*, *Pension Tuanake* and *Chez Lucien*. Allow 1500 CFP to 2500 CFP for a meal, without drinks. There are set menus.

It is also worth exploring hotel restaurants with à la carte menus. *Rangiroa Beach Club* offers a great range of meat, fish and poultry dishes at moderate prices. The chicken grilled in lime costs only 1250 CFP and there are seafood dishes from 1450 CFP to 3100 CFP. Excellent cocktails, such as maitais, cost 850 CFP.

The cuisine at *Kia Ora Village Hotel* is, of course, high class. The chef at the delightful over-water restaurant/bar offers a wide and appetising menu of Polynesian and French dishes. Try a lunchtime burger for 1250 CFP, tuna sashimi for 1450 CFP or other dishes for 1750 CFP to 2150 CFP. Desserts cost 600 CFP to 850 CFP. Dinner dishes start from 2000 CFP and there's a twice weekly barbecue buffet and Polynesian dance performance for 4250 CFP. Cocktails cost about 800 CFP.

Miki Miki Village has an open terrace looking over the lagoon and a set dinner menu for 2500 CFP.

In Tiputa, an unusual destination for lunch is the restaurant of the *CETAD* (☎ 96 72 96, 96 02 68). The students prepare and serve the food and there is a fixed menu for 1200 CFP. You can get a boat transfer from the wharf next to Chez Glorine, on the eastern end of the Avatoru string of islets, near the pass. Lunch is only available on Tuesday and Thursday and booking is essential at weekends.

Cafés & Snack Bars Each village has a few snack bars, where you can eat in or take away. There's also a bar at the airport that opens before every flight. The popular *Snack Manuragi* in Avatoru is pleasantly decorated in traditional style. It's owned by Moana of the adjacent Chez Punua & Moana. It's open at lunchtime and in the evening daily and turns out substantial fish specialities for 800 CFP.

Chez Béatrice (☎ 96 04 12), about 5km east of Avatoru, on the lagoonside and opposite the cultured-pearl school, is a little more formal. The décor is stark but the place is impeccably clean and the food is OK. It has vegetable omelette for 900 CFP, *maa tinito* (pork and red kidney beans), also for 900 CFP and prawns in curry for 1550 CFP. A Hinano beer costs 300 CFP. It's open daily from 11 am to 2 pm and 6 to 9 or 10 pm.

Pizzeria Vaimario (☎ 96 04 96), on the ocean side near the Rangiroa Beach Club, has a variety of pizzas for about 1000 CFP a slice. It'll even deliver! It's open for lunch and in the evening.

You can enjoy coconut-bread, fruit mousse (400 CFP) and *firifiri* (doughnuts) at the *Pâtisserie Afaro* (☎ 96 04 91), behind the Magasin Rochette (no sign), on the ocean side, less than 1.5km east of Avatoru village.

It's run by a Frenchman and orders must be placed the day before. It's closed on Monday.

Self-Catering Avatoru has a few well-stocked supermarkets including one next to the Catholic church and *Magasin Daniel* near the marina. *Magasin Rochette* is about 1.5km to the east, 150m past Paréo Carole, on the ocean side. In Tiputa you can buy provisions at *Magasin Tiputa* and *Magasin Maihiti*. In principle the shops are open Monday to Saturday and Sunday morning.

Entertainment

The only island entertainment is the twice weekly buffet with traditional dances organised by the *Kia Ora Village Hotel*. It's possible to skip the buffet and just catch the entertainment.

Shopping

A few shops around Avatoru sell souvenirs, postcards, handpainted *pareu* (sarongs), film and a few local handicrafts. Paréo Carole, about 1.5km east of the village, sells clothes, souvenirs, pharmacy items and French magazines and papers. Ocean Passion, near the Rangiroa Beach Club and beside the lagoon, has pretty handpainted pareu for 4000 CFP to 6000 CFP. There are shops in the Kia Ora Village and the Rangiroa Beach Club.

If you wish to buy pearls, contact the owners of the pearl farms directly (see the section on Pearl Farms earlier). There is also the modest Vai Boutique jewellery shop at the entrance to the village, 50m from Chez Henriette.

Getting There & Away

Air The airport is about 5.5km east of Avatoru village. The office of the Air Tahiti representative (☎ 96 03 41, 96 05 03) is inside the airport *fare*. It is open Monday to Thursday from 8 am to noon and 1 to 4.30 pm. On Friday it stays open until 5.30 pm; on weekends and public holidays, its hours vary according to flights. Tickets can be purchased with credit cards.

Rangiroa is connected to Tahiti, Bora Bora, the Marquesas and other atolls in the Tuamotus. There are several one hour flights daily between Papeete and Rangiroa. Rangiroa is also a centre for access to other Tuamotu atolls such as Tikehau, Manihi, Kaukura, Mataiva, Fakarava and Apataki. Tourists appreciate the direct connections with the Leeward Islands via the three or four-times weekly Bora Bora-Rangiroa-Manihi flight. In the other direction it only operates once weekly. There's a weekly Papeete-Rangiroa-Nuku Hiva (Marquesas) connection (only in that direction).

Fares are: Papeete-Rangiroa 13,600 CFP, Bora Bora-Rangiroa 20,700 CFP; Rangiroa-Tikehau, Kaukura or Fakarava all cost 4400 CFP, Rangiroa-Manihi 8800 CFP; and Rangiroa-Nuku Hiva 24,500 CFP.

Boat The *Dory*, *Mareva Nui*, *Vai-Aito*, *Saint Xavier Maris Stella* and *Rairoa Nui* serve Rangiroa. They load and unload freight at the wharf in Avatoru Pass and the wharf close to Chez Glorine on the other end of the motu string, as well as at the Tiputa wharf next to the mairie.

The *Aranui*, on the way back from the Marquesas, stops at Rangiroa for half a day, anchoring opposite the Kia Ora Village Hotel, the last stop before Papeete. For more information see the Getting Around chapter.

Getting Around

A sealed road that runs almost in a straight line links Avatoru village at the western end of the string of islets to the Tiputa Pass at the eastern extremity, some 10km apart. There is no regular service crossing the pass separating the Avatoru islets from Tiputa village, although from time to time speedboats travel between the wharf next to Chez Glorine, and the Tiputa landing-platform. During the school term you can take the school ferry for 500 CFP. It operates from 6 to 7 am and noon to 4 pm on weekdays. Or ask at Chez Glorine, where they'll organise a return trip for 1000 CFP.

To/From the Airport If you have booked accommodation, your hosts will be at the airport to welcome you. Transfers are not automatically included in the accommodation price.

Car, Fun Car, Scooter & Bicycle Rangi Location (☎ 96 03 28), part of the Europcar group, is 2.2km east of the village on the lagoonside and rents cars for 6000/7500 CFP a half/full day. Fun cars, those curious little three-wheeler devices, rent for 5000/6500 CFP, bicycles 850/1400 CFP, scooters 4500/5000 CFP or 2000 CFP an hour. Several guesthouses work with Rangi Location and have bicycles and scooters at the same rates. Credit cards are accepted.

Paréo Carole (☎ 96 82 45), about 800m east of the village, offers bicycles for 600/1200 CFP for a half/full day and scooters for 3300/4400 CFP. Paréo Carole is closed on Sunday and credit cards are accepted. Kia Ora Village Hotel has bicycles it hires out for 500 CFP for a half-day, and scooters for 4000/5500 CFP for a half/full day.

Boat For boat excursions on the lagoon see the earlier Organised Tours section.

Northern Tuamotus

Though Rangiroa is the main tourist destination in the Tuamotus, other atolls in the north of the archipelago are also equipped for tourism.

The northern group includes Makatea, south-west of Rangiroa; Tikehau and Mataiva in the west; and Manihi and Ahe in the northeast. Only the atolls of Tikehau, Mataiva and Manihi have airports and accommodation for travellers. Ahe has an airport but no official tourist lodging; it is, however, a popular stopover for cruising yachts.

Further to the east, Takaroa and Takapoto, both accessible by plane, both have accommodation facilities. The atolls to the east of Rangiroa, Aratua and Kaukura, are less well known. Further to the south-east, the giant Fakarava competes in size with Rangiroa. Anaa is a small atoll farther south.

MAKATEA
pop 84 • area 30 sq km

Flying between Papeete and Rangiroa, the pilot might draw your attention to the

THE TUAMOTUS

THE TUAMOTUS

Makatea – A Half-Century Industrial Epoch

It's difficult to imagine an island in the Tuamotus covered in mining installations and more than 1000 workers but for 50 years Makatea made French Polynesia an industrial centre.

The history of Makatea is intimately linked to the exploitation of phosphate, the presence of which was noted at the end of the 19th century. The Compagnie Française des Phosphates d'Océanie (CFPO) was created in 1908 to exploit the deposit on a grand scale. Infrastructure appeared from nowhere: industrial equipment (including a rail network), houses, schools, a cinema, places of worship and shops. Until the early 1950s labour came largely from Asia.

With 3071 inhabitants in 1962, Makatea was the most populated island in the Tuamotus. Vaitepaua mushroomed like a boomtown in a gold rush. The shallow waters and the absence of a lagoon forced the mineral ships to anchor some distance away from the harbour. Cargo was transferred by barge until 1954, when a 100m-long metal jetty was built.

Makatea phosphate became the core of the French Polynesian economy. From 12,000 tonnes in 1911, the extraction rate rose to 251,000 tonnes in 1929 and 400,000 tonnes in 1960, a record year. Until WWII, exports were mainly to Japan, New Zealand and Australia. In 1956, phosphate became the most valuable export, ahead of copra and vanilla.

By 1966, when the reserves were depleted, nearly 11 million tonnes of phosphate had been torn from the island. In the space of a few weeks, the workers packed everything up and Vaitepaua became a ghost town. Today only a few people live in Moumu, making their living from copra production and the sale of *kaveu* (coconut crabs) to passing tuna boats.

The cessation of mining on Makatea had little economic impact, because three years earlier the Centre d'Éxpérimentation du Pacifique (CEP) had been established on Moruroa and Fangataufa.

---

raised atoll of Makatea, 210km north-east of Tahiti. The only high island in the Tuamotus, Makatea is a bean-shaped plateau with 80m-high cliffs forming its outer edge. These cliffs used to be barrier reef and the plateau was once the basin of a lagoon, where vast amounts of phosphate accumulated (see the 'Makatea' boxed text in the Australs chapter). It is thought that the atoll may have emerged as an indirect consequence of the uplifting of Tahiti. It was 'discovered' by the Dutch navigator Roggeveen in 1722. For information on Makatea's role in the development of French Polynesia's economy, see the boxed text on this page.

TIKEHAU
pop 400 • lagoon area 461 sq km
reef passes 1
Tikehau, just 14km west of Rangiroa, was 'discovered' on 25 April 1816 by the Russian navigator Kotzebue. The atoll forms a ring, slightly oval-shaped, which is 26km on its longest axis. It's cut by Tuheiava Pass in the west and by more than 100 hoa. Dotting the lagoon are a number of motu that provide nesting grounds for birds.

The islanders are grouped in the village of Tuherahera, in the south-west of the atoll. Their livelihood is copra production and fishing (the variety and quantity of fish is exceptional). Frequent connections by plane and boat to Tahiti allow the transport of fresh fish to the markets of Papeete. The enchanting landscape of the motu and the quietness of Tuherahera, attractions disappearing on Rangiroa, mean that more and more Tahitians and tourists are choosing Tikehau as a holiday destination.

Information
There is no bank on Tikehau. The post office is open Monday, Wednesday and Friday from 7.30 to 9.30 am, and Tuesday and Thursday from 7.30 to 11.30 am. The

post office has fax facilities and sells phonecards. A card-operated telephone booth is in front of the post office. The hospital adjoins the mairie.

Things to See & Do

Tuherahera is a pretty and prosperous village, made colourful by rows of uru and coconut trees, bougainvillea and hibiscus. Two sand-covered tracks run straight for more than 1km along the lagoon on the south-western end of the atoll. The village has several places of worship including Catholic, Sanito, Adventist and Protestant churches.

Lagoon excursions allow visitors to explore a number of picturesque sites. The scattered motu are populated by several species of **ground-nesting birds** that construct their nests right on the ground, in *miki miki* bushes and even in trees. Brown noddies and *uaau* (red-footed boobies) are the most frequently encountered species. Motu Mauu to the south and Puarua and Oeoe to the north have the most nests. Guesthouses generally organise trips to **Île aux Oiseaux**, to the north-east, charging 4000 CFP to 5000 CFP per person.

Tuheiava Pass, to the west of the atoll, about 30 minutes by boat from the village, is another popular excursion. Fishers regularly come to the **fish parks** here as it's a pleasantly isolated area. Ask at your guesthouse about trips, which cost 3000 CFP to 4000 CFP. Motu picnic trips are also made for 2000 CFP to 3000 CFP.

Scuba **diving** is a great reason for a visit to Tikehau. The celebrated Raie Manta Club, based on Rangiroa, has an offshoot at Tikehau village, with a divemaster. Dives are made in the magnificent Tuheiava Pass. See the 'Diving' special section for details.

Places to Stay

Accommodation in Tikehau won't disappoint you. There are a few moderately priced but superior-standard guesthouses and you can choose between bungalows and rooms. The places in the village are not directly beside the lagoon, unlike those near the airport. Prices quoted are per person per day and include transfers to the airport but don't usually include VAT or the daily 50 CFP per-person room tax.

North of the village, close to the lagoon, *Chez Maxime* (☎ 96 22 38) offers four rooms for two people and one room for four people. It's satisfactory, with shared cold-water bathroom, and costs 3500/4500 CFP for half/full board. The food is fairly ordinary.

Chez Isidore & Nini (☎ 96 22 89), near the village entrance coming from the airport, belongs to the same family as Chez Maxime and charges the same prices: 3500/4500 CFP for half/full board plus an extra 2000 CFP for a one night stay. There are three spartan rooms for two people, with shared bathroom. The garden is beautiful, with uru, bougainvillea, kava, lemon, hibiscus and coconut trees all around the house.

Also in the village, *Chez Colette* (☎ 96 22 47), about 100m from Chez Isidore & Nini, right next to the grocer's shop Chez Maui, is brilliantly clean. The Huri family offers five two-person rooms in two buildings (one with cold-water bath) for 3000/5000 CFP half/full board. There's a 2500 CFP supplement for a one night stay. There is an equipped kitchen and meals are also served

THE TUAMOTUS

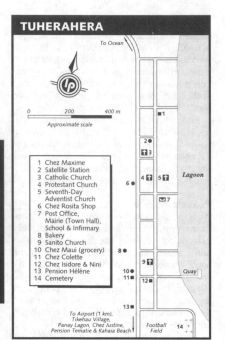

TUHERAHERA

To Ocean

0   200   400 m
Approximate scale

1 Chez Maxime
2 Satellite Station
3 Catholic Church
4 Protestant Church
5 Seventh-Day
   Adventist Church
6 Chez Rosita Shop
7 Post Office,
   Mairie (Town Hall),
   School & Infirmary
8 Bakery
9 Sanito Church
10 Chez Maui (grocery)
11 Chez Colette
12 Chez Isidore & Nini
13 Pension Hélène
14 Cemetery

Lagoon

Quay

Football
Field

To Airport (1 km),
Tikehau Village,
Panay Lagon, Chez Justine,
Pension Tematie & Kahaia Beach

in a comfortable outdoor dining room. Outrigger canoes can be rented for 1500 CFP, jetskis for 10,000 CFP for two hours.

For comfort and service, the immaculate **Pension Hélène** (*☎ 96 22 52, fax 96 22 00 at the post office*), at the village entrance on the left track coming from the airport, is hard to beat. For 4500/5500 CFP half/full board, Hélène offers four rooms with fan and shared cold-water bathroom for two or three people. There's also a room with attached bathroom for an extra 1000 CFP per person. Hélène also offers a night in a small chalet or a three room house on a private motu for 1500 CFP per person. Add 2000 CFP per day for provisions, or for 7000 CFP someone will stay on the motu and prepare meals. There's an outrigger canoe for guests' use.

Situated 600m from the village and 400m on the left coming from the airport, **Tikehau Village** (*☎ 96 22 86*), managed by Caroline and Paea Tefaiao, is an attractive place.

There are six two-person bungalows with cold-water bathroom, set on an enchanting beach, which cost 7000/8000 CFP per person half/full board, and three in a coconut grove for 6000/7000 CFP. Meals of local specialities are served in a large *fare potee* with a bar. There are bicycles for guests' use.

The popular **Pension Tematie** (*☎/fax 96 22 65*) is beside the lagoon, near the airport and Tikehau Village. There's a room with cold-water bathroom in the house and two bungalows sharing a bathroom made of coral blocks. The cost is 4500/6500 CFP per person for half/full board.

On the edge of the lagoon, 1.2km from the village entrance and 250m on the right coming from the airport, **Panau Lagon** (*☎/fax 96 22 99*) has five comfortable bungalows for two people and one bungalow for four people, with cold-water bathrooms and mosquito nets. Prices are 4500/6000 CFP for half/full board.

Chez Justine (*☎ 96 22 88*), on the edge of the lagoon, is 1.5km from the village entrance and 500m on the right coming from the airport. It has two bungalows for two and one family bungalow with cold-water bathroom for 5500/6500 CFP half/full board.

The most remote of the guesthouses is **Kahaia Beach** (*☎ 96 22 77, fax 96 22 81*), on a motu to the north-east of the airport. There are four lagoonside bungalows with their own cold-water bathrooms for 5000/7000 CFP half/full board.

Places to Eat
Apart from the guesthouses, there are not many places to eat. **Chez Maui** and **Chez Rosita** are shops with general supplies and village's only bakery often has coconut bread. **Chez Hélène** does meals for 2500 CFP, but you must book. **Tikehau Village** has a restaurant in a superbly situated beachfront *fare,* where lunch costs 1500 CFP and dinner 2000 CFP.

Getting There & Away
Air The airport is little more than 1km east of the village entrance. Air Tahiti (*☎ 96 22 66*) has four flights a week between Papeete and Tikehau direct, or via Rangiroa.

Grafting is a delicate operation that involves introducing a nucleus into the gonads of the pearl oyster.

A pearl farm, Manihi (Tuamotus)

Pearl-shell is used for making buttons.

Lustre and sheen contribute to a pearl's value.

Before the grafting operation the pearl oysters are washed and sorted.

Preparing the shells for the grafting operation

After grafting, the oysters are reimmersed.

Papeete-Tikehau costs 13,600 CFP, Tikehau-Rangiroa 4400 CFP.

Boat The *Rairoa Nui*, *Mareva Nui*, *Saint Xavier Maris Stella* and the *Dory* stop at Tikehau and tie up at the wharf on the lagoonside (see the Getting Around chapter).

Getting Around
A 10km track goes around the motu on which Tuherahera is situated, and passes by the airport. Your hosts can hire or lend you bicycles for about 500 CFP a day. See the Places to Stay section for lagoon boat-trip operators.

MATAIVA
pop 227 • lagoon area 25 sq km
reef passes 1
The first European to land on Mataiva, at the north-western end of the archipelago, was Bellingshausen, in 1820. There is a great risk that its appearance will change dramatically in the years to come, as there are plans to mine the lagoon substratum, which contains about 70 separate phosphate deposits. This would replace the Makatea deposits, which were exhausted in 1966 (see the boxed text 'Makatea – A Half-Century Industrial Epoch' for more information). The accessible part is estimated to contain 12 million tonnes, enough for 10 to 15 years of mining. Such large-scale industrial activity in such a restricted space will undoubtedly cause ecological problems.

Pahua, the village, is divided by a pass suitable only for very small boats; it's just a few metres wide and no deeper than 1.5m. A bridge spans the pass and links the two parts of the village. Nine hoa, thin trickles of water, provide small links between the lagoon and the ocean. Mataiva (literally, 'Nine Eyes') is named after these channels.

The structure of the Mataiva lagoon gives it a very special appearance: the coral constructions at the surface of the water create dividing walls of 50 to 300m that form about 70 basins of a maximum depth of 10m. Seen from a plane, the play of light on this underwater tessellation forms a mosaic of green.

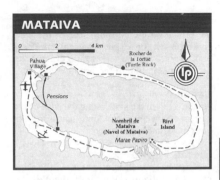

Despite the limited tourist infrastructure, visitors will find the atoll a delightful escape. There are superb beaches, numerous snorkelling spots, lots of fish and one of the few noteworthy archaeological sites in the Tuamotus. Air Tahiti flights make it a possiblity to spend a pleasant weekend on the island.

Information
There is no bank on the atoll. Pahua has two shops and a post office, south of the bridge. The post office is open Monday to Thursday from 7.30 to 11.30 am, Friday to 11 am. It has a fax service and sells phonecards. There are card-operated telephone booths opposite the post office and at the airport.

Pahua
For the 200 inhabitants of this peaceful village the prospect of the phosphate-mining project is like the sword of Damocles. For the time being, most of people live off fishing and copra production but in 1998 a huge wave partially ravaged the village. Repairs may still be underway.

Le Rocher de la Tortue
Called Ofai Tau Noa (Rock of the Turtle) by the inhabitants of the atoll, this rock is a remnant of an uplifted *feo* (coral reef), with the shape of a splayed mushroom. It gave rise to the cloud legend: if a cloud of the same shape as the rock appears above the pass, weather changes can be predicted and turtles will come to the surface. It will then be time to hunt them.

To get there, take the track that starts at the bridge on the northern side of the pass and follow it for 4.7km. Then take the secondary track on the left, which crosses the coconut plantation to the ocean.

Beaches

On the south of the atoll, along the edge of the lagoon, there are many fine beaches. Take your mask and fins along.

Marae Papiro

Mataiva has a well-kept marae on the edge of a hoa, about 14km from the village, south-east of the atoll at the end of the track. In the centre of this marae, you can clearly see the lithic-stone seat from which, according to the legend, the giant Tu guarded the pass against invasion. In case of attack from enemy tribes, he needed to take no more than three steps to push the assailants off the island and crush them. Tu is one of the gods in the Tahitian pantheon. It is also the name of a fierce warrior king from Anaa Atoll, an ancestor of the Pomares, who conquered the surrounding atolls as far as Fakarava.

The throne is surrounded by rectangular marae and bordered by little blocks of coral limestone driven into the ground. In the centre of each marae, two larger stones stand on their sides.

Île aux Oiseaux

A good place for nesting, east of the lagoon, this crescent-shaped coral tongue covered in small shrubs is a favourite place for oio, tara and red-footed boobies.

Nombril de Mataiva

According to legend, a rock on the surface of the lagoon, next to Île aux Oiseaux, called Mataiva Papa (The Navel of Mataiva), is the place where King Tu first set foot. Tradition has it that a foreigner reaching Mataiva should put a foot on this rock.

Fish Parks

Don't miss the chance to accompany the fishers on their way to trap fish in one of the numerous parks around the lagoon and the pass. A first fisher, wearing a mask, jumps into the water carrying fencing wire that is closed at one end in the form of a hoop net, while the other fisher splashes the surface. The frightened fish rush into the trap. All the fishers have to do is empty them into the boat and repeat the routine. The few big fish that escape the trap are harpooned. Sorted, scaled and gutted, they are sold in the village for around 500 CFP per kilogram. Balistes, mullets, parrotfish and jackfish are all part of the bounty.

Shipwreck

Stuck right in the middle of the coconut plantation, this rusted wreck, of which only a part of the bow remains, is a symbol of nature's violence. According to elders, this ship sank in the 1906 cyclone and was carried to the coconut plantation by cyclones in later years.

To get there, follow the track for about 3km, then take the secondary track that turns right towards the ocean. After 450m, you will come to a fork, from where you can catch a glimpse of the ocean. Don't head towards the ocean, but follow the other track to the left for 250m to reach the wreck.

Places to Stay & Eat

The people of Pahua hope that an increasing number of tourists will dissuade the government from setting up drilling sites on the lagoon. The three pensions are very similar, only the locations differ. Prices are per person per day and include airport transfers.

The only guesthouse north of the pass, 150m from the bridge and right on the pass, is Edgar's *Mataiva Village* (☎ 96 32 33, ☎/fax 96 32 95). The six two-person bungalows are clean, comfortable, have cold-water bathroom facilities and cost 4000/6000 CFP half/full board. Crayfish are a speciality in the large dining room on stilts, but ask for a mosquito coil.

Super Mataiva Cool (☎ 96 32 53) is south of the bridge, also right on the edge of the pass, and is run by the Huri family. The damage caused by the freak wave in 1998 has been repaired and the three units have cold-water bathrooms and cost 5500/7000

CFP half/full board for one person, 10,000/13,000 CFP for two.

Ava Hei Pension (☎ 96 32 39) is close to the lagoon, about 5km from the village. The beach location is perfect and the traditional-style bungalows (with thatch roofing and crushed-coral floor) have bathroom and fan and cost 7000 CFP per person including meals. There's a restaurant *fure* and a *fure potee* with a fully stocked bar.

Apart from the pensions there's really nowhere to eat, although there are several small *shops* with basic food supplies.

Getting There & Away
Mataiva is 350km north-east of Tahiti and 100km west of Rangiroa.

Air The Air Tahiti (☎ 96 32 48) representative is the proprietor of the Mataiva Village guesthouse. Papeete-Mataiva flights connect at least twice a week, via Rangiroa, usually on Thursday and Sunday. Papeete-Mataiva costs 13,600 CFP, Rangiroa-Mataiva 4400 CFP.

Boat Mataiva is on the route of the *Mareva Nui* and *Saint Xavier Maris Stella*. See the earlier Getting Around chapter for more information.

Getting Around
A track goes almost all the way around the island, in the middle of the coconut plantation. To the north, the track finishes at Marae Papiro, about 14km away. To the south, allow about 10km to the end. Cycling is an excellent way of getting around. The Mataiva Village and Super Mataiva Cool guesthouses rent out bicycles for about 1000 CFP per day. Cars can be rented for 2000 CFP to 3000 CFP per day, with driver. Inquire at the guesthouses. All the guesthouses have motor boats and will suggest a visit to the Île aux Oiseaux, the fish parks and the Nombril de Mataiva. Allow 2000 CFP to 3000 CFP for the day, including a picnic and the visit.

MANOLO MYLONAS

The arrival of a ship in port is an occasion of great excitement for islanders on the most remote of the Tuamotu atolls.

MANIHI

pop 769 • lagoon area 192 sq km
reef passes 1

Some 175km north-east of Rangiroa, Manihi has acquired an international reputation for pearl production. The big names in this business, Bréaud, Paul Yu and SPM, chose to set up here and the lagoon is now scattered with large-scale family and industrial pearl production farms.

Shaped like an ellipsis, the atoll is 28km long and 8km wide, with only one opening, the Tairapa Pass in the south-west. The exhilarating beauty of the lagoon and the riches of its underwater world were quickly recognised and an international hotel was built in 1977. Tourism and pearl production have created many jobs and provide work for most of the inhabitants; fishing and copra production provide a supplementary income.

Manihi is also a pioneer in the field of infrastructure. The second airstrip in the archipelago was built on the south-west of the atoll in 1969. A cyclone in February 1993 destroyed 70% of it but it was rebuilt and raised in order to avoid a similar disaster.

Information

There is no bank on the atoll but the Manihi Pearl Beach Resort may be able to change money in emergencies. The post office is in Paeua village opposite the marina. There are card-operated telephone booths on the ground floor of the post office building, at the airport and at the Manihi Pearl Beach Resort. The village also has a hospital.

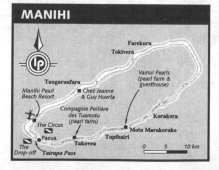

Paeua

This charmless, almost neglected village is in striking contrast to villages on other atolls and will not entice you to stay. The pace of life is set to the rhythm of work in the pearl farms, where most of the inhabitants are employed. Paeua has four places of worship: Sanito, Mormon, Protestant and Catholic.

Pearl Farms

The first pearl farm was set up on Manihi in 1968 and the atoll has steadily established itself as a principal centre for black pearls in the South Pacific. See the boxed text 'Black Pearl, Jewel of the Tuamotus' in this chapter for information on pearl production. For travellers, visiting a pearl farm is a must. The best idea is to visit to a small family farm and a larger industrial farm. Avoid holiday periods, particularly Christmas, when the workers may be away.

The Manihi Pearl Beach Resort is the main organiser of pearl-farm visits, usually combined with a picnic and village excursion; the tours visit the Compagnie Perlière des Tuamotus (CPDT) three times weekly and cost 2544 CFP. The fourth largest pearl farm on the atoll, CPDT employs just five people to produce 100,000 pearls a year. It's on Motu Takovea, 5km east of the village. The Manihi Pearl Beach Resort has a shop with mounted and unmounted black pearls directly from this farm. They both accept credit cards.

Vainui Pearls (☎ 96 42 89) is a family farm run by the Buniets, who also own a guesthouse on Motu Marakorako. They specialise in *mabe* (hollow mother-of-pearl) and make direct sales of pearls and mabe. Again, credit cards are accepted.

Nothing stops you from contacting the small firms directly. All you have to do is go to the village and ask; you may even find the pearl of your dreams at a very reasonable price. Remember, however, that a pearl farm is a business, not a tourist site. Remember also that the production centres may not be where you find the best pearls, as most pearls are quickly despatched to Papeete. Prices do tend to be about 30% lower than in Papeete or abroad, however.

Richard Steger (☎ 43 31 10 in Papeete) speaks English and will organise tours to Pai Moana Pearls if you contact him before leaving the capital.

Diving

A well-known dive centre operates from the Manihi Pearl Beach Resort and organises dives to a number of magnificent sites near the pass. See the 'Diving' special section in the Outdoor Activities chapter for details.

Places to Stay

Reasonably priced accommodation is difficult to find on Manihi and the facilities are scattered all over the atoll.

Budget *Chez Jeanne & Guy Huerta (☎ 96 42 90, fax 96 42 91)* is on the lagoonside on Motu Taugaraufara, about 9km north-east of the airport. It has well equipped bungalows with bathroom, two on the beach for 8000 CFP per person and one over-water for 12,000 CFP including airport transfers. These prices include all meals but it's wise to bring some food along just in case. The owners will take you shopping in the village. Credit cards are accepted and lagoon tours are organised.

Vainui Pearls (☎ 96 42 89, fax 96 42 00 at the post office) is on Motu Marakorako, east of the village and about half an hour by boat from the airport. The French-Tahitian couple that runs this guesthouse has six rooms with shared bathroom for 8000 CFP per person per day, including all meals, airport transfers and fishing and picnic excursions. The owners have a small pearl farm and sell mabe, keshi and pearls. If they are going to the village or airport they'll take you to the diving centre at Manihi Pearl Beach Resort for free; otherwise it costs 4500 CFP return. Credit cards are accepted.

Top End Two minutes from the airport, at the south-western end of the lagoon, *Manihi Pearl Beach Resort (☎ 96 42 73, fax 96 42 72; ☎ 43 16 10, fax 43 17 86 in Papeete)* has 41 units (22 on the beach and 10 over-water), providing tough competition for the most prestigious hotels in the archipelago.

The whole development is harmoniously integrated with the idyllic natural setting: airy coconut-groves, white-sand beaches, a sea-water swimming pool and the magnificent lagoon. Glass-bottomed tables for underwater viewing have become the norm in over-water bungalows, but here, even the bedside tables have glass bottoms! The beach bungalows have bathrooms with gardens. The Poe Rava Restaurant has a beachfront terrace and the bar, with its own terrace, directly overlooks the pool, the lagoon and the beach.

This luxury will cost you the trifling sum of 30,240/49,680 CFP for a beach/over-water bungalow. Add 6100/8400 CFP per person for half/full board. Lunches are à la carte. Organised activities include long-line fishing, snorkelling (1590 CFP), visits to a pearl farm and the village, picnic trips to a motu (5830 CFP) and game fishing (12,349 CFP per hour). Credit cards are accepted.

Places to Eat

Apart from the guesthouses and hotels, there are hardly any places to eat. In Paeua, the self-service *Jean-Marie*, near the marina, has good supplies.

The restaurant at the *Manihi Pearl Beach Resort* has reasonable prices, especially at lunchtime. The setting by the swimming pool and lagoon is delightful and entrees cost 800 CFP to 2000 CFP, main courses 1300 CFP to 2200 CFP, and desserts are around 900 CFP.

Getting There & Away

Air Air Tahiti's office (☎ 96 43 34 or ☎ 96 42 71 on flight days) is in Jean Marie's supermarket in Paeua. On flight days it's at the airport. There are near-daily flights between Papeete and Manihi, direct or via Ahe or Rangiroa. Papeete-Manihi costs 16,500 CFP, Rangiroa-Manihi 8800 CFP. Manihi is also linked to Bora Bora, via Rangiroa, three times weekly in the Bora Bora-Manihi direction and once weekly Manihi-Bora Bora (23,400 CFP).

Boat The *Mareva Nui*, *Saint Xavier Maris Stella* and *Vai-Aito* service Manihi (see the

Black Pearl, Jewel of the Tuamotus

The trump card of the Polynesian economy, the *poe rava* (black pearl) is the result of natural phenomena and complex human intervention. The main centres of production are on the Tuamotus and in the Gambier Archipelago. Manihi, Takapoto, Takaroa, Arutua, Makemo and Mangareva are the best-known. Their lagoons, studded with pearl farms standing on piles, look like lakeside towns. The size of the operations varies from one or two people, to more than 80 people on the industrial sites. The cause of this activity is an oyster, *Pinctada margaritifera*, found in abundance in Polynesian lagoons.

The shells of these bivalves were used in ancient times to make ceremonial jewellery, fish hooks and lures, and were once much sought-after by the European button industry. The overexploitation of natural beds and the decline of the button industry sounded the death knell in the 1960s, and the culture of oysters for pearl production took over, initially on Manihi.

The formation of a pearl results from the accidental or artificial introduction of a foreign body inside the oyster. In response to this intrusion, the epithelial cells of the mantle (the secretory organ) produce material to isolate the foreign body. In this way, the nucleus is gradually covered in *nacre* (mother-of-pearl). If the foreign body (eg a grain of sand or coral) is introduced by natural means, the result is an extremely rare natural pearl, known as a fine pearl.

The pearl farmer must reproduce this natural mechanism. Firstly, the oysters are methodically reared. At certain times of the year, they release sexual substances that are fertilised in the water. After swimming around for several weeks, the young oysters (seed oysters) attach themselves to the coral. The pearl farmer catches the seed oysters in artificial collectors sunk in the lagoon and then attaches them to underwater rearing lines.

The first stage consists of sacrificing a perfectly healthy mature oyster, known as the donor oyster. A fragment of its mantle is removed and divided into about 50 minute particles, called grafts. The second stage is the grafting proper, which takes just a few seconds. The recipient oyster is fixed to a support and held open with forceps. Using a scalpel, the grafter firstly incises the back of the gonad (reproductive organ) and inserts the graft. A perfectly spherical bead (the nucleus), about 6mm in diameter, is introduced into the gonad so that it is in contact with the graft. The graft cells develop around the nucleus to form the pearl sack which, once closed, secretes the nacreous material. The grafted oysters are placed inside keepnets (metal baskets) and lowered back into the lagoon. They are then regularly inspected and cleaned.

Getting Around chapter for details). Loading and unloading takes place at the Paeua wharf in the pass.

Getting Around

The only track on Manihi links Taugaraufara to the airport – covering a total distance of only about 9km. Getting around the atoll requires some ingenuity! The Manihi Pearl Beach Resort can suggest where you can rent a bicycle for around 500 CFP per day.

To/From the Airport The airport is at the south-western end of the atoll, two minutes away from Manihi Pearl Beach Resort. This hotel, Chez Jeanne & Guy Huerta and Vainui Pearls organise airport transfers. To get to the village you have no choice but to hitch a boat ride from the wharf, right next to the airport *fare*.

Boat To get to the dive centre from the village, you can use the Manihi Pearl Beach Resort staff shuttle, which generally leaves

Black Pearl, Jewel of the Tuamotus

Layer upon layer, the mother-of-pearl thickens around the nucleus at the rate of 1mm a year. Eighteen months later, the first harvest is gathered. A second nucleus may be implanted to obtain a second, larger (15 to 20mm) pearl 15 months later.

Grafting entails risks inherent to all surgical operations: of 100 grafted oysters, 25 to 30 do not survive the shock of the operation and another 25 to 30 reject the nucleus. When the time comes to harvest them, only five of the remaining 40 (just 2%) will have produced perfect pearls. When a second graft is performed, the success rate increases to just under 10%.

Until recently, the only grafters were Japanese. They were virtual superstars who had to be retained at great expense, but they are gradually being replaced by Polynesians who have allegedly discovered the 'secret' of the technique. A centre for the pearl-shell and pearl-culture professions has been established on Rangiroa and provides training for future pearl farmers. Nonetheless, the act of grafting is still partially veiled in mystery.

The pearls are mainly used for rings and pendants. Several factors determine their value: the diameter (from 8.5 to 18mm); shape (whether it's round, ie perfectly spherical; ringed, ie with visible rings; baroque, ie asymmetrical; pear-shaped); quality (absence of flaws or marks) and colour. 'Black pearl' is in fact an inaccurate term. The pearls produced by *Pinctada margaritifera* range in colour from pearly white to black, and include deep purple, champagne and grey. The orient (the pearl's iridescent reflection) and lustre (mirror effect) also enter into the equation. Jewellers generally classify pearls by using two letters followed by a figure: a pearl classed as RB 12 is perfectly round (R), has a few pits or surface flaws, a correct orient (B) and measures 12mm in diameter.

Less well known, *keshi* and *mabe* are two other products of pearl culture. Keshi is pure mother-of-pearl, a pearl without a nucleus. In some cases the nucleus is rejected but the secreting graft continues to produce mother-of-pearl. The resultant pearls vary from 2 to 8mm in diameter and are often baroque in shape; they are not discovered until harvesting and are used to make earrings or bracelets.

Mabe, by contrast, is the result of deliberate manipulation. The technician sticks a plastic mould on the inner surface of the shell. The mould is gradually covered in layers of mother-of-pearl. After a few months, the mother-of-pearl is cut off with a diamond disk and the mould is removed. The result is a pure, hollow mabe, which is filled with epoxy resin before a small mother-of-pearl plate is welded on to form the base. Mabe is highly valued in the jewellery trade for making pendants, brooches, earrings and cufflinks.

the Paeua marina at about 6 am and returns around 4 pm. It'll take you for free. If they're going to the airport or the village, resort owners will generally take you across to the dive centre. For other points around the atoll, talk to boat owners in the village.

AHE

pop 377 • lagoon area 170 sq km
reef passes 1
Situated 15km west of Manihi, Ahe was 'discovered' by Wilkes in 1839. The atoll is 20km long by 10km wide and is entered by the Tiareroa (or Reianui) Pass in the west. The village of Tenukupara is on the southwestern side. Cultured-pearl production is beginning to develop. Ahe is well known to yachties, who often pull in when sailing from the Marquesas.

Getting There & Away

Air Tahiti connects Ahe two to three times weekly with Papeete. The return flight sometimes goes via Manihi. Papeete-Ahe costs 16,500 CFP. The *Saint Xavier Maris Stella*, *Mareva Nui* and *Vai-Aito* are the ships that service Ahe. See the Getting Around chapter for information.

TAKAROA

pop 488 • lagoon area 113 sq km
reef passes 1

First seen by European eyes on 15 April 1616 by Le Maire, Takaroa (literally, Long Chin) and its close neighbour, Takapoto, form a pair. Marine maps have persisted in calling them the King George Islands, ever since Byron's visit in June 1765.

Takaroa is, along with Manihi and Tepoto, one of the northernmost islands in the Tuamotus. The rectangular atoll is 27km long by 6km wide and has only one pass, Teauonae, in the south-west. The only village, Teavaroa, was built on the edge of the pass. Takaroa's most singular feature is that it is a Mormon bastion, which contrasts with the traditional religious characteristics of the Tuamotus. The population is 90% Mormon and alcohol is prohibited on Takaroa. The inhabitants live off cultured-pearl production and, to a lesser extent, fishing and copra production.

Information

There is no bank on Takaroa. The post office, near the bridge at the end of the village and next to the hospital, has fax facilities and phonecards. There's a card-operated public telephone in front of the mairie and a first-aid room beside the post office.

Teavaroa

Sleepy quietness emanates from this village, which time seems to have passed by. Life takes a gently monotonous course, punctuated by fishing, copra production and work at the pearl farms. In the evening, young Paumotu gather near the pass and fish with long wooden rods to the sound of *kaina* (Polynesian) music. There is no danger of losing your way: you will inevitably see the Mormon church with its red steeple, built in 1891. A weather bureau, the most important in the northern Tuamotus, is near the mairie.

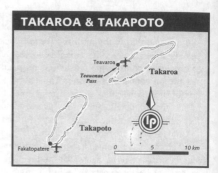

TAKAROA & TAKAPOTO

Marae

There are two marae close to the village, but they've been neglected and all you can see is a shapeless mass of rock, covered in bushes. The first is beside the bungalow that's owned by the Temanaha family, next to the north-eastern end of the airstrip, on the lagoonside.

The second marae is hidden under some bushes, about 500m from the bridge at the village exit, just on the left of the track towards the airport. Walk beyond the white house for 200m and you'll see the marae hidden on your left.

Shipwreck

The imposing wreck of a four-masted vessel, which ran into the coral reef at the beginning of the twentieth century, is an indication of how difficult sailing is in the Tuamotus and of how violent the cyclones can be. The rusted hull of the ship is now covered in graffiti. From the airport *fare*, it is 6km along the track, going in the opposite direction from the village.

Pearl Farms

Paul Yu, Giot and Vaimareva are the major pearl producers on Takaroa; there are also a host of small family businesses. The staff at place you stay will probably be delighted to show your their own pearl grafting operation or will direct you towards other pearl-farm operators.

Snorkelling

Takaroa's lagoon has numerous coral formations near the beach that are wonderful for snorkelling. Ask village kids about accompanying them when they go spear fishing.

Places to Stay & Eat

Chez Vahinerii (☎ 98 23 05) is run by the Temanaha family, who rent one of their impeccably clean bedrooms for 3000 CFP for one or two people. The house faces the Mormon temple and the bathroom is shared. Add another 800 CFP for breakfast, 1200 CFP for lunch and 1500 CFP for dinner. The bungalow with TV, bathroom and kitchen, beside the lagoon and about 800m from the airport, faces their pearl farm and costs 5000 CFP for two people, without meals. The coral heads breaking the surface close to the beach will entertain snorkelling enthusiasts.

Pension Poe Rangi (☎ 98 23 82 or ☎ 98 23 77 at the weather station) literally means 'pearls of heaven' and guests may think it's a good description. It's situated on the other side of the pass, 10 minutes by boat from the village. There are three bungalows with cold-water bathroom, one with a kitchenette. The per-person cost is 6000/7000 CFP half/full board including transfers from the airport. Meals include local specialities such as *maa paumotu* (Paumotu food) and Caribbean dishes and are served in the *fare potee*, where there's also a bar. You can rent a kayak (600 CFP an hour), go waterskiing (2000 CFP for 10 minutes), go snorkelling (2500 CFP), make a fishing trip (500 CFP), visit a pearl farm or take various atoll excursions (3000 CFP to 5000 CFP).

Apart from the guesthouses there's really nowhere to eat. The only *shop* is run by Austrian Manfred Ennemoser. It's in front of the Mormon temple and has basic supplies and canned food.

Getting There & Away

Takaroa is 575km north-east of Papeete and less than 100km east of Manihi.

Air The airport is 2.5km north-east of the village. The office of the Air Tahiti representative is in the village. There are at least three weekly flights Papeete-Takaroa (18,000 CFP) and Takaroa-Takapoto (4400 CFP) as well as less-frequent connections to Manihi. The Papeete-Takaroa trip takes just over 1½ hours.

Boat The *Mareva Nui* and *Saint Xavier Maris Stella* service the atoll; they draw up to the wharf in the pass. See the Getting Around chapter for details.

Getting Around

The only track goes from the village to Paul Yu's pearl farm, through the airport – about 10km. Your hosts will arrange picnics on the lagoon motu for 2500 CFP to 3500 CFP per person. To rent a bicycle, ask at the Pension Vahinerii.

TAKAPOTO

pop 612 • lagoon area 102 sq km

Takapoto (literally, Short Chin) Atoll is 9km south of Takaroa and was 'discovered' on 14 April 1616 by Le Maire. It's 20km long and 6km across at its widest point and doesn't have a pass. On a scientific level, this atoll is one of the best-known in the Tuamotus. Since 1974 it has been closely examined within the multidisciplinary studies of the UNESCO Man & Biosphere (MAB) program.

The second pearl farm in the Tuamotus was built on this atoll in the late 1960s. As this activity flourished at the beginning of the 1970s, the shore mushroomed with the characteristic huts on stilts. See the boxed text 'Black Pearl, Jewel of the Tuamotus' earlier in this chapter for information on the production of pearls. Apart from pearl production, the protected lagoon has maintained its traditional collection of young oysters. In 1985, 600,000 young oysters took to the underwater platforms on Manihi. Copra production and fishing are a further source of income for the inhabitants. Pearl farms, beaches and some archaeological remains could one day make the atoll a popular tourist attraction.

Information

There is no bank service on the atoll. The post office, next to the mairie, offers fax facilities and phonecards. There is a card-operated telephone in front of the mairie. The community clinic is also next to the post office.

THE TUAMOTUS

Fakatopatere

The appearance of this little village, on the south-west of the atoll and next to the airport, is quite surprising because it spreads across the entire width of the reef crown, and its streets (sand tracks, in fact) create a criss-cross pattern, with a Catholic church in the middle.

There is a Fakatopatere agency of EVAAM, an organisation whose purpose is to develop and promote aquaculture and maritime activities.

Pearl Farms

To see the whole process of pearl production (see the boxed text 'Black Pearl, Jewel of the Tuamotus' in this chapter) you'll have to make an appointment with the cultured-pearl producers. However, almost all guesthouse proprietors own a pearl farm and will suggest that you visit theirs. You can buy pearls directly from these producers.

Beaches

Takapoto has many idyllic and wild places, including numerous white-sand beaches around the lagoon, which are easily accessible by a track. In the village itself, there is a small beach close to Pimati Toti's house. During their stopover in Takapoto, *Aranui* tourists usually picnic on a beach 2km east of the village. Follow the track through the coconut grove until you come to the white building on the left, less than 5km from the village. Walk for 700m and turn off at the path on the left that crosses the coconut grove towards the lagoon. You'll find several fishers' *fare* and the beach of your dreams.

Marae Takai

This archaeological site is worth the long walk. It consists of three small marae surrounded by vertical coral slabs. According to the owner of the land it could be a funeral site containing bones. North-west of Fakatopatere, the marae is well hidden behind bushy vegetation. Follow the track that goes past the cemetery at the village exit for 15km. You will see a hoa, spanned by a stone bridge. Cross this bridge and immediately on the right walk 60m along the hoa towards the lagoon. Turn left for about 30m, clearing your way through bushes and coconut trees and you will come upon the three marae in a little clearing.

The walk to Marae Takai will take you through magnificent and beautifully maintained coconut plantations. The lagoon shore is festooned with pearl farms and white-sand beaches.

Fish Parks

Follow the north-eastern track to the end, about 9km, to Teavatika, a fish park built of coral blocks in a hoa. This public park is a rare example of its kind.

Fish Farms

Easily recognisable by their posts, which pierce the surface of the water in channels or lagoons, fish farms are a familiar part of the landscape on many of the Tuamotu atolls.

These enclosures enable fishers to regulate the numbers of fish taken according to the needs of the inhabitants, the arrival of the schooners or the availability of air freight.

The establishment of a fish farm takes into account the currents, where the fish usually pass by and the layout of the sea bed. Generally, they are set up near channels or inside the reef ring in 2 to 4m of water. Two collecting branches, arranged in a V-shape (*rauroa*) and open at varying angles, lead to a rounded chamber (*aua*). The aua is in turn connected by a narrower entrance to a secondary hoopnet (*tipua*), placed at the side. The fish that enter this maze are unable to turn back. The fishers simply have to harpoon them or catch them in a hoopnet.

The passages, made of wire netting fixed to metal or *kahaia*-wood posts, require constant maintenance. Piled-up blocks of coral were once used to fulfil the same functions.

Places to Stay & Eat

Étienne Heuea (☎ 96 65 09) is close to the post office and has a well equipped chalet with mezzanine. It costs 4000 CFP per person per day and is often rented to government officials.

Takapoto Village (☎ 98 65 44) is on a small yellow-sand beach beside the lagoon, south-east of the village and about 100m from the EVAAM building. It's run by the Totis, who you might first encounter making *ombrièreses* (the synthetic devices that are put out for pearl-oyster larvae to attach themselves to). There is a comfortable bungalow with cold-water bathroom for two people and a room, also for two, with shared bathroom in the main house. Per-person, the bungalow costs 4500/6000 CFP half/full board and the room is 3500/5000 CFP. Mr Toti is mayor of Takapoto and has a thorough knowledge of the history of the Tuamotus and can tell you stories about the frightening raids of the Anaa warriors.

Apart from the guesthouses, places to eat are scarce. The *Nadine* shop is near the wharf on the oceanside, and is relatively well supplied.

Getting There & Away

Takapoto is 560km north-east of Papeete and less than 100km east of Manihi.

Air The airport is just a stone's throw to the south-east of the village. Air Tahiti has three weekly flights, connecting Papeete, Takaroa and Takapoto and, on certain days, Manihi. Papeete-Takapoto costs 16,500 CFP, Takapoto-Takaroa 1100 CFP. The Papeete-Takapoto trip takes 1½ hours.

Boat The *Saint Xavier Maris Stella* and *Mareva Nui* serve Takapoto. *Taporo IV* and *Aranui*, en route to the Marquesas, also stop here (see the earlier Getting Around chapter). The transfers by bonitier take place at the landing stage next to the Nadine shop.

Getting Around

There are two tracks from the village. The first one goes in a north-easterly direction for about 9km, to the coral-block fish park.

The other goes in a north-westerly direction. It's fine as far as Marae Takai, 15km out, but then reaches a few hoa that are impossible to cross.

The ideal way to explore the atoll is by bicycle (500 CFP per day) or scooter (1500 CFP to 2000 CFP). Most guesthouses organise picnics on deserted motu, reached by speedboat. Allow 2000 CFP per person.

ARUTUA

**pop 620 • lagoon area 570 sq km
reef passes 1**

This almost circular atoll is nearly 25km in diameter. The lagoon waters meet the ocean through the small Porofai Pass in the east, near the village of **Rautini**. The village is on a motu south of the airport, half an hour away by boat.

The village, which was devastated by cyclones in 1983, has been entirely rebuilt. The lagoon has a reputation for being rich in fish and crayfish. Fishing, copra production and, most importantly, **cultured pearls** are the main economic activities on the atoll.

Places to Stay

Chez Neri (☎ 96 52 55) in Rautini is the only place to stay. There are two rooms in the house, a shared cold-water bathroom and it costs 6000 CFP per person per day, with all meals. The owners also have a pearl farm and will take you to lagoon fish-parks. Airport transfers cost 3000 CFP per person return.

Getting There & Away

Arutua is about 375km north east of Tahiti. To the west, only 30km separates it from the eastern extremity of Rangiroa.

Air There are three flights weekly between Papeete and Arutua (14,000 CFP) and two of the return flights stop at Rangiroa (4400 CFP). Getting to Rautini from the airport, at the west of Motu Tenihinihi, takes half an hour by boat.

Boat The *Saint Xavier Maris Stella*, *Mareva Nui*, *Dory* and *Cobia I* serve Arutua (see the Getting Around chapter).

THE TUAMOTUS

KAUKURA
pop 379 • lagoon area 546 sq km
reef passes 1
Kaukura was first reached by a European
on 28 May 1722, by Roggeveen, who also
'discovered' Easter Island. Oval-shaped
and measuring 50km by 14km at its widest
point, there is only one pass into the lagoon. Fishing is the atoll's main activity.
Kaukura, together with Tikehau, is the
biggest provider of fish to the Papeete markets from the Tuamotus. Transport is by
cargo boat and plane. The inhabitants live
in **Raitahiti** village, on the north-western
side of the lagoon.

Places to Stay
Pension Rekareka (☎ *96 62 40, 96 62 39),*
run by the Parker family in Raitahiti, is a
multistorey house with six two-person
rooms with shared bathroom for 6000 CFP
per person per day, full board. There are
also five bungalows for two people with
shared bathroom on Motu Tahunapona, 15
minutes by boat from the village. Transfers
from the airport are included. Excursions to
pearl farms and fish parks, and bicycle
rental can be organised.

Getting There & Away
Kaukura atoll is 55km south-east of Rangiroa and 340km north-east of Tahiti.

Air The airport is 2km from the village. Air
Tahiti flies Papeete-Kaukura twice weekly
via Rangiroa for 14,000 CFP. The trip takes
1 hour and 40 minutes. Rangiroa-Kaukura
costs 4400 CFP.

Boat The *Saint Xavier Maris Stella*,
Mareva Nui, *Cobia I* and *Dory* have
stopovers at Kaukura (see the Getting
Around chapter).

FAKARAVA
pop 467 • lagoon area 1121 sq km
reef passes 2
Fakarava is the second-largest atoll in the
Tuamotus. Roughly rectangular in shape, its
lagoon is 60km long and 25km wide. The lagoon waters merge with the ocean through

FAKARAVA

Garuae Pass in the north and Tumakohua
Pass in the south. The opening of a permanent airstrip in 1995, near the northern pass,
has helped to open up this magnificent atoll.
One day it could be a second Rangiroa but
in the meantime its huge tourist potential is
seriously underexploited! Visits to **pearl
farms** and picnics on idyllic **motu** are the
order of the day. Fakarava has amazing **diving** in the pass (see the 'Diving' special section) and it's also on the program for several
dive-cruise operators. See the Getting
Around chapter for details.

Most of the population is gathered in **Rotoava** village at the north-eastern end, 4km
east of the airport. A handful of inhabitants
also live in Tetamanu village, on the edge of
the southern pass. On the eastern edge, an
uninterrupted reef-strip stretches for 40km.
The western side, on the other hand, has a
few scattered islets. Copra and cultured-
pearl production and fishing are the main
industries.

THE TUAMOTUS

Places to Stay

Relais Marama (☎ 98 42 25), on the ocean side of the motu at Rotoava, has two rooms and two bungalows with shared bathroom. Costs are 4800/6500 CFP for half/full board and airport transfers cost 500 CFP per person.

Pension Paparara (☎ 98 42 40; *leave a message for M Ato Lissant*) is about 5km south of the village. Beside the lagoon there are several bungalows with shared bathroom for 6500 CFP per person full board plus 1000 CFP for airport transfers.

Tetamanu Village (☎ 43 92 40, fax 42 77 70) is managed by Sané Richmond, a shipowner on Tahiti. It's at the other end of the atoll, beside the Tumakohua Pass. Lovers of complete escape will find happiness in this idyllic setting – it's difficult to imagine a more remote location. The per-person cost, including all meals and transfers, is 40,000/50,000/70,000 CFP for three/five/seven days. There are four two-person bungalows with shared bathroom, meals are served in an over-water restaurant and activities such as fishing, motu picnics, pearl-farm visits and snorkelling in the pass are all included.

Getting There & Away

The atoll is 488km east-north-east of Tahiti and south-east of Rangiroa.

Air The airport is about 4km from the village, going west towards the pass. Air Tahiti flies Papeete-Fakarava three or four times a week for 14,700 CFP, via Rangiroa in each direction for 4400 CFP.

Boat The *Saint Xavier Maris Stella, Vai Aito* and *Marevu Nui* serve Fakarava. The *Auura'Nui 3* (whose owner is Sané Richmond, the owner of Tetamanu Village) stops at Tetamanu. See the earlier Getting Around chapter.

Getting Around

From Rotoava, a track goes to the southwest of the atoll for about 40km. Boat excursions are arranged by both guesthouses on the atoll.

ANAA

pop 425 • lagoon area 184 sq km

Anaa Atoll, which is oriented on a north-west/south-east axis, is just 28km long and 5km wide. It's made up of 11 islets scattered on the reef circumference and it doesn't have a pass. Anaa, which used to be densely populated, became known for the ferocity of its inhabitants, who extended their domination over the northern part of the archipelago, pillaging the atolls they conquered.

Cyclones have cost Anaa dearly. Tukuhora village, razed by a tidal wave in 1906 that left 100 people dead, was devastated again in the 1982-83 cyclone season. The inhabitants live off fishing and copra production.

Places to Stay

Pension Maui Nui (☎ 98 32 75) is close to the airport and the lagoon. There are two bungalows, one with cold-water bathroom, as well as a house with two rooms for 4000/6000 CFP per person half/full board.

Pension Toku Kaiga (☎ 98 32 69), also near the airport, has a bungalow and a *fare* with bathroom for 5500/6500 CFP half/full board.

Getting There & Away

Anaa is 450km east of Papeete. There are Papeete-Anaa flights once or twice a week for 15,000 CFP (1 hour and 10 minutes). It's also on the shipping route of the *Auura'Nui 3* and *Kura Ora*.

Southern & Eastern Tuamotus

If not for the presence of the nuclear-testing operations, the infamous CEP, this totally isolated region would have remained forgotten. CEP activities have made some of these atolls infamous.

Hao is the regional centre where cultured-pearl production, fishing and copra production are the major industries. The

THE TUAMOTUS

smallest atolls in the archipelago are in this region; some, like Tikei, Nukutavake, Pinaki and Akiaki, are barely 5 sq km. In this marginal world tourist facilities are rare and so are visitors.

RAROIA

pop 184 (with Makemo, Taenga and Katiu)
• lagoon area 440 sq km • reef passes 1
'Discovered' on 12 July 1820 by Bellings-hausen, Raroia is east of the central Tua-motus, 8km south-west of its nearest neighbour, Takume. The lagoon meets the ocean through only one pass, in the west.

Getting There & Away

Raroia is served by the *Auura'Nui 3* and *Kura Ora* (see the Getting Around chapter).

PUKA PUKA

pop 175 • lagoon area 16 sq km
Described by Magellan in 1521 and in 1616 by Le Maire, who called it Houden Eiland (Island of Dogs), this atoll, at the eastern-most boundary of the Tuamotus, has a la-goon in the process of filling in and drying up. Puka Puka was the first land seen by Thor Heyerdahl and the *Kon Tiki* adven-turers, on 30 July 1947 (see the boxed text for more information on the voyage).

The *Auura'Nui 3* and *Kura Ora* serve the atoll.

NUKUTAVAKE

pop 190 • lagoon area 5.5 sq km
Situated 1125km south-east of Tahiti, Nukutavake is the only inhabited atoll where the lagoon has been entirely filled in by sand and limestone particles from the external reef. It is entirely covered by a co-conut plantation.

Places to Stay

Pension Afou (☎ 98 72 53), in the village of Tavananui, 1km from the airport, has three local-style bungalows with shared bathroom. The cost is 7000 CFP full board per person and 1500 CFP for transfers to the airport. Fishing trips and boat rides around the island can be organised by your hosts.

The Kon Tiki Expedition

It was on the southern part of the Raroia reef that the *Kon Tiki* ran aground in 1947, putting an end to a great sea epic. Thor Heyerdahl and his unfortunate com-panions (including Swedish ethnologist Bengt Danielsson) had embarked on a mad enterprise 101 days earlier: to sail aboard a balsa and bamboo raft – a replica of the crafts used by Incas on Lake Titicaca and the Peruvian coast – to Mangareva in the Gambier Archipelago. The purpose of this expedition was to prove that Polyne-sia had been populated by the Incas.

The adventure was unsuccessful. The raft drifted much farther to the north than the route first predicted. Moreover, botanists, linguists and archaeologists have all invalidated the thesis of the Inca origin of the Polynesians.

Getting There & Away

Air Air Tahiti serves Nukutavake via Hao (change of plane) at least once a week. The Papeete-Nukutavake fare is 27,500 CFP.

HAO

pop 1317 • lagoon area 609 sq km
reef passes 1
The Spaniard Quirós was the first Euro-pean to set foot on this atoll in the centre of the Tuamotus in 1606. With only one pass and measuring nearly 60km in length, it has seen great demographic growth since the 1960s as an administration and transit centre for the CEP nuclear-testing organi-sation and the installations of the Com-missariat à l'Énergie Atomique (CEA). It has state-of-the-art infrastructure, includ-ing a 3300m runway built to handle the military transport planes carrying highly sensitive material destined for Moruroa, 500km to the south. When atmospheric tests were conducted, there were up to 5000 people busy on the atoll. With the switch to underground testing, most of the military staff were moved to Moruroa and Fangataufa.

Hao is also a regional centre and the centre for air traffic to the southern Tuamotus and Gambier Archipelago. It has a college and a medical centre and most inhabitants earn their living from cultured-pearl production in **Otepa**, a village on the north-east. The end of nuclear testing in 1996 has made major changes to the situation on the atoll.

Places to Stay

In Otepa, you can stay at *Chez Amélie* (☎ 97 03 42, fax 97 02 41). Amélie Danzer, the Air Tahiti representative, has four rooms in a house with attached hot-water bathrooms. Two have air-con and cost 6500 CFP per person; the rooms without air-con go for 5500 CFP. Count on another 1500 CFP for each meal.

Getting There & Away

Air Air Tahiti flies Papeete-Hao three or four times a week via Anaa or Makemo. The Papeete-Hao trip takes two hours and 20 minutes and costs 24,000 CFP. There are also connections to Takume, Fangataufa, Fakahina, Takakoto, Tureia, Vahitahi, Nukutavake, Pukarua and Reao. Inquire at Air Tahiti about flight schedules.

Boat The *Auura'Nui 3* and the *Kura Ora* serve Hao (see the earlier Getting Around chapter).

MORUROA

pop 20 • lagoon area 324 sq km
reef passes 1

Often mistakenly spelt 'Mururoa', this atoll, 1250km south-east of Tahiti, will forever be synonymous with nuclear tests (see the boxed text 'French Nuclear Testing' in the Facts about the Islands chapter). 'Discovered' in 1792 by the Englishman Weatherhead, it is 28km long and 11km wide and has only one pass.

The atoll was chosen for the tests because of its isolation from inhabited zones and its suitability for the necessary infrastructure. It was equipped with ultramodern electricity-production installations, a desalinisation plant and an airport for large aircraft. Entertainment facilities and an internal radio and TV channel were established for military staff. The atoll was ceded to the French state in 1964. With the final tests, jurisdiction was returned to the French Polynesian government and the installations were dismantled. Today there's just a small contingent of French legionnaires.

THE TUAMOTUS

THE
MARQUESAS

TIARE

MANOLO MYLONAS

The Marquesas

Te Henua Enana (Land of Men) is the Marquesans' name for their archipelago. These are the bewitching islands of legend, boasting a wealth of archaeological remains, many of which are still to be catalogued.

Four thousand kilometres south of Hawaii, 500km from the closest of the Tuamotu atolls and 1400km north-east of Papeete, this is the most northerly archipelago of French Polynesia. The 15 islands of the archipelago, which stretches diagonally about 350km from north-west to south-east, share a geographical isolation. The islands, only six of which are inhabited, are divided into two groups: northern and southern.

These unprotected blocks of lava rise abruptly from the vastness of the Pacific Ocean. Ragged and distorted, their rugged contours were formed by the erosion caused by sea and wind. Unlike the high Society islands, these islands have no sheltering reefs or lagoons to soften the assault of the waves. As a result, necks, needles and peaks towering more than 1000m stand side by side with high plateaus bordered by steep cliffs. This sharp relief is ridged with deep valleys covered with luxuriant tropical vegetation.

Partly sunken calderas have formed vast amphitheatres and it is in these more sheltered areas that the Marquesans chose to build their homes.

The archipelago is not affected by cyclones. Rainfall is quite variable, but is generally evenly spread throughout the year, with greatest precipitation between June and August. Torrential downpours are often followed by lengthy droughts. Temperatures vary and can be vastly different between one valley and another, but temperatures are slightly higher than those in Papeete.

The islands' flora and fauna differ little from those of the other archipelagos. The *nono*, a minute black or white fly with a painful bite, is endemic. The islands are also home to wild horses and goats, introduced by Europeans.

HIGHLIGHTS

- Inspect the tiki at Puamau (Hiva Oa) and the archaeological remains at Hatiheu (Nuku Hiva)

- Eat a *kaikai enana* (Marquesan meal)

- Ride a horse on Ua Huka

- Meet artists on all the islands

- Visit the bay and beach at Hanahevane (Tahuata)

- Walk from Omoa to Hanavave (Fatu Hiva)

- Dive with electra dolphins at Nuku Hiva

The six inhabited islands have a total of about 8000 inhabitants. The agricultural sector includes copra cultivation and recently *noni*, a fruit with interesting therapeutic properties, has become a major export to the USA. The public service (health, education, administrative services) is also an important source of employment.

Notoriously underdeveloped until the early 1980s, the Marquesas are beginning to catch up with technology. Projects aimed at reducing the islands' isolation and dependence on Tahiti are currently in effect, including the development of fishing and agricultural resources, construction of new schools, improvement of roads and inter-island transport, more-frequent flight connections and the promotion of tourism. The people of the Marquesas want to catch up with the modern world without losing their traditional lifestyle.

Ecotourism and the discovery of the islands' cultural, historic and natural heritage offer great potential but meanwhile, the small numbers of visitors are privileged to experience the mysterious ambience and warm welcome of a place that has to be experienced to be understood.

THE MARQUESAS

Motu One
Hatutu
Eiao
Motu Iti
Nuku Hiva
Ua Huka
0   50   100 km
NORTHERN GROUP
Ua Pou
Fatu Huku
SOUTHERN GROUP
Hiva Oa
Tahuata
Motane
Fatu Hiva

History

Early Settlers The Marquesas were amongst the first islands to be settled by the Polynesians during their great South Pacific migrations. The Marquesas served as a dispersal point for the whole Polynesian triangle, from Hawaii to Easter Island and New Zealand. The exact date of the islands' initial colonisation, however, has not been established. Estimates vary from prehistory to between 300 and 600 BC.

This initial period of settlement is characterised by the people's affirmation of a distinct cultural identity. Witness to this are the numerous archaeological remains which have survived to modern times, including *tohua* (meeting places), *meae* (the Marquesan equivalent of marae), *pae pae* (paved floors or platforms) and tiki. See the 'Civilisation & Archaeology' special section for information on traditional Marquesan culture.

European Contact The Marquesas' isolation was broken in 1595, when Spanish navigator Alvaro de Mendaña y Neira arrived in sight of Fatu Hiva by pure chance. The expedition had left Peru a month earlier with the aim of discovering the hypothetical

Terra Australis Incognita, a land which was believed to abound in gold and spices. This initial, unexpected contact ended in the death of several islanders. Mendaña's fleet then sailed along past Motane and Hiva Oa and anchored for around 10 days in Vaitahu Bay at Tahuata.

Mendaña christened these four islands Las Marquesas de Mendoza in honour of his sponsor the viceroy of Peru, García Hurtado de Mendoza, Marquis of Cañete.

In 1774, Captain Cook lingered for four days on Tahuata during his second great voyage. He managed to form a more cordial relationship with the islanders than did his European predecessors. Ingraham, the US commander of the *Hope*, came upon the northern group of the Marquesas in April 1791, arriving slightly ahead of Frenchman Étienne Marchand, captain of the merchant vessel *Le Solide*, which took on fresh supplies on Tahuata and then landed on Ua Pou in June 1791.

In 1797, a young Protestant pastor of the London Missionary Society (LMS), William Crook, landed at Tahuata and although his attempts at evangelism were unsuccessful, he recorded some irreplaceable impressions of Marquesan society. A Russian geographical and commercial mission took Admiral Krusenstern to Nuku Hiva in 1804. Aboard the vessel were men of science and artists, who published their observations when they returned to Europe.

From the early 19th century onwards, sea traffic increased in this area of the Pacific. A triangular trading route was established between the Marquesas, China and Australia, and it was during this time that the islands' precious sandalwood trees were plundered. This was also the period of the whalers, for which the Marquesas acted as a supply base. On board one of the vessels was the writer Herman Melville.

In 1813 Nuku Hiva was requisitioned by the American Captain Porter as a US naval base during the conflicts between the USA and Britain. The US presence was short-lived, however, as Porter's territorial designs were not supported by his government.

Haakakai O Te Henua Enana: the Legend of the Land of Men

This creation legend is one of the most important Marquesan myths. At the dawn of humanity, two deities, Oatea and Atuana, ruled over the vastness of the ocean. One day Atuana expressed the wish to live in a house. Oatea, her husband, decided to draw upon his divine powers and promised the house would be built by dawn the following day.

He devoted himself to incantations and chose a site on the ocean. He put up two posts, and exclaimed, 'This is Ua Pou!'. He then took a roof beam and placed it on the two posts. After tying it with coconut-fibre rope he cried, 'This is Hiva Oa!'. When fitting the rafters he said, 'This is Nuku Hiva!'. He made the roof from nine coconut-palms and cried, 'This is Fatu Hiva!'. To bury the leftover vegetation strewn over the ground, he dug a hole.

Atuana saw the glimmer of dawn on the horizon. 'This is Tahuata!', Oatea shouted. And when Atuana added impatiently, 'I can hear the morning birdsong!', Oatea replied, 'This is Motane!'. He quickly threw the scraps into the hole and said, 'This is Ua Huka!'. He felt his divine powers leaving him with the sunrise and with his last breath he murmured, 'This is Eiao!'.

This creation myth likens the birth of the archipelago to the construction of a *hae* (house). It relates only to those islands that were inhabited long ago; Motane and Eiao are no longer populated.

Annexation by France French interest in the region grew as a means of countering English expansion in the Pacific. After an initial reconnaissance voyage in 1838, Rear Admiral Abel Dupetit-Thouars took possession of Tahuata on 1 May 1842 in the name of King Louis-Philippe. The Marquesan chieftains, who didn't realise the ramifications of the act, did not oppose this transfer of sovereignty. Only Iotete, a chieftain from Tahuata, rebelled some months later, but his opposition was in vain.

The Marquesas were quickly marginalised in favour of Papeete for geographical, economic and strategic reasons. Only the Catholic missionaries, who had been active since their arrival on Tahuata in 1838, persevered. Their evangelising endeavours were more fruitful than those of their Protestant rivals from the LMS and Hawaiian Missionary Society who arrived in 1825 and 1831. Catholicism became firmly entrenched in the Marquesas.

Upon contact with western influences, the foundations of Marquesan society collapsed. Whaling crews brought alcohol, firearms and syphilis, and the colonial administration and missionaries paid little attention to the ancestral values of the Marquesan people. The stunning decline in population reflects the steady process of disintegration: from an estimated 18,000 in 1842, the population fell to 5264 in 1887 and 2096 in 1926.

Recent History Thanks to the efforts of Louis Rollin, the doctor appointed to the Marquesas from 1923 to 1930, the decline in population was stemmed. Vaccinations, sanitary measures and assistance for new arrivals also helped boost the population.

In the 20th century, the experiences of the painter Paul Gauguin and singer Jacques Brel drew world attention to the Marquesas (see the boxed texts 'Gauguin: the Wild & the Primitive' and 'The Last Song of Jacques Brel', under Hiva Oa later in this chapter). More recently, the development of transport and telecommunications infrastructures have helped to lessen the archipelago's isolation and archaeological discoveries have underlined the significance of Marquesan civilisation.

Activities

The Marquesas offer excursions to historic and archaeological sites on foot or by 4WD, opportunities to shop for high quality crafts, scuba diving at Nuku Hiva and, on a number of islands, there are walking and horse riding possibilities.

Accommodation

There are several good hotels on Nuku Hiva and Hiva Oa, particularly in Taiohae and Atuona, the main towns. More frequent flights and cheaper fares should spur more hotel-room construction. On Ua Huka, Ua Pou, Tahuata and Fatu Hiva there are guesthouses, rooms in family houses and, sometimes, independent bungalows.

Many villages have several guesthouses and although prices and standards vary, they do give you an opportunity to experience Marquesan life. Most places organise excursions and activities.

Getting There & Away

Air There are direct flights between Papeete and the Marquesas (three hours) and, once weekly, a direct flight from Rangiroa in the Tuamotus to Nuku Hiva. There are airports at Nuku Hiva, Hiva Oa, Ua Huka and Ua Pou but it's the Nuku Ataha (or Terre Déserte) airport on Nuku Hiva that gets the most traffic. There are three weekly flights from Nuku Hiva to the secondary airstrip at Ua Pou, and one to Ua Huka.

High airfares were once a major discouragement to tourist development in the Marquesas and although they have dropped, the costs are still very high. There are Air Tahiti representatives on each of the major islands. Don't forget that the Marquesas are half an hour ahead of Tahiti time.

Boat The *Taporo IV* and *Aranui* serve the Marquesas from Papeete via Rangiroa and/or Takapoto in the Tuamotus. The *Aranui* does about 15 trips a year while the *Taporo IV* departs every two weeks. Taiohae, Hakahau and Atuona are the only places with wharfs where the ships can actually dock; at other ports unloading is done with whaleboats. See the Getting Around chapter, and 'The *Aranui*' special section in this chapter for more details.

See the Outdoor Activities chapter for information about yachts in the Marquesas.

Getting Around

Getting around the Marquesas is difficult, whether by sea or land. The valleys are isolated, making it virtually impossible to do island tours by road and only the main towns and villages have sealed roads. Some villages have no landing stage and the sea is often rough, making landings difficult.

The introduction of helicopter shuttles within the northern and southern groups has improved inter-island transport, which was previously only possible with Air Tahiti or by irregularly passing boats.

Island to Island Problematic inter-island transport in the Marquesas is one of the major obstacles to tourist development. Visitors should be prepared for a certain amount of uncertainty and definitely should not expect things to go strictly to schedule.

There are various means of transport including Air Tahiti, helicopters, *bonitiers* (old whaleboats, from the term 'Boston whalers') and, as a last resort, the cargo ships *Taporo IV* and *Aranui*.

The inter-island links depend on the islands. Between the south and north Marquesas, there are reasonably regular links between Hiva Oa in the southern group and Nuku Hiva in the northern, plus there's a weekly flight between Hiva Oa and Ua Pou in the north. It's impossible to travel directly from Tahuata or Fatu Hiva in the south to Ua Pou or Ua Huka in the north without a transit stop on Nuku Hiva or Hiva Oa.

Traffic demands or mechanical breakdowns can complicate the situation. Travel between Nuku Hiva and Ua Pou in the northern group is generally fairly easy, because these two islands are linked several times a week by plane, helicopter or bonitier. Nor is there a problem between Hiva Oa and Tahuata in the southern group, but there is only a once-weekly service between Nuku Hiva and Ua Huka and, at the time of writing, Fatu Hiva in the southern group was virtually isolated. Nuku Hiva is the number one island in terms of transport infrastructure. It's linked to Hiva Oa, Ua Pou and Ua Huka and its airport can handle ATR 72s. It's also the headquarters

Marquesan Handicrafts·

Marquesan handicrafts enjoy an excellent reputation, particularly sculpture, for which a school has been opened at Taiohae on Nuku Hiva. Tiki, pestles, *umete* (bowls), adzes, spears, clubs, fishhooks and other items are done in *miro* (rosewood) or *tou* wood, bone or volcanic stone. You will also find necklaces, *umu hei* (Marquesan *monoi;* coconut oil and sandalwood-powder) and the famous *tapa* of Fatu Hiva, cloth made from beaten bark and decorated with traditional designs.

In most villages there are small craft *fare* with items for exhibition and sale but they may only be open when requested or, of course, when the *Aranui* is in port. These places have the most items for sale, but it's well worth approaching craftspeople directly. With a little luck you may see them working in their studios but be aware that the amount of stock is variable. The craftspeople participate twice a year, usually in June and November, in Marquesan craft exhibitions in Papeete and it takes some time to replenish their stocks. Some work is only done to order so if you stay several days on an island it's worth making a visit as soon as you arrive. Even at the worst, the craft *fare* will always have some items for sale.

Bring enough cash because you cannot pay with credit cards. Prices may be relatively high but they're still lower than in Papeete. Count on at least 1500 CFP to 2000 CFP for a small tapa piece (up to 10,000 CFP for a piece 1m long), 3000 CFP for a small 15cm-high tiki (perhaps 20,000 CFP for a large one), 5000 CFP for an umete or an adze of about 50cm. It's possible to bargain a little but this is not a Pacific tradition so don't expect much change. Several craftspeople on each island are listed here, but this is not an exhaustive list. Ask people you meet, and at your accommodation for suggestions.

Nuku Hiva

Several important names in sculpture work on Nuku Hiva.

In Taiohae, you can visit Pierrot Keuvahana (☎ 92 06 14), behind the football ground, who works in tou and miro wood and makes a variety of objects. You can buy clubs or spears from Edgar Tamarii (☎ 92 01 67) or from Mooroa Hutia, who lives nearby. Their workshop is about 100m behind the Chez Stella roulotte on the seafront.

The island's best-known sculptor is Damien Haturau (☎ 92 05 56), who lives in the Meau Valley, 300m from the Mauia *pae pae* (meeting platform) in the large house set back from the road. Among his most beautiful works are the statues in the cathedral and *Virgin with Child* at Vaitahu's church, on Tahuata.

Marcel Taupotini (☎ 92 02 42), known as Kehu, lives in the Hoata Valley; he works with stone, bone and wood and makes all types of objects from tiki to adzes. In the Français Valley, the Ah Scha family (☎ 92 02 46) has several famous sculptors who work in wood, stone and bone. One of them, Raphaël, is also a tattooist. During the school term you can visit the CETAD (technical school), to the east of the city.

In Taipivai contact Edmond Ah Scha and Firifiri (in the beige house with green door-frames 300m from the church, to the left of the Hatiheu track) or Jacob Teikitohe (☎ 92 01 25).

Ua Huka

Vaipaee, Hane and Hokatu villages each have a craft centre. In Hane, visit Joseph Vaatete (☎ 92 60 74), a well-known stone sculptor.

Marquesan Handicrafts

Ua Pou

Many of the region's most respected artisans come from Ua Pou. The craft *fare*, inspired by the one at Vaipaee on Ua Huka, is intended to function as a central distribution point for the island's artwork, a stone's throw from the quay.

In Hakahau, contact Alfred Hatuuku (☎ 92 52 39), one of the sculptors who carved the pulpit in the Catholic church. William Aka (☎ 92 53 90) has a huge repertoire including small tiki, jewellery boxes, umete, necklaces, turtles, lizards and small stools in tou or miro wood. Coming from the waterfront you will find his shop on the right, shortly before the Guéranger snack bar.

Eugene Hapipi (☎ 92 53 28 at his sister's, in the neighbouring house) is close to the *gendarmerie* (police station) and produces bone necklaces as well as work in tou, volcanic stone and in stone found at Hohoi.

Marcel Bruneau (☎ 92 50 02), known as Maté, lives in the south of the village. He carves volcanic rock, basalt and tuff as well as wood. Pestles for grinding *popoi* and *raau* (medicines) are one of his specialities.

In Hakahetau, Madame Hikutini (☎ 92 51 56) has an operation producing monoi, *peue* (braids) and hats in *niau* (plaited coconut-palm leaves). From the quay, facing the sea, go to the left for 100m. Also in Hakahetau, Tony Tereino (☎ 92 51 68) dedicates himself to stone sculpture; Yvonne Hokaupoko (who is married to Étienne) produces umu hei, and plaits pandanus to make braids or hats.

In Hakamaii, José Kaiha (☎ 92 50 07) lives in the *fare* with the carved posts in the lower part of the village, near the *mairie* (town hall). Tiki and clubs are his most common works.

In Hohoi, Uri Ah Lo shapes classic umete, tiki and spears and, in one week, small *pirogues* (outrigger canoes) in mango or banyan-tree wood. His blue house is on the right as you go towards the beach.

Hiva Oa

Hiva Oa has fewer artisans than other islands in the archipelago. There are two craft *fare* that do not have much stock and open mainly when the *Aranui* is in port. One is next to the museum and the other is opposite. Go directly to the artisans' homes.

Tuarae Peterano (☎ 92 75 16), a tattoo artist/sculptor well known to American yachties, can offer you finely worked tiki of tou or miro, spears, ukuleles and carved pigs' teeth and cattle bones. His house is on the edge of the road that goes along the Vaioa River, 50m on the right after the sign saying 'Piste Cavalière de Hanamenu' (Hanamenu Bridleway) and a 10 minute walk from the Hoa Nui restaurant in Atuona.

Jean-Marie Otomimi (☎ 92 70 55) makes tiki (from 5000 CFP), ukuleles (from 15,000 CFP), hair pins and bracelets. His wife plaits *keikaha*, coconut fibre for the cord that she connects to disks of coconut shell to make original belts for women (10,000 CFP). Take the road that goes up toward Pension Gauguin and continue on for 100m until the blue road-sign announcing 'Sculpture Traditionnelle sur Bois'.

In Hanaiapa, ask to meet the sculptor Riko.

Tahuata

Three top-rate Marquesan sculptors work in Vaitahu: Edwin and Félix Fii (☎ 92 93 04) and Teiki Barsinas (☎ 92 92 67).

THE MARQUESAS

Marquesan Handicrafts

To visit their studio, follow the street that borders the river for about 200m and turn at the second small bridge. They sculpt wood and bone indifferently, but make imposing adzes, paddles and bowls in tou, sandalwood or miro, earrings and fishhooks in cattle bone and even daggers of swordfish bone. They are also tattooists.

Ronald Teiefitu exhibits his work in the second house on the left coming from the quay. He specialises in women's jewellery (bracelets, brooches and necklaces) carved with Marquesan designs.

In Hapatoni contact Liliane Teikipupuni, who presides over the Mahakatauheipani Cultural & Craft Association. She will take you to the craft *fare*, where you can purchase carved animals (lizards or turtles), bowls, adzes, wickerwork and plaited articles.

Fatu Hiva

Arts and crafts are the island's major economic activity, and Fatu Hiva prides itself on being the only island in French Polynesia to have perpetuated the manufacture of tapa by traditional methods. Practically all the women make it, and the villages resound with the sound of *uru* (breadfruit) or mulberry bark being beaten into shape. They sell it to *Aranui* passengers, passing yachties, and craft outlets in Papeete. Guesthouse owners, such as Cécile Gilmore and Norma Ropati, are well known for their work.

In addition to tapa, you will find carved coconuts – small marvels of creativity. Charles Seigel in Omoa is one of the experts. There are also some wonderful wood carvings. In Omoa, Joseph Pavaouau is one of the last stone sculptors.

Umu hei is a speciality of Fatu Hiva. This is an assortment of gently fragrant plant material such as ylang-ylang, vanilla, pieces of pineapple covered in sandalwood powder, and various other fruits and plants. It is all held together with a plant fibre, which you can use to perfume a room or tie in your hair.

You will have no difficulty in finding the artisans, either at their homes or at the craft centre in each of the two villages. In Hanavave, contact the craft centre president, Edwige Pavaouau (☎ 92 80 48).

---

for Héli Inter Marquises, which provides helicopter services between different centres on the island and to Ua Pou and the town of Taiohae. From there you can get to the island of Hiva Oa and Ua Pou and onwards to Tahuata, Ua Huka and, finally, to Fatu Hiva.

See *'The Aranui'* special section and the Getting Around and Activities chapters for information about cruises in the Marquesas.

Around the Islands Transport around an island is generally very difficult. The roads are rough and the terrain spectacularly steep and divided by numerous valleys and the area really requires a 4WD. There's no pub-

lic transport and, as surprising as it may sound, on Nuku Hiva helicopters are the main means of getting around the island.

By sea, bonitiers and speedboats usually link the villages more rapidly than 4WDs. When there's not even a track these may be the only means of transport. At villages where there is no jetty, it's necessary to land on the beach.

Helicopter Based at Taiohae (Nuku Hiva), Héli Inter Marquises has been operating in the northern group since 1994. From Taiohae, an Ecureuil flies to Ua Huka and Ua Pou in a few minutes. It's a convenient service but very costly.

THE *ARANUI*

Exploring the Marquesas aboard the *Aranui* (Big Road) is one of the most popular Polynesian adventures. For nearly 20 years, the *Aranui* (there has been more than one) has been the umbilical cord between Tahiti and the Marquesas, an integral part of life in the archipelago. A real favourite with tourists, this 104m cargo-and-passenger vessel does 15 annual trips departing from Papeete. Its 16 day voyage takes it to Takapoto in the Tuamotus and the six inhabited islands of the Marquesas (some of them twice) before returning via Rangiroa in the Tuamotus.

An Unusual Formula

The *Aranui* is a real cargo vessel; it has been supplying the remote islands of the Marquesas since 1984 and that is still its primary mission. In 1990 the *Aranui*'s owners decided they could increase the operation's profitability if they took some tourists along for the ride. These passengers could make shore excursions while the ship was loading and unloading in each port. The idea worked; the passengers appreciated the conviviality and authenticity along with the good organisation and comfort levels.

The originality of this 'anti-cruise' isn't the only key to its success – the *Aranui* fills a real need. Unless you're on a yacht, there's simply no other way to visit so many islands in the Marquesas, with two Tuamotu atolls thrown in as a bonus. Furthermore the prices aren't excessive. Of course, 15 days to visit six islands and two atolls without a whole day (often only a half-day) on any of them can seem like a rush, but it does give visitors long enough to get a feel for the archipelago. Paul Theroux's *The Happy Isles of Oceania* has a good description of travelling on the *Aranui* (see Books in the Facts for the Visitor chapter).

Life on Board

Shipboard life has been a major contributor to the *Aranui*'s success. There isn't a barrier between the 42 crew and the hundred-odd passengers. You'll quickly get to know some of the sailors and these tattooed giants become the real stars of the operation. There's a captain, second in command, supercargo, bosun, cooks, engineers and ordinary sailors, as well as the bar and dining-room staff. Two or three multilingual guides, who know the locals well, are there for the shore excursions. Informal evening entertainment and buffets are organised, with music provided by the crew.

The stops are tied up with the loading and unloading of freight, a major event on the islands. You can watch the unceasing ballet of cranes offloading pallets of cement, crates of beer, children's bicycles, drums of fuel, loads of timber and even cars and motorcycles ashore. Locals will be waiting with their 4WDs to load the goods ordered from Papeete the previous month. In turn copra, sacks of citrus fruit and *noni*, the new wonder fruit, are loaded aboard.

Services & Facilities

The front half of the *Aranui* looks just like any other cargo boat of this size, with two cranes, and holds for all types of goods. The back, however, is more a like a cruise ship, with cabins, several decks, a mini-swimming pool, sundeck, dining room, bar, small lounge and library and a video room. There's nothing luxurious about it – everything is simple and functional. There's small shop with postcards, film, sunscreen, plastic sandals and the like. Foreign currency and travellers cheques can be changed and credit-card advances made, with appropriate commissions of course. There's a doctor permanently on board and an infirmary but no telephone service.

There are four classes of accommodation. The A-deluxe cabins have double beds and bathroom with bath, A-standard cabins have two single beds and bathroom with shower, the B cabins have two single beds and share bathroom facilities and the C-class accommodation is 22 dorm-style beds in groups of two with a locker, a curtain for some privacy and shared bathroom facilities. All the accommodation has air-con, towels are provided and there's a laundry service twice a week. In the restaurant there's a buffet breakfast and a set lunch and dinner with French and Polynesian dishes in copious quantities and, since this is *French* Polynesia, lots of wine.

There's also a rather spartan deck class used by local islanders, for whom the ship is a means of getting from one island to the next.

Shore Excursions

There are no nights ashore; all the shore visits last just a day or half-day and are accompanied by the *Aranui* guides. There are only three places – Nuku Hiva, Ua Pou and Hiva Oa – where the *Aranui* can tie up at a wharf. Elsewhere it has to transfer passengers and freight to *bonitiers* (whaleboats), hefty open boats which can carry about 30 people. Getting on the whaleboats can be tricky if the seas are rough but the crew are strong, efficient and well practised. The longest period at sea without a stop is three days.

While the ship is unloading and loading, passengers make excursions ashore, which may vary from one trip to the next but typically include:

Takapoto (Tuamotus): A pearl farm and a picnic on a lagoonside beach
Rangiroa (Tuamotus): Swimming, optional scuba dive, a snorkelling drift through the passes or a glass-bottom boat excursion
Ua Pou: The villages of Hakahetau and Hakahau
Nuku Hiva: A 4WD trip with a picnic-lunch stop from Taiohae to Taipivai and the archaeological site of Paeke; scuba diving at Taiohae; the village of Hatiheu; the archaeological sites of Hikokua and Kamuihei; an optional jaunt up to the Anaho Pass
Hiva Oa: The museum at Atuona and the Calvaire Cemetery (south coast); the archaeological site of Puamau and the village of Hanaiapa (north coast)

Tahuata: Vaitahu and sometimes Hapatoni
Fatu Hiva: Omoa followed by the (optional) 17km hike to Hanavave
Ua Huka: Vaipaee with its museum and botanical centre; an optional horse-riding excursion or a 4WD trip to Hane and the archaeological site of Meiaute; the village of Hokatu

In each village, stops are made at the craft centres, where you can meet the craftspeople and make purchases. Bring cash – nobody will accept credit cards. There is a demonstration of tapa-making on Fatu Hiva.

Lecturers – European and North American art-history experts, archaeologists and ethnologists – are invited on the cruise and bring some cultural insights.

Passengers do get to make culinary visits to the four best dining addresses in the Marquesas: Chez Rosalie on Ua Pou, Chez Yvonne on Nuku Hiva, Hoa Nui on Hiva Oa and Chez Fournier on Ua Huka, where a gargantuan *kaikai enana*, a traditional Marquesan meal with 10 or more dishes, is served.

The arrival of about 100 tourists in a village, far from being an incongruous invasion, is a major event for the local population, which really looks forward to it. Local operators rent out their 4WDs, crafts-people sell their work, dancers perform and restaurants do good business. The *Aranui* has played a particular role in the revitalisation of Marquesan culture and handicrafts.

Bring along good walking shoes, plastic sandals or thongs for the beach, an umbrella or raincoat for the inevitable rain and a daypack for the shore excursions.

The Passengers

The *Aranui* attracts a cosmopolitan clientele, with French and Americans the largest contingent. You may meet Californian retirees, French residents of Papeete or from France itself, archaeologists on vacation, writers looking for inspiration, students, civil servants, even Marquesan-tattoo enthusiasts. Perhaps the major warning is that getting off the ship and onto the whaleboats (remember there are only three landings at a wharf) can require some agility and physical effort. The cabins and shore excursions are not ideal for small children but if there are enough children on a given trip, a day nursery is organised.

The only disappointed customers are likely to be those misinformed by travel agents that this is some type of luxury cruise. If you're after gala balls, luxurious bars and a refined atmosphere, the *Paul Gauguin*, *Renaissance* or the luxury catamaran *Haumana* are more appropriate. See the Getting Around chapter for information.

Finally, this is an organised journey where things happen hour by hour. If you don't like to be tied to a schedule or forced to live with a group, then it may not be for you.

Prices & Bookings

The prices quoted are for an adult with all meals and taxes for a 15 or 16 day trip ex-Papeete but without any optional extras. Cabins are usually for two people; there are additional costs for solo occupancy.

An A-deluxe cabin costs 421,898 CFP (about US$3835), an A-standard cabin costs 356,353 CFP (US$3240), a B cabin costs 310,137 CFP (US$2819) and a bed in C class costs 193,800 CFP (US$1762). Children aged three to 15 sharing a cabin with adults pay 93,534 CFP (US$850) while children under 12 in C class pay 96,900 CFP (US$881). It is possible to join the *Aranui* on Nuku Hiva just for eight days in the Marquesas: A class costs 229,374 CFP (US$2088), B class 189,896 CFP (US$1726), C class 128,520 CFP (US$1168).

Officially visitors are dissuaded from using deck class, but if you are just going from one island to the next and there's room, there shouldn't be a problem. Contact the tour guides at the stopovers and count on about 20,000 CFP from Tahiti to the Marquesas or 3000 CFP from one island in the Marquesas to another. This doesn't include meals (so don't try and join the other passengers!) or excursions. Only a mattress is provided, so bring a sleeping bag.

Bookings are essential and peak periods (July-August and December) are booked out months in advance. Contact your travel agent or go directly to the shipowner, the Compagnie Polynésienne de Transport Maritime (CPTM; ☎ 42 62 40, 43 76 60, fax 43 48 89, email aranui@mail.pf), BP 220, Papeete. CPTM's Papeete office, at the entrance to the Motu Uta port zone, is open weekdays from 7.30 to 11.30 am and 1.30 to 5 pm. Take le truck No 3 from the *mairie* (town hall). You can find out more about the *Aranui* on its Web site at www.aranui.com.

In Europe, contact Quotidien Voyages (☎ 1 41 92 08 30, fax 1 46 24 34 88), 103 Ave Charles-de-Gaulle, 92200 Neuilly. In North America, contact CPTM (☎ 650-574 2575, 1-800 972 7268, email cptm@aranui.com), 2028 El Camino Real South, Suite B, San Mateo, CA 94403.

Other Operators

There are other operators with Marquesan cruises on yachts carrying eight to 10 passengers. Archipels Croisières, Club Med and Nouvelles Frontières are possibilities. See the Getting Around chapter for details.

MANOLO MYLONAS

Car The 4WD is the most common means of transport. With two exceptions (Atuona and Taiohae), they are hired with the services of a driver. Self-drive rental has been abandoned because most visitors are not used to such deplorable road conditions and inevitably damage the vehicles.

Enforced passenger status may seem restricting at first, but it has its advantages. You will soon notice that driving in such conditions is exhausting and dangerous. Distances are measured in hours, not kilometres, and drivers proceed with infinite caution at an average of 10 to 15km/h. They also seem to know everybody and can introduce you to local communities, as well as guide you to difficult-to-find locations such as archaeological sites.

The rental rates seem astronomical if you're by yourself, so try and get a group together or ask about excursion programs. Bookings for 4WD tours are essential. Your hotel or guesthouse will do this for you but it's wise to meet your driver and check if there will be any communication difficulties. Tours often take a full day so check that the vehicle isn't too crowded.

Hitching Although the traffic volume is very small, hitching is possible and for some solo travellers this is the only way to avoid the high cost of renting a 4WD. Position yourself at the edge of the road or approach 4WD or commercial-vehicle owners directly outside premises such as shops, the post office or *mairie* (town hall). Alternatively, you can try your luck with the valley dwellers, who come into the main towns on a regular basis. All the usual cautions apply.

Boat Speedboats and bonitiers are faster than 4WDs and can reach the entrances to all the valleys. Ask at your accommodation or go directly to the boat owners and enquire about finding other visitors to share the costs. Bonitiers can take up to 15 people. Tahuata and Fatu Hiva have a communal bonitier that runs a twice-weekly ferry service to Hiva Oa.

Boat hitching is possible; ask boat owners in the marinas, or passing yachts. Another

Nono a Gogo

Prepare to face a (nearly) invisible but (sort of) deadly enemy in the Marquesas: the *nono*. This tiny endemic sand midge is ready to bite any visitor willing to offer a blood transfusion. The bites are itchy and can easily become infected. White nono live on beaches, black ones in vegetation. Attempts to eradicate them have been unsuccessful but fortunately they are not found absolutely everywhere. The only prevention is to make liberal use of *monoi* (fragrant oil) or insect repellent, and to cover-up well.

possibility is to hitch a ride with medical or administrative personnel who regularly do a one-day round of the remote valleys by speedboat or 4WD.

The movements of the *Kaoha Nui*, a fairly large vessel that provides inter-island transport for sports tournaments, religious celebrations and school outings, are totally unpredictable. If it should happen to moor, jump on. Cargo ships pass at more-or-less regular intervals and may let you make a few short hops. Ask about arrival dates of the *Aranui* or *Taporo IV*.

The Northern Group

The northern group consists of three main inhabited islands – Nuku Hiva, Ua Huka and Ua Pou – and the deserted islets farther to the north – Motu Iti (Hatu Iti), Eiao, Hatutu (Hatutaa), Motu One (Sand Island) and the Clark Bank.

NUKU HIVA
pop 2372 • area 340 sq km
highest point Mt Tekao (1224m)
The main island of the northern group, and the largest in the archipelago, Nuku Hiva (The Chevrons) is the administrative and economic capital of the Marquesas.

THE MARQUESAS

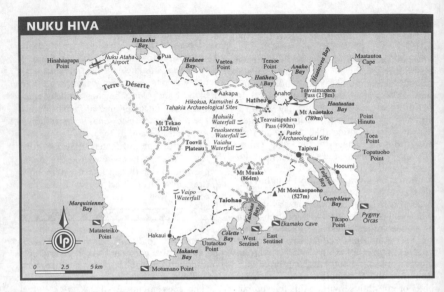

Nuku Hiva has the largest population but one of the lowest population densities. Settlement is concentrated in Taiohae on the south coast, Hatiheu on the north coast and Taipivai in the east. Hamlets such as Anaho, Hooumi, Aakapa and Pua are home to only a handful of people.

Nuku Hiva was formed from two volcanoes, stacked one on top of the other to form two concentric calderas. The top of the main caldera forms a jagged framework that surrounds the Toovii Plateau; the broken-mouthed caldera of the secondary volcano reaches its highest point at Mt Muake (864m) and outlines a huge natural amphitheatre. At its foot is a vast harbour, around which curls Taiohae, the main town on the island. Deep bays cut into the south and east coasts. On the north coast, erosion by wind and rain has shaped impressive basalt *aiguilles* (needles).

In 1791, the American Captain Ingraham was the first westerner to see Nuku Hiva. In the first half of the 19th century, sandal-wood merchants and whalers put into port in Taiohae Bay. One such sailor was Herman Melville, future author of *Moby Dick* and *Billy Budd*, who jumped ship and spent

three weeks at Taipivai (see the boxed text 'Polynesia & the Pen' and the Books section, in the Facts for the Visitor chapter). A fortress was built on Nuku Hiva in 1813 by the American Captain Porter. Catholic missionaries reached the island in 1839 and the religion took hold when the archipelago was seized by the French in 1842. During the second half of the 19th century the island was ravaged by disease.

Today there are frequent flight connections to Nuku Hiva from Papeete and the tourist future looks bright. The first luxury hotel opened in 1999 and the island offers magnificent landscapes, varied accommodation, high-quality handicrafts, interesting archaeological heritage and energetic activities.

Information

Tourist Offices The tourist office (☎/fax 92 03 73) in Taiohae is in the mairie. Deborah Kimitete speaks English and can provide you with information. Some free brochures are also available and the office is open weekdays from 7.30 to 11.30 am.

Rose Corser, head of the Keikahanui Nuku Hiva Pearl Lodge, has established a small museum of Marquesan culture and has several explanatory booklets. To get up to the hotel take the road just beyond the village; it's the second white house on the left.

Money Banque Socredo (☎ 92 03 63) is on the seafront, on the corner of the street that leads to Français Valley. Open weekdays from 7 to 11 am and 1 to 4 pm, it handles exchange and credit-card withdrawals. The last exchange is at 3.30 pm.

Post & Communications The post office (OPT) is on the eastern side of the bay, opposite the *gendarmerie* (police station). It is open Monday to Thursday from 7 am to 3 pm and on Friday to 2 pm. Phonecard telephone booths can be found at the marina, in front of the post office, at the cargo-ship wharf, close to the Kovivi restaurant, at the airport, in Taipivai and in Hatiheu.

Laundry Enquire at d'Archipels Croisières at the marina or the Marquesas Dive Centre.

Medical Services Several doctors, surgeons and dentists practise at the hospital (☎ 92 03 75, 92 04 79), 100m from the post office. Each village has an infirmary or first-aid post.

Taiohae

The economic and administrative capital of the archipelago, Taiohae has about 1700 inhabitants. The town hugs Taiohae Bay for nearly 3.5km, from the marina, in the east, to the Keikahanui Nuku Hiva Pearl Lodge, in the west. Nearly all the town's hotels, restaurants, shops and services are clustered together on the seashore.

Three roads run back from the seafront and climb up into valleys, one of them crossing the Pakiu Valley and continuing to Taipivai. The entrance to the bay is flanked by two islets, the East Sentinel and the West Sentinel. Dominating the marina is the promontory where the military buildings of Fort Collet, which have now disappeared, were built in 1842.

Climbing the Meau Valley for less than 1km, you reach a restored **meae**, with a small contemporary tiki figure. An enormous

banyan tree dominates the site. To the west of the town, between the cemetery and the nautical club, stands the **Herman Melville Memorial**, a magnificent wooden sculpture by Kahee Taupotini unveiled in 1992. Approaching the centre, 700m farther along, is the **Piki Vehine Pae Pae**, also known as Temehea. Rebuilt for the 1989 Marquesas Islands Festival (see the boxed text of the same name in the Ua Pou section later), this open-air museum in the form of a *hae* (traditional house) contains modern sculptures and a dozen magnificent tiki made by the island's sculptors and by artisans from Easter Island.

Before the hae, a **sculpture** representing a traditional Marquesan house is decorated with scenes symbolising unity, including one of five people eating from one *umete* (traditional Polynesian bowl). This same theme of communal activity is repeated on a sculpture farther to the east. Other images include a double-hulled war canoe with a hull like a legendary eel, a birdman and an egg with a tiki head and a *moai* (Easter Island tiki) head.

A hundred metres or so farther east stands a stone cross at a crossroad, marking the commencement of the Catholic mission. Take the road that turns left to **Notre-Dame Cathedral of the Marquesas Islands**, built on the Tohua Mauia, a sacred place venerated by the ancient Marquesans. Carved into a tree is a statue of Monsignor Dordillon, bishop of the Marquesas from 1848 to 1888, who was given the land by the traditional Moana chieftain to build a school here; the cathedral was built alongside in 1977. The stone used in the construction of the church comes from the archipelago's six inhabited islands

On the seafront, opposite the Kamake supermarket, is the **Monument to the Dead**, an obelisk which bears a commemorative plaque in honour of Étienne Marchand. This is a popular area for Sunday pastimes such as boules and bingo, played in the *fare* beside the shipping wharf.

The **Tohua Koueva** is 1.5km up the Pakiu Valley on the road to Taipivai. It takes about 15 minutes to reach by walking up to the machine that crushes stones for road-building,

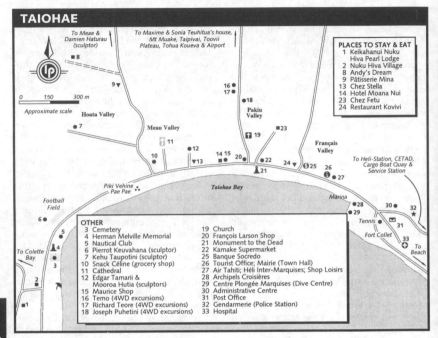

TAIOHAE

To Meae & Damien Haturau (sculptor)

To Maxime & Sonia Teuhitua's house, Mt Muake, Taipivai, Toovii Plateau, Tohua Koueva & Airport

0   150   300 m
Approximate scale

Hoata Valley

Pakiu Valley

Meau Valley

Français Valley

To Heli-Station, CETAD, Cargo Boat Quay & Service Station

Piki Vehine Pae Pae

Taiohae Bay

Marina

Football Field

Tennis

Fort Collet

To Colette Bay

To Beach

PLACES TO STAY & EAT
1 Keikahanui Nuku Hiva Pearl Lodge
2 Nuku Hiva Village
8 Andy's Dream
9 Pâtisserie Mina
13 Chez Stella
14 Hotel Moana Nui
23 Chez Fetu
24 Restaurant Kovivi

OTHER
3 Cemetery
4 Herman Melville Memorial
5 Nautical Club
6 Pierrot Keuvahana (sculptor)
7 Kehu Taupotini (sculptor)
10 Snack Céline (grocery shop)
11 Cathedral
12 Edgar Tamarii & Mooroa Hutia (sculptors)
15 Maurice Shop
16 Temo (4WD excursions)
17 Richard Teore (4WD excursions)
18 Joseph Puhetini (4WD excursions)
19 Church
20 François Larson Shop
21 Monument to the Dead
22 Kamake Supermarket
25 Banque Socredo
26 Tourist Office; Mairie (Town Hall)
27 Air Tahiti; Héli Inter-Marquises; Shop Loisirs
28 Archipels Croisières
29 Centre Plongée Marquises (Dive Centre)
30 Administrative Centre
31 Post Office
32 Gendarmerie (Police Station)
33 Hospital

crossing the stream and walking along the small track. Restoration began in 1998 and it was opened during the 1999-2000 Marquesas Islands Festival. It's believed this communal site, with its paved esplanade, belonged to the war chief Pakoko. During a confrontation with the French in 1845 he killed five soldiers on this tohua and was subsequently executed by the French.

Colette Bay

Colette Bay, a small cove beyond the western spur of Taiohae Bay, is also called Haaotupa, a derivative of Haeotupa (House of Tupa). According to legend, Tupa was a great builder, a sort of Marquesan Hercules. The enormous diamond-shaped rock on the hill between the bay and Taiohae is said to be his unfinished house. Tupa wanted his house to reach right up to heaven and, as he was afraid of the gods, he worked by night. Unfortunately, his sister, who was supposed to warn him at the first light of dawn, was

misled by the crowing of the cockerel and so the house remained earthbound.

Colette Bay is only 3.5km from the centre of Taiohae, and can be reached on foot, on horseback, by speedboat or by 4WD. To get there, take the track that goes up to the Keikahanui Inn, at the far-western side of the bay. Instead of branching left to go to the hotel, keep right and continue for about 2km. The track climbs along the western side of the cove and then descends to the beach at Colette Bay, an ideal place for a picnic, but take something to protect yourself from the nono.

Mt Muake

The grey mass of Mt Muake (864m), hewn by axe, forms the backdrop to Taiohae Bay and affords spectacular views. It is used as a takeoff site for hang-gliders.

Muake can be reached on foot or by 4WD along a picturesque track that takes you through tropical vegetation to conifers and

THE MARQUESAS

Aerial view of the outer reef of a Tuamotu atoll, with motu and passes clearly visible

Coconut palms, Rangiroa

Fishing in a fish park

A motu beach at Rangiroa

Traditional fishing at Mataiva (Tuamotus)

The Island of Reefs (L'Île aux Récifs), Rangiroa

Young Marquesan

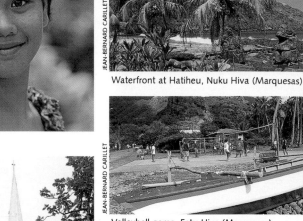

Waterfront at Hatiheu, Nuku Hiva (Marquesas)

Volleyball game, Fatu Hiva (Marquesas)

Church in Omoa, Fatu Hiva (Marquesas)

The Bay of Virgins, Fatu Hiva (Marquesas)

Semi-wild horses, Ua Huka (Marquesas)

Gauguin's tomb, Atuona, Hiva Oa (Marquesas)

resinous trees near the summit. From the seafront at Taiohae, by François Larson's shop, take the road that goes up towards Pakiu Valley. Continue just under 7km to the first fork, go left, and some 4km farther on to another fork. Turn left again into the forest (if you go straight you're heading towards Toovii and the airport) and continue for about 2km to the radio relay station. At the summit, be particularly careful because the rock is crumbly and the face vertical.

Toovii Plateau

Toovii Plateau, crossed by the Taiohae-Terre Déserte (airport) track, is at an average height of 800m. Partly surrounded by a chain of mountains, a welcome coolness can be enjoyed here, in marked contrast to the sweltering heat of the bay areas. With its plantations of conifers and resinous trees and vast pastures where cattle graze, this desolate place looks surprisingly like the mountains of Bavaria. Toovii supplies the whole archipelago with meat, dairy produce and timber.

Hakaui Valley

About 8km west of Taiohae as the crow flies, the Hakaui Valley is one of the most imposing sights on Nuku Hiva. On either side of the river, vertical walls rise to nearly 800m and **Vaipo Waterfall**, one of the highest in the world at 350m, flows vertically into a basin, through a natural narrow gutter. It's a fine natural swimming pool but during prolonged droughts it can be reduced to a mere trickle.

Numerous remains attest to ancient human occupation; the valley was once the fiefdom of King Te Moana and Queen Vaekehu. A paved road, which was an ancient royal way, goes up the valley following the river past **pae pae**, **tohua** and **tiki** hidden behind a tangle of vegetation.

From Taiohae, the valley can be reached by speedboat (about 20 minutes), on foot or on horseback by a 12km bridleway. Take a picnic, some plastic sandals, a swimming costume, mosquito repellent and a waterproof bag for your camera. From the bay where the boat anchors, allow two hours to reach the waterfall on foot. The path, which

is not particularly difficult except for a few fords, follows the river and includes stretches of the ancient paved royal-way. When you return to Hakaui Bay, walk 100m east to the magnificent **Hakatea Beach**.

Hatiheu

Scottish writer Robert Louis Stevenson succumbed to the charm of this village on the north of the island. Its focal point is the wooden church, with its yellow facade and twin symmetrical red steeples. To the rear, the cemetery encroaches on the hill behind the church. The seafront is planted with lawns and coconut palms and decorated with tiki, the recent work of local sculptors. On one of the peaks to the west, at a height of 300m, is a white **statue of the Virgin**, erected in 1872.

The tiny mairie on the seafront houses a small **museum** with a collection of traditional Marquesan artefacts. Yvonne Katupa, mayor of the village and owner of a guesthouse and restaurant, actively promotes Marquesan cultural heritage.

From Taipivai, follow the main road inland and west. The track deteriorates as it climbs to the impressive **Teavaitapuhiva Pass** (490m), 7.5km from Taipivai, from which there are magnificent views. Shortly before Hatiheu, 4km farther, **meae** are concealed under the vegetation to the right and left. See the 'Civilisation & Archaeology' special section for more information.

Taipivai

The ancient fiefdom of the Taipi tribes, Taipivai lies 16km north-east of Taiohae. The town carpets the floor of a river valley and its single street follows the river's course for nearly 2km. At the eastern end of the village the river rushes into Contrôleur Bay.

The majority of Taipivai's inhabitants are farmers and the village is filled with the subtle perfume of vanilla, the cultivation of which is well suited to this fertile alluvial plain. Pods can be purchased when stocks are available (1000 CFP to 1500 CFP for 100g). Try asking Monsieur Tava, whose blue house is on the Hooumi road, set back on the left after the school (take the little

THE MARQUESAS

road on the left); Edmond Ah Scha, who lives in the bamboo house just alongside; or Monsieur Teikitohe, who lives in a beige house on the left below the Hatiheu road, about 1km from the bridge. The production of copra is another important activity in Taipivai.

In the early 19th century, the people of Taipivai fiercely resisted the incursions of the American Captain Porter, who tried to annex the island in 1813. His soldiers used cannons to massacre the population.

Literature has also made Taipivai well known. In July 1842, the American whaler *Acushnet* put in at Taiohae and on board was a sailor named Herman Melville, who jumped ship and wrote of his unusual experiences in *Typee*, which was published in 1846. See the 'Polynesia & the Pen' boxed text in the Facts for the Visitor chapter for more information about Melville and other writers who have visited French Polynesia.

The place Melville is supposed to have lived is marked with a sign reading Cité Melville; it's about 4.5km from the bridge in the centre of Taipivai, on the left-hand side of the Hatiheu road.

Allow 1½ hours by 4WD to reach Taipivai from Taiohae; take the road at right angles to the seafront in front of François Larson's shop.

Hooumi

Once inhabited by the fierce Teavaaki, this charming hamlet is about 4km east of Taipivai. The track from Taipivai goes through the village, which features a row of **pae pae**, on which houses have now been built, and copra-drying sheds. The village also has a picturesque small timber **church**. The track was initially a cliff-top road, and affords marvellous views over Contrôleur Bay and ends at a stunning white-sand **beach** opposite one of the bay's two inlets. Unfortunately, the beach is plagued by nono and mosquitoes.

Anaho

In 1888, Robert Louis Stevenson moored in Anaho Bay while he was cruising the Pacific on the *Casco*. The setting inspired him

to write many pages eulogising the unsettling beauty of the place.

A few families live in this peaceful hamlet, which has been untouched by time. The long white-sand **beach**, sadly infested with nono, stretches for nearly 1km and the bay is perfectly sheltered from the wind and the swell, contrasting sharply with the coves on the other Marquesas. It's a popular anchorage for visiting yachts. The only **coral reef** on the Marquesas has formed here, creating a lagoon-like effect. The shore is edged by copra-drying sheds, a magnificent **coconut plantation** and a tiny chapel.

Anaho is less than 10 minutes by speedboat from Hatiheu, or walk along the picturesque track. Take walking shoes, water and mosquito repellent. At the crossroad 100m east of the Hinakonui restaurant, take the tar-sealed track up to the right. About 500m farther on, there's a small clearing and if you have a vehicle it's best to leave it here. The start of the path is on the left, beyond the little bridge, 100m uphill from the white house built on a pae pae. It's about a 45 minute walk to Anaho Beach.

From the **Teavaimaoaoa Pass** (218m) there's an unbroken view over Anaho Bay, and the descent, right through the middle of a huge coconut plantation, is quite steep.

Aakapa

On the north coast, this village is in a superb setting characterised by peaks forming a sharp-edged wall. Aakapa can be reached by the path from Hatiheu or by speedboat.

Beaches

Nuku Hiva has several beautiful white and black-sand beaches. Taiohae has two beaches, a not particularly attractive one to the west and another to the east. It's close to the tennis courts, below the medical centre. The beach at Colette Bay is remote and wild, like the one at Hakaui Bay.

The most beautiful beaches on the island are, without doubt, the ones to the north at Anaho and in the adjacent bay at Haatuatua. Unfortunately, nono will give you a hard time, so bring mosquito repellent.

Archaeological Sites

See the 'Civilisation & Archaeology' special section for more information.

Hikokua One of the most attractive archaeological sites in the Marquesas, Hikokua was discovered by the archaeologist R Suggs in 1957 and restored by Hatiheu locals from 1987. It dates from around 1250 AD and was in use until the 1800s. Once a place of ceremony and human sacrifice, today ancient sculptures stand alongside modern works.

The tohua, a vast, central, rectangular esplanade, stretches north-south and was used for dance performances at community festivals. It's flanked by tiers of small and flat basalt blocks that were once used as steps for the spectators. The lower caste sat below, the upper caste above.

On the terrace stand two fine sculptures, modern works by Uki Haiti, and a flat rock which was used as a rostrum for solo dances or for rituals associated with puberty.

To the south-east of the esplanade are nine Christian tombs. They probably date from the time of the first missionary's arrival, after the abandonment of the site.

The platform at the bottom, on the northern side of the esplanade towards the ocean, was the *tuu*, or ceremonial activity centre. It's flanked with *keetu* (volcanic rock) tiles and to the front are three relatively well preserved tiki. It was on this tuu that sacrifices and display of the victims' bodies took place. The chief's residence stood at the north-east corner of the esplanade.

On the platform immediately to the left, at the entrance to the site, is a metre-long tiki phallus. It's made of a natural stone not found in this area. Nearby is an *ua ma* (food pit). Today the site is regularly used for traditional dances, particularly the impressive Dance of the Pig (see the 'Ori Tahiti – Tahitian Dance' special section), which is often performed by the Hikokua group of Hatiheu for the passengers of the *Aranui*.

Coming from Taipivai, it's about 1km from the Chez Yvonne guesthouse, along a small track suitable for vehicles. Ask at the guesthouse for Alphonse Puhetini (also known as Rua) to accompany you, as he has worked with the archaeologists in this valley.

Kamuihei & Tahakia About 300m towards Taipivai from the Hikokua site, this vast site spreads across both sides of the track. A team led by the archaeologist Pierre Ottino began restoration in 1998. Several ceremonies took place in this magnificent setting during the 1999-2000 Marquesas Islands Festival.

It's thought the Puhioho clan lived here and the grand ensemble was built around a stream and assembled numerous tribal architectural elements: there are vestiges of pae pae, tohua, meae, petroglyphs, ua ma and sacred banyan trees. The importance and sheer number of these structures testifies to the dense population this valley once sheltered. The site is spectacular, the mysterious air emphasised by the large moss-covered basalt rocks and the enormous banyan trees. The site has not been dated.

Beside the track a hae has been rebuilt on the largest of the pae pae. Further along a meae stands at the foot of an immense banyan, along with a pit, presumably dug for the remains of sacrifices or for taboo objects necessary to avoid contact with. Other pits are scattered about the site; these ua ma may have stocked *popoi*, the dough fermented from *uru* (breadfruit) as a provision during times of scarcity. A little higher are two large rocks about 2.5m high by 3m wide and decorated with petroglyphs. There are clearly visible representations of turtles, fish, the eyes of a tiki and human figures that could be representations of ancestors or divinities. It's estimated that the valley contains more than 500 such images.

On the other side of the track is the restored Tahakia tohua, one of the biggest in the Marquesas, stretching 155m by 42m and pae pae. This was the site of the warrior Keikahanui's clan. The site is not easy to make out but a guide, such as Yvonne Katupa at Hatiheu, will be able to explain it. There are plans to erect banners and signs on the site to explain about the culture and flora.

THE MARQUESAS

Paeke This site features two well maintained meae, flanked by a set of brick-coloured tiki. Massive and squat, with well-developed lower limbs, they radiate a forbidding power that makes them look like petrified Cerberuses. The meae farther up the hill has a pit into which human remains were thrown.

To get to the site from the little bridge in the centre of Taipivai, take the road for Hatiheu (uphill) for about 1.5km until you leave the village. Then follow the path that passes the blue house on the right and goes up through the coconut plantation. It's a 20 or 30 minute steep walk uphill, so take some mosquito repellent, a hat and sunscreen.

Activities
Diving There's a centre at Taiohae that operates to a dozen magnificent sites which are very different to those of the Society group or the Tuamotus. See the 'Diving' special section for details.

Walking There are good walking tracks all over the island, including the hikes to the Hakaui waterfall, Colette Bay and from Hatiheu to Anaho.

Horse Riding From Taiohae, it is easy to reach Colette Bay on horseback. Other popular rides are to the Hakaui waterfall, along the track between Hatiheu and Aakapa and on the Taiohae ridgeline.

In Taiohae ask at your hotel or contact Patrice Tamarii at Le Ranch (☎ 92 06 35) directly. He's a guide for horse-riding and walking trips and has docile and very well trained horses with leather saddles. There are trips for all levels of riders, from one-hour rides in the Taiohae Valley to outings lasting several days. The island's flora, history and other aspects are explained along the way. Trips to the Taiohae ridge or the south-west coast are also offered. Costs are 1500 CFP an hour (1000 CFP for children) or 8000 CFP for a day, including guide. Le Ranch may be moving to Muake.

You can also contact Louis Teikiteetini (☎ 92 02 37); he asks 1500 CFP per hour for guided outings. In Hatiheu contact Yvonne Katupa at the Chez Yvonne guesthouse and count on 5000 CFP per day, including guide.

Parasailing The only *parapente* (parasailing) club in the Marquesas is in Taiohae. There's a take-off platform at the top of Mt Muake. Parasailers leap off the sheer cliff with its absolutely vertical drop. Beginners can take their first steps on the infinitely more reassuring slopes on the hills above the town. At the time of writing there was no instructor at Taiohae, so only experienced members of the club could join in; a three month membership costs 1500 CFP. A parasail costs 3000 CFP to rent. Phone Roland (☎ 92 05 30) for more details.

Cruises See the Outdoor Activities chapter for information about cruises from Nuku Hiva.

Helicopter Flights Héli Inter Marquises (☎/fax 92 02 17, ☎ 92 00 54 at the heli-station, ☎ 92 04 40 at the airport) operates scenic 20-minute flights for a minimum of five people at 14,500 CFP each.

The circuit makes a loop from Taiohae over the Hakaui Valley towards the Toovii Plateau, following the coastline north to the needles of Aakapa and the village of Hatiheu, passing Anaho Bay and the beach at Haatuatua, before turning south towards the Taipivai Valley and Mt Muake. Inquire as early as possible so a group can be organised. It's often possible to join a group from the *Aranui* when that ship is in port.

Organised Tours
Pua Excursions, run by Monsieur Taupotini (☎ 92 02 94, 92 06 12, fax 92 01 35), offers three and four-day tours with English-speaking guides. The itinerary includes Toovii, Taiohae, Taipivai, Hatiheu and Anaho (three days) and Hakaui (four days). The price, which decreases with the number of persons, does not include transport from Papeete nor accommodation and meals. Per-person costs are 58,500/33,500/25,500/21,000 CFP for one/two/three/four on a three day circuit.

Alternatively, contact André Teikiteetini of Andy's Dream in Taiohae (☎/fax 92 00 80), which also offers island tours with all meals.

Places to Stay

Nuku Hiva has accommodation ranging from guesthouses to good-quality hotels and traditional bungalows.

Taiohae In the budget category the only option worth noting is *Chez Fetu (☎ 92 03 66)*, BP 22, Taiohae, Nuku Hiva. Fetu has a fully equipped bungalow for three people with kitchen, cold-water bathroom and veranda, next to his house and a stone's throw from the Kamake store in the centre of Taiohae. The simple rooms costs 2000 CFP per person, plus 500/1000 CFP for breakfast/other meals. His son's *house* in the Meau Valley, about 1km from the sea, has three rooms with fan, lounge with TV, fully equipped kitchen, cold-water bathroom and a big veranda. If you don't mind being a little distance from the centre and you're happy with preparing your own meals, it's great value at 2000 CFP per person. Follow the small path that starts from the west side of the Kamake store for 200m.

Ideally situated right in the centre of Taiohae on the seafront, the more upmarket *Hôtel Moana Nui (☎ 92 03 30, fax 92 00 02)* is run by Charles Monbaerts. The seven spotless rooms have fan and hot-water bathroom and cost 5000/5500 CFP single/double with breakfast, 7500/10,500 CFP half-board (breakfast and dinner) and 10,000/13,500 CFP full board (three meals). Ask for room No 1 or 2, which directly overlook the seafront. Meals are served in the restaurant on the ground floor, credit cards are accepted and there's a laundry service.

At the western end of Taiohae Bay, facing the beach, *Nuku Hiva Village (☎ 92 01 94, fax 92 05 97)* is the rising star of Taiohae's hotel industry. Its 15 sparkling-clean *fare* on a lush green property sleep two to three people. They have hot-water bathroom, fan and small veranda and cost 7020/8100/9180 CFP for one/two/three people; add 3500/4700 CFP per person for half/full board. Meals are served in the large

restaurant *fare*, credit cards are accepted and laundry costs 1000 CFP.

Keikahanui Nuku Hiva Pearl Lodge (☎ 92 03 82, fax 92 00 74; in Papeete ☎ 43 90 04, fax 43 17 86, email info@spmhotels .pf) is the most luxurious establishment in the northern Marquesas. Overlooking the western extremity of Taiohae Bay, 20 bungalows for two with air-con cost 28,080 CFP to 37,800 CFP. Add 800/5300/7800 CFP per person for breakfast/half/full board. All sorts of activities are offered and there's a swimming pool.

Andy's Dream (☎/fax 92 00 80) is a little out of the centre in the peaceful Hoata Valley. There are two functional bungalows with equipped kitchen, cold-water bathroom and veranda, next to André Teikiteetini's house. One has one room, the other has two and they cost 2500 CFP per person with breakfast, 5000/7500 CFP half/full board. Packages for a minimum of two people including meals, village visits, horseback trips and even pig or goat-hunting trips are offered.

Taipivai *Chez Martine Haiti (☎ 92 01 19, fax 92 05 34)* is on the riverside, 400m after the church towards Contrôleur Bay. A charming bungalow with two rooms and hot-water bathroom costs 2000 CFP per person, including breakfast. A four bedroom house with shared bathroom and equipped kitchen costs the same. Other meals cost 2000 CFP. In general visitors prefer to stay in Hatiheu or Anaho, so give the owner several days warning.

Hatiheu Hatiheu has an excellent guesthouse, *Chez Yvonne (☎ 92 02 97, fax 92 01 28)*. The Katupa family has five bungalows for two people with shared cold-water bathroom, facing the seafront and at the entrance to the village as you come from Taipivai. It costs 2600 CFP per person with breakfast; meals are served in the Hinakonui restaurant a little farther on. Travellers cheques are accepted.

Places to Eat

Taiohae In the centre of Taiohae *Kamake*, *François Larson* and *Maurice* are three well stocked shops on the waterfront with everything from food to hardware. They are basically open Monday to Saturday from 7.30 to 11.30 am and 2.30 to 5.30 pm; Sunday morning after mass. Kamake also serves as a bakery from 5.30 am; the entrance is at the side. There's another *bakery* on the waterfront, about 200m west of Hôtel Moana Nui but there's no sign. Some pastries are on sale; count on 120 CFP for a *firifiri* (sweet fritter). *Snack Céline*, on the waterfront and very close to the river, is actually a grocery store.

On the waterfront, 200m west of the Hôtel Moana Nui, the permanently stationed roulotte attached to the small *Chez Stella fare* offers a dish of the day such as chow mein or chicken curry for 750 CFP to eat there or take away. Other snacks are 350 CFP to 700 CFP and there are refreshments and desserts. Crêpes are served on Friday and Saturday in this friendly, airy place. It's open for lunch and dinner weekdays and Saturday morning.

Pâtisserie Mina (☎ 92 00 86), 400m along the waterfront beside the road in the Meau Valley, stands in front of a pae pae and is pleasantly decorated with Marquesan motifs painted in blue. Mina is Italian and does excellent pizzas for 850 CFP to 1300 CFP, quiches, brioches and light meals such as hamburgers for 350 CFP, as well as drinks. Opening hours are generally Tuesday to Saturday from 8 am to noon and 2 to 5 pm and Sunday morning – or anytime there's a demand, if you phone.

Restaurant Kovivi (☎ 92 03 85) is hidden by lush vegetation beside Banque Socredo. The restaurant enjoys an excellent reputation with classic French cuisine crossed with tropical influences. There's a good set lunch for 1100 CFP or you can order à la carte. The chef's speciality is lobster smoked in hot coral sauce for 2800 CFP. Wine by the bottle is from 2200 CFP, half-litre carafes cost 550 CFP. The inside is a little gloomy so book a table on the terrace. It's open daily for lunch and dinner, except Sunday night and it's closed in July. The menu is in English, French and Marquesan and there's a children's menu for 1000 CFP.

The hotel restaurants are also worth exploring. The restaurant at *Hôtel Moana Nui* offers traditional cuisine in a pleasant setting with a terrace facing the seafront. The lunchtime dish of the day is 1000 CFP and salads cost from 600 CFP, pizzas from 1400 CFP, a generous *poisson cru* (raw fish) from 1100 CFP, fish and meat dishes from 1100 CFP to 2220 CFP and various snacks from 1000 CFP. It's open daily except Sunday for lunch and dinner and accepts credit cards.

At *Nuku Hiva Village*, to the west of the bay and right by the beach, the *fare*-restaurant is in an airy local style with a thatched roof supported by columns carved like tiki. The food is good and the prices reasonable; count on 800 CFP for tuna sashimi or 1100 CFP for grilled tuna, 1500 CFP for steak with pepper or mushroom sauce, 500 CFP to 900 CFP for a dessert. Prices on the small winelist start at 1550 CFP and a half-litre carafe costs 550 CFP. It's open daily for lunch and dinner, sometimes there's live music, and credit cards are accepted.

There's also a restaurant at the *Keikahanui Nuku Hiva Pearl Lodge*.

Taipivai *Chez Martine Haiti* has a restaurant that serves Marquesan specialities such as goat, pork, lobster and fish. Meals cost from 2000 CFP and bookings are essential.

Hatiheu *Hinakonui* restaurant at Chez Yvonne has a deservedly good reputation. Its magnificent terrace opens directly onto the seafront, 50m from the church. In this temple of fine Marquesan food, generously sized dishes range from a plate of poisson cru for 1200 CFP to a full meal for 2500 CFP. You need at least 10 people to try the excellent Marquesan oven, the house speciality, so contact Yvonne to see if the *Aranui* or some other group will be visiting. There's a popular bar and reservations are essential.

Shopping

In Taiohae, some curios and pareu are on sale at the Kanahau Shop and Shop Loisirs (which also sells photographic supplies).

Getting There & Away

Air The Air Tahiti office (☎ 92 03 41, 92 05 02) is on the eastern side of the cove, on the seafront. Marcelline, the company's representative, speaks good English and is on duty weekdays from 8 am to noon and 2 to 5 pm and on Saturday from 8 am to noon. These opening hours are somewhat theoretical as she is also on duty at the Nuku Ataha airport (☎ 92 01 45) on days when there is a flight. On those days there's a poster on the office door. Credit cards are accepted.

There are five to seven flights a week between Papeete and Nuku Hiva (three hours), one of which stops at Rangiroa in the Tuamotus in the Papeete-Nuku Hiva direction only.

Within the Marquesas there are flights from Nuku Hiva to Atuona (Hiva Oa), Ua Huka and Ua Pou. Frequencies vary with the season but there are four or five flights weekly Nuku Hiva-Atuona-Nuku Hiva. Nuku Hiva-Ua Huka-Nuku Hiva operates once a week, supposedly on Thursday, and Nuku Hiva-Ua Pou-Nuku Hiva three times weekly. All these flights connect to/from Papeete.

Papeete-Nuku Hiva costs 26,500 CFP, Nuku Hiva-Ua Huka and Nuku Hiva-Ua Pou cost 5100 CFP, Nuku Hiva-Atuona costs 8800 CFP.

Helicopter Héli Inter Marquises (☎/fax 92 02 17, ☎ 92 00 54 at the heli-station, ☎ 92 04 40 at the airport) is adjacent to the Air Tahiti office on the seafront at Taiohae, and opens weekdays from 7.30 am to noon and 12.30 to 4 pm (closing on Friday at 3 pm).

The helicopter provides regular shuttle services to Hakahau (Ua Pou; 15 minutes), supposedly on Wednesday, Friday and Sunday, in both directions for 12,000 CFP per person one way. The heliport, at the eastern end of Taiohae Bay, overhangs the cargoship wharf. Credit cards are accepted.

Boat In Taiohae, Xavier Curvat, the director of the dive centre (☎/fax 92 00 88) on the marina quay, operates a Taiohae-Hakahau (Ua Pou)-Taiohae (1¾ hours) ferry twice weekly. It leaves Taiohae on Friday at 5 pm

and returns from Hakahau at 7.30 pm. On Sunday it departs Taiohae at 2 pm and returns from Hakahau at 4.30 pm. One way/weekend return costs 5000/8000 CFP. The schedule is subject to alteration; make reservations and check in advance. It's also possible to charter the boat (maximum 15 passengers) for 45,000 CFP to Ua Pou or 50,000 CFP to Ua Huka.

Laurent (Teiki) Falchetto (☎ 92 05 78) is also in Taiohae and has a six to eight-passenger bonitier that can be chartered to Ua Pou for 45,000 CFP and to Ua Huka for 50,000 CFP. The owner of the speedboat *Dina* (☎ 92 04 78) charters his boat at the same rates.

The *Aranui* and the *Taporo IV* serve Nuku Hiva and dock at the end of the bay in Taiohae. The *Aranui* goes to Taipivai and Hatiheu as well as Taiohae (see the Getting Around chapter and 'The *Aranui*' special section in this chapter for details).

Getting Around

A network of tracks link the airport, Taiohae, Taipivai, Hooumi, Hatiheu and Aakapa.

To/From the Airport It takes at least two hours to reach the airport from Taiohae along a bumpy, winding track, longer if it has rained and the ground is muddy – and it's only 18km as the crow flies!

Approved 4WD taxis that carry four to six people generally wait for each flight. It is nevertheless wise to book, either through your hotel or guesthouse, or directly by contacting the taxi drivers: Joseph Puhetini (☎ 92 03 47), Maxime or Sonia Teuhitua (☎ 92 02 22), Temo (☎ 92 04 13), Marie-Jeanne Ah Scha (☎ 92 01 84), Uki Otto (☎ 92 04 89), Léonard Hokaupoko (☎ 92 00 16) or André Teikiteetini (☎ 92 00 80). The airport-Taiohae run costs 4000/5000 CFP by day/night per person (except with Maxime or Sonia, who charge 3500 by day). It's also possible to hitch.

Héli Inter Marquises (☎/fax 92 02 17, ☎ 92 00 54 at the heli-station, ☎ 92 04 40 at the airport) provides a helicopter-shuttle to each Air Tahiti Papeete connection. Between the airport and Taiohae costs 7000 CFP per person, half-fare for children under 11, and takes eight minutes. It also goes to Hatiheu and Taipivai. Reservations are necessary going to the airport, but not from it. The helicopter can also be chartered.

4WD 4WDs can be rented with or without driver. Taiohae has several 4WD operators who make excursions to the various tourist sites and villages. Your accommodation can make arrangements or you can book directly. In the Pakiu Valley, Temo's house is about 200m from the church on the left and Joseph Puhetini is in the red brick house on the other side of the road. Maxime and Sonia Teuhitua, who speaks a little English, live in the Meau Valley, behind the bridge from the Bigot store and are slightly cheaper than the others. Marie-Jeanne Ah Scha is behind the Moana Nui (ask Charles Monbaerts to show you the way). See To/From the Airport earlier for phone numbers. There's also Jean-Pierre Piriotua (☎ 92 00 17).

From Taiohae, for the whole vehicle, which will take four passengers, count on 3000 CFP to 5000 CFP to Muake, 12,000 CFP to Taipivai, 20,000 CFP to Hatiheu and 25,000 CFP to Aakapa. The hotels in Taiohae will try to group their customers. In Taipivai contact Henri Taata (☎ 92 01 36). In Hatiheu contact Yvonne Katupa (☎ 92 02 97). Count on 6000 CFP between Hatiheu and Aakapa.

Charles Monbaerts at the Hôtel Moana Nui has a two seater Suzuki available for 9000 CFP for 24 hours including insurance and unlimited distance. This is good value if you are alone but for two or more people it's cheaper and less stressful to get a vehicle with driver. There's a petrol station on the cargo-ship wharf at the eastern end of the bay in Taiohae.

Boat Speedboats take four to six people and cost around 12,000 CFP (flat rate) to visit such places as Hakaui Bay and the Vaipo Waterfall. Call the owner of the *Dina* (☎ 92 04 78), Léonard Hokaupoko (☎ 92 00 16) or Francis Falchetto (☎ 92 01 51).

Through Yvonne Katupa at Chez Yvonne, it costs 6000 CFP to make the Hatiheu-Anaho crossing, 7000 CFP for Hatiheu-Aakapa.

UA HUKA
pop 571 • area 83 sq km
highest point Mt Hitikau (855m)

Ua Huka (the 'leftover scraps' in the Marquesas Islands legend) lies 50km east of Nuku Hiva and 56km north-east of Ua Pou. Ua Huka's topography is quite different from these nearby islands, yet it rarely features in the itinerary of travellers, who tend to concentrate on its two neighbours.

The island consists of two stacked volcanoes. The caldera of the main volcano forms an amphitheatre facing south-west to south-east, while the secondary volcano occupies the south-eastern part of the large caldera. Vaikivi Plateau, covered with impenetrable clumps of vegetation, occupies the northern edge of the island, while the island's three villages – Vaipaee, Hane and Hokatu – nestle around the edges of steepsided valleys on the south coast.

Ua Huka, the driest island in all French Polynesia, has almost desert-like plains in the south. Between Hane and Vaipaee there are some wonderfully chaotic landscapes, accentuated by free-ranging herds of semi-wild horses (hence the nickname 'Island of Horses'). Goats also roam free and several offshore islets are home to thousands of nesting birds.

The island boasts archaeological treasures such as the Hane tiki and the Vaikivi petroglyphs and the Marquesas' first museum devoted entirely to archaeology. Each of the three villages has craft exhibition-and-sales centres and, surprisingly perhaps, a first-rate arboretum is the pride of the island.

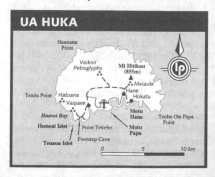

Information

There is no bank on Ua Huka. The post office is in Vaipaee, next to the museum (open weekdays from 7.30 to 11.30 am and 1 to 2.30 pm and when the *Aranui* calls in), and each village has phonecard telephone booths and an infirmary or first-aid post.

Vaipaee

The island's main town is at the end of a very deep narrow inlet, measuring about 1km and rightly named Invisible Bay. When the *Aranui* comes in, it manoeuvres in a space the size of a handkerchief and ties up to the rock face with hawsers.

The village stretches along the valley with the church, the museum, the post office and mairie constituting the centre. The rest of the township is in the adjacent valley to the east, while an incongruous housing development is a few kilometres away towards Hane.

Museum The museum, in the centre of Vaipaee, opened in 1987, largely due to the endeavours of Mayor Léon Lichtlé. Its size may be modest, but it has great symbolic value for the heritage-proud Marquesans.

The museum is in a group of buildings which also house the mairie, a craft centre and the post office. On the esplanade in front of the museum is a commemorative plaque dedicated to Captain Étienne Marchand, who landed in the northern group of the Marquesas in 1791. The museum includes pestles, tiki, finely carved sculptures, *pahu* (drums), a variety of jewellery and period photos as well as a hae. There are also scale reproductions of ancient sites and objects such as paddles, spears and clubs. Entry is free but donations are appreciated.

Arboretum This botanic garden, created in 1974, is well worth a short visit. It is beside the road, halfway between Vaipaee and Hane and includes dozens of species from around the world. There is a striking contrast between this wealth of plants and the relative aridity of the island. The fact that so many species have adapted to the dry Marquesan soil opens up great possibilities for local agriculture. The species best adapted to the climate are used for reforestation where the vegetation has been destroyed by wild goats and horses.

Hane

It's said that the first Polynesian settlement on the Marquesas was here, tucked away in a bay protected on the east by Motu Hane, an impressive islet shaped like a sugarloaf. The local personality is sculptor Joseph Vaatete, whose workshop is 200m from the beach.

The white house on the seafront houses the craft centre and a small **marine museum** that opened in 1995 and contains some traditional pirogues. Ask for the key from Joseph Vaatete.

Hokatu

This peaceful village lies about 3km east of Hane in a sheltered bay. The main street leads to the **craft *fare*** and the black-pebble beach.

Footstep Cave

Tupapau (ghosts) are said to haunt this cave, slightly west of Point Tekeho, between Vaipaee and Haavei Bay.

According to legend, a fisherman took refuge in the cave during a storm. He awoke to note large footprints on the sand. A few days later, when the tide should have washed them away, the footprints were still there. Today, people swear they are still there and we did indeed see footprints and the word *kaoha* (hello) written in the sand – the work of the village youngsters, no doubt.

The cave can be reached at low tide when there is not much swell. If you visit with a guide, the boat will stop about 30m from the crevice and you will have to swim to the edge, taking care not to be swept onto the reefs by the undertow. Take plastic sandals and ask your guide to bring a torch (flashlight).

Bird Islands

Thousands of sooty terns *(kaveka)* have taken up residence on the islets of **Hemeni** and **Teuaua**, near the south-western point of

Ua Huka. They lay thousands of eggs daily, which the islanders regularly gather.

Access to Hemeni is prohibited in order to protect the species. Teuaua, the neighbouring islet, is accessible by speedboat, but the boat isn't able to come in too close because of the swell. It's necessary to jump on to a rocky ledge and clamber up the rock using a length of permanently fixed rope, a rather perilous exercise.

There's a final test: the smell emanating from the thousands of birds. Their eggs, whitish and speckled with brown or black marks, are not all fit for eating and only an expert eye can spot which ones are suitable. The kaveka become infuriated and their cries are deafening. The more reckless among them are bold enough to swoop over your head and you will soon be reliving a scene from Hitchcock's *The Birds*.

If, despite all this, the experience still attracts you ... wear a hat.

Beaches

Ua Huka has the most beautiful beaches in the Marquesas, although the nono spoil the pleasure. Bring insect repellent. Accessible by speedboat or 4WD, **Manihina Beach**, between Vaipaee and the airport, is fringed with fine white sand. There are excellent opportunities for snorkelling, as the beach is sheltered by a bay. **Hatuana Beach** is in the west of the island; there are petroglyphs nearby. **Haavei Beach** is a beautiful inlet that belongs to the Lichtlé family. Ask the owners, who live on the coconut plantation, for permission before you plunge in.

Motu Papa

This island picnic-and-snorkelling spot is just offshore from the airport. It is a large block of volcanic rock which, at low tide, reveals a fairly wide rocky ledge where you can sit. As the speedboat cannot come alongside, you have to swim about 50m to the edge of the rock. Food and various items of equipment are loaded in a large floating bin and all you have to do is swim with it to the rock. Take sunscreen (there are few shady spots) and plastic sandals, as the rock is very slippery.

Archaeological Sites

Meiaute Less than 30 minutes walk from the village, this site is one of the major attractions on Ua Huka. It includes three red-tuff tiki a metre in height that watch over a group of stone structures, pae pae and meae, which have not yet been restored and are partly overgrown. Two of these tiki have very projecting ears, unlike most of their fellows. One has legs and sex organs, the other two only have head and trunk. The glade forms a natural lookout with magnificent views of Hane Bay on one side and the caldera on the other. There are plans to further develop this site.

To get there, follow the track from the Auberge Hitikau (see Places to Stay later) at the edge of the village for about 200m, heading in the direction of the mountain. At the crossroad, go straight; after about 20 minutes you will come to a cement stairway on your right, 30m after a sharp bend. Leave the main track at this point and climb the steep hill to the pae pae. A little higher up, in a clearing, you will find the tiki. From the stairway, arrows on trees indicate the path, but you need to look carefully.

Vaikivi Petroglyphs This little-visited archaeological site on the Vaikivi Plateau is worth the detour, if only for the walk or horse ride to get there. See Walking under Activities later. The well restored petroglyphs are engraved on a grey stone. They represent an octopus and a human face and there are other petroglyphs nearby. If they are covered with earth or moss, pour a little water on them and scrape them delicately with your hand to make them visible.

Activities

Walking It's a beautiful three hour walk inland to the Vaikivi petroglyphs. Take a guide because it's a long way and the trail is indistinct. The departure can be from Vaipaee or Hane.

From Hane follow the main road to the edge of the village on the mountain side and then take the track that branches to the left before the first house. A little farther on the route rejoins a small trail and the difficulties begin. The path climbs the steep volcano caldera (one to 1½ hours). From the glade at the ridge there are wonderful views over Hane Bay with Motu Hane visible to the west. When it's clear you can make out Fatu Huku to the south-east with the village a speckled ribbon of red and white.

The track continues inland and begins to descend gently, as the thick vegetation gives way to tree ferns. The contrast with the coastal scenery is striking. After about 30 or 45 minutes, branch left and hack your way through a forest of pandanus and other vegetation. Just over half an hour later you reach the petroglyphs.

Take good shoes and sufficient food and water. A guide will cost 3000 CFP to 5000 CFP; ask at your accommodation or contact Léonard Teatiu or Napoléon at Vaipaee mairie, Gilles Brown at Vaipaee or Patrick Teiki at Hokatu.

The coastal route between Haavei to the west and Hokatu to the east, offers spectacular views and is also worth doing.

Horse Riding Horses are an important part of activities on Ua Huka. There are varied itineraries but the most popular route is to ride from Vaipaee to Hane, passing the arboretum, airport and wind-swept arid plateaus before reaching the cliff road, which plunges down towards Hane. If the weather cooperates, this ride will certainly be one of the highlights of your stay on the Marquesas.

Ask at your accommodation about where to find horse owners. A ride typically costs 5000 CFP, including a guide. Wooden saddles are still quite commonly used, but fortunately, padding is provided to relieve the discomfort.

Places to Stay

Considering the small number of visitors, Ua Huka has a surprising number of guesthouses, with some of the most attractive tariffs in French Polynesia. Excursions by boat, 4WD and horse are often organised but credit cards are not accepted and the prices quoted generally do not include VAT.

Marquesan Horses

Domesticated or wild, horses are an integral part of the Marquesan landscape. Originally from Chile and mainly chestnut in colour, they were introduced by Dupetit Thouars, who gave them to Chief Iotete (of Tahuata) in 1842. In some valleys they serve as a means of transport and are even used to haul copra. Perfectly used to local conditions, they're ideal for exploring the wild Marquesan countryside. Ua Huka has the greatest number of horses; they are a pony-thoroughbred mix, and are renowned for their sense of balance. Excellent riders, the Marquesans are used to riding bareback. Most of the islands have horses for hire, with or without the services of a guide.

Vaipaee *Chez Alexis Scallamera* (☎ 92 60 19, 92 61 16) has four quiet, well kept doubles with shared cold-water bathroom for 1500 CFP per person or 3500/5000 CFP with half/full board including airport transfers. Guests can use the kitchen. The house, which is blue, is beside the main road, on the right as you come from the quay.

The prices at *Chez Christelle* (☎ 92 61 08, 92 60 34) are attractive, at 1500 CFP per person, 1000 CFP for breakfast, 1500 CFP for other meals; airport transfers are included. The four rooms with shared cold-water bathroom are sparkling clean and Mme Fournier prepares excellent and generously sized Marquesan dishes featuring lobster as the main ingredient.

At the exit from the village towards Hane, *Mana Tupuna Village* (☎/fax 92 60 08, email manatupuna@marquises.com) is perched on the side of the hill to the right. There are three local-style bungalows on stilts, elegantly arranged with covered veranda, mezzanine and hot-water bathroom. There are beautiful views over the valley below. The costs are 5500/10,000 CFP for one/two people with half-board. One of the bungalows is used as a restaurant.

THE MARQUESAS

Hane *Auberge Hitikau (☎ 92 60 68)*, run by Céline Fournier, doubles as a very good restaurant, adjoining which are four simple but clean double rooms with shared cold-water bathroom for 2000/3000 CFP for one/two people. Add 500 CFP for breakfast and 2000 CFP for other meals. To get to the guesthouse, go up the main street towards the mountain; it's 300m past the church, on the large ranch-like property.

Hokatu The Rootuehine family's excellent place, *Chez Maurice & Delphine (☎/fax 92 60 55, email delphine@marquises.com)*, is the first house on the left as you enter the village from Hane. In the owners' house there are two clean and welcoming double rooms with shared cold-water bathroom. One room has a fan. From the terrace, there's a beautiful view over the village and the bay and the prices are very reasonable – 1200 CFP per person, and 500/1000 CFP for breakfast/other meals. There are two more-private bungalows with verandas perched above the edge of town. One has a cold-water bathroom and a fridge and will accommodate six people. The other also has a small kitchen and sleeps three. They cost 2000/3000 CFP for one/two and have wonderful views of Motu Hane.

If you stay several days you will have the opportunity to enjoy a traditional meal from a Marquesan oven. Pork and fish are wrapped in aluminium foil, placed in an oven hollowed out of the ground, covered with earth and baked. Maurice is one of the best sculptors on the island. There's a small shop in the house's garage.

Haavei Haavei Bay, about 5km west of Vaipaee, belongs to the Lichtlé family. A track makes it accessible by 4WD. *Chez Joseph Lichtlé (☎ 92 60 72)* is near a very pretty beach. There are two bungalows with cold-water bathroom; one large three bedroom house with shared bathroom; and a solar-powered two bedroom house with shared bathroom. Joseph Lichtlé, a fine chef, features local specialities on his menu, and charges 5500 CFP a day for full board, including transfers to the airport.

Places to Eat

Apart from several small *snack bars* and *food shops*, the choice is restricted on Ua Huka. Fortunately, the food offered by the *guesthouses* is good and includes Marquesan specialities. Try to sample the succulent kaveka-egg omelette, the undisputed speciality of the island.

The only true restaurant is the *Auberge Hitikau* in Hane. Local specialities have pride of place: goat, pork, fish in coconut milk, kaveka-egg omelettes and delicious cakes made by Céline Fournier. It costs 2000 CFP for a set meal, excluding drinks, and bookings are essential.

Getting There & Away

Air On Thursday a Dornier flies Nuku Hiva-Ua Huka-Nuku Hiva, connecting with the flight linking Papeete with Nuku Hiva. Papeete-Ua Huka via Nuku Hiva costs 27,500 CFP, Nuku Hiva-Ua Huka is 5100 CFP. Marie-Louise Fournier is the Air Tahiti representative (☎ 92 60 85, 92 61 08) in Vaipaee. On Thursday she's on duty at the airport (☎ 92 60 44).

Boat Maurice Rootuehine (☎/fax 92 60 55) and Paul Teatiu (☎ 92 60 88), in Hokatu, have speedboats and can do the Ua Huka-Ua Pou/Nuku Hiva crossings for 50,000/60,000 CFP. Let them know you want a place. The *Aranui* and the *Taporo IV* serve Ua Huka (see the Getting Around chapter for details).

Getting Around

A 13km track links Vaipaee to Hokatu via Hane; the stretch from Vaipaee to Hane is surfaced. Haavei is also accessible by the track from Vaipaee.

To/From the Airport Airport transfers are usually included in guesthouse charges.

Car In Vaipaee, contact Alexis Scallamera at the guesthouse of the same name or Jean-Baptiste Brown (☎ 92 60 23). In Haavei, the Lichtlés also have a 4WD. In Hane, you can contact Céline Fournier at the Auberge Hitikau and, in Hokatu, Maurice Rootuehine at Chez Maurice & Delphine. See

Places to Stay earlier for contact details. A full day's hire, with a driver, will cost you 10,000 CFP (or 7000 CFP with Maurice Rootuehine).

Boat Contact the Fournier family in Vaipaee, Céline Fournier in Hane and Maurice Rootuehine in Hokatu. Bonitier hire comes to about 10,000 CFP a day.

UA POU
pop 2013 • area 125 sq km
highest point Mt Oave (1203m)
Lying 45km south of Nuku Hiva, Ua Pou was the site of a settlement estimated to have been established around 150 BC. Frenchman Étienne Marchand landed on the island in June 1791 and claimed it on behalf of France; American Ingraham, captain of the *Hope*, had noted its existence two months earlier.

Ua Pou ('the pillars' in the Marquesas Islands legend) is geologically the youngest

UA POU

Hakanai Bay
Hatukoemo Point
Aneou
Airport
Anahoa Beach
Motu Mokohe
Tepapaki Point
Hakahau
Hakahetau
Matatihotea Point
Panahu Point
Haakuti
Mt Poutemoka (685m)
Hakamoui Valley
Vaiehu Bay
Mt Oave (1203m)
Archaeological Site
Poava Point
Hakamaii
Hohoi
Tekotake Point
Hikeu
Paaukoheputa Point
Hakaohoka Archaeological Site
Hakataō
Mt Tekataihiko (433m)
Motu Papati
Motu Tamuko
Motu Takaae
Motu Tehuaki
Motu Oa
0   2.5   5 km

The Marquesas Islands Festival

The most important annual event in the archipelago, the festival is a clear indication of the strength of Marquesan culture. The Motu Haka (Gathering) Association was created in 1978 with the goal of protecting and promoting local culture. Its main battle at the time was to ensure that the Marquesan language was taught in schools. The association took a decisive step in 1985 when, in the wake of the Pacific Arts Festival on Tahiti, the idea to organise a similar program of dancing, singing, traditional sports, cuisine and arts and crafts took hold.

The first festival was held on Ua Pou in 1987. A second followed on Nuku Hiva in 1989, a third on Hiva Oa in 1991 and a fourth on Ua Pou in 1995. On each occasion archaeological sites were restored. The fifth, on Nuku Hiva, will be in 2000.

The festival is intended to strengthen the community memory of the value of ancestral practices. Of course the festival also encourages tourism, with archaeological sites being restored, small museums being created, handicrafts being encouraged and tourist infrastructure being improved.

island in the archipelago, with its sharp contours and 12 pointy pinnacles, obelisks or columns of basalt, often shrouded by cloud cover.

Hakahau, the island's main settlement, is home to most of the population. A few villages nestled in the steep-sided valleys are dotted along the east and west coasts.

Ua Pou is noted for its culture and arts. It was the birthplace of the Motu Haka Association and the revival of Marquesan identity (see the boxed text 'The Marquesas Islands Festival'). It is a breeding ground for talent: singing star Rataro, the Kanahau Trio musical group and most of the well known Marquesan dance groups are from Ua Pou and its wood and stone-sculptors have brought fame to the island.

Fascinating archaeological remains can be seen in the Hakamoui and Hohoi valleys.

Information

Tourist Offices Contact Rosita Teiki-tutoua (☎ 92 53 36), the head of the tourist office. You can also contact Tina Klima, the Air Tahiti representative (☎ 92 53 41), who is well informed and speaks English, or the Motu Haka Association (☎ 92 53 21).

Money Banque Socredo (☎ 92 53 63) is in one wing of the Hakahau mairie, not far from the post office. You can change currency and travellers cheques or get a cash advance with your credit card. The bank is open weekdays from 7.30 to 11 am and 1.30 to 4 pm.

Post & Communications The post office is to the west of the bay and is open Monday to Thursday from 7 am to 3 pm, Friday to 2 pm. There are phonecard telephone booths beside the post office, on the quay and opposite the Air Tahiti office.

Laundry Contact the Restaurant-Pension Pukuéé (☎/fax 92 50 83) and count on 1500 CFP per machine-load, washed and dried.

Medical Services In Hakahau, a small medical centre with a doctor and dentist is in the south of the village, halfway between the church and the museum. Every village has an infirmary or first-aid post.

Hakahau

The four north-south streets start at the seafront quay and run to the other end of the bay. The CETAD (technical school) and the secondary school, decorated with frescoes representing tiki, face the black-sand beach, which is frequented by young surfers fresh from school. Farther west, the market livens up each Sunday after mass.

Inaugurated for the 1995 Marquesas Islands Festival (see the boxed text 'The Marquesas Islands Festival' earlier in this chapter), the **Museum of Hakahau** faces the esplanade where the demonstrations were staged. Just as in Vaipaee's museum on Ua Huka, locals were encouraged to lend objects representative of Marquesan material culture to be displayed. Admission is free but, unfortunately, the museum remains empty.

As part of the festival, a team from the archaeological department of the Museum of Tahiti & Its Islands travelled to Hakahau to restore the **Pae Pae Tenei** right in the middle of the village. Admirably restored, this site is representative of the characteristic structure of traditional dwellings.

The recent stone-and-timber Catholic church in the south of the village, on the Hohoi road, houses some very noteworthy **sculptures** by local artisans. The monumental pulpit representing the bows of a boat balancing on a net full of miraculous fish is particularly interesting.

For a beautiful view of **Hakahau Bay** climb from the white cross to the east of the centre. Ascend to the Pension-Restaurant Pukuéé and continue along the track until you reach a small pass. At the pass, take the right fork and climb steeply for five to 10 minutes, until you reach a small flight of steps leading to the cross, which you can see from the quay. The view is magnificent: in addition to the jagged profile of Nuku Hiva to the north, you can also see blue Anahoa Bay and its white border of sand to the east. In clear weather, you can see Ua Huka to the north-east.

Hohoi

This picturesque little village on the southeast of the island is accessible from Hakahau. The 12km track passes numerous types of luxuriant vegetation, which contrasts strikingly with the aridity of the plateaus in the north-west of the island. There are some good views over the sea, particularly at Haakaunui Bay.

Time seems to stand still in Hohoi. You may pass a few locals returning to the village, leading horses laden with bunches of bananas or bags of coconuts. As you enter the village, 100m before the blue-roofed mairie on the left, you will spot two **pae pae**. On the corner beehives are lined up on a stone platform. The curious pagoda shape of the **church** is also noteworthy.

On the beach there are a few thatched fisher's huts. It's here that Hohoi's famous **flowering pebbles** can be found. They are pieces of phonolite that have crystallised to form amber-coloured flower shapes.

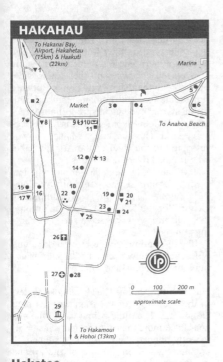

HAKAHAU

PLACES TO STAY & EAT
1 Chez Adrienne
2 Tepano Kohumoetini
6 Restaurant-Pension Pukuéé
8 Snack-Pâtisserie Vaitiare
11 Chez Marguerite Dordillon
17 Snack Guéranger
20 Pension Vehine
21 Snack Vehine
24 Chez Samuel & Jeanne-Marie
25 Chez Rosalie

OTHER
3 Secondary School
4 CETAD
5 Fare Artisanal
7 Honey for Sale
9 Banque Socredo; Mairie (Town Hall)
10 Post Office
12 Grocery Shop; Boutique
13 Gendarmerie (Police Station)
14 Eugène Hapipi (sculptor)
15 William Aka (sculptor)
16 Aimé Kohumoetini (sculptor)
18 Grocery Shop
19 Joseph B's Shop
22 Tenei Pae Pae (archaeological site)
23 Boutique; Air Tahiti
26 Church
27 Medical Centre
28 Fara Shop
29 Museum

Hakatao

This tiny village, on the south-west of the island, is accessible by boat or by the track from Hohoi.

Hakamaii

This one-street village, stretching along the Kahioa River, is only accessible by pirogue – the person paddling has to catch a wave at just the right moment so that the pirogue is gently propelled rather than dumped onto the shore.

The façade of the town's stone **church**, facing the ocean, has unusual yellow, blue and red painted wooden panels which replicate stained-glass windows. Seen from the ocean, the illusion is almost perfect.

There's a path along the river at the far end of the village; take some mosquito repellent.

Haakuti

The tiny village of Haakuti is the terminus of the 22km track from Hakahau, which will

one day be extended to Hakatao. Meanwhile, Haakuti feels deliciously like the end of the world. The one street links the stone **church**, built on a pae pae at the top of the village, with the tiny sea-swept quay some 600m below. At nightfall, don't miss the return of the **fishers**. Good-sized bonito and tuna form a large part of the catch.

Hakahetau

This charming village, noted for its red church-tower near the waterfront, was the residence of Monsignor Le Cleac'h, known for his translation of the Bible into Marquesan. Hakahetau's inhabitants live off copra production, fishing, and arts and crafts.

A 15km track snakes between the bare plateaus of the island's north-west and, along the section between Hakahau and Aneou airport, you will see wild horses and goats. In the background, due south, the slender profile of Mt Oave (1203m) appears, while in the north you can make out the contours of Nuku Hiva.

Motu Oa

South of the island, this motu is home to colonies of thousands of sea birds.

Beaches

Twenty-five minutes walk east of Hakahau, white-sand **Anahoa Beach** fringes Anahoa Cove and contrasts with the wildness of the neighbouring volcanic scenery. Go there on foot or by horseback to enjoy the panoramic view going down towards the bay. From the Hakahau quay, follow the direction indicated by the Restaurant Pukuéé signpost and take the track after the restaurant. About 10 minutes climb to the pass there's a superb view of Hakaheu Bay and its peaks.

Shortly after the airport at Aneou, 11km from Hakahau, is Hakanai Bay, below the track leading to Hakahetau. It's a popular local picnic spot. It's been named Plage aux Requins, **Shark Beach**, because of the many sharks seen in the cove.

The black-sand **Puamau Beach** is popular with young surfers. Wherever you go it's imperative to have mosquito repellent to cope with the horrible nono.

Archaeological Sites

See the 'Civilisation & Archaeology' special section for more information on archaeological sites.

Hakamoui Valley This valley, also known as the Valley of the Kings, is now deserted. Formerly inhabited by the dominant Atipapa tribe from which the island's chieftain came, it was one of the main centres of population on the island. Interest in Hakamoui has revived, thanks to the Marquesas Islands Festival (see the boxed text on the festival earlier in this chapter) in December 1995.

The valley is easily accessible from Hakahau. Follow the road to Hohoi for about 3km and take the left fork, which descends eastward towards the ocean. One kilometre farther on, on the right and set back from the track, is a **pae pae** that was used as the platform for a recent dwelling but now lies abandoned. You can see a clear bas-relief and hollowed-out carvings, one on the northern side and the other on a stone slab placed edgeways on the eastern side, both slightly hidden by vegetation. Both are representations of human features with round staring eyes and disproportionate rectangular mouths. Not far away is a well-preserved tiki. This site, called Mataautea, was restricted to the chief of the Atipapa tribe, who reigned over the whole island.

Two hundred metres farther on is the imposing **Temenaha pae pae**, built by Chief Puheputoka. This site was completely cleared for the festival. If you get up onto the platform, you will see a series of carvings on the stone.

If you continue for just over 1km, you will reach a pretty coconut plantation fringing a black pebble-and-sand beach.

Hakaohoka Valley The Hakaohoka Valley, in the south-east of the island, opens onto Hohoi Bay. From the pebbly shore the site goes back more than 2km inland. This until-recently populated area has been studied by archaeologist Pierre Ottino of the French oceanographic research institute ORSTOM.

According to a legend told by Jacques Dordillon, who owns the land, Heato, the last king of Ua Pou, wanted to marry the daughter of the chief of the Kaavahopeoa tribe who had taken up residence in Hakaohoka Valley. He was given a categorical refusal and the Kaavahopeoa fled aboard huge bamboo rafts to escape retribution, eventually settling on Napuka (Tuamotus).

More prosaically, it is known that this valley was deserted in the 1860s as the result of a smallpox epidemic, and the dwellings became ossified. For a stretch of 70m on each side of the main river bed, there are sandstone structures, the remains of ancient human occupation, consisting of pae pae, paving and low walls. Start your visit with **Chief Hamipohue's pae pae**, which is protected from run-off water and the sun by a corrugated-iron roof. At one end, you can see the chief's back-rest. At right angles to the terrace are some rough stone carvings.

The whole area is full of more pae pae, **tohua** and **meae**. The ghostly silhouette of the banyans, the islands' sacred trees, reinforces the mystical atmosphere of the place.

Hakaohoka site, accessible by the track, is 13km from Hakahau. At Hohoi, go down to the pebbly beach and follow it along the track bordered with *miro* (rosewood) and *tou* trees. After the first fishers' shelter, you will see a sign with a map of the site. Take the track up and walk for 15 minutes until you arrive in sight of the pae pae, on the right under the plant cover. At Hohoi, don't forget to give 1000 CFP to the custodian, Willy Hikutini, who can also act as your guide. This money is used to finance the upkeep of the track and restoration of the site.

Activities
Walking There are many hiking possibilities including simply following the tracks from one village to another. If you intend to leave the tracks it's advisable to take a guide.

Horse Riding Francis Aka (☎ 92 51 83) has three horses that he rents for 800/2500/5000 CFP an hour/half-day/day, not including a guide. In Hakahetau contact Tony Tereino or Étienne Hokaupoko (☎ 92 51 03) and count on 4000 CFP per day, 5000 CFP with a guide.

Places to Stay
Guesthouses are the only accommodation. Tariffs do not include VAT.

Hakahau Well known to the yachties who anchor in the bay below are Hélène and Doudou, who run *Restaurant-Pension Pukuéé* (☎/fax 92 50 83), ideally located away from the rest of the town at the eastern end of the bay. The building is on the hillside, looks like a chalet and has fine views over the bay. Singles/doubles cost 3000/5500 with shared cold-water bathroom. Add 500 CFP for breakfast. The owners have a restaurant, organise excursions and can arrange to do laundry for 500 CFP.

Chez Marguerite Dordillon (☎ 92 51 36) has two rooms with kitchen and bathroom for a very reasonable 2000/3000 CFP. It's right next to the post office.

Pension Vehine (☎ 92 53 22, 92 50 63) is next to Snack Vehine, 500m from the seafront. It's run by Toti Teikiehuupoko, the president of the Motu Haka cultural association. The functional building has two rooms, a lounge area, hot water and a veranda for 2000/3000 CFP. For a meal you only have a 20m walk to Snack Vehine.

Chez Samuel & Jeanne-Marie (☎ 92 53 16) is run by the same family as Pension Vehine. A very straightforward room with shared bathroom costs 4500 CFP per person with all meals.

Towards the western end of Hakahau Bay, on the bend in the road to the airport, *Tepano Kohumoetini* (☎ 92 53 88), BP 61, Hakahau, rents out four comfortable double rooms with shared cold-water bathroom for 2000 CFP per person.

Hakamaii There's no official guesthouse at Hakamaii but check with *Agnè Huuti* in the house overlooking the church.

Hakahetau You simply must see *Pension Vaekehu* (☎ 92 51 03), BP 120, Hakahetau, facing the telephone booth in the centre of the village, next to a pae pae. The chatty owner, Étienne Hokaupoko, is an active champion of Marquesan culture and a member of the Motu Haka Association. He knows all the legends of Henua Enana (see the 'Haakakai O Te Henua Enana: the Legend of the Land of Men' boxed text earlier) and has an excellent command of English. Three double rooms with shared bathroom each cost 2000 CFP per person and meals, taken with the family, cost 1000 CFP each. You will get the chance to try *kaikai enana*, a typical Marquesan dish of uru and *fei* (plantain-like banana). Étienne welcomes students, who help him in the garden or to break copra and he has a pirogue you can rent for 2000 CFP.

Also in Hakahetau, you can stay with sculptor *Apataroma Hikutini*, who has three rooms with shared bathroom for 1000 CFP per person. Add 300 CFP for breakfast and 500 CFP for lunch or dinner and you've found what may be the cheapest guesthouse in French Polynesia.

THE MARQUESAS

Places to Eat

The only real eating places are in Hakahau. In the other villages, you can go to a *guesthouse* or make do with a few provisions from the *shops* and *grocers*.

In Hakahau, you can stock up at *Joseph B's* shop opposite Snack Vehine, at one of the two grocers in the same street as the gendarmerie, or at the *Fara* shop, opposite the medical centre. *Snack Guéranger*, in the south-west of the village, is more of a grocer's but it also sells a few reasonably priced takeaway snacks.

If you are dying for a pastry, go to the *Snack-Pâtisserie Vaitiare*, run by a former legionnaire. It's beside the airport road, after the mairie. It has a pleasant little terrace and a shop and it's open daily at lunchtime and in the evening.

Chez Rosalie (☎ 92 51 77) only opens when the *Aranui* is in port. Don't hesitate to join in their feast, a full Marquesan meal for 3000 CFP.

You can eat cheaply at *Snack Vehine* (☎ 92 53 21, 92 50 63), opposite Joseph B's shop. Hamburgers with chips cost 669 CFP, steak and chips 824 CFP and poisson cru 721 CFP. On request only, you can have a full set menu for 2000 CFP. It's open Monday to Saturday for lunch and for dinner on demand.

The owners of *Restaurant-Pension Pukuéé* (☎/fax 92 50 83) do quite a lot for Marquesan cuisine. Hélène, who is from Ua Huka, excels at cooking lobster and shrimp and doesn't skimp on quantity. It costs 2000 CFP to 3000 CFP for a full meal. The terrace restaurant looks out over the seafront and the quay.

Chez Adrienne snack bar (☎ 92 53 60) is by the sea at the western end of Hakahau Bay, beside the airport road. It's the relaxed family atmosphere, as much as the food, that's the major attraction. Count on 500 CFP for a plate or 2000 CFP for a complete meal.

Getting There & Away

Air The Air Tahiti office (☎ 92 53 41) is in Hakahau, inside the shop hidden behind the clump of bougainvillea, opposite Chez Samuel & Jeanne-Marie. It's open Monday and Tuesday from 9 am to noon, Wednesday from 2 to 4 pm and Friday from 9 am to noon and 3 to 4 pm. On Thursday, Tina Klima is on duty at Aneou airport (☎ 92 51 08).

The island is served every Thursday by a 19-seater Dornier, which does the Nuku Hiva-Ua Pou-Nuku Hiva run and connects with the Papeete-Nuku Hiva link. It costs 27,500 CFP for the Papeete-Ua Pou via Nuku Hiva flight, 5100 CFP for Nuku Hiva-Ua Pou. There is also a connection Atuona-Ua Pou-Atuona via Nuku Hiva, two or three times a week for 8800 CFP.

Helicopter Héli Inter Marquises, based on Nuku Hiva (☎/fax 92 02 17, ☎ 92 00 54 at the heli-station, ☎ 92 04 40 at the airport), has regular Taiohae-Hakahau-Taiohae services, in principle on Wednesday, Friday and Sunday. The 15 minute flight costs 12,000 CFP per person, one way.

Boat The *Aranui* and *Taporo IV* serve Ua Pou. Sailing from Hakahau, the *Aranui* also stops at Hakahetau. See the Getting Around chapter earlier for details.

In Hakahau, contact Joseph Tamarii (☎ 92 52 14). He charges 40,000 CFP to charter his bonitier (for up to 10 people) for Taiohae; the Hakahau communal bonitier (☎ 92 53 17, 92 53 22) can also be hired at this rate. Manu Guéranger (☎ 92 51 49), at the snack bar of the same name, charges 45,000 CFP for the same service.

Getting Around

On the east cost, a track connects Hakahau with Hohoi (13km) and continues to Hakatao. On the west coast, Hakahau is connected to Hakahetau (15km), Haakuti (22km) and Hakamaii. The track doesn't make a complete circuit of the island but there is a plan to extend the track from Hakamaii to Hakatao.

To/From the Airport The airport is at Aneou, about 10km west of Hakahau, on the Hakahetau track. Your hosts will come to collect you if you have booked accommodation; it costs 500 CFP to 1000 CFP per person for the transfer.

Car In Hakahau, Patricia Guéranger (☎ 92 51 49) will drive you to Hakamoui and Hohoi on the east coast for 10,000 CFP or to Hakahetau and Haakuti on the west coast for 15,000 CFP. You can also contact Rudla Klima (☎ 92 53 86, 92 50 90), who offers the same rates, or the owners of the Restaurant-Pension Pukuéé. If you are so pressed for time that you wish to visit both coasts on the same day, negotiate the rate to 15,000 CFP.

In Hakahetau, get in touch with Étienne Hokaupoko (☎ 92 51 03), who charges 4000 CFP for the excursion to Haakuti and 8000 CFP to Hakahau (with the addition of Hohoi for an extra 7000 CFP). If you hire his services for at least three days you can negotiate a better rate. Apataroma Hikutini charges 14,000 CFP a day (see Hakahetau under Places to Stay earlier).

Boat Prices vary considerably. In Hakahau, Manu Guéranger (☎ 92 51 49) charges 20,000 CFP to charter his boat to Hakamaii or Hakatao and 35,000 CFP for an around-the-island trip. Joseph Tamarii's (☎ 92 52 14) services are less expensive at 15,000 CFP to Hakatao. Alain Alho's (☎ 92 52 80) rates are even better: 8000 CFP to Haakuti; 10,000 CFP to Hakamaii; 12,000 CFP to Hakatao; and 25,000 CFP around the island.

In Hakamaii, contact Jules and Charles Tissot or José Kautai. The transfer to Hakahau generally costs 8000 CFP.

UNINHABITED ISLANDS

Hatu Iti, Eiao, Hatutu, Motu One and the Clark Bank lie to the north of Nuku Hiva. Their waters are occasionally visited by fishing boats and Eiao was almost chosen for the French nuclear tests.

The Southern Group

The southern group comprises three inhabited islands – Hiva Oa, Tahuata and Fatu Hiva – and the four deserted islands of Motane (Mohotani), Fatu Huku, Terihi and Thomasset Rock.

HIVA OA
pop 1829 • area 320 sq km
highest point Mt Temetiu (1276m)

Formerly the administrative capital of the Marquesas, Hiva Oa (the 'roof beam' in the Marquesas Islands legend), in the south-east of the archipelago, is now overshadowed by Nuku Hiva in the northern group. However, it maintains its pre-eminence within the southern group.

The first European to see Hiva Oa was the Spanish navigator Mendaña, in July 1959. He contented himself with sailing along its coast and christened it Dominica because it was a Sunday.

Stretching 40km west to east and about 10km north to south, this hook-shaped island's distorted relief is evidence of former volcanic activity. A ridge forms a spine across the length of the island and has an average height of 800m. Steep ridges at right angles to this backbone separate each valley, making access difficult.

The slopes of Mt Temetiu (1276m) and Mt Feani (1126m) form a vast amphitheatre, at the base of which is Atuona, the island's capital. Atuona proudly cultivates the memory of its two distinguished guests: the painter Paul Gauguin and the Belgian singer-poet Jacques Brel, who both chose this small town as the last stop on their wanderings. See the boxed texts 'Gauguin: the Wild & the Primitive' and 'The Last Song of Jacques Brel' in this section.

On the north-east coast, Puamau, ringed by mountains more than 700m high, has the most important archaeological remains discovered to date on the Marquesas. The site at Taaoa, in the south-west, is also an archaeological treasure. The lush valleys of Hanaiapa, Hanapaaoa and Nahoe in the north, where the pace of life is set by the cargo ships, safeguard the traditional Marquesan way of life.

Information

Tourist Offices The Atuona Tourist Board (☎/fax 92 75 10) is in the craft *fare* behind the museum, in the centre of the village. The office is open weekdays from 7.30 to 11.30 am.

THE MARQUESAS

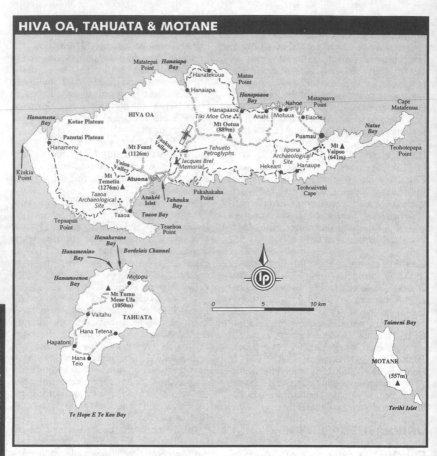

HIVA OA, TAHUATA & MOTANE

Money Banque Socredo (☎ 92 73 54) is next to the Air Tahiti office, across from Tohua Pepeu, right in the centre of Atuona. You can change currency and travellers cheques and make credit-card withdrawals. The bank is open weekdays from 7.30 to 11.30 am and 1.30 to 4 pm.

Post & Communications In Atuona, the post office is next to the mairie, 50m east of the gendarmerie. It's open weekdays from 7.30 to 11.30 am and 1.30 to 4.30 pm (3.30 pm on Friday) and Saturday from 7.30 to 8.30 am. It has a fax service and sells phonecards.

Phonecard telephone booths are in front of the post office and near the school in Atuona and at the harbour in Tahauku. There is another post office in Puamau. Some villages have phonecard telephone booths; if not, a telephone service can be provided by a private individual.

Laundry Contact Brigitte Chastel (☎ 92 71 27) or Kora, who lives in the white house to the right and below the first hairpin corner near the cemetery. Count on 1500 CFP per kilogram, washed and dried.

Medical Services In Atuona, the hospital (☎ 92 73 75) and the dental centre (☎ 92 73 58) are behind the mairie buildings. There is an infirmary or first-aid post in each village.

Atuona

This trim and tidy town of 1300 residents has the antiquated air of a tropical sub-prefecture, but Jacques Brel (1929-78), who lived there from 1975 to 1978, would no doubt be surprised to see the gleaming 4WDs and opulent American commercial vehicles driving through it today. The singer's shadow, as much as that of Paul Gauguin, still hovers over the town and both the museum and the Calvaire Cemetery, where he is buried, are great places of pilgrimage for his fans.

Atuona is at the north of Taaoa Bay, at the mouth of the Vaioa River and stretches back up the valley for about 1.5km. Three main sealed roads pass through the town and most of the shops and business are concentrated in Atuona's centre, near the Tohua Pepeu where the Marquesas Islands Festival took place in 1991 (see the boxed text 'The Marquesas Islands Festival' earlier in this chapter). To the west, the massive outline of

Mt Temetiu blocks off the horizon, while to the east, carefully maintained houses cling to the sides of the rocky promontory that separates Atuona from Tahauku Bay. Sometimes known as Traitors' Bay, this cove attracts sailing boats from the world over and is a landing stage for cargo ships. Beneath Atuona is a black-sand beach, a surfer's delight, fringing the bay. To the south-west stands the lookout post of Anakéé Islet.

Most of the town's working population is employed in tertiary industries, particularly local administration, at the hospital, in schools, at the Service Militaire Adapté (SMA) garrison or in small businesses. The medical and administrative services are housed together in attractively decorated traditional-style buildings in the east of the town. In the town centre, the Catholic church is next to the Sisters of Saint Joseph of Cluny school, founded in 1843. It is now one of the most important boarding schools in French Polynesia.

Museum Don't expect to see anything extraordinary in this small museum (☎ 92 75 10) in Atuona's centre. The collection has been revised several times and today

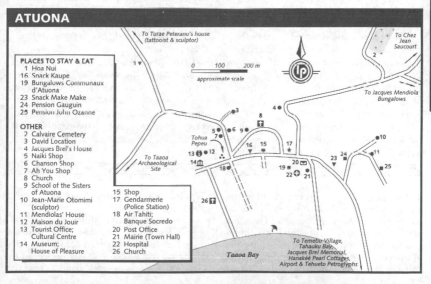

ATUONA

PLACES TO STAY & EAT
1 Hoa Nui
16 Snack Kaupe
19 Bungalows Communaux d'Atuona
23 Snack Make Make
24 Pension Gauguin
25 Pension John Ozanne

OTHER
2 Calvaire Cemetery
3 David Location
4 Jacques Brel's House
5 Naiki Shop
6 Chanson Shop
7 Ah You Shop
8 Church
9 School of the Sisters of Atuona
10 Jean-Marie Otomimi (sculptor)
11 Mendiolas' House
12 Maison du Jouir
13 Tourist Office; Cultural Centre
14 Museum; House of Pleasure
15 Shop
17 Gendarmerie (Police Station)
18 Air Tahiti; Banque Socredo
20 Post Office
21 Mairie (Town Hall)
22 Hospital
26 Church

To Turae Peterano's house (tattooist & sculptor)

To Chez Jean Saucourt

0   100   200 m
approximate scale

To Jacques Mendiola Bungalows

Tohua Pepeu

To Taaoa Archaeological Site

Taaoa Bay

To Temetiu Village, Tahauku Bay; Jacques Brel Memorial, Hanakéé Pearl Cottages, Airport & Tehueto Petroglyphs

Gauguin: the Wild & the Primitive

The evocative paintings of Paul Gauguin are largely responsible for Polynesia's enduring reputation as a paradise lost.

Born in 1848, Gauguin began to paint in his mid-20s. After a childhood in Peru he prepared for naval college, joined up as an officer cadet and, from 1868 to 1871, roamed the seas. He then worked as a stockbroker in Paris and began to paint his first landscapes. Having come to the notice of Camille Pissarro, he exhibited with the Impressionists in 1879. Gauguin gained the friendship of Edgar Degas, who supported him by buying his pictures. The collapse of the stock market in 1882 put an end to Gauguin's business career and, leaving his wife and children, he devoted himself exclusively to painting. Condemned to solitude by poverty, he took refuge in Pont-Aven, a small town in Finistère, before voyaging to Martinique and returning to Paris, where he met Vincent van Gogh.

Gauguin's second stay in Pont-Aven, in 1888, was artistically decisive. Influenced by Japanese prints, he adopted a new, simplified style, characterised by large flat areas of colour with clearly defined outlines: 'Pure colour, everything must be sacrificed to it!'.

After a two-month stay in Arles with van Gogh – it was during this period that van Gogh mutilated his ear – Gauguin painted a series of masterpieces *(Yellow Christ, Beautiful Angel)*, but could think only of escape. In a letter to the painter Odilon Redon in 1890, he wrote: 'I am going to Tahiti and hope to finish my life there. I consider that my art ... is just a seed and I hope to cultivate it there for myself, in its primitive and wild state'.

In Mataiea on Tahiti, where the Gauguin Museum now stands, he concentrated on capturing images of daily life and, in 1892 and 1893, experienced an exceptionally productive period, painting *Te Nave Nave Fenua* (Delicious Land), *Manao Tupapau* (Spirit of the Dead Watching) and *Arearea* (Amusements). Exuberant settings and flamboyant colours, with yellow, red and blue predominating, increasingly pervaded the artist's painting.

Gauguin sold few canvases and was again impoverished. He sailed for France in 1893 and in November of that year a large exhibition devoted solely to his work opened in Paris. He took up ceramics and embarked on writing a narrative, *Noa Noa*, which was inspired by his Tahitian period and designed to make the public understand his work. But the time was not ripe for his talent to be recognised and he set off for the South Seas again in 1895.

His most powerful compositions, *Te Arii Vahine* (The Royal Woman; 1896), *Nevermore* (1897) and *Where Do We Come From? What Are We? Where Are We Going?* (1897), date from this second and final stay in Polynesia, which was marked by illness and distress. After a failed suicide attempt, he took refuge on the island of Hiva Oa in the Marquesas, where he defended the inhabitants against the colonial administration and the all-powerful Catholic mission. Although weakened, he did not stop writing, drawing, sculpting and painting, and it was during this period that he produced one of his most beautiful nudes, *Barbaric Tales* (1902). Gauguin died in May 1903.

includes copies of Gauguin's paintings by a French forger including *Sur la Plage*, *La Sieste* and *La Femme Éventail*. There's a permanent exhibition of drawings, photographs, watercolours, letters and souvenirs of the painter Paul Gauguin and his friend and admirer, the writer-physician Victor Ségalen, who landed at Atuona in August 1903.

To one side is a faithful replica of Gauguin's **House of Pleasure**. The replica's main façade has been decorated with copies of the carved wooden panels fashioned by Gauguin. Carved in wood one can read the maxims the painter passed down to posterity: 'Be mysterious' and, 'Be in love and you will be happy.' The inside of the building has been stripped bare and at best you may find some work by craftspeople. See the boxed text 'Gauguin: the Wild & the Primitive' for more information about the painter's life.

There's an adjoining arts and crafts *fare* and the tourist office plus *Jojo*, Jacques Brel's personal plane, in which he used to fly to Papeete. The museum is open weekdays from 7.30 to 11.30 am. Admission costs 400/200 CFP for adults/children over 10. Books and videos are on sale.

Calvaire Cemetery Jacques Brel and Paul Gauguin were laid to rest a few dozen metres from each other in the small, outstandingly well-maintained Calvaire Cemetery.

Jacques Brel's grave is in the lower part of the cemetery, near the access steps on the left. The gravestone, partly hidden by vegetation, is adorned with a medallion depicting the artist with his companion, Madly. See the boxed text 'The Last Song of Jacques Brel' for information about this popular Belgian singer.

Two rows farther up, at the right-hand edge of the cemetery, is **Paul Gauguin's tomb**, with a replica of the statue *Oviri* (literally, 'wild') standing guard. Gauguin identified with the violent symbolism of this statue and chose it for his last resting place.

To get there, take the road up to the right next to the gendarmerie. After 200m you'll see Jacques Brel's house on the left by the first bend. Continue for another 400m until you reach a fork in the road: follow the direction indicated on the sign to the cemetery 100m farther on. It takes about 10 to 15 minutes on foot.

Tohua Pepeu Restored for the 1991 Marquesas Islands Festival, this tohua faces Banque Socredo in the centre of town. In includes a reconstructed hae.

Jacques Brel Memorial This memorial to the singer was erected in 1993 by the tourist office at the very place where the artist wished to build his house, some kilometres east of Atuona, not far from the airport. His illness prematurely interrupted the project. The site, a narrow tongue of land accessible by track, is magnificent and wild, with a superb view of Atuona Bay.

The memorial is a black marble plaque set into a large rock. Beside a portrait of the artist is his famous line: 'Do you want me to tell you, moaning is not acceptable ... on the Marquesas.' There are plans to built a Jacques Brel auditorium at the site.

There are two possible routes here. Follow the track that goes up to the airport. Pass the small access road to the Hanakéé

The Last Song of Jacques Brel

A fighter against hypocrisy and proudly iconoclastic, Belgian-born singer and songwriter Jacques Brel derided the flaws of society and left enduring masterpieces, such as 'Dans le Port d'Amsterdam' (In the Port of Amsterdam), ' Le Plat Pays' (The Flat Country) and 'Les Bigotes' (The Bigots).

Wishing to escape media pressure, he set out to sail around the world on the *Askoy*, his private ketch, accompanied by his companion, Madly, from Guadeloupe. In November 1975 they arrived at Atuona and, seduced by its serenity, Brel never left. In 1976 he and Madly set up a small home on the hillside above the village. He equipped himself with *Jojo*, a Beechcraft airplane in which he travelled between the islands of the northern group and as far as Papeete.

Jacques Brel and Madly became involved in village life and were well-liked by the locals. From time to time the artist would perform medical evacuations to Papeete in his plane.

Jacques Brel died of cancer in October 1978 at the age of 48. His last song, 'Les Marquises' (The Marquesas), resounds as a vibrant homage to this generous place. At Calvaire Cemetery, where he rests near Paulo (as he called Gauguin), Brel's tomb is lovingly decorated with flowers.

Pearl Cottages, which goes off to the left, and go straight for 400m. You will then see a track on your left leading to a private property. Go up here, past the front of the house (beware of the dogs!) and continue for about 200m. You will then come out at a small piece of open ground overlooking the Hotel Hanakéé. The path leading to the memorial bends to the left and goes 2km uphill to the hillside site.

Another possibility, which is considerably longer, is to follow the track leading to the airport and, 300m before the Rural Development Department buildings, turn left and continue along the path for approximately 2.5km.

It's better to walk to the site than try to get here by 4WD; the tracks are very narrow and some sections are in terrible condition.

Puamau

The village of Puamau is a 2½ hour drive from Atuona, in the north-east of the island. It occupies a coastal plain, bordered by a vast ring of mountains, and the elegant seafront is lined with ironwood trees and a black-sand **beach**. To enjoy the view over the whole bay, follow the track to the Iipona archaeological site and continue as far as the pass. The village has the most beautiful archaeological site in the Marquesas, if not all of French Polynesia. See Archaeological Sites later in this section.

Hanapaaoa & Surrounding Hamlets

This tiny village of 40 people is on the north coast of the island between Hanaiapa and Puamau. Far from the 'bustle' of Atuona, goat hunting, fishing and catching lobsters, copra and noni production are the rhythms of daily life. There's a small **church** with yellowed facade beside the river.

The area surrounding Hanapaaoa has a wild beauty. The secondary track that links Hanapaaoa to Anahi and Nahoe, a few kilometres to the east, winds through valleys covered in fruit trees. The track, which is partly a cliff road, also affords superb views over Fatu Huku and the north coast. Wild goats abound, scarcely frightened away by

your approach, and dozens of **pae pae** are covered by the vegetation.

It's a two hour journey by 4WD to Hanapaaoa from Atuona. The track, which is accessible to motor vehicles, passes the airport and shortly after it splits; the first turn-off goes to Hanaiapa, and the second leads to Hanapaaoa. Arm yourself with a map and/or guide and ask at the Atuona Tourist Board for further information. From Hanapaaoa to Anahi and Nahoe, the track is narrow, winding and steep. Great care is needed to prevent your vehicle veering off the road and into the ocean.

Hanaiapa

It is not difficult to succumb to the charm of this flower-bedecked village in the north of the island, accessible by track from Atuona and Puamau. It stretches for more than 1km along a single street, which follows the course of the Teheitahi River. Traditional copra-drying sheds are found scattered here and there.

In the centre of the village, opposite the reconstructed Marquesan hut, a remarkably well maintained **pae pae** has pride of place. One of its pavements has three cup-shaped structures, which are thought to have been designed to contain the substances used in tattooing. At the back of the pae pae, slabs of the island's red tuff indicate that the site was the abode of a chieftain or priest.

Beaches

Hiva Oa's beaches include the black-sand stretches at Atuona and Puamau. Those of Hanamenu and Hanatekuua can be reached by pirogue. As everywhere in the Marquesas, bring mosquito repellent because the nono are terrible.

Archaeological Sites

See the 'Civilisation & Archaeology' special section for more information.

Tehueto Petroglyphs The Tehueto site is in the Faakua Valley, near Atuona and features stylised, horizontal human figures, their arms in the air, which have been carved into an enormous basalt block.

The site makes a good walk from Atuona. Take the road towards Tahauku Bay and by the Tahauku snack bar go 100m along the unsealed road leading to the airport. You will then see a secondary track and the sign for the Tehueto Historic Site on the left. After about 1.4km, turn left at the fork. The petroglyphs are 800m away, in a clearing. The track is narrow, little used and includes a small ford.

Taaoa This site, 7km south-west of Atuona, has more than 1000 **pae pae**. It has been partially restored; the remainder lies buried under a tangle of vegetation.

Firstly, you will find yourself facing a vast **tohua** built on several levels. Continue for 100m and, on the right, is a well-preserved **tiki** more than a metre in height, sitting on a platform. From a distance, it looks like a plain block of basalt, but as you get closer you can clearly pick out the contours of the eyes and mouth. The shoulders and arms are truncated, compared to the large head.

To get to the site from the Atuona gendarmerie, follow the sealed road as far as Banque Socredo, turn right and continue for about 7km. Turn right at the telephone booth at the entrance to Taaoa village, 200m before the stone church and go up this secondary track for 1.4km; it's accessible by 4WD. You will then reach a clearing and the tohua is set back on the left.

Iipona Discovered in the 1800s by ethnologists and archaeologists, the Iipona site is one of the most important testimonies to pre-contact Marquesan civilisation. Under the leadership of French archaeologists Pierre and Marie-Noëlle Ottino, the site was extensively restored for the third Marquesas Islands Festival, in 1991.

Iipona is an exceptional collection of impressive and varied paving, platforms and stone sculptures. It is a meae arranged on two large main terraces covering 5000 sq m; a variety of trees form a shady fringe.

The area's topography played a key role in the meae's establishment and layout. Orientated along a north-south axis, the site is bordered on the west by Toea peak, a remarkable grey mass which pierces the tangle of vegetation. Until the 19th century it sheltered skulls and a funeral cave. To the east, the meae is bounded by the Ahonu stream. Between the peak and the stream, the site measures 120m in width and 150m in length.

At the end of the 19th century, the German ethnographer Karl von den Steinen learnt of the traditions associated with the site from the locals of Puamau. It is said that the valley was inhabited by the Naiki tribe, led by three nobles who captured and sacrificed a Hanapaaoa chieftain. To avenge his death, clans joined forces against the Naiki and drove them out. The victors transformed the residence of the three nobles into a meae and erected the large tiki. Archaeologists date these events to the 18th century.

The site's main attraction is its five monumental tiki. As you advance towards the first platform, your attention will be caught by the reclining tiki, or **Maki Taua Pepe**, representing a woman lying on her stomach, her head stretched out and arms pointing to the sky. Experts suppose she represents a woman giving birth. The petroglyphs on the pedestal represent dogs but their meaning is unknown.

A few metres farther on, the **Manuiotaa tiki** is in complete contrast to the others: less massive, its proportions are harmonious and balanced. The hands are clearly recognisable, as is its female sex. It was decapitated but its head has been replaced by archaeologists.

Takaii, the site's emblematic tiki, is named after a warrior chief renowned for his strength. Measuring 2.67m above the soil, it is the largest tiki in French Polynesia. It is the archetype of strength, balance and beauty.

The **Te Tovae E Noho tiki** is set to the left of Takaii, on a lower platform. Less finely worked than the others, its upper torso is hard to make out and the head has disappeared. Note that its hands each have six fingers. Further back stands the **Fau Poe tiki**. Measuring about 1.8m, it is sitting with its legs stretched out, a position typical of women when they work in the fields. Experts believe it to be Takaii's wife.

To reach the site from Puamau, follow the track directly back from the seafront, next to the football ground and continue for about 1.5km. You will need to pay 200 CFP to Madame Kahau, who maintains and guards the site.

Tohua Pehe Kua In Puamau, on the property of the Chez Marie-Antoinette guesthouse, shortly before the Iipona site, is the tomb of the valley's last chief and his partner, who died early in the 20th century. Interestingly they were buried according to Christian rituals, although some pagan elements are also present. One of the four tombs at the site is flanked by two tiki and to one side is an imposing pae pae.

Tiki Moe One About 15 minutes walk south-east of Hanapaaoa stands one of the strangest tiki in the Marquesas, the Moe One tiki, about 1m in height. The statue's head is adorned with a carved crown of flowers. According to legend, the inhabitants used to take the tiki down to the beach every year, where they bathed it and coated it with *monoi* (fragrant oil) before putting it back in place. It is believed to be endowed with strong *mana* (supernatural power). Nearby, some human bones and a *pu* (conch shell) are concealed at the foot of an enormous banyan. The sacred character of this place is almost palpable. Hidden in the vegetation on the slope of a hill, it is almost impossible to find this tiki on your own; ask some of the village children to take you there.

Activities
Walking The island's 4WD tracks are good for easy hikes, but don't venture off these tracks without a guide. In the immediate vicinity of Atuona there are easy jaunts to the Tehueto petroglyphs and to the Jacques Brel memorial.

Horse Riding Some old bridleways cross the western part of the island from Taaoa to Hanamenu, following the coast for some of the way. The route between Atuona and Hanamenu is also possible; allow two days for the round trip. Contact Colliano (☎ 92 71 04) to rent a horse.

In Puamau contact Étienne Heitaa (☎ 92 75 28), who rents horses for 3000 CFP for a

half-day. With a guide for up to six participants there's an extra charge of 3000 CFP.

Deep-Sea Fishing Ozanne Rohi can take you fishing for tuna, *mahi mahi* (dolphin fish), marlin or tazar aboard his bonitier for 15,000 CFP a day (flat rate), tackle included. Also contact Médéric Kaimuko (☎ 92 74 48).

Places to Stay
Accommodation is mainly concentrated in Atuona and its surrounding area, with the exception of one guesthouse in Puamau. Tariffs quoted generally do not include VAT.

Atuona *Bungalows Communaux d'Atuona* *(☎ 92 73 32 at the mairie, weekdays from 7.30 to 11.30 am and 1.30 to 4.30 pm – ask for Madame Terme; fax 92 74 95)* are next to the administrative centre in Atuona. The seven bungalows have cold-water bathroom, small equipped kitchen, refrigerator, fan and shower. Although reserved for administrative officials, if there's room they are available for visitors. A large two bedroom bungalow costs 2000 CFP for one person, 500 CFP for each additional person. The small bungalows cost 2500 CFP for the first person. Booking is recommended.

Jacques Mendiola (☎ 92 73 88), BP 60, Atuona, Hiva Oa, has two superb bungalows for two to three people in the Atuona hills. Equipped with bathroom with water heater, kitchenette, mezzanine and small terrace, they are particularly popular with local administrative staff, who hire them by the month or year. They offer a view like no other over Tahauku Bay and cost 5000 CFP a day. To get to the owners' residence, take the road that goes up to the Pension Gauguin, continue for about 100m and take the first sealed road on the right. The Mendiolas' house is on the left-hand corner.

Chez Jean Saucourt (☎/fax 92 73 33) has two double chalet-style bungalows with hot-water bathroom, fan and mosquito net for 4000 CFP. The owners prefer to rent by the month or, if necessary, by the week. If you stay for three weeks, the fourth is free. The bungalows are on the hillside in the east of Atuona, looking out over Taaoa Bay, the town and Anakéé Islet. To get there, take the road which goes up towards the Calvaire Cemetery. Turn left 500m after the cemetery and continue for 250m to the end of the cul de sac and you will come out right at the Saucourts' house.

Also in the east of Atuona and on the hillside is the wonderfully peaceful *Pension John Ozanne* (*☎/fax 92 73 43)*. Two simple, clean doubles with shared cold-water bathroom and fan cost 3500/5000 CFP per person for half/full board. There are also two fully equipped bungalows with an outstanding view over the black-sand beach below. Each has bathroom, TV and two balconies and costs 2500 CFP per day or, on a per-person basis, 4000/5000 CFP for half/full board. Meals, which are based on Marquesan specialities and fish, are taken with the family in a *fare potee* in front of the residence. To reach the pension, follow the road toward Pension Gauguin, walk about 100m and take the first road on the right. Continue for 150m and the Rohis' house is set back on the left, partly concealed behind an enormous avocado tree.

A very popular address with travellers is *Pension Gauguin* (*☎/fax 92 73 51)*, in the east of Atuona Bay, a stone's throw from the Make Make snack bar. Nestling in luxuriant vegetation, this elegant two-storey building comprises six spotlessly clean rooms, four of which have their own hot-water bathroom outside the room. A spacious terrace opens onto the bay and the food served there is stimulating and varied. The daily cost for half-board is 6000/11,000 CFP a single/double. André Teissier, the master of the house, organises numerous excursions to Hiva Oa and Tahuata, particularly to the Hanahevane Valley.

A 20 minute walk from Atuona, on the Tahauku Bay side, *Temetiu Village* (*☎/fax 92 73 02)*, also known as Chez Gaby, is the other popular choice for travellers. You will be warmly welcomed and Gaby's wife has a good command of English. The two double bungalows and the large family bungalow for five people with hot-water bathroom are faultless and half-board costs 6000/11,000 CFP a single/double. The bungalows look

directly over Tahauku Bay; meals are served on the restaurant terrace. Gaby offers excursions to Tahuata. From the centre of Atuona take the road towards Tahauku Bay for a little more than 1km and then take the first left after the AMA building, which flies the French flag. The road climbs for 400m to the pension. Credit cards are accepted.

The only luxury lodging on the island is *Hanakéé Pearl Cottages* (*☎ 43 90 04, fax 43 17 86, email info@spmhotels.pf)*. It's to be found perched on the hillside at Tahauku Bay, above the cargo-ship quay. Its 20 fine bungalows with air-con cost 28,080 CFP to 37,800 CFP. Add another 5600/7500 CFP for half/full board. There's an unforgettable view of the bay, a swimming pool and various activities can be organised.

Puamau *Chez Marie-Antoinette* (*☎ 92 72 27)* has two bare but clean double rooms with shared cold-water bathroom for 3500 CFP per person half-board. Add 2000 CFP for a lunch of local specialities. Bernard Heitaa, known as Vohi, is the *tavana* (mayor) of Puamau and took part in restoring the archaeological site in 1991. There's actually an archaeological site with several tombs and tiki on the guesthouse's land (see Archaeological Sites earlier).

To get there, follow the road which is at right angles to the track along the seafront, beside the football ground, for 700m. The house is on the corner of the road that branches off to the right.

Places to Eat

In Atuona, you will find well-stocked food shops such as *Naiki, Ah You* and *Chanson*. Ah You and Chanson are also bakeries from 6 am. There are two small *grocer shops* in Puamau.

Atuona On school days (in the morning) and on Sunday morning after mass, one or two roulottes take up position near the Tohua Pepeu and sell sandwiches, banana or coconut turnovers, chocolate cakes and simple meals at modest prices.

Near the administrative centre, on the inland side of the road, the owner of *Snack*

Make Make (☎ *92 74 26)* sells nice snacks at very reasonable prices. The inevitable poisson cru in coconut milk is 850 CFP, the lemon chicken is 900 CFP and shrimps with vegetables or curry are 1200 CFP. The grilled tazar, freshly caught and priced at 950 CFP, is tasty. You can eat there or take it away. Sandwiches are on sale at 150 CFP, but a bottle of mineral water is an exorbitant 300 CFP, a beer 400 CFP. It's open from 7 am to 6 pm (closed Saturday at 2 pm) as a rule, but hours are variable.

Snack Kaupe, in the centre of the town, is run by a couple of *popaa* (westerners) and offers pizzas from 1000 CFP to 1300 CFP, fish dishes from 900 CFP to 1400 CFP and some specialties from Réunion, such as tuna marsala for 1300 CFP. You can eat there or take it away and it's open Tuesday to Friday for lunch and on the weekend for dinner. The popular *Snack Tahauku*, 2km from the centre in Tahauku Bay, is currently closed but may be reopening.

Hoa Nui restaurant (☎ *92 73 63)* is concealed in vegetation to the left of the road that goes along the Vaioa River, to the north of the village. It specialises in Marquesan cuisine and you can try pork, fish or crustacean dishes. The atmosphere heats up several degrees when they put on a feast for *Aranui* passengers. A full meal costs 2200 CFP plus drinks, a single dish is 1000 CFP. It's open every lunchtime and in the evening on request only.

On the terrace of the restaurant at *Temetiu Village* you can have lunch or dinner while viewing Tahauku and Taaoa bays. Prices are quite acceptable: for the full meal (2000 CFP) you can enjoy local specialities such as poisson cru or goat in coconut milk. The restaurant is open daily at lunchtime and in the evening. Bookings are essential and credit cards are accepted.

Another tasty but more expensive option is the restaurant at *Hanakéé Pearl Cottages* at Tahauku Bay. French-Polynesian meat and fish costs around 1200 CFP to 1900 CFP.

Puamau Tourists staying in Atuona who spend the day at Puamau tend to have lunch at *Bernard Heitaa's*. The set menu based on

Marquesan specialities such as uru, *poe* bananas, poisson cru, wild pig, and goat or beef in coconut milk cost 2000 CFP.

Getting There & Away

Air Atuona has connections to Papeete, Nuku Hiva and Ua Pou (via Nuku Hiva). Papeete-Nuku Hiva-Atuona return flights go five times a week. One-way fares are: Papeete-Atuona 27,500 CFP, Nuku Hiva-Atuona 8800 CFP. Atuona-Ua Pou return flights operate two or three times a week (8800 CFP).

The Air Tahiti office in Atuona (☎ 92 73 41, or ☎ 92 72 31 at the airport) is next to Banque Socredo, opposite the Tohua Pepeu. It's open weekdays from 8.30 to 11.30 am and 2 to 4 pm. Credit cards are accepted.

Boat The *Aranui* and *Taporo IV* stop at Hiva Oa. The *Aranui* sometimes serves Atuona, Puamau, Hanaiapa and, less frequently, Hanapaaoa.

Ozanne Rohi (☎/fax 92 73 43) and Médéric Kaimuko (☎ 92 74 48), 200m behind Banque Socredo towards the beach, have bonitiers that can be chartered. It costs 20,000 CFP to 25,000 CFP for Atuona-Vaitahu/Hapatoni (Tahuata)-Atuona, about 15,000 CFP for Atuona-Motopu (Tahuata)-Atuona, 55,000 CFP for Atuona-Hanavave (Fatu Hiva)-Atuona. Keep informed of which charters are being organised during your stay.

The Tahuata communal bonitier connects Vaitahu with Atuona twice a week, usually on Tuesday and Thursday.

Getting Around

To/From the Airport The airport is 13km from Atuona. If you have booked your accommodation, your host will come and collect you for 1500 CFP to 1800 CFP; the journey takes about 25 minutes. It's also possible to hitch a ride.

Car Excursions by 4WD cost 8000 CFP to 9000 CFP to Taaoa, 12,000 CFP to Hanaiapa, 15,000 CFP to 20,000 CFP to Hanapaaoa and 15,000 CFP to 21,000 CFP to Puamau.

Contact André Teissier of the Pension Gauguin, Gaby Heitaa of the Temetiu Village guesthouse, Serge Lecordier of the Hanakéé

Pearl Cottages, Ozanne Rohi (see Places to Stay earlier for these people's contact information), or Ida Clark (☎ 92 71 33). In Puamau, ask for Étienne Heitaa (☎ 92 75 28).

The only exception to the seemingly fixed rule of hiring a 4WD with a driver is offered by David Location (☎ 92 72 87), in a small street a stone's throw from the Chanson, Ah You and Naiki shops. There's one Suzuki for hire at 12,000 CFP a day, with unlimited kilometres and insurance included. Read the contract carefully, particularly the clauses regarding responsibility in the case of an accident. You'll find him looking for business at the airport. There's a petrol station at the cargo-ship quay at Tahauku Bay.

TAHUATA
pop 637 • area 70 sq km
highest point Mt Tumu Meae Ufa (1050m)
Separated from Hiva Oa by the 4km-wide Bordelais Channel, Tahuata (`dawn' in the Marquesas Islands legend) is the smallest inhabited island in the archipelago. Orientated along a north-south ridgeline, it has numerous inlets, two of which shelter the island's main villages, Hapatoni and Vaitahu.

Vaitahu Bay was the scene of several important episodes in Marquesan history. In July 1595 the Spanish navigator Mendaña dropped anchor, naming the bay Madre de Dios and the island Santa Cristina. In 1774 Cook visited the bay and named it Resolution Bay. In 1791 the Frenchman Étienne Marchand lay at anchor nearby, off Hapatoni to the south.

The pastors of the LMS and the Picpus Fathers established a foothold in Vaitahu between 1797 and 1838 and the island became a bridgehead for the evangelisation of the Marquesas.

The year 1842 was a turning point in the islands' history: Dupetit-Thouars forced his former ally, Chief Iotete of Tahuata, to sign the treaty of annexation by France. Realising that he had just been duped, Iotete later opposed the transfer, but his rebellion was crushed by the French. It was also during this period that the island's reserves of sandalwood were plundered.

Tahuata lives in the shadow of its powerful neighbour, Hiva Oa and its economy is based on copra production and arts and crafts. Several commemorative monuments attest to the island's tumultuous past and are well worth visiting; its dreamlike scenery is another good reason to come. Enchanting Hanamoenoa Bay is a favourite anchorage for yachts from March to August – see Sailing in the Outdoor Activities chapter. Hanahevane Bay is also idyllic but it's private and, theoretically at least, you're not able to visit.

Information
For tourist information, contact the mairie (☎ 92 92 19) in Vaitahu.

Bring cash; there is no bank on Tahuata. The post office, open weekdays from 7.30 to 11.30 am, is in Vaitahu, as is the infirmary and phonecard telephone booth.

Vaitahu
This tiny village, built against the steep slopes of the central ridge, retains a few vestiges of its stormy past. On the seafront stands a modest **memorial** topped by a rusty anchor. It recalls the first meeting marked by the seal of friendship between Admiral Dupetit-Thouars and Chief Iotete on 4 August 1838. It was unveiled in November 1988 to commemorate the 150th anniversary of their meeting. Next to the post office, you can read an **epitaph** to Halley, a French lieutenant commander who perished at Tahuata on 17 September 1842 during the revolt by Iotete and his warriors.

On the hill that dominates the village to the south are a few remains of a building known as the **French Fort**, in an advanced state of decay.

The monumental stone **Catholic church** opposite the seafront was financed by the Vatican and opened with great pomp and ceremony on 22 August 1988 and recalls the importance of Tahuata in the evangelisation of the archipelago. The church has beautiful stained-glass windows, which diffuse an atmospheric halo above the altar. Outside, have a look at the imposing wooden statue *Virgin with Child*, nearly 4m in height, which was made by Damien Haturau of

Nuku Hiva. A masterpiece of Marquesan art, it combines Marquesan culture and Catholic archetypes: the Child Jesus is not curled up in his mother's lap but is held out in both hands, an attitude reminiscent of the posture of the tiki; he is also holding an uru as an offering, a symbol of the Marquesas.

There is a small Polynesian art and history **museum** in the mairie on the seafront. It has a collection of objects characteristic of the island, and admission is free.

Vaitahu is a good place to have a wander. Copra-drying sheds are dotted here and there, and brightly coloured traditional *vaka* (outrigger canoes) are lined up on the shore.

Hapatoni

Hapatoni curves around a wide bay, and is accessible from Vaitahu, several kilometres north, by boat in less than 15 minutes or by the bridleway.

The **royal road** is the village's main attraction. Built on a dike on the orders of Queen Vaekehu II in the 19th century, this paved road, lined with 100-year-old tamanu trees, extends along the shore. At the promontory a path leads up to a **lookout**, marked by a cross, with a magnificent view of the bay.

On the seafront, a **memorial** commemorates the peaceful visit of Étienne Marchand; it was inaugurated for the bicentennial of the event. In the middle of the village, a magnificent **meae** on several levels has been restored.

Other Villages

Motopu, to the north, has a few dozen inhabitants and is accessible by 4WD by the vehicle track that crosses the island's interior. A handful of people live in **Hana Tetena** to the east of the island.

Horse Riding

The track which joins Vaitahu and Motopu in the north-east, a distance of about 17km, is an ideal place for riders.

Simon Timau, known as Kiki, in Vaitahu, has several horses (with wooden saddles). His house is right behind the small yellow church, close to the seafront and quay. Check

also with the owner of the Chez Jeanne guesthouse. In Hapatoni, contact Frédéric Timau (☎ 92 92 55). Vaitahu-Hanahevane-Motopu and return costs 5000 CFP to 10,000 CFP, with a guide.

Places to Stay & Eat

Chez Jeanne (☎ 92 92 24 at the school or ☎ 92 92 19 at the mairie) is close to the seafront in Vaitahu. There are two rooms for 5000 CFP per person with full board but it's not open during the school vacations. At the edge of the village *Chez Nicolas Barsinas (☎ 92 92 01)* has a room available for 2000 CFP plus 1500 CFP for a meal.

Every village has one or two small shops.

Getting There & Away

Tahuata is not served by aircraft as it has no landing strip.

Boat The *Te Pua O Mioi* communal bonitier (☎ 92 92 19) runs a Vaitahu-Atuona-Vaitahu ferry service on Tuesday and Thursday for 1000 CFP per passenger return (about an hour). It departs at about 6.30 am and usually returns at around noon.

In Vaitahu, ask for Yves-Bertrand Barsinas (☎ 92 92 40) or Louis Timau (☎ 92 92 71). For Atuona see the Getting Around section in Hiva Oa. It costs between 20,000 CFP and 25,000 CFP to charter a boat between Vaitahu or Hapatoni and Atuona.

The *Aranui* and *Taporo IV* serve Tahuata. See the Getting Around chapter for details.

Getting Around

Car A 17km track, accessible to 4WD vehicles, crosses the island's interior to link Vaitahu with Motopu. It costs 15,000 CFP for one day's hire with driver. Contact Louis Timau (☎ 92 92 71), Yves-Bertrand Barsinas (☎ 92 92 40) or Philippe Tetahiotupa.

Boat Hapatoni is less than 15 minutes from Vaitahu by speedboat.

In Vaitahu, contact Célestin Teikipupuni (☎ 92 92 13), Yves-Bertrand Barsinas (☎ 92 92 40), Louis Timau (☎ 92 92 71), Donatiano Hikutini or Nicolas Barsinas. In Hapatoni, ask for Liliane Teikipupuni (☎ 92 92 46, 92

92 28) or Frédéric Timau. It costs about 6000 CFP to hire the boat between Vaitahu and Hapatoni return, 7000 CFP to 10,000 CFP between Vaitahu and Hanahevane.

FATU HIVA
pop 631 • area 80 sq km
highest point Mt Tauaouoho (960m)
Fatu Hiva (the 'roof' in the Marquesas Islands legend) is indisputably the island of superlatives: the most remote, the farthest south, the wettest, the lushest and the most authentic. It was also the first in the archipelago to be seen by the Spanish navigator Mendaña, on 21 July 1595. He christened it Santa Magdalena after the saint whose day it was.

About 75km south of Hiva Oa, Fatu Hiva consists of two craters, forming arcs open to the west. Between the flanks of the calderas are two valleys, in which nestle the only villages on the island: Hanavave in the north and Omoa in the south, 5km apart as the crow flies.

With no landing strip and only poorly serviced by the bonitiers, Fatu Hiva is a virtually intact, semi-wild paradise. Thanks to its plentiful rainfall, mango, banana, grapefruit, uru, orange and lemon trees thrive on the steep slopes of the island. Thor Heyerdahl, of *Kon Tiki* fame (see the boxed text 'The Kon Tiki Expedition' in the Tuamotus chapter), used his 1½-year stay on the island from 1937 as the basis for his evocatively titled work *Fatu Hiva, the Return to Nature*.

The jagged relief of the island has created some curiously shaped outcrops. The phallic protuberances of Hanavave Bay caused it to be named Baie des Verges (Bay of Penises). Outraged, the missionaries hastened to add a redeeming 'i' to make the name Baie des Vierges (Bay of Virgins). At sunset, it is drenched in purple and the surrounding peaks give off bronze reflections, forming an entrancing spectacle which has intoxicated hundreds of international yachties.

Fatu Hiva prides itself on its top-quality art and crafts, whose reputation has spread far beyond the Marquesas.

Information
There is a post office in Omoa and an infirmary or first-aid post in both villages. There is no bank on the island.

Omoa
In the south of the island, Omoa is dominated by the church with the red roof, white façade and slender spire. Facing the shore, which is partly obscured by a string of multicoloured canoes, the football ground forms a vast seaside esplanade.

Ask someone to take you to the giant **petroglyph** at the edge of the village, near the river: it's an enormous fish carved on a block of rock.

Hanavave
The village is set on the seashore, at the mouth of a steep-sided valley leading onto the beautiful **Bay of Virgins**. Near the shore, the town's sombre small white church with the blue door contrasts with the church in Omoa.

Walking & Horse Riding
A classic activity is to walk or ride to the Bay of Virgins from Omoa along the island's only existing track. On foot it's several hours walk, with no particular difficulties except the climb to the pass separating the two valleys. Take good shoes and sufficient water.

The first part of the walk goes up the Omoa Valley on a corniche with beautiful views over the village below. The trail then crosses through the interior of the island; the caldera is clearly visible and very impressive. It's a steep descent to Hanavave and there's not much shade along the way.

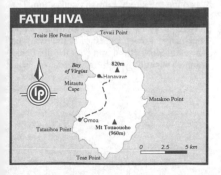

FATU HIVA

Teaite Hoe Point • Tevaii Point • Bay of Virgins • 820m • Hanavave • Matautu Cape • Matakoo Point • Omoa • Mt Touaouoho (960m) • Tataaihoa Point • Teao Point • 0 2.5 5 km

This route can be followed by horse or by 4WD if it's not too muddy. Roberto Mara-etaata (☎ 92 80 23 at the mairie) has two horses with leather saddles for 5000 CFP, without a guide. He needs several days warning.

Check with the place you stay about activities such as walks and canoe trips.

Places to Stay & Eat

Apart from the guesthouses, eating options on Fatu Hiva are limited to a few small grocers' shops.

Omoa *Pension Heimata (☎ 92 80 58)* has two well kept rooms with shared cold-water bathroom for 4000/5500 CFP half/full board per person.

Chez Norma Ropati (☎ 92 80 13) is near the beach. The six double rooms with shared hot-water bathroom cost 1500 CFP per person, 5000 CFP full board. You will be served fortifying traditional Marquesan dishes of poe and fei bananas, goat in coconut milk and poisson cru.

Chez Cécile Gilmore (☎ 92 80 54), in front of the previous guesthouse, has a bamboo house with two bedrooms, lounge, dining room and shared cold-water bathroom. Cost per person is 3500/5000 CFP half/full board.

Chez Marie-Claire (☎ 92 80 75 or ☎ 92 80 23 at the mairie – ask for Henri) has two doubles with shared cold-water bathroom and kitchen for 3000 CFP.

Chez Lionel Cantois (☎/fax 92 80 80) is the last house in the village, about 1.5km from the quay. It's a wild place, beside the river and in the middle of a beautiful tropical garden. A well designed and equipped bungalow with bathroom costs 4000 CFP for two people. Add 2500 CFP per person for full board.

Hanavave There is no official guesthouse, but try *Edwige Pavaouau (☎ 92 80 48, 92 80 94)*, the president of the craft centre, or *Agnès Kamia (☎ 92 80 78)*.

Getting There & Away

Fatu Hiva is the most difficult island to get to in the Marquesas. Theoretically, there's a weekly local catamaran between Omoa and Atuona, but it has not been operating for some time. That leaves the *Aranui* and the *Taporo IV* or a chartered private bonitier.

Getting Around

The only road, of beaten earth, is 17km long and links Hanavave with Omoa. As it is impassable in wet weather, journeys between villages are often by motorised pirogue.

4WD Ask at your accommodation about renting a 4WD; count on 8000 CFP a day with driver.

Boat On Fatu Hiva, speedboats have not yet ousted the traditional outrigger canoes, which take three to four people. The only concession to modern times are the low-powered outboard motors. Count on 4000 CFP to 5000 CFP between Omoa and Hanavave; contact your guesthouse family for information.

UNINHABITED ISLETS

The uninhabited island of **Motane** (Mohotani) lies south-east of Hiva Oa and east of Tahuata. With an area of 15 sq km and a peak height of 527m, this inhospitable island is now home to only wild goats but it was once the site of human occupation. The **Terihi Islet** is south of Motane.

Fatu Huku is to the north of Hiva Oa and **Thomasset Rock** lies east of Fatu Hiva. The waters of Fatu Huku and Motane are occasionally visited by fishing vessels.

THE
AUSTRALS

TIARE

The Australs

Well to the south of Tahiti and the Society Islands, the Austral group is effectively an extension of the same range of submerged peaks that make up the southern Cook Islands. Rurutu is a *makatea* island (see the 'Makatea' boxed text later in this chapter), like Atiu and Mangaia in the Cook group. There are five inhabited islands in the Australs: Rimatara, Rurutu, Tubuai, Raivavae and remote Rapa. There are also two uninhabited islands: Maria Island at the northwestern end of the chain, and Marotiri, also known as the Bass Rocks, at the southeastern end. The chain extends 1300km from end to end.

The islands lie along the Tropic of Capricorn and it's regularly remarked that the climate is much cooler than on the Society islands, although only Rapa is really far enough south to qualify as temperate. Nevertheless, the islands are not lush and fertile like the Society islands; their appearance is altogether more spartan. The population of the entire Austral group is just over 6000.

The Australs are remarkably varied and their features of interest include limestone caverns and ancient marae on Rurutu, reminders of the powerful artwork and massive stone tiki of Raivavae and the *pa* (hilltop fortresses) of Rapa. Tourism is little developed but there are guesthouses on the inhabited islands and modern phonecard-operated telephones from which you can direct-dial to anywhere in the world.

History

The Australs were the last of the Polynesian islands to be settled, and it is believed the first arrivals came from Tahiti between 1000 and 1300 AD. European sightings of the whole chain were a long and drawn-out affair. Cook first saw Rurutu in 1769, Gayangos and Varela 'found' Raivavae in 1775, Cook was back to make the first landing on Tubuai in 1777 and Vancouver 'found' remote Rapa in 1791. But it was not until Captain Samuel Pinder Henry chanced

upon Rimatara in 1811 that the last of the islands came to European attention.

Apart from a colourful chapter in the *Bounty* saga, when the mutineers unsuccessfully tried to establish themselves on Tubuai, contact with Europeans and the western world was remarkably limited until the 20th century. It was not until 1889 that the French established a protectorate over all the islands, and it was in 1900 and 1901 that the last of them were formally annexed. This long period during which English missionaries, or more frequently their native representatives, held sway has ensured that Protestantism remains strong to this day.

Getting There & Away

Two of the islands, Rurutu and Tubuai, are about 600km south of Tahiti and are visited by regular Air Tahiti flights. Rimatara and Raivavae can be fairly easily reached by ship, but getting to Rapa, over 1000km south of Tahiti, takes real effort.

Air Only Rurutu and Tubuai have airports and Air Tahiti flies to them about three times weekly in the low season, nearly every day in the high. One flight goes

THE AUSTRALS

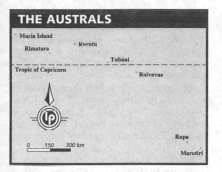

Tahiti-Rurutu-Tubuai-Tahiti while the next goes Tahiti-Tubuai-Rurutu-Tahiti. The one-way fare Tahiti-Rurutu is 16,500 CFP, Tahiti-Tubuai 18,500 CFP and Rurutu-Tubuai 8300 CFP.

Boat Two passenger-carrying cargo ships serve the Australs. The *Tuhaa Pae II* does three trips a month while the *Vaeanu II* does two. See the Getting Around chapter for details.

RURUTU

**pop 2015 • area 36 sq km • reef passes 1
• highest point Mt Taatioe (389m)**

Rurutu has a high plateau with great views from the hilltops; limestone caverns dotted around the coast and some ancient marae. The island is fringed by a continuous reef but it's rarely more than a stone's throw from the shoreline. Occasionally there are small pools between the shore and reef edge, but there's no lagoon as such. So even where there's a good beach, and there are some, particularly south of Arei Point and at the southern end of the island, there's little opportunity to swim.

History

Cook sailed by Rurutu in 1769 during his first great voyage, but the islanders' hostile reception prevented him from landing. Joseph Banks noted the high quality of their canoes and weapons. There was little contact with Europeans until well into the 19th century, when London Missionary Society (LMS) missionaries sent native teachers to

establish a mission. Christianity quickly took hold, but as on so many other islands in Polynesia, European diseases arrived at much the same time as European religion and the result was disastrous.

Rurutu has the most extensive marae site in the Australs, but, unfortunately, it is not well maintained. Although there are no longer any woodcarvers on Rurutu, the statue of the Rurutu ancestor god A'a is one of the most important Polynesian works of art on display in London – the pioneering missionary John Williams took it home.

Orientation & Information

Rurutu is about 10km long and averages about 5km wide. The population is concentrated in three main villages on the coast. Moerai is the largest, with the island's only dock for ocean-going ships, a post office, a Banque Socredo and several shops. A sealed road runs about a third of the way round the island, linking the airport with Moerai and

Hauti (also spelt Auti). Another sealed road climbs over the centre of the island to link Moerai with Avera, the third village.

Apart from the roads shown on the map, there is a network of minor tracks winding into the island's dense patchwork of plantations.

Around the Island

It's 36km around Rurutu, about the same distance as around Bora Bora. Pedalling yourself around Rurutu is, however, a whole different story because the road does not stick faithfully to the coast. Four times it drops right down to the coast, then climbs away, rising past the 100m level on three occasions and once reaching nearly 200m. Keep these altitude changes in mind before you blithely set off to cycle round the island. Nevertheless, it's an interesting ride and worth the effort. The road runs through a variety of plantations, passes beautiful stretches of coast and skirts rocky headlands. It's a very quiet route, particularly on the southern half of the island, where you'll probably see as many people on horseback as in cars and 4WDs.

Moerai The main town of the island is about 4km south-east of the airport. Tauraatua Pass, the only pass suitable for ocean-going ships, leads directly into the town's small artificial harbour. The picturesque little Protestant church, just back from the harbour, dates from 1865-72. Éric

de Bisschop, the island's most famous resident, was a French Thor Heyerdahl (see the boxed text 'The Kon Tiki Expedition' in the Tuamotus chapter), dedicated to perilous voyages in unsuitable craft. He's remembered solely by his simple gravestone, which, translated from French, states that he was 'born in Lille (France), died at Rakahana (Cook).' His **grave** is in the second cemetery, towards the mountainside, off the main road to the south of the village centre.

Moerai to Hauti The solid concrete road continues from Moerai along the coast to Arei Point, one of Rurutu's impressive elevated reef cliffs. Just before the point, a short path leads up to a large cliff-face **cavern**, complete with stalactites and stalagmites. There are similar caverns around the coast and the island has some other interesting cave systems waiting to be discovered.

From Arei Point the road runs directly south along the coast until it reaches the Te Vaipa River, running into the sea beside Mauo Point, another rocky cliff-face. Here the road climbs inland and skirts around the point before dropping down to Hauti, the second of the island's three villages.

Hauti to Avera Almost immediately out of Hauti the concrete road-surface ends and the dirt road climbs, drops back almost to sea level then climbs again to over 100m before dropping steeply down to the coast near the southern tip of the island, Toataratara Point. This road runs along what was the ancient lagoon bottom, before it was thrust up above sea level. The east coast of the island, about 500m east of the road, ends in steep cliffs, dropping 50m into the sea. This was once the reef (see the 'Makatea' boxed text).

Where the road turns right just before the coast, take a short diversion to the left and look for a small tin shed on the ocean side of the road. Nearby in the field is the small **Marae Poreopi**, with the spike-like vertical stones characteristic of Austral marae. A series of beautiful little **beaches** runs to the east of the point. As with everywhere around the island, however, there are just

---

Stone-Lifting Competition

In January each year the Amoraa Ofae stone-lifting competition takes place. There are rounds in each village and the finals are in a clearing beside the Hauti-Toataratara Point road, where the official stones are kept. During preliminary attempts the stone is greased with oil to make lifting it even more difficult! Male contestants must try to lift a 130kg stone; the female equivalent is 90kg (the original 110kg stone was dropped and broken).

Makatea

Rururu is the Austral island geologically most like the southern Cook islands – it is a textbook example of *makatea*. At some time in the past, a sudden upthrust raised the whole island above sea level and converted the fringing reef into a coastal cliff. The sheer, rocky cliff-faces around much of the island were once the outer face of the island's coral reef. The valley, along which the road south from Hauti to Toataratara Point runs, was once the lagoon between the island and its outer reef. That reef is now the ridgeline falling sheer into the sea along the south-east coast of the island. As on the makatea islands of the Cooks, Rurutu is riddled with limestone caverns, another reminder of the cataclysmic upheaval that raised what were once underwater caves to their new location.

shallow pools between the shoreline and the outer reef.

Clinging to the coast, the road rounds the point and heads north, passing a curious small garden beside the road. Leaving the coast the road climbs steeply, passing through pine forests and then, at the 190m high-point, a coffee plantation. Then it's down again, with superb views over the coast and, to the north, over Avera, the third village, to the three peaks of Teape, Taatioe and Manureva. The concrete road-surface recommences in Avera and runs over the central pass to Moerai, but continuing on the island-circuit route it soon goes back to dirt.

Avera to Moerai The road climbs round the edge of the headland then drops down to the coast again just beyond Parari Point. In the space between two houses, hidden from the road by a hedge and back among the coconut trees, is the remains of the **Marae Vitaria**, the marae of the last Rururu royal family. It's said that at one time the marae stretched for 1km and it's still an extensive site, with many of those spike-like vertical stones. Nearby is the huge **Teanaeo Grotto**,

also known as Mitterand Cave since the French president visited here in 1990. The coast road continues past the Rururu Village Hotel, finds the concrete surface again and skirts the airport runway before rounding one more impressive sheer cliff-face, at Anamaniana Point, and arriving back at Moerai.

Whale Watching

Whales come close to shore from July to October and the Raie Manta Club diving centre organises whale-watching trips during this period. See the 'Diving' special section following the Outdoor Activities chapter for details.

Walking

It's easy to climb the three highest peaks, arrayed along a ridgeline looking down on Avera. Starting from just beyond the Moerai end of the airport runway or from Moerai itself, the routes soon meet and climb steadily to the 200m Tetuanui Plateau, a fertile highland plantation area with everything from pineapples to taro. A network of tracks criss-cross the plateau, including a central one leading to some water reservoirs. Tracks to the left or the right will take you towards the summits and the easiest plan is simply to aim for Mt Manureva (385m), distinguished by the small TV-relay station at the top. The mountains are not cloaked in dense vegetation so finding a route is no problem. A narrow foot-trail leaves the larger track to head straight up the ridgeline to the top of Mt Manureva, with views over both Moerai and Avera. Follow the ridgeline a short distance to Mt Taatioe (389m) and down to Mt Teape (359m), with good views of the north-west coast. From there it's easy to make your way back down to the main track.

Places to Stay & Eat

Rururu's four accommodation centres provide free airport transfers.

Chez Catherine (☎ 94 02 43, fax 94 06 99) is right in the centre of Moerai, across from the docks area. This friendly and well-run place has 10 simple rooms with attached hot-water bathroom for 3000/4500 CFP a single/double, or with half-board (breakfast and dinner) 6500/10,000 CFP. Island tours are available for 4000 CFP per person, cave visits for 1000 CFP and credit cards are accepted. There's a good small restaurant and a popular bar.

Rurutu Village Hotel (☎ 94 03 92, fax 94 05 01) is not in one of the villages but right on the rocky north-west coast, about 1km from the airport. There are eight comfortable coral-block bungalows, with bathrooms with solar-heated water, and verandas. There's a large *fare* housing the restaurant, lounge area and bar beside the swimming pool. Singles/doubles are 4000/5000 CFP, and breakfast/lunch/dinner adds 800/1800/3000 CFP. Island tours cost 3500 CFP and credit cards are accepted.

Pension Ariana (☎ 94 06 69) is near Rurutu Village Hotel and has three rooms sharing two hot-water bathrooms, a lounge and a dining room. Rooms cost 4500 CFP for two; half-board for two adds another 10,000 CFP. A guided island-tour costs 5000 CFP for the car.

Pension Temarama (☎/fax 94 02 17) is about 1km from the village and has three rooms in a house with shared hot-water bathroom. Two of the rooms are 3000/4000 CFP, the third 4000/5000 CFP. Half-board adds 2500 CFP for one person, 4500 CFP for two.

There are various small shops, particularly in Moerai, where you will find *Snack Tetua* by the sports field.

Shopping

You can see hats being made at Artisanat Aerepau, near the waterfront in Moerai, but check out the amazing display at the airport. There are *peue* (mats), baskets, bags and other work but it's the huge selection of hats that dominates. Men's hats have a higher top and narrower rim, while women's hats are flatter on top and have a wider rim. Cheaper hats cost 1000 CFP to 2000 CFP and there are many mid-range ones for 2500 CFP to 4000 CFP, but the really fine hats, kept in glass showcases, are 10,000 CFP and more. For this work a special pandanus, *paeore*, is grown on shaded hillsides. The pandanus used for hats is bleached.

Getting There & Away

Rurutu is about 600km south of Tahiti and is the most accessible of the Australs, with regular flights and shipping services. Air Tahiti (☎ 94 03 57) is at the airport. It's a considerable feat fitting a ship into Moerai's small harbour-basin. See the Getting There & Away section at the start of this chapter for more details.

Getting Around

The airport is about 4km from the main village of Moerai. Your accommodation will pick you up at the airport and island and cave tours are offered. Rurutu Village Hotel, Chez Catherine and Pension Temarama rent out bicycles for around 1000 CFP a day; Chez Catherine and Pension Temarama also rent out cars for 6000 CFP a day.

TUBUAI

pop 2049 • area 45 sq km • reef passes 4
highest point Mt Taita (422m)

It's the largest of the Austral islands and is the administrative centre for the group, but Tubuai doesn't have the interesting geology, varied geography or ancient marae of Rurutu. Virtually the only unusual thing about Tubuai is that, unlike on other Polynesian islands, the *pirogues* (outrigger canoes) have their outriggers on the right. The *Bounty* mutineers did try, unsuccessfully, to establish themselves on Tubuai, as a remote centre far from the long reach of British naval justice, but there's barely any trace of that visit.

History

Captain Cook landed at Tubuai in 1777 en route to Tahiti on his third voyage. Some theories hold that it was only settled a few generations earlier, but the locals were certainly fiercely protective of their island, as the *Bounty* mutineers discovered when they attempted to settle there in 1789. Ships bound for Australia started to stop on Tubuai early in the 19th century and the LMS despatched native teachers to the island in 1822.

At about this time European diseases started to afflict the islanders and, in the few years to 1828, the population reportedly plummeted from 3000 to less than 300. It

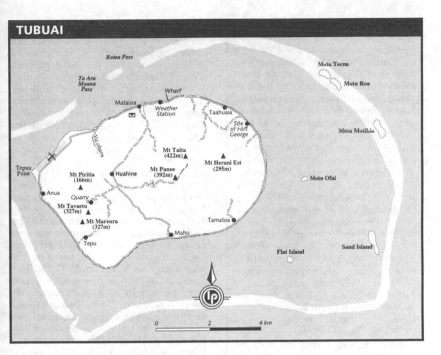

TUBUAI

Rotea Pass

Motu Toena

Motu Roa

Ta Ara
Moana
Pass

Wharf

Mataura

Weather
Station

Taahuaia

Site
of Fort
George

Motu Motiha

Vaahuru

Mt Taita
(422m) ▲

Mt Herani Est
(295m)

Motu Ofai

Tepuu
Point

Mt Piritia
(166m) ▲

● Huahine

Mt Panee
(392m) ▲

● Anua

Quarry

Mt Tavaetu
(327m) ▲

▲ Mt Mareura
(327m)

Tamatoa

Mahu

Tepu

Flat Island

Sand Island

0   2   4 km

was to fall further still before it began to recover. When Pomare II visited the Australs in 1819, the island chiefs ceded power to him, so when Tahiti came under France's wing in 1842, Tubuai followed. The island was formally annexed by France in 1880.

Orientation & Information

Compared to islands in the Society group, with their dramatic peninsulas and bays, the coast of Tubuai is rather boring. The 25km coast road only leaves the water's edge as it passes the airport. There are two mountain ranges sloping down to flat plains to the sea and separated by an equally low-lying central region. A cross-island road (the Route Traversière) bisects the island but even that doesn't rise very far above sea level. Mt Taita (422m) is the highest point on the island. The island is surrounded by a wide but very shallow lagoon with an outer reef dotted by a handful of motu at its eastern end. These motu are popular for beach excursions.

Mataura, about 4km from the airport, is the main village and has a post office, a Banque Socredo (open weekdays) and a couple of reasonably sized stores. A few smaller stores are dotted round the island.

Around the Island

One quick circuit of Tubuai and you've pretty much done it. From the centre of Mataura, proceeding clockwise, the 25km coast road runs past the Météo France meteorological station, the shipping wharf and through **Taahuaia**, the island's second village. Just past the village, on the inland side, an empty patch of green is the site of the *Bounty* mutineers' **Fort George**. There's no sign or memorial to the site's history, but if you look closely you may think you can make out the faint depression marking the foundations of two sides of the stockade.

The three larger motu are visible at the edge of the lagoon as you round the long, even curve of the island's eastern end. The

Hermit Crabs

Cycling round the coast road late one night I was astonished to find a busy traffic of hefty-sized hermit crabs scuttling across the road, all of them occupying the large brown shells of the giant African snails that have become a pest on a number of islands. Had they evicted the snails from their shells? It's a nice picture, a hermit crab hauling a reluctant snail out of its shell and leaving it shivering in the undergrowth while the crab settles into its new home.

Hermit crabs are common on many islands, and range from miniature little things to medium-sized snail-shell inhabitants and even larger. Hermit crabs live in shells to protect their fragile carapace. When a hermit crab outgrows its home it has to find a larger shell and make a swift move to its new mansion. Hermit-crab races are a popular activity with children on the beach. Just gather up a collection of crabs, put them down together, draw a large circle around them and wait for them to decide it's all clear, emerge from their shells and scuttle off. First across the outer circle wins.

Tony Wheeler

village of **Mahu** marks the southern end of the Route Traversière, and at the end of the village Nöel Ilari's **self-made tomb** stands in front of his home. Born in 1897, Ilari was a larger-than-life Frenchman who married a Tubuaian woman and became president of the French Polynesian Territorial Assembly in 1954. However, his squabbles with the French government led to a self-inflicted exile on Tubuai. He never forgave the government and the inscription recounts his indignation. Convinced his death was imminent, Ilari constructed the tomb in the 1970s, then lived until 1985! He also ran a guesthouse that he named L'Hermitage-Ste Hélène after Napoleon's place of exile on the remote South Atlantic island of Sainte Hélène.

From Mahu the road makes a sharp right turn at the island's south-west corner, another

sharp right at the airport and quickly ends up back in Mataura. The best **beaches** and **swimming** are along this stretch; the beach at the Ta Ara Moana Pass, just west of Mataura, is excellent and the water is deep.

The Mormons have made a major onslaught on Tubuai and their modern, functional churches, each with a floodlit basketball court, are sprinkled all around the island's coast road.

Walking

It's an easy climb to the summit of Mt Taita. From the Route Traversière, a track runs east along the ridgeline towards the peaks. The turn-off is just north of the very clear road west to the quarry on the western range. The track switchbacks up through pine plantations until it rounds the top of Mt Panee (392m), topped by the small hut of the TV-relay station. From here the 4WD track continues along the ridgeline until it finally terminates and a much more attractive walking path takes over. This pushes through small thickets and patches of fern until you eventually arrive at the tumble of boulders that tops Mt Taita (422m). It's a bit of a scramble over the moss-covered boulders to reach the summit but you're rewarded with superb views. It's the most picturesque spot on Tubuai, and there's lots of graffiti to confirm that you're not the first to enjoy it.

Places to Stay & Eat

There's a small *supermarket* and one good-sized *store* in Mataura, plus a scattering of smaller stores around the island. However, the choice of goods will be wider and the prices lower on Tahiti, so you may want to bring supplies with you. Come prepared for mosquitoes as well. Don't count on using credit cards on Tubuai.

Chez Doudou (☎/fax 95 06 71) is in Mataura, close to the shipping wharf, and has 20 rooms with hot-water bathroom for 3000/4500 CFP a single/double. Breakfast costs 500 CFP, lunch or dinner 1800 CFP and airport transfers 1000 CFP.

Pension Vaiteanui (☎/fax 95 04 19) is on the Route Traversière and has five rooms with hot-water bathrooms for

2500/4000 CFP. Add 2500 CFP per person for half-board. Activities can be organised including motu picnics (3180 CFP), island tours by boat (4240 CFP) or 4WD (2650 CFP) and guided walks (1060 CFP). Airport transfers are free.

Chez Sam & Yolande (☎/*fax 95 05 52*) is right by the sea in Mataura and has five rooms with hot water bathrooms for 6000/7500 CFP. A motu excursion costs 3500 CFP, an island tour 1000 CFP. In Taahuaia, *Le Bounty* (☎ *95 03 32, fax 95 05 58*) is connected with the college and has *fare* for 3000/5000 CFP.

Getting There & Away
Tubuai is 600km directly south of Tahiti and about midway between Rurutu to the north-west and Raivavae to the south-east. It can be reached by plane or cargo ship. Air Tahiti (☎ 94 03 57) is at the airport, and cargo ships enter through the large passes on the north-western edge of the reef and dock at Mataura. See the Getting There & Away section at the start of this chapter for more information.

Getting Around
The island pensions will collect you from the airport or dock if you book ahead. Bernard Le Guilloux (☎ 95 06 01) in Mataura has cars to rent for 4000 CFP a day, or ask at the guesthouses.

Other Australs

While Rurutu and Tubuai can be reached by air, the other islands in the group – three high islands and two uninhabited atolls – can only be reached by sea. Visitors are very few. Moving down the chain from the north-west, these less-frequented islands start with uninhabited Maria Island.

MARIA ISLAND
At the most north-west of the Austral chain, uninhabited Maria Island is an atoll with four motu on a triangular-shaped reef. The atoll is about 200km north-west of Rimatara and about 400km east of the Cook

Islands. The name comes from the whaler *Maria*, whose crew sighted the island in 1824, although it's also known as Hull Island. The *Tuhaa Pae II* makes occasional stops at Maria Island (see the Getting Around chapter) and visitors from Rurutu and Rimatara come here from time to time to harvest copra. The low-lying island has a very shallow lagoon but there is abundant **birdlife**.

RIMATARA
pop 929 • area 8 sq km • reef passes 1
highest point Mt Uahu (83m)
The tiny island of Rimatara is a rough circle 3km in diameter, rising to Mt Uahu (or Vahu; 83m) in the centre. Around this low mountain are the three villages of **Anapoto**, **Amaru** and **Mutua Ura**, linked by a road running some distance inland from the coast.

Like Rurutu, the island is circled by a fringing reef, and the narrow Hiava Pass lets small boats in to land on the beach in front of Amaru or Anapoto. The waterfront cemetery is the first thing visitors see on landing at Amaru. Traditionally, arriving visitors must pass through the smoke of a purifying fire as they step ashore.

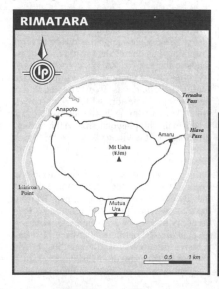

RIMATARA

Teruahu Pass

Anapoto

Amaru

Hiava Pass

Mt Uahu
(83m)

Iririroa Point

Mutua Ura

0   0.5   1 km

Rimatara is the most densely populated Austral island. Pandanus work and shell necklaces, plus the plantations, support the islanders, who have preserved their own distinct dialect.

History

Rimatara was the last of the Austral islands to be 'discovered'; Captain Samuel Pinder Henry spotted it in 1811. The first native missionary teachers were dropped on the island in 1821 and within two years it was reported that the entire population of 300 had been converted to Christianity.

Places to Stay

The only place to stay is **Umarere** (☎ 83 25 84 in Papeete), a two-room, fully equipped house for 2000 CFP per person. You've got to fend for yourself on Rimatara so bring supplies.

Getting There & Away

Rimatara is about 600km south-west of Tahiti, and about 150km west of Rurutu. Only small boats can enter Hiava Pass so goods are transferred to shore on whale-boats that land right on the beach.

RAIVAVAE

pop 1049 • area 16 sq km
reef passes 3 • highest point Mt Hiro (437m)
Proclaimed as one of the most beautiful islands in the Pacific, Raivavae (pronounced 'rye-vie-vie') is encircled by a motu-dotted reef. The island has five villages and a mountainous interior, which rises to Mt Hiro (437m). Rairua is the site of the island's main shipping quay but Mahanatoa is the largest of the villages.

History

Raivavae was noted for massive stone tiki that once stood in the island marae but, at the site of the principal marae, near Rairua, there is only one great tiki left today. It is certainly a very powerful figure, emanating great *mana* (supernatural power). Its impressive relations are now standing in the gardens of the Gauguin Museum on Tahiti. The Raivavae islanders also made unusual

sculpted drums, which have also become museum pieces.

Captain Thomas Gayangos of Spain was the first European to come upon Raivavae when he stopped there in 1775 en route to Peru. Like Tubuai, the island was ceded to Pomare II of Tahiti in 1819 and thus became a French protectorate in 1842 and was annexed by France in 1880.

At the time of the first European contact, Raivavae was a crowded island with around 3000 inhabitants, who had a highly developed social order and were unparalleled seafarers. It's said they regularly visited the Society Islands and even voyaged as far as New Zealand. Then in 1826 the same European fever that had devastated Tubuai reached Raivavae and killed almost the entire population. Only about 100 people survived, and the island's cultural and seafaring traditions were totally wiped out.

Today very little fishing is done around Raivavae and agriculture is the main activity. The cool climate and fertile soil are perfect for growing cabbage, carrots and potatoes as well as more-tropical crops such as coffee and oranges.

Archaeological Sites

Raivavae's famous **tiki** is nearly 2m high and stands neglected and overgrown a short stroll off the coast road, just to the west of Mahanatoa. At the other end of the island, inland from the road along the south coast, is the better-maintained **Marae Maunauto**. The name translates as something like Marae of the Sad (or Crying) Hero. Huge vertical slab-stones, many of them 2m high, surround the site, while nearby is another walled-in enclosure, said to be the grave of a princess.

Places to Stay

Chez Annie Flores (☎ 95 43 28) in Rairua village, where the boats dock, has two rooms, each with a double bed. There are bathroom facilities and an equipped kitchen for a daily cost of 2000 CFP per person. The house can be rented for 35,000 CFP per month.

Chez Vaite (☎ 95 42 85) in Mahanatoa has a house with three rooms, with lounge, dining room and equipped kitchen for

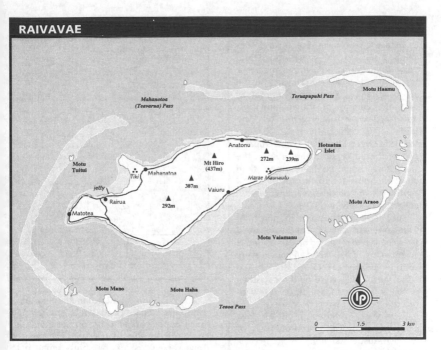

RAIVAVAE

4000/7000 CFP a single/double. The same type of lodging is offered by **Pension Moana** (☎ 95 42 66), also in Mahanatoa, for 2000 CFP per person, 4000 CFP with half-board.

Shopping

In the village of Matotea at the western end of the island, a craftsman produces exquisitely detailed models of pirogues. They're laid out for inspection on his veranda when any ship brings visitors to the island.

Getting There & Away

Raivavae is about 650km south-east of Tahiti and about 200km south-east from Tubuai. There is no airport but the ship *Tuhaa Pae II* comes by about twice a month.

RAPA

pop 521 • area 22 sq km
highest point Mt Perau (650m)
Rapa is the most remote and isolated island of French Polynesia – even its nearest

inhabited neighbour in the Australs, Raivavae, is over 500km away. This far south there are no coral reefs and no coconut palms, and temperatures as low as 5°C have been recorded in winter.

There are soaring and jagged-edged peaks, six of them reaching over 400m, the highest being Mt Perau (650m). The island is the remains of a gigantic volcano cone, with the eastern side of the cone breached so that the ancient crater is now the wide expanse of Haurei Bay. Numerous other bays indent the convoluted coastline.

The island is also known as Rapa Iti (Little Rapa) to distinguish it from Rapa Nui (Big Rapa), the Polynesian name for Easter Island. The population is concentrated in the villages of Haurei and Area, which are on opposite sides of Haurei Bay. They are generally linked by boat as there is only a rough road around the bay. At its peak there were about a dozen villages scattered across the island.

THE AUSTRALS

Austral Arts

Despite their isolation, the Australs developed some of the most vibrant and powerful artforms in Polynesia, including the giant stone tiki of Raivavae and the woodcarvings of Rurutu. Unfortunately, with the coming of the missionaries, these arts were totally wiped out and there is virtually nothing to be seen today. Even the largest and most impressive of the Raivavae tiki are now at the Gauguin Museum on Tahiti, rather than on their home island. Rurutu is still a centre for the production of wonderful cane and basketwork.

Both islands specialised in particular forms of wood carving. Delicately carved fly-whisks were produced on Rurutu, while ceremonial paddles, ladles and bowls were crafted on Raivavae. No-one is quite sure what the paddles were used for as they were too frail to paddle a canoe. A few intricately carved examples of these items have survived in museums, but the missionaries destroyed all examples of wooden Austral statuary.

RAPA

1 Tevaitau Pa
2 Morongo Uta Pa

History

Although it's believed that Rapa was only settled by Polynesians around 1000 to 1300 AD, it was once densely populated and divided into warring kingdoms whose mountain-top forts, or pa, were closely related to those of the warrior Maori of New Zealand. It is believed that land pressures, the result of overpopulation, were the cause of this perpetual warfare.

The island's first European visitor was George Vancouver, in 1791. Vancouver had already accompanied Cook to the Pacific on his second and third voyages. It was not until 1816 that another European visited Rapa, but this contact brought a series of disastrous epidemics that depopulated the island. From a crowded 2000 at the first contact, the population had plummeted to 500 by 1838 and in 1864 there were a mere 150 people on Rapa.

The final blow came when Peruvian slaving ships raided the islands and carried many people off to work on the guano islands off the Peruvian coast. The men of Rapa seized one of the ships, sailed it to Tahiti and demanded that the French take action. When the Peruvians attempted to return over 300 of the Polynesians they had enslaved, the vast majority of them died en route and the handful of survivors that landed on Rapa brought a terrible smallpox epidemic to the island.

When steamships began to operate across the Pacific, a coaling station was established on Rapa for ships crossing the Pacific Ocean to Australia and New Zealand. It was an attempt to combat the English influence in Polynesia that led to the French annexation of Rapa.

Today the Rapa islanders almost prize their isolation. Taro is the island's principal crop but some fine coffee, a variety of vegetables, and excellent oranges are also grown. There is also fishing, and the island is noted for its abundant goats, which are almost omnipresent; they even cling to the precipitous rocky peaks towering offshore from the main island.

Information

Rapa has some small shops and a post-office with a phonecard telephone.

Archaeological Sites

Morongo Uta, between Haurei and Hiri bays, is the best preserved of Rapa's ancient pa and was restored by a team led by Norwegian explorer Thor Heyerdahl and New Zealand archaeologist and anthropologist William Mulloy in 1956. Heyerdahl wrote about their work on Rapa in his book *Aku-Aku* (see Books in the Facts for the Visitor chapter). The great pa has terraces separated by deep moats around the central fortress, which has a perimeter of over 300m and is overlooked by a double-pyramid watchtower. Directly overlooking Haurei is the **Tevaitau Pa**, restored in 1960. Other pa can be found along the mountain ridge and at the passes from one valley to another. They typically have flat terraces and a lookout tower.

Places to Stay & Eat

Chez Cerdan Faraire (☎ 95 72 84), in Haurei, is the only family-run pension that takes guests; it costs 4000 CFP per person per day with all meals.

Getting There & Away

Rapa is more than 1000km south-east of Tahiti and more than 500km beyond Raivavae, its nearest inhabited neighbour. The *Tuhaa Pae II* visits Rapa about once a month. The wide Haurei Bay is the easiest to enter and most sheltered anchorage in the Australs.

MAROTIRI

Also known as Bass Rocks, the uninhabited rocky spires of Marotiri rise from the sea about 70km south-east of Rapa. Although even landing on the rocks is difficult, the largest one has a saddle between its two pinnacles – and this saddle is defended by a miniature **pa**!

THE GAMBIER ARCHIPELAGO

TIARE

MANOLO MYLONAS

The Gambier Archipelago

The most remote of the French Polynesian island groups, the Gambier Archipelago lies at the extreme south-eastern end of the long arc of the Tuamotus. On a map the islands appear to number among the many Tuamotu atolls, but in fact they are high islands and quite distinct from the neighbouring group. Well to the south, the climate is relatively mild and in winter it can actually get cool. The archipelago is one hour ahead of Tahiti.

The Gambier consists of high islands and motu within an encircling reef plus Temoe (or Timoe), a separate island to the south-east. Mangareva, which means 'floating mountain' in Polynesian, is the largest of the group and the only properly populated island. It was the centre for the obsessive missionary activities of Father Honoré Laval between 1834 and 1871, and the islands are almost a monument to his single-minded fervour.

History

The islands were populated in three waves around the 10th to the 13th centuries and there is much speculation that they may have been an important stopping point on the Polynesian migration routes to New Zealand or Easter Island.

Although the islands have such strong links with French Catholicism, the group was actually named in 1797 by James Wilson, captain of the *Duff*, who brought the pioneering London Missionary Society (LMS) missionaries to Tahiti in that year. He named the archipelago after Gambier, an English admiral who had supported the mission's activities. The islands' highest mountain is named after Wilson's ship. It wasn't until 1826, however, that FW Beechey, another Englishman, set the first European foot on the islands and made contact with the islanders. The islands soon became an important port for ships to replenish their supplies and trade for the abundant mother-of-pearl from the lagoon.

The first Catholic mission in Polynesia, the Sacred Heart Congregation, was established here in 1834 and quickly converted the entire

HIGHLIGHTS

pop: 1087
area: 27 sq km
reef passes: 3
highest point: Mt Duff (441m)

- Marvel at Father Honoré Laval's amazing Cathedral of St Michael
- Shudder at the ominous *maison nucleaire* fallout shelter
- Explore the many islands and motu on the huge lagoon

population. Father Honoré Laval, leader of the mission, and his assistant François Caret became virtual rulers of the archipelago. Until persistent complaints about his behaviour led to his exile on Tahiti in 1871, Laval ran the islands like his own personal fiefdom.

Laval transformed the islands, building wide roads, a massive cathedral, nine churches and chapels, monuments, lookout towers, wharves and a whole range of buildings, including a prison. Unfortunately, at the same time, the people of the Gambier Archipelago simply died out. When Laval arrived the population may have been 5000 to 6000, spread across the four main islands, but it quickly went into a free fall. In 1887, when the first official census was conducted, the population was only 463 and only recently has it once again passed 1000. Almost all of the inhabitants live on one island.

It's an open question how responsible Laval was for this disaster. The view that's most sympathetic towards Laval is that European diseases, imported by whalers and trading ships, caused the annihilation of the population and culture, and that Laval was merely an observer. The opposite view is that Laval was a single-minded bigot who wiped out native culture and then worked the islanders to death constructing a collection of absurdly over-ambitious monuments to his

THE GAMBIER ARCHIPELAGO

submerged and dangerously difficult to see around the southern half.

Within the lagoon there are 10 volcanic high islands. Apart from a handful of people on other islands, only Mangareva, the largest of them, is populated. Mangareva is 8km long but only 1.5km across at its narrowest point. The highest points are Mt Duff (441m) and Mt Mokoto (423m). The three other larger islands are Aukena, Akamaru and Taravai. The airport is on the largest motu, Totegegie, on the north-eastern side of the lagoon. About 50km south-east is the small island of Temoe.

Getting There & Away
The Gambier Archipelago is about 1700km south-east of Tahiti.

Air Air Tahiti (☎ 86 42 42, fax 86 40 69 on Tahiti) flies to the Gambier about once a week. The flight takes three hours 40 minutes, costs 27,500 CFP and sometimes goes via Hao. Check with Air Tahiti as this schedule is subject to change.

Boat From Tahiti, the cargo ship *Nuku Hau* sails via the eastern Tuamotus to the Gambier every three weeks. See the Getting Around chapter for details.

Getting Around
The airport is on Totegegie, a motu on the eastern side of the lagoon. Local boats meet every flight and charge 500 CFP for the 45 minute journey.

Chez Benoît & Bianca and Chez Pierre & Mariette organise island tours for 2500 CFP to 3000 CFP per person. Chez Benoît & Bianca also rents out bicycles for 1000 CFP per day while Chez Pierre & Mariette rents out cars for 5000 CFP per day. Chez Jojo can organise fishing trips.

MANGAREVA
In the dry season the grass-covered hills of Mangareva can take on a sombre brown appearance, but **Rikitea**, the sole village on the island, is a green, pleasant and quiet little place. At the upper part of the town stands the **Cathedral of St Michael**, the ultimate symbol

beliefs. Laval's own memoirs recount with delight the destruction of the idols and symbols of the old religion, along with the undeniable adventures of that time. Robert Lee Eskridge's *Manga Reva, the Forgotten Islands* tells the story of the missionary period.

Remarkably, Laval and Caret found time, soon after their arrival in the archipelago, to pop over to Tahiti and attempt to carry Catholicism to that bastion of Protestant missionary activity. Their subsequent clash with Queen Pomare IV and English missionaries was the excuse for the French takeover of Tahiti. Although France established a protectorate over the Gambier in 1844, it continued as a semi-independent entity and was not formally annexed until 1881.

Today Mangareva is more or less self-sufficient, raising livestock and growing fruit, root crops and a little coffee. The Gambier Archipelago is also an important centre for the production of black pearls.

Geography
The wide polygon-shaped lagoon is protected by a 90km coral barrier. There are 25 motu dotted along the reef around its northern half, but the reef edge is partly

of Laval's single-minded obsession. The cathedral can accommodate 1200 people – more than the population of the island today! It has twin blue-trimmed towers, is 54m long and was built between 1839 and 1848. The altar is decorated with mother-of-pearl and the woodwork is also inlaid with pearl shell.

Various other Laval constructions stand in the village, including the coastal watchtowers and the turret, which are all that remain of the 'palace' Laval built for the island's last king. The king, Maputeao, changed his name to Gregoria Stanislas for Laval and has a memorial in **St Peter's Cemetery**. The island's **Rouru Convent** once had 60 Mangarevan nuns, and it's said Laval would hide the entire female population of the island in the convent whenever a whaling ship paid a visit. An overgrown path built in Laval's era leads uphill to the convent, passing a hollowed-out rock pool known as the **Queen's Bath** on the way and finally entering the nunnery through a triumphal arch. Only the empty shells of the convent buildings remain.

A much more recent construction stands beside the coast road on the northern side of the island – the **maison nucleaire**. Moruroa lies just 400km north-west of Mangareva and during the period from 1966 to 1974, when above-ground nuclear tests were conducted, the entire population of the island was herded into this ugly metal-walled fallout shelter if contrary winds threatened to blow fallout towards the Gambier. Older island residents remember being squeezed into this windowless tomb for up to three days at a time. It's no wonder *faaore te atomi*, 'no to atomic testing', is painted on Mangarevan walls.

Places to Stay & Eat

Chez Pierre & Mariette Paemara (☎ 97 82 87) is just 100m from the docks in Mangareva. It has a house with three bedrooms, a living room, cold-water bathroom and kitchen. Rooms cost 2000 CFP per person, 4000 CFP with half-board (breakfast and dinner) or 6000 CFP with full board (all meals). Also in the village, *Chez Terii & Hélène Paemara* (☎ 97 82 80) offers similar facilities for a similar price, in a two bedroom house.

Chez Benoît & Bianca (☎/fax 97 83 76) is 1km from the quay and offers fine views across the bay to Aukena from its hillside location. There are three rooms with shared hot-water bathroom, for 5500/7350 CFP per person half/full board.

Chez Jojo (☎/fax 97 82 61) is by the water, 5km from the quay, and also has three rooms with shared hot-water bathroom. They cost 4500/6000 CFP half/full board and you can also camp here for 1000 CFP per day.

There's a small *bakery* by the waterfront in Rikitea, run by two former Foreign Legionnaires – one Portuguese and one Turkish!

TARAVAI & AUKENA

When the missionaries arrived, all the major islands in the group were populated and Taravai had a population of 2000. Today only a handful of people live on the island and the 1868 **Church of St Gabriel**, with its conch-shell decoration, is deserted. There are other buildings in **Agokono**, the all-but-empty village on the island.

Aukena also has reminders of the missionary period, including the 1839 **Church of St Raphaël** and the hexagonal **lookout tower**, still used as a landmark, on the south-western tip of the island.

AKAMARU & TEMOE

Akamaru was the island where Laval first arrived and his 1841 **Our Lady of Peace Church** still stands on the utterly deserted island. Occasional groups come over from Mangareva to maintain the church or to pick oranges in season.

The remote island of Temoe, 50km southeast, has a **marae** with some Marquesan features, leading to theories that canoes from the Marquesas may have paused here en route to Easter Island. Even this remote and tiny island was populated until 1838, when the missionaries shifted the people to Mangareva. Bishop Museum archaeologist Kenneth Emory carried out investigations here and on Mangareva in 1934, and in that same year James Norman Hall, coauthor of *Mutiny on the Bounty*, was shipwrecked on the island.

Language

TAHITIAN

Tahitian (also known as Maohi) belongs to the group of Polynesian languages which includes Samoan, Maori, Hawaiian, Rarotongan and Tongan. There are several dialects of Tahitian, including the Tuamotan or Paumotan dialect of the Tuamotus, the Marquesan dialect of the Marquesas and the Mangarevan dialect of the Gambier Archipelago. It was the spread of Christianity through French Polynesia that helped to make Tahitian, the dialect spoken on Tahiti, the most widespread dialect.

Few Tahitian words have managed to make their way into English or any other languages. The two familiar exceptions are 'tattoo' from the Tahitian *tatau* and 'taboo' from the Tahitian *tabu* (or *tapu*).

An interesting characteristic of Tahitian is the formation of words by agglutination. For 'helicopter', you say *manu tautau na te reva*, literally 'bird suspended in space'; 'television' is *afata teata*, literally 'theatre box', while 'refrigerator' is *afata fa'ato'e-to'eraa ma'a* or 'box for cooling food'. For more information on Tahitian, pick up a copy of Lonely Planet's *South Pacific phrasebook*, which also includes a useful section on Pacific French.

Tahitian grammar is pleasantly uncomplicated. There are no genders, declensions, conjugations or auxiliaries, and plural forms are denoted solely by the article: the definite article (the) is *te* in the singular and *te mau* in the plural. The notions of past, present and future are expressed by using prefixes or suffixes with the verb. A single word in Tahitian can be a verb, adjective or noun, eg *inu* can mean 'to drink', 'a drink' or 'drinkable', according to the context.

Pronunciation

Tahitian isn't a difficult language for English speakers to pronounce, as most Tahitian sounds are also found in English. Likewise, the Tahitian alphabet, devised in the 19th century, is fairly simple to use.

Vowels

As with all other Polynesian languages, there are five vowels, pronounced much as they are in Italian and Spanish:

a	as in 'father'
e	between the 'e' in 'bet' and the 'ay' in 'bay'
i	as in 'marine'
o	as the 'o' in 'more'
u	as the 'oo' in 'zoo'

Tahitian and most other Pacific languages have a second series of long vowels. The 'shape' of these is the same as their shorter counterparts, but they are held for approximately twice as long. You can get an idea of this concept by comparing the pronunciation of English 'icy' and 'I see' – both are distinguished only by the length of the final vowel.

The missionaries who devised the spelling system of Tahitian didn't account for vowel length, assuming that any native speakers would naturally know whether a given word had short or long vowels. However, for non-Polynesians the long vowel is indispensable, since vowel length can change the meaning of a word. Long vowels are indicated in this language guide by a macron over the vowel (ā, ē, ī, ō and ū).

Consonants

Consonants are pronounced much as they are in English, with a few modifications.

h	as in 'house' or as the 'sh' in 'shoe' when preceded by **i** and followed by **o**, eg *iho* (only/just)
p	as in 'sponge', not as the 'p' in 'path' (ie not followed by a puff of breath)
r	often rolled as in Scottish or Spanish
t	as in 'stand', not as the 't' in 'talk' (ie not followed by a puff of breath)
'	glottal stop. This sound occurs between two vowels and is like the sound you hear between the words

'uh-oh'. In Tahitian, this sound isn't indicated in the normal spelling (with a few minor exceptions), since native speakers know where they occur. Foreigners, however, aren't so lucky – the glottal stop is indicated by the apostrophe (') in this language guide.

FRENCH

All French nouns are either masculine or feminine and adjectives change their form to agree with the noun. In the following list of words and phrases, only the singular version of nouns and adjectives is given.

Basic French vowels are pronounced as they are in Tahitian, but there are a few other rules of pronunciation worth remembering:

ai	as the 'e' in 'pet'. Any following single consonant is usually silent.
eau/ au	as the 'au' in 'caught' but shorter
ll	as 'y', eg *billet* (ticket), pronounced 'bee-yeh'
ch	always pronounced as 'sh'
qu	as 'k'
r	pronounced from the back of the throat

There is a distinction between **u** (as in *tu*) and **ou** (as in *tout*). For both sounds, the lips are rounded and pushed forward, but for the 'u' sound try to say 'ee' while keeping the lips pursed. The 'ou' sound is pronounced as the 'oo' in 'cook'.

For nasal vowels the breath escapes partly through the nose. They occur where a syllable ends in a single **n** or **m**; the **n** or **m** is silent but indicates the nasalisation of the preceding vowel.

USEFUL WORDS & PHRASES

English French	Tahitian
Hello/Good morning.	
Bonjour.	*Ia ora na, nana.*
Goodbye.	
Au revoir.	*Pārahi, nana.*
Welcome.	
Bienvenue.	*Maeva, mānava.*

English French	Tahitian
How are you?	
Ça va?	*E aha te huru?*
My name is ...	
Je m'appelle ...	*To'u i'oa 'o ...*
Thank you.	
Merci.	*Māuruuru roa.*
Pardon?	
Comment?	*E aha?*
Excuse me/Sorry.	
Pardon.	*E'e, aue ho'i e.*
No problem/ Don't worry.	
Pas de problème.	*Aita pe'ape'a.*
Yes.	
Oui.	*E, 'oia.*
No.	
Non.	*Aita.*
Good luck!	
Bon courage!	*Fa'aitoito!*
I don't understand.	
Je ne comprends pas.	*Aita i ta'a ia'u.*
How much?	
Combien?	*E hia moni?*
How many?	
Combien?	*E hia?*
Where is ...?	
Où est ...?	*Tei hea ...?*
When?	
Quand?	*Afea?*
What time is it?	
Quelle heure est-il?	*E aha te hora i teie nei?*
Cheers! (for drinking)	
Santé!	*Manuia!*
I'm ill.	
Je suis malade.	*E ma'i to'u.*
address	
l'adresse	*i'oa fa'aeara'a*
bank	
la banque	*fare moni*
bathroom	
la salle de bain	*piha pape*
beach	
la plage	*tahatai*
bed	
le lit	*ro'i*

English French	Tahitian
beer	
la bière	*pia*
bicycle	
le vélo	*pereo'o tāta'ahi*
boat	*le bateau poti*
breakfast	
le petit déjeuner	*tafe poipoi*
bus	
l'autobus	*pereo'o mata'eina'a*
car	
la voiture	*pereo'o uira*
chemist/pharmacy	
la pharmacie	*fare ra'au*
coffee	
le café	*taofe*
country	
le pays	*'ai'a*
day	
le jour	*ao*
embassy	
l'ambassade	*fare tonitera rahi*
film (camera)	
la pellicule	*firimu*
food	
la nourriture	*ma'a*
map	
le plan	*hoho'a fenua*
menu	
la carte	*tāpura mā'a*
money	
l'argent	*moni*
now	
maintenant	*i teinei*
parents (extended family)	
les parents	*fēti'i*
plantation	
la plantation	*fa'a'apu*
police station	
le commissariat	*fare mūto'i*

English French	Tahitian
restaurant	
le restaurant	*fare tāmā'ara'a*
room	
la chambre	*piha*
shop	
le magasin	*fare toa*
telephone	
le téléphone	*niunu paraparau*
that	
cela	*terā*
today	
aujourd'hui	*i teie nei mahana*
tomorrow	
demain	*ānānahi*
tonight	
ce soir	*i teie pō*
water	
l'eau	*pape*

1	*un*	*hō'ē/tahi*
2	*deux*	*piti*
3	*trois*	*toru*
4	*quatre*	*māha*
5	*cinq*	*pae*
6	*six*	*ono*
7	*sept*	*hitu*
8	*huit*	*va'u*
9	*neuf*	*iva*
10	*dix*	*hō'ē 'ahuru*
20	*vingt*	*piti 'ahuru*
100	*cent*	*hō'ē hānere*
500	*cinq cents*	*pae hānere*
1000	*mille*	*hō'ē tauatini*
5000	*cinq mille*	*pae tauatini*
10,000	*dix mille*	*hō'ē 'ahuru tauatini*
one million		
un million	*hō'ē mirioni*	

Glossary

ahimaa – underground oven used for cooking traditional Polynesian food

ahu – altar in a *marae*; in French Polynesia the ahu was generally pyramid shaped

aito – ironwood

anuhe – fern

arii – high chief of the ancient Polynesian aristocracy; literally, 'king'

arioi – priest caste or religious society of the pre-European Society Islands

atoll – type of low island created by *coral* rising above sea level as an island gradually sinks; postcard atolls consist of a chain of small islands and reef enclosing a *lagoon*; see also *low island*

atua – collective term for Polynesian gods

barrier reef – *coral* reef forming a barrier between the shoreline and the open sea but separated from the land by a *lagoon*

belvédère – lookout

bonitier – whaleboat; used for fishing and for transferring passengers and cargo from ship to shore on islands that have no wharf or quay

boules – see *pétanque*

BP – *boîte postale*; post-office box

breadfruit – see *uru*

bringue – local festival or party, generally accompanied by lots of beer

caldera – volcano crater

capitainerie – harbour master's office

CEP – Centre d'Expérimentation du Pacifique; the French nuclear-testing program

CETAD – Centre d'Études des Techniques Adaptés au Développement; technical and vocational college

CFP – Cour de Franc Pacifique; currency of French Polynesia

ciguatera – illness caused by eating infected reef-fish

CMAS – Conféderation Mondiale des Activités Subaquatiques; scuba-diving qualification; the Francophile equivalent of *PADI*

copra – dried coconut meat, used to make an oil

coral – animal of the coelenterate group which, given the right conditions of water clarity, depth and temperature, grows to form a reef

croque-madame – toasted ham-and-cheese sandwich with a fried egg on top; also known as *croque-vahine*

croque-monsieur – toasted ham-and-cheese sandwich

cyclone – tropical storm rotating around a low-pressure 'eye'; 'typhoon' in the Pacific, 'hurricane' in the Caribbean

demi-pension – see *half-board*

demi – person of Polynesian-European or Polynesian-Chinese descent

DOM-TOM – Départements et Territoires d'Outre-Mer; French overseas departments and territories

ÉFO – Établissements Français d'Océanie; official acronym for French Polynesia from 1903 to 1946

emergence – geological activity that pushes land up above sea level

ÉVAAM – Établissement pour la Valorisation des Activités Aquacoles et Maritimes; marine-research organisation

faapu – small cultivated field

fare – traditional Polynesian house; hotel bungalow

fare atua – house for the gods on *marae*; actually a small chest in the form of a statue

fare potee – chief's house or community meeting place; open dining-area of a restaurant or hotel

fare tamoa – dining house

fare tupapau – shelter where dead bodies were laid out to decompose in pre-European Polynesia

fenua – country or region of origin

FFESSM – Féderation Française d'Etude et des Sports Sous-Marin; French diving association; see also *CMAS*, *PADI*

fringing reef – *coral* reef that is immediately alongside the shoreline, not separated from the shore by a *lagoon* as with a *barrier reef*

full board – accommodation and all meals; French: *pension complète*

gendarmerie – police station

goélette – schooner; inter-island cargo or freighter ships are commonly referred to as *goélettes* even though the age of sailing ships has long disappeared

hae – traditional Marquesan house

half-board – accommodation, breakfast and lunch or dinner; French: *demi-pension*;

heiva – festival; specifically refers to the series of festivals (Heiva I Tahiti) during July in Papeete that include dance and song competitions

high island – island created by volcanic action or geological upheaval; see also *low island*

himene – Tahitian-language hymn

Hiro – god of thieves who features in many Polynesian legends

hoa – shallow channel across the outer reef of an *atoll*, normally carrying water into or out of the central *lagoon* only at unusually high tides or when large swells are running; see also *pass*

honu – turtle

kaikai enana – Marquesan food; see also *maa*

kaina – Polynesian; Polynesian person; see also *popaa*, *demi*

kava – traditional mildly intoxicating drink made from the root of *Piper methysticum* (the pepper plant)

kaveu – coconut crab

keetu – characteristic red volcanic stone of the Marquesas

keshi – Japanese term for pearl formed from pure *nacre* (mother-of-pearl), when the *nucleus* has been expelled from the oyster

lagoon – the calmer waters enclosed by a reef; may be an enclosed area encircled by a *barrier reef* (eg Rangiroa and Tetiaroa) with or without *motu*, or may surround a *high island* (eg Bora Bora and Tahiti)

lagoon side – on the lagoon side of the coast road (not necessarily right by the lagoon); see also *mountain side*

LDS – Mormon; follower of the Church of Jesus Christ of the Latter-Day Saints

leeward – downwind; sheltered from the prevailing winds; see also *windward*

le truck – main form of public transport in French Polynesia; trucks with bench seats that operate a bus-like service

LMS – London Missionary Society; pioneering Protestant missionary organisation in Polynesia

low island – island created by the growth and erosion of *coral* or by the complete erosion of a *high island*; see also *atoll*

maa – food

maa tahiti – Tahitian or Polynesian food; Tahitian buffet

maa tinito – Chinese food

mabe – hollow cultured pearl

mahi mahi – dolphin fish (no relation to the dolphin, which is a mammal); one of the most popular eating fish in French Polynesia

mahu – transvestite or female impersonator; see also *rae rae*

mairie – town hall

makatea – *coral* island that has been thrust above sea level by a geological disturbance (eg Rurutu in the Australs and Makatea in the Tuamotus)

mana – spiritual power

manahune – peasant class or common people of pre-European Polynesia

mao – shark; French: *requin*

Maohi – French Polynesian

mape – Polynesian 'chestnut' tree found on the Society islands

maraamu – south-east tradewinds that blow from June to August

marae – traditional Polynesian temple generally constructed with an *ahu* at one end

marae arii – important 'national' marae

marae tupuna – ancestor or family marae

maro ura – feather belt worn by a chief as a symbol of his dynasty

meae – Marquesan word for *marae*

Melanesia – islands of the western Pacific including Papua New Guinea, the Solomons, Vanuatu, New Caledonia and Fiji

Micronesia – islands of the north-west Pacific including the Mariana, Caroline, Marshall and Kiribati groups, and Nauru

miro – *Thespesia populnea*; rosewood

monoi – oil made from coconut oil and perfumed with the *tiare* flower and/or other substances

motu – *coral* islet; small islet along the outer reef of an *atoll* or on a reef around a *high island*

mountain side – on the mountain side of the coast road (not neccessarily up in the mountains); see also *lagoon side*

mupe – skirt made from natural fibres and used in traditional dances

nacre – mother-of-pearl; iridescent substance secreted by pearl oysters to form the inner layer of the shell; shell of a pearl oyster

navette – shuttle boat

niau – sheets of plaited coconut-palm leaves, used for roof thatching

noni – fruit with therapeutic properties, grown in the Marquesas and popular in the USA

nono – very annoying biting gnat found on some beaches and particularly on islands in the Marquesas

nucleus – small sphere, made from shells found in the Mississippi River in the USA, which is introduced into the gonads of the pearl oyster to produce a cultured pearl

ono ono – barracuda

Oro – god of war; the cult that was superseding the *Taaroa* cult when the first Europeans arrived

ORSTOM – Office de Recherches Scientifiques et Techniques d'Outre Mer; oceanographic-research organisation

pa – hilltop fortress

PADI – Professional Association of Dive Instructors; the most popular international scuba-diving qualification

pae pae – paved floor of a traditional house; meeting platform

pahu – drum

pandanus – palm tree with aerial roots; the leaves are used for weaving hats, mats and bags

pareu – traditional sarong-like garment; also known as *paréo*

pass – channel into the *lagoon* through the outer reef of an *atoll* or the *barrier reef* around a *high island*; see also *hoa*

Paumoto – the Tuamotus; people from the Tuamotus

pension – guesthouse

pension complète – see *full board*

pétanque – French game in which metal balls are thrown to land as near as possible to a target ball; also known as *boules*

petroglyph – carving on a stone or rock

peue – mat

phonolite – type of volcanic rock

pirogue – outrigger canoe; Tahitian: *vaa*

PK – *pointe kilométrique*; distance markers found along the roads of some French Polynesian islands

plat du jour – daily special; literally 'plate of the day'

poisson cru – popular raw-fish dish

Polynesia – islands of the central and south-eastern Pacific including French Polynesia, Easter Island, Tonga and the Cook Islands

popaa – European; westerner; see also *kaina, demi*

poti marara – motorboat; used for fishing in the *lagoon*

raatira – middle rank of pre-European Polynesian society, above the lower class but below the *arii*

rae rae – *mahu*; sometimes applied to mahu who are homosexual, rather than just cross-dressers

requin – shark; Tahitian: *mao*

roulotte – mobile diner; van with flaps lowered and to be used as counters, stools outside for customers and staff inside to prepare food

Sanito – branch of the Mormon religion

seamount – underwater volcano that rises more than 1000m above the ocean floor but does not break the surface

seaward – side of an *atoll*, island or *motu* that faces the sea rather than the *lagoon*

sennit – string or material woven from coconut-husk fibre

Taaroa – supreme Polynesian god whose cult was being superseded by worship of *Oro*, god of war, at the time of the European arrival

tabu – see *tapu*

tahua – priest of the ancient Polynesian religion

tamaaraa – family meal

tamure – hip-jiggling version of traditional Polynesian dance

tane – man

tapa – bark-cloth beaten thin; traditional clothing worn by the people of pre-European Polynesia and much of the Pacific

tapu – sacred or forbidden; the English word 'taboo' comes from *tapu* or *tabu*

taro – root vegetable; a Polynesian staple food

tatau – tattoo; although tattoos were also known in Japan, it was on Tahiti that sailors first discovered them and adopted the word into European vocabularies

tiare – gardenia; fragrant flower that has become symbolic of Tahiti

tifaifai – colourful appliquéd or patchwork material used as bedspreads or cushion covers

tii – Society Islands term for the Marquesan word *tiki*

tiki – human-like sculpture usually made of wood or stone and sometimes standing more than 2m high; once found on many *marae*

Tinito – Chinese

tiputa – *tapa* poncho; traditional attire

tohua – meeting place or a place for festival gatherings in pre-European Polynesia, especially in the Marquesas

tou – *Cordia subcordata*; medium-sized tree, common in the Marquesas, that produces a dark, hard, grained wood popular with carvers

tuff – volcanic rock of Polynesia

tupapau – spirit ghosts of the ancient Polynesian religion, still much feared

tuu – ceremonial activities centre in the Marquesas

ua ma – Marquesan food pit

umete – traditional Tahitian wooden dish or bowl

umu hei – Marquesan *monoi*; packet of fragrant natural vegetable essences

uru – breadfruit; starchy staple food of Polynesia that grows on a tree as a football-sized fruit; breadfruit tree; French: *arbre à pain*

vaa – outrigger canoe; French: *pirogue*

vahine – Polynesian woman

VTT – *vélo à tout terrain*; mountain bike

windward – facing prevailing winds; see also *leeward*

LONELY PLANET

Guides by Region

Lonely Planet is known worldwide for publishing practical, reliable and no-nonsense travel information in our guides and on our Web site. The Lonely Planet list covers just about every accessible part of the world. Currently there are thirteen series: travel guides, shoestring guides, walking guides, city guides, phrasebooks, audio packs, city maps, travel atlases, diving & snorkeling guides, restaurant guides, first-time travel guides, healthy travel and travel literature.

AFRICA Africa on a shoestring • Africa – the South • Arabic (Egyptian) phrasebook • Arabic (Moroccan) phrasebook • Cairo • Cape Town • Cape Town city map• Central Africa • East Africa • Egypt • Egypt travel atlas • Ethiopian (Amharic) phrasebook • The Gambia & Senegal • Healthy Travel Africa • Kenya • Kenya travel atlas • Malawi, Mozambique & Zambia • Morocco • North Africa • South Africa, Lesotho & Swaziland • South Africa, Lesotho & Swaziland travel atlas • Swahili phrasebook • Tanzania, Zanzibar & Pemba • Trekking in East Africa • Tunisia • West Africa • Zimbabwe, Botswana & Namibia • Zimbabwe, Botswana & Namibia travel atlas
Travel Literature: The Rainbird: A Central African Journey • Songs to an African Sunset: A Zimbabwean Story • Mali Blues: Traveling to an African Beat

AUSTRALIA & THE PACIFIC Auckland • Australia • Australian phrasebook • Bushwalking in Australia • Bushwalking in Papua New Guinea • Fiji • Fijian phrasebook • Healthy Travel Australia, NZ and the Pacific • Islands of Australia's Great Barrier Reef • Melbourne • Melbourne city map • Micronesia • New Caledonia • New South Wales & the ACT • New Zealand • Northern Territory • Outback Australia • Out To Eat – Melbourne • Out to Eat – Sydney • Papua New Guinea • Pidgin phrasebook • Queensland • Rarotonga & the Cook Islands • Samoa • Solomon Islands • South Australia • South Pacific Languages phrasebook • Sydney • Sydney city map • Sydney Condensed • Tahiti & French Polynesia • Tasmania • Tonga • Tramping in New Zealand • Vanuatu • Victoria • Western Australia
Travel Literature: Islands in the Clouds • Kiwi Tracks: A New Zealand Journey • Sean & David's Long Drive

CENTRAL AMERICA & THE CARIBBEAN Bahamas, Turks & Caicos • Bermuda • Central America on a shoestring • Costa Rica • Cuba • Dominican Republic & Haiti • Eastern Caribbean • Guatemala, Belize & Yucatán: La Ruta Maya • Jamaica • Mexico • Mexico City • Panama • Puerto Rico
Travel Literature: Green Dreams: Travels in Central America

EUROPE Amsterdam • Amsterdam city map • Andalucía • Austria • Baltic States phrasebook • Barcelona • Berlin • Berlin city map • Britain • British phrasebook • Brussels, Bruges & Antwerp • Budapest city map • Canary Islands • Central Europe • Central Europe phrasebook • Corsica • Croatia • Czech & Slovak Republics • Denmark • Dublin • Eastern Europe • Eastern Europe phrasebook • Edinburgh • Estonia, Latvia & Lithuania • Europe on a shoestring • Finland • France • French phrasebook • Germany • German phrasebook • Greece • Greek Islands • Greek phrasebook • Hungary • Iceland, Greenland & the Faroe Islands • Ireland • Italian phrasebook • Italy • Krakow • Lisbon • London • London city map • London Condensed • Mediterranean Europe • Mediterranean Europe phrasebook • Norway • Paris • Paris city map • Poland • Portugal • Portugal travel atlas • Prague • Prague city map • Provence & the Côte d'Azur • Romania & Moldova • Rome • Russia, Ukraine & Belarus • Russian phrasebook • Scandinavian & Baltic Europe • Scandinavian Europe phrasebook • Scotland • Slovenia • Spain • Spanish phrasebook • St Petersburg • Switzerland • Trekking in Spain • Ukrainian phrasebook • Vienna • Walking in Britain • Walking in Ireland • Walking in Italy • Walking in Spain • Walking in Switzerland • Western Europe • Western Europe phrasebook
Travel Literature: The Olive Grove: Travels in Greece

INDIAN SUBCONTINENT Bangladesh • Bengali phrasebook • Bhutan • Delhi • Goa • Hindi & Urdu phrasebook • India • India & Bangladesh travel atlas • Indian Himalaya • Karakoram Highway • Kerala • Mumbai (Bombay) • Nepal • Nepali phrasebook • Pakistan • Rajasthan • Read This First: Asia & India • South India • Sri Lanka • Sri Lanka phrasebook • Trekking in the Indian Himalaya • Trekking in the Karakoram & Hindukush • Trekking in the Nepal Himalaya
Travel Literature: In Rajasthan • Shopping for Buddhas

LONELY PLANET

Mail Order

Lonely Planet products are distributed worldwide. They are also available by mail order from Lonely Planet, so if you have difficulty finding a title please write to us. North and South American residents should write to 150 Linden St, Oakland, CA 94607, USA; European and African residents should write to 10a Spring Place, London NW5 3BH, UK; and residents of other countries to PO Box 617, Hawthorn, Victoria 3122, Australia.

ISLANDS OF THE INDIAN OCEAN Madagascar & Comoros • Maldives • Mauritius, Réunion & Seychelles

MIDDLE EAST & CENTRAL ASIA Arab Gulf States • Central Asia • Central Asia phrasebook • Hebrew phrasebook • Iran • Israel & the Palestinian Territories • Israel & the Palestinian Territories travel atlas • Istanbul • Istanbul to Cairo • Jerusalem • Jordan & Syria • Jordan, Syria & Lebanon travel atlas • Lebanon • Middle East on a shoestring • Syria • Turkey • Turkey travel atlas • Turkish phrasebook • Yemen
Travel Literature: The Gates of Damascus • Kingdom of the Film Stars: Journey into Jordan

NORTH AMERICA Alaska • Backpacking in Alaska • Baja California • California & Nevada • Canada • Chicago • Chicago city map • Deep South • Florida • Hawaii • Honolulu • Las Vegas • Los Angeles • Miami • New England • New Orleans • New York City • New York city map • New York, New Jersey & Pennsylvania • Pacific Northwest USA • Puerto Rico • Rocky Mountain • San Francisco • San Francisco city map • Seattle • Southwest USA • Texas • USA • USA phrasebook • Vancouver • Washington, DC & the Capital Region • Washington DC city map
Travel Literature: Drive Thru America

NORTH-EAST ASIA Beijing • Cantonese phrasebook • China • Hong Kong • Hong Kong city map • Hong Kong, Macau & Guangzhou • Japan • Japanese phrasebook • Japanese audio pack • Korea • Korean phrasebook • Kyoto • Mandarin phrasebook • Mongolia • Mongolian phrasebook • North-East Asia on a shoestring • Seoul • South-West China • Taiwan • Tibet • Tibetan phrasebook • Tokyo
Travel Literature: Lost Japan

SOUTH AMERICA Argentina, Uruguay & Paraguay • Bolivia • Brazil • Brazilian phrasebook • Buenos Aires • Chile & Easter Island • Chile & Easter Island travel atlas • Colombia • Ecuador & the Galapagos Islands • Healthy Travel Central & South America • Latin American Spanish phrasebook • Peru • Quechua phrasebook • Rio de Janeiro • Rio de Janeiro city map • South America on a shoestring • Trekking in the Patagonian Andes • Venezuela
Travel Literature: Full Circle: A South American Journey

SOUTH-EAST ASIA Bali & Lombok • Bangkok • Bangkok city map • Burmese phrasebook • Cambodia • Hanoi • Healthy Travel Asia & India • Hill Tribes phrasebook • Ho Chi Minh City • Indonesia • Indonesia's Eastern Islands • Indonesian phrasebook • Indonesian audio pack • Jakarta • Java • Laos • Lao phrasebook • Laos travel atlas • Malay phrasebook • Malaysia, Singapore & Brunei • Myanmar (Burma) • Philippines • Pilipino (Tagalog) phrasebook • Singapore • South-East Asia on a shoestring • South-East Asia phrasebook • Thailand • Thailand's Islands & Beaches • Thailand travel atlas • Thai phrasebook • Thai audio pack • Vietnam • Vietnamese phrasebook • Vietnam travel atlas

ALSO AVAILABLE: Antarctica • The Arctic • Brief Encounters: Stories of Love, Sex & Travel • Chasing Rickshaws • Lonely Planet Unpacked • Not the Only Planet: Travel Stories from Science Fiction • Sacred India • Travel with Children • Traveller's Tales

Phrasebooks

Lonely Planet phrasebooks are packed with essential words and phrases to help travellers communicate with the locals. With colour tabs for quick reference, an extensive vocabulary and use of script, these handy pocket-sized language guides cover day-to-day travel situations.

- handy pocket-sized books
- easy to understand Pronunciation chapter
- clear & comprehensive Grammar chapter
- romanisation alongside script to allow ease of pronunciation
- script throughout so users can point to phrases for every situation
- full of cultural information and tips for the traveller

'... vital for a real DIY spirit and attitude in language learning'
– *Backpacker*

'the phrasebooks have good cultural backgrounders and offer solid advice for challenging situations in remote locations'
– *San Francisco Examiner*

Arabic (Egyptian) • Arabic (Moroccan) • Australian *(Australian English, Aboriginal and Torres Strait languages)* • Baltic States *(Estonian, Latvian, Lithuanian)* • Bengali • Brazilian • British • Burmese • Cantonese • Central Asia (Uyghur, Uzbek, Kyrghiz, Kazak, Pashto, Tadjik • Central Europe *(Czech, French, German, Hungarian, Italian, Slovak)* • Eastern Europe *(Bulgarian, Czech, Hungarian, Polish, Romanian, Slovak)* • Ethiopian (Amharic) • Fijian • French • German • Greek • Hebrew • Hill Tribes • Hindi & Urdu • Indonesian • Italian • Japanese • Korean • Lao • Latin American Spanish • Malay • Mandarin • Mediterranean Europe *(Albanian, Croatian, Greek, Italian, Macedonian, Maltese, Serbian, Slovene)* • Mongolian • Nepali • Pidgin • Pilipino (Tagalog) • Quechua • Russian • Scandinavian Europe *(Danish, Finnish, Icelandic, Norwegian, Swedish)* • South-East Asia *(Burmese, Indonesian, Khmer, Lao, Malay, Tagalog Pilipino, Thai, Vietnamese)* • South Pacific Languages • Spanish (Castilian) *(also includes Catalan, Galician and Basque)* • Sri Lanka • Swahili • Thai • Tibetan • Turkish • Ukrainian • USA *(US English, Vernacular, Native American languages, Hawaiian)* • Vietnamese • Western Europe *(Basque, Catalan, Dutch, French, German, Greek, Irish, Italian, Portuguese, Scottish Gaelic, Spanish (Castilian), Welsh)*

Lonely Planet Journeys

JOURNEYS is a unique collection of travel writing – published by the company that understands travel better than anyone else. It is a series for anyone who has ever experienced – or dreamed of – the magical moment when they encountered a strange culture or saw a place for the first time. They are tales to read while you're planning a trip, while you're on the road or while you're in an armchair in front of a fire.

These outstanding titles explore our planet through the eyes of a diverse group of international writers. JOURNEYS books catch the spirit of a place, illuminate a culture, recount a crazy adventure or introduce a fascinating way of life. They always entertain, and always enrich the experience of travel.

ISLANDS IN THE CLOUDS
Travels in the Highlands of New Guinea
Isabella Tree

This is the fascinating account of a journey to the remote and beautiful Highlands of Papua New Guinea and Irian Jaya: one of the most extraordinary and dangerous regions on the planet. Tree travels with a PNG Highlander who introduces her to his intriguing and complex world, changing rapidly as it collides with twentieth-century technology. *Islands in the Clouds* is a thoughtful, moving book.

SEAN & DAVID'S LONG DRIVE
Sean Condon

Sean and David are young townies who have rarely strayed beyond city limits. One day, for no good reason, they set out to discover their homeland, and what follows is a wildly entertaining adventure that covers half of Australia.

'a hilariously detailed log of two burned out friends' – *Rolling Stone*

DRIVE THRU AMERICA
Sean Condon

If you've ever wanted to drive across the USA but couldn't find the time (or afford the gas), *Drive Thru America* is perfect for you. In his search for American myths and realities – along with comfort, cable TV and good, reasonably priced coffee – Sean Condon paints a hilarious road-portrait of the USA.

'entertaining and laugh-out-loud funny' – *Alex Wilber, Travel editor, Amazon.com*

BRIEF ENCOUNTERS
Stories of Love, Sex & Travel
edited by Michelle de Kretser

Love affairs on the road, passionate holiday flings, disastrous pick-ups, erotic encounters … In this seductive collection of stories, 22 authors from around the world write about travel romances. Combining fiction and reportage, *Brief Encounters* is must-have reading – for everyone who has dreamt of escape with that perfect stranger.

Includes stories by Pico Iyer, Mary Morris, Emily Perkins, Mona Simpson, Lisa St Aubin de Terán, Paul Theroux and Sara Wheeler.

Lonely Planet Travel Atlases

L onely Planet has long been famous for the number and quality of its guidebook maps. Now we've gone one step further and produced a handy companion series: Lonely Planet travel atlases – maps of a country produced in book form.

Unlike other maps, which look good but lead travellers astray, our travel atlases have been researched on the road by Lonely Planet's experienced team of writers. All details are carefully checked to ensure the atlas corresponds with the equivalent Lonely Planet guidebook.

- full-colour throughout
- maps researched and checked by Lonely Planet authors
- place names correspond with Lonely Planet guidebooks
- no confusing spelling differences
- legend and travelling information in English, French, German, Japanese and Spanish
- size: 230 x 160 mm

Available now: Chile & Easter Island • Egypt • India & Bangladesh • Israel & the Palestinian Territories • Jordan, Syria & Lebanon • Kenya • Laos • Portugal • South Africa, Lesotho & Swaziland • Thailand • Turkey • Vietnam • Zimbabwe, Botswana & Namibia

Lonely Planet TV Series & Videos

L onely Planet travel guides have been brought to life on television screens around the world. Like our guides, the programs are based on the joy of independent travel and look honestly at some of the most exciting, picturesque and frustrating places in the world. Each show is presented by one of three travellers from Australia, England or the USA and combines an innovative mixture of video, Super-8 film, atmospheric soundscapes and original music.

Videos of each episode – containing additional footage not shown on television – are available from good book and video shops, but the availability of individual videos varies with regional screening schedules.

Video destinations include: Alaska • American Rockies • Argentina • Australia – The South-East • Baja California & the Copper Canyon • Brazil • Central Asia • Chile & Easter Island • Corsica, Sicily & Sardinia – The Mediterranean Islands • East Africa (Tanzania & Zanzibar) • Cuba • Ecuador & the Galapagos Islands • Ethiopia • Greenland & Iceland • Hungary & Romania • Indonesia • Israel & the Sinai Desert • Jamaica • Japan • La Ruta Maya • London • The Middle East (Syria, Jordan & Lebanon • Morocco • New York City • Northern Spain • North India • Outback Australia • Pacific Islands (Fiji, Solomon Islands & Vanuatu) • Pakistan • Peru • The Philippines • South Africa & Lesotho • South India • South West China • South West USA • Trekking in Uganda & Congo • Turkey • Vietnam • West Africa • Zimbabwe, Botswana & Namibia

The Lonely Planet TV series is produced by: Pilot Productions
The Old Studio
18 Middle Row
London W10 5AT, UK

Lonely Planet Online

Whether you've just begun planning your next trip, or you're chasing down specific info on currency regulations or visa requirements, check out Lonely Planet Online for up-to-the-minute travel information.

As well as miniguides to more than 250 destinations, you'll find maps, photos, travel news, health and visa updates, travel advisories and discussion of the ecological and political issues you need to be aware of as you travel. You'll also find timely upgrades to popular guidebooks that you can print out and stick in the back of your book.

There's an online travellers' forum (The Thorn Tree) where you can share your experience of life on the road, meet travel companions and ask other travellers for their recommendations and advice.

There's also a complete and up-to-date list of all Lonely Planet travel products including travel guides, diving and snorkeling guides, phrasebooks, atlases, travel literature and videos, and a simple online ordering facility if you can't find the book you want elsewhere.

Lonely Planet Diving & Snorkeling Guides

Beautifully illustrated with full-colour photos throughout, Lonely Planet's Pisces books explore the world's best diving and snorkeling areas and prepare divers for what to expect when they get there, both topside and underwater.

Dive sites are described in detail with specifics on depths, visibility, level of difficulty, special conditions, underwater photography tips and common and unusual marine life present. You'll also find practical logistical information and coverage on topside activities and attractions, sections on diving health and safety, plus listings for diving services, live-aboards, dive resorts and tourist offices.

FREE Lonely Planet Newsletters

We love hearing from you and think you'd like to hear from us.

Planet Talk

Our FREE quarterly printed newsletter is full of tips from travellers and anecdotes from Lonely Planet guidebook authors. Every issue is packed with up-to-date travel news and advice, and includes:

- a postcard from Lonely Planet co-founder Tony Wheeler
- a swag of mail from travellers
- a look at life on the road through the eyes of a Lonely Planet author
- topical health advice
- prizes for the best travel yarn
- news about forthcoming Lonely Planet events
- a complete list of Lonely Planet books and other titles

To join our mailing list, residents of the UK, Europe and Africa can email us at go@lonelyplanet.co.uk; residents of North and South America can email us at info@lonelyplanet.com; the rest of the world can email us at talk2us@lonelyplanet.com.au, or contact any Lonely Planet office.

Comet

Our FREE monthly email newsletter brings you all the latest travel news, τeatures, interviews, competitions, destination ideas, travellers' tips & tales, Q&As, raging debates and related links. Find out what's new on the Lonely Planet Web site and which books are about to hit the shelves.

Subscribe from your desktop: www.lonelyplanet.com/comet

Index

Text

MAP LEGEND

BOUNDARIES

—··—··—·· International
—··—··—·· State
— — — — Disputed

HYDROGRAPHY

Coastline
River, Creek
Lake
Intermittent Lake
Reef
Canal
Spring, Rapids
Waterfalls
Swamp

ROUTES & TRANSPORT

Freeway
Highway
Major Road
Minor Road
Unsealed Road
City Freeway
City Highway
City Road
City Street, Lane

Pedestrian Mall
Tunnel
Train Route & Station
Metro & Station
Tramway
Cable Car or Chairlift
Walking Track
Walking Tour
Ferry Route

AREA FEATURES

Building
Park, Gardens
Cemetery

Market
Beach, Desert
Urban Area

MAP SYMBOLS

◎ **CAPITAL** National Capital
◉ **CAPITAL** State Capital
■ **CITY** City
● **Town** Town
● **Village** Village
○ Point of Interest

■ Place to Stay
△ Camping Ground
▼ Place to Eat
☗ Pub or Bar

✈ ✕ Airport, Airfield
Ancient or City Wall

Archaeological Site
Bank
Beach
Cave
Church
Cliff or Escarpment
Dive Site, Snorkelling
Golf Course
Hospital
Lighthouse
Lookout
Monument
Mountain or Hill
Museum

Parking
Pass
Petrol
Police Station
Post Office
Shipwreck
Shopping Centre
Surfing
Swimming Pool
Synagogue
Temple, Taoist Temple
Tomb
Tourist Information
Transport

Note: not all symbols displayed above appear in this book

LONELY PLANET OFFICES

Australia
PO Box 617, Hawthorn, Victoria 3122
☎ 03 9819 1877 fax 03 9819 6459
email: talk2us@lonelyplanet.com.au

USA
150 Linden St, Oakland, CA 94607
☎ 510 893 8555 TOLL FREE: 800 275 8555
fax 510 893 8572
email: info@lonelyplanet.com

UK
10a Spring Place, London NW5 3BH
☎ 020 7428 4800 fax 020 7428 4828
email: go@lonelyplanet.co.uk

France
1 rue du Dahomey, 75011 Paris
☎ 01 55 25 33 00 fax 01 55 25 33 01
email: bip@lonelyplanet.fr
www.lonelyplanet.fr

World Wide Web: www.lonelyplanet.com *or* AOL keyword: lp
Lonely Planet Images: lpi@lonelyplanet.com.au

Boxed Text